W9-ADN-402

WITHDRAWN

Gramley Library
Salem College
Winston-Salem, NC 27108

EMERGING PERSPECTIVES

ON

AMA ATA AIDOO

EMERGING PERSPECTIVES
ON
AMA ATA AIDOO

EDITED AND INTRODUCED

BY

ADA UZOAMAKA AZODO & GAY WILENTZ

Africa World Press, Inc.

P.O. Box 1892		P.O. Box 48
Trenton, NJ 08607		Asmara, ERITREA

Gramley Library
Salem College
Winston-Salem, NC 27108

Africa World Press, Inc.

P.O. Box 1892
Trenton, NJ 08607

P.O. Box 48
Asmara, ERITREA

Copyright © 1999 Ada Uzoamaka Azodo & Gay Wilentz
First Printing 1999

All rights reserved. No part of this publication may be reproduced, stored in a retrieval system or transmitted in any form or by any means electronic, mechanical, photocopying, recording or otherwise without the prior written permission of the publisher.

Book design: Jonathan Gullery   Cover design: Linda Nickens

Library of Congress Cataloging-in-Publication Data
Emerging Perspectives on Ama Ata Aidoo / edited by Ada Uzoamaka Azodo
   & Gay Wilentz.
        p.   cm.
    Includes bibliographical references and index.
    ISBN 0-86543-580-4. -- ISBN 0-86543-581-2 (pbk.)
      1. Aidoo, Ama Ata, 1942- --Criticism and interpretation.
   2. Women and literature--Ghana--History--20th century.
   3. Developing countries--In literature. 4. Ghana--In literature.
   I. Azodo, Ada Uzoamaka, 1947- . II. Wilentz, Gay Alden, 1950- .
   PR9379.9.A35Z65   1998
   828--dc21   98-7823
                                               CIP

The editors and publishers of this book of essays are very grateful to the following individuals and institutions for their permissions to reprint formerly published materials or materials to which they hold or administer copyrights:

Heinemann, publishers of John S. Mbiti's *African Religions and Philosophy* (second edition, 1990) for permission to reprint a map of Africa showing the ethnic peoples of Africa.

Lynne Rienner, publishers of April A. Gordon and Donald L. Gordon's *Understanding Contemporary Africa* (second edition, 1996), for permission to reprint J. W. Neff's map: Countries and Capitals.

D. A. Heath for the map of Early States and Empires of Africa in *Understanding Contemporary Africa*.

Wiley and Sons Publishers for the map showing the political map of Africa in 1914 in *Understanding Contemporary Africa*.

The editors of *Studies in Twentieth Century Literature*, for the permission to reprint a previously published paper by Gay Wilentz, "The Politics of Exile: Ama Ata Aidoo's *Our Sister Killjoy*" as "The Politics of Exile: Reflections of a Black-Eyed Squint in *Our Sister Killjoy*."

Modern Photo Co. Ltd., Accra, Ghana, for the post-card pictures of "Elmina Castle, East Bank, S. Jor Jorge—Ghana" and "Cape Coast Castle from the Sea—Ghana."

Mrs. Alice J. Roberson for photographs taken by her during her 1993 travel to Ghana.

Thompson and Thompson, New York, NY, for the reprint of the first ten lines of Countee Cullen's poem, "Heritage."

Ernest N. Emenyonu, Editor, *Medium and Message*, University of Calabar, Nigeria for permission to reprint Aidoo's revised essay, "Unwelcome Pals and Decorative Slaves or Glimpses of Women as Writers and Characters in Contemporary African Literature."

Front Cover Photo: Ada Uzoamaka Azodo
Back Cover Photo: Marie L. Umeh

DEDICATION

With gratitude to my parents, Mr. B. Enuma (a.k.a. Ezeugo) and Mrs. B. Chineze (a.k.a. Ọchiọra) Oguejiofo, for inculcating early in me pride in myself; for impressing on me the necessity of equilibrium in whatever I do; for teaching me to balance the value of my Western formal education with a deep appreciation of my Igbo (African) heritage.

—Ada Uzoamaka Azodo

To the people of Sierra Leone and Nigeria who opened up a world to me, so that I could introduce a part of this world to my students; to Ama Ata Aidoo, who has presented for me a model for social activism and creative energy; and finally to my female ancestors, especially my mother Stevie, who taught me that there is a way out of every restriction.

—Gay Wilentz

CONTENTS

PART FOUR:
AFRICAN WOMAN AND RADICAL FEMINISM

PART FIVE:
CONVERSATIONS WITH AMA ATA AIDOO

Illustrations

Photographs (between pages 252-253)

Figure 1A: Interior of an Ashanti chief's palaquin.

Figure 1B: Ghanaian Ashanti chief riding in a palaquin.

A

Figure 2A: The Edina Bakatue fishing festival:
Opening of the Benya lagoon.

Figure 2B: Offering of sacred foods, including eggs and mashed
yams mixed with palm oil to the god of the river.

Figure 2C: Casting of the Omanhene's net three times signals the lifting of the fishing ban.

Figure2D: The fishing festival in full swing.

Figure 3A: The stool, symbol of personal salvation in Ashanti mythology, in the National Museum, Kumasi.

Figure 3B: Another view of stools in the National Museum, Ghana.

Figure 4. The Fifteenth-century Portuguese fort of Elmina,
the oldest of the historic slave forts in Ghana.

Figure 5A: "Male" dungeon
at the Cape Coast slave
fort, Ghana.

Figure 5B: "Female" dungeon at the Cape Coast slave fort, Ghana.

Figure 5C: Mrs. Alice J. Roberson
at the entrance door to a female dungeon.

Figure 5D: A panoramic view of the Cape Coast slave fort, Ghana.

Figure 6. The Cape Coast Castle, from the Atlantic Ocean.

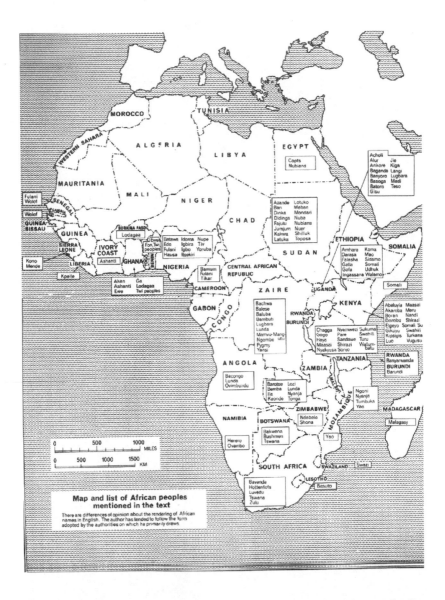

MAP 1: Reprinted from *African Religions and Philosophy*, 2nd edition, by John S. Mbiti. Copyright 1990 by Heinemann Publishers.

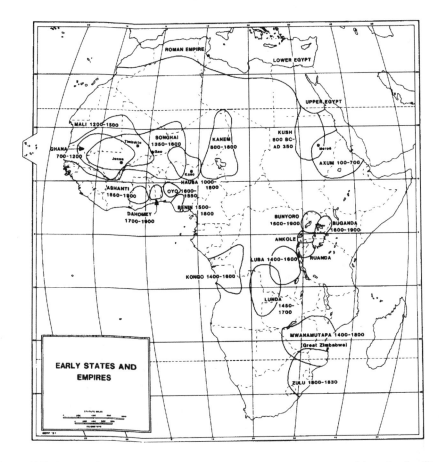

MAP 2: Reprinted from *Understanding Contemporary Africa*, 2nd edition, edited by April A. Gordon and Donald L. Gordon. Copyright 1996 by Wiley and Sons Publishers.

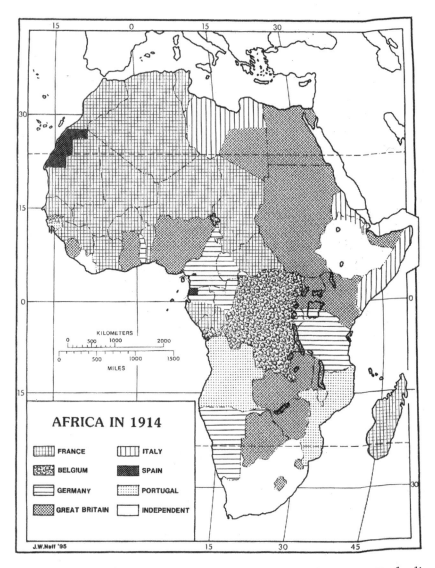

MAP 3: Reprinted from *Understanding Contemporary Africa*, 2nd edition, edited by April A. Gordon and Donald L. Gordon. Copyright 1996 by D. A. Heath.

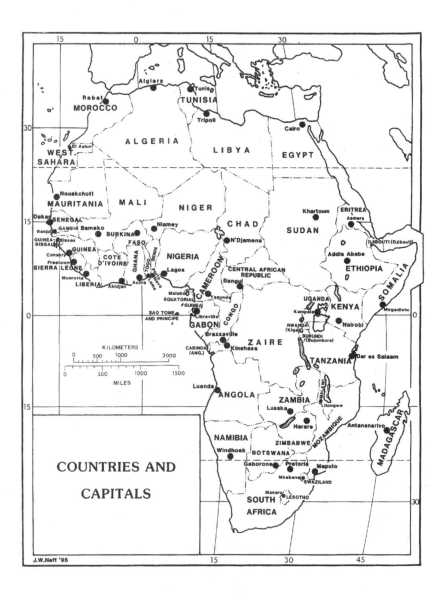

MAP 4: Reprinted from *Understanding Contemporary Africa*, 2nd edition, edited by April A. Gordon and Donald L. Gordon.
Copyright 1996 by Lynne Rienner Publishers, Inc. Reprinted with permission of the publisher. Note that Abuja, Dodoma and Yammassoukro, are the new capitals of Nigeria, Tanzania, and Cote d'Ivoire respectively..

Introduction:

A Breath of Fresh Air

Ada Uzoamaka Azodo and Gay Wilentz

This book of essays on the life and work of Ama Ata Aidoo is long deserved and long overdue. It is therefore a celebration and a success for scholars in this volume to come together to produce this work on Ama Ata Aidoo's contributions to human knowledge.

Aidoo is an unusual woman, a forerunner, for a simple reason. She is able to write comfortably the short story, novel, play, poetry, essay, letter, and criticism. Second, she is original in her ability to use any of these genres as the occasion demands, sometimes all in one text, to convey her thoughts to her readers. Third, like her personas, she holds divergent views from those of her community without yielding her ground, but rather all the time aiming at converting her people to her way of thinking. Fourth, due to her immersion in hard-core politics when writers of her generation dodge it in order to avoid negative criticism, Aidoo will always be remembered as a strong literary voice in African and international politics. Finally, her critical and creative writings have led to the development of a kind of African feminism based on the cultural traditions of the community and the region, which relates the political to the personal. She is one of the first women in African literature to address the fact that an acceptance of a Western feminism, born from the patriarchal societies of Europe and the US, may not be what feminism has been set up to be for all peoples at all times; rather she turned to her own Akan cultural milieu, and began to examine what in that culture could direct an indigenous women's movement that would make sense to the people, untainted by the biases of the colonial encounter. Speaking to an interviewer, she states clearly what all her writings invoke in terms of women's role pre-colonially and after:

> I'm not saying at all that sexism was introduced into Africa by colonial men. But it definitely seems that the kind of systematic exclusion that was practiced was born out of a total misunderstanding of how our societies operated .... Ours have a double quarrel. Not only as Africans, but also as women. Colonized by the colonizer, then by our men with their new power. (Maja-Pearce 1990:17)

For Ama Ata Aidoo, speaking her mind and doing so loudly is more acceptable to the person she is than any attempt to placate the world for her own personal gains. And Aidoo has paid dearly for it, for her boldness, her radicalism, and her commitment. A subtext of her writing could be: Towards a Decolonized, Non-patriarchal African Literature, a task left undone by the first work of that kind, *Towards the Decolonization of African Literature*, which managed to ignore, for the most part, women's contribution to African orature, literature and culture. Aidoo's vision is revolutionary since she refuses to take what she calls the "garbage" of the past, aiming instead to find a usable past, made up of "what was healthy in our society" (18). In a recent article that seems to support Aidoo's point of view, Kwaku Larbi Korang identifies this fine author's attempt to repair a post-colonial African psyche in *Our Sister Killjoy*:

> Aidoo proposes the ethno-cultural imperative of knowing and affirming an African self through a poetics of a will-to-power, a strong survivalist ethic, and the urgent task of recovering an Africanist mode of knowledge and being .... To the extent that a masculinist version of pan-Africanism has tended to overlook women's presence (of mind) in the nationalist undertaking, Aidoo's position as a woman enjoins her—and us—to complicate the nationalist address. (Korang 1992:52-53)

Korang forcefully links Aidoo's radical political vision for the repairing of the African psyche after colonialism (as she once said, "Post

what? We're not post anything!") with the demands of an indigenous African feminism, informed by a critical revision of the precolonial past. Taken together, Aidoo's *oeuvre* poses —and to some
extent, leads to—a resolution of problems concerning how to create a modern African (specifically, Ghanaian) society based on the
patterns and traditions of non-colonized African past within the
context of a present-day, technological society; how to engender a
rapprochement between Africans and Diasporans; how to maintain
the dignity of the African woman in her society.

Compared to other writers of her own generation and those of
the newer generation, Aidoo stands out both in terms of her
resilience as an artist, the newness of her subjects, and the invigorating quality of her work on the orature of the past. Here we have
an illustrious daughter of Africa who deserves to go down in the
annals of African literature as one of the most resourceful and
forceful writers the continent has ever known, and among women
writers comparable to Micere Mugo, Flora Nwapa, Buchi Emecheta,
Nadine Gordimer and Bessie Head in terms of her engagement in
the issues of the present affecting society. Aidoo brooks no non-
sense. Her women characters are radical on social, political, and
economic issues. They rail against the oppression of women without waiting for surrogates from elsewhere to do it for them.

Still, the author is at once an outsider and an insider in the
world of African literature. African male writers do not accept her
and other women writers as belonging to the guild of African writers. Theo Vincent, for example, has challenged Sissie's sagacious-
ness in politics, that is, her shrewdness or her keenly perceptive
or discerning mind as seen in *Our Sister Killjoy*. Although Vincent
would not call Sissie "a freak," he clearly questions Aidoo's imagination in creating her character (Vincent 1980). Within the context of this questioning is an inherent resistance to a woman writer
presenting a critique of self-exiles through the eyes of a young
woman. In her downright sarcastic, so-called apology on the first
page of *Changes: A Love Story*, Aidoo seems to be laughing in the
face of those critics who believe that women should eschew politics but only indulge in writing love stories, or those who are so
ignorant they imagine that love and social issues have nothing to
do with each other, nay that the personal is not also political:

> To the reader, a confession, and the critic, an apol-
> ogy. Several years ago when I was a little older than
> I am now, I said in a published interview that I could

never write about lovers in Accra. Because surely in our environment there are more important things to write about? Working on this story then was an exercise in words—eating! Because it is a slice from the life and loves of a somewhat privileged young woman and other fictional characters—in Accra. It is not meant to be a contribution to any debate, however current.

—AAA (Aidoo 1991:1)

The considerably large number of studies, analyses and interpretations in this book, realized from a relatively limited number of sources, demonstrates the genius of Aidoo as well as the scholarship of her critics. Aidoo's expert use of the oral narrative genre of the dilemma tale has allowed her to initiate issues and questions without guidance as to their resolutions, but allowing critics widely different interpretations of the same texts. Critics then seize the moment and the discussion continues. Still the essays in this volume have hardly exhausted all the possibilities, given that Aidoo's texts are, above all, about evolving life, and with evolving life no one knows what might happen next. Aidoo has ingrained the oral narrative technique into her work expressly to provide ambiguity, depth, and complexity. The reader's comprehension is expanded by her access to an overwhelming amount of information, a variety of perspectives without a privileged insight as to how the author wants her reader to think. Imitating the traditional African griotte, Aidoo offers the reader contrasting interpretations of events and characters past and present. Scenes and episodes contrast, each giving a different perspective and allowing a distinctive voice. In essence, the linear story is often subverted or challenged by gaps, complexities, contrasts, or ambiguities; hence the abundance of ellipses in Aidoo's work; hence the different approaches, interpretations, readings, insights, opinions, and analyses that Aidoo's work has provoked. What are Aidoo's works about? Why does she write the way she does?

There are inevitably tensions between the personal and the political in Aidoo's *oeuvre*; between the traditions of literary scholarship and the exigencies of African oral tradition. In both the personal and the artistic, Aidoo strives to overcome alienation, isolation and oppression engendered by colonization, imperialism, patriarchy and phallocentrism. Aidoo's heroines, as we have already suggested, refuse to be victimized. However, despite Aidoo's desire to transcend the limitations of a woman writer in our day, her fiction still has its origins in the dialectic between the personal and the political, as well as between the concerns of the literary circle and her personal need for self-realization promoting the merits and values of African oral tradition, which express women's contributions.

It is true that African women are presented in her works as intelligent, educated most of the time, enterprising, uninhibited. Still, Aidoo's fiction is the site of the dilemmas of modern African nations between the personal and the public, the individual and the community. The heroines embody their author's life tensions, ambitions, desires, and griefs. The more public the work appears, the more indeed it calls us back to the personal basis of the fiction: the effects of exile, alienation and isolation on personal lives; the role of family and society in forging human understanding; African oral tradition as expression of self, especially women's lives in a time of changes, conflicts, choices, crises, and the instinctual including sexuality. If we have not so far seen the entire journey of a woman writer expressed in her creative works, we prophesize here that we will not be kept too long waiting.

Therefore, we submit that Aidoo's writing is highly self-conscious of the craft of her art. It is also self-conscious of two opposing tendencies each of which has its own complexities and contradictions. The first tendency, which seems to be feminine, includes the personal, the instinctual, the socially and morally conscious. The second tendency, seemingly masculine, has to do with the rational, the public, and the dominating, and distinguishes between public politics and personal possessions. Apparently, Aidoo desires to bring these opposites together where the survival of the nation is conditioned on the survival of the woman and the community. The personal and the communal thus converge through politics. From this angle of vision, Aidoo joins the ranks of Thomas Sankara, Agostigno Neto, Amilcar Cabral, Samora Marchel (all males and feminists too!), who have at one time or another stated that there can be no liberation of Africa without the liberation of women. The tyranny of gender roles, they hold, hampers women's political, social, and economic contributions in Africa.

Aidoo's articulation of feminism is shaped by an awareness that the committed writer is responsible not only to promote the cause of women on the continent, but also to build the nation, the continent and the Diaspora. Hence Aidoo's anxiety to overcome the

narrowness of mind that comes with the ideology; hence her recommendation that the African woman reassert herself in history,
affirm herstory as an African or Diasporan, and commit as writer
and/or artist or some other professional, who is aware of her surroundings and her dilemma. Aidoo's fiction mirrors both the major
global political changes as they affect Africa since the European
chattel slavery and the colonization of African peoples through
imperialism. Moreover, her writing also reflects Africa's present
attempts to be economically viable in the global village. It is in this
particular global set-up that she attempts to function as a committed writer.

At the forefront of those writers creating neologisms and new
genres, which do not exactly tally with modern literary genres nor
traditional ones, Aidoo adapts traditional forms to modern versions,
sort of putting new wine into an old bottle. Although a realist, she
still has an unusual interest in the psychological, the symbolic, the
metaphysical, the spiritual, and the art of fiction.

While Aidoo often appears focused on hard-core ideas, especially about African and international politics as they affect human
relations, and national and regional revolutions, she has nonetheless given voice to the desires of the body, to the gaze and mind's
consciousness of the environment. Although her fiction is about
rebellion against oppressive institutional structures and explorations of alternative ways of living, she also attempts to bring
together the truth of the senses and the body with the demands of
the mind and moral consciousness in the turbulent cultural and
political vicissitudes of modern Africa. Aidoo's fiction evolves from
the search for a better relationship between Africa and the
Diaspora, which she believes will constitute the sole panacea for
a worthy place in the world community towards the millennium
for Africans and other African peoples.

The origins of Aidoo's early works—which include two plays
(*The Dilemma of a Ghost* and *Anowa*), a novel (*Our Sister Killjoy*), a
collection of short stories (*No Sweetness Here*), and two books of
poetry (*An Angry Letter in January* and *Someone Talking to
Sometime*)—is based in the lives of ordinary people. These people
she writes about (which include herself) are those she observed
during her sojourn at home in Ghana and her travels as a student
in Africa, Europe, and North America. These people are engaged
in quests of self-exploration. From this angle of vision Aidoo's
works are, at least partially, autobiographical. These writings
explore the dilemmas of Africans in contact with Europeans in

African and in their home countries, with African diasporans, or with other Africans after the euphoria of independence, and the difficulty of finding a path out of the quagmire of neocolonialism and imperialism.

Since those earlier works, Aidoo has brought forth a new novel (*Changes: A Love Story*) and a new collection of short stories (*The Girl Who Can And Other Stories*). A characteristic of this second wave of writing is that the author is multi-voiced on the subject matter of her fiction. The modern era and living in Africa towards the millennium is an oxymoron. It is the world of restless, rebellious, and revolutionary women discussing dreams, pursuing careers, projects, alternatives, choices, the commitment to self first and then to family, community, nation and their region of the globe. These are the faces of heightened tensions in Africa today. Still these tensions also emphasize personal relations, perceptions, morals and their effects on personal decisions and actions. Questions about personal preferences, individual will versus social traditional structures and norms, economic and social determinism, recall the reader to the era of complementary gender roles in traditional Africa. It is possible, for example, to see *Changes* and *The Girl Who Can* as a self-conscious examination of the merits of African oral tradition in writing for communal and national survival.

As her later writings replicate in some ways her earlier writings, we have come full circle: Africa needs to humanize its social structures; Africa needs to seize its space in the world to pursue development in its own way; women need to demand full reins to contribute their quota to society.

The structure we have imposed on this volume of essays arises from a desire to explore the full range of Aidoo's writings and the body of criticism on her work, including a personal interview and an essay. These divisions, we hope, will help the reader to grasp the finest and lasting aspects of Ama Ata Aidoo the African, the woman and the writer.

Part One, Writing Back: Aidoo's Critical Voice, begins by bringing together the creative and the critical and featuring "Unwelcome Pals and Decorative Slaves" (1981), one of Aidoo's own exegeses of theory. Although this essay is often referred to in critical works on Aidoo, we include it in its entirety in this book to serve our readers and future critics of the author. In addition, we need to contribute to the current debate and thus promote the necessity of a broad theoretical base in African literature, especially literature by women and/or for women.

Gay Wilentz frames this essay by a discussion of Aidoo's role as a critic and essayist in "Reading the Critical Writer." In "Unwelcome Pals and Decorative Slaves," Aidoo joins the ranks of other African writers, such as Chinua Achebe and Ngugi wa Thiong'o, examining not only the place of the writer in society, but also challenging the notion of the political writer in African societies as male.

Part Two, The Challenge of History, details Aidoo's views on what is and should be the relationship of Africa and its diaspora.

Angeletta Gourdine in "Slavery in the Diaspora Consciousness: Ama Ata Aidoo's Conversations," agrees with the Du Boisan tenet that diaspora consciousness should be repositioned within a larger pan-Africanist perspective, which includes the African, Caribbean, and African American worlds. Gourdine adds that Africans of the continent who have so far remained aloof should make sincere and fervent efforts towards the reestablishment of the broken lineage, as a way of effecting authentic liberation and making reparations for past errors of omission or commission.

Mildred A. Hill-Lubin's attack on Africans is more open, direct, and two-pronged. In "Ama Ata Aidoo and the African Diaspora: Things 'all Good Men and Women try to Forget,' but I will not Let Them," she charges Africans for their complicity with strangers in the dispersal of their kith and kin four hundred years ago. Then she gives to Africans the burden for the reaffirmation of African dignity through spearheading cross-cultural solidarity of Africans and Diasporans.

Using the metaphor of *Abiku* (Yoruba; *Ogbanje* in Igbo), Maureen Ngozi Eke in "Diasporic Ruptures and (Re)membering History: Africa as Home and Exile in *Anowa* and *The Dilemma of a Ghost*," examines the double tragedy (double yoke!) of Africans both as insiders and outsiders. Slavery and colonization constitute the *double rupture*, which have made Africans and Diasporans exiles both at home and abroad. What is expedient is the healing of the historical fractures so that "Abiku" can finally find solace on earth.

Still, regional politics is such that Africans often think that paradise is to be found in the Western center, ignorant that all spatial spheres have their own peculiar limitations. Critiquing contemporary theories of exile as a move into the knowledge of the *metropole*, Gay Wilentz examines Aidoo's own foray into the world of the colonizers and her challenge to the self-exiles through revisiting white supremacy and black inferiority myths in "The Politics of Exile: Reflections of a Black-Eyed Squint in *Our Sister Killjoy*." Although this paper had been published elsewhere, we reproduce it here in order to give a heightened attention to the problems of brain-drain and African exiles, which continue to preoccupy Ama Ata Aidoo.

Haiping Yan sees transnationality as a trope that contests and complements at the same time postcoloniality and postmodernism, in "Transnationality and Its Critique: Narrative Tropes of 'Borderland' in *Our Sister Killjoy*." This paper asserts that all that modern men and women try to do is make sense of their lives caught, as they are, at the confluence of transnational capitalism and its historical impacts.

Part Three, Creating an Indigenous Text, probes the nature of Aidoo's *oeuvre* and her commitment to create texts in English, which mirror her own development of an artistic awareness and consciousness about the nature of story telling and portrayal of life's drama through characters, and about the essential nature and conventions of the art of writing—what Gay Wilentz has called elsewhere "oraliterature." Aidoo manifests a penchant for finding her own way of deconstructing an established art or genre of the European tradition, making it new, entirely her own, because blended with new elements of the African oral tradition. She has taken the oral genre of the African dilemma tale and infused it with her own sensibilities, decentering present-day historical determinism, and analyzing the effects of slavery, colonization, regional and international politics and imperialism in Africa.

According to Naana Jane Opoku-Agyemang in "Narrative Turns in Ama Ata Aidoo's *No Sweetness Here*," Aidoo goes beyond the content of her writings to employ structures and stylistic devices from African oral tradition to respond to the pervading notions of nationhood and womanhood in Africa.

Linda Strong-Leek, in "Inverting the Institutions: Ama Ata Aidoo's *No Sweetness Here and Deconstructive Theory*," deconstructs and decenters patriarchy through her criticism of Lloyd Brown's views of Aidoo's works. Countering phallocentrism with gynocentrism, Strong-Leek observes that Aidoo's women are strong women who remain in hostile communities to fight for a place for themselves.

Do African women have a voice? Arlene Elder responds in "Ama Ata Aidoo: The Development of a Woman's Voice," that Aidoo uses the West African story-telling tradition to show that an abundance of cultural problems arise from people's inability or unwillingness to listen to one another. Aidoo's work, she affirms, is imbued with epic memory, which allows art, the artist and audience to participate together in the same celebration or pathos. She concludes that Aidoo empowers a woman's voice and reasserts orature's traditional moral dialectic between the artist and her audience.

Both Kenneth Harrow and Paula Morgan see travel as a motif for self-actualization. Focusing on the Homeland's relationship with the Caribbean, Harrow compares Aidoo with Derek Walcott even as Morgan compares her with Jamaica Kincaid. Harrow examines *other versions* of the epic story in "Of Those Who Went Before," challenging the Eurocentric design of the *Bildungsroman*, when the reason to leave is connected to slave trade. He identifies a counter-trope in Aidoo, dismantling this form of writing as a patriarchal narrative.

Paula Morgan, for her part, in "The Risk of (Re)membering My Name: Reading *Lucy* and *Our Sister Killjoy* as Travel Narratives," raises the question of return for the African and the Caribbean female subjects, who challenge and beat the colonizer or neo-colonizer in his own game, with her reading of Aidoo's peculiar reversal of the habitual form of the European travel narrative.

The speed of modern travel and relocation hamper the normal rhythm with which myths accumulate, thus requiring individuals to formulate their own personal myths. This is the premise from which Ada Uzoamaka Azodo explores Aidoo's mythic consciousness in *"The Dilemma of a Ghost*: Literature and Power of Myth," when Aidoo's first play is read as a form of travel literature which recalls Africans and Diasporans to their common heritage, and by extension, the entire humanity as *Homo Sapiens* to their common origin. This study affirms humankind's ability once more to attain a form of unification in diversity, if only reason would be allowed to reign.

Vincent Odamtten in "The Bird of the Wayside: From *An Angry Letter* ... to *The Girl Who Can*," closes this third section of the book by above all bringing into focus a lesser known work of Aidoo and also her most recent, and tracing the evolution and development of Aidoo's artistic sensibility from the beginning to the present. What emerges is a panoramic survey of Aidoo's commitment, not just to Africa and its diaspora, but also to her art and craft, and all women towards the twenty-first century.

Part Four, African Woman and Radical Feminism, treats the feminist side of Ama Ata Aidoo's writings. In the face of multivocal feminist voice today, Aidoo's feminism and her view of African feminism is a very important topic of discussion for the author that this volume would not have failed to explore.

Peter W. Stine in "The Language of Endurance in the Short Stories of Ama Ata Aidoo," categorizes Aidoo's women into active and passive endurers. The ones are hardened by experience and are prepared for the pain and absence of "sweetness" in their environment. The others are armed with the language of aggression and are ready to change the rules, if need be, to find a place for themselves in the burgeoning modern cities they find themselves.

In what might be considered an ironic twist, Gay Wilentz, in "African Woman's Domain: Demarcating Political Space in Nwapa, Sutherland, and Aidoo," examines the breakdown of generational continuity and the changing of the rules by the modern African woman in the city. By posing traditional models in contradistinction to the newly achieved "independence," the essay questions what kind of examples these city dwellers are setting for future generations of African women, when their freedom is seemingly achieved at the expense of their community and nation.

Juliana Makuchi Nfah-Abbenyi, for her part, in "Flabberwhelmed or Turning History on its Head?: The Postcolonial Woman-as-Subject in Aidoo's *Changes: A Love Story*," seemingly maintains that African feminism is about the new modern woman confronted with many problems attempting to re-write her history while making space for herself in the cultural scripts within which her identity and subjectivity are constructed and sustained.

Naana Banyiwa Horne's "The Politics of Mothering: Multiple Subjectivity and Gendered Discourse in Aidoo's Plays," affirms a multiple definition of female personhood. Furthermore, this essay interrogates aspects and manners of male hegemonic discourse, even in precolonial Africa, in subjugating women.

Sally McWilliams, in "Strange as It may Seem: African Feminism in Two Novels by Ama Ata Aidoo," redefines African feminism, positing compulsory heterosexuality as an institutionalized social system worthy of rejection, due to its inherent hierarchical and opposing qualities, and complicity with patriarchy and Western feminism to subordinate African women.

For Pauline O. Uwakweh, in "Free But Lost: Variations in the Militant's Song," African feminism is women electing to be subjects and doers, not objects that are acted upon. Marriage, more than heterosexuality, she asserts, robs women of their autonomy; hence divorce becomes a liberating option for resilient women, a gateway to self-determination, striking-out and achieving an alternative to the offensive *status quo*.

Whose truth is the *real* truth, the man's truth or the woman's truth?, asks Miriam C. Gyimah in "Sexual Politics and Phallocentric Gaze in *Changes: A Love Story.*" Not only are recent African feminist theorists making an impact, indeed, they are revisiting what so-called illiterate women had always done in experiential circumstances: break the boundaries that inhibit women in order to reclaim their subjectivity, which had been stolen by their men who erroneously hold that theory is a masculine domain where men are at home and where women should fear to tread.

In "The Multifaceted Aidoo: Ideologue, Scholar, Writer, and Woman," Ada Uzoamaka Azodo summarizes the life and works of Ama Ata Aidoo the versatile and multiple. This essay holds that as a veteran writer of some thirty years, for whom not a single work has ever been out of print, Aidoo presents as a woman of enduring ideas, an artist of considerable intellect, an activist of international repute, and a woman who cares about the interests of women as a significant and valuable sector of humanity.

Also in a recent interview, "Facing the Millennium: An Interview with Ama Ata Aidoo," recorded in 1996 at Hauppauge, New York, and which comprises **Part Five—Conversations with Ama Ata Aidoo**—the final part of this book of essays, Ada Uzoamaka Azodo captures Aidoo's voice along with that author's revelation of her destiny as a writer, intellectual, revolutionary and feminist, thanks to the benefits of modern technology.

In presenting the text of the interview, and subsequently the circumstances of the recording in "Afterword: Interviewing and Transcribing a Writer-Oral Artist," Azodo breaks with generally accepted interview norms by seeing the interviewee as an oral artist and the interviewer as a collector of oral tradition. There is as much interest in the process of recording the speech and transcribing the recorded text as in the presentation of the final edited version. What comes out of this experimentation is the observation that, perhaps, Aidoo's famed penchant for genre-crossing is no more than the exploitation by this knowledgeable and talented writer—perhaps unconsciously—of the art of storytelling as performance. Aidoo, apparently, simply sets down words as they come to her in the process of writing, as if they were segments of speech. Because we enjoy reading plays better if we are able to get glimpses of activities off stage and at the side, it seems that reporting interviews in the manner that it has been done here, that is allowing circumstantial elements to be included in the text, should make an interview a written text and therefore much more interesting to read. Furthermore, the treatment of interviews as a literary genre, which might develop from this experimentation, could also enlarge the definition of literature, which already includes less orthodox genres such as memoirs, letters, autobiographies and biographies.

This book, *Emerging Perspectives on Ama Ata Aidoo*, as we have mentioned earlier, has been designed to capture a broad spectrum of the latest scholarship on Ama Ata Aidoo. From the criticisms and interpretations of our contributors, we have been able to discern that Aidoo's work shows an author for whom literature has a double role of humanizing society and serving women's interests at the same time. For this reason, the habitual manner of distinguishing maleness from femaleness appears ridiculous before this woman who is fighting for the common good. Nor does masculinity automatically exclude femininity, rendering it inferior as far as Aidoo is concerned. Aidoo provides literary strong role-models for women whose identities do not depend on men and also who provide new possibilities for women engaged in seeking alternative lifestyles. She reverses preconscribed notions of femininity and masculinity, portraying androgynous female characters, women who feel deeply and respond to their emotions without violence, but who are nonetheless articulate, responsible, enlightened, enterprising, opinionated and self-confident. Their behavior and personality go hand in hand with their responsibilities at work and in their communities.

Aidoo's writings support the creation of a feeling of sisterhood, which promotes solidarity among women as a way of minimizing dependence on men. Sisterhood can be between mother and daughter or between best friends. What is important is to eschew hatred between women, hatred that only renders them vulnerable to male domination, and like a domino effect, reduces their potential for contributing constructively to their communities. We as readers and critics feel close to Aidoo's characters because we believe they must have gone through the experiences they portray.

Aidoo raises the consciousness of the reader as personal or recurring societal problems are fictionalized from an actual historical base. This includes what men usually say to other men to put them down when they treat their women as human beings; the realistic presentation of the political, social and economic situation of Africa in general, and also of particular countries like Nigeria, Burkina Faso and Ghana.

The variety of contributions in this volume is such that no one reading or theory, no matter how sophisticated and complex, would have been able to explain them all. What we have is an admixture of studies on nationalism, international politics, pan-Africanism, feminism, creative writing and literary theory, enabling us to confirm what has always been said about Aidoo's work, namely that the survival of the nation is predicated on the survival, liberation and progress of its women, and that the private and the public, the personal and the political must be fully integrated for human progress to be achieved. This brand of feminist ideology which combines the struggle for the common good with the fight for women's liberation is what Ada Uzoamaka Azodo calls here the "spirit of Aidooism." It is in that spirit that we offer this collection of essays, as a libation to Aidoo's own work and to the ensuing discussion that we, critics and activists, hope will continue.

There are, nonetheless, changing perspectives and awareness, which will keep emerging with social evolution; there will also be a constant revision of forms that will appropriately convey our author's visions. Then again, with the recent take-off of Aidoo's second wave of literary creativity, there will be room enough for our followers to try something new. The promise of more creative works by Aidoo is confirmed in a recent note to the editors, dated July 9, 1997, in which Aidoo had this to say on the present situation of her writing: "(I) confess that I have not had the time to do anything at all except write 3 short stories and a few long poems." Aidoo then added that work was still pending on a novel she shelved to begin and finish *Changes: A Love Story*. For now, we end by saying that the number of approaches, claims, readings, opinions and insights in this volume reveal that Aidoo brings into African literature today a breath of fresh air.

WORKS CITED

Aidoo, Ama Ata. *Changes: A Love Story*. New York: CUNY, The Feminist Press, 1991.

Korang, Kwaku Larbi. "Ama Ata Aidoo's Voyage Out: Mapping the Coordinates of Modernity and African Selfhood in *Our Sister Killjoy.*" *Kunapipi* (Aarhus Denmark) 14, 3 (1992):50-61.

Maja-Pearce, Adewale. "We Were Feminists in Africa First." *Index on Censorship*,19, 9 (October 1990):17-18.

Vincent, Theo. "Form in the Nigerian Novel: An Examination of Aidoo's *Our Sister Killjoy* and Okpewho's *The Last Duty*. Paper presented at the African Studies Association, Philadelphia, October 7, 1980.

Part One

WRITING BACK: AIDOO'S CRITICAL VOICE

READING THE CRITICAL WRITER

GAY WILENTZ

A recent article in *Human Rights Quarterly* raises prevalent questions concerning the nature of the contemporary women's rights movement globally by focusing on two well-known slogans of the women's movement: "the personal is political" (a well-known adage from US feminism) and "women's rights are human rights" (from the international arena). In juxtaposing these two slogans, developed in part by Western women, the authors place themselves as African women and explore what exactly these statements mean in regards to them. They note that challenging these two slogans is "particularly germane given the historical practice of western societies capturing, defining and transforming, or 'orientalizing' realities in the 'third world'" (Oloka-Onyango and Tamale 1995:693-94). Throughout the essay, they examine different anthologies and points of view in addressing the issue of cultural definitions of women and how local realities relate to "universal" notions of womanhood.

Their essay addresses significant questions in regards to these issues, but, like most socio-economic studies, it ignores the aspects of women's experience brought up by writers and artists. This leaves the essay a "dilemma tale" with an untenable opposition, lacking the visionary focus and input of women who write about these concerns on the most intimate level, the day-to-day existence of ordinary women's lives. Had the authors included the critical writings of Ama Ata Aidoo in that essay, they might have seen how such writings in general—and the creative efforts of one African woman in particular—demarcates *exactly how* human rights are women's rights.

Aidoo, as author and activist, truly integrates the personal with the political as she reaches back to inform us of women's roles throughout West Africa before the colonial era and compels us to envision another place for women, incorporating this past, in the future. Aidoo does not glorify the past; however, she is clear about the realities of an imposed feminism from outside that has its own problems. As she states succinctly in one interview,"I genuinely feel that one way to reclaim ourselves is to find out what exactly happened" (Maja-Pearce 1990:18). And in the attempt to find out "what exactly happened," Aidoo retells a version of African history from a female perspective. For Aidoo, the secret of how African women can function in the present is linked to a greater understanding of the past. In her view (and in agreement with Oloka-Onyango and Tamale), African women today are caught between the Western feminists with their imperial biases and the African male leadership, whose nationalist impulses have also incorporated Victorian notions of womanhood. Aidoo states sharply: "Over the last five hundred years we've had African men in leadership positions, certainly since Africa's collusion with the Western world. Isn't it clear that the African man alone isn't able to cope with our relationship with the West and the rest of the world?" (18). In her critical writings, Aidoo details what historian Cheik Anta Diop, social scientist Filomina Steady, and others have been exploring in other disciplines: that although women's role within a precolonial African world may not have been equal in any present-day conception of women's equality, there were many ways in which women maintained a position of political power and economic activity that was severely curtailed during colonization and has not changed with post/neocolonialism.

The body of Aidoo's works attests to the strength of Aidoo's vision in terms of developing a political role for women in the process of decolonization, and her own position as a leader in global feminism, rooted in the notion of female citizenry within an African continuum, as exemplified in her famous essay, "Unwelcome Pals and Decorative Slaves." Furthermore, her other critical writings identify her as a theoretician in leading the way to "transvalue the old values of Africa, and to bring them into a

4

meaningful relationship with the present and the future" (Korang 1992:60). From her early writings on African literature to later essays and interviews on the role of traditional culture in neo/post-colonialism, she has been unswerving in her aim to make sure that Africans do not continue to suffer from cultural "amnesia" concerning the past, either positive or negative. In speaking about contemporary drama in West Africa, Aidoo comments:

> I think any discussion of African drama has to start with the so-called oral traditions. Because if African theater is really going to gain any strength, some of it is going to have to come from there. Everybody needs a backbone. If we do not refer to the old traditions, it is almost like operating with amnesia (Aidoo 1976:124).

Aidoo's own plays have shown this attention to earlier traditions, and in roundtables and interviews, she has directed this consciousness toward her fellow writers and critics. However, Aidoo does not examine the past uncritically. She has chided African historians (both oral and written) and the population in general for "amnesia" concerning the Slave Trade, commenting wryly: "The oral traditions can tell you about migrations that happened about a thousand years, and yet events that happened two to three hundred years ago are completely blanketed over.... Why?" (Vincent 1981:7).

It is this voice of Aidoo, the one like her black-eyed squint, Sissie, that makes people uncomfortable and brands her a controversial figure in African literature. But it is also this same unflinching honesty about the West and the rest of us that has gained her admiration as well. In an early essay on Armah's *The Beautyful Ones Are Not Yet Born*, called "No Saviours," Aidoo begins to define herself in relation to her own political stance as a writer and critic, while critiquing this powerful work. In discussing the negative reactions to his book in relation to Armah's aims, Aidoo states: "Meanwhile it should be remembered that this type of purgative exposure, however painful it is, is absolutely necessary, depending whether or not one believes that truth as represented in writing can be in any way effective in helping social change" (Aidoo 1973:18). We can see, in the young Aidoo, two of the tenets that have governed all her writings, both critical and creative: that art can (and should) be used as a method of evoking social change, and when you are really committed to that vision, any truth—no matter how harsh—should be permissible in the face of oppression. It is, as Aidoo states, "absolutely necessary" to do so. For throughout her theoretical discussions on what the African nation-state—and the role of women in that state—is going to look like, Aidoo, like Armah, has never minced her words. As she has found her voice to become one of Africa's most important international women writers, Aidoo has never shied away from calling former colonialists, Western feminists, or African men to task.

In what may appear to be a personal response to the affront Aidoo felt by having *Our Sister Killjoy* ignored by African (male) critics of literature, she presented a paper at the International Conference on African Literature and the English Language, Calabar, Nigeria, in 1981, the basis for the essay, "Unwelcome Pals and Decorative Slaves," later included in the conference proceedings, *Medium and Message*. In "Unwelcome Pals," Aidoo turns the personal hurt she felt from the silence of the African community into a forceful critique of the problems of the woman writer in Africa, as well as the role that women must play in the decolonization of African literature, to paraphrase Chinweizu. It is not what it appears at first, a kind of "sour grapes," but rather a call to arms. Her critique of her fellow male writers for their presentation of women, albeit harsh, also poses a way to read women within culture, a way to transform the politics of African literature from the colonial hold of male dominance of language, evident in Western culture. For, as Aidoo notes, all the writers are "part of an articulate minority that handles the language of power" (Aidoo 1981:32), adding that the responsibility of the writers to improve the condition of the people falls on both the men *and* the women.

In "Unwelcome Pals" and other critical pieces since, Aidoo aims to fulfill that role of the responsible writer, especially in regards to women, pre- and postcolonial. Her own creative writings have dealt with the touchy subjects—Africa's complicity in the Atlantic Slave Trade, African self-exiles in the colonial capital, and what, often disparagingly, have been called "feminist concerns." Whatever her level of association with so-called "Western feminism," Aidoo has not been afraid to call herself a feminist, since her concerns are the ones she defines in "Unwelcome Pals," especially a desire to unfold "a revolutionary vision of the role of women tomorrow as dreamers, thinkers, and doers" (32). However, her revolutionary vision includes revisiting the past, with an eye to what women's role has been precolonially, and how we can glean from that position a way to envision a future for men and women together, finding a usable past away from the tainted recreation of African culture by the colonizers.

As I noted in the beginning of this essay, one of Aidoo's major contributions as an activist and critical thinker has been in the position of women and their role in the society. Aidoo, along with 'Molara Ogundipe-Leslie, Micere Mugo, Chikwenye Okonjo-Ogunyemi and others, have begun to develop an African feminism, which not only challenges prevailing notions of feminist theory, but also certain biases toward what it means to be an African woman. In her 1990 interview with Maja-Pearce, Aidoo makes it clear that feminism (however labeled) is not the prerogative of Western women. Moreover, as she states in the same interview, the position of West African women, especially precolonially, reflects/ed some of contemporary women's demands of citizenship within the community, despite the fact that one could not justifiably characterize that position as one of complete equality: "In that regard, we have been luckier than most women in the world, but when you look at us from inside our society we are no better off than women anywhere else vis-à-vis the patriarchy or at least the male orientation of society" (Aidoo 1990:17). Like Achebe, Aidoo does not glorify the precolonial Akan world, yet she is forceful in exposing the notions that these women were worse off than the women of the colonizers; in fact, she is very clear in stating that colonization was a double whammy for West African women: "[The colonizers] came from a patriarchal society, all those Victorian men who didn't understand their own women and definitely did not understand the women of the colonized." She further notes that the "advantages the colonial regimes gave to the African men have carried over into the present" (17), disrupting a more balanced system and further subjugating women.

Aidoo's brand of feminism focuses on the role of women as nation-builders, while also exploring ways to improve the condition of women worldwide, using indigenous, not imported, examples. As she states in her essay, "Literature, Feminism, and the African Woman Today": "Feminism is an essential tool in women's struggles everywhere. And that includes African women" (Aidoo 1996:10). To the point that both women and men within an African context should be feminists, she comments further:

> Especially if we believe that we Africans should take
> charge of our land and its wealth and our own lives
> and the burden of our reconstruction from colo-

nialism and slavery. For, with that belief comes
another awareness. That at least half of the entire
population of Africa are women: and therefore if
Africa is to develop, then first, African women too
must get the best that the environment can offer for
their well-being and development. (10)

By linking the aim to improve women's lives with the importance
of women in the overall development of their communities and
nations, Aidoo responds to the apparent dilemma posed by Oloka-
Onyango and Tamale, of how to integrate the personal/political
with the concept that women's rights are human rights. Her own
so-called "apology" at the beginning of *Changes*—a book, which on
one hand, deals with the lovers in Accra she felt she didn't have
time for earlier, but on the other hand, is still a critique on contemporary Ghanaian society—is another way of exploring how the
intimate experiences of women must be taken into account in relation to issues of national development. However, Aidoo is quick to
remind us that contemporary feminist theory cannot be viewed
uncritically, either. In "Literature, Feminism, and The African
Woman Today," Aidoo clearly states that the conflicts within feminism, especially the relationship with "white" feminists, including the feminist/womanist debate in the US, can often
"essentialize" the experiences of African women and women of
African descent, and may be "inadvertently limiting our capacity
to understand ourselves, which, in turn, could weaken our capacity to deal effectively with the predicament we find ourselves in"
(Aidoo 1996:9). Because part of Aidoo's aim as a critical writer is
to dislodge many of the preconceptions about African women and
look at them "properly": "Hoping that with some honesty, it would
be seen that vis-à-vis the rest of the world, the position of the
African woman was not only not that bad, but in actual fact, in
some of the societies, as in West Africa, she had been far better off
than women of so many other societies" (11). In other words, there
may be a model for women, born from the precolonial position of
women as citizens in their own right, that may help us to understand more fully women's role as "thinkers and doers" in the future.

There may be a slight irony in including "Unwelcome Pals" in
the present collection of essays on Aidoo, despite its relevance to
the problems faced by emerging women writers in Africa and elsewhere. At the end of "Literature, Feminism, and The African
Woman Today," Aidoo gives us an anecdotal tale in which she is

alerted by an American (white) woman about an interview with Kwame Anthony Appiah, who in a discussion of African writing fails to mention one woman writer. The woman asks Aidoo why she isn't "mad"? and Aidoo answers "quite calmly": "I and other African women writers are used to being ignored" (Aidoo 1996:12-13). However, Aidoo has never allowed those who might want to, to ignore her, and her voice has been clear and strong in compelling us to dismantle the stereotypes and see African women properly and the role they have always played in maintaining and improving their communities. Although it is still difficult for women writers, and while women everywhere still have a long way to go to achieve that elusive goal of equality and justice, one thing is certain: With this collection and others like it, Aidoo the writer and critic is no longer being ignored.

WORKS CITED

Aidoo, Ama Ata. *Changes: A Love Story*. New York: CUNY, The Feminist Press. 1991.

———. "Literature, Feminism, and the African Woman Today." African Literature Conference. Stony Brook, New York: March 1996.

———. "No Saviours." *African Writers on African Writing*, Ed. G. D. Killam. London: Heinemann, 1973.

———. *Our Sister Killjoy or Reflections from a Black-Eyed Squint*. Lagos/New York: Nok Publishers, 1979.

———."Roundtable Discussion," First African Literature Association Conference, Northwestern University, *Issue 6,1*(1976):124-127.

———. "Unwelcome Pals and Decorative Slaves or Glimpses of Women as Writers and Characters in Contemporary African Literature." In: *Medium and Message*. Proceedings of the International Conference on African Literature and the English Language. Calabar, Nigeria: University of Calabar Press (November 1981). Rpt. *Literature and Society: Selected Essays on African Literature*. Ed. Ernest Emenyonu. Lagos, Nigeria: Zim Pan-African Publishers, 1986.

Chinweizu, Jemie Onwuchekwa and Ihechukwu Madubuike. *Towards the Decolonization of African Literature*. Washington, D.C.: Howard University Press, 1983.

Korang, Kwaku Larbi. "Ama Ata Aidoo's Voyage out: Mapping the Coordinates of Modernity and African Selfhood in *Our Sister Killjoy*." Kunapipi: 14, 3, (1992):50-61.

Maja-Pearce, Adewale. "We Were Feminists in Africa First," Interview with Ama Ata Aidoo. *Index on Censorship* 19,9 (1990):17-18.

Oloka-Onyango, J. and Sylvia Tamale. "'The Personal is Political' or Why African Women's Rights are indeed Human Rights: An African Perspective on International Feminism." *Human Rights Quarterly* 17 (1995):691-731.

Vincent, Theo. "Interview with Ama Ata Aidoo." In: *Seventeen Black and African Writers*. Lagos: Three Continents Press, 1981. 1-8.

Unwelcome Pals and Decorative Slaves

OR

Glimpses of Women as Writers and Characters in Contemporary African Literature

Ama Ata Aidoo

I had sensed vaguely as a child living among adult females that everything that had to do exclusively with being a woman was regarded as being dirty or definitely setting them apart in some uncomplimentary respect or another.[1]

A girl's first menstrual flow was celebrated after a whole week of confinement.

We know now that the "celebration" was really a subtle broadcasting of the fact that she was ready for procreation, and interested parties could start thinking of coming forward to bid to be partners in that holy enterprise.

And once you, the young man, had been bold enough to go for-

Gramley Library
Salem College
Winston-Salem, NC 27108

ward and take her off her mother's back, you could also take it for granted, that you had acquired

> a sexual aid;
> a wet nurse and a
> nursemaid for your children;
> a cook-steward and
> general housekeeper;
> a listening-post;
> an economic and general consultant;
> a field-hand and,
> if you are that way inclined,
> a punch-ball.

No, the position of women in Africa has been no less ridiculous than anywhere else—the few details that differ are interesting only in terms of local color and particular family needs—unless you are lucky or unlucky to get born into one of those families that can see alternative lives for children, other than the ones adults live.

For instance, by the time I was born, my father had come to consider formal Western education as the answer to the problems of the limitations of the untrained mind, and the definite waste that was the sum of female lives.[2]

An aunt who had learnt to read only enough of our language to be a member of the church choir, and who never forgave the fate that had not given her more educational opportunities, once told me when I was in secondary school: My child, get as far as you can in this education. Go and go and go. Go until you yourself know you are tired. Because as for marriage, it is something a woman picks up along the way."

That was quite some time ago.

Therefore, is it any wonder that I should get plainly confused now, if in associating with both female and male undergraduates, graduates, lecturers and professors, I should learn that they think, believe and insist that basically, marriage is what a woman was created for?

And higher education for a woman is an unfortunate postponement of her self-fulfilment?

That any successful career outside the home is naturally for men, and a few rather "ugly" women?

That the only way for a woman to be and remain in the academic world is for her to also be married? And if she does not marry, then her basic unattractiveness is exposed? And if she is quite obviously an attractive person, in other respects then she is just being foolish, and making other people feel uncomfortable?

Clearly, proposing to be a university teacher and a writer in such an environment must betray an extreme case of some unmentionable psychosis.

And no one reassures you to the contrary.

Indeed, your male colleagues themselves seem to resent your professional standing with them, and punish your presumption in mean little ways. They blame your femininity for what one would have thought were evidence of regular human frailty, ill-health, laziness and any other excuses for poor productivity.

If they do not find you physically repulsive, they take a continued single state as an insult to their manhood.

If you remain single into your thirties, then you have no right to look well to wit, well-dressed (with a slight plumpness, or reedy thin) a good skin, a smiling face, because scholarly spinsters are normally sour with discontent and wizened for lack of semen in their system![3]

Besides, any proper woman's seeming well-being should be always recognized for what it is: a direct product of some man's affection and *his* successful career. But the real puzzle is where you got your nerve from, a woman, to encroach on male territory.

Married or unmarried, you are unwanted, period. And insulting you publicly is nothing if they can get away with it.

Legend: 1971: from a rather young lecturer to a crowded Senior Common Room, among those present, me!

> "... really, these independent academic bitches? They are incapable of love or affection. They realize their need for men only when they want babies."

In any case, as a woman, your persistence in staying in the academic field is a total waste of time: your own and everybody's, since articulateness and other manifestations of intelligence are all masculine.

So even here on the campus, within these so-called ivy-covered towers, no one expects a woman to perform well in any other areas apart form cooking, sewing and other so-called traditional feminine activities.

Legend: May 1980: after a hard morning of lecture and tutorials, I go to the Senior Common Room for my one-bottle ration of beer. A mature, final year student rushes to me, eyes shining and full of smiles.

Student: Hei you, shake my hand.
            And I take his extended right hand, all the while
            wondering why.
Student: It's all over the halls of residence that you gave
            two super lectures this morning.
            I smile, beginning to be pleased, obviously.
Student: As for you... but you know we like your lectures?...
            Of course! Except that we hear you outdid yourself
            this morning... They say your English was abso-
            lutely masculine ...

Now I speak English like a man? And they intend it for a com-
pliment. Yes.

They had always told me I wrote like a man. Read a bold and
legible script.

They had always told me I drove like a man. Read relaxed steer-
ing, near-perfect reflexes, a predilection for speed ...

Now I speak English like a man? Read an overall confident handling of the language, perhaps?[4]

So, the list of areas covered by female incompetence grows to
include linguistic aptitude?

And while you are about it, include political awareness, sensitivity to social issues, and vulnerability to mental and physical pain.

Legend: May 31st, 1980: At the end of a symposium organized
by the Students Union.

The panel and chairman consist of three members of the faculty, and a recent head of state.

The topic is: "Violence: Its Structure and Uses." When all the
major speeches have been given, the chairman calls a female student to the stage. Precisely at that moment, it occurs to me that all
the main participants have been males. And of course, strictly in
accordance with bourgeois intellectual practices, it is now fitting
that a girl should grace the occasion by giving the vote of thanks!

On an impulse, I comment on this to my nearest neighbor to
the right, also a university teacher.

Colleague: Yes, yes ... Now that you mention it ...
            But it is a-l-r-i-g-h-t.
Me: Is it?
Colleague: Sure ... in any case, what's wrong if the
            four main speakers are all men?
Me: Nothing, if they had not asked a girl to go
            and

give a vote of thanks.

Colleague: Hmm. I see what you mean.
But really my sister, what do you women
know about *violence*? (Emphasis mine, A.
A. A.)

And I wonder how I could have been so petty bringing up the issue.[5]

Since doing anything "like-a-man" implies that you are doing what it is impressively, it should be submitted that not only aptitude and skill, but also expertise, professionalism, diligence, perfection, talent, genius, are all masculine.

And it should be further submitted that since these are also precisely the criteria for measuring and judging human accomplishments, if they are exclusively masculine, then only men are human beings. Women are not human.

What is completely bewildering though is that having been reduced to non-persons, our genuine efforts to prove ourselves human by entering genuine fields of human endeavor should go so totally unappreciated. In fact, much worse than that, our attempts to do well in these fields almost inevitably provoke resentments, both overt and covert.[6]

A woman who tries to operate in the so-called men's world excites panic dismay in other women, and except her own father, arouses anger in all other men.[7]

And of course, the more exclusive the field, the greater the hatred.

Once in a while these days, I catch myself wondering whether I could have found the courage to write if I had not started to write when I was too young to know what was good for me. Frankly, I am glad the question is purely hypothetical.

For instance, in an argument on a national issue some professors from another Ghanaian university shouted that I am not fit to speak about public matters. That I should leave politics and such to those best qualified to handle them, and concentrate on doing what I normally do best, which is writing plays and short stories.[8]

Most certainly, my trials as a woman writer are heavier and much more painful than any I have to go through as university teacher. It is a condition so delicate, it almost cannot be handled. Like an internal wound and therefore immeasurably dangerous, it also causes a ceaseless emotional haemorrage.

You feel awful for seeing the situation the way you do, and terrible when you try to speak about it. Because this kind of resentment never even comes out in jokes. Certainly, people are unaware their attitudes and utterances can be judged as hostile. Therefore, the revelation itself excites hostility.

Yet, you have to speak out since your pain is also real, and in fact, the wound throbs more relentlessly and bleeds more profusely, when you are upset by people you care for, those nearer, those you respect.

So it is that the un-reception given my latest book is so difficult to contain.[9]

Legend: January 1980: My head of department, a good friend and a well known writer himself, and I are discussing the latest edition of the book which has just come out in New York. We are both going on about how well-laid out it is, the beautiful type used, the fact that it is altogether a neat volume. Then I remark that unfortunately, my impression is that the publishers don't seem to care whether they sell it or not.

"What a shame," says he, "because there are all these women studies programmes springing in universities all over the United States of America. *They* would be interested in it..."

And I bled. Because although the only protagonist of the story is a young woman, anybody who tries to read the book would realize that her concerns are only partially feminist, if at all. In any case, what if they are? Feminism is about half of the human inhabitants of this earth?

Legend: mid-1978: a group of us together one evening.

They are all males except me. One has come from another country to visit. He is a well-known writer. We are discussing the political situation with some fervour and at the same time, trying to listen to some jazz music.

For some reason, there are about five minutes when the others are not in the room or were rather absorbed in the music. The writer who is incidentally sitting by me whispers in my ear, rather conspiratorially.

"I've read your latest book and I like it very much." I probably murmur some thanks and begin to bleed inside again.

I was visiting the United States when I finished writing this same book.

So I sent a copy of the same full typescript to a friend who is a known critic and also edits a respectable campus journal of the Arts and Humanities. When I returned to the campus later in the year, he did not say a word about the manuscript. But that was all right.

What has never been all right is the following.

Legend: 1976: a mutual friend volunteers to read the printer's proofs for me. He does a first class job, he being not only a famous author himself, but also a rather meticulous individual. Later, someone asks him what he thinks of the contents. The author replies that the book is like what a designer of aeroplane would condescend to put together, if such a person was asked to design a car. When I press him for his opinion about the book, he charges me with hypocrisy, calls me some other names, and has not spoken to me since.

And all of this happens in the house of my critic-and-editor friend, who meanwhile holds his peace. Occasionally since then, he would murmur something about *Killjoy* and feminism. In passing.

I am convinced that if *Killjoy* or anything like it had been written by a man, as we say in these parts, no one would have been able to sleep a wink these couple of years. (That is from all the noise that would have been made about it).

If *Killjoy* has received recognition some place else, it is gratifying. But there is no salve for the hurt that my own house has put a freeze on it.

For surely, my friends and brothers know that the only important question is the critical reception of a book's existence, not necessarily approbation. When a critic refuses to talk about your work, that is violence. He is willing you to die—as a creative person.

And when someone whom you consider a friend refuses to talk to you because of a book you've written, then he is trying to drive you insane with speculation. For

1) is he angry with you for daring to write that book? Or

2) is he ashamed of you because you wrote that book? Or

3) is he jealous because he wishes he had written that book?

This was not meant to be a catalogue of slights suffered and bitterly stored over the years. Nothing in my background had prepared me for them, and until I actually sat down to do this paper, I was not aware that when the need arose, I would find so much evidence to prove a point.

An inquiry of this nature runs the risk of getting charged with pettiness. Yet petty or not, it is also legitimate. The ancients have said that if you assume indifference at a meat sharing, you end up

with bones.... No matter that the hooks that dragged away our attention came coated with sugar and sprayed over with honey.[10]
It is uncomfortable. This fairly new feeling of being under pressure to talk about oneself ....[11] But it is there, the product of a curiosity in others. To know about the freak that is you, and of your own need to declare your existence... or your right to exist. To be. But before anyone begins to feel that this individual is just making weather of absolutely nothing, I'd like to quote Gloria Wade-Gayles, a black American woman writer whose poem, "Sometimes As Women Only," has become for me the definitive statement on the pain, the frustrations and almost despair exclusive to being an African (or black), a woman, and a writer:

We know the hard heavy pull of
weights riveted to our dreams
and yet
sometimes as women only
do we gasp in narrow spaces
and remain locked behind walls
too rough for etchings from our soul.
We are now queens of ebony
celebrating ourselves in
diadems of natural beauty
feeling the swing of large gold hoops
around our tight-skinned smoothness
walking a regal dance and singing the music
of a clear struggle that names us well.

But
as women
are sometimes marked beyond adornment
for we have seen white lines run
east west north south cracking on our flesh
like earthquakes that no longer tremor
and we have felt the pressure of rigid staves
peaking breasts grown limp from the pull
of hungry mouths we alone can feed
we
are
fragile figurines
whose neurosis comes and goes
with the pull of the moon

black sturdy shoulders
we are monuments that refuse to crumble
deep-rooted oaks from which the generations
like thick-leaved branches grow and thrive
we are the strong ones
having balanced the weight of the tribe
having made our planting as deep as any man's
and yet
as women
we have known only meager harvests
we sing strong songs
and the world hums a sweet lullaby
we write rich poems
and the world offers muted applause
for a jingling rhyme ...

Sometimes as women only
do we weep
we are taught to whisper
when we wish to scream
assent
when we wish to deftly
dance pretty
                    (On tiptoe)
when we would raise circles of dust
before the charge.

According to Femi Ojo-Ade, "African literature is a male-created, male-oriented chauvinistic art. The male writer, like the male social animal, is more fortunate than the female. His presence is taken for granted. The publisher seeks him out. Unlike the woman whose silence is also taken for granted."[12] Ojo-Ade is a man. A university teacher. And I suspect he is making us uncomfortable with his clarity, especially his honesty.

But I could assure him that the real horror is not in the feeling of not belonging. Of being excluded. Of not counting. For that you grow up with being female. As a woman writer, you learn solidly to accept that no critic automatically remembers that you are around. If you come in, you come in as an after-thought. Your name an echo from a discussion held some other place. At some forgotten time.

Some times, there is a measure of popularity. But full of cold comfort. When you realize that your general reader, student or even mature critic expects you, the woman writer, to provide them with more male heroes and anti-heroes: Okonkwo, Baako Onipa, The Man, The Boy, The Old Man ... Jero.

How come you write about women, meaning, how come your main characters are female?

And yet, they know that there are men where your tales come from. They live. But of course, they do not occupy center stage.

Indeed as there are women where Achebe's tales come from. But they do not occupy center-stage either, women who exist in perfect accord with tradition, for the he-males to bully, snob and terrorize. Okonkwo feels out of sorts at the approach of a festival. So naturally he takes his wife and gives her "a sound beating" while his other women hover around, whimpering, "Okonkwo, it's enough ... Okonkwo, it's enough."[13] Very traditional. Very realistic.

Women people the world of Soyinka. Nimble-footed, wicked-witted women whose rules are only to serve men:

Sadiku pathetically dancing to the fictional loss of her male's manhood after a lifetime's slavery;[14]

Amope, whose vitality is employed solely in demonstrating what a fraud the great Jero is;[15]

And Sidi. Our lovely, tragic Sidi. A sunbeam created and condemned between chaos and hell. Sidi thinks she is too smart for the clown that is Lakunle? Well baby, there just ain't no other dudes around, but th' dirty ole feudal bully they call Baroka ...[16]

And you wait to rage, rage.

And who says Soyinka is the only one who creates great women to service men, or worse just to frustrate?

Armah is the expert here. Oyo is a whiner, unreasonable, plain unreasonable. Her mother is a greedy ageing bitch and Estella, your perfumed indolent whore.[17] But it's the fate of Araba Jesiwa which sends you stark raving mad.

She is a wonderful human being. Introspective, philosophical, articulate. But all that was in the past. Learned through flashbacks for the unfolding of the main story. Armah wilfully puts her out of circulation. "...supine... her limbs gave an impression of heaviness. Each hand was covered tightly in a massive clay cast wrapped round with thick cloth. Each leg was similarly sheated only the leg casts were heavier...!"[18] Preposterous, no? Maybe we are being unfair. But some of us suspect that encasing her so ridiculously was the only way the author could make sure she would not steal the limelight from Densu, the good man who is the hero. Therefore,

Jesiwa is kept down until the very end of the story, when she is released and produced, a veritable *deus ex machina* to come and set our hero free.

And still, they query why a woman writer would want to create women characters whose lives are valid, however tragic, on their own terms? Women must not be main characters.

Whom am I to write about? Man? But why? Do you ask your male writers why they write about men? It should be natural for a man to probe, to mourn, to celebrate the human male. He is a male. In the image of himself in a mirror he meets man every morning. More often than he meets women. And that should go for women writers.

I have been suffering an on-going shock. Confronting the notion that people—including some highly respectable academics—consider me a feminist simply because I write about women. Or rather, I shall insist—my major characters are generally female.

I shall not protest if you call me a feminist. But I am not a feminist because I write about women. Are men writers male chauvinists just because they write about men? Or is a writer an African nationalist just by writing about Africans? Or is a revolutionary such for writing about poor oppressed humanity? Obviously not.

We are being forced to state the obvious. And that is very sad.

Unless indeed, as one suspects, women are not supposed to be proper subjects for tragedy or a celebration.

In fact, some male writers have thought so, and dared, at safer times, to express it.

Says John Donne, the great English metaphysical poet:

> It is agreed that we have not so much from them [women] as any part of either our mortal souls [or]sense of growth...[19]

Otherwise, no writer, female or male, is a feminist just by writing about women. Unless a particular writer commits his or her energies, actively, to exposing the sexist tragedy of women's history; protesting the on-going degradation of women; celebrating their physical and intellectual capabilities; and above all, unfolding a revolutionary vision of the role of women tomorrow, as dreamers, thinkers and doers; they cannot be described as feminist writers.

In the meantime, women are half of humanity. Our lives too are simple songs that can be sung simply and ordinary tales that can be told, ordinarily.

Life for the African woman writer is definitely "no crystal stair." it is a most peculiar predicament. But we also share all, or nearly all, the problems of male African writers.

We have to cope with chaotic personal lives that drain us of energy and abolish precious creative time.

We are also part of an articulate minority that handles the language of power. Therefore we are expected and expect ourselves to articulate even subjects we would rather not hold opinions on. We expect ourselves to act powerful.

There are the inevitable flirtations with bourgeois politics or for some of us our inability to keep from leadership positions in revolutionary struggles: Amilcar Cabral, Dennis Brutus, Flora Nwapa, Kofi Awoonor. And sometimes we lose more than writing time: Christopher Okigbo, Deolinda Rodriques Francisco de Almeida.... We have entered the 1980s still burdened with foreign versions of the principal instruments of our profession. Language. And there dosen't seem to be an easy solution to it in sight. Unless like Ignazio Silone's peasants of Fontamara, we learn to accept that since we must speak, any language will do.

Then even after all these, there are still the horrible dilemmas of publishing. If you are a Ghanaian now, you still have not got local publishing avenues on the one hand. And on the other, in response to the general collapse of your country's economy, foreign publishing houses are now treating you like a poor relation of the writing world....

The list of problems is endless. And we women don't miss out on any of them. We have the same ridiculous sense of responsibility and frustration.

What is clear though, is that right now, over and above all the others we share with our brothers, we suffer those aspects of being—yes—an oppressed section of society: If not always, sometimes, as women only.

Calabar, 19 March 1981

NOTES

(The first part of this paper forms the general introduction to a paper first presented to a seminar on *Creative Women in Changing Societies* organized by UNITAR in Oslo, 9-13 July 1980).

1. At definite traditional landmarks in a woman's life cycle, she was regarded literally as untouchable. The scope and frequency of the restrictions depended on such factors as the family's mode of ancestral worship and the propinquity of the women's domicile to private and public shrines. These landmarks included the first menstruation and (for some) all other menstruations; all of the postpartum 40 days for the first born and subsequent births; a whole year of widowhood (compare 40 days at most for a widower), and dying pregnant; in which latter case it was the corpse of the woman that was exposed to humiliation!

2. It was from my father I first heard of the rather famous quotation from Dr. Kwegyir Aggrey: "If you educate a woman, you educate a nation."

3. Sure, we are looking for an African version of the bluestocking!!!

4. Obviously, my colleague had never heard of all-female battalions in the armies of the kings of Dahomey; of the Anglo-Saxon, Boadecia; of the Asantewas of the Ashantis; of Joan of Arc of France; of Rosa Luxemburg or Fanny Lou Hamer; of Deolinda Rodriques Francisco de Almeida.... But if this colleague had not always struck me as a gentle type of human being, this remark alone would have automatically betrayed him as a secret wife-basher!

5. The existence and ever-increasing popularity of a magazine like *Ms* proves that even in the highly technologically advanced societies of the world, women have not had it easy.

6. Except for a few rather exceptional individuals, any male that is close to any high-achieving female betrays some jealousy at some time or other. A most sad and outstanding example was the rather vulgar ridiculing of Shirley Chisolm by the male black community when she tried in 1972 to run for the Presidency of the U.S.

7. See "LSNA Statement to our Detractors," *The Legon Observer*, 14th July, 1972. Re-reading the relevant papers on the controversy, for the purpose of this reference, I am appalled by the vulgarity and venom with which they met an ordinary intellectual challenge.

8. *Our Sister Killjoy: Or Reflections From a Black-Eyed Squint.*

9. Any heterosexual would tell you that, at least during courtship.

10. And let's face it. If you are a writer and you are any good at all, then the lives of the characters you create must inevitably be more and more interesting and more exciting than your own. So why bore people with stories about yourself?

11. Roseann P. Bell, Betty J. Parker and Beverley Guy-Sheftall. Eds. *Sturdy Black Bridges.*

12. Femi Ojo-Ade, "Female Writers, Male Critics: Criticism, Chauvinism, Cynicism ... and Commitment" (unpublished).

13. Chinua Achebe, *Things Fall Apart*, 27.

14. Wole Soyinka, *The Lion and the Jewel.*

15. Wole Soyinka, *Brother Jero.*
16. Wole Soyinka, *The Lion and the Jewel.*
17. Ayi Kwei Armah, *The Beautyful Ones are not Yet Born.*
18. Ayi Kwei Armah, *The Healers*, 38.
19. *Problem IV: Paradoxes and Problems*, 914.

WORKS CITED

Achebe, Chinua. *Things Fall Apart.* London: Heinemann, 1976. 1992.

Aidoo, Ama Ata. *Our Sister Killjoy: Or Reflections From a Black-Eyed Squint,* Harlow, U.K.: Longman, 1977.

---. "Ghana: To Be a Woman." In: *Creative Women in Changing Societies.* Conference proceedings of UNITAR Seminar. Oslo, Norway: July 9-13 (1980).

Armah, Ayi Kwei. *The Beautyful Ones are not Yet Born.* Portsmouth, N.H.: Heinemann, 1968.

---. *The Healers.* London: Heinemann, 1979.

Bell, Roseann P, Betty J. Parker and Beverley Guy-Sheftall. Eds. *Sturdy Black Bridges.* New York: Anchor Press, 1979.

Donne, John. *Problem IV: Paradoxes and Problems.* New York: Norton, 1968.

Ojo-Ade, Femi. "Female Writers, Male Critics: Criticism, Chauvinism, Cynicism ... and Commitment" (unpublished).

Wole Soyinka, *The Lion and the Jewel.* London/New York: Oxford Univ. Press, 1973.

---. *Brother Jero.* London: Eyre Metheun, 1984.

Part Two

THE CHALLENGE
OF HISTORY

Slavery in the Diaspora Consciousness: Ama Ata Aidoo's Conversations

Angeletta KM Gourdine

What is Africa to me:
Copper sun, or scarlet sea,
Jungle star or jungle track,
Strong bronzed men or regal black
Women from whose loins I sprang
When the birds of Eden sang?
One three centuries removed
From the scenes his fathers loved,
Spicy grove, cinnamon tree,
What is Africa to me?

- Countee Cullen, "Heritage"

The epigraph above from Countee Cullen's poem "Heritage" poses a critical question, which can easily serve as the point of departure for contemporary African diaspora studies in the United States. While I do not intend to make that argument here, noting its viability contextualizes my selection of this verse to introduce a discussion of Ama Ata Aidoo and her dramatic contributions to conversations about the diaspora as well as how her contributions help us to define and awaken a diaspora consciousness. In constructing my idea of a diaspora consciousness, I refer to Vévé Clark's argument that the New Negro, Indigenist, and Négritude movements in the 1920s and 1930s United States, Caribbean, and Africa, respectively, "invented a construct, the African diaspora, referring to the phenomenon and history of African American [sic!] displacement in the New World" (Clark 1991:41).

Clark outlines what she terms diaspora literacy, referring to readers' knowledge of African, African American and Caribbean literatures, and this literacy includes a comprehension of the texts from an "informed, indigenous perspective," a perspective engendered by awareness of the "historical, social, cultural and political development generated by lived and textual experiences" (42). She identifies several discursive strategies and it is her third, "reformation of form," that best sustains my discussion of Aidoo. This principle is a "reduplicative posture which assumes and revises Du Bois' double consciousness" (42). It seems clear to me that this process of revision is deliberate and directed towards not simply exploring the diaspora, but creating a space for negotiation of the historical, social, cultural and political consequences of diaspora membership. Thus, an engaged identity consciousness is constructed, one which revolves around a diaspora politic. Hence, this essay's primary assertion is that, through a revision of Du Boisian "double consciousness" and Nkrumahan pan-Africanism, Aidoo constructs a diasporically conscious voice, which vocalizes her commitment to not only Clark's notion of diaspora literacy, but also a diaspora politic.

From as early as the 1880 census, when "Negroes" was used to replace "Coloreds" as an identity marker, to the questions surrounding why the NAACP was not the NAANP or even the NAAAP (National Association of African People), black people in America have attempted to reconcile and articulate their historical and cultural past in concert with their geographical present. Cullen's poem epitomizes, in one line, this struggle for cultural identity and cultural positionality as the black American speaker attempts to negotiate identity in relation to Africa as cultural mooring place, their socio-cultural, historical past. Furthermore, the italicized refrain stresses this disconnected connectedness, a struggle for a consciousness of place. The speaker accepts that there is an ancestral connection, patri- and matrilineal, but ponders how that connection should be continued, reestablished, represented, if you will, in the present, and maintained.

The selection from Cullen's poem makes literarily manifest Du Bois' "double consciousness." Cullen asks, in the first line of the poem, "What is Africa to me?" The "me" in this context is the Negro, black American, now African American. Cullen's poem captures the sentiment of approximately 150 years of black American psychological and cultural struggle. As such, a cursory examination of the thinking of W. E. B. Du Bois, the acknowledged "father of Pan-Africanism," is useful.[1]

Du Bois argued prophetically that the difficulty of the twentieth century would be "the problem of the color line" (Du Bois 1989: 13). For him, color was race, or at least indicative of it. Color was the visible marker, and the color line was a racial boundary, the perimeter and/or parameter of racial differences. Having established the color line, the frame of racial division, Du Bois predicted that racial strife and struggle would be the crucible of the future. In 1897, Du Bois submitted that "the history of the world is the history, not of individuals, but of groups, not of nations, but of races" (Du Bois 1971a:21). He further added that anyone "who ignores or seeks to override the race idea in human history ignores and overrides the central thought of all human history" (21). Races afforded Du Bois a tangible way to talk about historical evolution. For Du Bois, race "is a vast family of human beings" defined, in part, by "purely physical characteristics" (21;20). While the significance of his claims have been critically proven in terms of large racial relations, how he prophesies the internal African identity struggle is uncanny. In these ideas surrounding the idea of race as family, we get the beginning of a diaspora consciousness, and a need for a definition of same, and an exploration of its manifestations. Clearly, Du Bois was forging a belief in race as superseding geographical and/or national boundaries, and suggesting cultural ones, a racial/cultural family.

Du Bois' articulated belief in a race family is a grounding for discussions of the diaspora, of blackness. Du Bois argued that each race was "striving, each in their own way, to develop for civilization its particular message, its particular ideal," the

> English nation stood for constitutional liberty and commercial freedom; the German nation stood for science and philosophy; the romance nations stood for literature and art. (24).

Here, he attempts to "mobilize the advance guard of the Negro people" into developing and perpetuating the message of the race, the family ideal. One means of demonstrating what we stand for is the development of cultural traditions. Hence, the constructs of "race" as family, "race" as nation, require not only a biological and sociological explanation for racial divisions, but also a cultural and historical one. This call to arms, as it were, reflects a later plea by Nkrumah to Africanists [see below], but while Nkrumah's focus was consigned to the continental family, Du Bois' was delegated to the "race" family, a wider net, a broader agenda.

Most clearly, Aidoo's work intersects with perhaps the most known portion of Du Bois' almost century of work and commitment to "the autobiography of a race concept." Du Bois articulates this principle in his definition of the Negro:

> [T]he Negro is a sort of seventh son, born with a veil, and gifted with a second sight in this American world . . . . It is a peculiar sensation, this double consciousness . . . . One ever feels his twoness, — an American, a Negro; two souls, two thoughts, two unreconciled strivings; two warring ideals in one dark body, whose dogged strength alone keeps it from being torn asunder.

(Du Bois 1989:5)

Du Bois' description of the Negro as two beings begs the question of what the two are—American and what else. I believe that to define this double consciousness as "American *and* Negro" is necessarily to implicate Africa, implicate *an* Other space, for the roots of the Negro in America are the consequences of routes out of Africa, this merging of roots and routes that makes an African an American.[2] The development of a diaspora consciousness, then, requires that the black American and the African separately, but in relation to each other:

> merge [their] double self into a better and truer self. In this merging [they wish] neither of the older selves to be lost. (5)

In other words, the Negro should not strive toward Africa more than toward America. The Negro's space is equally both. The Negro should strive to be African [and] American, a recognition of duality and a confirmation of cultural routes and roots. Moreover, the African should struggle to reclaim their affiliation with the new Negro members of their race family and understand the interconnectedness of their conditions and struggles. Such conflated identity seeks to not only define but also connect peoples across time and space. This merging of the cultural past with the geographical, political, cultural and social present, Africa with America, and the idea of a "double consciousness" accounts for the historical origin and present day location of Africans in the Americas and Europe, speaks the silence and slowly fills the historical void.

Aidoo engages this syncretism in her first play *Dilemma of a Ghost*, which deals with the problematic marriage between a Ghanaian been-to, Ato Yawson, and Eulalie Rush. While studying in the United States, Ato meets and falls in love with Eulalie, a black American student. They marry and subsequently return to his village. The obvious dilemma to which the play's title refers is Ato's inability to reconcile his American education and its ideas and values with the values and expectations of his family (Berrian 1987: 156). However, on another level, the dilemma of the play can be defined as the reconciling of historical dissonance. The ghost of the title is an explicit reference to a children's folk song about a ghost lingering at the crossroads between Cape Coast and Elmina, pondering to which city it should travel. Unable to decide, it simply repeats, "I don't know, I can't tell" (Aidoo 1965: 23). This ghost returns to Ato in a dream, from which he awakens exclaiming "Damn this ghost at the junction . . . I used to wonder what the ghost was doing there. . . . But why should I dream about all these things now?" (24) The ghost has been read as reminiscent of Ato's own dilemma, balancing his Western acquired ideas with the traditional expectations he meets when he returns to Ghana. In other words, it is the dilemma of the been-to (Wilentz 1992: 45). The ghost clearly revisits Ato because he has invoked the ghost of hidden history, personified in the person of Eulalie, an African American woman. In fact, Cape Coast and Elmina were very active ports before and during the Atlantic slave trade (Busia 1987:35; Odamtten 1994: 44).

In this respect, the ghost in the play's title refers to the haunting and silent history of African involvement in the slave trade. The ghost read this way initiates a conversation which hopefully can expose the lack of information and understanding that Africans and African Americans have of one another. Ato can serve as a potential bridge spanning the Middle Passage, for he is the only character who has made a life on both sides of the Atlantic. Unfortunately, Ato fails in this respect, because even though Eulalie "returns" to Africa, she has yet to establish her life there, a life amongst Ato and his people. As a result, the necessary dialogue across the silence and the distance is deferred.

When Ato informs his family that he has married an American, they fear that she is white. Upon hearing that Eulalie is black, but belongs to no tribe, Nana, Ato's grandmother responds, "[s]ince I was born, I have not heard of a human being born out of the womb of a woman who has no tribe. Are there trees which never have any roots?" (Aidoo 1965:11). Ato explains that Eulalie's family was amongst the Africans taken to America as slaves. Hence, Ato awakens the African dilemma of how to deal with this past, to incorporate into their historical narrative:

> Nana: My spirit mother ought to have come for me earlier. Now what shall I tell them who are gone? The daughter of slaves who came from the white man's land. Someone should advise me on how to tell my story. (14)

Because Nana serves as the link between her living relatives and their ancestors who have passed on, it is her responsibility to narrate her family's history to account for their actions. Eulalie's presence complicates her narration because to include Eulalie in the story she must speak, or write, what has yet to be acknowledged. Like Beloved's story (Morrison 1988:193), this was not one to be passed on. However, Ato has forced Africa to confront this past, or at least include it in the telling of its present.

While Ato's family initially rejects Eulalie, Aidoo does not cast Eulalie as totally responsible for the bad communication and poor relations she has with her in-laws. Ato as well must bear that responsibility for not having "dealt well with" his family and his wife. Ato had not clearly explained to Eulalie what would be expected of her in Ghana as his wife and a member of his tribe. In part, Ato's silence is due to Africans' failure to acknowledge their historical implication in the slave trade, which bore upon Eulalie's predicament. Secondly, Eulalie's conflicting emotions toward Africa represent the African American end of the dilemma. Her expectations are akin to those described by Alex Haley in *Roots*. She tells Ato that she will relax among the "palm trees, the azure sea, the sun and golden beaches" (Aidoo 1965:36). She describes Africa in terms of storybook myths, and, as Ato tells her, "a tourist brochure" (36). More directly, she speaks to her dead mother's spirit and tells her, "I've come to the very source. I've come to Africa and I hope that where'er you are, you sort of know and approve"

(19). Eulalie has married Ato with as much information about Africa as Ato has of African Americans. Importantly, Eulalie attempts not only to address her double consciousness but to reconcile the two parts of herself. Instead of existing as a "native stranger" in Ato's land, Eulalie yearns to be simply native, to annihilate her strangeness; for once she is going to be at home.

Eulalie's vision of Africa epitomizes a double consciousness: she recognizes that part of her is linked to Africa as geographical and cultural space, yet her knowledge is encoded in an Other discourse. Much like the speaker in Cullen's "Heritage" identifies Africa with exotic scenes of a "copper sun, or scarlet sea" and "spicy grove, cinnamon tree," Eulalie's idyllic Eden constructs an exotic African text. Though Eulalie's desire had been to find peace and harmony in her new marriage, in her new home with her new family, her ignorance of Africa and Ghana's lived reality brings only chaos. However, having brought Eulalie to Africa, Ato perpetuates her ignorance by not providing her with adequate information; he has not taken the time to educate his new wife to his family's ways. For instance, Eulalie agrees with Ato's proposition that they should not have children. Ato tells her that he would be jealous of the children taking up so much time, and furthermore, that they "shall be free to love each other.... and that is all [Eulalie] should understand about Africa" (37). However, the tradition amongst Ato's people is clearly that marriage is not a two person affair, but involves families.

Hence, Nana confronts Ato with his and Eulalie's secrecy surrounding the issue of having children, over her desire to become a great-grandmother. Ato refuses to admit that they are using birth control, but instead, leaves Eulalie to explain and bear the responsibility as well as the scorn. Eulalie's reaction is to pose the question, "Ato, who married me, you or your goddamn people?" (87). The climax of the play comes when Eulalie and Ato battle over their crumbling marriage and his failure to communicate to her what his people expected of her as a wife. Eulalie accuses Ato's people of only understanding "their own savage customs and standards," to which Ato responds, "Shut up! How much does the American Negro know?" (87) Eulalie storms out, and Ato goes to his mother to complain about Eulalie's insult:

> Ato: She said that my people have no understanding, that they are uncivilized.

> Esi: Is that it? My child, and why should your wife
> say this about us?

> Ato: I don't know. (90)

Esi scolds Ato for he "never seems to know anything" in spite of all that they have sacrificed for his schooling. Ato attempts to explain, retorting "in these days of civilization," but Esi Kom interrupts him and admonishes him:

> Esi: In these days of civilization, what? Now I know
> that you have been teaching your wife to insult us.
> No stranger ever breaks the law... my son. You have
> not dealt well with your wife in this. (90-91)

At this point, Eulalie enters, stumbling, and Esi Kom embraces her reminding Ato that "[her] mother is dead [and] if she had any tenderness, [h]er ghost must be keeping watch over [a]ll that happens to her" (92). Because Eulalie has married a family instead of an individual, she is saved. However, dilemma tales very seldom end with an instructional moral and when they do the moral is often so "divisive and open-ended" that further discussion is always necessary (Abrahams 1983:17).

This tale ends with Ato alone and the ghost repeating, "I don't know. I can't tell." Though Esi Kom embraces Eulalie and says "Come my child," it is not clear that her embrace is one of acceptance as some critics have claimed (Berrian 1987:158; Wilentz 1992: 56). I believe the embrace signifies an embrace of the responsibility to tackle the issue, to discuss the silent history. The readings thus far have indicated that what Ato does not know and thus cannot tell is which way he should go. However, I submit that Ato lacks a diaspora consciousness. He does not know how to reconcile himself with his family and his wife, how to fashion their relationship. He lacks historical, cultural and social text and thus he cannot make pragmatic choices and informed decisions to govern his lived experience. Aidoo's voice here (250) echoes another verse from Cullen's "Heritage" when the speaker refers to "Africa? A book one thumbs/ Listlessly till slumber comes."

This reference to textual reality recalls for us several textual histories, one which I argue Aidoo creates with her literature, but also an already existing one in need of revisioning and revisiting. Specifically, Aidoo provides us a way to examine how the syncretic process of diasporization evidences itself in literary production and consumption. One such veiled appearance is as a "cultural presence" (Holloway 1992:12). Karla Holloway reminds us that cultural identity "operates in fictive places in [black texts]; in the imaginative realms, [ethnicity] becomes the ultimate signifier as it plays within the imaginative domains of fictional language" (12).[3] It is precisely because this blackness permeates the "fictive places," "imaginative realms" and "imaginative domains" of Ama Ata Aidoo's fiction and plays that I find her work most helpful as we attempt to understand the manifestations of diaspora consciousness in black women's literature, texts which examine the relationships between members of Du Bois' race family.

Even more compelling, Aidoo manages, through her fictive constructs to draw our attention to historical lived spaces as well, and I am sure that it is of great historical and literary consequence that Aidoo launches these inquiries from Ghana. Ghana, the first black African nation to gain independence from colonialism was also the home of Kwame Nkrumah, its first national president. Setting aside other political debates surrounding Nkrumah's leadership, he is noted for his treatises on and commitment to pan-Africanism. What is most interesting in this context, though, is how Nkrumah expressed his pan-Africanist vision, his firm belief that "the independence of Ghana [was] meaningless unless it [was] linked with the total liberation of the African continent" (Nkrumah 1968:10).

Nkrumah clearly indicates that his ideas about pan-Africanism were guided and informed by the "work of the early pioneers of pan-Africanism such as H. Sylvester William, Dr. W. E. B. Du Bois, Marcus Garvey, and George Padmore, none of whom were born in Africa [but their work has] become a treasured part of Africa's history" (5). Nkrumah forged a platform which aligned historical, intellectual, and political struggles. He notes that part of moving Africa toward a productive and independent future requires a "recovery and reawakening" of its past. In his address to the First International Congress of Africans, Nkrumah charges that those gathered:

> [must be] determined to pool [their] immense knowledge of Africa for the progress of Africans. [Their] efforts mark a renascence of scientific curiosity in the study of Africa and should be directed at an objective, impartial scrutiny and assessment of things African. While some of [them were]

engaged with political unification of Africa, Africans everywhere must also help in building the spiritual and cultural foundations for the Unity of [the] continent. (Nkrumah 1962:5)

Hence the dilemma for the African becomes a reclaiming of historical and cultural space, a "regeneration of Africa" (11). Although Africans are not a "homogeneous race, [they] possess a common fundamental sentiment which is everywhere manifest, crystallizing itself into one common controlling idea" (10)—Pan-Africanism: "the spectre of black power."[4] Though Nkrumah's counsel with black American intellectuals is very well-known and acknowledged, his direct focus for Pan-Africanism was continental, with ramifications and implications for the diaspora. Nonetheless, it seems fair to suggest that his dilemma was how to unite and liberate Africa, a vast project indeed, while simultaneously directing that unified attention to related liberatory struggles elsewhere.

Aidoo's literature clearly manifests Nkrumah's position and his ideological quandary. In *Anowa*, her second play, Aidoo briefly tells the tale of the slave trade and the dissemination of Africans across the globe. In *Dilemma of a Ghost*, we see a child returning. Aidoo returns as well to imagine and create Eulalie's history. And as Odamtten suggests, this movement back defines her second play, *Anowa,* as the reconstruction of a past from which the life narratives of *Dilemma of a Ghost* evolves. *Anowa* in itself is dialogic, its voices speak to the various intricacies involved in the institution of slavery. As well, it provides us with an insight into why Africans sold their brothers and sisters to the whites.

Anowa is set in the late nineteenth century, approximately 1870, and with such historical contextualization Aidoo opens the Pandora's box, which contains the history of slavery both within and without Africa. The play focuses on Anowa, a beautiful woman who rejects societal authority and expectation in order to marry a man she has chosen, Kofi Ako. They gain wealth in trading, but soon Kofi expands their trading to include human cargo: "[Kofi] is buying men and women as though they were only worth each a handful of sand on the shore" (Aidoo 1970:39). Anowa refuses any of the benefits from her husband's business in stocking and selling slaves, for she finds it an immoral as well as inhumane enterprise. For Anowa, there was "something unwholesome about making slaves of men" (39).

While Odamtten makes a convincing argument that *Anowa* is

historically contextualized within "a specific piece of Ghana's colonial past," and chooses the backdrop of rising British colonialism in Fantiland as the point of departure for his discussion, one cannot deny the African participation in the Atlantic slave trade which the play invokes. In this vein, we have Anowa recounting to the reader a story told to her by her grandmother, Nana, wherein the "truth" is revealed as to how "the pale men" came to own Africans.

Nana tells of her travels to lands far and away from Africa, a land across a "sea that is bigger than any river and boils without being hot" (44). In these new lands she sees "houses whose foundations are wider than the biggest roads" in Africa (44). These houses were built large, she tells Anowa, to house the slaves—"[those] who are bought and sold" (45). Anowa questions Nana, and their exchange highlights several key facets of my argument:

Where did the white men get slaves?
I asked.
You frighten me child.
You must be a witch, child.
They got them from the land.
Did the men of the land sell other men of the land,
and women and children to pale men from beyond
the horizon who looked like you or me peeled, like
lobsters boiled or roasted?

I don't know, child.
You are frightening me, child.
I was not there!
It is too long ago!
No one talks of these things anymore.
All good men and women try to forget;
They have forgotten! (46)

Anowa reclaims those who have been "forgotten," those dispersed Africans and names them her own. She becomes mother [Africa] and the mo[u]ther of unspeakable things. Just as she is named witch—one with a power to haunt, one associating with a haunting visionary power—she awakens the ghosts from the past, gives voice to the silenced cries of those whose bodies were torn asunder and now lie under the waters of the middle passage. When Anowa goes to sleep that night she dreams that she, like Africa, gave birth to the men and women who were captured into slavery:

I dreamt that I was a big, big woman. And from my insides were huge holes out of which poured men, women and children. And the sea was boiling hot and steaming. And as it boiled, it threw many, many giant lobsters, boiled lobsters, each of whom as it fell turned into a man or woman, but keeping its lobster head and claws. And they rushed to where I sat and seized the men and women as they poured out of me, and they tore them apart, and dashed them to the ground and stamped upon them. (46)

Odamtten, in his attempt to restrict our reading of Anowa/*Anowa* to a localized context, further testifies to the power of Aidoo's diaspora consciousness. The tale of Anowa, Aidoo says, "grew directly out of a story" her mother told her, but "as the play has come out, [her mother] cannot even recognize the story" (James 1990:19). This typifies the reduplicative and reconstructionist craft of a conscious diaspora storyteller. Anowa evolves from a local narrative and constitutes in that space a very compelling myth, articulating a metaphor which defines a wide range of social roles. Yet, the replicated tale touches upon issues of a more globally black nature, those of cultural and historical destruction and rebirth. The play identifies destruction with Kofi's maleness, but it also crystallizes how destructive forces in the hands of women can be reconstituted as creative, regenerative. Anowa's witchery identifies her as a revolutionary, a source of transformational female power.[5] Most directly, she identifies her politics as diasporan cultural critic and its concomitant struggle toward diasporan consciousness raising.

While this attention to excavating an African past, an investigation of diasporan textual realities, has been a recurrent theme for black American writers, in the main, African writers have not shown as much concentrated interest in exploring this historical connection. Besides Syl Cheney Coker's 1991 *Last Harmattan of Alusine Dunbar*, a notable exception to this pattern of indifference is Ama Ata Aidoo.[6] In her crafting of African women and in discussions of their status in Africa, she has found it useful to investigate how Africans in the diaspora fit into her analysis of the African woman's condition and the inextricable connection between this condition and the whole condition of Africa, evidencing her diaspora consciousness. Aidoo defines her literary commitment as an extension of her social vision:

[her] commitment as an African, the need for [her]

to be an African nationalist, to be a little more pressing. It seems that there are things relating to our
world, as African people, which are of a more throbbing nature in an immediate sense. (James 1990:15)

And a significant aspect of this commitment, one "throbbing" issue
to which she has devoted attention is to the silence of history
regarding why and how Africans came to be displaced and dispersed across the globe. She resolves that this void must be overcome if Africa is to come to terms with its past and move toward
the future. Aidoo recalls that "go[ing] to places where there are concentrations of other black peoples" aided her resolution to "face
the question," in her literature and by other means available to her,
to explain just why "so many [African peoples] are in Harlem and
so many in the West Indies" (Vincent 1981:35). Consequently, in
all of her fiction and plays there are allusions to the diasporic relationship, particularly as it relates to Africans and African
Americans, and her characters encourage a collective conscious
conversation.

Drama works well for Aidoo as she attempts to investigate this
multi-spaced history and literary tradition. It allows her to present
the issues through a heteroglossia, which is also perplexing.
Relatedly, most of Aidoo's work can be characterized as resembling
dilemma tales, a narrative which "throw[s] the floor open to debate,
demonstrating yet again that in the African context the function
of storytelling is to initiate" (Abrahams 1983:16-17). A poignant
recurrent dilemma is that invoked by the legacy of Du Boisian "double consciousness"; Nkrumahan pan-Africanism; the question of
"Heritage," and its shadow; contemporary Africentricism, that is
critical, analytical and historical focus on what and who are these
black people all over the world. More specifically, how can
Nkrumah's commitment to a unified Africa speak to Africa's own
defined concern for a pragmatic and historically conscious dialogue
on black peoples' relations to and relationships with one another?
Here, Aidoo reifies centuries of conversation amongst African
American scholars, writers and intellectuals.

Correspondingly, the history of racialized discourse in the US
offered us the idea of blackness[7] as "a cultural umbilical cord connecting [African American peoples] to Africa" (Marable 1992:295).
Here, blackness becomes the clear indication that we—in this particular case, Africans and African Americans—are of one continuous blood and cultural line, no matter how diffused. Within this

39

framework, to be black is to be African and American particularly, but also African and Caribbean, African and Brazilian or African and English. Thus, blackness has less to do with race, *per se*, than with culture; it names a collectivity and defines its cultural milieu. [B]lackness is metonymic. It at once names a larger population while representing a specific segment of that population. The objective is to organize a sociopolitical body around the tenet that first and foremost, blackness signifies "all people of African descent—the Latin, the Jamaican, the Haitian, the Brazilian, the Caribbean, and the African American" (Kouyate B8).[8] Because D'Jimo Kouyate further suggests, "although they were not born in Africa, they are still African people" (B8), this cultural syncretism has led to the development, and intellectual and creative exploration, of pragmatic consequences of this history. In Aidoo's *Dilemma of a Ghost* a child inscribed by blackness renavigates the middle passage and claims her metonymic blackness, and the history of her blackness, of her cultural (re)invention, is embodied in/by Anowa.

Aidoo also speaks to problematics engendered by diaspora textual and lived history and its consequent search for knowledge in her first novel. At the end of *Our Sister Killjoy*, just before Sissie's long letter addressing the behavior of her fellow Africans abroad, the inquiry is couched in the brief exchange between an African American student who questions a visiting African Professor about African history:

> "Sir, please tell me: is Egypt in Africa? . . . . I mean Sir, I don't mean to harass you or anything," pressed the student, "but did the Egyptians who built the pyramids, you know, the Pharaohs and all, were they African?" (Aidoo 1966:111)

The Professor responds quite exasperatedly:

> "My dear young man . . . to give you the decent answer that your anxiety demands, I would have to tell you a detailed history of the African continent. And to do that, I shall have to speak every day, twenty-four hours a day, for at least three thousand years. And I don't mean to be rude to you or anything, but who has that kind of time?" (111)

Though this only occupies about thirteen lines of the text, it serves to introduce Sissie's letter which voices her concerns over violations against Africa by non-Africans and Africans alike. In this textual moment, Aidoo recalls Nkrumah's charge to the Africanist to regenerate and make accessible Africa's historical legacies. Also, the student invokes Du Bois' idea that the Negro must reconcile his Negroness/Africanness with his Americanness, know both selves so as to merge them and become a better self. Presumably, if a successful attempt to rewrite Africa into its deserved historical role had manifested, the questions (the student's, Ato's and Anowa's) would not have been necessary. Indicatively, Sissie questions "[her] Precious Something," about why they "were never able to discuss some of [the] matters relating to their group survival" (114). Among these is the "old story" and a "painful one" about how Africans were made slaves and exploited as free labor. This violence was committed, Sissie discloses:

> with the help of the gun and some of our own relatives . . . . [and] we were made slaves because we are stronger, and can work longer hours in the sun and other such nonsenses . . . . (114)

Without a doubt this passage speaks to the forced labor of Africans during the colonial period, but the literature of Africa also informs us that though this violence is a painful story, it has not been one untold.[9] However, as evidenced by Anowa and her "dream," the role of Africans in the slave trade is an old, painful and *untold* story. The "love letter" demonstrates that Aidoo is furiously working to raise a historically and politically charged diaspora consciousness. On a corresponding note, Rachel Blau DuPleiss tells us that narratives "produce representations by which we imagine the world as it is" (DuPleiss 1985:3). For Ama Ata Aidoo, the black world as she imagines it, lived and textual, requires a space for pasts, presents and futures to face one another.

Notes

1. This essay can by no means present in totality Du Bois' views on Pan Africanism; recognizing the magnanity of that endeavor, I resign myself to selecting portions of his writing which best reflect the historical backdrop against which I place Aidoo's inquiries.

2. The semantic and homophonic relationship between routes and roots were first explored by Paul Gilroy in his "It's a Family Affair" in Gina Dent's *Black Popular Culture* (Seattle: Bay Press, 1992).

3. Though the position I take here, in terms of diaspora consciousness vis-

à-vis existing ideas of blackness, is not explicitly stated or argued by Holloway in *Moorings and Metaphors*, the implications of her discussion are such that my configuration of her analysis does not undermine the spirit of her project.

4. Note Ranu Samantrai's reading of Aidoo's *Our Sister Killjoy* as an unabashed appeal to "Africans' sense of loyalty and obligation to Africa" (Samantrai 1995:142). This reading corresponds with my suggestion here that Aidoo is influenced by Nkrumah's political legacy. However, Samantrai—like Odamtten in his readings of Aidoo's work—relegates Aidoo's politics to her native Ghana, while I infer more far-reaching implications.

5. The reference to Anowa as a witch allows for other interesting interpretations of her character. There are multiple meanings of "witch" in the context of African women's fiction; however, to go beyond what I have briefly mentioned here moves my discussion beyond its direct foci. For more discussion of Anowa as witch, see Carole Boyce Davies' 1995 chapter on Anowa; pay particular attention to pages 74-8, "Witchery and Madness and Anowa's Desertion of Self-Empowerment."

6. Though some male writers have addressed the dispersal of Africans during the slave trade, at this writing, their response has not been as focal as Aidoo's. Wole Soyinka, for example, has an African American school teacher, Joe Golder, in his *Interpreters*, and mentions Africans selling Africans during the Atlantic slave trade in *A Dance of the Forests*. There is a mention of black Americans in Ngugi wa Thiong'o's *Devil on the Cross*, and Ayi Kwei Armah explores the experiences of black Americans traveling to Africa in his *Fragments* and *Two Thousand Seasons*. In film, Sembène Ousmane's *Ceddo* (1976) discusses the slave trade and his *Camp de Thiaroye* (1987) brings an African and an African American face to face in a moment of shared history, with blues playing in the background. In a short story, "Tribal Scars or Voltaïque," Ousmane presents his version of how Africans, pushed to the wall by sheer force of circumstances, were forced to collaborate with the enemy in the slave trade. Nonetheless, compared to African American writings on the historical connections between these two peoples, African discussion is limited. See Bernth Lindfors, "The Image of the Afro-American in African Literature" and Jacob Drachler's edited collection, *Black Homeland, Black Diaspora*, for further detailed discussions.

7. Here I want to note my varying capitalizations of the word "blackness." As rules of standard English usage tell us, capitalization indicates a certain way we should read and understand written language. Hence "Blackness" indicates a reference to, discussion of, raced ideas while "blackness" refers to culturally infused notions of identity and positionality.

8. See the "Introduction" to Carole Boyce Davies' *Black Women, Writing and Identity*, wherein she discusses the United State-ness of these ideas of blackness and the specific significance in the US context.

9. See the Introduction to Ken Harrow's *Thresholds of Change* (Portsmouth, N.H.: Heinemann, 1994).

WORKS CITED

Abrahams, Roger. *African Folktales.* New York: Pantheon, 1983.

Aidoo, Ama Ata. *Anowa.* London: Longman, 1970.

——. *Dilemma of a Ghost.* London: Longman, 1965.

——. *Our Sister Killjoy: Or Reflections from a Black-Eyed Squint.* London: Longman, 1966.

Armah, Ayi Kwei. *Fragments.* New York: Collier Books, 1971.

——. *Two Thousand Seasons.* Chicago: Third World Press, 1979.

Berrian, Brenda, "The Afro-American West African Marriage Question: Its Literary and Historical Contexts." *Woman in African Literature Today.* 15, (1987).

Bond, Horace Mann. "The Relations Between American Negroes, African Students in the United States, and Africans." Paper Presented at American Negro Leadership Conference on Africa. 24-17 September 1964. Washington D.C., Moorland-Spingarn Research Center, Howard University, Washington D.C.; Dabu Gizenga Collection on Kwame Nkrumah 128-23:518.

Busia, Abena, "Words Whispered over the Voids: A Context for Black Women's Rebellious Voices in the Novel of the African Diaspora." *Black Feminist Criticism and Critical Theory.* Eds. Houston A. Baker and Joe Weixelmann Studies in Black American Literature, Vol. 3. Greenville, Fla.: Penkewill 1987. 1-41.

Clark, VèVè. "Developing Diaspora Literacy and Marasa Consciousness." *Comparative American Identities: Race, Sex and Nationality in the Modern Text.* Ed. Hortense Spillers. New York: Routledge, 40-61, 1991.

Cullen, Countee, "Heritage." In: *The New Negro: Voices of the Harlem Renaissance.* Ed. Alain Locke. New York: 1925. Rpt. New York: Macmillan, 1992. 250-253.

Davies, Carole Boyce, *Black Women, Writing and Identity: Migrations of the Subject.* New York: Routledge, 1995.

Dent, Gina. *Black Popular Culture.* Seattle: Bay Press, 1992.

Drachler, Jacob. *Black Homeland/Black Diaspora,* Port Washington, N.Y.: National Univ. Press, 1975.

Du Bois, W. E. B., "The Conservation of the Races." *W. E .B. Du Bois: A Reader.* Ed. Andrew Paschal. New York: MacMillan, 19-30, 1971a.

—. "Pan-Africanism: A Mission in my Life." *W. E. B. Du Bois: A Reader.* Ed. Andrew Paschal, New York: MacMillan, 241-52, 1971b.

—. *The Souls of Black Folk.* New York: A. C. McClurg. 1903. Rpt. New York: Viking, 1989 (1903).

Du Plessis, Rachel Blau. *Writing Beyond the Ending: Narrative Strategies of Twentieth Century Women Writers.* Bloomington: Indiana University Press, 1985.

Gilroy, Paul. "Its a Family Affair." In: *Black Popular Culture* Ed. Gina Dent. Seattle: Bay Press, 1992.

Holloway, Karla FC. *Moorings and Metaphors. Figures of Culture and Gender in Black Women's Literature.* New Brunswick, N.J.: Rutgers Univ. Press, 1992.

James, Adeola. *In Their Own Voices: African Women Writers Talk*. Portsmouth, N.H.: Heinemann, 1990.

Kouyate, D'Jimo. "African Holocaust." *Michigan Citizen*, Oct 2 (1989): B8.

Lindfors, Bernth. "Images of the Afro American in African Literature." *Association for Commonwealth Literature and Languages Studies Bulletin* 4,3 (1975):19-26.

Marable, Manning. "Race, Identity, and Political Culture." *Black Popular Culture*. Ed. Gina Dent. Seattle: Bay Press, 1992.

Morrison, Toni, *Beloved*. New York: Plume, 1988.

Nkrumah, Kwame. "Africa's Glorious Past." Address Delivered at Opening of First International Congress of Africanists. 12 December 1962. University of Ghana, Legon. Moorland-Spingarn Research Center, Howard University, Washington D.C. Kwame Nkrumah Papers 154-17:18.

——. *The Spectre of Black Power*. London: Panaf Moorland-Spingarn Research Center, 1968. Howard University, Washington D.C. Dabu Gizenga Collection on Kwame Nkrumah 128-5:83.

Odamtten, Vincent O. *The Art of Ama Ata Aidoo: Polylectics and Reading Against Neocolonialism*. Gainesville: Univ. of Florida Press, 1994.

Ousmane, Sembene. *Ceddo*. Santa Barbara, Calif.: *Newsreel*, 1976. Film.

——. *Camp de Thiaroye*, Santa Barbara, Calif.: Newsreel, 1988. Film.

Samantrai, Ranu. "Caught at the Confluence of History: Ama Ata Aidoo's Necessary Nationalism." *Research in African Literatures* 26,2: (1995):140-57.

Smitherman, Geneva. "What is Africa to me?: Language Ideology and African American. *American Speech. 66,3* (1991) 115-132.

Soyinka, Wole. *A Dance of the Forests*. London/New York, Oxford University Press, 1973.

——. *Interpreters*. London: Eyre Metheun, 1984.

Vincent, Theo. *Seventeen Black and African Writers on Literature and Life*. Lagos: Cross Continent Press, 1981.

Wa Thiong'o, Ngugi. *Devil on the Cross*. London. Heinemann, 1982.

Wilentz, Gay, *Binding Cultures: Black Women Writers in Africa and the Diaspora*. Bloomington: Indiana University Press, 1992.

Vincent, Theo. "Interview with Ama Ata Aidoo." In: *Seventeen Black and African Writers*. Lagos: Three Continents Press, 1981. 1-8.

AMA ATA AIDOO
AND THE AFRICAN DIASPORA:
THINGS, "ALL GOOD MEN AND WOMEN TRY TO FORGET,"
BUT I WILL NOT LET THEM

MILDRED A. HILL-LUBIN

Tell me Nana........
Did the men of the land sell other men of the land, and
women and children to pale men from beyond the horizon who
looked like you or me peeled, like lobsters boiled or roasted?
I do not know, child.
You are frightening me, child.
I was not there!
It is too long ago!
All good men and women try to forget;
They have forgotten!
What happened to those who were taken away?

Do people hear from them?
How are they?
Shut up child.
It is too late child.
Sleep well, child.
All good men and women try to forget;
They have forgotten!

-Anowa

These are the words of Anowa, the main character in the play of the same name by Ama Ata Aidoo. Taken from a memory poem embedded in the third phase of the play, the monologue recalls the childhood dialogue that Anowa and her grandmother had regarding the symbolic forts which haunt the coastline of Ghana. These "big houses" as they are called remain as reminders of what Aidoo refers to as a "bigger crime" in which the people of the land played the game of "dipping with the stranger" (Aidoo 1987:66). But as the protagonist of the play relates, according to her Grandmother, "All good men and women try to forget."

Aidoo, however, in a voice repetitive and as dominant as the forts, is determined to let neither them nor their children forget. Furthermore, as concerned as the young character in her play, Aidoo demonstrates that she as writer is equally troubled about what has happened to the men, women, and children who were taken "beyond the horizon." She not only seeks information about them, but her texts indicate that she has visited them and has been sensitive to their condition. Above all, she recognizes and acknowledges a special kinship. As she has stated in an interview with Adeola James in *In Their Own Voices*:

> I think that the whole question of how it was that
> so many people could be enslaved and sold is very
> important. I've always thought that it is an area that
> must be probed. It holds one of the keys to our
> future.... Until we have actually sorted out this
> whole question of African people, both on the con-
> tinent and in the diaspora, we may be joking, sim-
> ply going round in circles (James 1990:21).

The statement invites us to remember Paule Marshall, the Barbadian American writer who has done so much with the theme of the re-connection of African peoples with their history, their past, and with each other. Most works of Marshall's have emphasized the need of the African in exile to make the journey back through history in order to achieve wholeness.[1]

The theme of "The Return Home," with its variations of "Back to Africa," and "Roots in Africa," has been a common one among diaspora writers.[2] Most often, it has espoused the romantic notion of the lost child returning to find "home" but, as Jonathan Ngate (1986:557) argues, in many texts the return home has not always brought wholeness. Instead, for some writers' characters, particularly women, Africa has meant a "prison house."[3]

Back in 1982, I published a paper entitled "The Relationship of African-Americans and Africans: A Recurring Theme in the Works of [Ama] Ata Aidoo." It continued a search that Bernth Lindfors had described in 1975 in which he had discovered that the "Afro-American is nearly an invisible man" in the literature of Africans. I pointed out also, that only a few African writers had even mentioned anything about Africans in the diaspora;[4] Aidoo, however, holds a singular distinction—that of being a major African author who has made this subject of Africans and/in the diaspora a central issue. While she modifies her position about this relationship in her writings, she continues to be the only African author who treats this subject with depth and passion. As this discussion will demonstrate, it is possible that her voice has challenged other African authors to take up "the blood stained banner."

My earlier paper focused on the treatment of this theme in *The Dilemma of a Ghost*, Aidoo's first published play and a work which (though it does not make the Afro-American "man" visible) introduces an African American female who has wed one of the "been-to" Ghanaian males who has taken his bride "home". Aidoo's development of the topic continues in *Anowa* and in the collection of the short stories, *No Sweetness Here* (especially in "Other Versions"); and it re-appears in the extended work of fiction, *Our Sister Killjoy: Or Reflections from a Black-Eyed Squint*. While acknowledging Aidoo's early treatment of the subject, what Lemuel Johnson calls "situating of black diaspora origins in a nightmare of dismembering parturition"(Johnson 1990:112), the present paper concentrates on the African diaspora theme in the collection of poetry, *Someone Talking to Sometime*, published in 1985. Aidoo's most recently published novel, entitled *Changes: A Love Story* (1991) contains little on this subject.

The collection of poetry and the play, *Anowa*, provide an overview of the threads which this author emphasizes: first, the historical involvement of Africans in the dispersal; second, the commonality in the condition, suffering, and plight of Africans every where, and, third, the recognition and use of the cross-cultural influences between Africans and their kin in the Diaspora. Linked closely to the first in which this Ghanaian chides Africans for selling off the men, women and children at an earlier period is her similar anger and contempt for those African brothers and sisters who leave the continent to study but do not return, remaining in a different type of diaspora. She labels these individuals as "the academic-pseudo-intellectual version" whom she declares is more dangerous, because, as she proclaims, "in the face of reality that is more tangible than the massive walls of the slave forts standing along our beaches, [they] still talk of universal truth, universal art, universal literature and the Gross National product" (Aidoo 1979:6). As Esi Sutherland-Addy points out, Aidoo defines herself as a committed writer whose "works represent an ongoing process of reflecting on, exploring and promoting an idea" (Sutherland-Addy 1989:52). As a traditional artist, Aidoo sees herself in the service of her community. Her role does not permit her to be only the praise singer who brings a favorable message, but also the voice who will call the wrong doings of the people to their attention with the notion that they will find a way of achieving harmony again. All of her works are quite complex; they reach out on many levels, exploring the inter-relationship of the individual and the community, the public and the private, the political and the social. She is most concerned with the interlocking nature of gender, economics, history, and race, especially as these impact on the life of the African woman.

In examining the literature of Aidoo, one notes the close similarity of the protagonists or the narrators of her works to the author. Most often, the figure is a sensitive, independent, thought-provoking, angry young woman. She appears to be extremely wise for her age and recognizes the foolishness, cruelty, harshness, injustices that humans inflict upon one another. As Kofi, the male figure in *Anowa* says about his mate, "You bare our wounds. You are too fond of looking for the common pain and the general wrong" (Aidoo 1987:99). Aidoo "bares the wounds," especially of her people. In one of the poems in *Someone Talking to Sometime*, according to the narrator, one of the brothers has said to her, "Stop shouldering the world's troubles, learn to laugh and live! Her answer: "laughing,/ That's easy:/ it's all we do instead of crying/ and since there's so much to cry about/ we laugh /and laugh and laugh. But living?"

(Aidoo 1987:61). Many of Aidoo's works ridicule the absurdity and the silly actions of humans; therefore, as readers, we are forced to laugh. The dominant tone, however, is one of anger and accusations, most often distilled through irony. Although Aidoo lashes out most vociferously, especially in the poetry, she will come back in another poem or sometimes in the same piece to acknowledge that neither she nor her narrators are exempted. The speaker always includes herself with such words or statements as in the poem "For Kinna 1": "But think, my child,/ what kinds of fools were we/" or as in "A Salute to African Universities.": "No,/ I am not cursing you/... Besides,/ we are all/ beginning to learn/ the wisdom of those we do/ not respect" (Aidoo 1985:26).

In addition, as suggested above, while this very involved author most often presents the "pains," "wounds," "absurdities" in terms of African situations, especially of her country, Ghana; they reflect "the common pain and the general wrong" because her greatest indictment is that we, humans, seem unable to learn from history. We always find a way to keep repeating our silly deeds and cruel acts; nor do we recognize that the acts and deeds reverberate. Therefore, Aidoo considers it as her responsibility to make sure all "good men and women" do not forget.

Although *Anowa* is Aidoo's second published work, it precedes the story in *Dilemma*, the first play, in terms of setting and history. Both are works about Africans and their relationship with the diaspora. *Anowa*, set in the late nineteenth century, thirty years after the Bond Treaty of 1844, combines the political and the personal and demonstrates the interconnectedness of race, gender, and economic oppressions. It reveals the complicity of Africans in the slave trade, notes the cover-up in terms of silence. As the Grandmother says that everyone has forgotten, she encourages Anowa to forget also.

The "wise" Anowa, however, re-members her childhood visit with her grandmother who had reluctantly unraveled the story of the "pale men from beyond the horizon" who had taken the men, women and children of the land away. The tale was so shocking to her as a twelve year old that even then, she had dreamed that she was "the mother" of these men, women, children who were then seized by "giant lobsters, boiled lobsters" who tore them apart, dashed them to the ground and stamped upon them"(Aidoo 1987: 106). She relates that she became ill over the dream, and at that time "the women of the house" warned her not to mention the dream again. However as she says, "any time there is a mention of a slave, I see a woman who is me and a bursting... " (107). When she hears that her husband, Kofi Ako, wants to have slaves or repeat a similar kind of crime, that of enslaving another, she is repulsed. The scene invokes two major themes of this writer, that of the dispersal of Africans to the diaspora and the notion of the repetition of history. To reinforce the first, Aidoo instructs that the spiritual, "Swing Low, Sweet Chariot" should be sung by an "unseen wearied multitude" (107) and for the second, the protagonist refuses to be a part of her husband's new movement to enslave to make himself feel important. Her response: "I shall not feel happy with slaves around... Kofi, no man made a slave of his friend and came to much himself. It is wrong. It is evil" (90).

That the husband would insist on getting slaves adds another strain to their relationship and contributes to the personal tragedies of the two main characters, but it invites the linking up of history, that is the past, present, and the future. Earlier in the "Prologue," the Old Man, one of the pair of "The-Mouth-That-Eats-Salt-And-Pepper," in his chronicle of the state of Abura, informs us of the "bigger crime/ We have inherited from the clans incorporate." He suggests that the clans had participated in a "game of dipping with the stranger"/ but he states that "Kofi was, is, and shall always be/ One of us," which suggests that Kofi is "dipping or will dip" in the present; but his explanation or remark is written as if to point out that there will be some who will continue in the future. Although the play reflects the beginning of colonialism in Ghana, it hints to, perhaps, personalities in post-independence and neo-colonial Ghana and Africa:

> If there be some among us that have found
> a common sauce-bowl
> In which they play a game of dipping
> with the stranger,
> Who shall complain?
> Out of one womb can always come a disparate breed
> (66).

Vincent Odamtten makes a similar reading of Aidoo's texts in his *The Art of Ama Ata Aidoo*. While the Old Man may seek our sympathies at the beginning of the play, as the drama unfolds, we see the results and note the irony and ask, "Shouldn't one complain?"

Someone Talking to Sometime, Aidoo's first volume of poetry, brings us into the diaspora to explore the ramifications of Africans selling other Africans. Following the publication of the book of short stories, *No Sweetness Here* (1972), in which the author includes African Americans in the United States in "Other Versions" and her first long, fictional piece, *Our Sister Killjoy: Or Reflections from a Black-Eyed Squint*(1979), in which she relates that Africans on the continent and in the diaspora suffer similar oppressions, she published the poetry collection in 1985.

Organized in two parts, Section Two of Part One of *Someone* is entitled, "New Orleans: Mid-1970s . . . some tropics are cold." Biographical references tell us that Aidoo came to the United States to study at both Harvard and Stanford.[5] In addition, she also participated as a visiting writer/professor to many of the predominantly Black colleges as part of the Phelps-Stokes program, which encouraged exchanges among African and Black colleges.[6]

The poems in the heart of *Someone* confirm that Aidoo has had a personal visit or visits in the diaspora, particularly the cities of New Orleans and Boston in the United States. The narrator of the poems indicates that she is an African sister who has a reunion with many of her kin. Many of the pieces have names of individuals, which suggest that the speaker is acquainted with the other characters. For example, the first poem is entitled, "The City—An Apology to Patricia." In it the narrator pokes fun at New Orleans, which comprises a mixture of cultures. To dramatize this unusual place, the poet includes phrases from various languages—"this city was parleyed depuis/ longtemps": "hombres," "gringo,"—mixed with southern speech: "It's 'cos we still feel so cold inside." Haute cuisine mixed with cheap wine and stale cheese; "pickaninnies pour the hot sauce" and the "big House" with Miss Ann; "jazz," "brown waters of the/Mississippi." She mocks the city of New Orleans, even pointing out that: "Polygamy is referred to as an African Disease, but, Bourbon Street could be named "Confusion Whoring Incorporated" (Aidoo 1985:41-42). Then, she addresses the listener, perhaps Patricia as "My Sister," and asks her to forgive a traveler "who was in search of a dream place."

New Orleans is made into Little Africa, USA, in the poem "Mardi Gras." The problem, according to our angry narrator, is that people have learned not to see Africa, although it is everywhere; therefore they give all the African borrowings such as the food, "gumbo" in particular, to the French or Spanish; but as the speaker laments, Africa has been hurting for so long and things are so crazy such as "Black Men in New Orleans/ play[ing]/ Zulus/ in black face" that one cannot really mind. Nevertheless, she cannot help wondering that in a land of "determined name-calling," no one has come up with names for "kinky-haired/thick-lipped/honkies, or the straight-nosed/ blue-eyed spooks..." (43-44).

The reference to the hurt and suffering, neglect of Africa, and the killing of black people furthers this subject which permeates the long fictional piece, *Our Sister Killjoy*. As the following excerpt relates, this abuse is not limited to New Orleans but is spread all over the Western world:

> Beautiful black bodies
> Change into elephant-grey corpses
> Littered all over the Western world
> Thrown across railway tracks for
> Midnight expresses to mangle
> Just a little bit more—
> Offered to cold flowing water
> Buried in thickets and snow
> Their penises cut. (Aidoo 1979:62)

As we return to the poems in *Someone*, the famous soul-food restaurant "Dooky's" in New Orleans provides the setting for the speaker to remind a degree-conscious sister that Boston may be a good place to stop but we can never call it home. This poem also has the name of an individual, "Lunch at Dooky's for Violet." The language and tone suggest a sisterhood between the two, but with a gentle reminder that the American sister needs to be more politically conscious, since it seems that she has not seen that Boston is trying to catch up with Birmingham, Alabama. Surely, the allusion refers to the children who were killed in the church bombing during the Civil Rights struggle of the sixties. The poem probably was written during or as a response to the period when Boston was up in arms about school desegregation in the following decade.

Another poem, "Carolyn," deconstructs the concept of "home." This time, the setting is someplace in Africa, perhaps Ghana. The speaker begins with one of the nostalgic familiar tourist scenes in which she describes, "African peasant farmers taking a holiday, costumed and seated with drums and creating a ceremony to welcome African American relatives" back home after four centuries/ or/ three/or/ two.../Who cares?"(Aidoo 1985:46-47). At the same time she juxtaposes the idea that perhaps in America, one works a number of jobs to buy a home. Although very critical of the "brothers," somewhat indicting the men in Africa as well as the United States, the speaker steps back to say, "Not their fault either." Nevertheless, she reminds us:

we are
still
looking for our
scattered belongings from among
the ruins of the havoc
that it
caused. (48)

One can almost hear the response from an African American church group, "Lord, have mercy." The narrator responds herself and says,

But
keep cool, My Sister
keep cool...
—in spite of dangerous men—
A tight body and a strong mind can
weather storms. (48)

The poem concludes again with warm feelings of sisterhood, not only for the person addressed, but for all the sisters:

With no effort
I think of
you and your sisters
tenderly...

The speaker adds her wish for lots of blessings upon the listener's house. This piece represents one of Aidoo's strongest statements on the relationship of Africans and African Americans of the United States. It speaks about the history, the implications of the "first crime," but it also looks to the future with hope.

Most of the poems address women, although there is one with an "apology to Ronald" and another entitled "for a Zulu in the Bayous," with the opening line to "Robert."

These seven poems in *Someone Talking to Sometime* certainly demonstrate that Aidoo maintains a strong interest in Africans in the diaspora, and she shares a special bond with them. The New Orleans poems also reveal that Aidoo is knowledgeable about the happenings, the treatment, and the history of Blacks in America. Unlike the representation in *The Dilemma of a Ghost*, these poems indicate deeper insights and more knowledge about African Americans in the United States.

The New Orleans visit plays a major role in this book of poetry, but Aidoo borrows in another way from the diaspora. She expands the diaspora to include African Caribbeans. Her essays, poems, and works disclose that she reads and rewrites or responds to African American writers, and African Caribbeans and that she recognizes the cross-cultural influences or threads which exist among the two groups. A noteworthy example would be her "Fontamara" poems. There are two poems in *Sometime*, "Reply to Fontamara I"(75) and "Reply to Fontamara II"(76-77) which are responses to the poem, "Love Letter" by Haitian poet, Fadrin [Fardin].[7] At the beginning of the collection, there is a note stating that "Every effort has been made to trace the copyright holder of the poem "Love Letter" by Fadrin of Haiti, reproduced in the Notes." The poem appears in translation in the Notes. It is obvious that this piece by the Haitian stirs her imagination, for in addition to the two poems in the text, the end notes states that these were written as a "reaction against an earlier personal response to 'Love Letter.'"

"Reply to Fontamara" serves as the title for Section Two of Part Two, which contains poems that speak of betrayal, a reversal of expectations. In "Love Letter," the Haitian poet warns a traveler, "my love" perhaps from Haiti, a beautiful summer environment, that life may be awful in a cold, freezing, strange "white man's country"; but she should remember to return to the paradise "country" of warmth and beauty if the situation becomes too terrible. Aidoo in her poems destroys the romantic image by pointing out that even in these warm sun shiny places, "life is not too sweet," and she addresses the poet, Fadrin, as "My Brother." She even entitles one poem, "Now that the weather man has gone crazy..." because people are doing some of the same awful, crazy, terrible things in sunshiny, beautiful places, and she suggests in one poem that perhaps, "the sun has been up so long... we no more/know/ the difference between / a mild morning and a hot noon" (76-77).

In one of the poems in Part One, Section One, there is the piece, "Of Love and Commitment," of which Aidoo states that it began as a love poem, but became one of her most political (James 1990:14). There are references to "Malcolm's Autobiology" and "Stokely" (11). Surely, the first is a play on *The Autobiography of Malcolm X* and the other to Stokely Carmichael, both of whom were militants of the Black Power movement of the sixties. With the inclusion of the hope placed in "Nkrumah," and a play on his name too, "they say he was a /Kruman you know," African and African American revolutionary movements are intertwined and also illustrate Aidoo's creativity in language.

In an essay, "Unwelcome Pals and Decorative Slaves," Aidoo quotes in its entirety "Sometimes as Women Only," a long poem by Gloria Wade-Gayles, a Black American woman poet of the United States. She inscribes it as "a definitive statement on the pain, the frustrations and almost despair exclusive to being an African (or black) woman and a writer." (Aidoo, 1981:19) So clearly, does Gayles identify with being a Black, (African) woman writer that she paraphrases a line from Langston Hughes's poem, "Mother to Son," life for the African woman writer is definitely 'no crystal stair'" (Aidoo 1981:21).

Finally, although, I am not aware that Aidoo has indicated any influence from Alice Walker, in some ways, they are similar in theme, form, technique, and commitment. As indicated at the beginning of this essay, there is this determination in Aidoo to teach, to make sure that the reader has knowledge that she believes is essential. Walker has a similar goal, so much so that, at times, she appears to be the preacher, giving a sermon. As Aidoo connects African Americans with Africans in many of her texts, Alice Walker makes similar connections of Africans and African Americans. Nettie's letters in *The Color Purple* serve to provide information about life and the missionary work in Africa by African Americans from the United States. The discussions about "scarification" and how people in America will think Tashi, the African young woman, is different are other examples of the lessons. This theme of mutilation of the body of the African woman and even Tashi's re-appearance in *Possessing the Secret of Joy* continues Walker's involvement with Africa.

As stated earlier in Aidoo's latest novel, *Changes* (1991), she makes only one statement about slavery or the diaspora. In addition to connecting Africans, it picks up on the issue detailed in the "New Orleans" poems of *Someone Talking to Sometime* that no one wants to give credit to Africa for anything. In this case, the speaker blames "racist historians and lazy African academics suffering from the same disease: allergy to serious and honest research." She points out that they sustain the theory that "plantains," "cassava," and other African staples came from Asia or the Americas. She answers with the question: "And incidentally, what did the slaves take there with them by way of something to grow and eat?" (Aidoo 1991:12). This passage also illustrates similarities between the Alice Walker-type teaching and that which punctuates the texts of Aidoo. One of the most enlightening and perhaps the longest representation of this Ghanian author's intervention is the one which delin-eates the situations which lead "twentieth-century Africans and other world women elite and neo-elite to use tranquillizers":

> telephone calls that never came;
> cosy week-ends that never materialized;
> Knowing your best friend wants your boyfriend instead of the
> one she was going out with;
> knowing your best friend's date was so much smarter than the inarticulate somebody who was dating you;
> not knowing how to handle male-chauvinist lec-turers who
> didn't even make the effort to read your essays properly
> because
> you were a woman;
> wanting to be a nuclear physicist but everyone telling you it's much safer to go into teaching because you know, isn't that too much for a woman? ... and wouldn't that be too exotic for Africa? (143-144).

Known for her experimental poetry-prose style which character-izes Aidoo's writing, both the prose and poetry, she continues in this vein in *Someone Talking to Sometime*. It reflects her interest in including the oral in the written. Significantly, this issue of racist, "male-chauvinist lecturers" also forms the core theme in Paule Marshall's latest novel, *Daughters*.

Although *Changes* is not as unconventional as *Sister Killjoy*, it still possesses much of the powerful, invigorating, innovative style that may be seen in the writing of many of the contemporary African American women writers.

It is not necessary to argue here that the women writers of Africa and the diaspora influence one another. The similarity in themes and stylistic features supports their common heritage, both as daughters of Africa and as individuals who share similar expe-riences and hopes. As Andree Nicola McLaughlin states, their "lit-erary upsurge... unveils a renaissance of the spirit inspired by those who have refused to surrender. Those who have resisted oppres-sion. Those who have undertaken to remake the universe to own their future" (McLaughlin 1990:XXXI). Aidoo emphatically belongs to this impressive and determined sisterhood.

We do know, however, that Aidoo's courageous, bold form and strong tone inspired another African Caribbean female writer to pen her first work. Michelle Cliff credits this African author for helping her to gain the confidence to write:

> After reading *Our Sister Killjoy*, something was set
> loose in me, I directed rage outward rather
> than inward, and I was able to write a piece
> I called "If I Could Write This in Fire I Would
> Write This in Fire." In it I let myself go, any thought
> of approval for my words vanished;
> I strung together myth, dream, historical detail,
> observation, as I had done before, but I added native
> language, tore into the indoctrination of the colo-
> nizers, surprised myself with the violence
> of words." (Cliff 1985:16)

The strongest manifestation of Aidoo's investment in addressing the relationship of Africa and its diaspora comes in the work of another female writer from Ghana who is now in exile in the United States, Abena P. Busia. In an insightful article, Susan Andrade persuasively shows how Buchi Emecheta's *Joys of Motherhood* rewrites Flora Nwapa's *Efuru* and the two rewrite the history of the Women's War in Nigeria and thereby naming an African women's literary tradition. Busia, with her poem, "Achimota: From the Story My Mother Taught Me," accomplishes a similar achievement through her re-writing of Aidoo's memory poem from *Anowa*, which begins this paper. Busia re-assures Aidoo that "Sometimes it seems we are forgetting/ but so long as there are people alive who remember/ we will remember the meaning." (Busia 1990:30-31). What these "people" are remembering is that the "famous school," "A-chee-mo-ta-no," that is now there and what people talk about most, was once an "underground railroad"(31). She reveals that once the "forest" beside the school served as a shel-ter to hide those fleeing to escape the chains and lash. Busia links this hiding place/ in Africa as a precursor/ long before, on this side of the world with the "underground railroad" in America (30). She echoes the words of Aidoo from Anowa:

> No one will tell you that today.
> We too have been taught forgetting.(31)

The irony is that Busia continues the song that her literary fore-mother, Aidoo, has sung, as well as re-tells "the story my Mother taught me." On one hand, their remembering, re-visiting, and reconnecting African history and people, provide the outline for defining a Ghanaian woman's literary canon, which shares similar concerns with the works of other women authors, especially, those who are in the African Diaspora. On the other hand, and perhaps more important, Busia's contribution indicates that the challenge to break the silence regarding Africa and the diaspora which Aidoo alludes to in practically all of her creations, is being heeded.

"All good men and women have not forgotten."

NOTES

1. See her three novels and short stories which address this journey: *Brown Girl, Brownstones* (1959); *The Chosen Place, The Timeless People* 1969); culminating with *Praisesong for the Widow*, 1983). In an early essay, "The Negro Woman in American Literature" (1966), Marshall also makes this pronouncement. In the short story, "Reena," it is discussed in terms of a return to Africa in the physical sense, but her later works suggest that the journey can be a spiritual one.

2. The best known proponent of this theme is Marcus Garvey with the "Back to Africa" Movement of the early part of the twentieth century. Many Harlem Renaissance writers adopted this theme also: Countee Cullen, with his poem "Heritage"; Langston Hughes, in several poems reflecting on Africa; and his first published poem, "I Have Known Rivers" take the Negro back to the continent. Claude McKay's "Banjo" brings together Africans from the continent and from the diaspora. W.E.B. Du Bois, Carter G. Woodson, and Joel A. Rogers are early African American Africanists who maintained that Blacks in the Americas retained much of their African heritage. This theme also appears in the texts of the sixties and is receiving considerable attention with the *Black Atlantic* movement in contemporary criticism.

3. While Ngate addresses the Afro-Caribbean woman as the figure who returns, he links her with Eulalie, the African American from the United States in Ama Ata Aidoo's play, *The Dilemma of a Ghost*. Ngate's thesis reveals that these texts deal with the problem of a foreign woman (African or European) who cannot fit well into her African husband's family.

4. In a note, I cited a few African anglophone authors, Wole Soyinka, John Pepper Clarke, Taban Lo Liyong, Keorapetse Kgositsile, and Ayi Kwei Armah. A number of others may be added, particularly Ngugi wa Thiong'o and South African poets.

5. See Jahn et al 1972:25-26. Herdeck (1973):29-30; and Horne 1992:34-40.

6. Information given to author while a visiting writer at the University of Florida, 1979.

7. Aidoo spells the name, "Fadrin." Maurice A. Lubin, an Haitian who has written much on Haitian poetry, also editor of the Haitian bio-bibliography in Herdeck et al. 1979, believes the reference is to Fardin, Dieudoone (pseudonym from Louis Marie Pierre Benoit) who is included in the above anthology as a "Poet, novelist, storyteller, anthologist, editor" (381).

WORKS CITED

Aidoo, Ama Ata. *Changes: A Love Story*. London: The Woman's Press, 1991.

_____. *No Sweetness Here*. Essex, England: Longman, 1989.

_____. *Our Sister Killjoy or Reflections from a Black-Eyed Squint*. New York: NOK, 1979.

_____. *Someone Talking to Sometime*. Harare, Zimbabwe: The College Press, 1985.

_____. *The Dilemma of a Ghost and Anowa*. Essex, England: Longman, 1987.

_____. "Unwelcome Pals and Decorative Slaves." *AFA Journal of Creative Writing*. November (1982):I:34-43.

Andrade, Susan. "Rewriting History, Motherhood, and Rebellion: Naming an African Woman's Literary Tradition." *Research in African Literatures* 21, I (Spring 1990):91-110.

Busia, Abena. *Testimonies of Exiles*. Trenton, N.J.: Africa World Press, 1990.

Cliff, Michelle. *The Land of Look Behind: Prose and Poetry*. Ithaca, N.Y.: Firebrand, 1985.

Cullen Countee. "Heritage." In: *Colar*. New York/London: Harper and Brothers (1925).36-41.

Emecheta, Buchi. *The Joys of Motherhood*. London: George Brazillier, 1979.

Herdeck, Donald, Ed. *African Authors*. Washington, D.C.: Black Orpheus Press, 1973.

Herdeck Donald, Maurice A. Lubin, John Figueroa, et al. *Caribbean Writers: Bio-Bibliographical-Critical Encyclopedia*. Washington, D.C.: Three Continents Press, 1979.

Hill-Lubin, Mildred A. "The Relationship of African-Americans: A Recurring Theme in the Works of Ama Ata Aidoo." *Presence Africaine* 124, 4 (1982):190- 201.

Horne, Naana Banyiwa. "Ama Ata Aidoo." *Dictionary of Literary Biography* 117. Detroit: Gale, 1992:34-40.

Jahn, J., Ulla Schild, and Almut Nordman. Eds. *Who's Who in African Literature*. Tubingen, Germany: Erdmenn Publishers, 1972.

James, Adeola. "Ama Ata Aidoo." In: *In Their Own Voices: African Women Writers Talk*. London: Heinemann, 1990.

Johnson, Lemuel. "A-Beng: (Re) Calling the Body In(to) Question." *Out of the Kumbla: Caribbean Women and Literature*. Eds. Carole Boyce Davies and Elaine Savory Fido. Trenton, N.J.: Africa World Press, 1990.

Lindfors, Bernth. "The Image of the Afro-American in African Literature." *Association for Commonwealth Literature and Language Studies Bulliten* 4,3 (1975):19-26.

Marshall, Paule. *Daughters*. New York: Atheneum Macmillan, 1991.

_____. *Brown Girl, Brownstones*. New York: Random House Publishers, 1959.

Rpt. CUNY, The Feminist Press, 1981.

_____. *The Chosen Place, The Timeless People*. New York: Harcourt Brace Jovanivich, 1969.

_____. *Praisesong for the Widow*. New York: CUNY, The Feminist Press and Putman's, 1983.

_____. "The Negro Woman in American Literature." *Freedomways* vi (Winter 1966). 20-25.

McKay, Claude. *Banjo*. New York: Harper and Brothers, 1929. Rpt. 1970.

McLaughlin, Andree Nicola. "A Renaissance of the Spirit: Black Women Remaking the Universe." In: *Wild Women in the Whirl wind: Afro-American Culture and the Contemporary Literary Renaissance*. Eds. Joanne Braxton and Andree Nicola McLaughlin. New Brunswick, N.J.: Rutgers University Press, 1990.

Ngate, Jonathan. "Reading Warner-Vieyra's *Juletane."* *Callaloo 9,4* (Fall 1986): 557.

Sutherland-Addy, Esi, "Narrative Technique and the Role of Commentators in Ama Ata Aidoo's Works." *Institute of African Studies Research Review* 5,2. Legon, Ghana: University of Ghana. (1989). 67-70

Walker, Alice. *Possessing the Secret of Joy*. New York: Pocket Star Books, 1992.

_____. *The Color Purple*. New York: Washington Square Press, 1983.

Diasporic Ruptures and (Re)membering History:

Africa as Home and Exile in *Anowa*

and *The Dilemma of a Ghost*

Maureen N. Eke

I am only a wayfarer, with no belongings either here or there. —*Anowa*

A Wayfarer is a traveller. Therefore to call someone a wayfarer is a painless way of saying he does not belong. That he has no home, no family, no village, no stool of his own, has no feast days, no holidays, no state, no territory. —*Anowa*

Wanderer child. It is the same child who dies and returns again and again to plague the mother— Yoruba belief. —Wole Soyinka, "Abiku"

In the first two epigraphs above, Aidoo's character Anowa, in the play of the same name, signifies her identity as a "stranger," both as a gendered person, a woman who is unlike any other woman, and as an individual, estranged from her community because of her social and psychic visions. In this paper, I propose to use the term "abiku," the identification for the Yoruba "spirit" or wanderer child who returns again and again from the dead to plague its mother, to signify Anowa's identity as a "wanderer," a migratory and alienated character. This paper will examine Aidoo's use of these two women characters: Anowa in *Anowa* and Eulalie in *The Dilemma of a Ghost*, paying special attention to their "abikuness," as tropes for exploring Africa's violent rupturing by the slave trade and European colonization, as well as social attitudes towards that past, particularly the continent's self-imposed "amnesia" or silence about that past. In using these women as catalysts of social criticism, communal (re)membering, and healing, Aidoo also introduces a discussion of societal biases against women and the marginalization of women in her society. The term "trope" is used here in its general meaning to identify a "rhetorical or figurative device" (Cuddon 1991:107) and used repetitively and sometimes with a variance (Gates 1988). Thus, the figure of "abiku" represents both Anowa's spiritual migrations (the returning spirit child) as well as her spatial location as outsider and insider among her people.

Because of the spirit's migratory nature and connection with multiple temporal and spatial phases—the past, the present, "here, there, everywhere"—it also simultaneously possesses visions of both the past and the present. It is old and young, transgressing borders and all strictures. In her attempt to define the "abiku" character, Chikwenye Okonjo Ogunyemi (1996) borrows from both Yoruba and Igbo sources, defining the figure as "*ogbanje*" among the Igbo and "*abiku*" among the Yoruba. According to Ogunyemi: "Canceling temporal, spatial, and artificial boundaries by traveling to engender infinite possibilities is liberatingly *Abiku's* metier"(66). She adds, "Simultaneously old, young, 'ageless,' and waiting to be born, while belonging to here, there, and everywhere, *Abiku* emerges as the arch-magician and master creator, a shape shifter adept at playing many roles" (66-67). Consequently, according to Osundare, abiku is "the grand fusion of time" (qtd. in Ogunyemi 1996:67).

The primary source of Anowa's difference is her "abiku" nature as suggested by various characters in the play, including her mother, the old man and woman, and Kofi. The opening epithets, therefore, address this difference which dislocates Anowa from her people. Anowa's "otherness" is further heightened by her subjectivity as a woman who is preoccupied with (re)membering and examining her people's history—particularly, African diasporic ruptures stemming from the slave trade and European colonization—as well as her people's complicity in the dismemberment of the continent. Like Anowa, Eulalie, the African American character, in *The Dilemma of a Ghost,* is also an "abiku" figure, a sojourner migrating between two worlds, the past (dead) and the present (living), the world of her ancestors and historical past (Africa) and that of her present reality and contemporary history (the United States of America). For Ato's people, she represents the ghost from their past come to haunt them in the present. In these two plays, therefore, both women are simultaneously at home and exiled in Africa, marginalized because of particular connections to a shared historical past and/or an obsession with examining that past, or because of their (en)gendered positions as women. The figure of "abiku," therefore, serves in this paper as a discursive metaphor for the characters' dislocation and migratory nature.

In the "Prologue" to the play, the Old Man inscribes Anowa as "a child of several incarnations." Later, her mother identifies her as the returned spirit of a formerly dead child, hence, her restlessness. As the migratory spirit who travels between the dead and the living, Anowa is linked to the past (dead) and present (living) of her people's life, temporally and psychically. She carries the group's mythic consciousness, and for Aidoo, she becomes the visionary who "prompts" her people to confront their collective guilt and amnesia about the past. Like Anowa, Eulalie is also a migratory spirit, but, whereas she does not possess Anowa's visions, as a child of the African diasporic experience, Eulalie shares the group's psychic anxiety and for Ato's people, she becomes a physicalization of that schismatic past. For Aidoo, then, Eulalie helps to activate the African community's exploration of its relationship with its historical past and diasporic children.

As one of Africa's foremost women writers, Ama Ata Aidoo has become known for her combatant perspectives on issues concerning Africa, especially African diasporic history and oppressive attitudes towards women on the continent. In her literary works, she champions the causes of African liberation and like the first president of her country, Kwame Nkrumah, articulates a pan-Africanist or pan-African diasporic vision of this liberation. As such, Aidoo's social vision, states Wilentz (1992), is centered around the "betterment of women's position as well as a global concern for the liberation of Black peoples everywhere" (38). History and the healing of historical fractures are some of the themes Aidoo tries to address in her works.

DIASPORIC RUPTURE: ANOWA AND AFRICA'S PAINFUL HISTORY

Aidoo believes that an awareness of diasporic history and the historical connections among African peoples globally are necessary for understanding Africa's future. In her response to Adeola James' question about the significance of an appeal to "the sentiment of historical connection between Africans and Africans in the diaspora," Aidoo states:

> Maybe it is because I come from a people from whom, for some reason, the connection with African-America or the Caribbean was a living thing, something of which we were always aware. In Nkrumah's Ghana one met African-Americans and people from the Caribbean. In my father's house we were always getting visitors from all over. I think that the whole question of how it was that so many of our people could be enslaved and sold is very important. I've always thought that it is an area that must be probed. It probably holds one of the keys to our future. (James 1990:20-21)

Aidoo's sentiments about African history and the slave trade are also shared by her character, Anowa, whose source of anguish is the knowledge that many Africans were sold into slavery and used as cheap labor for Western civilization.

In one of Anowa's speeches, perhaps her longest, towards the end of the play, she recounts a conversation with her grandmother concerning the slave trade. The grandmother's story about the "huge houses rising to touch the skies, houses whose foundations were wider than the biggest roads" (Aidoo 1985:104) prompts the precocious Anowa to further investigate the history of her people. The houses she refers to are the slave forts at Elmina and along the West African coast, those "great places" to which Nana had traveled, but which according to the Old Man of the "Prologue" "shall remind our children" that "there is a bigger crime" (66), the community's complicity in the slave trade. Anowa's request for more details from her grandmother: "Tell me Nana, who built the houses?" (104) encourages the grandmother to tell a more elaborate, but often muted story of the horror of the slave trade: "The pale men.... They are white men" (104 -105) who were said to have "built the big houses to keep/ the slaves" (105). However, Anowa's inquiry: "What is a slave, Nana?" (105) draws an angry response from her grandmother who cautions her to "Shut up! It is not good that a child should ask /big questions./ A slave is one who bought and sold" (105).

It is clear that Anowa's determination, even as a child of eight, to uncover the truth about her people and their history sets her apart from others in the community, a difference which frightens the grandmother, who labels the child a "witch." But, for Anowa, the story of her people's bondage and crime against their own people becomes the source of her psychic schism. Her trauma is actualized in the nightmare she has on the night after she heard the story. But, unlike Nana, who discourages her granddaughter from interrogating her history, Aidoo sees Anowa as a catalyst for initiating such investigation into Africa's past in order to understand why so many millions of Africans were taken away from the continent. Speaking for the author, Anowa asks: "'What happened to those who were taken away?/ Do people hear from them?/ How are they?'" (106). These are questions which frighten Nana even further and to which she does not provide adequate answers. Rather, she encourages Anowa to sleep, stating, "All good men and women try to forget;/ They have forgotten'" (106). Like her community, Anowa is encouraged to sleep the sleep of silence and forgetfulness. However, contrary to Nana's claim, some people remember and there are reminders, as the Old Man of the "Prologue" cautions, that "there is a bigger crime/ We have inherited from the clans incorporated/ Of which, lest we forget when the time does come,/ Those forts standing at the door/ Of the great ocean shall remind our children/ And the sea shall bear witness" (66). The Old Man's comment references the group's complicity in a trade, similar to Kofi's present merchandising of his people, as well as the physical evidence of the forts and the ocean which serves as communal grave for many Africans who died during the trans-Atlantic voyage. Lloyd Brown observes that the Prologue "offers pointed reminders about the complicity of an earlier generation in the arrival of colonialism (by virtue of having signed the Bond Treaty) and less excusably, in the trans-Atlantic slave trade" (1987:91).

For Aidoo, therefore, the importance of uncovering historical "truths" cannot be over looked. In fact, the play is set in the 1870s, "approximately thirty years after the Bond Treaty with the British opened up the door to European hegemony in the Fanti area of what was then called the Gold Coast" (91). Brown adds that:

> The historical events which Aidoo interweaves with her legendary materials are also important in the play's themes. In recalling the Bond Treaty which bound the Fanti to British rule, the old man of the prologue introduces the familiar theme of change, encouraging the audience in this case to recognize links between the arrival of an alien and hostile culture and the cold-bloodedness of the new generation represented by Kofi. (91)

Anowa is a lone voice in the community, for she alone wishes to uncover the truth so that others may remember and learn from the past. Nana, however, is representative of the collective consciousness whose guilt overwhelms it to forget, and by forgetting denies the inhumanity of which her people are guilty, and consequently, encourages such inhumanity in the new generation. Thus, Brown correctly concludes: "The inhumanity which leads the greedy Kofi to own slaves is a part of the brutishness that flowed from the Bond Treaty and its consequences, but it also represents the continuation of a long-standing 'crime' in Kofi's society" (92). Like her author, Anowa is engaged in the type of social criticism which Aidoo hopes would lead to consciousness raising about African diasporic history. Aidoo's attitude is best summarized in an interview with Theo Vincent, where she states: "I don't know how people react when they leave Africa and go to places outside where there are concentrations of other Black people," she says, "but for me it was incredible" (qtd. in Wilentz 1992:39). Then she adds, pointing at the presence of African peoples across the Atlantic: "I just couldn't believe that I could cross the whole of the Atlantic and go and find all of these people who are like people at home" (39). "But definitely," she continues, "this is the reason I keep coming back to this because I think it is part of what is eating us up. You can't cover up history.... It is time we faced the question of what happened that so many of us are in Harlem and so many in the West Indies.... You see, grief accepted is grief overcome" (39). But, grief denied causes the type of psychic schism which disempowers Anowa and leads to her tragedy.

GENDER AND PSYCHIC SCHISM IN *ANOWA*

Even as a lone voice, Anowa experiences the psychic fracturing and anguish of her community in particular, and of the continent, in general. In fact, the story of Africa's subjugation, colonization, and resulting fragmentation is told through Anowa's body. In the nightmare which she has on the night after her grandmother's tale, Anowa metamorphoses into a "big woman," from whose "insides were huge holes out of which poured men, women, and children" (106) who are subjugated by a hybrid of giant, lobster-like men and women. Her haunting dream is permeated with imagery of destruction and violence carried out against her children and the land. She narrates:

> And the sea was boiling hot and steaming. And as it boiled, it threw out many, many giant lobsters, boiled lobsters, each of whom as it fell turned into a man or woman, but keeping its lobster head and claws. And they rushed to where I sat and seized the men and women as they poured out of me, and they tore them apart, and dashed them to the ground and stamped upon them. And from their huge court-yards, the women ground my men and women and children on mountains of stone. But there was never a cry or murmur; only a bursting, as of ripe tomato or a swollen pod. And everything went on and on and on. (106)

Anowa's nightmare is imbued with metaphors of power, conquest and domination, empire and colony. The nightmare is symbolic and is framed as Anowa's reconstruction of the story of Africa's fragmentation as a result of foreign intrusion into the continent. In the dream, Anowa becomes a metaphor for "Mother Africa," whose children are being subjugated, torn, and dispersed globally. Like mother Africa, Anowa experiences the anguish of watching helplessly while her children are destroyed or dispersed. This dispersion and the subsequent emergence of African children world-wide in Anowa's dream is represented as a "bursting, as of a ripe tomato or a pod" (106). While it is true that this dispersal led to the emergence of African cultures and people in the diaspora, it also suggests a destruction of the originating culture—the ripe "mother tomato" or "mother Africa," as well as the "rupturing" of African female "subjects" under slavery and colonial domination. The image of Mother Africa which Aidoo evokes is not idealized or idolized; rather, it is all too close to the lived reality of many African women who are marginalized, physically and psychically abused, and exploited. In conflating Anowa with Mother Africa, Aidoo endows her character with the collective consciousness or mythic memory of her people, heightening Anowa's significance, as female subjectivity, in the (re)membering, as in putting together and recollecting, of Africa's history. Therefore, symbolically, through Anowa's (re)membering, Africa as female subjectivity (re)members "herself."

The conflation of Anowa and Mother Africa enables us to read the two subjectivities as texts, on whose bodies the acts of colonial violence, rupture, and cultural transformations can be perceived. According to Carole Boyce Davies (1994), Anowa "refigures the New World/Old World signs of rupture, schism, opening and othering as it simultaneously embodies the critique of constructions of the woman in society" (59). Like Africa, husbanded, thrust, and scripted into economic and social marginality by Europe, Anowa is driven into exile, a state of "otherness" by her community's rigid strictures and exploited by her husband, Kofi. Also, like Africa, Anowa is haunted by the scars of a past whose memory she has repressed, although it is continually activated by events in the present. "I was very ill and did not recover for weeks" (107), she informs the audience in her soliloquy. Then she continues, "When I told my dream, the women of the house were very frightened. They cried and cried and told me not to mention the dream again" (107). But silencing Anowa does not heal her schism, neither does it mute the memories. She informs the audience further that "since then, any time there is mention of a slave, I see a woman who is me and a bursting of a ripe tomato or a swollen pod" (107). Notice that Anowa's nightmare weaves together images of pregnancy and shared violent birthing. Anowa's ripened pregnancy bursts (violently) to give birth to African diasporic cultures and peoples.

For Anowa, although the dream is frightening and painful, it functions as a gateway to the past, to understanding history or communicating with it. It is an act of "re-memory," to borrow Toni Morrison's term for recuperating history/memory or the past in order to use it for the present. However, as is evidenced by Anowa's anguish, the repression or muting of the possibility of remembering history or of recalling stories of the past is both tragic and painful. According to Maggi Phillips (1994), "the play's tragic force is derived from the repression of dream as a channel for genuine communication" and connections. (94) These historical and spiritual connections of Africans world-wide are affirmed theatrically in the play through "the voices of an unseen wearied multitude" which begins to sing the spiritual, "Swing Low, Sweet Chariot" on stage after Anowa tells her tale of horror (107).

The song is a call for liberation. It calls for both spiritual and physical flight from bondage to a paradise, a haven. For colonized Africans, it is a call for freedom from colonial domination, and for diasporic Africans, in bondage, the song suggests hope of both physical and psychic liberation either in the diaspora or hope of when "the people could fly" back home to Africa, a theme also explored by Virginia Hamilton in *The People Could Fly* and Toni Morrison in *Song of Solomon*. This spiritual or physical return to Africa is explored in Aidoo's *The Dilemma of a Ghost* through Eulalie's return "home" to Africa, the land of her ancestors. In the play, Aidoo provides answers to the questions which Anowa poses to Nana: "what happened to those who were taken away? Do people hear from them?" (106).

BACK TO AFRICA: RETURN TO THE SOURCE?

From a pan-Africanist perspective *The Dilemma of a Ghost* represents Aidoo's attempts to fulfill one of the goals of Marcus Garvey's "Back to Africa" movement, that is, the return of diasporic Africans to a continental homeland. This attitude also articulated by other pan-Africanists like W.E.B. Du Bois and Kwame Nkrumah, Ghana's first president, emphasizes a unification of Africans through exploration of shared historical and cultural experiences, as well as the relocation of diasporic Africans in the continent. In fact, Aidoo states that her social and literary visions are informed by her experiences in the United States and in Nkrumah's Ghana, which encouraged the explorations of diasporic connections.

Like Anowa, Eulalie in *The Dilemma of a Ghost* becomes a trope for Aidoo's exploration of the implications of the trans-Atlantic slave trade for Africans and African Americans. Eulalie, who is also an "abiku" figure, is a "ghost" from the past and has come to haunt the community in the "present" by confronting Ato's people with the consequences of their involvement in the slave trade, which fragmented the continent. As a transgressive spirit, Eulalie's presence unearths the community's sense of guilt, fear, pain, and discomfort associated with a history of "horror," cultural dismemberment, and secrecy. One of the central themes in this play is how to address the community's "amnesia," or silence, what people have forgotten about the past so that the community in the present may heal. As Aidoo has stated, "until we have actually sorted out this whole question of African people, both on the continent and in the diaspora, we may well be joking, simply going round in circles" (James 1990: 21). It would not be erroneous to conclude that Eulalie's presence among Ato's people helps them and the audience of the play to reassess their feelings and attitudes towards African diasporic history. The return is a journey back to origins to seek a nation of her own, a "lost homeland and lost mother" (Innes 1992:34). In a sense, it is to reconcile her American self with her African heritage. This purpose is articulated in her exchange with Ato at the beginning of the play when she asks: "And your Pa mine?.... And your gods my gods" (Aidoo 1985:9). Later in her soliloquy she tells her mother, "I've come to the source" (24), expressing a feeling of contentment over her newly found nation. Identifying an originary home for herself in Africa is important, for a home signifies belonging to a people, a nation. Whereas Eulalie refers to the United States as her birth place, it is still a place of "exile" filled with memories of her racial and gender marginalization. These painful memories are recounted in her recollection of her mother's admonition about the unattainable dreams of black girls:

> 'Sugar, don't let them do you in'....'Sugar, don't sort
> of curse me and your Pa every morning you look
> your face in the mirror and see yourself black. Kill
> the sort of dreams silly girls dream that they are
> going to wake up one morning and find their skins
> milk white and their hairs soft blonde like them
> Hollywood tarts. Sugar, the dear God made you just
> black and you canna do nothing about it.' (24)

But, a return to the "source" is not as glorious as Eulalie may have perceived it, for contrary to her expectations, she has not returned to her *"pays natal"* as demonstrated in Ato's people's attitude towards their new daughter. Rather, Eulalie is seen as a stranger, "a wayfarer" who has neither kin, tribe, nor people of her own to establish or confirm her roots. The community privileges one's "known" heritage, and Ato's people do not hesitate to assert this as they ask him probing questions about his wife's origins. Mansa asks, "Who is your wife?" to which Monka adds, "What is her name?" and then, Esi extending their questions, queries, "Where does she come from?" (16). Indeed, Eulalie's lack of "known" familial connections is seen as an aberration because according to Nana, Ato's grandmother, Eulalie "has no tribe." Further, expressing her dismay, Nana states, "The story you are telling us is too sweet, my grand-child. Since I was born, I have not heard of a human being born out of the womb of a woman who has not tribe. Are there trees which never have roots?" (17) To Nana, any individual's lack of rootedness is incomprehensible, for as she and other members of her village suggest, one is one's history, one's heritage. One's identity can only be determined by reference to one's roots, people, and tribe; to be without those roots is to be lost, to be forgotten. Consequently, Nana perceives Eulalie's lack of "known" heritage as a contamination of Ato's familial history and a threat to the survival and maintenance of his family's cohesion and continuity into the future. In one of her outcries, a repudiation of the marriage between her grandson and Eulalie, Nana bemoans her dilemma as tragic and one which she could not tell her ancestors because of the "strangeness" of her daughter-in-law:

> My spirit mother ought to have come
> for me earlier.
> Now what shall I tell them who are gone?
> The daughter of slaves who come from the white
>   man's land.
> Someone should advise me on how to tell my
> story.
> My children, I am dreading my arrival there
> Where they will ask me news of home.
> Shall I tell them or shall I not?
> Someone should lend me a tongue
> Light enough with which to tell
> My Royal Dead
> That one of their stock
> Has gone away and brought to their sacred precincts
> The wayfarer! (19)

Yes, Nana's cry centers on her fear that the sanctity of her ancestors' "precincts" have been violated. But, while the reality of Ato's actions may be painful to Nana, her outcry and fear also underscore the community's fear and denial of their ties to Eulalie, whose history begins in Africa.

By returning Eulalie "back to Africa," then, Aidoo problematizes the implications of that "return" to both continental and diasporic Africans. Indeed, the attitudinal responses and cultural conflicts represented in the play underscore divergent and sometimes contested interpretations of the identity and nationality of diasporic Africans. Who are they? What is their nation? In her introduction to Aidoo's 1971 edition of *The Dilemma of a Ghost*, Karen C. Chapman rightly points to these attitudinal realities which the play problematizes when she states:

> The experience of a black American is inevitably different from that of an African, despite their common ancestry. In the eyes of many Africans, particularly those in the countryside, black Americans have more in common culturally with white Americans than with Africans. The American black has been removed from Africa for a long time; contrary to what many romantically inclined Garveyites would like to believe, a return to the 'source' is a much more difficult task than its fascination may suggest, for it would mean returning to a culture never experienced in fact. (Chapman 1971:14)

The immanent tensions activated by a return to the source cannot be mistaken. Certainly, such a return would set in motion various forms of cultural conflict as Berth Lindfors (qtd. in Wilentz 1992:40) and Gay Wilentz have pointed out. Yes, too, Wilentz correctly asserts that "since the conflict is between two cultures with similar ancestry, the encounter takes on more significance than if Eulalie had been a white American" (40). She adds, "precisely because Eulalie is a Black American, the play explores more than marital discord and cultural conflicts by examining what Aidoo feels has been covered up by a denial of history—Africa's relationship to its descendants in the Americas"(40). But, for Ato's people, an acknowledgment of this relationship threatens the community's conceptualization of a cohesive identity. To them, Eulalie's inclusion challenges precisely their idea of communal and, perhaps, national "purity," primarily because she is perceived as someone of tainted heritage, as "a white woman" (Aidoo 1985:17), "a slave" (18), "the offspring of slaves" (19), and finally, "a wayfarer" (19). The gradations of identities constructed for her are astonishing. It is thus Africa's contemplation or fashioning of a "pure" national/communal identity and Africa's location of her diasporic children at the fringes that Aidoo interrogates. Therefore, implicated in the idea of a return to the "source" is the question of nationality, which becomes even more contested when female subjectivities are involved as with Eulalie and Anowa.

CONTESTED IDENTITIES: WHAT IS THY NATION?

One of the areas in which women's subjectivities are constantly being contested relates to nationalism. Many African women who were involved in several African nationalist movements (Angola, Guinea Bissau, Mozambique, and South Africa) have claimed, and justifiably, that they were "fighting two colonialisms," the first being European colonialism, and the second being African patriarchal structures, which tend to exclude women from post-liberation politics. These women's dilemmas can also be extended to other African women, whose voices are often muted in nationalist debates. In her interview with Adeola James, Aidoo addresses the position of women in African societies, drawing parallels between the treatment of African women writers and general social attitudes towards women. She insists that "the question of the woman writer's voice being muted has to do with the position of women in the society in general," adding that "Women writers are just receiving the writer's version of the general neglect and disregard that woman in the larger society receive" (James 1990:11). Then she adds, "I am definitely committed, in my own way to the development of women" (18).The choice of two women characters whose views are different from those of their societies as voices for the author's critique of African history is not accidental. Like Aidoo, Eulalie and Anowa share a social vision which is concerned with both the unearthing of truths about African history and interrogating traditional constructions of women's subjectivities, especially, in the formation of national identity.

Aidoo's rendering of the land as "progenitress" or "mother of the nation," in Anowa ironically draws upon nationalist and even colonialist symbolization of the land or nation as female, although nationalist politics often excludes women. The muting of women's voices as significant perspectives on communal and national issues is emphasized through Anowa's silencing when she attempts to persuade Kofi to abandon his quest to trade in humans. Kofi responds to her outrage by interrogating her authority, asking: "Who are you to tell me what I must do or not do?" (Aidoo 1985:89). Then he adds, "Besides, you are only talking like a woman"(90), suggesting that her gender denies her a voice or right to speak or

73

challenge such traditions.

In *The Dilemma of a Ghost*, Aidoo gives her audience intermittent glimpses into the African community's dilemma as it tries to wrestle with and resolve the question of Eulalie's gendered/racial identity. The difficulty of naming Eulalie correctly, especially in terms of Ato's people's conceptualization of nationality is underscored by Ato's muddled efforts to explain his wife's history to his people. He identifies Eulalie as an American, to which Esi Kom, his mother, appends, "a white woman," an appellation which emphasizes Eulalie's racial and geographic difference from continental Africans. Ato, however, insists on a shared racial identity and asserts, "I say my wife is as black as we all are" (17). For him, a shared historical past (slavery) and racial commonality (blackness) are unifying factors in the creation of a national, a pan-Africanist, or pan-black identity. He further explains to his people later: "Eulalie's ancestors were of our ancestors, But [warming up] as you all know, the white people came and took some away in ships to be slaves" (18). However, Ato also realizes the ambiguities inherent in his wife's identity. To redress the ambiguities which his blundered definitions have introduced, he adds, "But she was not a slave. It was her grandfathers and grandmothers who were slaves" (18). Needless to say, his community thinks differently, insisting that one's nationhood or 'belongingness" can only be ascertained through one's geo-ethnic location as well as communal heritage and values. Nana and her people, therefore, reject Eulalie because she is a "wayfarer" and the "offspring of slaves." Besides her ancestry is a tabooed subject, for as another Nana tells Anowa in *Anowa*, "none talks of these things anymore" (106). Besides, Ato's people's overwhelming need to maintain national, or in this case, communal cohesion, in the face of potential threat outweighs any loyalty to a "prodigal" daughter. For Ato's people, it is less traumatic to deny Eulalie's connection to Africa than to admit her as their offspring or even acknowledge any role in making her history.

Ato's marriage confronts him and his people with a social and ethical dilemma, that of determining the "correct" attitude towards their relationship with their diasporic daughter. This, indeed, is a dilemma which all Africans face and must address, Aidoo suggests. Her choice of the African dilemma tale as a framing device and a medium for communicating this message in her play, therefore, is appropriate. By using the tradition of the dilemma tale, Aidoo succeeds in posing ethical and social questions which Ato and his community, as well as Africans and the audiences must address. Such questions demand that both individuals and the community thoroughly assess their choices or responses to the problems they face. The tale is "presented in the communal context of the oral tradition to which it belongs...thereby juxtaposing Ato's dilemma as a contemporary Ghanaian with the communal customs which insist upon the need to deal with moral and social dilemmas" (Brown 1987:87). Although the dilemma is often generally interpreted as Ato's, it is, nevertheless, a situation which Ato and his community confront, for the community, as a group, must resolve the question of Eulalie's nationality and choose whether to claim her as one of its own, or subordinate her to their desire for a "pure" and cohesive communal identity.

In his article, "What is a nation?" Ernest Renan defines a nation as "a soul, a principle" which is constituted of "two things," "the possession in common of a rich legacy of memories" and "present-day consent, the desire to live together, the will to perpetuate the value of the heritage that one has received in an undivided form" (Renan 1994:19). But Renan's framework excludes Anowa and Eulalie. Eulalie, for instance, cannot claim Ato's nationality because she does not share with his community a "common ... rich legacy of memories" and she has not articulated, before them, a desire to "perpetuate the value of the heritage." Unlike Eulalie, Anowa shares her community's heritage, but refuses to participate in its glorification or to perpetuate its values. Rather, she engages in its dismemberment by questioning her people's past injustice against their own kind when the community participated in the slave trade. She condemns Kofi who, although he is representative of the future generation, has inherited the "great crime" committed by his people in the past when they participated in the sale of humans. Consequently, she prefers to remain as Badua puts it, "a stranger in other people's lands" (91), "her soul hovering on the outer fringes of life and always searching for something" (93).

Unlike Anowa, Eulalie is an "unrelated" kin. She is only marginally affiliated with Ato's people because of her marriage to Ato. Yet, like Anowa, Eulalie discovers that marriage does not confirm freedom, citizenship, nationality, or empowerment. Rather, as Chikwenye Okonjo Ogunyemi suggests, marriage often marginalizes women in new ways, for a married woman is marginalized first as a daughter in her father's home and as a wife in the husband's home. Indeed, "woman is not only a 'native' born in her father's house," Ogunyemi points out, but is born again as a "slave in her master/husband's house" (Ogunyemi 1996:8). Ogunyemi's remark underscores the implications of nativization for women. Because nativization is gendered and often male, both Eulalie and Anowa are outsiders in their own communities and within their husband's homes. Elleke Boehmer underscores this gendering of nationality and nationalism when she states: "Gender informs nationalism and nationalism in its turn consolidates and legitimates itself through a variety of gendered structures and shapes which, either as ideologies or as political movements, are clearly tagged: the idea of nationhood bears a masculine identity though national ideals may wear a feminine face" (Boehmer 1992: 6). Although Anowa's story is conflated with that of the nation, national politics still exclude her. Similarly, although Eulalie claims Ato's Pa and gods as hers, she is not considered native born by Ato's people. In fact, at the end of the play, the issue of her nationality remains unresolved. Aidoo's resolution addresses only the misunderstanding activated by the question of Eulalie's "delayed" motherhood.

As migratory figures, located at the fringes of their societies, Anowa and Eulalie occupy those spaces where identity, history, and memory are contested. They do not find what Patricia Collins describes as "safe spaces" either in their husbands' houses or in the socially constructed and masculinized idea of "fatherland." Collins describes a "safe space" as "that social space where Black women speak freely" (95) without hegemonic domination. Included in Collins' definition are "extended families, churches," and community organizations. According to Collins, this space "is not only safe—it forms a prime location for resisting objectification as Other" (1991:95). But neither Anowa nor Eulalie can enter and speak freely within their communities. Eulalie is objectified and her identity is gendered, racialized, and contested as an "other." Likewise, Anowa's subjectivity is challenged by objectifying her as a "stranger," "not a girl to meet everyday." She is likened to a "girl in a folk tale," a figure from the folk imagination, whose reality deviates from that of "other normal people." In her people's construction of their identity, Anowa and her children will not have a home. Osam articulates this dislocation succinctly when he states: "The children of women like Anowa and their children-after-them never find their ways back. They get lost. For they often do not know the names of the founders of their houses" (Aidoo 1985:92). And, even when they return, "they do not know what to tell you if you asked them for just the names of their clans" (92). One such child is

Eulalie who cannot identify her clan or its founders, partly because the clan has rejected her and partly because the clan has forgotten or silenced its own stories and "truths." However, as Aidoo suggests in these plays, such "truths" and stories can be recuperated for the future through (re)memory and reevaluation.

In attempting to inscribe the reality of Africa's imperfect history, Aidoo unearths those social and "ethical" issues that were buried or muted in her community. This attempt to (re)cover, (re)member, or (re)memory Africa's history underscores Aidoo's desire to fill in those spaces in the received knowledge of her people. For Aidoo, the stories of Africa's unglamorous past and of the continent's attitude towards that history, must be reconstructed and told so that others may hear and learn from them. The telling for her is cathartic and the first step towards self healing and "wholeness." Some of that healing can be attained by returning to Africa, to a past and a present which are continually fused. The figure of "abiku" as the wandering spirit or ghost from the past living in the present encapsulates this fusion of various temporal and spatial realities of African diasporic history and experiences. "Abiku" as a literary trope, thus enables new readings not only of works by Africans, but also of those by other African diasporic writers which suggest a return to Africa or which address issues of temporal and spatial, as well as historical, cultural, and psychic connections to the continent.

WORKS CITED

Aidoo, Ama Ata. *The Dilemma of a Ghost and Anowa*. White Plains, N.Y.: Longman, 1985. All subsequent references will refer to this edition.

Boehmer, Elleke. *Colonial and Postcolonial Literature*. New York: Oxford University Press, 1995.

—-. "Stories of Women and Mothers." In: *Motherlands: Black Women's Writing from Africa, the Caribbean and South Asia*. Ed. Susheila Nasta. New Brunswick N. J.: Rutgers University Press, 1992.

Brown, Lloyd. *Women Writers in Black Africa*. Westport, Conn.: Greenwood Press, 1987.

Chapman, Karen C. "Introduction." *The Dilemma of a Ghost*. By Christiana Ama Ata Aidoo. New York: Collier, 1965. Rpt. 1971.

Collins, Patricia Hill. *Black Feminist Thought*. New York: Routledge, 1991.

Cuddon, J. A. *The Penguin Dictionary of Literary Term and Literary Theory*. New York: Penguin Books, 1991.

Davies, Carole Boyce. *Black Women, Writing and Identity: Migrations of the Subject*. New York: Routledge, 1994.

Gates Jr., Henry Louis. *The Signifying Monkey*. New York: Oxford University Press, 1988.

Hamilton, Virginia. *The People Could Fly: American Black Folktales.* New York: Alfred A. Knopf, 1985.

Innes, C L. "Mothers or Sisters? Identity, Discourse and Audience in the Writing of Ama Ata Aidoo and Mariama Ba." In: *Motherlands.* Ed. Susheila Nasta. New Brunswick N. J.: Rutgers University Press, 1992.

James, Adeola. Ed. *In Their Own Voices: African Women Writers Talk.* Portsmouth, N.H.: Heinemann, 1990.

Lindfors, Bernth. "The Image of the Afro-American in African Literature." *Association for Commonwealth Literature and Language Studies Bulletin* 4,3 (1975): 19-26.

Morrison, Toni. *Song of Solomon.* New York: Plume, 1977.

Ogunyemi, Chikwenye Okonjo. *Africa Wo/man Palava.* Chicago: University of Chicago Press, 1996.

Phillips, Maggi. "Engaging Dreams: Alternative Perspectives on Flora Nwapa, Buchi Emecheta, Ama Ata Aidoo, Bessie Head, and Tsitsi Dangarembga's Writing." *Research in African Literatures* 25,4 (1994):89-103.

Renan, Ernest. "What is a Nation?" *Nation and Narration.* Ed. Homi Bhabha. New York: Routledge, 1994.

Soyinka, Wole. *Idanre and Other Poems.* London: Eyre Methuen, 1967.

Wilentz, Gay. *Binding Cultures: Black Women Writers in Africa and the Diaspora.* Bloomington: Indiana University Press, 1992.

THE POLITICS OF EXILE:

REFLECTIONS OF A BLACK-EYED SQUINT IN *OUR SISTER KILLJOY*

GAY WILENTZ

The term "politics of exile" calls to mind those sufferers who must leave their homeland for political reasons. But there is another aspect of the politics associated with exile—that of the so-called Third World colonial who seeks the benefits and opportunities in a European country, perceived as culturally superior, thus avoiding the socio-political situation at home. Ama Ata Aidoo's *Our Sister Killjoy or Reflections from a Black-Eyed Squint* (1979) is a relentless attack on the notions of exile as relief from the societal constraints of national development and freedom to live in a cultural environment suitable for creativity. In this work, Aidoo questions certain prescribed theories of exile including the reasons for exile—particularly among African men. The novel exposes a rarely heard viewpoint in literature in English—that of the African woman exile; Aidoo's protagonist Sissie, as the "eye" of her people, is a sojourner in the "civilized" world of the colonizers. *Our Sister Killjoy*, which reflects Aidoo's own travels abroad, was written partially in the United States. Moreover, although it was published in 1979, first editions carry a 1966 copyright, closer to the time in which she was traveling. Although Aidoo experienced the supposed freedom of exile herself, her personalized prose-poem-novel illustrates her commitment to rebuild her former colonized home and confront those who have forgotten their duty to their native land.

Most critical reactions to the novel have ranged, predictably, from negative responses to silence and non-recognition. What has disturbed Aidoo most is not the negative criticism but the "unre-ception" of the novel—the refusal of many African critics to discuss it at all. In an essay titled "Unwelcome Pals and Decorative Slaves," Aidoo refers to the attitude of her male colleagues towards her involvement in political issues, expressed at a meeting on national development: "[Some professors] shouted that I am not fit to speak on public matters. That I should leave politics and such to those [men] most qualified to handle it" (Aidoo 1980:23). Later in this essay she comments: "I am convinced that if *Killjoy* or any-thing like it had been written by a man, as we say in these parts, no one would have been able to sleep a wink these couple of years" (38). Clearly, the fact that Aidoo is a woman has made this novel unacceptable to the predominantly male and/or eurocentric crit-ical community, but because she rejects male-oriented theories of exile and synthesizes feminist and *afrocentric* perspectives, *Our Sister Killjoy* could hardly have been written by a man. Here I exam-ine Aidoo's challenge to prevailing theories of exile, her question-ing of the supposed superiority of European culture for the colonial subject, and her expose of the politics of exile for African self-exiles. Through a combination of prose, poetry, oral voicing and letter writing, Aidoo's Sissie reports back to her home community what she sees in the land of the colonizers and responds to those exiles who have chosen, as Frantz Fanon says, to stand with the white world (perceived as the "real world") in opposition to their own world, the black world of the colonized (Fanon 1967:37).

A discussion of some relevant theories of exile may be of use here. Although I am not going to explore the distinction between exile and expatriation, I do exclude from this discussion those who were forced to leave as banishment (on penalty of prison or possi-bly death); rather, I focus on those who seek exile for personal and/or cultural reasons. Many of the theories concerning these self-exiles (as I call them) entertain the notion that the exile chooses to escape limitations at home. Whether seeking freedom from the small town in the metropolis or from the colonial province in the colonizer's capital, the exile, particularly the exiled writer, sees him-self—and I use this term advisedly—as freed from the constraints at home and open to a world of cultural expression and diversity (Gurr 1981:13-17). In *Exiles and Emigres*, Terry Eagleton clearly confirms this view in relation to the writers Henry James and Joseph Conrad: "James and Conrad chose England [for] its order, its manners, its settled, varied and traditionalist status.... [They] settled in England in flight from a lack of established order and civilized manners elsewhere" (Eagleton 1970:14). For the white American James, as for other colonials, there exists the cultural means of "compensating for that sense of cultural subservience" (Gurr 1981:8). For colonial exiles of the non-industrialized "Third World," both the difference of color and the lack of so-called development augment these feelings of cultural inferiority. The Caribbean writer George Lamming suggests that for colonial exiles, especially those living in the "country which has colonized [their] history," the exiles' sense of culture is intricately related to the self-interpretation of the dominant culture. In fact, for those educated in the colonial language, "their whole introduction to something called culture, all of it, in the form of words, came from outside" (Lamming 1984:27).

Although generally stated, most theories of exile and its political implications are based on male experience and are therefore male-oriented in approach. This male-oriented approach ignores women sojourners like Sissie, who are not fooled by the neo-colonial lie, but see the land of exile as it is. In giving voice to Sissie's viewpoint, Aidoo not only overturns the assumptions of cultural superiority that the self-exiles bring with them in expatriation; she also exposes the sham behind the self-exile's reason for leaving from a polemically female perspective. The African men Sissie meets fit these theories of colonial exile, but Sissie does not. She is the "squint" who, rather than being isolated from her home, becomes the eye of her community in the land of the exiles.

Sissie's reflections open with a section, "Into a Bad Dream," which prepares us for her shamanistic journey to the land of the colonizers. Before we are even introduced to our squint, Aidoo deconstructs the structure of the novel by opening it with a four-page poem/political statement, an attack on the world into which Sissie will descend:

> Yes, my brother
> The worst of them
> these days supply local
> statistics for those population studies, and

toy with
genocidal formulations.
That's where the latest crumbs
are being thrown! (Aidoo 1979:7)

In fact, it is hard to call this compilation of poetic anger, political commentary, journal entries, oral voicings, and letter writings a "novel" in the traditional sense. Rather, it appears to be a formulation of an African prose poem which reverberates with sounds of the orature in the written language and personal dialogue—illustrating Aidoo's comment that "we don't always have to write for readers, we can write for listeners" (Lautre 1972:24). Furthermore, Aidoo's breakdown of the novelistic structure exemplifies one aspect of exile that Lamming suggests affects most writers from colonized lands—the problem of writing in the colonial language. For the anglophone African author, writing in English, "home is in a different language. It is a double exile, in culture and in the tongue" (Gurr 28). In wrestling with this conflict, Aidoo manages to inject the colonial language with the substance and structure of her own Akan. Linguistically, she challenges the sense of double exile that comes with the colonial experience.

"Our Sister" does not choose exile but is picked as a promising student and is given scholarship to attend an international work-study program in Germany and to visit her colonial "capital"—London. As in a bad dream, Sissie boards a plane to Germany. In a mixture of prose and poetry, Sissie reports her feelings of being seen as an "exotic" by the people of Germany, her experiences with an unhappy German housewife, and her questions concerning the cultural superiority of Europe and its corresponding cruelty. Then, in journal entry form, she recounts her encounter with the colonial power that changed the history of her Ghanaian home—England. While in London, she faces Ghanaian and other African self-exiles, confronts them for deserting their homelands, and in a final "love letter" she berates a lover who has decided to remain in exile as she returns home.

Aidoo comments that her protagonist Sissie sees everything "through the filter of her memories of Africa" (Vincent 1981:2). Moreover, as "Our Sister," Sissie is rooted in her African communal society and all her responses are oriented toward decolonization and the education of this community. Unlike other exiles who have lost that sense of identity that comes from belonging to a community, Sissie becomes the eyes of her community, reporting on those lost ones who have forgotten maternal, familial, and community ties, and squinting at these men—young and old—who refuse to return home to face national realities and rebuild their countries. It is no mistake that Sissie is female; she is the representative of all the mothers and sisters and daughters who have been left behind on this elusive search for artistic, political, cultural and perhaps even sexual freedom.

In the statement on Conrad and James quoted above, Terry Eagleton focuses on their belief that culture and order existed only in Western Europe, most specifically in England, and by going there one could be freed from the lack of civilization elsewhere—most often, in the colonies. Sissie rejects these notions of civilization in her scathing attack on Western culture and in what she sees and contemplates in Germany. Critic Anita Kern, in a fairly negative review of *Our Sister Killjoy*, comments that Aidoo "seems to 'have it out for the west'" (Kern 1978:57), but clearly Sissie's angry language and shocked thoughts reflect a young woman who has expected to find a cultural paradise yet sees something far different. Sissie's first encounter with the Germans on the street reminds me of Frantz Fanon's remembrances of the little boy on a train from Paris who shouted "Look, a Negro" a few times, and then finally, "Mama, see the Negro! I'm frightened" (Fanon 1967:111-12). For Sissie, response to her blackness is not as extreme, but certainly as disconcerting:

> Suddenly, she realized a woman was telling a young girl who must have been her daughter: 'Ja das Schwartze Machen'.... [sic] And it hit her. That all the crowd of people going and coming in all sorts of directions had the colour of pickled pig parts....
> (Aidoo 1979:12)

Visibly, through her own crude description, Sissie is striking back at the Europeans who see her skin as unnatural, and she is later ashamed of her mocking words; but it is also evident that being black and female makes her an oddity for the Germans who are fascinated by this showpiece, this "African Miss" (43).

Ironically, the one person who sees beyond Sissie's blackness is Marija, the unhappy housewife, and through their friendship Sissie is exposed to what she sees not as cultural superiority, but as an example of the West's societal degeneration—the breakdown of the family. Marija, who befriends Sissie, lives in a cold, stone house with her son and a husband who never comes home. And lest we miss the point, both father and son are named "Adolf"—albeit a common German name, but certainly a loaded one. Sissie feels compassion as well as affection for this lonely, frail woman, yet at the same time, she is suspicious, uncomfortable, and angry at their mutual historicity. In her thought poems, Sissie spills out these feelings "Who was Marija Sommer?":

> A daughter of mankind's
> Self-appointed most royal line,
> The House of Aryan—
> An heiress to some
> Legacy that would make you
> Bow
> Down
> Your head in
> Shame and
> Cry. (48)

This section of the novel called "The Plums"—a European delicacy not available in Ghana—reflects Sissie's (and perhaps Aidoo's) conflicting feelings for the women of this dominant culture. On one hand, they are intricately connected to the values and privileges of this society, retaining many of the culture's prejudices towards the "other"—male or female—yet, on the other hand, they are also victims of this society. For Sissie, her comprehension of the emptiness of this isolated woman's life is exacerbated by Marija's attempt to reach out for her sexually. And, although this section may be problematic for some feminist scholars, it is evident that Aidoo—however sympathetically—sees this attempt at a lesbian relationship as a perversion of womanlove and part of the degeneration of European family life:

> Sissie thought of home. To the time when she was
> a child in the village.... Oo, to be wrapped up in
> mother's cloth while it rained. Every time it rained.

> And now where was she? How did she get
> there...where now a young Aryan housewife kisses
> a young black woman with such desperation, right
> in the middle of her own nuptial chamber.... (64)

Through Sissie's perceptions, we witness this sexual affection arising from the despair of a western-style, isolated, loveless family life. However, it is also clear that Marija is seen as a fellow sufferer, and her home situation is one that many women deal with in some way or another throughout the world. For Sissie sees Marija's weeping not only as personal loneliness but also as part of a larger political discourse—the "collective loss" (67) that women within the context of an aggressive patriarchy must endure. Moreover, as she watches older "Bavarian ladies" in black dresses walking through town, she envisions them as war widows, "The blood of their young men was/Needed to mix the concrete for/Building the walls of/ The Third Reich" (36).

If our squint Sissie sees the plight of the German woman sympathetically for the most part, she has very little compassion for German culture as a whole. She sees the notion of Aryan superiority as symptomatic of Europe's mandate to colonize and oppress, and she connects the attempted genocide of the Jews to the murder of oppressed peoples everywhere. When Marija tells Sissie she must see Munich, Sissie thinks in her poetic/polemical voice that Munich is the home of the "Original Adolf" and then her thoughts jump from images of "freshly widowed Yiddisher Mamas" to the Rhodesian concentration camp-like system of apartheid after the country's 1965 so-called independence (81). The workings of Sissie's mind on the colonizer and the colonized filter through her experiences in this supposed paradise for the exile; her thoughts strike back while her words remain polite. The division between the polite exchange student and the angry woman inside is revealed in Sissie's meeting with the German-born American professor. He tells her that the one thing Germans and Africans have in common is that they have both been oppressed. Amazed, she is unable to respond:

> Yes, so frozen was her mind with this icy brilliance
> of this master discovery, she could not ask him
> whether after the Germans, the Irish and Africans—
> indisputably in that order—there are or could have
> been some other oppressed people on the earth, like
> Afro-Americans or Amerindians or Jews. (93)

But she also realizes that "the world is not filled with folks who shared our sister's black-eyed squint at things" (93).

If our black-eyed squint mentally reprimands the colonizers because of their history of domination, she looks equally askance at the African self-exiles who have bought the colonial line. In Germany, our sojourner reacts to the various Europeans she meets and plays off her memories of home against this alien environment. But it is her trip to England that conjures up a personal response to colonialism and compels her to issue a direct attack on her countrymen who have considered it politically expedient to remain in exile. In the opening of this diary-like section, "From Our Sister Killjoy," she comments: "If anyone had told her that she would want to pass through England because it was her colonial home, she would have laughed.... But to London she had gone anyway" (85). This section, compiled like so many journal entries, is a report to family and community (those mothers left behind) on the state of the self-exiles who have not only forgotten to return to help with the process of decolonization, but who forget even to answer the letters pleading to learn of their health and whereabouts.

For the African self-exiles in England, Our Sister really is a killjoy. She confronts the life she sees there, not the one which has been paraded before the folks at home. For many exiles, "the desire to lose oneself in the [European] world was understandable: a naive faith that this is the way to escape the feeling of exile" (Dorsinville 1976:63). But Sissie does not become caught up in the exiles' dream; she sees the life they lead with clarity. Her piercing look exposes the lies that have been sent back to the provinces. Her amazement at finding so many black people in London is painfully accentuated by her acknowledgment of their poverty:

> Above all, what hurt Our Sister as she ... watched her people was how badly dressed they were. They were all poorly clothed. The women especially were pitiful. She saw women who at home would have been dignified matrons as well as young, attractive girls.... She wondered why they never told the truth of their travels at home. (Aidoo 1979:88-89)

Although Sissie focuses on the women when she looks at the poor people in the street, she centers on the men when she explores the psychological poverty of those who feel there is nothing left for them in the colonial provinces, that life in London is where all "culture" begins.

In *Black Skins, White Masks*, Fanon explains the delusion of cultural superiority that the exile in the colonial "mother country" suffers from: "The colonized is elevated above his jungle status in proportion to his adoption of the mother country's cultural standards. He becomes whiter as he renounces his blackness, his jungle" (Fanon 1967:18). As I have mentioned earlier, many of the theories of exile focus on a sort of freedom felt by separating oneself from the constraints of the home country; this feeling of freedom is linked with a distorted sense of importance for the colonial exile. Furthermore, for the third world exile, as Fanon points out, this freedom also involves a rejection of both racial and cultural identification. Again, although this example may extend to women self-exiles, Fanon appears to be using the term "he" not as gender-inclusive, but as a specific aspect of the psychological disturbances of these male self-exiles. Aidoo underscores this point in her discussion of a Ghanaian self-exile Kunle, who believes that the problems of apartheid will be solved by Western technology. He illustrates his point by citing the fact that a "good Christian" white South African doctor used the heart of a young Black man for a transplant to keep an old white man alive. When confronted by the confused Sissie and her friend on which hearts were used in earlier attempts at transplants, he answers eagerly, "He must have experimented on the hearts of dogs and cats" (Aidoo 1979:97). Kunle, caught up in his identification with the dominant culture's "advances," has no comprehension of the irony of his own comments. For Sissie, Kunle not only represents the self-exile who values the colonizers' world more than his own, he also represents the "been-to" who comes home with an exile's consciousness to complain and exploit rather than help build the nation. His identification with the culture of his exile makes him unable to confront the political realities at home. Although he returns to his native land, as Aime Cesaire calls it, he is not willing to sacrifice and utilize his skills to improve conditions. Instead:

> Kunle, like so many of us, wished he had had the courage to be a coward enough to stay forever in England. Though life 'home' has its compensations. The aura of having been overseas at all. Belonging to the elite, whatever that is. The sweet pain of getting a fairly big income which can never half support one's own style of living.... (107)

Kunle's death, his chauffeur-driven car "burnt to its original skeleton," illustrates the wastefulness of the African elite, both materially and spiritually. But Kunle's attitude also clarifies, for Sissie, the reasons why many others are "coward enough" to remain in England.

Some of the early novels of Africans in exile (Peter Abraham's *A Wreath for Udomo* comes to mind) examine the conflicting feelings even the forced exiles faced in terms of their life in England versus what they had to confront at home. For the self-exiles who

can return, remaining in Europe represents another political decision—to deny the needs of their homeland and ignore the hardships faced by those left at home. Our Sister Killjoy forces us to
look not only at what happens to those who are cowardly enough
to remain isolated from their community, but what happens to the
mothers and other family members who await their return.
Perhaps it is because more men have experienced exile—unham-
pered by children and often chosen by community leaders—that
Aidoo focuses on them as examples, but with the exception of
Sissie's comments about the poverty of the women's clothes, Aidoo
does not critique the role of the African women exiled overseas.
Sissie, although a student-exile herself, is clearly attached to her
homeland, especially the women who are waiting for some word
from their errant men. As she remembers these women left
behind, Sissie's thought-poems construct the mostly unanswered
letters from home, asking the sons Kofi, Bragou, Obi, and others
when they are coming home. The letters—"for which we died
expecting and/Which/Buried us when they came"—underscore the
financial and emotional hardship the families face when most of
their resources have gone into the training of the "One Scholar."
However, the letters also emphasize the love and confusion of these
women who have lost their children to false dreams of the dominant culture's ideology:

> There is nothing bad here
> ... except our family is
> drowning in debts....
> Now,
> it is me,
> Your Own Mother
> speaking.
> There is nothing bad here
> And I am not complaining
> My child
> You also know
> we are proud
> that
> you are Overseas. (104-50)

The pathos of these letters interspersed with the insensitivity of
the exiles themselves illustrates the socio-political effects of the
exile experience on those at home. Moreover, the letters critique
those feelings of freedom and notions of cultural superiority for

the self-exiles who have forgotten their duty to their emerging nations.

In the final section of this prose-poem-novel, Aidoo jumps from the snatches of letters cited above to what Chimalum Nwankwo has rightly called a "confrontational" love letter. Sissie writes this letter to her lover who decided to remain in exile. Although I am unable to agree that this love letter necessarily indicates "communication between man and woman" as "a way out of morass" as Nwankwo suggests (1986:58), we can see that Sissie clearly speaks her mind. The irony of this section's title is that Sissie's epistle ends up more a political statement than a traditional love letter. To her lover and the other African self-exiles, Sissie is the killjoy who refuses to allow them to live in their delusions and forces them to acknowledge the duties they have ignored towards their native land and families. "A Love Letter" is less angry than the earlier sections of this work. Rather, it is filled with remorse for a relationship that cannot last and for a world that has profoundly lost its way. She softens her language in writing to this lover, yet the use of colonial language as her medium exiles her from her deepest speech: "[How can I] give voice to my soul and still have her heard? Since so far, I have only been able to use a language that enslaved me, and therefore, the messengers of my mind always come shackled?" (112). Sissie's resistance to the language she writes in mirrors the concerns of many writing in the colonial language—a "language which sought to deny" them.[1] Moreover, the realization that Sissie cannot speak to her lover in anything but the colonial language, distancing her from him, is exacerbated by the fact that he does not see this as a problem. What he considers a problem is that she is too aggressive, too outspoken, "too serious" (112). This love letter is composed of her polemical voicings—possibly re-arguing points with this unseen lover. She compels him to address the problems colonial rule has left these countries with and the frightening loss of perspective and lack of leadership at home. At the same time, the letter is full of her wishing that she could stop confronting him, that he would hold her once again. For Sissie, her desire for this man comes in direct opposition to her strength as an African woman as she states:

> They say that any female in my position would have
> thrown away everything to be with you, and remain
> with you: first her opinions and then her own plans.
> But ... what did I rather do but daily and loudly crit-

icise you and your friends for wanting to stay forever in alien places?... Maybe I regret that I could
not shut up and meekly look up to you...But you
see, no one had taught me such meekness. (117)

In further incorporation of the dominant culture's values, the self-
exiled men demand what Sissie calls "hashed-up Victorian notions"
for their women, in spite of the fact that they should understand
that African women were not brought up to be like "dolls of the
colonizers" (117). In her other works, Aidoo has concentrated on
the strength of the African woman as well as the domination—both
male and colonial—over her. In *Killjoy*, she confronts the colonized
male's notion of the ideal African woman (all softness and meekness) when these men have forgotten the real African women at
home.

In this love letter, Sissie recounts her most direct confrontation
with the African self-exiles. Sissie speaks out at an African student
union meeting. They spend hours discussing the political situation
in the home countries but do not see the denial of their services
as part of the problem. Tired of the "beautiful radical analyses of
the situation at home," Sissie asks these exiles why they just don't
hurry back and do something about it (121). She examines each of
their reasons for exile and calls them excuses. Her greatest distress,
however, is directed at a doctor who stays in exile because he feels
that his sophisticated medical skills would be wasted in his country. Rather than dealing with the reality that many doctors are
needed in Africa, he is proud that he can remain to educate the
Europeans to "recognize our worth" (129). This, of course, is what
Fanon indicates as the final stage of internal colonization—to iso-
late oneself from one's own society and identify totally with the
colonizer. Only in this world are one's skills valuable; the self-exile
"congratulates himself" on the fact that "his race no longer understands him" or appreciates his skills (Fanon 1967:14). To Sissie, this
"brilliant" doctor becomes the symbol of everything "distasteful
about all the folks who have decided to stay overseas" (Aidoo
1979:126). He and others like him, who consider their only duty
to the country is to send some money home to their mothers, deny
a deeper commitment to their family and land of their birth; they
squander their talents on their colonizers, who would rather see
them "run, jump and sing" (129).

In the final line of Sissie's love letter, she recalls what her lover
asked her when they met: "I know everyone calls you Sissie, but

what is your name?" (131). We, as readers, do not find out her name (nor the name of her lover), but as Our Sister she is the messenger of the people, her kin, to the land of the exiles. For Sissie, "the tale is not done being told" and, as the eyes of her community, she will return to tell this tale to the mothers and other family members (121). Here is where the self-exiles are most nakedly exposed: they are afraid to go home. Sissie's tale, as a sister, is for the community as a whole but especially for the African mother who, as both the self-exiles and Sissie agree, has suffered. But she cannot be appeased—nor can "Mother Africa"—by a paltry sum. She needs to see her children face-to-face, bringing their skills for national development that she "scrimped and saved and mortgaged her dignity for" back home (123). Sissie ends her letter as her plane starts to descend to the West African coast. She decides not to send it. Writing it was all that was necessary—and later telling the tale to those at home: "Besides, she was back in Africa. And that felt like fresh wild honey on the tongue: a mixture of complete sweetness and smoky roughage. Below was home with its unavoidable warmth and even after all these thousands of years, its uncertainties"(133). Although Sissie's lover does not learn from her experience, those who read her thoughts do. This collective novel of political thought, poems and personal perceptions ends on a positive note; happy to be back from her shamanistic journey, Sissie is ready to tell her tale, dispel the myth, and go to work for her nation.

In an interview, Nigerian critic Theo Vincent questions Aidoo's use of an African woman as the protagonist of *Killjoy*, one as politically astute as Our Sister. Aidoo responds: "But will this kind of vision be part of any African man's awareness of Europe?.... What makes you think that our men are more politically aware than our women?" (3). Certainly, in this novel, it is the protagonist's social vision that differs from her male counterpart's; she discerns exactly what the politics of exile is. And like her protagonist, Aidoo saw through the false paradise of the exile during her stays in the United States and Europe, and she has remained, for the most part, in Ghana to be part of its national development. As an African woman writer, Aidoo questions the freedom of the exile who denies both familial and community ties; furthermore, she—as well as other African women writers such as Flora Nwapa, Efua Sutherland, 'Zulu Sofola, and Aminata Sow Fall—is committed to her homeland, in spite of the "uncertainties" that exist there, because of her ties to the land and its people. Aidoo and other women writers like her feel bonded to their larger national communities, as they do to their extended families. In

Killjoy, she presents an African woman who does not flee the constraints on her and her society, but instead takes the responsibility to be the "eyes" of her community and exposes the world of self-exiles who have forsaken their familial land.

NOTES

1. This phrase is taken from the introduction to an unpublished manuscript by the Trinidadian poet, Marlene Nourbese Philip, *She Tried her Tongue, Her Silence Breaks Slowly* (1988). See also: Lamming (1984) for the essay, "A Monster, a Child, a Slave" in *The Pleasures of Exile*: 95-117.

WORKS CITED

Abrahams, Peter. *A Wreath for Udomo*. London: Faber and Faber, 1956.

Aidoo, Ama Ata. Anowa. London: Longman, 1970.

_____. *The Dilemma of a Ghost*. London: Longman, 1965.

_____. *No Sweetness Here*. London: Longman, 1970.

_____. *Our Sister Killjoy: Or Reflections from a Black-Eyed Squint*. Lagos and New York: Nok Publishers, 1979.

_____. "Unwelcome Pals and Decorative Slaves." *Medium and Message*. Proceedings of the International Conference on African Literature and the English Language, Calabar, Nigeria: University of Calabar Press, 1980.

Dorsinville, Max. "Senghor and the Song of Exile." In *Exile and Tradition: Studies in African and Caribbean Literature*. Ed. Rowland Smith. New York: Africana Publishing, 1976. 62-73.

Eagleton, Terry. *Exiles and Emigres*. New York: Schocken Books, 1970.

Fanon, Frantz. *Black Skins, White Masks*, New York: Grove Press, 1967.

Gurr, Andrew. *Writers in Exile*. Sussex/Atlantic Highlands, N.J.: Harvester/Humanities Press, 1981.

Kern, Anita. "Review of *Our Sister Killjoy.*" World Literature Written in English 17,1 (1978):56-57.

Lamming, George. *The Pleasures of Exile*. London: Allison and Busby, 1984.

Lautre, Maxine. "Interview with Ama Ata Aidoo." In *African Writers Talking*. Eds. Dennis Duerden and Cosmo Pierterse. New York: Africana Publishers, 1972.

Ngara, John. "Review of *Our Sister Killjoy.*" *Africa Woman* 12 (1977):65-66.

Nwankwo, Chimalum. "The Feminist Impulse and Social Realism in Ama Ata Aidoo's *No Sweetness Here* and *Our Sister Killjoy.*" In *Ngambika*. Eds. Carole Boyce Davies and Ann Adams Graves. Trenton, N.J.: Africa World Press, 1986. 151-59.

Philip, Marlene Nourbese. *She Tried Her Tongue, Her Silence Breaks Slowly*. Unpublished (MS), 1988.

Vincent, Theo. *Seventeen Black and African Writers on Literature and Life*. Lagos: Cross Continent Press, 1981.

TRANSNATIONALITY AND ITS CRITIQUE:

NARRATIVE TROPES OF "BORDERLAND"

IN *OUR SISTER KILLJOY*

HAIPING YAN

The past decade or so has witnessed the irruption of the consciousness of border-crossings into literary, cultural, and sociopolitical analyses. As various narrative tropings[1] of the transforming human geography in the late Twentieth century have been redefining the organizing features of contemporary literatures, articulations of "borderlands" and their "in-between-inhabitants" have been rapidly developing.[2] Embraced by some critics as liberatory discourses that have "shifted the traditional boundaries of subjectivities profoundly,"[3] those discursive enactments of "hybrids" are contested by others as problematic sites where the globalized asymmetry of power relations in contemporary cultural productions under the dictates of transnational capital is displaced or written off.[4] The fluid formations of "in-between hybrids" and their critiques, one may argue, indicate the high significance of the tropes of "borderland subjectivity" as much as their real or potential pitfalls in an era of transnationality. It is precisely such significance of and pitfalls in the making of "transnational subjects" that are enacted and probed with penetrating insights in Ama Ata Aidoo's *Our Sister Killjoy*[5] (1977), one of the most prominent texts of twentieth century world literatures.

I invoke the term "transnational" here as a category that is at once supplementary to and contesting of "postmodern" and "postcolonial"; it is a term that designates the more spatially characterized, highly fluid, still formative and increasingly form-giving human activities that develop and differ from the temporally characterized human activities categorized under the rubrics of "postmodern" and "postcolonial" in scholarly discourse. "Transnationality" in my evocation, furthermore, implicates two other terms, "transnationalization" and "transnationalism," and their historical and discursive relations are understood in the way that Fredric Jameson demonstrates in his explication on the relation among modernization, modernism, and modernity. "If modernization is something that happens to the base, and modernism the form the superstructure takes in relation to that ambivalent development," Jameson (1991) suggests in his writing on postmodernism, "then perhaps modernity characterizes the attempt to make something coherent out of their relationship. Modernity would then in that case describe the way 'modern people' feel about themselves"(310). As a dialectical process that attempts to make "something coherent" out of the transnationalization of modern capitalism and the emerging transnationalisms as its various and relational narratives, transnationality, similarly, is about how human subjects caught in this historical confluence "feel about themselves."

It is this "structure of feelings"[6] and its critique that I explore in this essay. By conducting a close reading of Ama Ata Aidoo's *Our Sister Killjoy*, I intend to articulate the structure of Aidoo's tropings of "borderland" in which the category of subjectivity is recast through a critical writing of the conditions of transnationality and the meanings of "borderland-inhabitants" yielded under such conditions. By working through such a critical writing of "borderland" and "borderland subjectivity," I attempt to show that Aidoo's tropological narrative is simultaneously constitutive of the culture of transnational capital and contradictory to its structural aspirations. By explicating aspects of Aidoo's transnational poetics of people in the periphery, I touch, in the end of this essay, on the question of transnational agency.

REDRAWING THE BOUNDARIES: THE MULTIPLE CONDITIONING OF "BORDERLAND" INHABITANTS

A highly poetic narrative performance, *Our Sister Killjoy* enacts the journey of a young African woman, Sissie, which connects and differentiates Africa and Europe with their respective and intertwined histories. "It is a long way from home to Europe. A cruel past, a funny present, a major desert or two, a sea, an ocean, several different languages apart, airplanes bridge the skies" (Aidoo 1994:8), the narrative begins. As if heralding what is to follow, this passage embodies certain prominent organizing features of Aidoo's narrative: Time and space are evoked as two inseparable systems of measurement and signification, and the multiple times and spaces are brought into dynamic connections, differentiations, and contentions. The geomorphologic configurations of the world are designated as both contiguous and disjunctive—"a major desert or two, a sea, an ocean," just as the human skies of "several different languages apart" with "a cruel past" are "bridged" into "a funny present" by airplanes in a transnational moment of modern temporality. Moving through "bridged" spaces and times of differences, Sissie's body is to be spatialized into a site where multiple modes of human geography are inscribed and contested; her mind is to be temporalized into a moment in which multiple writings of human history interact and contradict. As Sissie's body and mind mark such a spatial-temporal "borderland," her journey becomes the locus for figurative mappings of the "borderland inhabitants," their trajectories that indicate how and where the boundaries of the modern world are being crossed and/or redrawn, and their dynamic multiplicity of existence and consciousness.

Such a multiplicity is constitutive of the very conditioning of Sissie in traveling—the conditioning of her process of becoming. As Aidoo narrates immediately after the opening passage, Sissie's journey was initiated in a specific time and place that she as a young Ghanaian woman occupied, yet such initiation was also constituted with certain forces operating elsewhere. "[Her trip] must have had something to do with a people's efforts 'to make good again,'" Aidoo's narrative continues, intimating that it was linked with a past that had gone somewhat "bad" and left such unfulfilled desires to redress it. This "redressing" project provided sponsorship for selected, young, and educated Africans to travel to Europe for a summer camping program in Germany, run by "an international volunteer organization" (INVOLOU). Yet far more important it seems than an INVOLOU activity, the project directly involved "the embassy"—the institutional extension of a much empowered European state: "Right from the beginning the embassy had shown a lot of interest" (8) and treated it as a matter of "international relations."

The image of the "embassy" in action, however, is evoked with more connotations than its appellation would usually evoke for a reader of the era of modernist nation-states. Rather than being an institution that represented a single national identity, the embassy which made its move for the project is described as follows: "The minute her [Sissie's] name had been submitted, they had come to the campus looking for her in a black Mercedes-Benz, its flag furled" (8). What is most visible here about the embassy is not its symbolic representation of a national identity—the national flag is unidentifiable, it is "furled." The strikingly recognizable and definitive features of the embassy, instead, consist in the significant materiality of the "black Mercedes-Benz," a "superyeoman" of an industrial and mobile capital.[7] It is German, of course; but it designates much more and much less than the German nation-state represented in the form of what Benedict Anderson terms "an imagined community" with human faces. The "Mercedes-Benz" asserts a humanly faceless form of material, materializing, and materialized powers, German-owned and globally assembled, distributed, and consumed—it is transnational; it embodies a whole range of transnational financing, managing, manufacturing, marketing, and trading networks and institutions. In E. M. Forster's time, it was a modernist driving force "ever in motion, hop[ing] to inherit the earth" (Forster 1921:323). In Ama Ata Aidoo's and Sissie's times, it has moved over and across the five continents, redrawing all the boundaries that define the relations among and across all the human inhabitants of the earth.

Such powers of transnational mobility, as much of the recent scholarship has shown, are at the same time local.[8] Indeed, the transnational "Mercedes-Benz" has made its way into the economic landscapes and psychic textures of Latin America, the Middle East, Asia, and Africa, adding to its old claims in metropolitan centers of Europe and North America. The metropolitan forces crystallized and asserted in this ever mobile instrument now are penetrating and intermingling with the time and place that Sissie inhabits as a Ghanaian woman—evidenced in the fact that they are part of the initiation of Sissie's journey. In effect, what sends the German, European, or North American elite into motion asserts similar functions in the formation and operation of present Africa's "chosen few" with, of course, hidden or overt differential effects. Such similarities and differences are troped most vividly by Aidoo in her enactment of Sissie's fellow countryman, Sammy. As one of those who "had obviously been to their country [Germany/Europe] before and seemed to have stayed for a long time" (Aidoo 1994:9), Sammy was introduced to Sissie when she was being "prepared" by the embassy for her prospective journey. It was at a cocktail party of the finest European style, one of the special hospitalities the embassy bestowed upon her, that Sissie met "this African, a single man" (8). Speaking with a fine European finish, Sammy not only "mingled" well with Mr. Ambassador, the First Secretary, and their wives, but performed his "invited function" smoothly at the dinner by singing "the wonders of Europe." He was very anxious to get Sissie to realize that she was unbelievably lucky to have been chosen for the trip. "And that, somehow, going to Europe was altogether more like a dress rehearsal for a journey to paradise" (9). Solid, loyal, polished, proper, and certainly efficient, Sammy, in Sissie's eyes, appeared to be a superb "Mercedes-Benz" at the embassy's service.

Yet he was not quite one of them, obviously not quite. The name by which "they referred to him throughout the evening"—Sammy—instantly reminds one of the Euroamerican practice of slavery and the white master's power to "name" their human possessions. Such association poignantly comments on Sammy's somewhat excessive display of love for the national-origins of those who named him: "his voice, as he spoke of that far-off land, was wet with longing" (9). Under his well-polished persona, moreover, something seems hidden like an invisible scar of human wound that human-made masks would often make if not inevitably cut when one wears them too tightly for too long: Sammy "laughed all the time even when there was nothing to laugh at. And when he was not laughing loudly, he carried a somewhat permanent look of well-being on his face, supported by a fixed smile" (9). This "fixed smile," like the name "Sammy" and its hidden double, as much conceals as it reveals the connections and differences between him as an "invited function" of "the black Mercedes-Benz" and those who own and run the Mercedes-Benz empires. While the full implication of Sammy's peculiar smile remains to be gradually and painfully revealed to Sissie throughout her journey, it is clear at this moment of the narrative that such a "fixed smile" marked a deep problematic of a "hybrid" nature that dialectically generated irrepressible impulses of resistance in Sissie: "Saliva rose into her mouth every time her eyes fell on his face," and "more saliva rushing into her mouth every time he spoke." As "time was to bring Sissie many many Sammys" (9), they only further intensified in her potent desires of a different structural orientation, desires for a different form of being in her border-crossing becoming.

Contextualized by the Mercedes-Benz Empire, its embassy and its Sammys, and by their different and interlinked energies and operations, Sissie appeared acutely aware of the multiple conditioning of her journey. Working through such conditions, Sissie conducted her movement which overlapped and contradicted that of the Sammys, and those who invited Sammys to function transnationally. When she flies from Accra to Lagos to take a Europe-bound plane since "at the time, many airlines were not allowed to stop at Accra, because Johannesburg and other Afrikaaner cities formed a backbone to their business" (10), she re-writes "South Africa" into its haunting Other: "Some of us," her gentle voice utters, "called it Azania." The intertwinedness and contestation between these two discursive formations of the land, in one short sentence, crystallize the trial of the entire African continent (10). Similarly, as she crossed the Mediterranean Sea and saw the "first streaks of glorious summer sunshine" dawning on Europe, she firmly held the sight of its double—the moon "that had been traveling at eye level with them all night. Silent, deathly pale" (11). Commenting and complementing one another, those images are evoked in such a way that they signify the double nature of the culture of European modernity. When the European Alps "at six o'clock in the morning" rising into and beyond the sky was noted by Sissie to be wondrous and awe-inspiring, the Great Rift Valley in Kenya, "two miles deep in the bowels of the Earth," was immediately summoned in her mind and heart as its African counterpart (11), each recast the other with a "second" sight and a "secondary comment."[9] As if a music made of differentiality (Bhabha 1994:174), Sissie's body and mind in this "traveling becoming" operated with a spatial and temporal multiplicity that registered and reconstituted the very conditioning of her being and seeing.

The structure of such multiplicity is illuminated in various moments of Sissie's boundary-crossing journey. After she and her group landed in Frankfurt, a German government official greeted them at the airport, treated them with an abundant breakfast, and then took them by a taxi to a railway station, "they were going to take a train from there to a small town where they would stay for two weeks"(Aidoo 1994:11). Sissie decided to use the waiting time for a train to stroll around inside the station. As she looked at the things on display in many shops in rows, her consciousness of a spatial-temporal multiplicity reached one of its active moments:

> [T]here seemed to be more shops right inside the station than in the whole of her country....
> So she walked along in her gay, gold and leafy brown cloth, looking, feasting her village eyes.
> Cloths. Perfume. Flowers. Fruits.
> Then polished steel. Polished tin. Polished brass. Cut glass. Plastic.
> As Sissie moved among what was around, saw their shine and their glitter, she told herself that this must be where those "Consumer Goods" trickled from, to delight so much the hearts of the folks at home. Except that here, there were not only a million times more, but also a thousand times better. (12)

This awareness of differentiated and interlinked spaces and times that are manifested in the textures of material goods, assumes a complex dynamic which interrupts—while working through—the much naturalized representation of modernity. Inhabiting multiple spaces and times, a gently strolling Sissie, in her "gay, gold, leafy brown cloth," illuminated the constructedness and the signification of the machine-processed "shine and glitter" on display in the space of the metropolis. In the very process of her strolling, she was in effect crossing the material and symbolic "borders" that differentiated while connecting the First and Third Worlds in an era of unfolding transnationality. The "consumer goods" here were recognized by Sissie's "village eyes" to be both very similar to and very different from those "at home" in Accra, Lagos, and other places in West Africa. Such differential similarity and disjunctive connection between "here" and "at home" were revealed in the presence of her disjunctively spatialized body and her "time-lagged"[10] gaze in motion: It is the presence of her spatial-temporal multiplicity that designated the asymmetrical relations between the locations where the "Consumer Goods/trickled from" and the locations where the poorest duplications of such goods "trickled to." In the process of Sissie's strolling, in short, a trans-boundary recognition of the power relations between different localities in the presently changing human geography and world order was staged. A strolling Sissie becomes a trope of transnational mapping.

The asymmetrical relations of transnational proportions that is illuminated by a strolling Sissie, it is important to note, has been structurally hidden from the sight of "the subjects of the imperial power" and their various far-flung "colonized others" (Jameson 1991:50) when both had been confined to often violent modernist divides.[11] The image of a Sissie strolling across those divides then, can be argued to be a figurative designation and a historical enunciation of a "new era," a liberatory trope of the rapidly emerging borderland inhabitants in the late twentieth century who are transgressing, illuminating, and redrawing the boundaries of modernity. Yet the implications of this "Sissie trope" configuring a "new era" in history and its representational crisis cannot be simply or neatly assigned to the modes of "hybridized in-betweens" (Bhabha 1994: 173) or "postmodern crossovers" (Hall 1977:186). Those intensely theorized modes of subjectivity in the making tend to skirt the complex conditions of "borderland" as transnational spaces and, in many instances, turned their formative inhabitants into boundary-free individuals. And as Norma Alarcon articulates in her important discussion on La Malinche, social, cultural, and epistemological liberatory moments do not necessarily occur if the "crossing over by 'choice' or by force" is viewed as the terrains of "sporadic individual arrangements" (Alarcon 1997:294). How historical and structural conditions differentiate transnational travelers from one another, in other words, is a crucial question that has to be raised in our attempt to explore borderland and borderland activity; borderland inhabitants of the late twentieth century need to be explored in their profoundly differential engagements with the structural forces of their multiple conditioning. Without confronting the very multiplicity of Sissie's conditioning and the differential energy that her borderland mode of being and becoming asserts in relation to such multiplicity, specifically, one may well turn blind to the crucial distinctions among the global operations of the Mercedes-Benz Empires, "many many" Sammys' transnational trajectories, and the critical border-crossing and its form-giving forces that Sissie displayed and developed through her traveling. How Sissie, with her awareness of the spatial-temporal multiplicity of her own existence and consciousness unfolding throughout her journey, works with, through, and against those multiple conditionings of structural magnitude, in other words, is necessary for us to examine.

"VOYAGE-IN" AS "VOYAGE-OUT":
TRANSNATIONALITY AND ITS CONTRADICTIONS

The multiple conditions of transnationality for Sissie are, first of all, full of real or potential crisis. As she was strolling in the Frankfurt train station and "feasting her village eyes" on the "shine and glitter" in the midst of mixed urban noises, for instance, a voice suddenly penetrated her ear, body, mind, and heart:

> ... she realized a woman was telling a young girl who must have been her daughter: *'Ja, das Schwartze Madchen.'* From the little German that she had been advised to study for the trip, she knew that 'das Schwartze Madchen' meant 'black girl.' She was somewhat puzzled. Black girl? Black girl? So she looked around her, really well this time. And it hit her.... For the rest of her life, she was to regret this moment when she was made to notice differences in human coloring. (Aidoo 1994:12)

Despite the fact that the modernist boundaries—which were once structurally impossible to cross—are being crossed by Sissie, this moment of crisis indicates that boundaries continue to exist and in effect are intensified in the very moments of being crossed. It is certainly significant that Sissie is traumatically racialized ("Black girl? Black girl?") while she is precisely crossing the boundaries of race, and the race-lines are activated in the moment of her crossing them. Contesting the postmodern utopia of borderless transnationality espoused by some critics (Hicks 1991:xxxix), Aidoo shows how Sissie's body is inscribed by the boundaries that she crosses and how her consciousness of those boundaries is heightened with a critical double: The mode and motion of her being and seeing illuminate the boundaries in a process of deconstructing them, at once designating and challenging the asymmetrical power relations in the moment of an otherwise much celebrated "postnational deterritorialization."

Sissie hence becomes the locus of the contradictory dynamics inherent in the process of transnationalizing, a process that changes while repeating what it changes: She stands in a tropological relation to the structural forces that break the modernist divides while also re-erecting them, plunging the once codified human orderings into a turbulence of historical change which, at the same time, activates repetition. In the following piece titled

"The Plums," such contradictions are played out with a great deal of emotional subtlety around Sissie's encounter with Marija, a white, German, lower middle class, lesbian house-wife. Sissie's reflective experience and developing reading of such an encounter, narrated by Aidoo with potency and insights, trope the critical formation of an Aidooian subjectivity that persistently interacts with and significantly differs from "the hybridized transnationals" that have received so much discursive promotion and negation.

The narrative starts with Sissie's unexpected meeting with Marija at a site of once "one of the largest castles in all Germany" in a Bavarian town from where one can "look at the town and the river," contemplating. The medieval past of Europe is carved in this site as a time and space where and when the Prince-Lord-Master possessed "the biggest land, the greatest number of serfs," and "unvirgined" the virgins "on their nuptial nights for their husbands" (Aidoo 1994:19). The naked class and gender hierarchy which legitimized master's rape of the land and humans into legal, moral, and institutional "rights," however, seems to have been displaced into rather different modes of human connections: The site is turned into a flexible "youth hostel" for fluid groups of "international volunteers" (19). Hence one day Sissie appeared there whose presence generated obvious tensions by redefining the texture and coloring of the location. "Are you an Indian?" Marija asked, responding to the tensions of such redefinition through her nebulous sense of its sources, "I like zem weri much. Zey verkt in ze supermarket. Zey ver weri nice" (20).

Sissie's answer to this question was a simple "no"; yet at another level she instantly recognized the implied structural connections among various borderland inhabitants of a global proportion informed by Marija's significant misreading of her identity. Two nameless Indians and a journey from Calcutta to Munich, "it is a long way" to look for means of subsistence and a painfully familiar story for the displaced throughout the century. Sissie knew that she could be "an Indian" just like them working in an European supermarket or some such places for minimum pay, and she remembered her "West Indian neighbours," their similarly dispossessed conditions and displaced trajectories across Ontario, Liverpool, New Jersey, Canada, Britain, the U.S.A., and their various physical or psychic traumatizations and disintegrations (21-23). Her mind's eye was made almost audible through Aidoo's intensely fluid narrative that follows "migrant birds of the world" moving across "many seas and lands" (23) while searching for means to be human and human subject in a world where humanity and subjectivity are sealed with the signatures of "the chosen ones"—however differently such signatures are legitimized from the times and places of the princely Europe or its other modern versions.

Standing among the ruins of a once large castle with her baby in a pram, Marija of late twentieth-century Germany could not see the disjunctive spatiality and temporality of the migrant humanity illuminated in Sissie's mind and registered by her body. Marija could not know that this is a human geography of structural hierarchy in which the boundaries of modernist divides are intensified in the very moment of being crossed, and that in this human hierarchy she has been assigned to a "positional superiority" to those multiracial migrant souls that she recognized in and confused with Sissie. A wife and mother of two "Adolfs" (23), Marija's mode of being and seeing is inextricably implicated in and inscribed by the forces which define her husband and son with that at once ordinary and egregious name in modern world history: Adolf Hitler, indeed, was once from the numerous "Adolfs" on this land aspiring to join the European scramble of the richest riches of modernity. The structural effect of her racial, national, and ethnic location is glaringly shown when Marija was completely puzzled upon learning that Sissie was baptized as "Mary:" "You an African?" she exclaimed, "but that is a German name!" (24). As "Janes," "Ingrids," or "Michelles" "naturally," "naturellement," and "natürlich" did, Marija took the name of "Mary" as an exclusive signifier for European whiteness, since "dear Lord, Your Angels, like You, are Western, White, English, to be precise" (26).

Marija's intense incomprehension of Sissie and Sissie's intense lack of communication with Marija, meanwhile, are dynamic indications of their connection. Such impossible connections designate the contradictory features of the moment in which modernist divides turn particularly visible as they are precisely being crossed. Indeed, it is no longer the time of complete "spatial disjuncture" explicated by Jameson; after all, Marija has met "the Indians" and Sissie has arrived in Germany. The racial, national, ethnic, and historical divides which structurally separated Marija and Sissie have apparently been complicated, shifted, or broken in the transnationalizing—albeit tension-ridden—space in which they have encountered each other. Operating with and against their differential modes of being and seeing, they begin to tease out their connections. Their need to talk to each other as women free and at peace (49), their shared recognition of the meanings hidden in "mothers' old wishes" for having male babies (51), and their exposures of the forces that rendered the female gender into "a curse" under the sun (51), brings them closer. Then, there were the plums. Marija's garden were full of "real fruit trees" with apples, apricots, pears, plums; she wanted to share them all, and Sissie responded particularly to the plums:

> [So] she had good reason to feel fascinated by the character of Marija's plums. They were of a size, sheen and succulence she had not encountered anywhere else in those foreign lands.... What she was...not aware of, though, was that those Bavarian plums owed their glory in her eyes and on her tongue not only to that beautiful and black Bavarian soil, but also to other qualities that she herself possessed at that material time: Youthfulness/Peace of mind/Feeling free:/Knowing you are a rare article,/Being/Loved. So she sat, Our Sister, her tongue caressing the plums berries with skin-color almost like her own, while Marija told her how she had selected them specially for her, off the single tree in the garden. (40)

Marija, each day, prepared the plums for Sissie and her fellow campers. She picked each lot about twenty-four hours ahead and kept them overnight in a polythene bag, a process that softened the plums and rid them of their fresh tangy taste, preserving a soothing sweetness. "Yes, work is love made visible" (41), and such work of love is where humanity finds its most tender sharing and most potent articulation. This is the first moment in Aidoo's narrative where Sissie is co-named as "Our Sister"—a further development of "one of the very few ways where an original [African] concept from our old ways has been given expression successfully in English" (28). The "plums" that Sissie enjoyed with Marija—a profound connection of profound differences through "work of love"—becomes a significant indication for the transnational path that she would further chart through her traveling, a path of transnationality that overcomes and transforms divides, nourishes and transfigures differences, enlarges and deepens humanity. Hence Sissie develops into Our Sister from this moment on throughout the remaining narrative of this piece, with all the qualities and meanings of the beauty of "The Plums."

Such a moment of connection, recognition, and enlargement of humanity, yet again, is doubled by the other dimension of the border-crossing contradiction. Throughout all the moments of their connectedness, Marija's incomprehension of Sissie and Our Sister's lack of communication with Marija persist with a structural constancy. When Our Sister was visiting Marija's garden and enjoyed recognizing the trees and fruits there, she was simultaneously remembering "textbook illustrations at home" and how she was trained to internalize the landscapes of "Australia," "Eurasia," or "America" yet without seeing "outside in the African sun, giant trees stood for centuries and little plans bloomed and died, all unmentioned in geography notes" (37-38). As they took their evening walk together along the main street of the Bavarian town, enacting and sharing another moment of transboundary humanity, Aidoo's narrative immediately evokes the structural disjunction underlining their individual conjunction:

> Who was Marija Sommer?/A daughter of
> mankind's/Self-appointed most royal line,/The
> House of Aryan-/An heiress to some/Legacy that
> would make you/Bow/Down/ Your head
> in/Shame and/Cry./And Our Sister?/A little/
> Black/Woman who/If things were what they
> should have been,/And time had not a way
> of/Making nonsense of Man's/Dreams,
> would/Not/Have been/There/Walking/Where
> the/Fuhrer's feet had trod!/A-C-H-T-U-N-G! (48)

Even in their most intimate moment, when Marija embraced Our Sister with tears in her bedroom—"a sanctuary for shrouded dreams," Our Sister's recognition of Marija's desperation in need for human love is doubled. Through a tearful Marija, she sees, "against the background of the thick smoke that was like a rain cloud over the chimneys of Europe, LONELINESS forever falling like a tear out of a woman's eye" (65). Yet as her mind goes out to Marija, her heart is seized by the throbbing agony of the African continent inflicted upon by the same forces that brought tears of loneliness into Marija's life. Marija's isolation and Sissie's alienation, in other words, are shown to be compelled by the same mobile forces that localized Marija and displaced Our Sister, but the possible connections between the two are suspended at the moment when they are suggested. Indeed, the unhappiness of the metropolis is gendered with a class fix, the tear is from the economic and cultural marginals within the metropolitan centers of modernity. Yet such "unhappiness" is historically specified with its own implication in the structural violence visited upon the globally peripherized by the metropolitan powers. "'Ver do you come from?' Marija asked. 'Ghana.' 'Is that near Canada?'" (23-24). Such ignorance, while revealing Marija's lack of access to education and mobility due to her gendered marginalization within the metropolitan body politic (61), shows her sharing of the fruits that such a body politic has reaped globally: The lack of knowledge about the traumatized human geography beyond her own garden of abundance marks and masks her given "positional superiority." With structurally reaped and given material resources, one does not have to confront let alone map one's own location in relation to the magnitude of the structurally dispossessed and displaced.

Blind to her own location in the asymmetrical human relations of the world, Marija crossed the modernist divides only to reinscribe them as she reached out to Our Sister. When Our Sister was to leave Bavaria and Germany by train, Marija thrust a bag of plums into her hands as the train whistled its departure, speaking hurriedly:

> Sissie, if you have time, in Munich, if your train have ze time, Sissie, before you go norz please don't miss it, stop in Munich, if only spend a little time ... please, Sissie, maybe for only two hours. Maybe zis morning. Zen you leave in ze afternoon, yes? Because Munchen, Sissie, is our city, Bavaria. Our own city ... So beautiful you must see it, Sissie. I was going to take you zer. Ze two of us. To spend a day. Please, Sissie, see Munchen. (79)

With those deeply felt words Marija stood on the platform as the train moved, "smiling smiling smiling, while one big tear trickled out of one of her eyes" (79). Our Sister sat by the window of a leaving train, gazing at the receding image of Marija, agonizing with all the silent words burning in her chest: "No Marija, there is no where in the Western world is a must—No city is sacred, no spot is holy, not Rome, not Paris, not London, nor Munich, Marija. No. And the whys and wherefores should be obvious" (80). But they were not obvious to Marija, "to those for whom things were only what they seemed" (79), and, one may add, to those who can afford to see things as "only what they seem." Marija did not seem to know that her dream journey of "just ze two of us" required no less than structurally changed conditions for developing humanity free from asymmetrical power relations. Struggling with her mode of spatial-temporal multiplicity, on the other hand, Our Sister was forced to see such asymmetricality of a transnational scale and its effects on human efforts to reach for love and connection; yet she had no language to articulate what she saw to Marija. The images of Marija and Our Sister "staring at each other, not finding words" (78), with which their encounter finally ends, crystallize the most challenging problematic that "borderland inhabitants" in the era of transnationality have to confront: if the structural forces that condition, differentiate, regulate, and indeed police the hybrid dynamics of border-crossings are not recognized and worked through, the "borderlander" impulses to move beyond the modernist divides would remain to be individual dreams and social impossibilities. "Hybridized subjectivity," in other words, may well remain as an imaginary without social content when its formation is removed from its structural conditions.

Such structural forces that condition borderland activities, it is important to point out here, are rendered strikingly visible in "The Plums" through the poetic dimensions of its overall prose narrative. As if a return of what was silenced between the two women and their aborted connection, moments of bursting lyricism punctuate the story telling, in which an imaginary dialogue that Sissie has with Marija about Africa, Europe, and the world, about the past, the present, and the future unfolds and resounds with charged emotions. Consisting of fifty-eight verses that enact such lyrical moments and suspend the flow of the prose throughout "The Plums" piece, this imaginary dialogue moves through, from, away, beyond, and back to the Sissie-Marija encounter, branching into and bringing back multidimensional cognitive mappings of the structural forces that are interweaving the local with the transnational and the individual journeys with motions of global history. The implications of Marija-Sissie encounter are thereby rendered into a contextualization by which the individual is revealed as the structural, and the structural is mapped out as the double of the individual.

Some of the narrative moments discussed earlier are worth revisiting here. When Marija mistook Sissie as one of the "Indians" from Calcutta, for instance, the narrative shifts to verses and branches into the vast world of the "migrant birds" unfolding in Sissie's mind's eye, showing how she saw in this individual misidentification the collective existence of the structurally dispossessed and displaced searching for survival across the globe. When Our Sister was appreciating Marija's garden, the narrative once again dances through her mind's wanderings which move deep into the memories and experiences of colonial Africa and the Third World: How the colonized had been made to recognize the physical and mental landscapes of their colonizers and turned blind to the lives on their own continent including, above all, themselves. On both occasions, structural forces of a global proportion are inarticulable to Sissie and unrecognized to Marija, yet connect and differentiate their lives; these forces are mapped out through beautiful verses that articulate the inarticulable and visualize the invisible.

This dual-narrative that comprises shifts between individual encounters represented in prose and structural mappings evoked through poetry runs through the entire texture of "The Plums," which assumes two prominent organizing features. First, the prose narrative of Our Sister's encounter with Marija enacts her "voyage" from Africa into Europe with an individual specificity. Sissie's crossing over into the other side of modernist divides, in other words, is narrated through her concrete, intimate, and individual experiences. Second, the narrative of an individual "voyage-in" provides a rich texture of human experiences that touches off a poetic narrative configuring a historical and structural map of a global situation in which the "voyage-in" takes place; such a mapping becomes a process which contextualizes, penetrates, comments, illuminates, and defines the "voyage-in" of the individual. Being constantly doubled by such mappings, Our Sister's "voyage-in" is shot through with critical energies of a "voyage out," a historically informed and structurally conditioned "spiral away from" the material and symbolic centrality of "Europe and the West" (Said 1994: 239).

This dual-dynamics of Our Sister's "voyage-in" as "voyage-out" of European modernist enterprises, furthermore, is doubled by the dual-dynamics of her "voyage-out" of the land of Africa as "voyage-into" a reconfiguration of this "old continent" (133). Marija's question about "who pays for all the travel" (59) compelled Sissie to reflect on her boundary-crossing journey in relation to the continent that she seemed to be leaving behind. As the Europe-bound "voyage" moves her from and beyond Africa, Our Sister finds herself in effect "voyaging" into its operations of an ever transnationalizing nature. The role that contemporary Africa plays in the drama of an unfolding transnationality—and her own participation in it as a chosen member of the "future African leadership"—

became thereby visible and questionable. Her "village eyes" takes on their previously unknown powers to read, to question, to unmask, to connect, and to illuminate. The "innocent" consumption of excessive food by "darling teenage pigs" from different parts of the world in the INVOLOU ("They were required to be there, eating ...and eating. Above all eating" [35]) for instance, is connected through Our Sister's village eyes with the starved men, women, and children on the African continent; the differentiations between those "chosen ones" and the multitude of their home countries who have to "pick tiny bits of undigested food from the offal of the industrial world" (53) is illuminated through such connection:

> *They* felt no need to worry over who should want
> them to be there eating. Why should *they*? Even if
> the world is rough, it's still fine to get paid to have
> an orgasm... or isn't it? Of course, later on when
> *we* have become Diplomats/Visiting
> Professors/Local experts in sensitive
> areas/Or/Some such hustlers/*We* would have lost
> even this small awareness, that *in the first place,*
> *an invitation was sent* .... (35, my emphasis)

This is an "invitation," one is reminded, extended in the first place by the transnational Mercedes-Benz empires to Sissie to cross the national boundaries for the privileges of consuming limitless material abundance, transnationally. With such a desire-inducing license, Sissie sees how, spatialized and temporalized by the transnationally mobile feasts, those "they" who at first had wondered why they want to consume boundlessly are processed into "we"—institutional functionaries with no reflection how "our" professional formations were tied into the current "world feasts" in their intensifying mobility. The pronoun shift in the above-quoted passage from "they" to "we" establishes a distinct syntax rupture of historical and structural significance: Between the two collective pronouns "they" and "we," there emerges a locus where the global forces that choose, invite, induce, and produce those "we" through unlimited consumption are designated, and a multinational elite in the making is revealed.

It is at this discursive level that the poetic moments of Aidoo's narration operate not only as an imaginary dialogue of Sissie and Marija but an implicit dialogue that the narrator has with her readers. The narrator delineates for Marija, for audience-readers, as for

Sissie herself, how this new elite in the making assumes a "rain-bow" appearance that has tempering effect on the human geography transforming under the sun. As active components of this elite, those of "sable countenances" mediate between the rich resources of the African continent with its laboring humanity and the rapid globalization of "the world powers" (60), fulfilling their trained function in moving the monopoly capital across the nations for borderless profits. The formerly colonized and now "independent" nations have been so re-structured that the draining of their natural wealth and the bleeding of their humanity knows endless new forms but no endings (57). Such draining and bleeding, required as necessary conditions for reorganizing the scope and motion of the transnational capital and its human agency, turned the continent into a sign of throbbing human agony, the agony that shapes the other side of the transnational elite—the other constitutive components of transnational capitalism in contradiction:

> Nigeria./Nigeria our love/Nigeria our grief../A big mirror to/Our problems/Our tragedies/Our glories./ Ghana? A/Tiny piece of beautiful territory in/ Africa—had/Greatness thrust upon her/Once...Now she picks tiny bits of/Undigested food from the/Offal of the industrial world../Oh Ghana./Poor Upper Volta too/Another familiar tale./There are/Richer, much/ Richer countries on this continent/Where graver national problems/Stay/Unseen while/Big men live their/Big lives/Within." (55)

It is certainly worth noting that although such structural mappings of a continental agony co-authored by transcontinental forces is made possible by Our Sister's implication in the making of the transnational elite, her inside knowledge of such elite and its operations designates her as a part of the "we." Furthermore, such mappings are enacted in the poetic space of Our Sister's imaginary dialogue with Marija, doubled by an implicit communication—also in the form of verses—that the author of Our Sister has with her readers. Emblematic of the changing conditions of the world and its representation, Aidoo seems to suggest through her literary creations and narrative performance that the contradictions between the transnationalized elites and their massive others can be traced most effectively in the bodies of borderland existence; but articulations of such contradictions cannot be carried out in ready-made representational styles. It is hence through the most unique combination of prose and poetry that Aidoo enacts Our Sister's "voyage into" Europe as a "voyage out" of its boundaries, and her "voyage out" of the African land as a "voyage into" the core of the African [his]story: carrying with her body and mind an Africa of agonizing mass humanity into the modernist landscape of European style, Our Sister turned her transnational trajectory of an elite origin into a process of revealing the ground of such landscaping, namely, the asymmetrical relations of production that render Africa's laboring humanity dispossessed, unrecognized, and peripherized.

It is such peripherized massive humanity that is troped in Our Sister as constitutive component and structural contradiction to the transnational capital. Those massive human casualties, in other words, are foregrounded by Aidoo through Our Sister's irreducible corporeal and mental constitution. The "invited" Sissie by the transnational elite to join the selected "we," dialectically, brought this materiality of massive human lives with her and inscribed "their" agonies firmly onto the joy of the "mobile feasts" reaped for this elite. Turning into a conscious "killjoy," Our Sister embodies the critical energy contradictory to, while constitutive of, the transnational capital and its human agency. A borderland subjectivity, she enunciates that "borderless feasts" have exclusive borders, and "for the sufferers" in this unprecedented moment of modern drama, the release from modernity is not necessarily a release from human "tragedy" (79).

This "voyage-in" as "voyage-out" of metropolitan boundaries doubled by a "voyage-out" as "voyage-into" peripherized humanity, operates within, through, and against the movement of the transnational capital, bears witness to the structural effect of such movement globally, and designates the tensions and ruptures in any transnational border-crossings conditioned by such movement. At once crossing over into the material and symbolic space of the transnational elite and anchoring herself with the magnitude of its peripherized others, Our Sister lives such tensions and ruptures. Working through the mechanisms of the ever mobile capital which renders anything in its way to globalization redundant, she embodies its human casualties that are "the essential other components"(Jameson 1991:50) of its ever expanding projects. Through Our Sister, those "components" are enacted as contradictions not only in their function but in their very origins: They are not only human inconveniences that the transnational capital simply needs to overcome in realizing its expanding, form-giving projects, but human lives that this "overcoming" and "expanding" ambition and process necessarily generates.

This structural contradiction troped by Our Sister with her "in-and-out" dynamics, one can hardly overemphasize, is not the borderland subjectivity explicated by some postcolonialism of hybridity that thrives on the ambivalence of indeterminism (Bhabha 1994:102). As Our Sister contests the movement and projects of the transnational capital, the process of her invited "voyage-in" compels her to be acutely aware of, rather than ambivalent about, the problematic inherent in her own mode of being and becoming: A borderland inhabitant who contests the transnationalized elite is, at the same time, its built-in component. Such awareness moves Our Sister to turn much of her reflection and contestation onto her own mode of being and becoming under the conditions of transnationality and its contradictions. The mapping and critique of transnationality and its contradictions then also means looking into one's own mode of existence and consciousness as constitutive of what is mapped and criticized, and the transnationalization of one's mode of being and seeing is also the very conditions of such mappings and critiques. By living her own borderland location in the confluence of border-crossing dynamics as a site for reflection, contestation, critique, and transfiguration, Our Sister turns her own existence into a human cognition of a profound dialectic: One's implications in the mechanisms of the transnational capital are the constitutive conditions for one's counter-actions to such mechanisms. This dialectic "turning upon" her own mode of existence is an undercurrent in the texture of "The Plums." It is in the final two pieces of the novel—"From Our Sister Killjoy" and "A Love Letter"—that this "implication-counter-action" dynamics and its dialectic are developed with promises to transfigure such "in-and-out" simultaneity and contradiction into possible forms of alternative transnational subjectivity.

"RETURNING TO AFRICA":
THE POETICS OF THE TRANSNATIONALIZED PERIPHERY

The piece "From Our Sister Killjoy" opens with Our Sister's arrival in England, "her colonial home," after Germany. Constitutive of a much larger confluence of historical forces while having become fully aware of it, Our Sister who is crossing the borders this time is visibly different from a strolling Sissie in the Frankfurt train sta-

tion. If previously Sissie had been largely unaware of the signification of her history-making strolling, this time Our Sister crosses
the borders with a profound understanding of what it meant for a
formerly colonized, black, Ghanaian, female, to enter the boundaries of London, a moment that would make her journey "abroad"
recognizable for "people at home": Being "Overseas" (85). Knowing
that the conditions under which the modernist divides were certainly not removed but shifted into a differential temporality and
spatiality where transnational confluence appeared fluid enough
to tolerate and even display a formerly colonized, black, Ghanaian,
female, Our Sister observes her own fluid and contested location
in this transnationalized space and time closely. As she walks into
London, Our Sister immediately notes "so many Black people
there. Men, women, children. The place seemed full of them" (85).
The visual registration of the quantity of those who left the tropi-
cal Africa and stayed in chilly England is quickly deepened into a
recognition of the conditions of those lives in such a large quantity. As Our Sister "stood on the pavements of London and watched
her people," one thing is immediately clear to her: "They were all
poorly clothed" (88). In "a cold land" where "poverty shows as
nowhere else" (89), such "poor clothing" marked certain depriva-
tion of life resources—material or otherwise—with particular patterns and significations:

> The women especially were pitiful.... Unused to the
> cold and thoroughly inefficient at dealing with it.
> They smothered their bodies in raiments of diverse
> lengths, hues, and quality—in a desperate effort to
> keep warm: A blue scarf/to cover the head and the
> ears,/A brown coat lined with/Cream synthetic
> fibre./Some frilly blouse,/its original whiteness
> compromised./A red sweater/with a button miss-
> ing./An inch or two of black skirting/showing under
> the coat./An umbrella,/chequered green, red, and
> blue./A pair of stockings that are too light for/A
> chocolate skin,/A pair of cheap shoes/Never-mind-
> what-color,/ But/Cheap. (88-89)

This is one of the most illuminating tropological narratives in twentieth century African and indeed world literatures which crystallizes the predicament of the otherwise much acclaimed "liberatory
postmodern" or "postcolonial": The formerly colonized, black,
female bodies "smothered" in a radically discontinuous "motley of

fabrics and colors" (88), the wretched of the displaced. In such a "motley," Our Sister clearly sees a historical tragedy and not a post-modern parody. She "bled as she tries to take the scene in" (85), as she recognizes in those bodies her very self "smothered" in a violently altered shape of being and representation. How many of them were once Sissies in "gay, gold, and leafy brown cloth" and with lucid eyes? How many Sissies now are walking on the London pavements in those "shoes" that are "always cheap. Cheap plastic versions of the latest middle-class fashions?" (89). How far those feet could go and what kind of paths they would follow in those "always cheap" copies of transnational modernity? Is it possible that they are "running very fast just to remain where they are?" (89). And is it possible that border-crossers are crossing the borders just to reinscribe them in somewhat "diverse" ways?

The question of "border-crossing" then is hereby rephrased as a question of the structured contents of both borders and the activities of crossing them. While any "border-crossing" could be a activity of challenging, destabilizing, and collapsing modernist divides and hegemony in a transnational mutation, it could also be a moment of masquerading "running fast" while in effect remaining on "square one" (130). Such a masquerade can be seen when Our Sister notes that "mothers pushing their babies in second-hand carriages while their men toiled the long day through as bus drivers, porters, construction workers, scavengers. Mostly scavengers" (85), yet every man and woman she talks to claim that s/he was a student, "the men were studying engineering or medicine or law. The women were taking courses in dressmaking and hairdressing. They said" (86). Between their location in the changing landscape of London and the representations of their location, there emerges a structural disjunction where a process of transnational recolonization masquerades as postcoloniality.[12] Enforced or induced by the high fluidity of transnational capital, such masquerade operates with a structural disjuncture between its perceived forms and masked contents—contradictions between being and representation. Such disjuncture and contradictions are poignantly revealed in the story of Kunle and his reading of the "Great News" of his times: the success of inter-racial "Heart Transplant."

A relative of Our Sister's friend from West Africa now living in London, Kunle was "practically a Londoner" (95). When the three of them met, Our Sister learnt that her friend and Kunle had a "great news" on their minds which weighed much heavier than the war raging on in Nigeria at the time: A black young man's heart was successfully transplanted into an old and dying white man's chest and restored the latter to his "new life." Unlike Our Sister, Kunle does not pause for a moment to question the claim that the black young man just collapsed one day on the beach and failed to respond to any efforts at resuscitation while his heart was therefore taken out as a human material for achieving scientific feats, let alone to ponder how many such "scientific feats" are made in the modernist medical history through experimentations upon the "colored bodies." Kunle embraced this successful "Heart Transplant" as "the Type of Development" that would solve "the Whole of the Color Problem" (96). The old divide of modernity is to be finally removed: it was proved and demonstrated that different races were after all the "same," and a black man's heart throbbed in a white man's body and turned "a new lease" in the history of the latter's "health or longevity" (100). With his eager and yet unseeing eyes, Kunle does not recognize in this "success of transplanting" a masquerade for human equality, masking the structural content—the asymmetrical power relations—that are reproduced in these scientific redrawings of the old master-slave divide, this success of relocating humanity. The question about whose life was torn out, uprooted, transplanted, and displaced into whose enterprises of "health and longevity" is never raised let alone explored, by Kunle.

Yet his own humanity palpitating in the body of London, as Aidoo's narrative continues to dissect, seems to be precisely a component of such a heart that was torn out of its formerly colonized body and transplanted into certain transracial and transnational enterprises that do not yield anything to cure the bleeding, open chest of the African continent. Following Kunle's bursts of happiness about the "great success" of inter-racial "Heart Transplant," Aidoo inserts a series of most poignant letters from Kunle's mother and family, from many Kunles' mothers and families struggling in that vast world of the peripherized and dispossessed. "THOSE LETTERS FROM HOME" (104) that take up a full four-page length of the narrative enact a historical sculpture of the magnitude of the loses and agony of a heartbroken humanity:

> *Kofi*, when are you coming?/*Bragou*, there is nothing bad here …except our family is drowning in debts;/ *Dede*, we did not finish dividing the expenses from your grandmother's funeral and libation observances before your small aunt …was discovered

with The Big Cough./*Obi*, please keep this to yourself and bear it like a man. And maybe it is not true,
but I hear they shelled your father's compound in
the night/But please *Kunle*, if only you were
here/now/it is me/Your Own Mother/speaking./
There is nothing bad here/and I am not complain-
ing/My child, you also know/we are proud/that/you
are Overseas. (104-5, my emphasis)

Meanwhile, the Kofis, Bragous, Dedes, Obis, and Kunles who
embraced the "Heart Transplant" as the sign of their future are rendering the land of chilly wind into its newly acquired wealth and
beauty of multiple human colorings. This multi-colored masquerade for the life-mirage of a "global village" characterized by its puta-
tively postmodern, postcolonial, or postnational "borderlessness"
—physically or otherwise—is not performed in London only, of
course. Munich, New York, Milan, Toronto, Paris, even Tokyo. The
masquerading Kunles are certainly not Africans only either: the
Indians, the Philippines, the Chinese, and all the other "ethnics"
who have "a common heritage" of a global scale and hope to find
in the present conditions of transnationality the "wonders" of their
transplanting opportunity. "Gambian ophthalmologist, Brazilian
lung specialist, Indian cancer expert" (32), and may I add, Chinese
eye surgeon, among others, "littered all over the western world"
(62), following "a dubious bargain that left us/plundered of our
gold/our tongue/our life/- while our/Dead fingers clutch/English
- a/Doubtful weapon fashioned/Elsewhere to give might to a/Soul
that is already/ Fled" (28-29).

Such masqueraders that dress the movement of recolonization
into a moment heralding the arrival of a "borderless post-history,"
however, are also the registers of the structural disjuncture and
contradiction between their living conditions under transnationality and its ideology. Their journeys are full of "incidents" during
which their homes could suddenly liquidize into borders by
transnational capital, and those borderlands that they inhabit could
be instantly closed up into "walls" which prison their mind and
body, solidifying into mechanisms that reengender, reracialize, and
recolonize their humanity. Those black women "poorly clothed"
(88) in the coldness of London, those black men toiling through
their heavy days as "mostly scavengers" for the cleanliness of the
Western world, those "wretched of the displaced" with the claims
to be "students of modernization" "since the beginning of time,"

these and other images powerfully evoked in Aidoo's narrative, testify to the constant dangers of crises in the representation of forced and/or induced enterprises of "transplanting"—hearts, bodies, minds, or souls. Our Sister knew such devastating crisis through her own journey "Overseas": A strolling Sissie in the Frankfurt train station was plunged into precisely such a crisis when she realized that a woman was pointing to her: "Ja, das Schwartze Madchen" (13). From such crisis Sissie learns that "any kind of difference" would always be used by "someone somewhere" as means to acquire, maintain, and legitimize domination and exploitation in modernist material, human, and knowledge reproduction. "Power, Child, Power. Power to decide who is to live, who is to die, where, when, how" (13-16).

It is precisely under the hegemony of such power about life and death that the Kunles work themselves into masquerading for its changing shows, its changing representations. While many Kunles have received "post-graduate awards" that induce and perpetuate their displacement in London, Munich, or New York, Our Sister renames such "awards" as "the leftovers of imperial handouts," and reads in these handouts a "most merciless, most formalized, open, thorough, spy system of all time: For a few pennies now and a/Doctoral degree later,/Tell us about/Your people/Your history/Your mind/Your mind/Your mind./Tell us/Boy/How/We can make you/Weak/Weaker than you've already/Been" (86-87. When the Kunles become adequately skilled in supplying "local data for population studies," or statistics surrounding "sensitive areas" (7) and, moreover, become thoroughly grateful to the opportunity to be such "specialists," they culminate into Sammy whom Sissie met at the beginning of her journey. Here is the answer to the riddle that lies in the initial "invitation" extended by the new bodies of the old empires such as the Transnational Mercedes-Benz to a tender-aged Sissie to "go transnational": to be another Kunle-Sammy—the "enlightened representatives" of those "developing nations and peoples"—who would and could function as the "service agencies" for, "witnesses" to, and "validation" of the globalizing world powers and their transmuting project of modernity.

Like the masquerading performance that appeals to the Kunles, however, the success of processing Kunles and turning the Kunles into Sammys for the transnational capital is not always guaranteed, because the constant dangers of crises in such processing are generated by its structural disjuncture and contradictions between its perceived forms and hidden content, between its conditional dynamics and representation. Kunle in the "Heart Transplant" story died at the end of this processing, died of what he embraced: he died of a car crash—a modernist death which was however refused to be recognized and covered by the policy he had taken with "a very reliable insurance company: Foreign, English, with the original branch in London and cousins in Ottawa" (108), an agency of the transnational capital. When the profit-centered project of transnational capitalism has to claim "necessary human casualties" including, in moment of crisis, the Kunles and Sammys to acquire its "global village," how can such doomed human casualties as its contradictions ever disappear just to convenience its motion and ambition—if the very motion of the ambition that demand such casualties does not change its logic of structural violence? As if an embodiment of the unerasable contradictions with indomitable strength, Sissie—who is "caught at the confluence of history" (118) and is implicated in the same project that has manufactured the Kunles and Sammys—works through the grip of its logic, turns its power mechanisms inside out, appropriates its space and time into her tropological mappings, and reconstructs her own transnational subjectivity. She develops into Our Sister Killjoy. The project designed to process Kunle-Sammy, Kunle-Sammy's Africa, and Kunle-Sammy's world, in other words, also generates Our Sister Killjoy—her Africa, and her world. She is at once constitutive of and contradictory to this project of the transnational capital. While Kunles and Sammys condition her traveling, Our Sister Killjoy maps and rewrites their trajectories by critically constructing her own paths as their contradiction.

Our Sister Killjoy, like the Kunles and Sammys, does cross borders transnationally and inhabit borderlands in an era of transnationality, with the "invitation" by the transnational capital as a pass for entrance into the ranks of multiracial "witnesses" to its legitimation. As an intellectual from the Third World implicated in the dynamics of the transnational capital and its project for exploiting material, human, and knowledge surplus-values, however, she refuses to be the Kunles or the Sammys by taking the mode of her own being and seeing as another site of dialectical criticism: Never losing her mode of spatial-temporal multiplicity, never allowing her mind, body, heart and soul be severed from that torn open, bleeding chest of the African continent—the land of her own humanity—while crossing over into the metropolis, and never loosening up her grips of the complex connections between material-psychic mechanisms of the transnational capital and their massive

human casualties, Our Sister Killjoy in her trans-boundary journey turns herself into a living map that illuminates the multi-lay-
ered correlation between the human magnitude of the peripherized
and the powers that peripherize humanity. Such a crossing is made
possible by Our Sister's implications in the mechanisms that need
human casualties as their necessary lubricating oils; but it is made
critically potent by Our Sister Killjoy's choice to turn on her own
mode of being and seeing as a historical locus and human resource
for critical agency. She is a dialectical crossover in her own making under the conditions that are not made by herself.

In the last piece of the book, "A Love Letter," Our Sister Killjoy
as a dialectical crossover is crystallized into a vision of transnational subjectivity shaped in the form of a lyrical first-person. Ama
Ata Aidoo and Our Sister Killjoy—the author-position and charac-
ter-position—finally merge into one voice operating with the pronoun "I," calling for a poetics of "returning to Africa." "My
Sweetheart," the letter goes, "was it not part of the original idea
that we should come to these alien places, study what we can of
what they know and then go back home?" (120). This "returning"
issued in the final pages of the book, unlike some critics seem to
argue,[13] is not envisioned at merely a geographical level let alone
as a simple reversal of the dichotomy between a cold whiteness
and warm blackness, of the fixed divide between the West and the
Rest. And this "home" is certainly not naturalized either. Kunle of
the "Heart Transplant" story after all did return in a literal geographical sense to Nigeria, his birth place, and he died on the
African soil but died of the same causes that rendered him "a ghost"
of his "former self" (89) in London, with a distinctly postcolonial
turn: His "native" chauffeur was driving the car because "what is
the point in owning a special car in Africa if you are going to drive
yourself to your village?" (107), and the car had an accident.
"Trapped between the door on his side and a tyre, screaming,
screaming unheard, his heart vigorous, long after his voice had
gone" (107). He is just one more casualty of the modernist mobility transplanted into a postcolonial-transnational time and space,
the casualty designates a moment of crisis in the post-neo-re-colo-
nial masquerading of modernity in transition. "The car itself had
burnt to its original skeleton, its passengers to ashes" (107). This is
not what the "returning to Africa" means for Our Sister Killjoy and
Ama Ata Aidoo, clearly. When she left Accra, she was a tender-
aged Sissie; by the time she left London, she had turned into a
transnationally learned Black-Eyed Squint—Our Sister Killjoy. For

her, "returning to Africa" fundamentally means not to die as the Kunles and Sammys—physically or symbolically, not and never to "die so uselessly!" (108). In its tropological sense as enacted in the book, such a "returning" is in essence a returning to life, to "running very fast" in order not to remain where one is or has been, to go beyond any "younger versions of the old bankruptcy" (121), and to live a life relevant to reproductive humanity and conducive to the development of transformative human subjectivities (129).

And it is a process of rethinking and rewriting the history of modernity in its ever expanding transnational variations, the "history" that has produced the conditions under which categories of "the centered elite and the peripherized multitude"—old and new, are drawn with ever multiplied complexities. It is a process of creating historical agencies with alternative languages to rewrite and rethink humanity in the era of transnationality:

> My Precious Something, First of all, there is this language. This language. ... Of course, I agree with you about letting time move. But, My Darling, we have got to give it something to carry. Time by itself means nothing, no matter how fast it moves. Unless we give it something to carry for us; something we value. Because it is such a precious vehicle, is time. ...the question is not just the past or the present, but which factor out of both the past and the present represent for us the most dynamic forces for the future. That is why, above all, we have to have our secret language. We must create this language. It is high time we did. We are too old a people not to. We can. We must. So that we shall make love with words and not fear of being overheard. (112-116)

For those who have been written off from the structurally dominating narrative of modernity in its constant expanding and transmuting motions, creating this "language" means to create their own forms of humanity and subjectivity, their own forms of being and seeing in the world, their own forms of being creators of their own histories. In this sense, it is also a monumental "returning of the peripherized" which, in Our Sister Killjoy's view as in Ama Ata Aidoo's vision, involves a profound re-making of both the center and the periphery across the globe, and the logic that has forced us to see and inhabit the globe and its asymmetrical human power relations organized through such categories and their various reinscriptions. Such a profound remaking process activates the factors out of both the center and the periphery, as "out of both the past and the present that represent for us the most dynamic forces for the future" (116). It is in this remaking that Africa—along with all the other peripherized in the modern world—regains and remakes its time and space in and as future. "Returning to Africa," in this sense, is a returning of the contradictions in modernist history with a historical imaginary and poetics which resist the structural violence of the transnational capital in all the localities in the world human geography, while rendering the politics of such resistance into a dialectical narrative of human hope. "When hope dies, what else lives?" (10), Our Sister Killjoy insists. Her multiply inscribed body and multiply informed mind configure a poetic trope which generates and shapes precisely such creative discourse and consciousness[14] that are constitutive of the relentless dynamics of the expanding transnational capital on the one hand, and its structural critiques and contradictions on the other—a borderland troping that is a manifesto of inexhaustible human strength of the globally dispossessed, displaced, and peripherized, of their limitless creativity as transnational agency, a poetics of the periphery.

Such poetics turns the ever mobile project of transnational capitalism and its human agency into a locus for cognitive and critical mapping, and a site for contesting the power relations enforced through its mechanisms, while enacting a cultural monument of transformative border-crossing that is simultaneously constituting, criticizing, and sublating the conditions of transnationality. Without constitutively working through the mechanisms of the transnational capital and its culture, such criticizing and sublating praxis would not be possible; yet without turning one's own constitutive implications in the cultural productions of the transnational capital into a contested site for structural mapping and counter narrative, announcements to be liberated from the modernist boundaries in the unfolding era of transnationality may well remain an imaginary without being empowered into social consciousness that make historical agencies. In her narrative, the space and time of the "in-between" fluidity are fully activated but are not allowed to be sublimed into a metaphysics of "indeterminism," and the transnational moment of modern capitalism is fully inhabited, but is not allowed to be "translated" into an unconditional "liberatory" sign for posthistory. Working with, within, through, and against the transnational capital and its culture, she turns the formative "hybridizing borderlands" into form-giving terrains for historical mapping and contestation by means of turning her own borderland mode of being and seeing into a human site of dialectical criticism. Troped as a borderland inhabitant, a dialectic crossover, and a transformative contradiction within the confluence of transnationality, such a praxis enacts a potent mode of cognition for illuminating the conditions of transnational capitalism and its structural contradictions, and for activating critical energies of transnational agency that may bring significant differences into the present human world in a moment of an unprecedented historical uncertainty.

NOTES AND REFERENCES

1. I use the term here in the way that Hayden White explicates in his seminal book *Tropics of Discourse* (1978)
2. See Prakash 1992, Bhabha 1994, and Appadurai 1997.
3. Stuart Hall, "Interview: *Critical Dialogues in Cultural Studies*" In: *Stuart Hall: Critical Dialogues in Cultural Studies* Eds. David Morley and Kuan-Hsing Chen. London: Routledge, 1996: 408.
4. See, among others, Shohat 1992, O'Hanlon and Washbrook 1992, and Dirlik 1997.
5. Ama Ata Aidoo, *Our Sister Killjoy* (New York: Longman Group Limited, 1994 edition) All the subsequent quotations from this work are from this edition.
6. I use the term "structure of feelings" in the way that Raymond Williams proposes and explicates it in his *Drama from Ibsen to Bretcht* (1969).
7. Fredric Jameson takes the term "yeoman" from E M. Forster and explicates it in his "Modernism and Imperialism" in Eagleton et al. 1990: 57.
8. Arik Dirlik's recent essay "Place-based Imagination: Globalism and the Politics of Place" (forthcoming), for instance, traces the interactive dynamics of the global and the local with illuminating insights.
9. Here I use the word "second" as a Freudian "secondary revision" Hayden White's "Introduction" to his *Tropics of Discourse* offers an interesting reading of this notion (White 1978:13-14).
10. I use the word in the sense that Homi Bhabha uses it in his "The Postcolonial and the Postmodern: The Question of Agency" in his *The Location of Culture* with the difference that, in my reading of Aidoo, the "time-lag" must be viewed as being structurally interwoven with "spatial disjunctures."
11. And, according to Jameson, it is due to the impossibility of crossing such modernist divides and hence the impossibility for the human minds on both ends of the divide to "know" "the whole," modernist aesthetics was called forth to mark and mask the crisis of modernist representation. See Eagleton et al. 1990:50-51.
12. Gayatri Spivak's comment that "postcoloniality" is "a failure of decolonization" is pertinent here See "Teaching for the Times" in McClintock et al. 1997:469.
13. See, for instance, Brenda Cooper, "Chaiba the Algerian versus Our Sister

Killjoy: The Case of a Materialist Black Aesthetic, *"English in Africa"* 12,2 (1985):21-51
14. Vincent O. Odamtten offers an illuminating discussion on Aidoo's calling to create "a new language" and on Aidoo's own narrative performance of such "new language" and consciousness. See Odamtten 1994:116-132.

WORKS CITED

Aidoo, Ama Ata. *Our Sister Killjoy*. New York: Longman Group Limited, 1994.
Ahmad, Aijaz. "The Politics of Literary Postcoloniality." *Race and Class* 36,3 (1995).
Alarcon, Norma. "Tradutora, Traditora: A Paradigmatic Figure of Chicana Feminism." In McClintock et al., *Dangerous Liaisons*. Minneapolis: University of Minnesota Press, 1997.
Anderson, Benedict. *Imagined Community: Reflections on the Origin and Spread of Nationalism*. London: Verso, 1983.
Anzaldúa, Gloria. *Borderlands/La Fromtera: The New Mestiza*. San Francisco: Spinsters/Aunt Lute, 1987.
Appadurai, Arjun. *Modernity at Large: Cultural Dimensions of Globalization*. Minneapolis: University of Minnesota Press, 1996.
Appiah, Kwame Anthony. "Is the 'Post-' in 'Postcolonial' the 'Post-in 'Postmodern?", In McClintock et al., *Dangerous Liaisons*. Minneapolis: University of Minnesota Press, 1997.
Bhabha, Homi. *The Location of Culture*. London/New York: Routledge, 1994.
Cooper, Brenda. "Chaiba the Algerian" versus *Our Sister Killjoy*: The Case for a Materialist Black Aesthetic." *English in Africa* 12, 2 (1985):21-51.
Dirlik, Arif. "Place-based Imagination: Globalism and the Politics of Place" (forthcoming).
———. "The Postcolonial Aura: Third World Criticism in the Age of Global Capitalism," In: *Dangerous Liaisons*. Minneapolis. University of Minnesota Press, 1997.
Eagleton, Terry, Frederic Jameson and Edward Said. *Nationalism, Colonialism, Literature*, Minneapolis: University of Minnesota Press, 1990.
Forster, E. M. *Howard's End*. New York: Vintage Books, 1921.
Hall, Stuart. "The Local and the Global: Globalization and Ethnicity." In: McClintock et al., *Dangerous Liaisons*. Minnesota: University of Minneapolis Press, 1977.
———. "Interview: Critical Dialogues in Cultural Studies." In: *Stuart Hall: Critical Dialogues in Cultural Studies*. Eds. David Morley and Kuan-Hsing Chen. London: Routledge, 1996.
Hicks, D. Emily. *Border Writing: The Multidimensional Text*. Minneapolis: University of Minnesota Press, 1991.
Jameson, Fredric."Modernism and Imperialism." In: *Nationalism, Colonialism, and Literatures*. Eds. Terry Eagleton, Frederic Jameson, and Edward Said. Minneapolis: University of Minnesota Press, 1990:50-57.
———. *Postmodernism Or, The Cultural Logic of Later Capitalism*. Durham: Duke University Press, 1991.
Michel Foucault. *Language, Counter-Memory, Practice*, New York: Cornell

University, 1977.

McClintock, Anne. et al., Eds. *Dangerous Liaisons: Gender, Nation, & Postcolonial Perspectives*. Minneapolis: University of Minnesota Press, 1997.

Morley, David and Kuan-Hsing Chen, Eds. *Stuart Hall: Critical Dialogues in Cultural Studies*. London: Routledge, 1996.

Odamtten, Vincent O. *The Art of Ama Ata Aidoo: Polylectics and Reading Against Neocolonialism*. Gainesville: University Press of Florida, 1994.

O'Hanlon, Rosalind and David Washbrook. "After Orientalism: Culture, Criticism, and Politics in the Third World." *Comparative Studies in Society and History* 34,1 (January 1992).

Prakash, Gyan. "Postcolonial Criticism and Indian Historiography." *Social Text* 31/32 (1992).

Saïd, Edward. *Culture and Imperialism*. New York: Vintage Books, 1994.

Samantrai, Ranu. "Caught at the Confluence of History: Ama Ata Aidoo's Necessary Nationalism," *Research in African Literatures* (Spring 1995).

Schwab, Gabriele. "The Anthropological Turn in Literary Studies."*REAL: Yearbook of Research in English and American Literature*. Tubingen, Germany: Gunter Narr Verlag, 1996.

Shohat, Ella. "Notes on the Post-Colonial." *Social Text* 31/32.(1992).

Spivak, Gayatri. "Teaching for the Times," In *McClintock et al.,Dangerous Liaisons*. Minnesota: University of Minneapolis Press, 1997:469

White, Hayden. *Tropics of Discourse: Essays in Cultural Criticism*. Baltimore: The Johns Hopkins University Press, 1978

Williams, Raymond. *Drama from Ibsen to Bretcht*. New York: Oxford University Press, 1969.

Part Three

CREATING AN INDIGENOUS TEXT

NARRATIVE TURNS IN AMA ATA AIDOO'S *NO SWEETNESS HERE*

NAANA JANE OPOKU-AGYEMANG

Storytelling is perhaps the most ancient of the literary-verbal and dramatic-art forms of the world. It creates the much needed artistic distancing that would allow for entertainment and social commentary. This form has survived over the years in the cultures of Ghana and its functions have not changed much, whether in oral or written form. Along with other forms of orature, the tale provides a passageway through which society confirms its strengths and growth strategies, while inducting new members into its lifeflow. Women have traditionally been active storytellers in most Ghanaian cultures, either as narrators who operate within the domestic sphere or as members of a professional performing group. Women writers from Ghana confirm this role. Lily Baeta's title to her 1951 work, *Da To Gli Nam (Tell Me a Story, Mother),* demonstrates the central role that women play in story-telling. The dedication to Aidoo's *Anowa* (1970) recognizes a female member of the family, "who told a story and sang a song." Or, did the tale originate from this woman's "garden"? Efua Sutherland reportedly bases her play, *The Marriage of Anansewa* (1975), on a tale from Ghana. In the Akan culture, the Ananse tales with their pointed morals and exaggerated plots and characterization are handy, literary sources for socializing young minds. The tales help to emphasize or challenge acquired methods of interpreting the world.[1]

Interest in Ghanaian traditional tales has expanded into the mass media, such as television and motion picture. The Ghana Television popular children's program, "By The Fireside," performs the tale on a stage created to approximate the traditional setting, thus preserving as closely as possible the traditional form of the tale with the usual music, dance, other para-linguistic devices and active audience. Kwaw Ansah's film, "Love Brewed in an African Pot," which is based on a popular tale, draws large audiences. However, unlike the aforementioned writers and film-maker, who rely heavily on the content of the tale, Ama Ata Aidoo goes beyond content to employ aspects of the form of oral tradition. In her collection of short stories titled *No Sweetness Here*, one can decipher a significant use of the stylistic devices of Ghanaian oral narrative.

Aidoo focuses specifically on the position of women in Ghana and more generally on the Ghanaian society. The subjects and concerns raised more than twenty-five years ago—of women and their place in society—are as relevant today as they were then. The variety of ways in which Aidoo tells the stories, and the images of women and society she conveys in her tales, call known paradigms for conceiving selfhood into question. These stories suggest possibilities and alternate models to existing modes of seeing.[2]

The eleven stories in *No Sweetness Here* deal with marriage, exploitation of women, and the problem of jobs for women. *No Sweetness Here*, as a text, is important not so much because the stories uniformly deal with issues that shape the lives of women, but rather because of the artistic manner in which the writer discusses the contents of the stories. There is the experimental fusion of oral traditional forms, sharp dialogue and commentary, vivid imagery and adept use of language, which make it a unique collection. This paper will analyze the ways in which *No Sweetness Here* uses both form and content to question pervading notions of womanhood.

Ama Ata Aidoo excels, principally, in her methods of narration and in the creation of powerful scenes. There are shifting points of view and narrative turns in *No Sweetness Here* that bear testimony to exciting and successful artistic innovations. We recognize nine different methods of narration. There is the story as *amanee*, in "In the Cutting of a Drink." "Something To Talk About On the Way to the Funeral" is a *dramatic* short story. There is *a slice of life* in "For Whom Things Did Not Change." "A Gift From Somewhere" is a *soliloquy*. The title short story, "No Sweetness Here," though also a soliloquy, is delivered from a *dual perspective*. The use of *parallelism* is obvious in "Certain Winds From the South" and "Something to Talk About on the Way to the Funeral." Both "The Late Bud" and "Two Sisters" employ *direct contrast* in the telling of the stories. "Other Versions" is a *three-tiered* story, a variation of a theme. The structure of "Everything Counts" can be termed a *reminiscence*.

Amanee is an Akan word for message. This message usually functions like a narrative. The sequential arrangement of episodes and incidents in the plot of *amanee* takes the audience from the immediate past to the present, working its way through a clearly defined linear thread of narration. It employs suspense, humor and other stylistic devices that would allow for a graphic rendering of relevant information. The person who delivers the *amanee* must have a good memory and be skillful in the use of language. The speaker completes his message before the audience asks questions. However, the message is rendered in such a way that the audience can clearly imagine what the messenger has experienced. A good delivery of *amanee* allows the audience to comment on the delivery as well as contribute to the discussion that inevitably follows.

In "In the Cutting of a Drink," the brother who narrates to his family how he found his sister, Mansa, relates the story in a "you-won't-believe-this" tone of voice, as he tells the family about the unfamiliar customs he witnessed in the city of Accra. The narrator's eagerness to convey to his relatives the dynamics of city life and his family's shock at and utter disbelief of the contents of his message, reveal the significant difference between urban and rural lifestyles. This distinction is necessary for the narrator and author to deliver effectively the message and convey the final shock of the narrative—the discovery of Mansa who, now grown up, works as a prostitute.

The opening lines of the story establish the context for the narration and reveal the structure of *amanee*:

> I say, my uncles, if you are going to Accra and any-
> one tells you that the best place for you to drop
> down is at the Circle, then he has done you good,
> but . . . Hm . . . I even do not know how to describe
> it . . .
> 'Are all these beings that are passing this way and
> that way human? Did men buy all these cars with

money . . .? But my elders, I do not want to waste
your time. (Aidoo 1970:30)

We are presented with an envoy who is speaking to a clearly identified audience, his family. After a brief opening, he raises curiosity by announcing the end of the introduction and the beginning
of the more direct and serious import of his mission. The reader
from then on suspects that the narrator may not stick to the linear
progression of the *amanee*, but would create something new out of
a known form.

Through flashback, we as readers, along with the audience, join
the messenger on the dramatic trip to Accra. When the driver says
to the narrator to "jump in" we do so with him, "round the thing
which was like a big bowl on a very huge stump of wood" (30). In
the city, we understand the source of his confusion in relation to
life in the city and the norms that govern conjugal and gender relations. The reader also feels like an active participant in his merri-
ment as he dances at a night club, perhaps for the first time. We
laugh with him when he admits he is "shaking like water in a brass
bowl" (35). We also share his trepidations at the prospects of inviting people he does not even know for a dance. We feel his pain
when Mansa fails to recognize him, and his shock when she tells
him without qualification, that "any kind of work is work"(37). This
close and active relationship between the narrator and the audience is a distinctive feature of the oral performance of the tale.

It is nonetheless paradoxical that the monologue is simultaneously interactive, not only between the speaker and the audience,
but also between the speaker and the reader. The narrator extrap-
olates the expectations, emotions and thoughts of his audience and
works them into his message. He stretches his report to cover
Duayaw, a member of the extended family, who helped him in the
city. When he gets to the section of his narrative, which touches
on the educational background of the lost sister, he anticipates his
mother's reaction. He quickly reassures her that the community
has not forgotten her efforts to make her daughter stay in school.
He also interrupts his narration to comment on the emotional state
of his audience: "These are useless tears you have started to weep,
my mother. Have I said anything to show that she was dead?" (32).
Or, in anticipation of his uncles' emotions he adds: "Do not be surprised, uncles" (34). He continues with great insight into the psychology of these men:

> My uncle, do not say that instead of concerning
> myself with the business for which I had gone to the
> city, I went dancing. Oh, if you only knew what hap-
> pened at this place, you would not be saying this. I
> would not like to stop somewhere and tell you the
> end . . . I would rather like to put a rod under the
> story, as it were, clear off every little creeper in the
> bush . . . (35)

Narrator-audience interaction is sometimes made possible by a response to a direct question reported by the narrator: "Ei! my little sister, are you asking me a question? Oh! you want to know whether I found Mansa?" (35). Sometimes as well, interaction is brought on by a request from the speaker to the audience, as when he asks that someone "cut him a drink." This "cutting of a drink" occurs three times in the story. Audience and reader are thus more actively involved in the narration. The first cutting of a drink occurs when, not sure if he is going to make any headway in his quest, he solicits the reader's support. The second happens towards the end of his *amanee*, when he tells his audience: "I was sent to find a lost child. I found her a woman" (37). The third takes place when the narrator demonstrates how city women claim freedom for themselves, cutting drinks like men. In these instances, the narrator invites the reader to share directly in his emotion of bewilderment. By the end of the narration, both the *amanee* proper and the question and answer that follow have been covered in what we may call an interactive monologue.

The story of Mansa speaks about the position of women in a rapidly changing society. Mansa had dropped out of school after grade three and had been apprenticed to a relative in the city to learn a trade. For a reason that she is not allowed to articulate by herself, Mansa becomes lost to her relatives who are determined to find her. The weakness of this eyewitness account is that the narrative is generally restricted to the point of view of her brother. As a result, the reader cannot hear Mansa's story in her own voice. However, textual evidence saves the story from losing its complete powerful effect, since important information about her earlier life implies her motive for behavior. After only three years of basic education and no further training there is very little option allowed a young woman in the city. This information allows the reader to understand how a young woman in Mansa's circumstances could end up as a prostitute. The anonymity of the city had allowed her to modify her morals and admit to her confused brother that "any kind of work is work" (37). The fact that she decides to go home and that her family looks forward to receiving her despite what she has become, makes interesting revelations about strong family ties. Another story in the collection, the tale of Mercy in "Two Sisters" adds to that of Mansa to highlight reasons that draw women into prostitution.[3] Mercy wants things she has not worked hard for, and she lacks the critical mind to assess even her own situation. Sex becomes, for her, one easy way of finding material things like shoes with which she symbolically walks further away from lasting solutions. In Mansa's it appears that prostitution was one of few alternatives for survival.

The second narrative turn that Aidoo employs is the dramatic story, which has two distinctive features in "Something To Talk About On the Way to the Funeral." Firstly, we have a dialogue between two women friends, even though only one of them does most of the talking. The other participates with interjections, questions and comments all of which nonetheless spur on the narration, sometimes to the irritation of the major speaker. Once, she tells off her listener by resorting to the use of a proverb: "I am taking you to birdtown so I can't understand why you insist on searching for eggs from the suburb!" (118). The second feature of this story is that characters are continuously in motion, walking toward the funeral home. The reader is obliged to tag along, conscious of the fact that s/he is not really expected to listen to the conversation, especially when the major narrator says: "One only speaks of it in whispers. Let me turn my head and look behind me . . . And don't go standing in the river telling people. Or if you do, you better not say that you heard it from me" (115). Through this conversation, Auntie Araba's biography is played before the reader. The past is interspersed with the present, even as the structure of the story moves back and forth, sweeping the details of the lives of the narrators into its flow. In the end, thanks to the technique of the narration, we have more than the biography of the deceased; we also know something about the lives of the narrators.

Auntie Araba was a successful and an innovative baker, turning the white flour into products that the original producers of the commodity may never have imagined. We are informed that she worked six out of the seven days in the week, that she "rolled her dough far into the night and with the first cock-crow got up to light her fires" (118). This woman had picked up her trade informally in the household in which she was sexually exploited. She passed it on to the younger woman she had hoped would be her daughter-in-law. Auntie Araba would have gone even farther in life, had her circumstances been more favorable. For the younger woman, it looked like her career was something she was doing to while away time. Her more important concern was to set her life "right," by getting married to the man whose child she was raising while he himself had an education. In this respect, the narrative takes a brief swipe at the debilitating effects of romantic love. Auntie Araba is devastated into inaction by her disappointment at the failed relationship with the father of her child.

The third narrative turn employed by Aidoo is a slice of life. Dialogue is the predominant narrative mode. In "For Whom Things Did Not Change," conversation takes place between Zirigu the housekeeper and Setu his wife and petty-trader. Dialogue also occurs between Zirigu and the guest, Kobina, who is a member of the middle class of a newly independent nation. In the first conversation, the speakers hop from a discussion of domestic and family obligations, to a commentary on the morals of the middle class male, onto ownership, and finally to downright exploitation. This discussion qualifies as *tranche de vie*, a slice of life, because of the smooth manner in which one topic blends into the other. The second conversation between Zirigu and Robina covers a wider portion of the story. The subjects are not ordered and are focused on the implications of political independence. After an initial hesitation, Zirigu relaxes with Kobina, who makes efforts to identify with the lower middle-class couple by asking to share in their meal and drink. The technique of dialogue used in presenting the slice of life implies some measure of equality.[4] It questions the barriers that exist between these characters and the groups that they represent. Through the conversations, barriers are broken. The "master" becomes the "student" at the feet of the housekeeper. By allowing a discussion on how political independence has not changed anything, the narrative is suggesting a reexamination of the heritage of structures that govern how the master is to relate to his subordinates.

The fourth narrative structure, seen in "A Gift from Somewhere," is a variation of soliloquy. There is an omniscient narrator who sets the stage and allows the major character to take over. The story is about the traditional healer who absconds when the baby of the narrator, Abena Gyaawa, dies in his hands, before ever he is made to face the music. Abena, for her part, is portrayed as one lost in contemplation of her loss. The position of the reader is made more tenuous given that the form of soliloquy is by definition private. Here, the woman wants to be alone with her memory and the reader is the unwitting observer of this emotion. Abena's stance reveals important information about her state of mind and heart, as well as her intimate thoughts and feelings about her marital situation. Yet the reader is not passive! At the end of the narrative, s/he is placed in the position not of a judge, but of a sympathetic listener.

Abena Gyaawa's husband is unfair and treats their children harshly. She has physical evidence in the form of a scar to buttress her case. However, she accepts her situation, consoled that she is a mother. One cannot judge the father because his testimony is presented wholly from the thoughts of his disenchanted wife. She is the only narrator and the principal actor in this story. It is possible that the narrator simply wanted to contemplate part of her life, and is satisfied with the opportunity to do so. After all, she appears to harbor little bitterness. However, the two sections of the soliloquy also contain much drama. The first section shows the medicine man go through his antics and run away before things get too complex. The scene is pierced with the shrill cries of a mother plagued by infant mortality. The second section takes us through the brutal assault of Abena's son, Nyamekye. Aidoo, the expert story teller, has taken the narrative form of the soliloquy and has artistically reversed it, achieving audience participation.

Abena Gyaawa blames her bad marriage principally on her husband's relations and co-wives: "Something tells me it's his people and his wives who prevent him from having good thoughts about me and mine"(83). Her major concern here is the absence of fairness by the husband and his people. The reader gets the impression that polygamy in itself is not the issue. Perhaps, if the men were not "bullies" like Kodwo Fi; if Abena's husband could show a little more warmth and understanding towards their children and stop physically abusing them in the name of discipline; and if he would call them "their" and not "her" children, marriage might be more tolerable. Like Abena Gyaawa, Maami Ama, takes refuge in motherhood as a source of consolation for a marriage without "sweetness".

When Aidoo treats the technique of soliloquy from a dual perspective, we have quite a modification of that narrative turn, and possibly a fifth structure. The eponymous short story "No Sweetness Here," comes from a dual perspective, from both the points of view of Chicha (Fantse for "teacher") and Maami Ama.

Chicha is a narrator and a commentator, while Maami Ama is a narrator of her own story, and an autobiographer. The close relationship between the two is important. It allows Chicha to take over the narration of Maami Ama, when the death of Kwesi does not allow the latter to be sufficiently distanced emotionally to continue the narration. The powerful scene in which the mother clutches at the school books of her dead child and the scene at the family gathering where the divorce proceedings take place could hardly have been adequately painted by Maami Ama, the principal actor in both dramas. Chicha's role is also important in taking us to the school compound where Maami Ama does not belong, thus broadening the canvas of the narrative.

The story is about Maami Ama on the verge of divorce after an unhappy marriage in a polygamous context. Chicha, a young woman teacher of the village school, is the major narrator of this story and the confidant of Maami Ama. Through their conversation, we learn that Maami Ama is separated from her husband. She recounts some unpleasant details of their seven-year marriage: "Seven years is a long time to bear ill-treatment from a man coupled with contempt and insults from his wives" (60). The problem goes beyond the wives to touch the personality of her husband, "a selfish and bullying man, whom no decent woman ought to have married" (60). This authorial comment does not probe the structures that allow the types of Kofi Fi to be "selfish" and "bullying." Rather, it reveals the attitude of the author toward Maami Ama who now makes a claim to her "decency" by speaking out, although only in parenthesis. Although she is the first wife, Maami Ama is given the most unproductive portion of land for her agricultural activity. Further more, all manner of interaction with her co-wives and in-laws is forbidden to her. This suggests two important things. First, the fact that the woman gets land through her husband shows that although she farms for a living, she has no free access to the major factor of her production—land. Therefore, it is not possible for Maami Ama to see her farming career as an option for unrestrained self-expression in her life. Second, the women uniformly lack space for verbal expression of their dissatisfaction. This need bursts at its seams and acts itself out in the frustrations they direct at one another in their polygamous context. The absence of freedom for these women is seen through their point of view, and is confined to the interior monologue of the narrator (with a restricted audience).

Maami Ama had occasion to complain to her mother about her plight, and the older woman gave her this advice: "In marriage, a woman must sometimes be a fool" (61). Maami Ama bears out the correctness of this admonition through her conduct in tolerating all manner of abuse. Obviously, the mothers of her co-wives must have had other guiding metaphors: hence their daughters' aggressive behavior. By asking for a divorce, Maami Ama shows there is a way out of a bad marriage. This outlet exists even if it means giving back whatever the man had given her as gift, dowry or medical expenses. She trades her freedom for all those material items—"I have been a fool for too long a time," she confides in Chicha. During the divorce proceedings, Maami Ama does not actively participate in the trading of accusations between the in-laws of both sides. Women from both sides give vent to their frustrations, calling one another "witches" among other unsavory epithets. This is, perhaps, one of the few stories in African literature to confront head on the issue of divorce.[5]

What comes out of this story is the picture of a woman stripped of that perceived important dual status that the society upholds for a woman—wifehood and motherhood. Maami Ama herself places motherhood above wifehood, and so she is not very interested in turning divorce into a money-making venture as does her ex-husband who haggles over gifts many years old. Her aunts, on the other hand, fail to share in her priorities and so they blame her for allowing Kodwo Fi to have the better of her. Maami Ama would be very happy out of marriage, if only she could be left alone to care for her child, whom she does not fight to keep though she has the right to keep him. Custody therefore goes to her ex-husband. It is possible to see Maami Ama as a weak character who loses sight of her rights even within a context that allows women some liberties. It is also possible to see her behavior, dominated by silence and inaction, as teaming up with the narrative technique to make a statement about the plight of some economically and socially deprived members of society. Our discussion of "The Late Bud" later, we hope, might throw further light on how disadvantaged women like Maami Ama are formed in society.[6]

"Something To Talk About" and "Certain Winds From the South" employ parallelism, the sixth narrative device, to recount their respective themes. In "Something to Talk about, Araba's life closely parallels that of Mansa, the young woman she had hoped her son would marry. Araba had come back to the village after her protégé's husband had made her pregnant. The son she bears in turn gets a young woman pregnant. Her life is thus played out all over in that of this younger woman. Both women feel disgraced and abandoned. In "Certain Winds From the South," both Mma Asana and her daughter Hawa share in common the pain of being left alone with newborn babies. As in the previous story, both women survive by lending support to each other. These two stories show four women, who for different reasons, become single parents who must "decide to grow up" (52), if they are to overcome their immediate hardships. The use of parallelism suggests the absence of qualitative change in the lives of women of different generations. This lack of improvement is due to the dominant, unaltered structures that govern their lives.

The two women in "Certain Winds From the South" are compelled by difficult circumstances to separate from their husbands and look after their children without any male support. The older woman, Mma Asana, lost her husband who had been recruited "to travel to the lands beyond the sea and fight . . . in other people's war." The confused wife had asked her husband: "What has all that got to do with you and me?" (54). This information is important in lending a human touch to the plight of the colonized male and showing the degree of loss of freedom, generally. It reveals to us the extent of the sacrifice made by the colonized people who fought in the oppressor's wars. Ironically, that was a time when one was badly needed at home to redress the problem of colonial hegemony and its attendant devaluation of human life. The younger woman, Hawa, is compelled to separate from her husband who has decided to travel south of the country "to cut grass" (50). This is considered a demeaning way to earn a living. The older woman lost her husband, and the younger one has no idea when she will see her husband again. The parallel between the lives of women is extended to describe the lives of men and women in similar deprived situations. This is important in avoiding an over-simplification of the debate of the genders. Here, it is broadened to include class.

For these women and some of their men, marriage is definitely not sweet since the precarious political and economic contexts in which they find themselves make it impossible for them to have any certainty even about their marital lives. Their husbands are not irresponsible. They are not bullies like Kodjo Fi. They are neither violent nor mean. They wish they could do right by their women, but the debilitating circumstances make it impossible for them to show ordinary strengths and weaknesses like ordinary human beings. Their portrait provides a balance to the one-dimensional, negative portraits of male adults who people the world of

No Sweetness Here. The story also shows women who, faced with a difficult future, commit themselves to do the best they can.

Direct contrast, as the seventh narrative device, is used in the telling of both "The Late Bud" and "Two Sisters." The sisters, in both stories, are very much unlike each other. In "The Late Bud" Yaaba loves the outdoors and refuses to cooperate in her mother's socializing mission of making a woman of her. Her sister, Adwoa, is the model child who never contradicts her mother. In the "Two Sisters," Mercy is single, trades sex for money and loses no sleep over her behavior, which causes her married sister, Connie, much anguish. Mercy believes the only solution to a wandering husband is for the wife to grab some freedom for herself. Connie, on the other hand, cannot see herself expressing her disapproval in like manner. Connie constantly worries about something, real or imagined. The list includes her sister, her husband's infidelity, the government ruling over new salaries and the possibility of transfer. Mercy, for her part, worries about new shoes and clothes and about finding a male companion to provide these items and others that she considers to be central to her existence.

"The Two Sisters" further suggests that there is no [automatic] sweetness in monogamy either. The extramarital escapade of James is a case in point. Connie is the only wife of her husband, James. The latter does little to hide his extramarital affairs. Connie appears helpless in the face of his misconduct. Although she reveals she has "reliable information" (90) about his misbehavior, her response is simply to act weak and cry. She makes lame efforts to state her displeasure. It is predictable that James "always tries to deal with these nightly funeral parlor doings by pretending not to know what they are about" (96). Her younger sister Mercy's solution is for women to seize "some freedom for themselves," while Connie meekly responds: "But I am sure that even if we were free to carry on in the same way, I wouldn't make use of it.... Because I love James and I am not interested in any other man" (90).

It is evident that the socialization factor is at the base of women's unhappiness. "The Late Bud" is important in this collection for two reasons. First, it is the only story to deal with the conflict that can result from the process that turns the young person child (Yaaba), into a woman. The story of Yaaba serves as a flashback to the kind of women we find in Connie of "Two Sisters," Maami Ama of "No Sweetness Here" and Gyaawa of "A Gift From Somewhere." In "The Late Bud," specifically, Yaaba wants to express herself outside the modes deemed appropriate for a growing young person. For example, she wants to climb trees and play outside the hearth, much to the consternation of her mother, the major socializing agent in her young life. Her mother discourages her through all manners of ways including withholding food, teasing her, and concealing her affection for her. The problem is that the older woman equates her daughter's love for the outdoors with lack of concern. She commends the virtue of showing affection, as amply displayed by her other daughter, Adwoa, who conforms to her vision of an ideal daughter—one who constantly squats by the hearth.

Then, Yaaba accidentally causes commotion in the middle of the night as she wanted to surprise her mother by providing her with clay she needed. Through this drama that wakes up the entire neighborhood, the point is made that the demonstration of consideration and understanding on the one hand, and the love for natural self-expression on the other, are not mutually exclusive. In other words, the young woman can express herself outside the confines of society's ideas of girlhood and still retain her fundamental humanity of caring. The fact that the whole community bears witness to Yaaba's efforts is important in making a public statement about the need to revise set ways of evaluating behavior. Aidoo's choice of the two daughters are shown to be complementary rather than exclusive.

"Other Versions" presents us with the three-tiered, and the eighth narrative structure, employed by Aidoo. It narrates the stories of three women. The connecting thread to these tales is the theme of huge sacrifice for varying degrees of returns. In the first, the mother of the narrator sells cloth to help raise her children. When the narrator brings part of his income to compensate her for her pains while he was growing up, she rather directs him to give the money to his father. In the second story, Mrs. Hye is the cook at the household of the Merrows who invited the narrator for dinner. Mrs Hye appears very briefly in the story, but the fact that she neither shared in the meal nor was acknowledged except as an afterthought, speaks volumes about her status and the life of sacrifice with little reward that women of her type go through everyday. The third woman also appears briefly, in the subway this time, with her thin coat, old handbag and her age which appears above what it is in reality, thanks to overwork with negligible returns. The portraits of these three women speak about shared experiences and problems despite geographical locations and states of the economy.

Finally, the opening story of *No Sweetness Here*, "Everything Counts," and the ninth in the series we have highlighted for study, is cast narratively as reminiscence. Sissie casts her mind back and remembers her first week as a university teacher. There is no other narrator and not even an implied audience. The narrative makes no conscious effort at secrecy and so the reader feels entirely free to assume the position of audience. A series of scenes make this story look like a picture album. The first scene takes us to the classroom where the topic of discussion does not come from the course of study but from the physical appearance of the women students who uniformly wear wigs of various sizes and shapes, "blatantly, aggressively, crudely" (3). These varieties cover a few pages of this album. There is a small picture that makes a big statement about the behavior of some "brothers" who make some African sisters imitate white women. One picture shows the dismay of the narrator who wonders how to tell her people that "cars and fridges are ropes with which we are hanging ourselves" (6). Her relatives, who probably own nothing, hope that she would save them the embarrassment of driving around in a "little coconut shell with two doors" (a Volkswagen Beetle) in the form of a car (6). The third picture covers the beauty pageant that finally selected "the most light skinned" of the competitors; "her hair, a mulatto's, quite simply, quite naturally, fell in a luxuriant mane on her shoulders" (7). A final picture shows Sissie throwing up and crying in the bathroom. It is a powerful scene which sums up the state of the nation she had come home to discover. These pictures are not arranged in any perceived logical order, suggesting the confused state in which Sissie finds her newly independent country. The twisted priorities of the women students who model themselves after people who neither recognize nor respect them; her relatives who equate the importation of items they have no plans to ever produce by themselves with well-being; and her nation that has its head full of "misguided foolishness." All push her to vomit. The fact that people hardly remember the past in a logical, sequential and chronological order is carried into this story whose checkered plot of unconnected episodes calls for a reevaluation of assumptions about modernity, nationhood, and womanhood. The suggestion is that there is something illogical about the ways in which society perceives these issues.

Sissie, the university teacher, is the most conscious of all of Aidoo's women characters, in terms of her awareness of the position of her country in relation to the outer world. She is everything

Mercy in "Two Sisters" is not. Sissie is married and does not display the dependency syndrome in which Mercy has entrapped herself. She enjoys her work even if the quality of thinking in her country, which translates itself in the physical make up of her students, upsets her. While Mercy, for example, has no detached critical attitude toward the shoes and rides in cars she can never dream of affording, Sissie sees all these imported items as traps of modern living. She is disturbed by the portrait of the educated woman she has come to find. The wigs of all shades are artificial, imported items, which symbolize the whole dependency of the country on values others have designed for them. Even the criteria for judging beauty contests is foreign, being seen that light skin and straightened hair are preferable to African features. Perhaps Mercy and these women are only victims. Sissie herself does not play the role of an innocent by-stander, for as a teacher, she makes no effort to understand the academic potential of her students, rather she is more interested in their wigs than in their minds.

Aidoo has experimented with various methods of telling the story in *No Sweetness Here*. The texts imply, through the manner of telling, ways of reviewing established modes of seeing. New forms are suggested to respond to present realities. This collection of short stories confirms Aidoo's artistic talents as one who constructs her narratives by exploring various forms of the short story, and at the same time providing a variety of women in different contexts. These women are not superhuman. They are ordinary people who survive difficult circumstances. In using innovative forms to convey their plight, Aidoo shows artistic strength, pointing at possibilities and alternate ways of telling old tales to confront new problems.

NOTES

1. Women writers from Ghana who have committed the tale into writing include Felicia Acolatse (1961), Peggy Appiah (1966; 1967; 1968; 1969; 1977; 1992), Susan Alhassan (1965), Hannah Dankwa-Smith (1975), Grace Omaboe (1995), Jane Osafoa Dankyi (1972; 1990), Grace Osei Mensah (1965), and Juliana Tetteh (1961a; 1961b). Others, such as Mercy Owusu-Nimoh (1977) and Peggy Appiah (1971; 1972; 1976a; and 1976b) make use of the rich sources of the tale in creating new texts (Opoku-Agyemang 1995).

2. To the list of women writers from Ghana who have used the genre of the short story to raise concerns about the position of women in society we may add Mabel Dove-Danquah, perhaps the first Ghanaian woman writer. She published stories about women between 1931 and 1969. Ajoa

141

Yeboah-Afari published stories in various sources between 1970 and 1974. These stories now appear in a single collection called *The Sound of Pestles* (1986).

3. Unlike Mansa, Mercy does not solicit clients in a drinking spot, but she trades sex for material things, thus functioning somewhat as a prostitute. Mercy has a "respectable" job in the city, and, unlike Mansa, she has family in a sister and her husband who provide emotional and economic support. Her problem is lack of confidence that will enable her visualize herself as the one to work toward improving her status. All she sees of herself is a typist who works her fingers numb and who cannot afford the good clothing of her co-workers. She believes all of those things can only be provided by a man. This thinking informs her sexual affairs with rich grandfathers and government bureaucrats. Mercy fits the portrait of the "little girls" of Zirigu's description in "Everything Counts" who are attracted to the "big men... they have the money . . . They have all the nice things, like big cars . . . And the little girls sleep with them because they like these things" (10).

4. The equality implied in dialogue is to be seen in the personal relationship between the classes and spouses. "For Whom Things Did Not Change" is the only story in this collection in which the male narrator openly appreciates the qualities of his wife: "Setu is a good wife...a good woman" (26). This "good" wife is a very small scale trader, the kind described in Ghanaian English as a "petty trader" who, in this context, sells cooked food. It is significant that the only support she has for her business—both financial and moral—comes from her husband. This arrangement underscores her precarious position in the economy that has sidelined people of her class and gender. We may recall the concern of the educated lower middle class worker, James, in "Two Sisters," to get credit from the bank. As a member of the Cocoa Brokers' Union, Father of "Other Versions" has access to a scholarship for his son. These options do not even enter the orbit of intelligent, uneducated and economically deprived Setu. In other words male and female characters have unequal access to institutional credit.

5. One may recall an earlier story, "Evidence of Passion," published in 1969 by Mabel Dove Danquah. This story takes the reader into the court room of a divorce case where the reader is also privy to the actual ramifications of the procedure.

6. We can see Maami Ama's desire to work, along with the women of "Something To Talk About On The Way To The Funeral" who throw their weights into their careers, as the beginning of women characters in Aidoo's work whose definition of womanhood would fall outside biological constructs. Perhaps the fact that she loses her only child is an indication of this assertion. This portrait is given full attention in *Changes: A Love Story* where motherhood is not central to Esi Sekyi's ways of conceiving her world.

WORKS CITED

Acolatse, Felicity. "Blessing Turns Into a Doom." *Daily Graphic*, September 10, 1961.

Aidoo, Ama Ata. *The Dilemma of a Ghost and Anowa*. Harlow, U.K.: Longman, 1965, 1987.

―――. *No Sweetness Here*. Harlow, U.K.: Longman, 1970.

―――. *Our Sister Killjoy: Or Reflections From a Black-Eyed Squint*. Harlow: Longman, 1977.

―――. *Changes: A Love Story*. London: Women's Press, 1991.

Alhassan, Susan. *Two Tales*. Accra: N.P., 1965.

Appiah, Peggy. *Ananse the Spider: Tales of an Ashanti Village*. New York: Pantheon Books, 1966.

―――. *Tales of an Ashanti Father*. London: Andre Deutsh, 1967.

―――. *The Children of Ananse*. London: Evans Brothers, 1968.

―――. *The Pineapple Child and Other Tales From Ashanti*. London: Andre Deutsch, 1969.

―――. *A Smell of Onions*. London: Longman, 1971.

―――. *Gift of the Mmoatia*. Tema: Ghana Publishing Corporation, 1972.

―――. *A Dirge Too Soon*. Tema: Ghana Publishing Corporation, 1976a.

―――. *Ring of Gold*. London: Andre Deutsch, 1976b.

―――. *Why the Hyena Does Not Care For Fish and other Tales From the Ashanti Gold Weights*. London: Andre Deutsch, 1977.

―――. *Kyekyekule: Grandmother's Tales*. Accra: Quick Service Books Ltd, 1992.

Baeta, Lily. *Da To Gli Nam (Tell Me a Story, Mother)*. London/Accra: Longman Vernacular Literature Bureau, 1951.

Burness, Donald Bayer."Womanhood in the Short Stories of Ama Ata Aidoo" *Studies in Black Literature* 4,2, (Summer 1993):21-23.

Dankwa-Smith, Hannah. *Some Popular Ananse Stories*. Accra: Waterville Publishing House, 1975.

Dankyi, Jane Osafoa, and Kitty Lloyd-Lawrence. *Firelight Fables*. London: Longman, 1972.

Dankyi, Jane Osafoa. *Tortoise Flies to a Funeral and Other Stories*. Accra: Sedco Publications Ltd, 1990.

―――. *Ananse Searches For a Fool and Other Stories*. Accra; Sedco Publications Ltd, 1994.

Dove Danquah, Mabel. *The Torn Veil and Other Stories*. London: Evans Brothers, 1975.

Korang, Charity. "Kweku and the Magic Pot." *Daily Graphic*. November 5, 1961.

Nwankwo, Chimalum. "The Feminist Impulse in Ama Ata Aidoo's *No Sweetness Here* and *Our Sister Killjoy*" In: Eds. Carole Boyce Davies and Anne Adams Graves. *Ngambika: Studies of Women in African Literature*, Trenton, New Jersey: Africa World Press, Inc., 1986:151-159.

Odamtten V. O. *The Art of Ama Ata Aidoo: Polylectics and Reading Against Neocolonialism*. Gainesville: University Press of Florida, 1994.

Omaboe, Grace. *By the Fireside*. Tema: Ghana Publishing Corporation, 1995.

Opoku-Agyemang, Naana Jane. "Lest we Forget: A Critical Survey of

Ghanaian Women's Literature." *Asemka* 8 (1995):61-84.

———. "A Girl Marries a Monkey: The Folktale as an Expression of Value and Change in Society" *Asemka* 7 (1992):5-12.

———. "Recovering Lost Voices: The Short Stories of Mabel Dove-Danquah." In: *Writing African Women: Gender, Popular Culture and Literature in West Africa.* Ed. Stephanie Newell. London: Zed, 1997.

Osei Mensah, Grace. *Eight Delightful Folktales.* Accra: Waterville, 1965.

Sutherland, Efua. *The Marriage of Anansewa.* Washington D.C.: Three Continents Press, 1975.

Tetteh, Juliana. "Stolen Food Makes Kweku Bald." *Daily Graphic*, October 22, 1961a.

———. "Kweku's Six Charming Wives." *Daily Graphic*, November 19, 1961b.

Yeboah-Afari, Ajoa. *The Sound of Pestles and Other Stories.* Accra: Afram Publications [Gh] Ltd., 1986.

INVERTING THE INSTITUTIONS:

AMA ATA AIDOO'S *NO SWEETNESS HERE* AND DECONSTRUCTIVE THEORY

LINDA STRONG-LEEK

Most certainly, my trials as a woman writer are heavier and more painful than any condition I have to go through as a university teacher. It is a condition so delicate that it almost cannot be handled. Like an internal wound and therefore immeasurably dangerous, it also causes a ceaseless emotional hemorrhage. You feel awful for seeing the situation the way you do, and terrible when you try to speak about it. Because this kind of resentment never even comes out in jokes. Yet you have to speak out since your pain is also real, and in fact the wound bleeds more profusely when you are upset by people you care for, those you respect.

-Ama Ata Aidoo, "Ghana: To Be A Woman."

In the volume of short stories collectively titled *No Sweetness Here*, Aidoo articulates the queries and concerns of womanhood presented in this brief quote above. She is "speaking about" many of the "painful" situations faced by African women in her stories, such as being wives, mothers, prostitutes, cooks and children, or all these conditions combined, from the colonizers, and the Africans who replaced the colonizers after independence.

Women's circumstances have been historically and traditionally limited by societal formations of womanhood, but within this selection of short stories Aidoo deconstructs these perceptions and challenges these conventions. She begins to *invert the institutions*, as Jonathan Culler has noted, in order to question the very foundations of patriarchy which has held women hostage for centuries:

> The claim is that because deconstruction is never concerned only with signified content but especially with the conditions and assumptions of discourse, with frameworks of enquiry, it engages the institutional structures governing our practices, competencies, performances. The questioning of these structures, whatever the consequences—can be seen as a politicizing of what might otherwise be thought a neutral framework." (Culler 1989:156)

Thus, utilizing Culler's discussion of the *inversion of institutions*, this analysis will articulate the manner in which Aidoo engages patriarchy, bringing the issue of African "womanism" to the forefront, and the socio-political ramifications of her arguments within deconstructive analyses. This work will engage, as example, the work of Lloyd Brown and his early examination of Aidoo, which, although initially bringing the works and concerns of African women into the critical purview of academe, also misrepresents much of her womanist illustrations.

What happens to women when they find the courage to address the injustices of their lives? Are women's lives still governed by society's biased perceptions of the positions of women? The women in Aidoo's stories are strong, independent, and often willfully detached from society; yet they remain susceptible to the community's rules and definitions of womanhood. Although she seems to offer no final analysis or any definitive solution, Aidoo continually poses questions pertaining to how and why African women are subjugated, abused, neglected, and mistreated by postcolonial societies, and often by those they love. Culler continues:

> Deconstructive analyses, the claim is, have poten-
> tially radical implications, but these implications,
> often distant and incalculable, are no substitute for
> immediate critical and political action.... Their rad-
> ical potential may depend on the surprising
> resources they reveal in an excessive, uncalculating
> theoretical pursuit. (159)

What are the "radical implications" presented by Aidoo in her work? Is she "deconstructing" the African patriarchy, as well as the new social order instituted by the colonizers and their African replacements? What "resources" will Aidoo's work in these issues reveal in this "uncalculating theoretical pursuit"? Through an analysis of three short stories, "Everything Counts," "No Sweetness Here," and "Two Sisters," this work will address these and other questions as they pertain to the "institutions" which are "inverted" by the writings of Aidoo. This analysis will illustrate that the women represented in these stories either challenge or succumb to the institutions and structures within which they live, and that as they exist or refuse to abide within these confines, their reactions challenge the very organizations on which their societies are established.

For example, in "Everything Counts," Aidoo discusses the effects of colonization on African perceptions of self and beauty. The story begins with a young female lecturer arguing with her male counterparts about the new utilization of European wigs by African women. "Not to struggle to look like the white girls. Not straightening one's hair. And above all, not to wear the wig" (1). However, to her dismay, the young lecturer finds not only herself, but also many of the young women in her classes wearing the dreaded wig—the artificial fiber—the "hair of dead white folks." What has happened within society that would make it not only acceptable, but also, moreover, necessary, for young, African women to adorn their heads with styles and colors in no way becoming to their natural African heritage? This wig is but one example of the perverting of society and the disruption caused by colonization. In an analysis of the work of Franz Fanon on the colonial experience and the consequences of that encounter, Abiola Irele notes that:

Fanon's analysis of the colonial situation is inscribed within this humanistic perspective. More concretely, he saw colonialism as the elevation of one set of men at the expense of another set. In the same measure that the colonial master extends his human dimension... in that same measure is the colonized slave impoverished in body and soul, depersonalized, reduced in his human stature and even nature. Colonial rule tends to drive a wedge between colonized native and his normal adherence to his essential humanity. (140)

Thus, the women now adhere to standards of beauty that have nothing to do with their reality—their own essential humanity. This point is even more dramatically exhibited when the beauty pageant takes place:

She should have known that it would turn out like that. She had not thought any of the girls beautiful. But her opinions were not really asked for, were they? She just recalled that all the contestants had worn wigs except one. The winner. The most light-skinned of them all. No, she didn't wear a wig. Her hair, a mulatto's quite simply, quite naturally, fell in a luxuriant mane on her shoulder's.... She hurried home and into the bathroom where she vomited and cried and cried... (6-7)

Hence, although the African woman has progressed in many ways beyond the traditional roles of wife and mother and into the realm of academia, it is with a price—the loss of appreciation for the natural beauty of the African, and the desire not only to be like, but even more disturbing, to *look* like the colonizer. The young lecturer vomits and cries in an attempt to purge herself of those perceptions, but ends with the knowledge that it will continue, that she will proceed in her pursuit of higher education, and that other Africans like her will continue to sell themselves and their souls for the "good life"—the life represented by the wigs, the big cars, the refrigerators—the European life. In this instance, Africans on the continent had just begun to confront the demons that their African counterparts in the Diaspora had battled since they were forced to "immigrate" to the "New World," the love/hate relationship with the colonizer, the attempt to imitate, but somehow to remain true to one's self, usually to the detriment of the colonized. Culler observes:

> If the force of theory depends upon possibilities of institutionalization—it becomes politically effective insofar as it can inform the practices by which we constitute, administer, and transmit a world—its most radical aspects are threatened by institutionalization and emerge precisely in a theoretical reflection that contests particular institutionalization of a theoretical discourse." (159)

Hence, Aidoo's critique of the traditional Western standards of beauty and their acceptance by a part of African society attacks the institution upon which this ideology is defined—the Western patriarchy—but now in the hands of the formerly colonized, because colonization is much more than a stark exploitation of the body: it achieves its ultimate success in the destruction of the human soul that results as a matter of the psychological destruction of those it seeks to enslave. Aidoo is both "informing" the West and criticizing those in Africa who have accepted this practice of attempting to conform to European standards of beauty. The beauty contest is then a farce, and the most notable losers are the winners—those who have "achieved" non-African status—the mulatto and those who believe that her beauty is more natural, more beautiful than her darker-skinned sisters. Aidoo acknowledges that certain aspects of colonization have proved catastrophic for all Africans.

Notably, in the title short story, "No Sweetness Here," Aidoo discusses the relationship between two women who choose to live without men (except for the young boy Kwesi) and outside of the normal constraints of their society. Chicha, the single school teacher, and Maami Ama, the soon-to-be divorced woman, forge a bond through their love for Maami Ama's son, Kwesi. They seem to be two women alone, but because of this shared love, and an intimate connection of the spirit, they find solace and support in each other. Although their society is quite respectful toward the young school teacher, this reverence is not transferred to Maami Ama, and it is clear during the divorce proceedings which party they will support—the man, Maami Ama's husband.

> 'The elders certainly have settled the case fairly,' someone was saying. 'But it seemed as if Kodjo Fi had no strong proofs of his argument,' another was

saying. 'Well, they both have been sensible. If one feels one can't live with a woman, one might as well divorce her. And I hate a woman who cringes to a man,' a third said. (66)

Moreover, although one in the crowd is willing to admit that Kodjo Fi is without substantial evidence to prove his claim and support his reason for desiring a divorce (which is never revealed to the reader), it is clear that it is *really* Maami Ama who desires a divorce. Furthermore, and even though one went so far as to say that "they both have been sensible," the conclusion is still the same: it is the man who should divorce his wife when he cannot live with her, not the woman who should divorce the man whom she cannot and will not live with because of his cruelty and indifference.

Note here that Brown's analysis of this story seems a bit askew, particularly when he writes: "If Maami is the victim of Kodjo's selfish and bullying temper, she is also victimized by her own weakness and by her lack of self-confidence" (Brown 1981:115). Is it a lack of confidence when Maami insists on divorcing her husband, knowing that she may lose everything, even the child she loves so dearly? Is it her own personal weakness when she refuses to beg for the money that she is rightly entitled to from her husband? And is it weakness when she does not fall down and die when the elders tell her that she must give up her son, whom she describes as "my husband, my brother, my father, my all-in-all," to a husband who has taken no interest in his son until the time of the trial? Perhaps Maami Ama's true weakness lies within her total dependence on her child. However, Brown's reaction to Maami Ama may be an "institutional" reaction, which points to his analysis of Maami Ama as a helpless woman rather than the powerful person represented by Aidoo. Culler (1989) continues: "Readings of Freud have taken up a further opposition that is deeply sedimented in our thinking and the deconstruction of which may have more immediate social and political consequences: the hierarchical opposition of *man* and *woman* (165, Culler's emphasis). And if it is true that, as Culler proceeds, "this is the primordial opposition on which all others are based" (165), then by her unwillingness to remain in an abusive, neglected, and bitter marriage, does Maami Ama invert the patriarchal institution in such a way that it must attack and demean her self-esteem and her very existence as woman? Is Brown's reaction, like those of the women in the story after the divorce proceedings, grounded in the feelings of superiority that patriarchy thrives upon?

Brown continues his discussion of "No Sweetness Here," with another characterization that is problematic—that of the young school teacher, Chicha:

> The irony is that the progressive, liberated, and sophisticated image of the Western-educated woman is really a mask: underneath there is the familiar vulnerability to the power of the male, and a new insecurity bred by the conflict between two cultural traditions. (117)

But does Chicha present the "familiar vulnerability" of African women, or is there something more? Speaking of her own experience as a lecturer, Aidoo writes:

> Is it any wonder that I get plainly confused now if, in associating with both female and male undergraduates, graduates, lecturers, and professors, I learn that they believe basically that marriage is what woman was created for? And that higher education for a woman is an unfortunate postponement of her self-fulfillment? (259)

At one point, Chicha says, "but I was a teacher, and I went the white man's way" (50). Could this be Chicha's way of vocalizing her rejection of the traditions of her society, and instead choosing the "white man's way" as a means of self-assertion? And by expressing this, is her happy, single life not the most prodigious danger to the patriarchal institution that exists in many African (as well as Western) societies? Aidoo continues to submit these and other questions in the story, "Two Sisters."

The two sisters in this story represent two vastly different lifestyle choices on the part of two African women who have come to live in the city. One sister, Mercy, has decided to gain financial security and happiness by making herself available to the African "big men," those in the government who have come to replace the white colonizers after "independence." Connie (Sissie), the other sister, has chosen a very conventional path. She is the "traditional" wife and mother. Mercy's decision to become like a "prostitute" is, thus, very unsettling for her sister:

> Please little sister, I am not trying to interfere in your private life. You said yourself a little while ago that you wanted a man of your own. That

man belongs to so many women already.... That silence again. Then there was only Mercy's footsteps as she went to put her plate in the kitchen sink, running water as she washed her plate and her hands. She drank some water and coughed. Then as tears streamed down her sister's averted face, there was the sound of her footsteps as she left the kitchen. (52)

At this point, acknowledging that Brown's work is an initial attempt to analyze the works of African women within a Western ideological context, I again question Brown's reading of the text. He writes that the story of the sisters is one of their "tragedy as women, and the tragedy of their social milieu as a whole, (which) consists of the fact that they are all living stereotypes whose experiences are a succession of second-hand clichés..." (Brown 1981:119). But are their lives merely "second-hand clichés"? Is Connie not fully aware of the implications of her choice to remain in a marriage that is not without flaws (as are most marriages), but that brings her happiness nevertheless? And is Mercy not aware of her choices? Does she not merely get another, "bigger" man after the overthrow of the government and her lover, Mensah Arthur? Could this new man be the one who would carry her away from her life in the home of her sister and eventually into a form of precarious independence? Who can declare whether or not Mercy will remain with this man after she achieves financial emancipation? She is aware of the marriage and children of her lover, yet she illustrates no regret when she brings him to the home of her sister. Are Brown's limitations then, once again, related to his reading of women's experiences as insignificant? Culler writes:

This is what one finds... in the case of Freudian theory: its power is linked to the ability of its hierarchical reversals to transform thought and behavior, but the institutions of psychoanalysis have arguably been quite conservative, and the radical force of Freudian theory is linked not to those institutions but to the resources it provides for a continuing theoretical critique—a critique of institutions and assumptions....(Culler 1989:159)

With a similar deconstructionist view of "Two Sisters," one may note that Mercy and Connie are not only making the most of their limited choices, but that they are both, in different ways, choosing their own route to happiness—Connie through marriage and family; mercy through sex, money, and powerful friends in high places. They are not like the women Aidoo describes as those who are "owned like property, abused and brutalized like serfs, privately corrected and, like children, publicly scolded, overworked, underpaid, and...thoroughly exploited," (263). They are, on the contrary, actively participating in their lives and they choose their individual avenues. They are neither blind nor deaf, but they vigorously participate and define their situations. Aidoo writes:

> The arrival of the new baby has magically waved away the difficulties between James and Connie. He is that kind of man, and she that kind of woman.... Who heard something like the sound of a car pulling into the drive? Ah, but the footsteps are unmistakably Mercy's. Are those shoes the old pair which were new a couple of months ago? Or are they the newest pair? And here she is herself, the pretty one. A gay Mercy. (99, 101)

Thus, rather than allowing the affairs of her husband to destroy her marriage and her family (though many feminists/womanist theorists may have difficulty comprehending or accepting this decision), Connie remains in the situation until the birth of her child, a symbol of the union of love between her and James, which seems to bring order to their lives. Mercy, also a survivor, finds this new "bigger" man, and comes home to visit her sister and the new baby with those (new) shoes on (although the reader cannot ascertain whether or not the shoes are new or old), notably "gay." Whether old or new, the shoes represent Mercy's upscale, elaborate life. Brown's observation concerning "Mercy's obsession with sexy clothes, uniformed chauffeurs, and vulgarly large American cars, and Connie's desperate determination to be respectably, even happily married, and her hackneyed conviction that the new baby will somehow restore the marriage" (Brown 1989:119), simply ignores the potential for Connie and Mercy to survive in the face of immense barriers. Culler states that the "understanding of the marginal or deviant term becomes a condition for understanding the supposedly prior term. The most general operations of the psyche are discovered, for example, through investigations of patho-

EMERGING PERSPECTIVES ON AMA ATA AIDOO

logical cases (Culler 1989:160). Brown neglects the "marginal terms" here by focusing only on what he can see—the negation of African womanhood by submission to the new rules imposed by colonialism, rather than viewing the marginal as the central theme. For this reader, the peripheral, underlying theme of courage and the logical, although somewhat dubious choices of the sisters remains the focal point of the story. It is not merely that the women are acted upon, but that they do act, react and affect the stimuli in their environment.

Therefore, Aidoo is able to create a new reality in her work, *No Sweetness Here*, through the development of many absorbing, multi-faceted characters. Though some may choose, like Brown, to focus only on the "institutions" within the work, a more in-depth analysis of the marginal subjects may facilitate a preferable understanding of the work. By reevaluating the position of the institutions, we gain an understanding that these must be inverted, (the marginal must become the focus), so that one may examine this work in an alternative framework dissimilar to Brown's. Aidoo creates characters who are not merely supporting actors, but who are, instead, those whose endeavors influence theirs, and the lives of others in her fictional world. They are actively involved in the critique of the new order, and many refuse to allow the former dictates of society to limit their activities. They are but a small representation of Aidoo's cast of multi-faceted, complicated female characters.

WORKS CITED

Aidoo, Ama Ata. *Our Sister Killjoy*. London: Longman, 1977.
———. *No Sweetness Here*. London: Longman, 1988.
———. *"Ghana: To Be a Woman."* UNITAR Seminar: Creative Women In Changing Societies, Oslo, July 9-13, 1980.
———. *Changes: A Love Story*. London: The Women's Press Fiction, 1991.
Brown, Lloyd. *Women Writers in Black Africa*. Greenwood Press, Westport, 1981.
Culler, Jonathan. *On Deconstruction: Theory and Criticism after Structuralism*. Ithaca: Cornell University Press, 1989.
Innes, C.L. "Mothers or Sisters? Identity, Discourse and Audience in the Writing of Ama Ata Aidoo and Mariama Bâ." In: *Motherlands: Black Women's Writing from Africa, the Caribbean, and South Asia*. Ed. Susheila Nasta. New Brunswick, N.J.: Rutgers University Press, 1991.
Irele, Abiola. *The African Experience in Literature and Ideology*. Bloomington: Indiana University Press, 1990.
Rooney, Caroline. "'Dangerous Knowledge' and the Poetics of Survival: A

154

Reading of *Our Sister Killjoy* and *A Question of Power.*" In: *Motherlands: Black Women's Writing from Africa, The Caribbean, and South Asia.* Ed. Susheila Nasta. New Brunswick, N. J.: Rutgers University Press, 1991.

Ogundipe-Leslie, 'Molara. *Recreating Ourselves: African Women and Critical Transformations.* Trenton: Africa World Press, 1994.

AMA ATA AIDOO:
THE DEVELOPMENT OF A
WOMAN'S VOICE

ARLENE A. ELDER

I would like to go
Where
In days of old
The Aged
Sharp-eyed
Hard-Knuckled
Sages of our race
Left silent grove and dark,
The sacred lore.
Mum the sage,
Mum the lore
No stray sigh from a dying breath
Flutters down the years
To guide my wandering
Feet to truth
                    -Ama Ata Aidoo, "Sebonwoma"

An aunt who had learnt to read only enough of our language to be a member of the church choir, and who never forgave the fate that had not given her more educational opportunities, once told me when I was in secondary school: "My child get as far as you can into this education. Go and go and go. Go until you yourself know you are tired. Because as for marriage, it is something a woman picks up along the way.'"

- Ama Ata Aidoo, "Unwelcome Pals and Decorative Slaves."

These two statements by Aidoo, one poetic, one explicitly autobiographical, may be interpreted as expressing the colonial and neocolonial dilemma of African women writers in general: their sense of displacement from the aesthetic/spiritual terrain of their heritage—a condition shared by their male counterparts, as the Negritude movement indicates—and their need to sound their own public voices in the non-traditional New World imposed by Western education. Western feminist discourse, too, concerns itself with a lost heritage—most often in speculations about the nature of matriarchal cultures and women's aesthetics (Gottner-Abendroff 1986) —and with Western society's historical silencing of alternative voices. For women writers of color, the issues sharpen to focus upon the dilemma of the contemporary woman artist with allegiances to both Western individualism and traditional communalism. In Aidoo's work, specifically, the resolution of this dialectic moves from the permanent silencing of the artist by hostile voices, as in *Anowa,* to *Our Sister Killjoy's* promise of a continuing female voice speaking, at least for the present, only to herself, yet, paradoxically conveyed by the oral strategies of the artist. From her earlier play, *The Dilemma of a Ghost*, to her latest novel, *Changes*, she continues to explore these themes and techniques.

Aidoo's grounding in orality and her sensitivity to the morality of communication is evident in her first play, *The Dilemma of a Ghost*, which was written and staged in 1965. While critics note structural flaws in the play, most of them praise Aidoo's use of language (Nagenda 1969; Adelugba 1974; Brown 1981). Dapo Adelugba even discerns "six levels of language" in the work and "within this spectrum... [a] wide variety of linguistic usage" (72). As the title of the play suggests, Aidoo is working within the West African storytelling tradition of dilemma tales, " an integral part of moral and ethical training in many Africa societies ... [that] point out that in human affairs there are often no answers, but only difficult choices which call into play conflicting moral values" (Bascomb 97: vii). All of Aidoo's works can be viewed as modern samples of this traditional genre, especially those concerned with the conflicting choices imposed on the woman artist.

Even her first published work serves the feminist and traditional purpose. The plot of *The Dilemma of a Ghost* can be summarized quickly: A "been-to," Ato, returns to his family with an African American wife, Eulalie, whose rejection of the customs of the Odumna clan is matched only by the horror of her Western attitudes and behavior. One of Aidoo's principal points is that Ato fails to prepare either party for the strangeness of the other, and family harmony is saved only by the sympathy of Esi Kom, his mother, who finally welcomes Eulalie as a daughter. In addition to this feminist twist on the frequently examined cultural clashes of "been-to" in African literature, Aidoo is also at pains to express the moral interconnectedness of artist, art and audience, specifically, the morality of the acts of telling and listening. Moreover, through traditional characterization, she reinforces the active role of the spectator/participant of orature.

The Bird of the Wayside of the Prologue, who at once represents the apparently meaningless or, at least, incomprehensive continuum of human life, paradoxically, is also, like the playwright herself, an interpreter who can "furnish you with reasons why/this and that and other things/Happened" (Aidoo 1965:1). Significantly, the Bird of the Wayside, a literal translation from the Akan, referring to the unseen eye of public opinion [Aidoo, interview with author], also serves as a dramatic device to engage the audience with the subject of the play and to invite it to make up its mind about the transpiring events:

> Look around you
> For the mouth must not tell everything
> Sometimes the eye can see
> And the ear should hear (1)

Throughout the play, there is continued emphasis on "telling" and "listening." The two women, one fruitful, one barren, in addition to being developed as individual characters, serve, in their role as chorus, the purpose of audience surrogates. They constantly observe the behavior of the Odumna clan, listen to the voices coming from its compound, and speculate aloud about its fate. The barren woman complains of being cut off from information and forced to rely on her friend for news:

> But you know, my sister,
> that my name is Lonesome.
> I have no one to go and listen
> To come back and tell me. (33)

When she asks how her friend knows all is not well between Ato and Eulalie, the other woman replies:

> Oh, I could tell you.
> The Bird of the Wayside
> Never tires of chirping
> But this is no secret
> My sons tell me this. (33)

In Aidoo's view, their eagerness to learn about and discuss the world around them transcends mere gossip, just as the presence of the audience at the play transcends mere curiosity or voyeurism. This distinction implies a public educative function for story telling that is made moral through the serious involvement of teller and listener, artist and audience.

One of the play's themes, as a matter of fact, is about the failure of many people to really listen to one another. Ato's downfall is not the frequently posited, inescapable dilemma of being a "been-to," but that he fails to communicate the expectations of African culture to Eulalie or of African American culture to the Odumna clan. He is a faulty medium, the failed voice who should have served as intermediary between two cultures, as Sissie of Killjoy, more courageously, attempts to do. Naively, he expects both sides to perceive instinctively the value in each other, without the kind of thoughtful scrutiny and speculation in which the two women habitually engage. When he does make an attempt at explanation, it is too late, the mutual mistrust has advanced too far, and he complains in frustration, "But no one is prepared to listen to me...," "But you will not listen to me...." "Please, I beg you all, listen..." (12).

Aidoo's understanding of the moral nature of "telling" and "listening" becomes completely clear by the end. Ato, bewildered by the consequences of his poorly-thought-out-actions, is left alone and hopeless. The voices of the children introduced earlier in the play, one of whom represents the youthful Ato, and foreshadows his impotent, ghost-like state, are heard by the audience "like an echo from [Ato's] own mind":

> Shall I go to Cape Coast?
> Shall I go to Elmina?
> I can't tell
> Shall I?
> I can't tell
> I can't tell
> I can't tell. (50)

Clearly for Aidoo, to be unable to "tell" is to be unable to understand and to be unable to act. The morality of story telling and the moral function of the artist synthesizes contemplation, communication, and action. As Ato's complaint suggests, however, and as Anowa's and Sissie's dilemmas demonstrate, the letter must have receptive listeners; that is, the artist must be perceived as part of the same society as her audience and represent its basic values.

In *Anowa*, Aidoo extends her examination of strong female characters like Esi Kom in *Dilemma*, by dramatizing the problems afflicting a woman who clashes with her society. Like the earlier play, this work, too, is a dilemma tale, concerned with not just the female character of its title, alone, but, through the extensive function of orature, with the impossible situation of any woman in a repressive society. Critic Carole Boyce Davies praises *Anowa* because, through its heteroglossic and fluid structure, "the writer, the play, the readers are able to traverse the boundaries of orality, writing and performance" (Davies 1994:61). It is the interweaving of genres and perspective that allows Aidoo's own understanding of the connection between colonialism and sexism to ring out.

Aidoo says, "The position of women in Africa has been no less ridiculous than anywhere else. The few details that differ are interesting only in terms of local color and particular family needs" (Aidoo 1982:34). One of the most devastating results of such sexism is the silencing of the woman artist. The discouragement with which Aidoo herself has met she describes as "an internal wound... [causing] a ceaseless emotional hemorrhage, so severe that I catch myself wondering whether I would have found courage to write if I had not started to write when I was too young to know what was good for me" (Aidoo 1982:38). A traditional reflection of such patriarchal control appears in the version of a Ghanaian legend told her by her mother, which becomes the kernel of Anowa's story:

A girl married a man her people did not approve of: she helped him become fantastically rich, and he turns round to sort of drive her away. The original story I heard, which in a way was in the form of a song, didn't say why he did this, and I myself provide an answer in this, a clue..." (Pierterse and Duerden 1972:23).

Aidoo's "answer" in her version of this traditional story, which is set in Ghana during the 1870s, is that Anowa cannot give Kofi Ako children: nevertheless, her suicide at the end of the play remains richly ambiguous. Does Anowa kill herself because she is barren? Because she feels guilty for Kofi Ako killing himself?: Because she wishes she had never married him? Because she feels responsible for his taking slaves? Because she cannot return to Yebi? To fulfill the conventions of a well-known folktale? Or, because of a more modern, feminist sense of confusion related to her conflicted sense of self-image? Since the explanations of her final act rest in the opposed interpretations of The-Mouth-That-Eats-Salt-And-Pepper, we must sort through all these possibilities to understand Anowa's death and, by extension, the meaning of her unusual life as an early embodiment of Aidoo's image of the woman artist. As Carole Boyce Davies notes, the Old Man and Old Woman designated by The-Mouth-That-Eats-Salt-And-Pepper "function as representative spokes-people of the community" and also "as intermediary readers of the text of Anowa's life, standing between the readers/viewers reading the play and Anowa and allowing us to do a double reading [of] the text and of their responses to the text of Anowa's life" (Davies 1994:60).

Aidoo's artistic source for her drama, the stories and songs she heard as a child from her mother, provide a context for our judgement. Examples of West African orature like, "The Beautiful Girl and the Fish," "Abena and the Python," and "Large Eyes Produce Many Tears," warn willful young women like Anowa—who reject their parents' choice of suitors—with disasters ranging from imprisonment to death to transformation into non-human forms. In a very real sense, Anowa's society relegates her to the realm of the non-human throughout her life by its repeated attempts, especially by the women in her life, to silence her: "A child like you should not ask questions"; "What devil has entered you child?"; "You frighten me child. You must be a witch, child" (46); "A good brain does not have a brain or mouth" (33). Anowa herself laments, "Someone should have taught me how to grow up to be a woman... In order for her to be a man, she must not think, she must not talk" (52). Demonstrating the cultural validity of this observation, Aidoo has Kofi Ako warn Anowa about his impotence. "If you do not leave me quietly, but go consulting everybody about this affair, I shall brand you a witch" (59). However, when his slaves overhear her questioning his manhood, Kofi does not attack Anowa; instead, he kills himself. Like their female counterparts, the unacceptable husbands in the folk tales also come to bad ends.

The Old Woman of The-Mouth-That-Eats-Sail-And-Pepper, Aidoo's chorus, reflecting the public opinion of the events taking place, correctly concludes, "This is the type of happening out of which we get stories and legends, and judges that, like a witch, 'Anowa ate Kofi Ato up!'" (63). The Old Woman, like the other women in the play, represents female conservatism and acceptance of the cultural limitations on their power. Consequently, she and the others are enraged by Anowa whose unorthodoxy and self-determination threatens social stability, especially patriarchal authority. Unlike her meaning for The Bird of The Wayside in *Dilemma*, Aidoo's treatment of The-Mouth-That-Eats-Salt-And-Pepper demonstrates that all talk is not good talk: some probing of other's lives might be malicious and destructive. Like most destructive characters of the folk tradition, the Old Woman looks her part of the typical village gossip. She "is wizened, leans on a stick, and her voice is raspy with asthma and a lifetime of putting her mouth into other people's affairs" (22).

The Old Man realizes:

> Anowa is not a girl to meet everyday.
> A child of several incarnations,
> She listens to her own tales,
> Laughs at her own jokes and
> Follows her own advice. (13)

Her father's recommendation that her unusual qualities be acknowledged and she be apprenticed to a priestess is met with Anowa's mother's conservative refusal: "I am not going to turn my only daughter into a dancer priestess.... In the end they are not people. They become too much like the gods they interpret ... a priestess lives too much in her own and other people's minds" (11, 12, 13). Indeed, as expressed here, the life of the priestess is remarkably like that of the artist. Instead, Badua wishes her daughter:

To be a human woman
Marry a man,
Tend a farm
And be happy to see her
Peppers and onions grow
A woman like her
Should bear children. (12)

The alternative to Anowa's half-hearted attempt at an ordinary woman's life would have been her own and society's acceptance of her as extraordinary and its willingness to listen to her ideas.

Ironically, more sensitive to his daughter's unique personality than his tradition-bound wife, Anowa's father warns, "a prophet with a locked mouth is neither a prophet nor a man" (13). Despite his gendered identification of prophet here, he provides the crucial connection between knowledge and voicing that Anowa later realizes she cannot do without. The Old Man agrees about Anowa's larger-than life personality: "They used to say around here that Anowa behaved as though she were a heroine in a story" (64). But he places the blame for her tragedy directly upon society: "It is men who make me mad. Who knows if Anowa would have been a better woman, a better person if we had not been what we are?" (64). His position is fairer to Aidoo's heroine than the condemnation of his female counterpart, in that he recognizes the limitations that society can inflict upon an individual, significantly, in this case, an imaginative woman.

Nevertheless, neither the Old Man's interpretation of Anowa's tragedy nor the resolution of the play's action resolves Aidoo's dilemma about the voicing of the woman artist. As she realizes, for Anowa to be "a better woman," she would have had to have been silent. In all probability, it is her final realization that there is no way for her to communicate to her society her outspoken opposition to slavery and materialism, embodied in Kofi's activities, her need for self-determination, and her insistence upon being heard, which leads directly to her drowning.

Both Anowa and the subsequent Sissie, of Our Sister Killjoy, reverse mirror images, reflect Aidoo's sense of the developing situation for the female artist from traditional to post-colonial societies. Significantly, both are silenced. Anowa, however, is wise, self-determined, and out-spoken from birth, hence, marginalized as a female individualist in a conservative culture. In contrast, the bright but inexperienced Sissie leads us on a maturation journey into a European "bush of ghosts," resulting in her development of a critical voice, like that of the *Abentia* [player of old], but one which requires the intervention of the narrator to be heard. She is ready, after visiting the "Dead's Land" of England, to speak out for the good of her community but would be restricted to an audience of one, herself, were it not for the interpretation of *Killjoy's* narrator. Throughout her creative work and in public statements, Aidoo has connected the importance of her heritage of Ghanaian orature and the woman artist's role in continuing this artistic/political tradition.

Nowhere is her appreciation of orature's "unity of the arts," more pronounced than in *Our Sister Killjoy* (1979). With its blending of poetry and prose and reliance on heteroglossia to convey different stages of a developing consciousness that reflects 'Molara Ogundipe-Leslie's (1994) concept of "STIWA," the privileging equally of women's freedom and overall African development that encompasses both genders, Aidoo remains concerned with the woman with the "locked mouth" and, also, with the locked minds of Sissie's listeners. On her way home to Africa after her experience in Europe, Sissie destroys her explanatory letter because she realizes it is futile to send it to her Westernized, individualistic African lover in England, who has accused her of being too political and idealistic. The ending of *Our Sister Killjoy*, then, offers both a thematic and formal ambiguity. Its last lines do not close the narrative but, instead, connect the story back to the text's hopeful beginning: in contrast, the unposted love letter represents yet another silencing of a woman by an unresponsive male hegemony, this time, the "been-tos" in Europe. As Chimalum Nwankwo observes of this text: "Many African women accept inferiority, many African men accept mastery as the norm" (Davies 1994: 156). We know, however, that neither Aidoo nor Sissie accepts inferiority, therefore, we must assume the implications of this open-ended text.

Despite the mute letter, like the young Anowa, Sissie promises to continue speaking out and espousing the traditional value of working for the good of her African community. We place our trust, however, not in her intentions alone, but in the voice of the narrator, always more perceptive and experienced than that of the young, maturing Sissie. As if initiating a performance cycle, this voice circles back thematically from the end to the beginning, not just promising but delivering continued communication, and we, through Aidoo's skillful maturing of her readers as well as her protagonist, are willing listeners. The book's last observation—"Sissie wondered whether she had spoken aloud to herself. Then she decided she didn't care anyway" (13-34)—returns us to the optimistic first line of the book: "Things are working out" (3). Possibly, Aidoo feels less constrained in this work than in *Anowa* by the sad fates of the heroines of the West African folk tales about disobedient young women. Or, it could be that the difference between Anowa's and Sissie's fates rests less with sources in orature than with Aidoo's adoption of her omniscient narrator who, unlike the Chorus of the play, clearly represents the author's own feminist perceptions. The narrative indeterminacy of *Our Sister Killjoy*, and especially, its heteroglossic structure that can be used to highlight particular feminist and cultural points of view, provide a flexibility that can accommodate multiple philosophies and stages of feminist consciousness but privilege Aidoo's own. The "defiant artistic form" of the work, then, enhances and represents its themes: We guess immediately that the writer has no sympathy for any form of traditional structure when such structures are used for inhibiting people or artistic expression (Davies 1994:155).

Changes, too, Aidoo's latest novel, her "love story," continues her focus on women's issues and the formal connections of contemporary writing in traditional orature. In the course of her story, Esi copes with the demands of raising a daughter; divorces her oppressive husband; introduces the revolutionary concept of "married rape" into her own, if not her people's vocabulary; benefits from a long-lasting, female friendship; freely chooses to enter into a polygamous marriage, a love match; thrives in her active, professional life; and, although disappointed with her womanizing, new husband, modifies her ideals for marriage and accepts a continuing, casual relationship with him, an arrangement actually suited to her need for time for herself as a professional woman. This feminist story of Esi's developing sense of self is told with a blending of forms from Western fiction—a lengthy narrative focused on one protagonist and passages of character analysis, for example—with elements of oral performance. Interspersed throughout the narrative are proverbial comments on the action. The following example is separated by indentation from the rest of the prose text and sounds a collective "wisdom" more extensive, even, than the voice of *Changes'* third-person narrator: "In any case, everyone know's that a man's relationship with women other than his wife, however innocent, can always help ruin a marriage. And that includes his love for his own mother" (44). Sections of the novel are couched in play form, the two-page dialogue between Aba and Ama (101-102), for instance, or between Ena and Nana (112-114), with no description of setting or character development at all, the form imitating a performance script. Passages of poetry celebrating ordinary people and their activities also abound:

> They know that art well
> Who trade in food—
> pad up
> where resources are scarce, or
> just for cool profit:
> grains for sausages
> some worms for burgers
> more leaves for Kenkey! (3)

Clearly, then, Aidoo's latest work reflects the dual concerns, thematic and formal, of her first.

As I have attempted to show, throughout her work, Ama Ata Aidoo has demonstrated a dual, yet synthesizing, interest in the moral function of Ghanaian orature and the woman artist's role in continuing this tradition. She insists in an interview with Maxine McGregor, "all the art of the speaking voice could be brought back so easily. We are not that far from our traditions" (Pieterse and Duerden 1972:24). Ironically, she reports being "complimented" by a student after a lecture, "your English was absolutely masculine" (Aidoo 1982:36), but shouted down by some professors from another Ghanaian university during a political debate on the grounds that "I am not fit to speak about public matters. That I should leave politics and such to those best qualified to handle it, and concentrate on doing what I normally do best, which is writing plays and short stories (37). She sarcastically lists the roles her society expects an African woman to play:

> A sexual aid:
> a wet nurse and a
> nursemaid for your children:
> a cook-steward and
> general housekeeper:
> a listening-post:
> an economic and general consultant:
> a field-hand and

if you are that way inclined
a punch-ball. (34)

Her understanding of the limitation reflects feminist critic Ogundipe-Leslie's analysis that sexism in Africa is "systemic" (Ogundipe-Leslie 1994:228-9). Aidoo's focus upon women and their struggle to achieve a voice is, clearly, based both on her grounding in Ghanaian orature and her personal experience. She relies heavily on the techniques of oral performance to examine issues concerning empowering a woman's voice, and to reassert orature's traditional moral dialectic between artist and audience. Aidoo's work consistently creates an aesthetic and political synthesis of the old and the new and asserts the authenticity of the woman artist.

WORKS CITED

Adelugba, Dapo. "No Sweetness Here: Literature as Social Criticism." *Ba Shiro* 6, 6, (1974).

Aidoo, Ama Ata. *Anowa*, London: Longman Drumbeat, 1970.

———. *Changes: A Love story*. New York: CUNY, The Feminist Press, 1991.

———. *Our Sister Killjoy: Or Reflections from a Black-Eyed Squint*. USA: Nok Publishers. 1979.

———.*The Dilemma of a Ghost*. Accra: Longman, 1965.

———. "Unwelcome Pals and Decorative Slaves," *AFA, Journal of Creative Writing* 1 (November 1982):34-38.

Bascomb, William R. *African Dilemma Tales*. The Hague: Mouton Publishers, 1975.

Brown, Lloyd W. *Women Writers in Black Africa*. Westport, Conn: Greenwood Press, 1981.

Davies, Carole Boyce. *Black Women, Writing and Identity*, London and New York: Routledge, 1994.

Gottner-Abendroth, Heide. "Nine Principles of a Matriarchal Aesthetic." *Feminist Aesthetics*. Ed. Gisela Ecker. Trans. by Harriet Anderson. Boston: Beacon Press, 1986.

McGregor, Maxine. "Interview with Ama Ata Aidoo." In: *African Writers Talking: A Collection of Radio Interviews*. Eds. Cosmo Pierterse and Dennis Duerden. New York: Africana Publishing Co., 1972.

Nagenda, John. "Generations in Conflict: Ama Ata Aidoo, J. C. deGraft and R. Sharif Eamon." In: *Protest and Conflict in African Literature*. Eds. Cosmo Pieterse and Donald Monro. London: Heinemann, 1969. 101-108.

Nwankwo, Chimalum. "The Feminist Impulse and Social Realism in Ama Ata Aidoo's *No Sweetness Here* and *Our Sister Killjoy*." In: *Ngambika: Studies of Women in African Literature*. Eds. Carole Boyce Davies and Anne Adams Graves. Trenton, N.J. Africa World Press, 1986. 151-159.

Ogundipe-Leslie, 'Molara. Re-Creating *Ourselves: African Women and Critical*

Arlene A. Elder

Transformations. Trenton, N.J.: Africa World Press, 1994.
Pierterse, Cosmo and Dennis Duerden. Eds. *African Writers Talking: A Collection of Radio Interviews*. New York: Africana Publishing Co., 1972.

OF THOSE
WHO WENT BEFORE

KENNETH W. HARROW

Daniel Kunene (1991), like Wilfred Cartey (1969) and Harold Scheub (1985), gives us the model of the typical African narrative pattern in which the protagonist journeys outward from home, going to a foreign land, experiencing what pangs and travails life intends for the African away from home. At the propitious moment the hero returns, wiser, perhaps sadder, perhaps even ready for death, like Shaka (Masizi Kunene 1979) or Samba Diallo in *L'Aventure ambiguë* (Kane 1961), but usually ready to assume the position of ruler, like Sundiata.[1] We can identify this pattern as that of the male hero, with its emphasis upon the quest and identity, and the correspondence between the hero's success and the rise of the state over which he rules. It is not so much the gender of the hero that defines this pattern as patriarchal as it is the construction of a phallocentric model that naturalizes hegemonic patterns of state or social control.

In contemporary written African literature, the meaning of the journey isn't as clear as for the oral epic. For the novel, there is the

European archetypical model for this type of narrative, the *Bildungsroman*, that conventionally ends with the hero learning that the object of the quest out into a greater world was always already to be found at home. In this model, the journey appears as a preparation or initiation experience that sets the stage for the eventual self-discovery. But what of the stories in which there is no return, no preparation for the inculcation of traditional values, no recognition of home truths—no initiation into the society of one's own? What of those stories that thematize exile and dramatize the permanence of that condition? These are the stories of a middle passage for which there is no return.

Kunene's model of the archetypical journey of initiation is neatly circular with an outward movement away from home culminating in a transformation of the hero—his death and rebirth—ultimately followed by a triumphant return home and legitimate accession to power. In contrast to this model of satisfied, authenticated rule, much contemporary written African literature presents us with an uncompleted fragment of this journey—voyages outward without return; deaths without rebirth; failed initiations, riddled with contradiction, frustration and despair.[2] A journey that concludes when it is halfway over is not a voyage of discovery and regeneration, but an exile, at the limit a permanent exile from self as from home—tales with "no sweetness," tales still awaiting the appearance of the "beautyful ones."

If the passage of Africans from the continent into slavery abroad was the journey outward, then the dream of returning to Africa, as figured in much Caribbean literature, must be the voyage home.[3] Misery of outbound voyage, joy of imagined return—the *Bildungsroman* is reversed in this African-Caribbean joint narrative because the original excitement of departure and adventure is betrayed by enslavement, while the anticipated return of the enlightened, homesick voyager is realized only as a dream, as a ghostly voyage undertaken in fantasy, in the spaces outside of harsh reality and its dilemmas, after death, when the likes of Sugarman (Morrison 1977) can finally fly home.

In her short story, "Other Versions" (1971), Ama Ata Aidoo sends the young scholar, Kofi, out to cross the Atlantic on a voyage to America. There he will pursue a course of education that will enable him to return to Africa equipped with a university degree. This new diaspora of young African students is built upon the historical shadow of the earlier, involuntary passage of millions of African slaves, which sets the stage for the encounter between

Kofi and a maternal African-American woman whom he meets in the subway. For Aidoo, the dynamic of this meeting is framed by Kofi's attachment to his mother, his great distance from home, and his introduction to racism in the United States.

In *Omeros* (1990) Walcott sends his protagonist, Achille, in the opposite direction. In a delirious dream, Achille, a fisherman, reverses the Middle Passage, returning to his African past. Upon his arrival in a mangrove swamp in Africa, he encounters his father and his paternal village. There he undergoes the dreaded experience of seeing the originary slave raid that led to the capture of his ancestors occur without being able to do anything about it. His quest to discover his origins, his meeting with his father, and his experience of the historical fate of his ancestors remain blocked.

Thus we have with Walcott the Caribbean dream of the return to a paternal truth, and with Aidoo the African dream of repeating the diaspora voyage in the name of the mother. Seen together the two narratives form a strangely complementary whole and sketch out the contours of the epic journey, rewritten according to the new exigencies of each. In the process, the patriarchal pattern is fractured, the epic of triumph supplanted by "other versions."

I. DEREK WALCOTT, *OMEROS*

"and there was a figure
framed in the quiet window for whom this was home,

tracing its dust, rubbing thumb and middle finger,
then coming to me, not past, but through the machines,
clear as a film and as perfectly projected

as a wall cut by the jalousies' slanted lines.
He had done a self-portrait, it was accurate.
In his transparent hand there was a book I had read.

'In this pale blue notebook when you had found my verses'—
my father smiled—'I appeared to make your life's choice,
and the calling that you practice both reverses

and honours mine from the moment it blent with yours.
Now that you are twice my age, which is the boy's,
which the father's?'

'Sir'—I swallowed—'they are one voice'." (68)
(Derek Walcott, *Omeros*)

Moving in the direction opposite to that of the outbound slave ships of the Middle Passage, Derek Walcott's Achille is sent us from St. Lucia across to Africa, the son now in quest of his father. The vehicle for this journey is hallucination. Whereas Aidoo presents us with a voyage without return, Walcott designs a voyage of the mind, carried on the wings of a sea-swift, across centuries, past sunken hulks whose ribs remain as signposts of slavery's cruel means of transportation—transporting us back across an ocean, the Middle Passage run in dream reverse, ending in a return to the beginning among the mangroves.

Walcott's account of Achille's voyage to Africa could be read as the return portion of the epic hero's quest, thus completing the cycle begun by the centripetal departure from Africa—Kofi's outward journey. Again to borrow Kunene's model, if the hero departs because of a character flaw, or an insurmountable obstacle at home (such as Shaka's corruption by Isanusi, or Sundiata's usurpation by his brother, Dankaran Touman), then Achille departs because he has lost the key to Helen's affections, or, in a larger sense, because he is threatened by the loss of his deepest cultural moorings. The felling of the giant laurier cannelles trees at the beginning of *Omeros*, is intended to remind us of the cutting off of the Aruac foundation to Caribbean culture. That the felled tree trunks then serve to provide Achille and his mates with their canoes and fishing boats underscores the irony that the loss of the first inhabitants of the islands is the price of the survival of their successors.

Achille's voyage, like that of Kofi or even Sister Killjoy, may be viewed as that of the epic hero as long as the story of his life, his love, even his culture is focused on his own individual person. However, the voyage of diaspora is not the story of romantic heroism, of the struggle of self-overcoming and of triumphant return, but of community loss, of severance and of survival. It is also, and perhaps more importantly, the story of those left behind who also, paradoxically, went before. Thus the completion of the epic cycle, consisting of departure-adventure-return, can also be seen in terms of the ghostly ones who have gone before. In the case of *Omeros* it is Achille's father who fills this role. The cycle seems complete as Aidoo's figure of the mother, anticipating her son's arrival abroad in "Other Versions," is replaced by Achille's father, who proceeds his son's arrival in St. Lucia as well as his return to Africa. In short, the story of Achille's reversal of the Middle Passage, taking him back to Africa, is anticipated by the presence of his father, Achille-Afolabe, whose place in Africa lies both before as well as behind him. The story of the voyaging hero is thus supplanted by that of the abandoned parent who paradoxically travels before his or her child.

If this appears complicated, one can simplify it by saying that the child does not travel alone, is not simply a precursor or a pioneer, but that he or she follows the path of those who have gone before, much as they may seem to have been left behind . . . and that the story is as much that of those left behind as those who undertake the voyage. The voyager travels like a signifier whose way has already been prepared, whose articulation is a repetition, as much as a new turn—the trope of irony.

The reversal of perspectives in the hero's quest story, which turns our attention to the neglected, abandoned ones left behind, can be seen as a parallel to the story of the invisible slaves, the maids or cooks hidden in the kitchen, not invited to the table for the feast, while the slave owners and masters fight out the glorious wars of conquest and fame. This was already the story of Achille's ancestor who served along with the other "black warrior ants" (83) to haul the cannon to the heights of the cliff, insuring the British victory in the 18th century battles against the Spanish. At first this anonymous slave is identified solely as "Achille's ancestor" (82), but as he succeeds in the monumental task of winching the cannon up the cliff, he is baptized anew by the British admiral: "It was then that the small admiral with a cloud on his head renamed Afolabe 'Achilles,' which, to keep things simple, he let himself be called" (83).

In the narrator's autobiographical portrait of his own father, Walcott also presents us with the image of a father whose presence lies both before and behind his son. Echoing the sentiment found in Wordsworth's famous line, "the son is father of the child," Walcott characterizes his father's poetry as a foreshadowing of his own work as well as being his father's creation in his own right. His father speaks to him across the distance of his son's memory, and says:

> I appeared to make your life's choice,
> and the calling that you practice both reverses
> and honours mine from the moment it blent with yours.
> Now that you are twice my age, which is the boy's,
> which the father's? (68)

Walcott's response is that they are one. As Kunene puts it, the epic hero's quest leads him to search for the answer to the question, "Who am I?" The answer lies in the name of the father. "Who am

I" presupposes the notion of a unified self, as we would expect from the male-centered epic—the self that has a hero-identity and that can be expanded to macrocosmic proportions so as to assume the dimensions of the empire. "Who am I" assumes the identity of the nation is waiting to be discovered that will provide the answer. As Walcott's father explains, their name, Walcott, derives from Warwick(shire), their roots going back to the English countryside, to the master's homeland. But as he looks out upon the landscape before them, in memorable terms he assigns his son the task of giving his voice to the voiceless, the black ants, "those Helens from an earlier time," who could not memorialize their fate. As his voice is "blent" with that of his son's, so is his sense of duty communicated by his son's commitment: speaking with the women toiling up a hill, bearing heavy loads, he says to his son, "as a child [you were] wounded by their power and beauty . . . . [Your duty is] to give those feet a voice" (76).

The poetry, then, reaches back to those who had toiled, had seen, had written before, to carry their burden forward. It is not surprising that the poem's protagonist, Achille, journeys back to Africa, following the hallucinating path of the sea-swift, should also bear the name of that original slave progenitor who had lost his name, Afolabe, when the admiral named him Achilles. Achille is the mythical fisher-warrior whose glorious fate is now to be Helen's lost lover. Both he and she seem to live out a fate, joined in their names—joined to a fate that is not their own, that is handed down to them by the master-admirals, the noble scions of Warwickshire, who somehow missed the point that the real force that hewed the trees, that hauled the cannon, the real beauty that launched a thousand ships, was transported in anonymity and despair across an endless sea whose track must be retraced backward for the epic voyage to be complete. If Aidoo's Kofi is ever to return home, Walcott's Achille must first voyage back to his origins, retrace his name back to the lost language of Afolabe.

Standing before his African father, this is the issue to which the two of them are joined:

His father said:
"Afolabe,"
touching his own heart.
"In the place that you come from
what do they call you?" (137)

We wonder at this communication. What is the language they are speaking? Where is this mangrove swamp, this village situated up-river? All that we have to situate it is the father's Yoruba name, Afolabe, while his son's response, given by "tapping his chest," is Achille, a name that means nothing to the villagers, or to Achille himself. His father asks:

> Achille. What does that name mean? I have forgotten the one that I gave you. But it was, it seems, many years ago. What does it mean? (137)

The son's response is that he, too, has forgotten. We don't know whether he is referring to his own name or to the meaning of "Achille," but the larger loss of meaning is made clear, as clear as the usurpation by Warwick of an originary title of African descent.

> The deaf sea has changed around every name
> that you gave us;
> trees, men, we yearn for a sound that is missing. (137)

Here we have come to the heart of the darkness. The search for self, the retracing of the sea lanes back through the past, the encounter with the primeval village, the original father, the one who assigned the name, and who gave with that name the meaning of the child's existence, all conclude with the loss. The "sound that is missing" is forgotten by the son and his father who can only enlighten his son about the meaning of the loss. "A name, " he tells Achille, "means something...."

> The qualities desired in a son,
> and even a girl-child; so even the shadows who called
> you expected one virtue, since every name is a blessing.
> (137)

Afolabe, whose own name means "born into wealth," can attest to this significance of names. But he cannot make the passage from Afolabe to Achille, cannot join his life to that of the black ant worker rebaptized by the admiral, and most of all cannot pass beyond the shadowy existence of dream-palimpsest into an actual portrait. The return is a sham, an echo of loss, remembered only as an absence.

The hollow, empty space of a forgotten name gives definition to diaspora existence. Achille's father asks him, "Did they think you were nothing in that other kingdom?" (137). Yet out of the loss and the absence, Achille can make his own sense, and that is in the act of finding before him the one who had been there behind him, of tracing the echo or loss back to its original form, so that in the act of looking ahead he can find the image of what was lost. This is his blessing: In answer to his father's question as to what his response would be to hearing his own name, he says:

> What would it be? I can only tell you what I believe,
> or had to believe. *It was prediction, and memory,*
> to bear myself back, to be carried here by a swift,
>
> or the shadow of a swift making its cross on water,
> with the same sign I was blessed with, with the gift
> of this sound whose meaning I still do not care
>   to know. (138)

If the epic quest cannot be completed until the hero's mettle is tested and the last obstacle overcome, this, then, must be that ultimate trial in the diaspora's journey outward—the trial of the son's forgotten name, the trial of the parent's forgotten loss. For the father, a son without name has lost his existence because another existence cannot be conceived in front of his son. Just as the son holds his father before him as the goal toward which he is moving, so does the father hold his son's absence before him as an effect without a cause, a being whose absence testifies to the loss of the cause of that absence. "Are you the smoke from a fire that never burned?" he asks (139). More, he acknowledges his son's loss as coming only at the moment when, too late, he becomes aware of that loss:

> Why did I never miss you until you returned?
> Why haven't I missed you, my son, until you
>   were lost? (139)

The son's loss meets that of his father here, as past loss blends into future loss. Achille sees both in this encounter with his father, and can only respond with tears:

> There was no answer to this, as in life. Achille nodded,
> the tears glazed his eyes, where the past was reflected
> as well as the future. (139)

II. Ama Ata Aidoo, "Other Versions"

> "Instead of going straight home, I had stayed in town
> to work."
> —Ama Ata Aidoo, "Other Versions"

In "Other Versions" (1971), Kofi sets out to cross the Atlantic as if he were merely extending the schoolboy's stay in town, away from home, after the exams were over. Already early in the story the dangers of this stay away from home, as well as the youth's insouciant ignorance of the perils, were foreshadowed: "Bekoe and I were going to stay in a small room in his uncle's house. The room was like a coffin but who cared?" (157).

The real exile from home for Kofi lies in his separation from his mother. After he's begun to work and earn money, he returns home with the idea of giving some of it to his mother, as she had sustained him in his school years while his father had only begrudgingly paid for his school fees and basic board. But his mother continues the pattern of her martyrdom, insisting that Kofi pay the extra money to his father. When Kofi wins a scholarship for America, it is still the thought of sending money to his mother that haunts him. Leaving home, then, is made painful due to his separation from his mother and nothing else.

"Other Versions" reads like a letter—not an oral account (despite the orality of the narrative voice)—a letter written as if its point were to be gleaned in the account given of one special event. More importantly, it frames that event by presenting itself as a letter written home from abroad. The first indication of the letter writer's distance from the events is given in the past perfect tense utilized in the opening narration: "The whole thing had started after the school certificate exams. Instead of going straight home, I had stayed in town to work" (157). The present narrative moment is set off by the use of this tense.

The second indication of distance, this time given in terms of space, is presented, abruptly, as soon as Kofi indicates that he had won a scholarship to study in America. He tells us immediately that it is from abroad that the narration is being made: "There were endless forms to fill out but I got the scholarship. And I came *here*" (163; my stress). Already angry about having to give a portion of his income to his father instead of his mother, already concerned about his hard working mother, his exile is tinged by the twin emotions of exhilarating success, or liberation, and nostalgic frustration. The first reaction he reports after going abroad is the latter: "Somehow I never forgot the money for Mother" (163). Once overseas, Kofi tells us nothing about the hardships of adaptation, the excitement in voyaging from one land to the other. Most important, he doesn't recount the traveler's principal story, how the new and different land strikes him as a foreigner. In short, the displacement, its thrills and its defamiliarizing effects, is glossed over. In its place, Kofi holds up the image of his mother whose sacrifices he cannot repay.

Perhaps the sense we have of a frozen action stems from Kofi's success. He is on a scholarship in a wealthy country, while his mother still struggles at home and his father still gripes about the need to finance his younger siblings' education. Kofi's success brings him guilt as long as he remembers the situation back home; and it brings frustration as long as he cannot funnel support back to his mother. His is not the agony of the slave, then, who went unwillingly, whose labor enriched a master, and who was rejected as inferior. He is a scholarship winner, and the key incident that he chooses to recount begins with his receiving an invitation to a dinner party held by the "chairman" of the syndicate, "or one of its top men" (164), responsible for bringing him to America. His observations are cryptic and mocking: the house to which he is brought is "a high and mighty hut" (164).

Again, the scene might have provided the occasion for Kofi to describe all that was new and different, the high and mighty "hut" and its strange denizens. Instead there is a brief ironic reference to the Americans' curiosity, which they express in somewhat insensitive fashion: "What did I think of America? How do I plan to use this unique opportunity in the service of Africa? How many wives does my father have?" (164). His feelings of being ill at ease are attenuated by the epistolarian's irony as Kofi the narrator comments, "I was the main course" (164). Still, the potential discomfort of this situation is underplayed. It is not till he leaves that we understand his earlier comment, "I had assumed that everyone in the household was there at the dinner table" (164), or that we comprehend the conventional compliments paid the hostess for her cooking. As Kofi leaves to be driven home by his host, he is surprised to learn that another person is also to be driven halfway home, and that is the black woman who cooked the meal for dinner, but who did not share it at the table with the guests, and who did not receive the compliments for the cooking.

At this point in her story Aidoo has assumed the mantle

Walcott's father assigned to his son to be the voice for the anonymous women who slaved like black ants:

> From here, in his boyhood, he had seen women climb
> like ants up a white flower-pot, baskets of coal
> balanced on their torchoned heads, without touching them,
>
> up the black pyramids, each spine straight as a pole,
> and with a strength that never altered its rhythm.
> He spoke for those Helens from an earlier time:
>
> Hell was built on those hills. In that country of coal
> without fire, that inferno the same colour
> as their skins and shadows, every labouring soul
>
> climbed with her hundredweight basket, every load for
> one copper penny, balanced erect on their necks
> that were tight as the liner's hawsers from the weight.
>
> The carriers were women, not the fair, gentler sex.
> Instead, they were darker and stronger, and their gait
> was made beautiful by balance.... (73-74)

Where the obvious tensions of being a black African in wealthy
white America are downplayed or ignored in the story, in the presence of the black woman cook Kofi is touched, guilty, and vulnerable: "In the car seat I smiled nervously at the other . . . . I tried
not to feel agitated" (165).

Some days later, as he takes a subway home at night, he again
encounters a middle aged black woman, again experiencing feelings of agitation; this time he strikes up a conversation and offers
her money, only to have her refuse it, as did his mother. He is
moved again, as he had been the night of the dinner party, and as
he had been when he had offered his mother the money at home,
only to be told he had to give it to his father instead. His emotional reaction to the encounter on the subway is based on the repetition of his rejected offer to his mother—an offer and rejection
framed by the sense of closeness between mother and child.

Aidoo has often presented us with this portrait of caring, devoted mothers, of children emerging from under the wing of the hen,
of the poignancy and pain of a mother's loss, and of the telling in
which there is no sweetness. "The Late Bud" and "No Sweetness
Here" are two such examples from the collection *No Sweetness Here*

(1970). The child's cry for his mother—here presented as the final words of "Other Versions" ("I heard myself mutter, "O Mother" [166])—echoes the earlier calls of students living abroad, in exile, in France in the 1930s or, a generation later, in the 1950s, those like Senghor, Laye, and even Mongo Beti, for whom a nostalgia for Africa could not be separated from the love of a mother. For some, the mother is joined to the son in a common condition of subordination to a domineering pater familias. Indeed, Aidoo is not unfamiliar with the feeling of the student experiencing the alienating effects of life abroad, as we have seen in her first novel, *Our Sister Killjoy* (1979), where the radical rejection of Western culture and assimilation are foregrounded.

Given the opportunity to make a strong statement on these same issues here, one wonders why Aidoo chose the more sentimental emotion of the child who misses and cares for his mother. If there is a key to this shift away from the radical posture of *Killjoy*, it is to be found in the figures of the overworked, fatigued middle aged black American women, invisible presences in wealthy white homes who must return alone at night, crossing the path of their lost African son. They are the ghosts in these stories of no return, and their function is not to present the nostalgia or sentiment of their own situation, now beyond the scope of their African relatives, but to act as catalysts to remind the new generation of successful Africans that the diasporic voyage, situated long before the modern period and its own exiles, could still bring together distant mothers and their long lost children.

What is the relationship between Kofi (who journeys) and Mother (who stays behind)? It is *his* journey, his adventure. If the epic hero departs so as to overcome a flaw, to undergo initiation, transformation, unwillingly leaving the home (like Mwindo or Sundiata), Kofi willingly goes, like Camara Laye in *L'Enfant Noir* (1953), having applied for and won a scholarship to study abroad. If there is a flaw that mars this departure, it is not to be seen in Western terms (in which scholarships are signs of success), but in African terms, in which separation from family is a loss, not a gain. The flaw, then, lies in the substitution of Western for African values. Kofi's fate is to become a been-to.

Though Kofi's scholarly successes and journey might appear to concern only him, this is on only one level, that is, the level that presents the hero's journey as the story of an individual fate. In fact, Kofi's journey is inseparable from his mother's loss. Laye poignantly describes his mother's anguish at his departure; Kofi has no such scene in his narration, and shows more concern over his long-suffering mother's refusal to accept any of his money for herself. But in another short story, "A Certain Wind From the South" (1971), Aidoo presents us with the plight of the women left behind while the adventuring husband, son or father departs in search of exploits, money, and glory. The trajectory of the epic hero's journey, then, is not complete without the account of the impact on the abandoned mothers-wives-daughters.

The significance of the diaspora "mothers" encountered by Kofi can now be seen in a new light. On the one hand, from his perspective, they are reminders of home and his ties to his family. That is their function within *his* story. However, from the point of view of the mother, they form part of the story of abandonment, or even, less dramatically but more fundamentally, of the ambivalent story of weaning in which the mother must separate herself from the one she loves in order that the loved one might have the space to grow, and in order that she herself might continue to live and to love. And the price she pays for this weaning is her child's anguished, pained sense of betrayal.

Caught between the emotions of a maternal love that maintains its hold, and one that releases its hold on the child, the mother is left abandoned by the child she herself sends away. In this case she literally cooperates in the process that leads to her child's departure by financing his schooling, and by encouraging his progress. Yet she is not left out of the picture. A magical transference occurs, whereby the abandoned mother reappears twice in the form of the wise, middle-aged black women encountered by Kofi in America. The mother goes before the child whom she sends out. His voyage without return is an encounter with his abandoned mother; his story flips into hers, which becomes a tale of survival, perseverance, and continuity as she declines his proffered guilt money with the same gesture of motherly concern, "Son, keep them dollars. I sure know you need them more than I do" (166).

These were her only words to Kofi, and she leaves with him a gesture of warmth and a smile that acknowledges not only the strength of the diasporic bond, of the mother-child bond, but even more of the survival instincts of the mother who knows how to wean her child as well as how to nurse him. In the face of her silent, understated role, Kofi's three-D drama of success and nostalgia pales to insignificance.

Aidoo's recasting of the male epic, unlike that of Walcott who continues to play the stops of the identity theme, relies upon the centrality of the mother's story—we might say, of the mothers' stories. In a sense they were always there—behind Mwindo, behind Sundiata whose return home and fulfillment of his destiny could not begin until his mother had died. But where the epic takes up the central narrative of the hero's quest after Sogolon, the Buffalo Woman's death, Aidoo has chosen to linger over those stories of struggle and survival in which the drama of the children cannot be recounted without recalling the words of their mothers. While the sons, fathers, husbands, were caught by the shine on the soldiers' shoes, enlisting for foreign adventures, ready to begin the story, there were always those who had gone ahead, and who had to stay behind to tend to the children.

III. CONCLUSION

"Then I remembered what Mother had told me."

—(Ama Ata Aidoo, "Other Versions")

"Along this coal-blackened wharf, what Time decided to do with my treacherous body after this,"
he said, watching the women, "will stay in your head

as long as a question you have no right to ask,
only to doubt, not hate our infuriating
silence."

—(Derek Walcott, *Omeros*)

What is there about these images of repetition, absence, and reversal that gives them such portentous weight? In part, we sense in them the haunted echo of the great epic motions, mocked in the gestures of unfulfillment. But more, they respond to our times—they are the epics of scholarships, and of an age in which it is infinitely more natural for children to leave home as a sign of success than for a people to conquer old kingdoms and establish the legitimacy of new rule. But more profoundly, they are the epics of those reaching across the boundless space of diasporic distance to find meaning in the paradoxical presence of those who have gone before—a reaching out, an outward motion, a going forward that is translated into a voyage back.

I cannot dare conclude that there is anything like self-discovery that lies at the end of this itinerary. Where does the self lie for

Achille, one whose present name is a meaningless gift, and whose original, meaningful name is lost? There is no real name for Achille, no return to Afolabe, and Kofi's mother will always refuse the money. Yet the encounters of Achille with Afolabe, and of Kofi with his surrogate mother, hold a meaning whose ineffable, poignant, painful sense becomes our own. The shadowed epic of diaspora is the epic of our times.

NOTES

1. Whereas Kunene, Scheub, and Cartey have emphasized a general pattern of the hero's voyage, a pattern the first two applied to the epic, others have been more circumspect. In particular, Stephen Belcher (1993) warns against generalizations that obscure the differences in traditions and performances. In particular he takes to task Okpewho's work in which for "specific differences in place, occasion, or even form, are subsumed under the greater unity of the `oral performance'" (498). Elsewhere Belcher (forthcoming) emphasizes the differences between Ozidi, Mwindo, Lianjo, and Sundiata: "Isidore Okpewho (1979) blends all these heroes in their orality: Christiane Seydou (1982) has advanced more convincing arguments for distinguishing between West and Central African epic traditions . . . on performance and stylistic grounds. The question of the difference in narrative patterns is a broad one, which has not yet been addressed, to the best of my knowledge" (chapter 5, n.3).
2. Ironically it is Wole Soyinka, much criticized by feminist critics for his depictions of women, who problematized the paradigm of the complete initiation in much of his early work, such as *The Strong Breed* (1973), *Death and the King's Horseman* (1975) [see my chapter on Soyinka in *Threshold of Change in African Literature* (1994)]. For example of the fragmented or incomplete journey, see Armah's *Fragments* (1970), Aidoo's *Our Sister Killjoy* (1977), and a number of the stories in *No Sweetness Here* (1970). The few examples of African literature that thematize the return of the diaspora African community include Syl Cheney-Coker's *The Last Harmattan of Alusine Dunbar* (1990) and Kofi Awoonor's *Come the Voyager at Last* (1992). Finally, on the scholarship of the journey, with its accompanying themes of exile and migration, see the two volumes of *Yale French Studies* 82 and 83, on "Post/Colonial Conditions; Exiles, Migrations, and Nomadisms."
3. Clarisse Zimra (1986) has pointed out that the early Caribbean novel, based on "the determination to write history as so many national counter-histories," took on a typically male perspective. The rewriting of the original loss/disaster, the "wrenching from Africa, the primal mother," turned into a quest story: "the quest of the writer-son is always for the undiscovered father. In the Caribbean the father is always absent, hence undiscoverable. The son is always a bastard" (230). The heading for the section of the essay in which these words appear is "Did Caliban Have a Sister?" Zimra goes on to examine the works of Maryse Condé, Marie Chauvet, and Jeanne Hyvrard

for the ways in which the women's accounts succeed in "standing on its head" the underlying topos of the conventional male Caribbean narrative.

WORKS CITED

Aidoo, Ama Ata. *No Sweetness Here.* Garden City, New York: Anchor Books, Doubleday, 1970; 1972.

———. *Our Sister Killjoy.* New York: Nok, 1979.

Armah, Ayi Kwei. *Fragments.* Boston: Houghton Mifflin, 1970.

Awoonor, Kofi. *Come the Voyager at Last.* Trenton, N.J.: Africa World Press, 1992.

Belcher, Stephen. Review of *African Oral Literature* by Isidore Okpewho. *Journal of American Folklore* 106 (Fall 1993):497-99.

———. "Sinimogo—The Man For Tomorrow." In: *In Search of Sundiata.* Ed. Ralph Austin. Indiana University Press (forthcoming).

Cartey, Wilfred. *Whispers from a Continent.* New York: Vintage, 1969.

Cheney-Coker, Syl. *The Last Harmattan of Alusine Dunbar.* Portsmouth, N.H.: Heinemann, 1990.

Harrow, Kenneth. *Threshold of Change in African Literature.* Portsmouth, N.H.: Heinemann, 1994.

Kane, Cheikh Hamidou. *L'Aventure ambiguë.* Paris: Juillard, 1961.

Kunene, Daniel. "Journey in the African Epic." *Research in African Literatures* XX, 2 (Summer 1991):205-223.

Kunene, Masizi. *Emperor Shaka the Great.* London: Heinemann, 1979.

Laye Camara. *L'Enfant noir.* Paris: Plon, 1953.

Lionnet, Françoise and Ronnie Scharfman, eds. "Post/Colonial Conditions; Exiles, Migrations, and Nomadisms." *Yale French Studies* 1/ 2, 82/ 83 (1993).

Morrison, Toni. *Song of Solomon.* New York: Knopf, 1977.

Okpewho, Isidore. *The Epic in Africa.* New York: Columbia University Press, 1979.

Scheub, Harold. "Review of African Oral Traditions and Literature." *African Studies Review* 28, 2-3 (1985):1-72.

Seydou, Christiane. "Comment définir le genre épique? un exemple: l'épopée africaine." In: *Genres, Forms, Meanings: Essays in African Oral Literature.* Ed. Veronika Görög-Karady. Journal of the Anthropological Society of Oxford, Occasional Papers, (1982) 84-98.

Soyinka, Wole. *Death and the King's Horseman.* New York: Hill and Wang, 1975.

———. *The Strong Breed.* In: *Collected Plays.* Vol.1. London: Oxford University Press, 1973.

Walcott, Derek. *Omeros.* New York: Farrar, Straus, Giroux, 1990.

Zimra, Clarisse. "W/Righting His/tory: Versions of Things Past in Contemporary Caribbean Women Writers." In: *Explorations.* Ed. Makoto Ueda. Lanham: University Press of America, 1986.

THE RISK OF (RE)MEMBERING MY NAME:

READING *LUCY* AND *OUR SISTER KILLJOY* AS TRAVEL NARRATIVES

PAULA MORGAN

To the ever-journeying peoples of the African diaspora, travel has assumed a multiplicity of resonances: domination and servitude; enforced physical/cultural penetration and cross-fertilization; resistance and accommodation; rejection and assimilation; paradise lost and edenic space reconstructed. The fictions are replete with travelers—islanders and continent dwellers alike—who each grope towards a new sense of self in new geographic and psychic landscapes. Travel, of necessity, spells confrontation of difference, within cultures and peoples and ethnicities. Travel spells acknowledgment of the essential sameness of the human condition. To some, like Ama Ata Aidoo, travel defines the imperative of return; to others, like Jamaica Kincaid it defines its impossibility. This paper reads Aidoo's novel, *Our Sister Killjoy* and Kincaid's *Lucy* against the background of traditional travel narratives and postcolonial adaptations of that form and seeks to make connections between the gendered subjectivity of each persona as traveler, her relationship to her socio/cultural/psychic environments, the nature of her journey and the narrative mode employed.

The travel narrative is an ancient mode of expression which has persisted in all oral and literate cultures, arguably because of its capacity for sustaining allegorical spheres of meaning and because it speaks so convincingly of and to the human spirit. Predictably, in the service of the nineteenth-century imperialist enterprise, travel with the agenda of discovery of new worlds in order to sweep them into Europe's civilizing ambit became an over-riding objective of the Western hero, both in life and in literature. The texts justified European domination and entrenched the normative value of Western culture. Seamus Deane in *Imperialism and Nationalism* argues that European success in the imperial endeavor "was achieved over nature, but a nature inhabited by peoples whose defeat, expropriation, enslavement, or extermination has to be justified in a series of theoretical formulations that relied on categories paraded as fundamental and universal" (Deane 1990:355).

In the novel of empire, the narration of journey was rooted in the need to theorize and often to recuperate failure and villainy as forms of success. The fictionalization of a racially, culturally, economically supremacist code was inextricably linked therefore with the romanticization of journey, falsification of its underlying intent. The subsequent canonization of these novels as classics—and more so, as children's literature—placed them in that exalted non-contested, non-discursive space in the Western imagination, and, through the colonial education system, in the mental structures of the colonized.

A major ideological objective of the novel of Empire was the denigration of the Other. Brian Street, writing on race and ideology in the classic European adventure tale, points out: "Behind the apparently trivial and harmless exotica of the tales of adventure lie deep preconceptions about the nature of humankind, about how the variety of human societies can be conceived of, described and understood and about the role of different cultures and "races in the world order" (Street 1985:95). Novelists exploiting the authority of narrative fleshed out deficient anthropological theories of Social Darwinism in lurid detail which captured the popular imagination entrenching stereotypes, which were more pervasive than

Paula Morgan

facts. Griffith argues in *Travel Narrative as Cultural Critique*:

> Travel narrative participates in this complex
> power/knowledge nexus, and each literate/literary
> representation of a people and a culture may be
> seen for the most part as a consolidation of old
> stereotypes or alternately, as an examination and
> denaturalization of stereotype. The consolidated
> stereotype informs and is also informed by the par-
> ticular way of seeing the world and the power rela-
> tions in it. The stereotype naturalizes the world and
> makes it familiar to the narrating subject who rep-
> resents this world through narrative.... But stereo-
> typical narrative representations of peoples and
> cultures can also serve as a significant ontological
> strategy....These stereotypical representations are
> the canvas upon which he foregrounds his selfhood.
> (Griffith 1993:88)

Crucial to the reception of these texts was the acceptance of their claims of heroism and mastery. The subtext was the construction of false identities based on communal deception promoted through the manipulation of narrative subjectivity—the location of the eye and the centrality of the perceiving self within the fictional universe as its singular signifier. The "gaze" was significant to Europe's civilizing discourse because, to borrow Conrad's terminology, "The conquest of the earth, which mostly means the taking it away from those who have a different complexion or slightly flatter noses than ourselves, is not a pretty thing when you look at it too much. What redeems it is the idea only" (Conrad 1975:10). As the travel narrative was pressed into the service of deception, so too was it pressed into the act of unveiling. It is the vehicle which reveals Marlow's ambivalent position in relation to the equally ambivalent "horror" the lie at the essence of Europe's civilizing mission, the nature of the masculinist quest and the complicity of the Western woman.

For the colonial to engage narrative was to engage the lie, for to enter into literacy, that is to read, was to read the self as inscribed at the margins of the text.[1] To appropriate narrative for a cross-section of the postcolonial writers, required bringing the colonized self from the margins to the center of the text. A crucial step was displacing the figure at the center. This was the agenda of Derek Walcott's reconfiguration of the discovery trope and deconstruction of the Crusoe myth within *Remembrance and Pantomime*

(1980). The Crusoe figure "Massa" Harry Trewe is unmasked as the vulnerable, emasculated male traumatized by his wife's success. And Jackson/man Friday declares "Bwana, Effendi, Bacara, Sahid...in that sun that never set on your empire I was your shadow" (112), yet he insists on exposing the lie. A similar impulse lies behind Lamming's deflation of the heroic conquistador in *Natives of my Person*, a psycho-cultural study of the forces which shaped imperialism.[2] Significantly, in both of these narratives, a significant dimension of the unmasking of the colonizer was the revelation of his inadequacy in relation to his woman. The shift in the nature of the gaze was not inevitable. Eurocentrism flourishes in the satirical travel narratives of V. S. Naipaul who affirms the lie in his well-known indictment of Caribbean society "(h)istory is built around achievement and creation; and nothing was created in the West Indies" (Naipaul 1962:29).[3]

Whereas the reconfiguration of these journeys are sited within the colony, another type of reconfiguration engaged the colonizer on his home turf and constituted a physical return to the metropolitan centre, to the locus of imposed meaning, to the heart of the lie, so to speak. Yet another necessary step in the maturing process then seems to be the rejection of any illusion of a sustaining relationship with the colonial motherland. How do Jamaica Kincaid and Ama Ata Aidoo engage the colonizer on his home turf? Korang argues in relation to *Our Sister Killjoy*:

> The metaphor of a shipwrecked history becomes a useful mnemonic with which to characterize the Ghanaian writer's reflection on the conditions under which the modernity of Africa is purchased. From a perspective that interprets a modern Africa in terms of her cannibalization into an alienating universe of discourse, Aidoo brings a skeptical feminine intelligence to an examination of her place within a unbroken continuum or a history of colonialism and neo-colonialism. The African woman writer seizes the initiative on Africa's behalf to make a timely intervention into the discourses that a European cultural apparatus writes over her homeland. (Korang 1992:52).

And the displacement and disillusionment of the exile within the mother country was a common concern for the early creative writers of the Caribbean. It is within a rich literary heritage that Kincaid intervenes into the discourses of Western cultural apparatus (in reason however to find the United States as the neo-imperial colossus). *Lucy* rehearses bleak themes of alienation, impossiblility of atonement with her past, rejection of mother and adopted mother, natal land and adoptive land—but with a significant new dimension. Commonly, the exile of the Caribbean person in the metropolis is the bittersweet loss of a home from which escape was crucial, if not inevitable. Lamming's Boy G of *In The Castle of My Skin* reflects on his impending departure as an irreconcilable loss conveyed metaphorically as the tongue probing the space left by an extraction. And Walcott's unsung returning poet/persona rues the day that he learns that there could be "homecoming without home" as seen in *A Kind of Homecoming*. Kincaid's exploration of exile differs in this crucial way—it is nonbelonging of an individual who, having lost the mindless cocoon of the womb, has never learned to negotiate the strange new outer worlds. Embedded within Kincaid's account of metropolitan exile is her grief of all other sites of disruption, dislocation in her stark portrayal of unaccomodated woman.

On the surface, it would be well nigh impossible to write from more widely divergent points of embarkation as Jamaica Kincaid and Ama Ata Aidoo. *Our Sister Killjoy* deals with a young girl's attempt to come to terms with the severe needs of postcolonial African society and the role of Africans in the Diaspora. Sissie travels to Europe and England on a European government grant intended for redress but also to strengthen sinewy ropes of obligation. With a squint, which brings to mind the perspective of Swift's Gulliver, she offers stringent critical insight on the mores of European culture and the vast gaps which can separate cultures as seen in *Gulliver's Travels*. Predictably, this travel narrative makes the Westerner uncomfortable in a manner that the "exotic" portrayals of the African tribal world do not, and it has been criticized for the looseness of its structure and the sour note imparted by the unending stream of criticism against Western culture. Much of this discomfort is rooted in the fact that the native/other has dared to transform "itself" into an autonomous perceiving eye and to appropriate the travel narrative for a satiric *exposé* of cultural and ethnic differences. Aidoo adopts the superciliousness, contempt, and tendency towards reductive stereotyping that Europeans had hitherto embraced as an exclusive birthright.

The flip side of her rejection of things European is her framing of a gendered nationalist discourse inserting the woman as agent where she had been placed by the majority of male African writers in the passive role as symbol. The narrative like the traveler/protagonist is restless—constantly shifting in time and space; within symbolic structures and frames of meaning. This woman refuses to be fixed in spatial, temporal and epistemological terms. Aidoo is careful to overturn the conflation of the female with mother Africa; rather than a mother calling her errant children home, she is the sibling—our sister, the sister of the collectivity encouraging the brothers set adrift to perceive their reality from a different vantage point.

Yet, Aidoo writes out of a settled inner sense of place and belonging which shapes her alien and alienating perspective of strange European lands. Sissie's essential rootedness in the ancestral landscape is as firm as Lucy's dispossession. The narrative voice is that of the tribal griot, a wise elder who tracks the journey of our Sissie assessing her situation and measuring her responses with eagle eye. The story teller mediates even into the reality which will be conveyed, determining the shape of the story Sissie will tell when she returns. The very naming of Aidoo's protagonist testifies to her favored position within community. Conversely, Kincaid's island home is the most tangible locus of her alienation— the alienation which she experiences in America is a mere shadow of the discomfort of "skin does not fitness." For Kincaid's protagonist also, the permutations of her name Lucy after Lucifer the quintessential outsider defines her non-belonging. Her intensely personal burden is to re-member a self from which to confront new realities.

Significantly, both narratives are semi-autobiographical in nature. Aidoo states that it is "not auto-biographical in the sense of being a faithful recording of the experiences I have been through. *Sissie* is a composite creation. Definitely there is a lot of me in her. Sure, some of the things she went through, I went through" (James 1990:16). In this respect *Our Sister Killjoy* joins numerous other narratives of development, in which there is no clear demarcation between autobiography and *Bildungsroman*. These veils raise interesting issues related to the intersections between self-representation, representative characterization and fiction, a major consideration being the manner in which such intersections are expressed in societies which are newly emergent from preliterate orality and others which have fully emerged into literacy but remain subject to varying stages of influence from the oral traditions.

Aidoo's subtitle *Reflections from a Black-Eyed Squint* suggests the underlying ambiguities of the text. The narrative is presented through a distorted vision, but the very distortion is meant as a corrective—to adjust the myopia of a colonial legacy. The issue is how can one replace a white-eyed (Eurocentric) perspective with a black-eyed (Afrocentric) perspective and more relevantly how can one work towards twenty-twenty vision. Such a challenge is announced in the onset of the narrative:

> what ticky tackies we have
> saddled and surrounded ourselves with,
> blocked our views,
> cluttered our brains (Aidoo 1977:5).

The tensions inherent in the fictional statement are manifest from the beginning. They hinge on the space between that early optimistic assertion that "things are working out their dazzling conclusion" (15) and the juxtaposed semantic gymnastics which displays the blindness of the educated assembly. As it seeks to press through into new modes of perception, it evolves into a protest narrative—complex, rich in allusion, in which the boundaries between prose and verse are blurred.[4] The subversion of the fixed form challenges Western conventions of narrative appropriacy and the tacit reader/writer contracts which were used to promulgate the original lie under the banner of universal truth. Aidoo not only challenges the content of the Western scribal convention, she dislocates its forms as well.

The third person omniscient narrator, aligned with Sissie's consciousness is constantly shifting between the perception of the young experiencing self and the older more experienced self who recalls the events in the light of "knowledge gained since" (this phrase functions like a refrain in the narrative), and the shifts in the perspective, experience and time often correspond with genre shift from prose to poetry. More often than not the prose segments deal with the present and the youthful experiences. The poetry segments tend to deal with the broader philosophical, sociological and historical issues—in other words they present an interpretative framework for the events of time present of the narrative. Like Kincaid, Aidoo is about an act of re-membering the self but with a far greater emphasis on restructuring an affirming framework of public and communal meaning.

What is the most significant basis of comparison between Aidoo and Kincaid? It is the unrelenting probing of the nature of the civilizations which they interrogate. It is the issues which they pose.

How can manifestly decaying cultures successfully masquerade as superior cultures? How can a people in crisis maintain the facade of exemplars? When norms at the so-called center are steadily being eroded, how can one convince the recuperated mimic men of the so-called marginal cultures of their inherent superiority? Even more basic—where is the margin and where is the center?

Kincaid and Aidoo share a propensity to constantly locate the personal experiences within their socio-political and cultural frameworks and within complex sequences of cause and effect relations. The texts represent a relentless exposé of individual complicity in unjust power systems in ways which players invariably prefer to ignore; moreover, they refuse to focus on black/white colonizer/colonized interactions as the only and the ultimate injustice. The result is that the narratives simultaneously center and de-center this pivotal though solitary incident of history and thereby rob it of a fixed sense of inevitability and historical continuity. While Lucy's political statement emanates from an intensely individual perspective, Aidoo pushes relentlessly beyond the individual illumination towards social imperatives and solutions.

Lucy zeroes in on the young immigrant's need to craft an appropriate identity within a metropolitan landscape—"I understood that I was inventing myself, and that I was doing this more in the way of a painter than in the way of a scientist." What are her tools? "I had memory, I had anger, I had despair" (Kincaid 1990:133). Her recreation comprises an examination of a multiple identity, has elicited a multiple anguish and a multiple rejection. What are these identities? She is a colonial who since puberty has refused to sing Rule Britannia. She early rejects a public face which requires a false hypocritical identification with the motherland and its immoral effort at civilization. It is her ongoing determination to reject the identity of the subaltern which imparts her needle sharp understanding of the albeit veiled oppressions which she encounters daily and her determination to repeatedly uncover the disguises at every turn. This Lucy and by extension Kincaid does with unrelenting passion and integrity.

Lucy refuses to get caught in the bad dream into which the generous patronage of her rich, liberal, white, employer threatens to lure her. She identifies with the black workers when they appear fleetingly in a dining car on a train in which all the servers looked like Lucy's relatives and all the people being served looked like Mariah's. There is a significant difference intended to signify on the apparent passivity of the black America working class. Lucy perceives: "On closer observation they were not at all like my relatives; they only looked like them. My relatives always give backchat."[5]

Lucy rejects this correlation between silence and objectification. Her potential positioning as an imported labor device, an *au pair* girl as reflected in the title of the opening chapter entitled, "Poor Visitor," is manifested in her accommodation: "The ceiling was very high and the walls went all the way up to the ceiling enclosing the room like a box in which cargo should be shipped. But I was not cargo," she asserts and proceeds to backchat with a vengeance, affirming her subjectivity as a seeing I/eye, and a speaking subject who consistently opens her mouth to deconstruct any impression of passive collusion with alien and alienating concepts of knowing and embodiment. In a far more extreme sense, Aidoo questions the ongoing appropriation of the black man's body when she rejects the view that the planting of the blackman's heart into the white man's body may be seen as an act of assimilation. She prefers to read this as the use of technological advance to continue to commoditize the black man, this time pillaging him for his body parts.

Kincaid insists then on a view of reality which recognizes the cause and effect relationships between the wealth of a privileged class and the oppression and environmental exploitation on which it is invariably built. And because Kincaid is deliberately, provocatively complex, eschewing hypocrisy at every turn, she introduces the varied determinants of interface with race to create a web of unjust power relations. Ethnicity emerges as a factor when Mariah boasts about proficiency in the natural world as a feature of her Indian ancestry. In response, Lucy interrogates the process by which persons of privilege align themselves with the powerless and lay claim to the positive, so-called inherent capacities of the vanquished group: "How do you get to be the sort of victor who can claim to be vanquished also?" (41).

In both narratives, power relations based on class and race and ethnicities form the macrocosmic design. At the start of each text, picture perfect domesticity seems intact. Iconography associated with the family is a recurrent theme in postcolonial literatures, not surprisingly because a major agenda of the colonial enterprise was imposition of idealized patterns of intimate relations and the politicization and racialization of desire and pleasure.[6] In *Lucy*, the symbol of the still photograph with the five heads is associated with the other civilizing icon—Wordworth's daffodil. Like this family, the photograph is two dimensional, flat, still, lifeless, and trapped in celluloid. The insistence with which the photographs are strewn all around the house suggests the creation of a representation in an effort in turn to create a reality. "In photographs of themselves, which they placed all over the house, their six yellow-haired heads of various sizes were bunched as if they were a bouquet of flowers tied together by an unseen string" (12). As a socializing avenue, the family as presently constituted produces sameness, lack of distinctiveness, the sterile togetherness of bunching. Lucy superintends the dissolution of marriage which amounts to an intrusion of reality into representation.

Aidoo's chronicle of the decay of European civilization plays itself out against the background of a castle turned youth hostel and again in relation to picture-perfect domesticity. Indeed, we first encounter Marija, the ideal housewife in the round sentry pot gazing at the town and the river. She is placed squarely within the framework of ancient authority structures. Her positioning is contradictory. She is both co-conspirator and victim. Sissie names this castle turned hostel from inception as a site of unjust power relations which manifest themselves through abusive sexual interactions against women. For here is the seed of the very atrocities which flourished in the colonial encounter:

> How many
> Virgins had
> Our Sovereign Lord and Master
> Unvirgined on their nuptial nights
> For their young
> Husbands in
> Red-eyed teeth-gnashing
> Agony, their manhoods
> Hurting... (Aidoo 1977:19)

The abusive relations are manifested through a male/male pecking order based on class with the woman as objectified as a site of ascendancy. Curiously even in this female-authored narrative, the virgins are erased. The narrative focus is on the pain of the young husbands as if they are the ones being raped. The ache of the turgid penises becoming a symbol of the agony of dispossession, displacement and humiliation. The message is that unjust power relations were from inception built into Western civilization and the terms of its subsequent manifestation in the African Slave trade is merely an outgrowth from this root. As we say in the Caribbean

Paula Morgan

"Goat doh make sheep."

Moreover these systems of power relations were inextricably connected to external structures which in turn masquerade as the glory of the civilization.

> Prince, This Lord and Master
> who had built one of
> The largest castles of them all,
> Possessed the
> Biggest
> Land, the
> Greatest number of
> Serfs? (19)

Aidoo is bringing into question here entire legacy of Hamlettian castles and fairy tales as a symbolic receptacle for cultural assumptions. The poem begins the second line of the formulaic opening of the fairy tale "there was a castle." The end of the poem predictably revises the formulaic close "and they lived happily ever after." Instead, it signifies on the events which are about to unfold "But 'all the days are not equal,' said the old village wall." (19) It is left to Marija to announce the inception of the formulaic romantic fairy tale, draw it into the recent past, change the cast of players if not the pattern of interaction "ONCE UPON A TIME, she said,/I too had met an Indian" (29). A central issue of the narrative is whether Sissie will take her part in the fairy tale romance. The stage is set in this perfect environment for "puppy love, European style"; the cast comprises children of the globe engaged in nurturing icons of European fantasy—"prospective Christmas Tree."

Lucy also rejects the opportunity to locate herself within the storybook reality of the other. Her first perceptions, when she is transplanted into the metropolitan landscape, lead her to reassess the location of herself as marginalized within Western narratives. These narratives conveyed that, given the absence of ruins of the Caribbean environment, simply to take one's place within a metropolitan city/land scape would validate one's existence and impart meaning. She dismantles from the onset these "fixtures of fantasy" constructed by a colonial education. Reality dispels the recurrent dream that simply entering and leaving famous buildings and important streets would become lifeboats to her drowning soul, would heal the pain of non-being.

In response to the physical landscape, Lucy's heart does leap when she beholds Wordworth's daffodil—it leaps with contempt, even rage that a simple natural flower should be emblematic of scenes of conquered and conquests, with the establishment of canonical Western texts which told us nothing about ourselves. Indeed they were primary instruments of narrative erasure of the colonized as a valid subject. The threat posed to the emerging self of the then ten-year-old school girl is mediated through a dream of being chased and buried beneath a mound of daffodils (Kincaid 1990:18).

The ultimate quest is the search for psychic space and a valid mode of being within a people who come to the metropolis already burdened by a response to natal and ancestral landscape which has been subverted by the imperial encounter. In inimitable simplicity, Lucy's experience of the cold metropolitan sun is linked with her ontological reality, her perception of her being in the world, her embodiment in the castle of her skin; as well as her epistemological reality—her way of knowing which is in turn associated with the act of naming:

> But I did not know that the sun could shine and the air remain cold; no one had ever told me. What a feeling that was! How can I explain? Something I had always known—the way I knew my skin was the color brown of a nut rubbed repeatedly with a soft cloth, or the way I knew my own name—something I took completely for granted, "the sun was shining, the air is warm" was not so. (5)

What avenues do these travel narratives use to reverse the process of erasure and ontological displacement? In her affirmation of her protagonist's subjectivity as a perceiving I/eye, Aidoo employs reductive stereotyping vicious enough to rival the efforts of the travel writers who documented the initial encounters between Europeans and Africans. Invoking the propensity within the genre to conflate physical characteristics with mental and moral qualities, she describes the children of the nations using a preponderance of animal imagery which intersects with oral imagery. Their propensity to imbibe an over excess of food suggests fixation at the oral stage. The "darling teenage pigs of Europe" are constantly stuffing themselves to the point of gluttony, to the point of oblivion. The swine imagery conflates the behavior patterns of the young white people with their physical features which Sissie earlier associates with a major dietary import imposed by the colonizer—"the colour of the pickled pig parts...[t]rotters, pig tails, pig ears" (Aidoo 1977:20). Signifying on the travel writers' collusion with the assumptions of social Darwinism which placed the black man on the lowest rung of the evolutionary ladder, closest to the ape, Aidoo chooses for the white a resemblance to pigs, with all of the less-than-savory connotations of this association.[7]

The European tour constitutes an orgasmic binge in which overindulgence and environment combine to seduce the children of the globe into a mass romantic delusion. The animalistic imagery remains constant. For those whose skin color does not qualify them to be pigs, Aidoo reserves the appellation of dogs. Some develop a taste for puppy love—"hand-holding, wet kissing along ancient cobbled corridors; hounds, they would jump on her, seize on the inevitable brown bags and devour their contents" (42). And, using the shift of genre, the long-term objective is defined:

> At nine a showpiece
> At eighteen a darling
> What shall you be
> At thirty?
> A dog among the masters, the
> Most orderly of the
> Dogs (42)

The *assimilé* is thereby trained to become the watchdog of the Empire—fierce, eternally dependent, loyal, and fawning.

Images of eating also take on a deeper mythic and psychological function. Food has always been a pivotal way of initiating and enhancing intimacy; of binding lovers; of creating dependency; of conveying love; of exacting revenge. Marija is constantly trying to seduce Sissie through offerings of food. Significantly, the only food which Sissie will accept with fervor are plums which she eats with orgasmic pleasure:

> They were of sheen and succulence she had not encountered anywhere else in those foreign lands.... What she was also not aware of, though, was that those Bavarian plums owed their glory in her eyes and on her tongue not only to that beautiful and black Bavarian soil, but also to the other qualities that she herself possessed at that material time...
> Knowing you are a rare article
> Being

Loved.
So she sat, Our Sister, her tongue caressing the plump berries
with skin-colour almost like her own, while Marija
told her how she had selected them especially for
her, off the single tree in the garden. (40)

The obsession with the plums comes to be associated with the narcissistic love of the "black and beautiful self" which blossoms on the black and beautiful Bavarian soil. This identity is being mirrored for Sissie everywhere she goes but most consistently so in Marija's eyes. Marija, in her attempt to carry the link between feeding, orgasmic satiation, power, and dependency further, seeks to enhance Sissie's diet with plum cake and cold flesh. The rejection of sliced cold meats which she finds distasteful—"in the end she decided that it had something to do with white skins, corn silk hair and very cold weather" (68)—coincides with rejection of Marija's cold pig trotter pink flesh reaching for the warm purple plums of Sissie's breasts. Significantly, the night of the rejection of the sexual advances is the night that they both forget customary gifts of plums.

The sexual rejection shadows at a deeper level a rejection of the developmental pathways outlined in Western mythic narratives—the received texts which were fundamental to colonial education. Mythic allusions shroud the journey which the *assimilé* Sammy, portrays as "a dress rehearsal for a journey to paradise." In fact it becomes a trip into the heartland of Europe into the garden of fairy land: "An ancient ruined castle at the edge of a / Brooding pine forest. Here she encounters Marija/Mary—the wife and mother of Adolf/Eve who attempts to seduce her into carnal knowledge with carefully selected and ripened plums from 'the single tree in the garden.'" The ascent into the sterile, deserted nuptial chamber/cave is conveyed in terms of Persephone's descent into the underworld against constant cajoling to seal the enchantment by eating. The dream, which has captured the aspirations of many an African traveler, is nothing short of a nightmare that has entrapped the spirit of the people in the shadowy underworld. It is imperative that Sissie shakes off the bad dream and surfaces into the real world. The stakes are high—the natural order of the seasons, productivity, fertility. This formulation recalls Erna Brodber's summation of the colonizing process as spirit theft leading to zombification. Healing of this dis/ease requires an unearthing of the submerged identities, collection of the scattered skeletons and a re-membering of all of the dimensions of the self.

In both texts, the excision of the possibility of psychic assimilation into the alienating society is connected to their perception of the physical landscape. Aidoo and Kincaid reverse the propensity demonstrated from "eighteenth to nineteenth century travel accounts and nature writing in the twentieth century tourist literature and development literature" to appropriate, sentimentalize and aesthetize the landscape by filtering it through what Susan Comfort in First World Garden/ Third World Plantation terms in relation to the Caribbean, a "sovereign objectifying perspective," the objective being to "conceal the massive oppression and exploitations imposed by the plantation system and neo-colonial resource extraction" (Comfort 1995:1-2). Going beyond the politicized fantasies of Third World gardens, Kincaid and Aidoo reject concepts of innocuous, pristine, First World landscapes. The freshly plowed fields extolled by Mariah elicits from Lucy a snide expose of the appropriating agendas behind many an agricultural enterprise: "Well, thank God I didn't have to do that" (Kincaid 1990:33). And, as the nineteenth century travel narrative served to expiate guilt as engendered by the nature of the imperial enterprise by invoking idyllic paradigms of landscape, so too Aidoo's narrative seeks to elicit guilt by invoking landscape. There is a constant unmasking in *Our Sister Killjoy* of the idyllic landscape as the site of the Jewish Holocaust, which is rooted in the same impulse as the imperial experiment. Deane argues that the experience of violence and exploitation generated by imperialism has not invoked the same response as that generated by Nazism:

> The catastrophe experienced by the subject races was a mediated experience for Europe, at least until the Nazi extermination of Jews and others during the Second World War. In the light of that particular holocaust, Europe has undergone a series of possibilities of representing such horror, the morality of attempting to do so, the complicity with it that any rendering of apocalypse as discourse might involve. There has been no comparable anxiety about the representation of imperialism's crimes. Instead, the West has discovered in postcoloniality a form of discourse that is irrepressibly given to misrepresentation of the Other. (Deane 1990:356)

Aidoo penetrates beneath the beautiful surface gardens of fairy land to unearth the subterranean reality of a landscape watered with blood, planted with bodies continually threatening to erupt from the defiled earth:

Widows all
From knowledge gained since
The blood of their young men was
Needed to mix the concrete for
Building the walls of
The Third Reich. But
Its foundations collapsed before the walls were com-
pleted.
Dear Lord...
That's why
They wonder,
They wonder, if should they
Stop cultivating the little pine trees, would
Something else,
Sown there,
Many many years ago
In
Those Bavarian woods
SPROUT? (Aidoo 1977:37)

Both protagonists armed with this view of the physical landscape exuviate the locations offered to them within the alien landscapes.

Yet the insitutionalized patterns of power relations which engineered colonial interactions and which mushroomed in domestic relations lie dangerously close to the surface. Aidoo implies that there is nothing sacrosanct about female sexual interaction. Having analyzed the injustice of the power relations which underlay serfdom and the manner in which it manifests itself in sexual interactions, Sissie becomes in psyche the cold, impenetrable, destructive male to the vulnerable Marija's impossible longings for love and pitiful attempts to secure it through the age-old female offerings of food. Aidoo hints that the individual's propensity to buy into socially entrenched patterns of inequity is locked up within the human heart and simply awaiting an avenue for manifestation. "It hit me like stone, the knowledge that there is pleasure in hurting. A strong three-dimensional pleasure, an exclusive masculine delight that is exhilarating beyond all measure" (76). This potential which transcends gender, nationality, and race is simply a legacy of the human condition.

Where does the white woman constructed as the ultimate cultural icon of desirability fit into the mosaic? How has the mighty fallen? In Aidoo's textual reversal, it is the black woman who rejects the white woman of impeccable lineage. The texts powerfully invoke the power of naming. Significantly the Caucasian women of both texts are named derivatives of the archetypal virgin. "My name is Marija. But me, I like ze English name Mary. Please call me Mary. Vas is your name?" Marija seeks to align herself with the Virgin Mary, the Western icon. She is the representation which Sissie rejected earlier when she resisted being renamed as Mary, she rejected attempts to impose the identity of "the true woman" on the black woman—who, after all is said and done, could only be a shadow version. The result of this virgin creates that gap between intellect and instinct, flesh and spirit. In Marija it results in a damned-up libido, which eventually surfaces in a raging hunger that seeks illicit expression, but can lead to no true mating of the mind or body, only an exploitation of the stranger/foreigner/other in a futile attempt to fill the spaces in the deficient self. In that sense Marija carries her share of the impulse behind the miscegenation practiced on the slave plantation and its subsequent vestiges and reformations.

Aidoo's Marija is the young housewife deprived of pivotal roles, of cooking, lonely, isolated, desperately seeking the sexual attention of exotic strangers, while Kincaid's Mariah is the emerging feminist-gentile, beautiful, generous-spirited—who is seeking to share with her black, younger sister her newly emerging insights on gender relations. In the interaction between the women, Mariah, though older by two decades, remains a lost babe in the woods. Lucy consistently demonstrates her ability "to read page." She possesses piercing prophetic insight into character and situation, especially those which presage ill-winds and deceit in human interaction. These propensities are veiled by excessive politeness, false aspirations, elaborate ritualized patterns of interaction within the social milieu. Compared to the twenty-year old's perception of gender relations learned in the rigorous school of Caribbean family life, Mariah emerges as an incurable innocent, if not a fool. The same judgement can be made of the feminist texts with which she pointlessly continually seeks to educate Lucy. Although Lucy aligns herself with Mariah as opposed to Lewis on the basis of gender, Lucy also tortures her because of her naive inability to see persistent daily manifestation of oppression based on class, race and money; her lack of insight into the affairs of her own daily life; her inability to see her husband and best friend for what they really are; her intense and counter-productive self-scrutinizing contemplation of her navel.

Yet this dissonance within Lucy's identity—her way of knowing and way of being—go beyond the strangeness of the travel encounter. While Aidoo locates the problem of exile in social, political, cultural realities, for Kincaid the issue is also a philosophical and metaphysical puzzle. And it is at this juncture that the texts part company. Kincaid journeys into the inner-self, individual and collective, in search of a core. The correlation between being, knowing, and naming are consistent throughout Kincaid's narratives, in which she slides often simultaneously along multiple continuums of inner and outer time and space—prehistoric, primeval space/time, pregestation space/time, measurable space and chronological time, and unfathomable supernatural space/time(lessness).[8]

The depth of Lucy's existential anguish is inscribed on the last pages of the text. "I wish I could love someone so much that I would die from it" (Kincaid 1990:164). Her craving is for engulfment through love, for release from the challenge and responsibility of charting a unique course and constructing a viable identity. The dilemma she faces is that of paradise lost and the challenge of remembering a self, outside of the safety beauty orders of its confines and this whether one defines paradise as mother, motherland, surrogate mother, adoptive land, the womb, the grave. And this dilemma underlies all of Kincaid's interrelated narrative—Is it possible for the human consciousness to exist in a state of undifferentiated unity with the other? Is this a state of light or a state of darkness? Is it a safe space to be embraced or a perilous terrain to be avoided? After embodiment, what nature of being, knowing and naming is possible? Is embodiment a fixed state which remains after one dies? Does the human being survive as a unique, and aware, being after death?[9]

This psychic journey is charted in Kincaid's other texts and alluded to in Lucy. In her interrelated fictional universe, the human consciousness faces the challenge of individuation at several junctures—when the person initially emerges from the undifferentiated evolutionary mass; when the infant emerges from the process of gestation to separate from the maternal body; when the child emerges from paradisaical innocence at puberty to confront carnal knowledge and the terrible necessity of death; and when the young adult investigates the power of love and sexuality to alleviate the aloneness of the human condition; when the young immigrant uses the guise of anonymity of the metropolitan space to explore alien modes of being.

Every stage of the journey is high risk. In "Wingless" in *At the Bottom of the River*, the narrating consciousness fantasizes about inhabiting a pupa stage of existence, primitive and wingless. In this stage there is great light, great transparency, and the possibility of knowing and being known with great thoroughness: "But again I swim in a shaft of light, upside down, and I can see myself clearly through and through from every angle. Over there, I stand on the brink of a great discovery, and it is possible that like an ancient piece of history my presence will leave room for theories" (Kincaid 1983:25) The pre-incarnate self at this stage of the journey perceives that the potential to inhabit all light is also potential to encounter all blackness which can engulf and erase the individual entity. "The blackness enters my many-tiered spaces and soon the significant world and event recede and eventually vanish; in this way I am annihilated and my form becomes formless and I am absorbed into a vastness of free-flowing matter. In the blackness, than I have been erased. I can no longer say my own name. I can no longer point to myself and say 'I'" (47).

It is within this framework of existential anguish that one can interpret Lucy's sexual adventurism. A crucial dimension of the quest to end the essential aloneness of the human condition is in the intimate, sexual intertwining in an attempt to create one flesh. It is this dimension that is a primary focus in *Lucy*. The young woman's sexual mores extends way beyond the rebellion against the sexual restraint and discretion required of a well-educated colonial girl. Rather it is an attempt to alleviate the sense of jealousy at not becoming a youthful target of sexual abuse perpetrated on her friend, when Mr. Thomas regularly inserts his middle finger into the young girl's vagina; for which privilege, he rewards her with coins. Having been betrayed into separation from the cherished/hated mother who until now has been the ultimate signifier of her being in the world, she toys with the option of halting her growing sense of disembodiment by the sexual abuse in an equation which reads "I feel therefore I am." This propensity matures into a violent sexual relationship with a so-called perverted young man.[10]

Invariably, Lucy's propensity towards violent sexuality is accompanied by a consistent symbolic identification between genital sexuality, a skeletal hand, and death. This appears initially with her intrusion on her parents' sexual intimacies and her mother's hand which had laid out a dead girl making circles on her father's

back (*Annie John*) with the contumacious coveting of digital penetration at the hands of a man now dead; and with the delicious
pleasure enjoyed at the hands of the pervert, whose hand was rendered skeletal as if groped in the fish tank.

Although sexuality in Kincaid's writing is a crucial dimension
of self-discovery, an attempt perhaps to deny the imposed meanings and resonances of her embodiment within her female, nut-
brown-colored skin, it never leads to oneness with the other. At
puberty, her sexual capacity is likened to Pandora's box and a
"black-haired beast emerging from the open lid." In the wake of
her acquisition of a party dress of this pattern, the contents of the
box are let loose—underarm and genital hair, menstruation. In each
of the relationships described—her sexual initiation with Tanner,
her masturbatory encounter with the unnamed boy in the library,
her affair with Hugh and later with Paul—she is careful to retain
the upper hand. The process involves a refusal to fall in love
because falling in love spells vulnerability and need and Lucy's
ego-boundaries are far too fragile to give herself to a love relationship. In the episode with Tanner, she short-circuits any triumph
he may feel at having taken her virginity into horror at having
come into contact with potentially castrating menstrual blood. In
response to Hugh, she is careful to clarify: "If I enjoyed myself
beyond anything I had known so far, it must have been because I
was so far from home. I was not in love" (Kincaid 1990:67). She
comments further: "Why because love would complicate my life
just now. I was only half-a-year free of some almost unbreakable
bonds, and it was not in my heart to make new ones" (71).
Moreover, having faced the devastating necessity to separate from
the romantic liaisons rather than have them broken, the result is
hollow victories—sexual adventurism without any sense of connectedness, which leads to an even greater sense of alienation within the castle of the skin.

Predictably, as the contradictory nature of her embodiment
remains unresolved and the object of her journey remains unreach-
able, so too the naming remains a point of contention in *Lucy*.
Annie John, facing separation from the maternal presence at
puberty, identifies with Lucifer the archetypal outcast during his
fall from grace. *Lucy* and Lucy are derived from this association as
the "true true name," which conveys the essence of her character
and the nature of her destiny. This is a quest which our Sissie need
not undertake—securely rooted as she is within culture and community. Sissie's individual self comes to fruition within the group

identity; our Sissie's name is unchanged and unchangeable.

Clearly for Lucy there can be no quest for community. But her inability to find a niche within the metropolitan community remains an extension of her myriad rejections—of biological mother and natal land and later surrogate white mother and her unadopted land. The text nevertheless remains as far as it conceivably can for Kincaid an act of appropriation. By the process of inscription, she writes for herself a space and claims for herself a name. Lucy's naming comes from a recognition that despite potential sites of dislocation, fragmentation and loss, despite the inevitability of non-arrival, the fundamental lack of a psychic port, a home, life is indeed worth living. Indeed, the ancient power of naming emerges for the nameless protagonist of Kincaid's early work, *At the Bottom of the River,* out of epiphany—the capacity to perceive beneath the surface of everyday nature of human life:

> In the light of the lamp, I see some books, I see a chair, I see a table, I see a pen.... And as I see these things in the light of the lamp, all perishable and transient, how bound up I know I am to all that is human endeavour, to all that is past and to all that shall be, to all that shall be lost and leave no trace. I claim these things then—mine—and now feel myself grow solid and complete, my name filling up my mouth. (Kincaid 1983:82)

How does a poor visitor learn a name, craft a resilient identity, cast off the nightmarish shadow of a bad dream? And beyond the individual emergence are there prospects for communal awakening, tenable national and ethnic identities and social solutions. Although Lucy insists on recognition of that link between personal privilege and collective exploitation and oppression based on race, class and gender, this text does not go beyond an intensely individual interrogation. Aidoo pushes relentlessly beyond the individual illumination, in a search for viable communal solutions. Aidoo's protagonist heads back to the warmth and uncertainties of Africa retaining the hope which she expresses early in her narrative that "things are working out towards their dazzling conclusion." Ultimately Kincaid can present no balm for an exile so all consuming, and an anguish so profound. Instead, she offers a finely crafted, in-depth diagnosis of "skin does not fitness" which enriches perspectives on Caribbean women in the Diaspora.

Finally, what do we glean from reading these texts as travel narratives? Kincaid's major triumph is located in her evocation of psychic space despite the unrelenting simplicity of her poetic prose. Aidoo's accomplishments is her sustained satirical probe of the colonizer's culture, wielded as a tool for calling "defectors" back to Africa. One wonders whether Aidoo's perspective can be linked to the enhanced potential for clarity of vision and cultural cohesion, which stand to be retained more effectively when indigenous peoples have been colonized within their own territories. And, by extension, to what extent does the mind-set and sense of inferiority imparted by more violent and disruptive patterns of colonization preclude such a vigorous debunking of the alienating culture?

Yet Aidoo's gaze, like that of the nineteenth-century travel writer, remains a distorted one? If one of the major objectives of the travel narrative has been the exploitation of the polarity between the self and the other, as Deane terms it "between a cultural formation that is fine and intricately articulated and one that is inchoate and amorphous... the definition of the self is produced in and through the appalling recognition of the Other's delinquent and savage formlessness" (Deane 1990:356). The other here is a lost princess in fairy land, a fairy land strewn with the ashes of those who stoked their own funeral pyres, with human bodies and whose princes have been transformed into archetypal Adolfs. Now, it is the European who enjoys the position of otherness, demonstrates the physical features of symbolically unwholesome animals, who is naive, incredulous, whose naive daughter speaks "broken english" in the simple syntax befitting a child. The agenda seems to have been to deconstruct the master's house using his tools, or put another way, to dig up the master's gardens using his spade. The limitation of Aidoo's travel narrative is that it does not push far enough. Despite the rich allusiveness of Aidoo's shape shifting prose, the ideological confrontation between the self and the other through the travel encounter has merely been reversed. The black-eyed squint does not go much beyond overturning the white-eyed vision.

NOTES AND REFERENCES

1. Toni Morrison explores this dynamic in her use of the Dick and Jane narrative for *The Bluest Eye*. Morrison, by running the syntax into a mass, strips words of their representational value and undermines their function of erasing her black girl from the "reality" represented on the page.

2. Ironically, in both of these narratives the stripping of these heroic types is accomplished in relation to their women.

3. For a discussion on Naipaul's travel narratives See Glynne Griffith's *Travel Narrative as Cultural Critique: V. S. Naipaul's Traveling Theory*. Griffith notes a connection between Naipaul's Eurocentric ideological position and the literary choices he makes: "Satire and irony become the major literary devices which he employs in his narratives, and his non-fiction is structured by an authorial voice which gains legitimacy by mimicking the anthropologist and ethnographer" (91).

4. Aidoo comments "I never describe it as a novel myself. When I have been forced to describe *Killjoy*, I have said it is fiction in four episodes" (James 1990:15).

5. Significantly, backchat as an act of resistance is the weapon identified by Paule Marshall whose army of Bajan domestic immigrants to the United States take their mouths to make guns. Zora Neale Hurston, in *Their Eyes Were Watching God*, affirms Kincaid's analysis indirectly in her description of eyeless and earless conveniences who after working hours withdraw in their communal space to assert their humanity, the validity of their ways of knowing and their power to pass judgement with "Mouf Almighty."

6. A most amusing evocation is the resistant poster of the blond ideal family in Hodge's classroom, in *For the Life of Laetitia*, which refuses to stay on the walls and insists on literally falling—a construct which cannot bear the symbolic burden which is placed on it.

7. According to Street, the early travel writers used a form of ethnographic fiction which went as far as to footnote the findings of anthropologists to aid in the willing suspension of disbelief. The novels of John Buchan, H. Rider Haggard, R. M. Ballantyne, Edgar Rice Burroughs, and countless others brought to a wider public, in vivid imaginative form, the ideas and debates being conducted in scientific circles at the time regarding the nature of society in general and of the "primitive" society in particular. In many cases, they drew on the writings of anthropologists for their underlying concepts and they claimed a "seriousness" and accuracy that was designed to transcend their status as "fiction" (Street 1985:104; cf., Street 1975 for a more detailed and extended treatment of the same topic).

8. The surrealistic narrative, *At the Bottom of the River*, which gains its power by the powerful dream/fantasy associations of childhood, explores the process of separation at various levels—the mother and child "merge and separate merge and separate" as they undergo the various stages of their evolution. The phases of the journey are the emergence of the individual human consciousness from the indistinct evolutionary pool, the separation of two distinct human entities at birth and the separation at puberty and the maturation of the young into her own productivity "A humming bird has nested on my stomach, a sign of my fertileness" (Kincaid 1983:61).

9. Kincaid interrogates the assumptions of decay and disembodiment in her portrayal of a dead man in *At the Bottom of the River*: "There is Mr Guishard, standing under a cedar tree which is in full bloom, wearing that nice white suit, which is as fresh as the day he was buried in it" (70).

Clearly narrative moves in favor of the survival of the individual clothed in his body and in its inviolate white suit. And this state is applied to creatures on the lower levels of existence—the rotting skin of an orange or a frog. In the face of the persistent terror posed by disembodiment, disconnection, and exile, she questions the link between the maternal presence and the power to name and thereby validate the existence of its offspring. "Will the hen, stripped of its flesh, its feathers scattered to the four corners of the earth, its bones molten and sterilized, one day speak? And what will it say? I was a hen? I had twelve chicks? One of my chicks named Beryl, took a fall? ("At Last" 18). This is that curse which haunts Annie John—the shame of a girl losing her mother, a vulnerable child cut loose from the umbilical cord seems to have no space in the world, no name, no identity. The result is that, as the pubescent Annie hates her mother for insisting on separation, were she to wish her mother dead, then she the child would be annihilated.

10. The equation "I feel therefore I exist" is also explored in "Holidays" (*At The Bottom of the River*): the narrating consciousness seeks to affirm the individual's power over death by embarking on a series of sensory experiences, some decidedly unpleasant, which affirm embodiment through the power to feel.

WORKS CITED

Aidoo, Ama Ata. *Our Sister Killjoy: Or, Reflections From a Black-Eyed Squint*. Harlow: Longman, 1977.

Comfort, Susan. "First World Garden/Third World Plantation." Unpublished paper, 1995.

Conrad, Joseph. *Heart of Darkness*. England: Penguin, 1975.

Davies, Carole Boyce & Anne Adams Graves, Eds. *Ngambika: Studies of Women in African Literature*. Trenton, N.J.: Africa World Press, 1986.

Davies, Carole Boyce and Elaine Savory Fido. Eds. *Out of the Kumbla: Caribbean Women and Literature*. Trenton, N.J.: Africa World Press, 1990.

Deane, Seamus. "Imperialism and Nationalism." In *Critical Terms for Literary Study*. Ed. Frank Lentricchia and Thomas McLaughlin. Chicago: University of Chicago Press, 1990. Rpt. 1995.

Griffith, Glynne. "Travel Narrative as Cultural Critique: V. S. Naipaul's Traveling Theory." *Journal of Commonwealth Literature*, 29, 2, (1993): 87-92.

Hodge, Merle. "Challenges of the Struggle for Sovereignty: Changing the World Versus Writing Stories." In: *Caribbean Women Writers: Essays from the First International Conference*. Ed. Selwyn R. Cudjoe Wellesley, M.A.: Calaloux Publications, 1990.202-208.

———. *Crick Crack Monkey*. London: Andre Deutsch, 1970.

———. *For the Life of Laetitia*. New York: Farrar, Strauss, Giroux, 1993.

Hurston, Zola Neale. *Their Eyes Were Watching God* (Foreword by Shirley Anne Williams), Urbana: University of Illinois Press, 1978.

James, Adeola. "Ama Ata Aidoo Interview." In: *In Their Own Voices: African Women Writers Talk*. London: Heinemann Educational Books, 1990.

Kincaid, Jamaica. *Annie John*. New York: Farrar, Strauss and Giroux, 1983.

———. *At the Bottom of the River*. New York: Farrar, Strauss and Giroux, 1983.Rpt. USA Plume, 1992. 13-19.

———. *A Small Place*. London: Virago Press Ltd, 1988.

———. *Lucy*. New York: Farrar, Strauss and Giroux, 1990.

Korang Kwaku Larbi."Ama Ata Aidoo's Voyage Out: Mapping the Coordinates of Modernity and African Selfhood in *Our Sister Killjoy*." Kunapipi 14, 3 (1992):50- 61.

Lamming, George, *In the Castle of My Skin*, London: Longman Caribbean. 1953. Rpt. 1970.

———. *Natives of My Person*. London: Pan Books, 1972 (1974).

———. *The Pleasures of Exile*. London: Michael Morgan, 1960.

Marshall, Paule. *Brown Girl, Brownstones*. New Jersey: The Chatham Bookseller, 1959.

Naipaul Vidiadhar Surajprasad. *The Middle Passage; Impressions of Five Societies: British, French and Dutch in the West Indies and South America*. New York: Macmillan, (1962).

Nasta, Susheila, Ed. *Motherlands: Black Women's Writing from Africa, the Caribbean and South Asia*. New Brunswick, N.J.: Rutgers University Press, 1991.

Phillips, Maggi. "Engaging Dreams: Alternative Perspectives on Flora Nwapa, Buchi Emecheta, Ama Ata Aidoo, Bessie Head and Tsitsi Dangarembga." *Research in African Literature* 25, 4, 4, (1994):89-103.

Schipper, Mineke, Ed., *Unheard Words: Women and Literature in Africa, the Arab World, Asia, the Caribbean and Latin America*. London: Allison and Busby Ltd., 1985.

Street, Brian V. "Reading the Novels of Empire: Race and Ideology in the Classic Tale of Adventure." In: *The Black Presence in English Literature* Ed. David Dabydeen. Great Britain: Manchester University Press, 1985. 95-111.

———. *The Savage in Literature: Representations of 'Primitive' Society in English Fiction 1858-1920*. London/Boston: Routledge & Kegan Paul, 1975.

Stout, Janis P. *The Journey Narrative in American Literature*. Westport. Conn: Greenwood Press, 1983.

Walcott, Derek. *Remembrance and Pantomine*. New York: Farrar, Strauss and Giroux, 1980.

THE DILEMMA OF A GHOST:

LITERATURE AND POWER OF MYTH

ADA UZOAMAKA AZODO

> And when the writer sends a dart of the true word,
> it hurts. But it goes with love. This is what [Thomas]
> Mann called "erotic irony," the love for that which
> you are killing with your cruel, analytical word.
> -Joseph Campbell

We re-echo Joseph Campbell, above, in order to put into perspective the commitment of Ama Ata Aidoo as a fiction writer who loves her people enough to subject them to severe criticism. Her art reflects on the past, present, and future of her people even as it reveals the truth about the world's unequal and separate societies. The quality of Aidoo's writing as good literature cannot be overemphasized. But, what do we understand by good literature?

A literature is good, due to the value and power of the word inherent in it, and for this reason it merits to be part and parcel of our daily lives. By making well written texts part of our daily living, we maintain above all else a tradition of mythological knowledge, which could otherwise be lost (Flowers 1989). Aidoo's writing, for this reason, is important as good literature.

Today, the world moves at such a jet speed that it is practically difficult for myths to have adequate time to form. Behind the words in a text, however, could be found mythological allusions and other anthropological structures that explain the social life, religion, economy, politics and philosophy—in one word, the culture—of a people. This is the thesis expounded by the French anthropologist Gilbert Durand in his seminal work, *Les Structures Anthropologiques de L'imaginaire*, which gave rise to his experimental and equally well-known critical analysis of the novel, *La Chartreuse de Palme* by Henri Beyle (also known as Stendhal). Other authors have confirmed this thesis, including this writer in a recent study of the novels of Guinean author, Camara Laye, entitled *L'imaginaire dans les romans de Camara Laye*. When we remember the story of an author's text, then we see the relevance in our individual and collective lives of the power of myth. We get to know or remember the traditions that govern our lives or governed the lives of those who have gone before us. When an author like Aidoo writes good literature, she assumes the responsibility to tell fictional stories, to teach, but always with the intention to reconcile our world, that is, harmonize our lives with the reality around us (Flowers 1988:4). At times, the author's stance may be such that the written word appears cruel to her people. It is therein, however, that lies the love, dedication and commitment to transform, to change the *status quo*. Aidoo is so struck by the subjects of her writing that she has indulged in self-sacrifice to save her people. By tracing the origins of some of the most relevant myths in Aidoo's work, we examine at the same time the potent force of these myths and how they continue to influence the thinking of many about peoples of African descent, about life, living and loving. Therefore, our exploration of Aidoo's mythic consciousness in *The Dilemma of a Ghost* mandates once again a review of Aidoo's commitment as a writer and the relevance of myths in our lives.

The text of *The Dilemma of a Ghost*, along with asides and stage directions, will serve as the poetics of our study of Aidoo's fictional commitment. By investigating the *mythème* (a term coined in 1970 by Ives Durand on the analogy of the term "phoneme" in linguistics), meaning the smallest unit of discourse that is mythically meaningful, we hope to arrive at a mythical understanding of the play. The *mythème* could be a motif, an emblem, image, symbol, word, phrase, sentence, paragraph or whole chapter or text, an issue or a subject. In the final analysis, our goal is to achieve a convergence of earlier criticisms of this play and our own understanding of Ama Ata Aidoo's merit as a writer.

Aidoo's imaginary story of the dilemma of a Ghanaian man of the '60s is both for entertainment and teaching purposes. If read simply as a modern adaptation of an African dilemma tale, it seems to teach young people to be aware that jumping into marriage with the first stranger has its rough implications and problems. If read as a cosmogonic myth, it tends to teach about the mythical, semi-historical, even legendary forefathers of the Ashanti—the "three elders" as Odamtten calls them: Oburumankuma, Odapadjan, and Osun—among other ancestors, supernatural and primordial beings. These three "wise men" as it were, led the Fanti in their push southwards after they broke away from the Ashanti and moved towards the sea (Odamtten 1994:27). Aidoo wants to provoke, above all else, the understanding of the Ashanti (and, by extension, Ghanaians and all Africans) as a people, and an appreciation of their world view through the power of myth. The ability of Africans as a people to get ahead today seems to have a lot to do with their understanding of the actions, gestures, attitudes and behaviors of other peoples and those peoples' particular cultures and being able to cope with them.

Mythology becomes in Aidoo's hands an aggressive tool against the frustrations she feels before the effects of European chattel slavery, colonization, neo-colonization and imperialism on the lives of Africans both at home and abroad. Aidoo's goal seems to be the realization of a Pan-African and human consciousness of self. First of all, she resurrects the personage myth of the Ashanti, a sort of culture hero or Messiah named Akonfo Anokye (pronounced phonetically; [Akonfo Anotchi]. As mythical time combines with concrete time, they foreground Aidoo's goal of abstracting history, idealizing its content in order to teach her readers the value of myth and history in their lives. L. V. Thomas clarifies the relationship between myth and history thus:

> In a sense, every myth is historical because it is a moment—sometimes fundamental—of the history of thought, the fruit of a political, economic, and even metaphysical conjuncture. In a more restricted manner, if history explains the present by way of the past, then myth merits being qualified as historical (...). If the past (indefinite) is stamped with

the invention of metaphysical and etiological myths, the present epoch will be characterized by myths which lay claims and which are justificative. This evolution depends upon a combination of circumstances, but more exactly, the conditional factor belongs to history just as do the psychological factors which result from it. (Thomas 1961:77)

It is the Ashanti myth-turned-legend of the Golden Stool which, in part, inspired Aidoo to undertake a great intellectual and creative enterprise in writing *The Dilemma of a Ghost*. This play deals with the conflict between a people's tradition and a new outlook on life. The Golden Stool gives rise, subsequently, to a whole schema of myths, having to do with African thought systems, history and human psychology in dealing with strangers. It is a metaphor for what happens in human society when xenophobia is allowed to become the slogan of human existence. The play could be seen as an urgent call to pay attention to the very act of living, that is to be deeply aware of our interconnections, to be alert and awake to our moral obligations toward the Other. This is the domain of mythology. Aidoo uses myths to teach the imperatives of history and the need for love, compassion and reason in our lives. The Omanhene's palaquin (see Figure 1) during the annual Edina Bakatue fishing festival in Ghana (see Figure 2) is today, perhaps, a public exteriorization of the symbolism of the Golden Stool.

The stool (see Figure 3) as a mytheme is a symbol of regeneration, restoration, and harmony, which is present in the play from the beginning. In the opening pages, we learn that Ato Yawson, the protagonist, has returned from the United States of America where he earned a university degree, and is living in the capital city of Accra for employment reasons:

> And certainly, he must come home for blessings when the new yam has been harvested and the stools sprinkled. The ghosts of the dead ancestors are invoked and there is no discord, only harmony and a restoration of that which needs to be restored. (Aidoo 1965:8)

Later in an aside, Esi Kom, Ato's mother, is seen arranging a set of six stools in the center of the stage for what appears to be an impending family reunion. Stools are commonly regarded as not only seats, but indeed also as symbols of the spirituality of the people. A man's personal stool is his shrine. In funeral ceremonies, stools are carried into the family shrine, often known as stool house, where offerings and sacrifices are made to the ancestors for at-one-ment and thanksgiving (Parrinder 1986:104). In case of other misfortunes, like infertility, people worship together in the stool house to drive away the spirit of infertility. It is for this second reason that the Odumna clan, to which Ato belongs, is gathering together. Eulalie, his African American wife, is not yet pregnant, and something must be done to placate the spirits holding shut her womb. In the absence of Ato's father, whom we presume dead, his uncle explains this African tradition:

> ... as you know, on this day, we try to drive away all evil spirits, ill luck and unkind feelings which might have invaded our home during the past year. You know also, that we invoke our sacred dead to bring us blessings. Therefore, we are asking you to tell us what is wrong with you and your wife, so that first we will wash her stomach with this, then pour the libation to ask the dead to come and remove the spirit of the evil around you and pray them bring you a child. (44)

Indeed, ceremonies which involve the feeding of and prayers to ancestors form a great part of Akan religion, and Aidoo has aptly invoked it here as part of the celebration of Ato's homecoming. Among the Akan people of Ghana, the Adae festival, celebrated twice every forty-two days, honors the living dead, referred to as stool ancestors—that is, those who once occupied stools as part of their official paraphenalia before they died. A stool ancestor must not have been dethroned during his life time, meaning that above all, he must have lived an examplary life and governed well. At his death, he is placed on his personal stool and bathed before he is laid in state. His personal stool is subsequently kept in a safe place until the time comes for blackening it. The ceremony of the blackening of the stool takes place during the last funeral celebrations, led by the chief stool-bearer and other stool-bearers. The blackening of the stool is done in the sacred grove at night, out of sight of unauthorized persons and in the presence of the Golden Stool. Once blackened, the stool is kept in the stool-house in memory of the dead chief. Peter Sarpong explains the process of blackening and their spiritual implications, stressing its washing in a brass basin used for washing other stools (before the latest addition), as a way of incorporating the new comer into the fold of the ancestors. Then the new stool is blackened by smearing it with soot mixed with egg yolk, and later on with the blood of sheep, and a piece of animal fat placed on the center support of the stool. It is then taken to the stool-house for safe-keeping. The Akan believe that the blackened stool is saturated with the spirit of the dead chief and therefore is a shrine or abode of the spirit of this ancestor. It is around this stool that the important Adae festival is celebrated, once on a Sunday, and called the Akwasidae (the public feast and a bigger occasion celebrated with talking drums) and later on a Wednesday, and called the Wukudae (the more private ceremony in the stool-house for the extended family) to offer food and drink to the ancestor as well as pray him for protection for the family and all the members therein (Sarpong 1971). It was a similar occasion that brought Ato and Eulalie down from Accra to join the rest of the Odumna clan for a spiritual revival, though in their case it was an annual ritual to usher in the New Year, which marks a sort of new beginning in the Akan cosmology (Aidoo 1977:44).

To return to Ashanti mythology, the people under the Supreme Deity, Nyame, received the Golden Stool, which brought them power and influence over their neighbors and enemies, as well as wealth and plenty. This myth slowly turned into a legend, so that the people could more closely feel the legacy of the lesson of the myth. According to legend, then, in the Eighteenth century, Osei Tutu, the fourth king of the Ashanti, turned his people into a great kingdom by listening to the revelation of a great seer and defector from a neighboring enemy country whose king and people had been a thorn in the flesh of the Ashanti. Akonfo Anokye, for that was the name of the seer, revealed that Nyame had bestowed a golden stool on the Ashanti. By means of his spiritual power, he brought the golden stool from the sky, in the midst of a black cloud, thunder and dust. This stool descended slowly until it rested on the king's knees. Osei Tutu had four bells made to hang on each side of the stool.

This stool, which became known as the Golden Stool, contained the soul of the Ashanti people, that is their essence as a people, their wealth and welfare. The king, queen, and chiefs made a binding covenant with hairs from their bodies, which were made into a potion that they all drank. They poured some of the potion on the stool. The stool was never to be sat upon, though on great occasions the king might pretend to sit on it three times and rest his hand on it. The Golden Stool went out in a procession once a year when it was carried under umbrellas and attended with royal state. The Ashanti were able to rebel against their oppressors, totally routing them and killing their king and queen. The Ashanti fastened their golden chains to the stool. Another king who dared to make a copy of the stool was reportedly killed and two golden masks made from his face were fastened to the Golden Stool as trophies.

It was with the British invasion of Ghana in 1896 that the Golden Stool entered into Ashanti history. It was hidden away to save it from destruction. In 1921, it reappeared and was finally given a resting place in the royal house at Kumasi. In 1922, when Princess Mary of England got married, the Queen Mother of the Ashanti sent her a silver stool, declaring that their love, her's and her husband's, were "bound to the stool with silver fetters, just as we are accustomed to bind our own spirits to the base of our stools" (Parrinder 1986:168).

At least one follower of Aidoo, Kojo Laing, has also exploited the myth of the Golden Stool in his creative writing in his effort to recall his people to their spiritual and mythic beginnings. In a provocative short story with an eloquent title, "Vacancy for the Post of Jesus Christ," Laing decries the rupture of the Ghanaian people from their God, to the point that were there to be "A Third Coming" of Jesus Christ, there would be no single individual rich or poor, young or old, educated or illiterate, who would be found worthy to fill the position left vacant by the death of the Messiah.[1] Laing is making allusion to the beginning when Anokye as Nyame's messenger brought salvation to a people. It is in the same way that Aidoo recalls her people to their origins in the face of the current vicissitudes of history.

In *The Dilemma of a Ghost*, Aidoo assumes the persona of four mythical figures to reinforce the need for myths in human lives. Four as a mythical symbol is a sign of plenitude. We often refer to the four corners of the earth, for example, meaning the totality of people in the world. Most African peoples have four-day weeks and count their numbers in batches of four. Thus, the number four is a sort of magic number with a symbolic meaning. Aidoo is thus able to comment on life and living in the modern era by speaking through her four personas, while at the same time remaining effaced. She is at once a bird, an aged woman of destiny, reminiscent of the spider woman of the Amerindian mythology, and two archetypal women with no proper names, women who are simply called Woman using the common noun that designates the other kind of human being who is of the female sex. One is barren and the other has very many children. Together, they both symbolize a complementarity. Aidoo says:

> I am the Bird of the Wayside...
> The sudden scampering in the undergrowth,
> Or the trunkless head
> Of the shadow in the corner.
> I am an asthmatic old hag (sic!)
> Eternally breaking the nuts
> Whose soup, alas,
> Nourished a bundle of whitened bones...
> Or a pair of women, your neighbours
> Chattering their lives away. (Aidoo 1965:7)

An explanation of the mythemes—bird, aged woman, and the two women—is necessary. In many world mythologies, the bird is an aerial symbol of progress. The bird is able to soar very high into the sky, well above tree tops, where it is held to commune with spirits and God the Most High. African mythology is replete with stories of birds who participated in the work of creation of the beginning. Many times, the bird is sent by the Most High to humans on earth with one message or another. According to a Yoruba cosmogonic myth, for example, a set of two birds, a pigeon and a hen with five toes spread the first mound of earth in the marshy waste, thus creating a firm land on which humans and other creatures were placed by the gods. This tiny earth was initially sent in a snail shell by Olorun, the God of the sky, to Orisha his earthly executive who then asked the birds to spread it (Parrinder 1986:21-23). Another story, from Ghana, states that once upon a time, a woman had a beautiful daughter, Foriwa, whom she protected from living by barring everyone from having anything to do with her. She built her a house in the middle of the forest and sent her food every day. When she visited, she would sing a particular song which the daughter recognized. Thereupon, she would open the door to be fed by her mother. One day, the leopard broke the secret code by eavesdropping and learning the song. After the woman left, it taught the song to the tortoise who gained entry into the girl's abode by singing the song perfectly, as if it was the mother. The leopard attacked the girl, killed her, gave her blood to the tortoise and shared her flesh with all the other animals and they ate her up. A weaver bird, the Heavenly messenger, disclosed the moral of the tale to the possessive mother: "...there is danger in trying to protect children from all the evil in the world. Parents do not own children" (Berry and Spears 1991:160). The little weaver bird sitting in a palm tree kept warning the mother that her daughter was dead but she would not believe it until, not having a response from her daughter, she forced the door open.

In the image of the Bird at the Wayside, Aidoo injects her visionary insights into the affairs of humans. By implication then, she claims to understand how the exigencies of modern living compel the young to travel far away from home, resulting in a generation gap between parents and their children. Age-old traditions and morality get sidetracked in the process. How do we adapt so that human lives do not get ruined in the process? The Bird of the Wayside, from this angle of vision, may not be seen as an insignificant stranger, a wayfarer, and its attributes as given by Aidoo have nothing to do with their "immateriality" (Odamtten 1994:24). On the contrary, from the bird's position at the wayside or lookout, sort of crossroads, nothing escapes its eagle eye. Everything that comes into and goes out of the clan is subjected to its strict scrutiny. All the expressions further describing the bird's activities are, from our manner of interpretation, mere characteristics of birds in general. Birds delight in hiding under foliage like "shadow(s) in the corner," only to "scamper" out at the faintest footsteps of humans and fly away. Birds delight in picking their food from the ground, momentarily seeming like "trunkless heads." At least one children's rhyme records some others of these innate characteristics of all birds: "Once I saw a little bird/Come hop, hop, hop,/ Then, I said, little bird,/ will you stop, stop, stop?'/ As I was going to the window to say 'how do you do?'/But he shook his little tail and away he flew!" As an image of progress then, the Bird at the Wayside—or is it Aidoo?—brings in intuitive knowledge and wise counsel made possible by its ability to get into privileged corners to fish out hidden secrets to be used as teaching resources.

As an asthmatic hag whose longevity is the source of her enormous wisdom, the author-narrator undergoes a metamorphosis, becoming Nana Kum, the octogenarian, who already meditates on death and dreams of joining the ancestors who have preceded her (Aidoo 1965:19). One of the issues which she undertakes to explain is how to balance traditional and modern living, that is how to cope with the demands of cross-cultural understanding and communication (19-20).

Lastly, in the third and fourth images of the two community women with no proper names, Aidoo is able to get opinions from all walks of life. First Woman and Second Woman, as they are called, represent unity of opposites, as do The Old Woman and The

Old Man in *Anowa*. They enjoy a complementarity, as we have already intimated, in that the first is childless and the second has a house full of children. The two women act like chorus and summarize for the reader what is happening on and off stage, from the circumstances of Ato's birth through his education and travel abroad, to his return with a foreign wife whose priority is not children, much contrary to African tradition. The hopes and dreams of the Odumna clan have been dashed after they spent enormously to train the One Scholar whom they hoped would get them out of poverty. Instead of their spirit of communalism, Ato has imbibed the spirit of individualism from abroad. Marriage for him is an individual affair, not a communal one: "But those days are over/When it was expedient for two deer/To walk together./Since anyone can see and remove/The beam in his eye with a mirror" (22). The point needs to be made that when the Second Woman calls herself Aba, that naming must be seen as the equivalent of the English Tom, Dick and Harry to stand for just anyone. "If the courtyard must be swept,/It is Aba's job./ If the *ampesi* must be cooked, / It is Aba's job" (11).

From all four personas the author, Aidoo, is everywhere yet effaced at all times. She is able to look critically at the past, make commentaries about the present in order to guide the future.

AIDOO ON THE PAST

Aidoo recalls the European chattel slavery, which gave rise to the African diaspora. Eulalie, the African American wife of Ato, serves as an effective and economical resource for garnering the myths surrounding the fact of being African or African American, two "distant cousins" who speak to each other without communicating, much like those mythical beings in the Tower of Babel, according to the Hebrew mythology recorded in the Old Testament of the Bible.

When the curtain first rises, the reader sees that the relationship of Ato and Eulalie had degenerated into a shouting match. The pseudo-politeness couched in "if you please," does not blind anyone to the fact that these young people are going through a difficult time and a tremendous strain in their marriage relationship:

> EU: Don't shout at me, if you please.
> ATO: Do keep your mouth shut, if you please.
> EU: I suppose African women don't talk.
> ATO: How often do you want to go on

about African women. Leave them alone,
will you... Ah, yes they talk. But Christ,
they don't run on in this way.
This running tap drawl gets on my nerves. (9-10)

So, within the first few pages of the play, we already are confronted
with two erroneous myths about Africans and African Americans.
This is Aidoo's artistic way of drawing the reader's attention to the
seriousness of the problem at hand. It is common, albeit erroneous,
knowledge that African women are supposed to be subservient,
weak, dependent, and subordinate. In reality, the truth is far from
that myth, which needs to be exploded once and for all. In colonial times, such an erroneous myth started as a result of the wives
of the colonial administrators who, having not much with which
to occupy themselves, spent their days lounging around as house-
wives. Joyce Cary's *Mister Johnson* also helped to perpetuate this
image, which now was imposed on the African woman as dependent and unproductive. More recently, such an error is again
repeated by a film, *Coming to America*, in which James Earl Jones
stars as an African king and Eddie Murphy, his spoilt African
prince, has a bevy of naked young maidens bathing him in a pool
while scheming individually for his attention. Ngozi Onwurah's
Monday Girls also depicts young maidens in the process of the circumcision rite of initiation baring their breasts to the community
who judge their morality quite openly. A person not quite familiar with Africa who takes at face value these pseudo-myths propagated by the mass media is likely to conclude that African women
were always subjugated, unless such a person is also familiar with
African legends-turned-myth about Queens, Queen Mothers and
co-regents, and warrior women, which also abound. Loth explains:

Matrilinearity and matriarchy do not necessarily go
together, but some women as the holders of secular
or religious offices do point to conditions which were
characterized originally by matrilinearity. "Female
kings" and armies of women (Amazons) in systems
which were otherwise patrilineal are often transitional forms which mark the passing of a matrilineal system. Such transitional forms—relatively
isolated pointers to former times—ensured the continued existence of special rights for individual
groups of women within certain peoples for many
centuries. Old accounts of voyages make occasional

reference to Amazons, female army commanders and regiments consisting of women.... In the western parts of Libya, at the frontiers of the world, there is supposed to have been a nation ruled by women; they waged war, served for a defined period in the army during which period they had to exist without men. When their years of service were past, they get together with men in order to perpetuate their race. Public office and general administration are, however, retained as their exclusive domain. Men live domestic lives like women in our society, and obey the orders of their spouses; they play no role in war, government and other matters of state, as such activities might make them rebel against their wives. Straight after birth, male offspring is handed over to the father, who feeds him with milk and other foods according to his age. If the child is female, however, her breasts are burned so that they do not grow in puberty, for it is regarded as an encumbrance for the carrying of weapons if the breasts project from the body; for this reason they are called Amazons (Breastless).... (Loth 1987:61)

Amazons are said to have existed in West Africa in the former Dahomey, now the Republic of Benin. The value of recalling here the myths and history of past powerful African women is not to reopen the battle of the sexes, but rather to debunk the erroneous myth that African women had always been subservient to their men, as Eulalie implies in her statement. If African women are today battling to regain their past glory, lost with colonization, it is thanks to an innate survival instinct which empowers them to refuse to stay down forever.

The other erroneous myth cited by Ato Yawson states that African Americans slur their words. This calls to mind the current war of words raging about whether Ebonics, an African American dialect of English, should be considered as a foreign language. The implication still is that African Americans do not pronounce properly. The story actually dates back to four hundred years ago, during the slavery period when African slaves brought to the New World learned, through a survival instinct, to disguise their speech in order to confuse the white slave masters whom they did not want to be privy to their conversations. Slaves could have been planning an escape, as many of them tried to do! We shall revisit this matter in due course.

For now, however, a third myth revolves around the words "native" and "boy." Eulalie refers to her husband as "Native boy" and perhaps "the blackest you ever saw" (25), in reference to the myth that Ghanaians with their position right on the Equator are the darkest skinned Africans on the continent. "Native" as a term was used by colonialists to refer to Africans as tribal peoples who are not "civilized," who are "primitive" and "bush," as opposed to Europeans who themselves do not belong to a tribe or ethnic group, who are civilized and who live in cities. Anthropology is therefore a study of native peoples even as sociology is a study of civilized peoples. Joseph Conrad's derogatory novel, *Heart of Darkness*, appeared to foster such a myth. On the other hand, such early novels as Chinua Achebe's *Things Fall Apart*, Camara Laye's *L'Enfant noir* and Amos Tutuola's *The Palm-Wine Drinkard* set out to erase the myth that Africans were not civilized and further to argue that advanced technology is not necessarily synonymous with civilization. The term "boy" recalls the colonial meaning of this term when used in reference to an African, to mean someone who is supposed to be an adult but who remains childlike in his ways. Colonialists often treated Africans as eternal children in order to justify their imposition of power on them. Cameroonian writer, Ferdinand Oyono, fully examined the miserable life of a colonial houseboy in his novel, *Une vie de boy*, translated into English as *Houseboy*. "Native boy" put together as a phrase reminds one of Richard Wright's protest novel, *Native Son*, set in the 1940s, and James Baldwin's *Notes of a Native Son*, set in the 1950s, also depicting the reality of being African American in the South of the United States of America. The 1950s literary period coincides with the beginning of the African novel protesting the presentation of Africans in novels by Westerners as less than human beings, as people with neither culture nor civilization.

As the play evolves, Aidoo seizes on a fourth myth, the myth surrounding African drums, and effectively puts Western understanding of it to ridicule. The drums were often targets for racist remarks. Joseph Conrad, the self-exiled Polish man living in nineteenth-century England, visited his cultural inadequacy on Africans and their drums thus in *Heart of Darkness:*

> At night sometimes the roll of drums behind the curtain of trees would run up the river and remain sus-

tained faintly, as if hovering in the air high over our heads, till the first break of day. Whether it meant war, peace, or prayer we could not tell.... We were wanderers on a prehistoric earth, on an earth that wore the aspect of an unknown planet. We could have fancied ourselves the first of men taking possession of an accursed inheritance, to be subdued at the cost of profound anguish and excessive toll. But suddenly, as we struggled around a bend, there would be a glimpse of rush walls, of peaked grass-roofs, a burst of yells, a whirl of black limbs, a mass of hands clapping, of feet stamping, of bodies swaying, of eyes rolling, under the droop of heavy and motionless foliage. The steamer toiled along slowly on the edge of a black and incomprehensible frenzy. The prehistoric man was cursing us, praying for us, welcoming us—who could tell? We were cut off from the comprehension of our surroundings; we glided past like phantoms, wondering and secretly appalled, as sane men would be before an enthusiastic outbreak in a mad house (Conrad 1910:14).

Eulalie re-echoes this myth when she freaks out at the sound of drums while she was visiting her African in-laws. Aidoo did not miss the opportunity that presented itself to debunk the erroneous myth about African drums: "(*Suddenly the drums just roll and roll. EULALIE throws away her cigarette, her eyes pop out. She is really scared. She mutters "Christ, Christ", like a caged animal. She rushes towards the room and crashes into Ato's arms.*)" The cause of this mighty consternation is later discovered to be only the sound of funeral drums, which Eulalie believes to be some villagers engaged in witch hunting (Aidoo 1965:25; see also Nketia 1963). Eulalie seems to have accepted as well the erroneous myth that Africans are witches, wizards and witch hunters.

Only temporarily does she bask in the feeling that the African continent she had arrived on was a long, exotic land of exotic fruits, drinks, coconut trees, palm trees, azure seas, sun, and golden beaches, and we have the sixth erroneos myth. She makes allusions to the Triangular Trade and the New World when she dreams of wearing cotton and watching palm trees sway their full and elegant bodies in the wind. It does not matter that she cannot tell a coconut tree from a palm tree, as she confesses. Africa is the "source" of the living fountain, of clean, refreshing and life-giving water, the paradise of the past, which the traveler seeks when the present becomes unbearable (9). Soon she foregoes these positive myths to return to the negative ones.

Once again, we are confronted with a seventh erroneous myth, according to which Africans are "primitive people," who eat "crawling things," ignorant and bastardly people, stupid narrow-minded savages, "more savage than dinosaurs," and "living a prehistoric existence" (47-48). Aidoo refutes here the notion that a non-writing people have no history, are pre-historic. It is ironical that even as recently as thirty years ago an Oxford professor, Hugh Trevor-Roper, was teaching English students in England to disregard any craving to understand Africa because Africa does not exist, has never existed:

> Undergraduates, seduced as always by the changing breath of journalistic fashion, demand that they should be taught the history of black Africa. Perhaps, in the future there will be some African history to teach. But at present there is none, or very little: there is only the history of Europeans in Africa. The rest is darkness.... And darkness is not a subject for history.... [There are only] the unrewarding gyrations of barbarous tribes in picturesque but irrelevant corners of the globe. (Trevor-Roper 1965:1)

Even the myth that Africans had no writing has since been refuted by discoveries of early African writing: the hieroglyphics in Egypt, picture writing in Somalia, and among the Efik of Nigeria the Nsibisi script. Thomas O'Toole, for his part, finds it ridiculous that anyone should think that even in literate cultures *all* peoples of those cultures are literate: "... even in those complex urban-centered societies called civilizations, which have had written records for more than 5,000 years, only a small minority of people were literate and most people did not live in cities. Certainly in Africa this prehistoric-historic distinction has little value" (Gordon and Gordon 1996:30). Aidoo is decidedly against the Western notion that Africa was a *tabula rasa* when the white man came. In addition, she seizes the opportunity to chide at the same time those Africans who are still ignorant of their illustrious past and who still do not recognize the common destiny they have with African Americans. According to the Western idea, Africa had no history, no inventions, no existence, more or less, when the white man came (Masolo 1994; Mudimbe 1988). When the Europeans arrived, the African continent became the "white man's grave," the "heart of darkness," to repeat yet again that infamous title of Conrad's novel. Greg Palmer explains the origins of the myth of African inferiority since slavery which, ironically, was indeed their intelligent and ingenious manner of coping with the impossible:

> To justify slavery philosophically, plantation owners needed to believe their possessions were child-like people of such limited intelligence and sensitivity that the onerous work, appalling conditions, and injustice of slave life didn't bother them. So the masters wanted to see their chattel singing, dancing and joking in ways that reinforced their belief that the slaves were naive children who needed white "protection." At the same time, the slaves were both laughing at their masters behind their backs and moderating their humor in the master's presence to make life easier. Being slow and lazy would get you beating. But if you were slow and lazy and *funny* about it, you could avoid punishment, as well as hard work. (Palmer 1994:27)

We had shelved part of our comment about the myth that African Americans slur their words in order to revisit it at this time. The above quotation explains the origin of that myth. The slaves found that they could make plans in front of the master if they adopted a modified form of the English language which the slave-master would find hard to decode simply because he had not learnt it. It did not mean at all that the slaves did not know how to talk, and Ato was callous in suggesting that African Americans do not know how to speak good English.

But to return to the loss of identity for many African Americans as a result of slavery, the knowledge of the truth did not stop many a black girl from dreaming that one day she would transform into a white woman with silky blond hair and blue or green eyes. Toni Morrison's *The Bluest Eye* recalls this myth. Eulalie, for her part, in *The Dilemma of a Ghost*, during a day-dream-turned-interior-monologue /soliloquy, hears her dead mother's admonition on the subject of passing:

Kill the sort of dreams silly girls dream
that they are going to wake up one
morning and find their skin's milk white
and their hairs soft blond like them
Hollywood tarts. (24)

In a way, African American women of light skin trying to pass for white women resembles the myth of Africans attempting to fly back to Africa. Both are mechanisms of the psyche attempting to escape from the unbearable present. The myth of Africans who can fly has inspired Toni Morrison's *Song of Solomon*, Paule Marshall's *Praisesong for the Widow* and Virginia Hamilton's *The People Could Fly*.

In the final analysis, we can say that the myth of the Golden Stool has inspired Ama Ata Aidoo to reexamine various myths about African and African American past. It appears that Aidoo is teaching her people where they have been before, so that they may live a better life of awareness in the present.

AIDOO ON THE PRESENT

In *The Dilemma of a Ghost*, perhaps the most significant preoccupation of Africans and African Americans in the present centers on love and marriage. Love and marriage are also primary subjects that enter the domain of mythology. World mythologies often speak of heroes and monsters who behave in every way like human beings. They go to war, they quarrel, avenge their loved ones, and enjoy themselves or others close to them. Specifically, they love and get married. In Africa, Egyptian mythology is rife with stories of jealous gods and goddesses, even brothers, who get involved in love triangles. Seth usurps his elder brother's, Osiris', marriage bed, seducing his wife Isis, while Osiris is traveling around the world spreading human civilization. Seth gets very jealous and angry when his big brother returns. In a fit of rage, Seth kills Osiris, cutting him up into sixty pieces, which he strew everywhere. He cuts off his penis and throws it into the river Nile where it is presumed that sea animals found it and ate it. Isis, who has the gift of medicine and healing, with the help of Anubis the embalmer, picks up all the sixty pieces of her husband and puts him together again. She fashions him a golden replacement penis with which he is able to give her a son, Horus (Ions 1983). Osiris becomes the paragon of all dead kings and all dead people in his image of the sun which dies each day and rises again at dawn. Cashford puts it succinctly thus, in order to exhort humans on the essence of their earthly journey:

> The appeal of the myth of Isis and Osiris lay in the fact that people could identify with them as sharing the fate of human beings, yet they also transcended the limitations of the human condition. Isis lost her husband but found him and revived him. She brought her child up alone, overcame his sickness, and he grew up to take his father's place. When the ancient Egyptians lost their loved ones they married like Isis, and they imagined that when they died they became like Osiris, continuing to live in another realm as he did. So the Egyptians also saw in the death and revival of Osiris an analogy for human life and death. (Cashford 1993:viii)

If there is any value in recounting the Seth-Isis-Osiris love triangle here, it is to show that human existence cannot be divorced from amorous entanglements. If gods and goddesses can do it, then humans can as well and do often do it. Aidoo shows an understanding of the place of myth in African oral tradition when she makes the living feel the presence of the dead through mythology. African reality is subjective though still unable to dispense with the need for reason as well in whatever we do and in the African world-view. It is for this reason that Aidoo seems to approach the issue of love and marriage with sympathy. The object is viewed as nominal but sacred, but full of its own essence. All that is left really is to determine where reason can be placed in relationship with myth.

In studying Aidoo's treatment of Ato and Eulalie relationship, it is necessary to recall Joseph Campbell's distinction of three kinds of love: Eros, Agape, and Amor. Eros and Agape are impersonal loves. Eros is sheer sexual desire comparable to lust. Ato and Eulalie's relationship is not about this. Agape is community love and the kind that could lead to an arranged marriage. Arranged marriages were common in Africa. Families went in search of wives for their sons, sometimes without much input from the would-be husbands. It is worthy of note that the fact that a marriage is arranged does not automatically preclude the possibility of the two partners ever falling in love. Even when they do not fall in love with each other, it must be understood that the relationship of marriage is different from that of romantic love. When an arranged marriage lasts till the death of one of the partners in harmony, it is because the couple understand the contract that brought them together. The man is supposed to fend for the family as the woman is supposed to take care of the husband and children and entertain visitors and the extended family, according to African tradition. A marriage based on romantic love falls apart after a number of years if the couple individually or severally does not graduate to the next level of sublimating themselves in the other. When the couple sublimates themselves to the other partner, they think more about the survival of the union, rather than about their own particular interests as individuals (see Flowers 1988:186).

When Ato's people lament the marriage of their son to a stranger, one could say that they are singing simultaneously praises to Agape. Had their son married a girl chosen for him from the neighborhood, from a family approved by them, their marriage would have been a love feast, an arranged affair between two young people by two families who know each other and are very friendly:

> 1st W: These are sad sayings, my sister.
> But where is his wife?
> 2nd W: I do not know, my sister.
> But I heard them say that his mother
> Had gone to knock the door of Yaw Mensa
> To ask for the hand of his daughter for him.
> 1st W: Oh, he would have had a good woman.
> I saw that girl when she came home for Christmas.
> School has not spoilt her, I think.
> 2nd W: And that is the sad part of it, my sister.
> He has not taken this girl
> Whom we all know and like,
> But has gone for this
> Black-White woman,
> A stranger and a slave. (Aidoo 1965:22)

By bringing up the issue of arranged marriage here in opposition to romantic love, Aidoo seems to invite her readers to revisit the issue of love and marriage in Africa, especially cross-cultural marriages between Africans and African Americans. In this regard, it is also pertinent to note that in Africa, traditionally speaking, any attempt by a married couple to become romantically involved is usually discouraged by the extended family who fear that they might be excluded in the love act. Aidoo, like a true traditional artist, makes no attempt to supply an answer to the dilemma tale she has told. The question remains open and readers are invited to participate in finding an answer to the issue of love and marriage cross-culturally.

Amor, contrary to Eros and Agape, is about romantic love, the kind of love practiced by the French Troubadours of the Provence in the Twelfth century. It is about personal love, says Campbell, in which there is an attraction of two people to each other to the exclusion of all others:

> You see, the experience of Amor is a kind of seizure. In India, the god of love is a big, vigorous youth with a bow and a quiver of arrows. The names of the arrows are "Death-bringing Agony" and "Open-up" and so forth. Ready, he just drives this thing into you so that it's a total physiological, psychological explosion.... This kind of seizure that comes from the meeting of the eyes, as they say in the troubadour tradition, is a person-to-person experience (Flowers 1988:186).

The relationship of Ato and Eulalie resembles very much a case of Amor. It was a mutual attraction in which they were the principal players, which at the beginning excluded everyone else: "But it all began on a University Campus; never mind where. The evening was cool as evenings are. Darkness was approaching when I heard the voices of a man and a woman speaking" (Aidoo 1965:8). Back in Ghana, amidst oppositions to his choice of marriage partner, for the second time Ato creates his own myth when he goes out of his way to reassure Eulalie that it will be all right for them to hold off on having children until she is ready. This is despite his awareness that Africans expect newly married couples to start a family as a matter of priority. The principal reason for marriage in traditional Africa has always been children. He utterly disregards his family's opinion on the issue and says to Eulalie: "Eulalie Rush and Ato Yawson shall be free to love each other, eh? This is all that you understand or should understand about Africa" (10).

Ato's problem, as Campbell would say, is that having decided to follow his "bliss" (read his individualism), he is incapable of embracing or accepting the pain that goes with it (Flowers 1988:190-191). Ato fails to prepare his people with knowledge about what direction he had chosen to give his life. His unconscious speaks to him in a dream in the middle of the afternoon, an ominous time when the overhead sun casts a person's shortest shadow, rendering him vulnerable to the spells of the evil genii. The two young children, a boy and a girl, are miniatures of Ato and Eulalie (Odamtten 1994:28).They are singing the song of the ghost in a dilemma at the junction who does not know which way to go. Ato is agitated at the sound of this song because instinctively he recognizes himself as that ghost:

> ATO:(*Looking right and left and searching with great agitation*).
> Where are they? Where are those urchins? Heavens! Those scruffy urchins and the racket of noise they were making. Why should they come here? But... Where are they? Or was it a dream? (*Panting*) Ugh! That's why I hate siesta. Afternoon sleep always brings me afternoon dreams, horrid, disgusting, enigmatic dreams. Damn this ghost at the junction. I loved to sing that song. Oh yes, I did. But it is all so long ago. I used to wonder too what it finally... Did it go to Elmina or to Cape Coast? And I used to wonder, oh, I used to wonder about so many things then. But why should I dream about all these things now? (Aidoo 1965:29)

In the final act of the play, the specter of Ato Yawson in the center of the stage behaving in every way like the ghost at the crossroads, or indeed a neurotic, constitutes the final image that lingers in the mind of the reader as the curtain falls:

> (ESI Kom *supports* EULALIE *through the door that leads into the old house.* ATO *merely stares after them. When they finally disappear, he crosses to his own door, pauses for a second, then runs back towards the door leading to the family house, stands there for some time and finally moves to the middle of the courtyard. He looks bewildered and lost. Then suddenly, like an echo from his own mind the voices of the children break out*). (52-53)[2]

Ato has not decided whether he should follow African tradition or the practice in modern times. For failing to make up his mind, he falls short of being an action hero. He becomes instead an anti-hero who allows things to happen to him. He married Eulalie out of love, but tries to make her do things according to the expectations and wishes of his people. This caused Eulalie to ask him whether he was the one who married her or his people:

> "My people... My people ...
> Damned rotten coward of a Moses.... I have been
> drinking in spite of what your people say.... Who
> married me, you or your goddam people?" (47).

From this point of view, Ato's marriage to Eulalie is a failure. Not only that, being an elite, and much like his Biblical counterpart who failed to lead the Israelites into the land of Canaan, he is guilty of failure to lead his people in the reconciliation of their past, so that the push forward might be started. The Elmina slave fort, built in 1482 by the Portuguese, is the oldest European fort in Ghana (see Figure 4). It also served as a conduit through which slaves were taken out to the Americas. (see Figure 5). In other words, it was the first symbol of Ghana's exposure to Western capitalism and menace. Elmina is thus a symbol of a brutal and physical encounter which Ghanaians (read Africans in general) would like to forget. But is forgetting synonymous with healing? And the Cape Coast Castle (see Figure 6), built in 1653 by the Swedes, is itself a symbol of the colonial encounter that came later. Cape Coast was the former colonial capital of the Gold Coast. By extension it is a symbol of European missionary work, brutal suppression by the colonial administration and mental enslavement through the schools. By looking, then, at Elmina and Cape Coast as options, the ghost that is Ato has not been able to grow beyond his past history. Worse, seen from his personal point of view, he has not been able to arrive at any kind of decision about what to do for the present nor for the future.

From the community's point of view, for failing to balance his love, desire, impulse, intuition and libido, Ato is the cause of communication breakdown between all the people. To achieve harmony that eluded the community, Ato only needed to have done five things which would have ensured that he got his people on his side and, at the same time, not transgressed the norms of his clan. The five virtues Ato needed were love, loyalty, courage, courtesy and temperance (Flowers 1987:192-193).[3] He, contrary to expectations, exposes his clan and culture to ridicule before his American wife when his courage fails him to tell his people that he and his wife are practicing birth control. This is the main source of Eulalie's dismay towards the end of the play when she asks Ato: "Why don't you tell them you promised me we would start having kids when

I wanted it?" (Aidoo 1965:47). It is also the reason for his mother's indignation at the end: "Is this not the truth? Why did you not tell us that you and your wife are gods and you can create your own children when you want them?... You do not even tell us about anything and we assemble our medicines together. While all the time your wife laughs at us because we do not understand such things... yes, and she laughs at us because we do not understand such things... and we are angry because we think you are both not doing what is good for yourselves" (Aidoo 1965:51). Ato does not show love for his community beyond the *clichés* he mouths from time to time. Eulalie calls him a coward for that. He does not show loyalty to his people who paid his fees and generally supported him while he was a student. The two women inform us that the Odumna clan has become poorer since his return and yet he would not help in their time of need. He lacked temperance for he is unable to make a choice.

In the end, Ato is the only one left unreconciled with the community. Not only is he a spineless ghost because of his ambivalence about his role as culture bridge, he is also a ghost for foreshadowing the dilemma of the educated African youth today who seem not to have learnt from the lessons of the past. He shows no evidence of coping with life in the present. Ama Ata Aidoo through the characters of the couple, Ato-Eulalie, has raised love and marriage to mythical heights in *The Dilemma of a Ghost*. In addition, Ato's dreams about the ghost at the junction are archetypal and they have mythic dimensions, going from the personal to the communal.[4]

AIDOO ON THE FUTURE

The future concerns itself with the important questions that all world mythologies ask: Who am I? Where am I going? How can the individual relate to her or his community? How can one people, one culture, relate to another people or another culture? How does one relate one's society to the world of nature and the cosmos?

In the first instance, destinies are no longer communal. In the present era of globalization, with its attendant movement of capital across national and cultural boundaries, we are witnessing the death of the nation-state and the birth, simultaneously, of a new kind of ethnicity where, especially in the so-called Third World, the fate of the individual is nearly entirely in her or his hands for the state cannot do much anymore (Ansell-Pearson, Benita Parry, and Judith Squires, 1998). That seems to be one of the great lessons that *The Dilemma of a Ghost* imparts. Individuals need to create their own myths with which to guide their actions and behaviors, seen that travel and education and jobs have dispersed people all over the world. The problem with creating new myths, however, is that individuals will have to follow up on their creations, and will be required to supply explanations and reasons for the myths, if need be.

Next, at the level of community, a people should relate to other people through emphasizing the interdependency of all peoples. They also need to create new myths fit for the present. The myth of the Golden Stool, for example, served its people when they needed it. Today, in multicultural settings and the prevalence of borderlands and hybridity, one needs the type of myths that are inclusive, not exclusive.[5] Wars, quarrels and bickerings should be eschewed among peoples, if humanity hopes to endure in the twenty-first century.

Thirdly and lastly, to relate one's society to another society and to the world of nature and the cosmos, it is necessary to emphasize the interconnectedness of all creatures, animate and inanimate, living and dead. This is what with regard to African spirituality, is referred to as animism. The term has absolutely nothing to do with the derogatory interpretation the word is given in racial circles, that of Africans who bow to rocks and stones believing them to be their gods. On the contrary, it is rather what Joseph Campbell calls a " trans-theological power," that is vital energy, or Father Tempels' *"force vitale,"* "that which is" (Masolo 1994: 150), which guides the world and all the creatures in it.[6] When Esi Kom invites Eulalie in at the end of the play without asking further questions, it is with seeming *prise de conscience* of this spiritual phenomenon.

> Yes, and I know
> They will tell you that
> Before the stranger should dip his finger
> Into the thick palm nut soup
> It is a townsman
> Must have told him to.
> And we must be careful with your wife
> You tell us her mother is dead.
> If she had any tenderness,
> Her ghost must be keeping watch over

All which happen to her...
Come, my child. (Aidoo 1965:52).

Aidoo certainly makes a differentiation between self, Other and community. Through Esi Kom, she accomplishes an emphatic agency by reconciling the "gentile" (read outsider and slave) into the community, nature and cosmos. It is a positive statement about the future of humanity.

* * * * * *

We have tried to demonstrate how Ama Ata Aidoo, perhaps unconsciously, has made use of myths to convey her anxieties for better human understanding in our time. For a play which lasts only about thirty minutes in production, *The Dilemma of a Ghost* has proven much denser and much more valuable as good literature than its author could have imagined. The adoption of the pedagogical notion of myth, which emphasizes reason, seems to be the way that human beings can promote the ground for being and the fundamental structuring of order in society (Masolo 1994:194-146).[7] What happens at present is that of all the cardinal functions of myths—cosmological, sociological, pedagogical, and mystical—the sociological seems to predominate, even though it sees only divisions in the beliefs and psychology of people, resulting in the isolation and alienation of people who do not belong to a particular ethnic group (McClintock et al. 1997).

As far as the African and African American question is concerned, it means those that Ato represents meeting those that Eulalie represents half-way and vice-versa, and both parties carrying their peoples along with them. On the global scene, it is either the individual adapts her or his dreams to society or society sweeps her or him aside (Achebe 1958).[8]

NOTES AND REFERENCES

1. Kojo Laing, "Vacancy for the post of Jesus Christ." In Achebe and Innes 1992:185-196. "A Third Coming" is used here in allusion to Irish poet William Butler Yeats' poem "A Second Coming," from which Chinua Achebe took the title of his first novel *Things Fall Apart*.
2. Flowers 1988: 41. In response to the question why heros, leaders and visionaries of this world come close to the edge of neurosis, Campbell says:

   "They've moved out of the society that would have protected

them, and into the dark forest, into the world of fire, of spiritual experience. Original experience has not been interpreted for you and so you've got to work out your life for yourself. Either you can take it or you can't. You don't have to go far off the interpreted paths to find yourself in very difficult situations. The courage to face the trials and bring a whole new body of possibilities into the field of interpreted experience for other peoples to see—that is the hero's deed."

3. Joseph Campbell refers to the five virtues as the qualities of the Medieval knights, which ensure harmony between the individual and society.

4. Flowers 1988:39-40. This is Sigmund Freud's own view on the interpretation of dreams. Joseph Campbell, however, gives it an anthropological bent when he says that a person's dreams could be transformed into a society's myth. Archetypal myths, says he, stem "from the realization of some kind that have then to find expression in symbolic form."

5. Flowers 1988: 33-34. Joseph Campbell quotes Chief Seattle as having said to Washington, in reply to his letter requesting that some land be sold to him:

   "This we know: The earth does not belong to man, man belongs to the earth. All things are connected like the blood that unites us all. Man did not weave the web of life, he is merely a strand in it. Whatever he does to the web, he does to himself."

   Cf., Camara Laye 1953:201

   "Ce que je fais pour mon prochain, je le fais pour moi-même et pour Dieu."

6. Flowers 1988:31. Joseph Campbell calls this

   "the source and end and supporting ground of all life and being. It is getting back into accord (all humans on one side) with the wisdom of nature and realize(ing) again our brotherhood with the animals and with the water and the sea."

   See also Gershoni Yekutiel 1997 and Johnson, Sally and Ulrike Hanna Meinhoff 1997.

7. The Ghanaian philosopher, Kwasi Wiredu, argues in Part Three of his book, *Philosophy and an African Culture*, that knowledge, action and evaluation are essentially connected, each leading to the other. Evaluating the role of reason in dealing with tradition and modernity, Wiredu states that, in order to verify if we have learnt anything from any knowledge, first of all, it is absolutely necessary to see if one has been able to derive any action from the knowledge. Then, she or he must subject the action to the test of experience. We can thus infer that if present practices cause more problems than they solve, then reason dictates that they should be discarded for more progressive ideas and practices. See also Flowers 1988: 7. Joseph Campbell argues that the sociological function of myth should be avoided due to its divisiveness, which has been proven by expe-

rience. Rather, the pedagogical function of teaching reason should be embraced as the new myth for the future:

"Yes this is the ground of what the myth is to be, It's already here: the eye of reason, not of my individuality; the eye of reason, not of my religious community; the eye of reason, not of my linguistic community...."

8. Mbiti 1990:7, 8, 56, 240. Mbiti explains that animism is a term invented by E. B. Taylor in 1886, which defines African religion as a "belief in spirit beings," from *animus* meaning the breath of life, soul or spirit.
    See also Bâ 1972:119. He explains this phenomenon in the context of "person," "culture," and "religion" in the tradition of the Peul and the Bambara, neighbors of the Akan. According to him, Africans recognize the existence of a force—*Puissance-Source,* which motivates the actions of all creatures of God. It is this force in every being which gives it life, sees to its development and, eventually, its reproduction. This animating, sacred force is almost indescribable, but it is there and gives rise to all kinds of religious beliefs and practices among Africans. Western ethnologists refer to it as "animism," understanding by that that Africans invest every creature with a soul, a sort of vital-force that they seek to placate with all manner of religious practices.

WORKS CITED

Achebe, Chinua. *Things Fall Apart.* New York: Fawcett Crest, 1993.

Achebe, Chinua, and C. L. Innes. *The Heinemann Book of Contemporary African Short Stories.* Portsmouth N. H.: Heinemann, 1992.

Aidoo, Ama Ata. *The Dilemma of a Ghost and Anowa.* London: Longman, 1965.

Ansell-Pearson, Keith, Benita Parry, and Judith Squires. Eds. *Cultural Readings of Imperialism: Edward Saïd and the Gravity of History.* New York: St Martin's Press, 1998.

Azodo, Ada Uzoamaka. *L'imaginaire dans les romans de Camara Laye.* New York: Peter Lang Publishers, Inc., 1993

Bâ, Hampaté A. *Aspects de la civilisation africaine.* Paris: Présence Africaine, 1972.

Baldwin, James. *Notes of A Native Son.* Boston: Beacon Press, 1955.

Berry, Jack, and Richard Spears. *West African Folktales.* Evanston: Northwestern University Press, 1991.

Cary, Joyce. *Mister Johnson.* New York: Harper and Brothers, 1962.

Cashford, Jules. *The Myth of Isis and Osiris.* New York: Random House, 1993.

Conrad, Joseph. *Heart of Darkness and The Secret Sharer.* New York: Penguin, 1983.

Durand, Gilbert. *Les Structures Anthropologiques de L'imaginaire.* Paris: Berg International, 1970.

Flowers, Betty Sue. Ed. *Joseph Campbell: The Power of Myth, Interview by Bill Moyers.* New York: Doubleday, 1988.

Gershoni, Yekutiel. *Africans on African Americans.* Washington Square, New York: New York University Press, 1997.

Gordon, April A. and Donald L. Gordon. Eds. *Understanding Contemporary Africa*. Boulder/London: Lynne Reinner Publishers, 1996.

Hamilton, Virginia. *The People Could Fly*. New York: Knopf, 1985.

Ions, Veronica. *Egyptian Mythology*. New York: P. Bedrick Books, 1983.

Johnson, Sally and Ulrike Hanna Meinhof, *Language and Masculinity*. Cambridge, Mass.: Blackwell Publishers, 1997.

Knappert, Jan. *African Mythology*. London: Diamond Books, 1995.

Laing, Kojo. "Vacancy for the post of Jesus Christ." In: *The Heinemann Book of Contemporary African Short Stories*. Eds. Chinua Achebe and C. L. Innes. Portsmouth, N.H.: Heinemann, 1992. 186-196.

Laye, Camara. *Dramouss*. Paris: Plon, 1966.

Leeming, David Adams. *The World of Myth*. New York/Oxford: Oxford University Press, 1990.

Loth, Heinrich. *Woman in Ancient Africa*. Translated by Sheila Marnie. Westport, Conn.: Lawrence Hill and Company, 1987.

Madu, Raphael Okechukwu. *African Symbols, Proverbs and Myths: The Hermeneutics of Destiny*. New York: Peter Lang Publishing, Inc., 1992

Martineau, Henri. *Stendhal: La Chartreause de Parme*. Paris: Editions Garnier Frères, 1961.

Masolo, D. A. *African Philosophy in Search of Identity*. Bloomington: Indiana University Press, 1994

Mbiti, John S. *African Religions and Philosophy*. Portsmouth, N. H.: Heinemann, 1990.

McClintock, Anne, Aamir Mufti and Ella Shobat. Eds. *Dangerous Liaisons*. Minneapolis/London: University of Minnesota Press, 1997.

Miller, Christopher. *Blank Darkness*. Chicago: University of Chicago Press, 1990.

Morrison, Toni. *The Bluest Eye*. New York: Random House, 1970.

Mudimbe, V. Y. *The Invention of Africa*. Bloomington, Indiana: Indiana Univerity Press, 1988.

Nketia, J. H. Kwabena. *Drumming in Akan Communities of Ghana*. London: Thomas Nelson Publishing, 1963. 6-10.

Odamtten, Vincent, O. *The Art of Ama Ata Aidoo: Polylectics and Reading Against Neocolonialism*. Gainesville and Tampa: University Press of Florida, 1994.

Palmer, Greg. *Eastsideweek*, April 20, 1994, p. 27.

Parrinder, Geoffrey. *African Mythology*. London: Hamlyn, 1986.

Pinkey, Alphonso. *The Myth of Black Progress*. Cambridge: Cambridge University Press, 1991.

Sarpong, Peter A. *The Sacred Stools of the Akan*. Teman: Ghana Publishing Corporation, 1971.

Thomas, L. V. "Time and Myth and History in West Africa," *Présence Africaine* (English Edition). 11, 39 (Fourth Quarterly 1961).

Trevor-Roper, Hugh. *The Rise of Christian Europe*. New York: Harcourt, Brace and World, 1965.

Wiredu, Kwasi. *Philosophy and an African Culture*. Cambridge, U.K.: Cambridge University Press, 1980.

THE BIRD OF THE WAYSIDE: FROM *AN ANGRY LETTER*... TO *THE GIRL WHO CAN*

VINCENT OKPOTI ODAMTTEN

Over the years, we have been constantly reminded, by sudden tragedies or startling revelations, of the precarious nature of the careers of our African writers, men and women, on the continent or in the diaspora, whose works have appeared like shooting stars to briefly illumine our readerly lives and, all too quickly, fade from our memories. Yet, there are writers whose works valiantly resist our lapses into a collective amnesia, our willful desire to dis(re)member the work of our literary producers. "For Bessie Head" from Ama Ata Aidoo's second volume of poetry, *An Angry letter in January*, attempts to not only remember a particularly talented, gifted, and insightful African griotte/writer, but also place her, as "such a fresh ancestress," in dynamic relationship between our pre-apartheid/colonial and spiritual histories and our conscious desire to marshall all our resources toward the transformation of our lives. To that end, our familiar poetic narrator-guide, The Bird of the Wayside, articulates our inarticulate keening:

Come
benevolent,
Dear fresh Spirit,
that rejoining
The Others
you can tell them
now more than ever,
do we need
the support
the energy
To create
recreate and
celebrate...
Nothing more
absolutely
nothing less ("For Bessie Head," Aidoo 1992:53-54)

The creation of the Bird-of-the-Wayside, that protean narrative voice which was first heard in *The Dilemma of a Ghost*, has undergone various metamorphoses: from the historically rooted "Mouth-that-Eats-Salt-and-Pepper" (*Anowa*), through the wise but slightly squinting Sister Killjoy, to the insistent personal voice of *Someone Talking to Sometime* and beyond, allowing us better to follow Aidoo's varied literary and ideological explorations.

It is in the context of what has happened to that voice, since that *Sometime*, that demands our attention in this essay. Changes in narrative tone and focus, set in and against the history of significant local and global political and economic transformations, make an examination of the most recent of Aidoo's publications particularly appropriate. If, as we suggested, in *The Art of Ama Ata Aidoo*, the poems in her first volume of poems "constitute an intermission, a retrospective and prospective contemplation ... [on] the problem of finding a language, an effective medium for communicating something relevant, in regard to the struggles of the wretched of Africa and, by extension, of the world" (Odamtten 1994:133-34); then, The-Bird-of-the-Wayside, in the second volume of poems, has found something "relevant," in a language which is well suited to the task of depicting the actions of people responding to globalization, to old and new (neo-)colonial and gendered relationships. The poetic voices in *An Angry Letter in January* act as choral response to and extension of the thematic concerns so poignantly expressed by Sissie in "A Love Letter" at the end of *Our Sister Killjoy*, and structurally and formally *Someone Talking to Sometime*. Yet, even as we start with an examination of, perhaps, the least acknowledged of the multiple genres Aidoo utilizes in her authorial project,[1] we are immediately made aware of the betrayal of critical silence:

> I have nightmared of
> different gatherings
> —after we parted—
> where too
> you sit at centre-stage
>
> where they call up
> characters to assassinate
> plot our on-doings, (sic!)
>
> And
>
> you do not say anything.
> ("As Always a Painful Declaration of
> Independence," Aidoo 1992:10)

This betrayal is at once personal, academic, political and global. The-Bird-of-the-Wayside, our poet-narrator, makes "As Always, a Painful Declaration of Independence." This opening poem delineates the partiality of relationships and the problematic discourses which, although intended to facilitate reciprocal communication, prevent the possible realization of their intentions and thus result in the dehumanizing of all subjects. The rejection of *this* relationship between lovers and others, between colonizer and colonized, between man and woman, between the-Bird-of-the-Wayside and her partial reader-audience is necessitated by the changed realities in the last quarter of the twentieth century, a period which is more often than not, described as both *post-colonial* and *post-modern*.

Curiously, it seems that both the title of Aidoo's second published volume of poetry, *An Angry Letter in January*, and the titular poem, even as they suggest a previous narrative into which we are entering just now, also pick up and iterate the concerns of her first volume, *Someone Talking To Sometime*, through an equal number of poems, forty-five, written between 1985-1990. Part One, "Images of Africa at Century's End" consists of twenty-five poems which explore our present predicament and our past heritage in relation to the ideas and realities of home and exile, self and other on the Continent and in the Diaspora. Part Two, while a natural extension of the first section, shifts our perspective to one which allows us to more clearly appreciate "Women's Conferences and Other Wonders." The nineteen poems in this part, even as they focus our attention on "A Young Woman's Voice Doesn't Break," in *Motherhood* and *Womanhood*, the processes of teaching and learning, ultimately document a w(rite) of passage: "A Young Woman's Voice Doesn't Break. It Gets Firmer." The quiet assurance of this poem reflects the maturity of the-Bird-of-the-Wayside's poetic voice and vision, her true independence from the hegemonic discourses that claim ownership of her/our past, even as "The Man [tries] / to grab our future too" ("Images of Africa at Century's End" 15–17). The work as a whole, like her earlier projects, insists on engaging and interrogating the historical legacy with which we have to deal.

The titular poem of the opening section, coming immediately after the pessoptomistic declaration of independence, continues, in theme and tone, the mixture of "sweetness and smoky roughage" (Aidoo 1988:133) which comes from the consciousness of *being*, in this case, rooted in Africa's blackness, with its history of compromises, contradictions, victories and continuing struggles. Even as the poem, "Images of Africa at Century's End" (15–17), looks to the near future we are aware from its content, its thematic concerns that the-Bird-of-the-Wayside will not allow us to forget the lessons of our historical encounters; nor the complex relationships which have arisen because of these encounters. Neither are we to be seduced by the new age of advertizing and consumerism into forgetting our past. The span of the poet's embrace is often Ancient Egypt till this very moment, *this Time*. This is truly someone not just *talking* to someone this time, but *asking* fundamental questions of existence beyond mere survival or subsistence. "The reason why / you never see / Black Folks properly" (Aidoo 1992:15) is not only an aesthetic "Problem," but an intricate part of the web of related ontological (material) realities and epistemological choices which help to explain:

> why The Princess Nefertiti
> and the youthful King Tut
> were dragged to
> Michael Jackson's beauty doctor
> long before

Young Michael was born
("Images of Africa at Century's End,"
Aidoo 1992:16).

The-Bird-of-the-Wayside has moved us to a more complex ground
on which to reclaim our sense of pride, of being-in-the-world, since:

"Home"
Can also be anyplace anywhere
where someone or other
is not trying to

Fry your mind,

Roast your arse, or

Waste you and yours altogether.

Hm???
("In Memoriam: The Ghana Drama Studio," Aidoo
1992:20)

Whether, like the-Bird-of-the-Wayside, we try to acknowledge those
"ancient graces," to keep the hope alive which was born "in this
truly ? No man's land" and find "whom ... we thank for Women's
Conferences" (Aidoo 1992:84-85)? Or, in the wonderfully affirma-
tive and disconcerting poems and testimonies of womanhood,
which constitute Part Two of this volume, *An Angry Letter in
January*, leaves us

Anxious
angry
sleepless—
Blissfully anxious
happily angry and
nervously fulfilled
that

I
too
am
a mother!

("Motherhood and the Numbers Game," Aidoo 1992:
82-83)

The-Bird-of-the-Wayside looks at the world without bitterness or ungrounded hope. She recognizes that there are possibilities that we can realize, and she seems to sense that there are people, men, boys, and more especially, young women and girls who are listening, who need the encouragement and clear affirming voice of "Woman" which ends the second volume and brings together body, mind and spirit in the struggle and quest to be.

A quarter century after the publication of Aidoo's collection of short stories, *No Sweetness Here* (1970), we are, fortunately, able to read *The Girl Who Can And Other Stories* (1996), the second collection of stories which engage us in what can only be described as the vintage "black-eyed squint" of a pessoptomistic Bird-of-the-Wayside. With regard to the earlier collection, we had described Aidoo's authorial project as:

> [one which] examines in greater detail the lived consequences of those problems [that arose from the historical confluence of local and foreign domination and were played out in the dilemmas between] ...personal choices and public imperative. She draws attention to the predicament of women's marginalization and oppression; however, as she stresses, both in the short stories and elsewhere, these injustices are part of a larger pattern of practices which affront human dignity and self-worth .... (Odamtten 1994:81).

The new collection, as the title suggests, is more overtly concerned with woman's achievement, of her overcoming the patterns of habit that have been reinforced by the historical consequences of patriarchy's pre-colonial and colonial strategies of exclusion, marginalization and outright oppression dramatically represented in Aidoo's play, *Anowa*. From the opening *fefewo*,[2] or "talking-story,"[3] "She-Who-Would-be-King "to the last, "Nowhere Cool," the familiar narrator of Aidoo's works takes us into some regions which are simultaneously uncharted yet, much traveled. These paths and byways mark the contours of our so-called post-colonial era, and which some would have us believe are indicators of a new post-modern and, perhaps, a post-neocolonial order.

The Girl Who Can and Other Stories, like Aidoo's previous collection of short fictions, consists of eleven stories which have a distinct inter-textual relationship. While the stories may be read separately themselves,[4] they may also be read with Aidoo's previous collection of short stories and her work in general. Unlike *No Sweetness Here*, the divisions that mark specific groups of related storytelling events, or episodes are more fluid—reflecting a paradoxical characteristic of this age addressed in the story, "Newly-Opened Doors." With the exception of four of the stories in this collection, all the others have been published before.[5] The confident pessoptimism we alluded to with regard to where *An Angry Letter* leaves us, manifests itself in the first three stories. Even as the stories, especially in their telling, display an unshaken conviction that the transformation of this world is possible, probable, and inevitable; because, as the narratives reveal, we have evidence of such trends and occurrences before our very eyes in large political, small private, and the everyday public sphere of work.

"She-Who-Would-Be-King" takes place on Africa Day in the year 2026: as such, it is a story of possibilities, suggesting that we may transcend the limitations of the present to see not only a "confederation of African States"; but, more importantly, the election of a woman as the President of such a union. What the *fefewo* enjoins us to do is a radical revisioning of Africa's capabilities, to challenge ourselves to consider seriously an Africa and its people—women and men—beyond the tired stereotypes. In many ways, this opening episode sets the transgressive and iconoclastic tone of the rest of the stories in the collection. From the near future, we return to the present of "The Girl Who Can" and "Heavy Moments." Both of these stories , like the opening one, ask us to ponder the assumptions we make about gender roles, about the relationship(s) between our biology and the social constructions we erect and believe to be essential for our definitions of ourselves-in-the-world. "The Girl Who Can" is told by Adjoa, the seven year old "Girl" of the title, who, although reliant on the world and discourse of adults from whom she gets knowledge, is not fully persuaded that they really have all the answers to her young life's problems. Indeed, Adjoa is very quick to realize that even though her grandmother, Nana, and her mother, Maami, may talk of "problems" or "the problem," there is a fundamental one neither of the adults are prepared to engage:

> As far as I could see, there was only one problem.... And my problem is that at this seven years of age, there are things I can think in my head, but which, maybe, I do not have the proper language to speak them out with. (Aidoo 1996:7)

Adjoa's "problem" and the tale she takes upon herself to tell seems to be a reply to the rhetorical questions raised in the final chapter of *The Art of Ama Ata Aidoo*:

> Perhaps the most important character and victim [of the novel, *Changes*], is the one from whom we hear the least—Ogyaanowa [the daughter of the protagonist]. So we might begin our "interminable palavers" by asking... what kind of world are we leaving for those unable to articulate, in "a more grownup language" (5), their concerns, when we so often and so blatantly refuse to consult them? ...what about the children who swell the "ranks of the wretched"? (Odamtten 1994:172-73)

The "problem" which confronts our young storyteller is her mother's fixation with the thinness of her legs, because "Legs that have meat on them: with good calves .... support solid hips ... to be able to have children" (9). Yet, it was those much maligned legs which enabled Adjoa to finally articulate, to demonstrate through action, her answer to the so-called "Problem." After she had won the prize cup for being "the best all-round junior athlete," her grandmother was elated and her mother "speechless": "surely, one should be able to do things with legs as well as have them because they can support hips that make babies" (11). Action transforms the world and silences criticism, it would seem.

The final story in this opening trilogy, "Heavy Moments," is not only a "salute to Millicent Melody Danquah, Joanna Araba Maana Dickson, and Ayele Kome, the three Women who dared join the Ghana Air Force as Pilots," but rather to all those whose courage and actions break these deprecating socially constructed barriers of exclusion. The story begins with a situation which we have all had to confront at one time or another, male or female (although for males it may appear easier to solve):

> She was now having to do a little *tinawale jig*. Left foot down, right foot up.... She struggled off the trousers of her uniform..., she was sitting on the toilet, and peeing what appeared to be all the clear fluids from her body. [And as Akuba relieves herself she remembers the saying:] "If they want to imitate men, fine. They'll find out whether they should wear trousers when they want to urinate!" ("Heavy

Moments." Aidoo 1996:12-13)

But Akuba Baidoo is more than prepared for the task, and she and her fellow cadet, Sarah Larbi, protest chauvinistic remarks even as they support each other through their harrowing apprenticeship at the academy. The-Bird-Of-The-Wayside particularizes Akuba's life and struggle to be recognized as Air Force pilot, so that we understand that the moment of triumph is not just a happy instance, but the culmination of many lives, many struggles over the years.

"Some Global News" and the stories that follow seriously interrogate what this "new world order" really means for those who are among the wretched of the earth. The-Bird-Of-The-Wayside takes us on a journey between the larger questions of how Yaa-Yaa Mensah and her NGO, "Venture 16" should respond to the globalization of self-help. No longer is one able to contribute in one's own wretched corner of the earth without being on show, an exotic/odd ambassador traveling to Europe or North America as Yaa-Yaa finds out: "'Yes, girl,' says her inner voice, 'in this global village, nothing is the same for everyone: and that includes languages.... Especially language' the voice corrects itself" (30). "About the Wedding Feast" is the story, told from the grandmother's perspective, of the culinary preparations and animosities that arise on the occasion of her grand-daughter's wedding. Like Aidoo's second published novel, *Changes: A Love Story*, this *fefewo* centers on the private changes that have arisen in this new age, like the forgetting of traditional, past modes of behavior, or the rules of etiquette. Yet, in the telling of this story, the grandmother is as accomplished as the narrator of "In the Cutting of a Drink" from Aidoo's first collection of stories, *No Sweetness Here*. The apparent tone of resignation evidenced at the end of the grandmother's narrative, "What is food anyway? Once it goes down the throat" (Aidoo 1970:35), recalls Zigiru's final question: "... what does 'Independence' mean?" (Aidoo 1970:29). The pivotal narrative in the collection "Lice" is, as we have suggested, arguably the most depressing of the eleven. However, in so far as it charts the attempted suicide, infanticide, and near nervous breakdown of a young mother, Sissie, it is a narrative unrivaled for its emotional power and its ability to link this desperate moment to the reader's own life. The irony of the situation is that contrary to the internal claims of the narrative, "To end the news, these were the main headlines: 'President Reagan...'" (44); rather, the affirmation of life, Sissie's decision to bring "her left foot [down] on the glowing match" (44) is the real headline.

Where can we go from here? The stories that follow this plumbing of the depths of the human soul keep us on a trajectory that allows a fish-seller, the narrator of the next tale, to regain her sense of self-worth by exacting "Payment" from a wicked nurse and speaking in her own voice at her own pace. The *fefewo* is very similar to "Something to Talk About on the Way to the Funeral." "Maleing Names in the Sun" consists of a series of three interlocked tales which explore how the arbitrariness of historical events have such serious consequences. The *tolis* each explores the linguistic impact of the colonial encounter, the first struggle for independence and our declarations of autonomy at the century's end. "Choosing" continues the linguistic explorations in terms of a meta-critical narratological exploration of what it means to be a writer/storyteller.

The next *fefewo*, is told by a cleaner and is very close in tone and spirit to "For Whom Things Did Not Change"; but it becomes all the more poignant, because it occurs so long after the nominal, "flag" independence of mid-twentieth century Africa. Sadly, the issues are all too familiar as they have that familiar scent of human weakness to them. The cleaner, doing her job one evening, walks through the open door of her boss, the "Chief" to find, "on a couch somewhere near the centre of the room, there was this man on top of a woman..." (89)! It seems that the moral decay, the lack of propriety is just a symptom of the age. This so-called post-colonial, post-modern age only means that the doors which were once closed; or behind which we did as our biological natures might prompt; or from a more cynical perspective, the corruption that had always been practiced was now done without shame, because of these "Newly-Opened Doors." The final storytelling performance by the-Bird-Of-The-Wayside returns to our familiar protagonist, Sissie. In this narrative, we contemplate with Sissie, the significance of globalization on relationships. Sissie has to leave her home and family, not to explore "the blank of whiteness" (Odamtten 1994: 120), but to further her education. To be away from her children and her husband is a venture which encourages paranoia; yet, like Bertolt Bretcht's Mother Courage, Sissie willingly follows the logic of her life's choices. Sissie is recast as "Sweet Sister Courage" (101), because she is both like her Bretchtian model and much more. The problem of leaving family is not a matter to be taken lightly:

Hei, Hei, Hei
Sweet Sister Courage, hei:
Courage to welcome death who bears lives...
So that then are two or three years?
Isn't absence bearable for those who know the ultimate
Togetherness?

And time does fly so?
Hei, Hei, Hei

Maybe its courage is all, and for the rest,
grief is part of
the theatre? And tears are orgasmic?

Dear Mother Courage:
my mother silk.
Hei... ("No Where Cool," Aidoo 1996:76)

She is conscious of the conflictual relationships and the forces, historical and political, that have led her to this time and place. Unlike her former manifestations, this Sissie is confident, an African woman for the twenty-first century.

NOTES

1. See Vincent Odamtten, "For Her Own (Works') Quality': A Brief on the Poetry Of Ama Ata Aidoo," *Matatu*, Special Issue (forthcoming).
2. *Fefewo* is an Ewe word which signifies the totality of a storytelling event —both the performance *and* reception. See *The Art of Ama Ata Aidoo*, chapter three.
3. The most appropriate term, used by the African-American writer Gayl Jones, was quoted in "The Storyteller and the Audience in the works of Ama Ata Aidoo" by Mildred Hill-Lubin, *Neohelicon* 16, 2, (1989):221-245. Many of Hill-Lubin's conclusions about Aidoo's practice as a storyteller, are also reflected in *The Art of Ama Ata Aidoo*; although the latter arrives at those conclusions from a different perspective.
4. While most of the stories are narrated from the third person perspective of the omniscient Bird-Of-The-Wayside, four are first person narratives. What is also interesting about these latter narratives, is that Aidoo has arranged the order of the narratives so that they mirror each other (the 2nd, 5th, 7th, and 10th tales) as they pivot on either side of what is arguably the most depressing story in the collection: "Lice."
5. "She-Who-Would-Be-King," *Matatu* (Leiden, The Netherlands, Summer 1993); "Heavy Moments", *Soho Square* (Bloomsbury Publishing, London,

England, 1992); "Lice" was published for the first time as 'Loos' (in a Swedish translation in *Rapport* the in-house magazine of SIDA Goteburg, May 1986) and for the first time in English in *West Africa*, (London, England, March 1987):"The Girl Who Can" *MS Magazine* (New York, March 1985); "No Where Cool" was originally published in *Asemka*, a journal of the University of Cape Coast, Ghana 1974. This completely restructured version first appeared in *Callaloo* (1990); "Payments" was originally published as "Satisfaction?" in the English Department's *Departmental Workpapers* (University of Cape Coast, Ghana, 1971); and "Male-ing Names in The Sun" was a contribution to *Unbecoming Daughters of the Empire*, edited by Shirely Chew and Anna Rutherford. London/ Sydney/Aarhus: Dangaroo Press, February 1993.

WORKS CITED

Aidoo, Ama Ata. *An Angry Letter in January*. Coventry, U.K.: Dangaroo Press, 1992.

———. *The Dilemma of a Ghost and Anowa*. Harlow, U.K.:Longman, 1965, 1970, 1985, 1987.

———. *Our Sister Killjoy*. Harlow, U. K.: Longman, 1977, 1988.

———. *Someone Talking to Sometime*. Harare, Zimbabwe: College Press, 1985.

———.. *No Sweetness Here*. Harlow, U.K.: Longman, 1970; Garden City: Doubleday and Co., 1971.

———.. *The Girl Who Can And Other Stories*. Legon, Ghana: Sub-Saharan Publishers, 1996.

Hill-Lubin, Mildred. "The Storyteller and the Audience in the Works of Ama Ata Aidoo." *Neohelicon*. 16, 2 (1989):221-245.

Odamtten, Vincent O. *The Art of Ama Ata Aidoo: Polylectics and Reading Against Neocolonialism*, Gainesville, Fla.: University Press of Florida, 1994.

Photo 1: From left to right: Buchi Emecheta, Micere Mugo, Ama Ata Aidoo and Mildred Hill-Lubin, African Literature Association Annual Conference, 1988, University of Pittsburgh, Pennsylvania. *Photo by Naana Banyiwa Horne.*

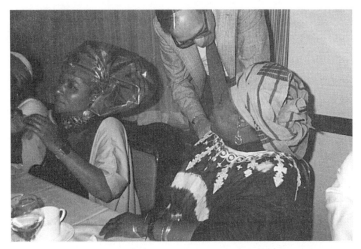

Photo 2:. Ama Ata Aidoo chats with a man from the audience after the Women Writers Plenary Session, African Literature Association Annual Conference, 1988, University of Pittsburgh, Pennsylvania. *Photo by Naana Banyiwa Horne.*

Photo 3: Ama Ata Aidoo relaxes at the end of the African Women Writers Plenary Session. *Photo by Naana Banyiwa Horne.*

Photo 4: A poster advertising the production of *The Dilemma of a Ghost*, African Literature Association Annual Conference, 1988, University of Pittsburgh, Pennsylvania. *Photo by Naana Banyiwa Horne.*

M

Photo 5: Ama Ata Aidoo on stage with the director/producer and cast of the Kuntu Repertory Theatre, following the performance of *The Dilemma of a Ghost*, University of Pittsburgh, Pennsylvania. *Photo by Naana Banyiwa Horne.*

Photo 6: Ama Ata Aidoo and the Caribbean writer Toni Martin at the Pan-African Book Fest sponsored by the African American Caribbean Cultural Arts Council, Community College North/Dale Campus, Miami, Florida, 1993. *Photo by Naana Banyiwa Horne.*

N

Photo 7: Ama Ata Aidoo, flanked on the left and right respectively by Vincent Okpoti Odamtten and Naana Banyiwa Horne, at a three-day conference sponsored by the Florida Humanities Council, the Santa Fe Community College, Gainesville, Florida, March 16–18, 1995.

Photo 8: After Ama Ata Aidoo's presentation at the 1995 Florida Humanities Council-sponsored talk, some members of the audience come forward for questions.

Photo 9: Ada Uzoamaka Azodo, Ama Ata Aidoo, and Katwiwa Mule at the 19th African Literature Association Annual Conference, Hauppauge, New York, March 27-30, 1996. *Photo by Aïssata Sidikou.*

Photo 10: Ada Uzoamaka Azodo, Ama Ata Aidoo, and Aïssata Sidikou at the 19th African Literature Association Annual Conference, Hauppauge, New York, March 27-30, 1996. *Photo by Katwiwa Mule.*

Photo 11: Ama Ata Aidoo and Ada Uzoamaka Azodo at the Yari Yari-Black Women Writers and the Future Conference, New York University, New York, October 15-18, 1997.

Photo 12: Ama Ata Aidoo acknowledges with humility and gratitude the standing ovation and loud applause, New York University, October 15-18, 1997. *Photo by Ada Uzoamaka Azodo.*

Photo 13: Ama Ata Aidoo and members of the roundtable on the craft, joys and travails of women writers of African descent in contemporary times, Yari Yari-Black Women Writers and the Future, New York University, New York, October 15-18, 1997. *Photo by Ada Uzoamaka Azodo.*

Photo 14: Gay Wilentz with Contributor Linda Strong-Leek, presenting at Stony Brook ALA on West African authors, Ama Ata Aidoo and Flora Nwapa

R

Part Four

AFRICAN WOMAN
AND RADICAL FEMINISM

THE LANGUAGE OF ENDURANCE
IN THE SHORT STORIES
OF AMA ATA AIDOO

PETER WILFRED STINE

In an appendix to *The Sound and Fury* added several years after the publication of the original text, William Faulkner (1956) includes long introductory descriptions of the members of the Compson family, that degenerate remnant of a once-proud Southern white family. When he comes to describe the Compsons' black servants, he uses fewer but kinder words. The very last character he considers is Dilsey, the Negro housekeeper, about whom he simply says, "They [she] endured." While the white family was thinning its ranks with suicide, incest, idiocy, and lack of issue, Dilsey (and her family) "endured"—she was strong, the bed rock of the household, the only one with a clear vision of the realities of life. Without using the same word "endure", Ama Ata Aidoo, from the collection *No Sweetness Here*, creates characters who surely "endure," who are survivors in the midst of poverty, travail, abandonment, disease, ostracism. The language Aidoo uses to describe them and their survival techniques give her readers clues about her intent and her support, especially as so many of her "endurers" are women.

For lack of better or more precise terms, we might divide the Aidoo survivors into "active" and "passive" endurers. The "active" endurers are often unattached younger women finding their way in post-colonial Ghana and the "new life"; the "passive" endurers are usually older, often from the villages, for whom life has not always been kind and gentle. A good example of a woman active in her destiny, whether we approve of her choices or not, is Mansa, the object of her brother's search in "In the Cutting of a Drink." The story is in the form of a monologue told upon his return home by a man who went to the city to find his wayward sister. He is telling this story to his uncles, aunts, and cousins, and he pauses from time to time to answer their objections or to address their questions, neither of which we hear stated. By leaving the entire narrative in the mouth of the seeking brother, Aidoo makes the story and our involvement in it more immediate. The language of the country-mouse brother seeking the city-mouse sister reveals his innocence, something his sister will have lost by the time he finds her. He admits to being surprised by things he sees: "I sat with my mouth open and watched the daughter of a woman cut beer like a man" (Aidoo 1995:34). The speaker, whose main function as narrator is so central that we never learn his name, is fascinated by life in the city bar and dances with one girl and then another. To the second, who speaks his dialect, he says, "Young woman is this the work you do? She claims not to understand him and when he persists with his moralizing, the harsh language of an active endurer breaks out: "And who are you to ask me such questions? I say, who are you? Let me tell you that *any kind of work is work*. You villager, you villager, who are you?" (36; my emphasis). The speaker asks if she knows him and she says, " I think you are my brother." The women to whom he is telling the story break into weeping at this point but he stops them. The language of "active endurance," of survival in the city, has convinced him for he tells his listeners, " What is there to weep about? I was sent to find a lost child. I found her a woman." It is a simple matter of economic expediency, he decides. " Any kind of work ... This is what Mansa told me with a mouth that looked like clotted blood. Any kind of work is work ... so do not weep. She will come home this Christmas" (37). Mansa has endured; she is a survivor. She may have defied the mores of her village and turned her back on her family and old friends, but she is "working" and her language is strong and even defensive but is that of one who has found a way to endure.

A second active "endurer" is Mercy, the younger sister in the story "Two Sisters." As the story opens, Mercy is frustrated: caught in an office job, living with her married sister and her family. She has men who would want her but they are poor and have little to offer. To tell this story, Aidoo again constructs a unique narrative mode, this time a mixture of first person by the sister and an omniscient narrator. We first hear Connie, the married sister, ruminating about her sister's contradictory finances and her new shoes: "And she said only last week that she didn't have a penny on her. And I believed her because I know what they pay her is just not enough to last anyone through any month, even minus rent ... I have been thinking she manages very well. But these shoes" (90). The shoes turn out to be a gift from an older man, well-placed in the government, and become then a symbol of this "active" endurance, this instinct for survival, which Aidoo gives so freely to her women characters.

Mercy may have a dull, low-paying job, but she has found a way to have new shoes and to get a ride in a nice car with "Mensar-Arthur." He is of parliamentary fame. Connie is not sure of the propriety of all this—she does not recognize it as survival but as sin; after all, their parents had been Presbyterians and she is sure that "running around with an old and depraved public man would have been considered an abomination by the parents" (93). James, her husband, on the other hand, thinks Mercy's approach to survival and self-employment is perfectly all right. He is much more pragmatic than his wife: "Since every other girl she knows has ruined herself prosperously, why shouldn't she? ... every morning her friends who don't earn any more than she does wear new dresses, shoes, wigs, and what-have-you to work. What would you have her do? (98). Things were going well: Mercy moved into a new apartment, Connie got a new washing machine motor, and James had the promise of a new car. Then came the coup, a nice touch by Aidoo to signify change. Where does this leave Mercy now that Mensar-Arthur is in jail for backing the wrong side? Never fear, this Mercy woman is a genuine "endurer," not to be deprived by a mere change in governments. As the story ends, Mercy stops by to visit Connie and James with a new boyfriend in town: Captain Ashey, an important figure in the new government. Connie makes one last desperate attempt to rescue her sister by humiliating her: "Wasn't there a picture in *The Crystal* over the weekend about his daughter's wedding? And another one of him with his wife and children and grandchildren?" (101). But Mercy simply answers "yes" and the story ends with the two sisters still in their separate worlds.

It may be objected that the two Aidoo women we have designated as "active endurers" have become so at the expense of conventional morality, that to Mansa and Mercy, "enduring" meant being an elegant whore, a kept woman who was no better than she should be. But Aidoo makes no such value judgment; she allows the women to rise above their circumstances to achieve material comfort without objection. She recognized that the economic position of most African women is precarious enough to warrant nearly any method or strategy available and gives them the strength to achieve what most others only dream about.

While these "active endurers" are enjoying some measure of material success because of their boldness and disregard for convention, it is those we will call the "passive endurers" who are the real heroines in Aidoo's stories. Here are people, usually middle-aged or older, mostly female [Kibira in "For Whom Things Did Not Change" may be an exception], who have been buffeted by the severe winds of life, have faced grief, loss, humiliation, and worse but have done so with a grace that is often a model for the younger people around them. The language of "passive endurance" is softer, less sharp, and less concerned with advancement than it is with survival. I have chosen three of Aidoo's women as examples of this inner strength, this ability to look adversity in the face without blinking: Amfoa in "The Message," Asana in "Certain Winds from the South," and Maami Ama in "No Sweetness Here," all of whom have learned the skills of enduring in the crucible of poverty and pain.

The first of these, Amfoa, is not entirely passive but reacts to a situation she does not completely understand with action and concern. If we are not careful, "The Message" could be read as a slightly comic story in which an old country grandmother, who does not understand the techniques of modern medicine, overreacts, but this reading would underestimate the story and its central figure. Amfoa's only child, a son, died in the white man's war and left a daughter for her to watch over. Since Amfoa was a woman "with whom infant mortality pledged friendship" (42), she has only her granddaughter who has now grown into womanhood and lives on the coast. As Amfoa hears it, she has been taken to the hospital, has been "opened up" (38), and has had her baby removed. This is the "message" of the title and is all Amfoa needs to know—she is off to see her only kin to claim her body if necessary, and to do what has to be done. She has lived long enough to know that death is never far away abut she will not leave her granddaughter's remains in the hands of those people from the Cape Coast. So off she goes. The driver of the truck who at first is reluctant to take her finally makes room for her. During the trip the determined lan-

guage of this "passive endurer" is expressed in an interior monologue:

> The scholar who read this telegram thing, said it was
> made about three days ago. God, that is too long ago.
> Have they buried her. . . . where? Or did they cut
> her up. . . . I should not think about it or something
> will happen to me. . . . ah, I hate this nausea. But it
> is the smell of petrol. Now I have remembered I
> never could travel in a lorry. I always was so sick.
> But now I hope that at least will not happen. These
> young people will think it is because I am old and
> they will laugh. At least if I knew the child of my
> child was alive, it would have been good. . . . I will
> give her that set of earrings, bracelet and chain
> which Adwumfo Ata made for me. It does not hurt
> me to think that I am going to die very soon. . . .
> Now, that is the end of me and my roots. . . . Eternal
> death has worked like a warrior rat, with diabolical
> sense of duty, to gnaw my bottom. Everything is fin-
> ished now. The vacant lot is swept and the scraps of
> old sugar-cane pulp dry sticks and bunches of hair
> burnt. . . . How it reeks the smoke! (42-43)

The story is in the traveling, the anticipation, and not in the arrival.
Amfoa arrives at the hospital certain that her grand daughter is
dead. We know better because we know what a Caesarian delivery
is, but the old lady does not. Even when she enters the room she
assumes her loved one is dead or, in one of Aidoo's metaphors, her
"last pot was broken." But it isn't and when the new mother spoke,
the now great-grandmother wept for joy. What if she was acting
like a villager, amusing and infuriating the hospital staff? Here was
a double endurance: the old and young women alike, made of the
same hard clay—the final sentence says it well and bears the mark
of this "passive endurance": "And by the bed the old woman was
trying hard to rise and look at the only pot which had refused to
get broken" (46).

In "Certain Winds from the South," one of Aidoo's most anthol-
ogized stories, another "passive endurer" rises from the hard soil of
the African village. The structure of the story is deceptively simple:
a woman has a late night visitor, her son-in-law, who has come to
tell her that he is leaving his wife and new baby to "go South" to find
work. She has had that experience before, with her own husband,

who left many years earlier, went South, then joined the army and never returned. She, M'ma Asana, now questions this new would-be wanderer with a directness which indicates she has been this way before and is suspicious of what is happening. When Issa, the son-in-law, inquires about the health of the ten-day-old son, she answers him appropriately: "Aah, my son. For what are you troubling yourself so much? Fuseni is a new baby who was born not more than ten days. How can I tell you he is very well? When a grown-up goes to live in other people's village ... will you say after the first few days that you are perfectly well?" (49). With this double entendre of going to another village which refers, of course, to the new arrival of the baby and to the move she is afraid her son-in-law might be making, M'ma Asana speaks the language of experience, of an endurer who has known this situation before and now recognizes abandonment, for the sake of work or even patriotism, for what it really is: abandonment. She still cannot, after all these years, understand why her husband had to go to fight in another peoples' war—she only understands that it left her alone with an infant and that now she is seeing this same scenario repeated. She has endured and must now use the language of that endurance to help her own daughter:

> Then the news [of her husband's death] came.... The news was like fire which settled in the pit of my belly. And from time to time, some would shoot up, searing my womb, singeing my intestines and burning up and up and up until I screamed with madness when it entered my head.
>
> I had told myself when you were born that it did not matter you were a girl, all gifts from Allah are good and anyway he was coming back and we were going to have many more children, lots of sons.
>
> Hawa, you had a lot of strength, for how you managed to live I do not know. Three days you were and suddenly like a rivulet that is hit by an early harmattan, my breasts were dry. . . . Hawa, you have a lot of strength.
>
> Later, they told me that if I could go South and prove to the government's people that I was his wife, I would get a lot of money.
>
> But I did not go. It was him I wanted, not his body turned into gold.
>
> I never saw the South. (54-55)

After this wrenching admission of sorrow and vulnerability, M'ma Asana knows what must come next, what has helped her endure all these years—a return to the routine of everyday life—and she does this in the paragraph with which Aidoo ends the story:

> I am going to the market now. Get up early to wash Fuseni. I hope to get something for those miserable colas. There is enough rice to make *tuo*, is there not? Good. Today even if it takes all the money, I hope to get us some smoked fish, the biggest I can find, to make us a real good sauce...." (55)

Taking refuge in the ordinary—going to market, selling colas—will be the key to their survival, and if Issa never returns, Hawa will become a passive endurer too, and will know the value of keeping life as stable and predictable as possible.

And finally, to the title story of Aidoo's collection, "No Sweetness Here," and to the plight of Maami Ama. Her son, Kwesi, was an ideal boy: good in sports, smart in school, and beautiful of face. He was clearly the apple of his mother's eye and a bright spot in Ama's life while she is in the midst of an ugly and acrimonious divorce. Chided and rejected by her husband's family, she depended on her handsome son for comfort and solace, even though he was only ten years old. There is, indeed, "no sweetness here," as witnessed by some of the things Maami says to the young school teacher who narrates the story. The language of endurance here is slightly bitter. When Chicha, the teacher, comments on Maami's fine colas, the farmer-woman replies: "Do you think so? Well, they're the best of the lot. My daughter, when life fails you, it fails you totally. One's yams reflect the sum total of one's life. And mine looks wretched enough" (59). Again, her bitterness spills over: "You don't know, but I've been the topic of gossip for many years. Now, I only want to live on my own looking after my child. I don't think I will ever get any more children. Our people say a bad marriage kills the soul. Mine is ready for burial" (62). Aidoo, at this point, brings in Kwesi and his mother's bitterness ceases: "All at once, for the care-worn village woman, the sun might well have been rising from the east instead of setting behind the coconut palms. Her eyes shone" (63).

And so Maami Ama's life goes: the weariness of the farm and the rancor of her husband is set aside by the presence of Kwesi, the beautiful boy. All the humiliation heaped on her by her mother's sisters who wanted the jewelry her mother had given her; all the name calling her husband's family insisted on whenever they saw her—all this she was able to endure as long as she had Kwesi. But then one day—and it seems as if Aidoo is giving Maami Ama an unbearable load—while playing football at school, Kwesi was bitten by a snake and, in spite of everyone's efforts, died, the first boy to die in the six-year history of the school. And the village all knew: "he was his mother's only child. She has no one now? We do not understand it. Life is not sweet" (71). The language of her endurance had been the expressions of her love for her son. But what will she do now? Aidoo does not tell us that for we see her last wearing the same dress she had worn to the divorce proceedings, kneeling "like one drowning" (74), clutching Kwesi's books and school uniform to herself. Our hope is that she has learned the way of endurance in this less than sweet world and she will, in spite of her great loss, survive and endure. We can only wish that this would be the case; Aidoo gives us no clue except the modes of endurance which all or most of her women seem to have.

And so the "language of endurance" takes many forms—bitter, sharp, defensive, patient, even hopeful. The tension between just surviving and enduring is clear in Aidoo's short stories for her women are strong and either in their active seeking to change things and make their lives better, or passively accepting what comes their way with steadiness and strength we have examined here. They are good models on how to avoid being swallowed by situation and ravaged by circumstances. It is usually the young women who are "active" in their endurance, eager to cut new paths, to make their own destiny even if it means to ignore conventional morality. And Aidoo recognizes that this new generation of African women have ways of their own to deal with the demands of life. However, it is clear that Aidoo's deepest affection is reserved for what we have called the "passive endurers," those older women hardened by time and circumstance, who have looked life directly in the face and have not wavered. It is they who speak the language of perseverance and survival, who are anchors of their families and the inspiration of their children. They are, although they would not recognize this, true role models and their appearance in Aidoo's short stories give us reason to be optimistic about the tenacity of the human spirit. They help us to see that we, too, can endure.

WORKS CITED

Aidoo, Ama Ata. *No Sweetness Here.* New York: CUNY, The Feminist Press, 1993.

Faulkner, William. *The Sound and Fury.* New York: Random House Press, 1956.

AFRICAN WOMAN'S DOMAIN:

DEMARCATING POLITICAL SPACE IN

NWAPA, SUTHERLAND AND AIDOO

GAY WILENTZ

There is a tradition in West African literature, beginning with the earliest (male) writers such as Achebe and Laye, to try to recreate (no matter how different the approach) an African historical past before the colonizers, and by doing this, to somehow strip away the biases and prejudices of the presentation of African cultures through the eyes of the colonizers who had, according V. Y. Mudimbe, "invented" it. And some of the first women writing in English in West Africa—Flora Nwapa, Efua Sutherland, and Ama Ata Aidoo—were also involved in a reclamation project, but one that critiqued both the colonizers and their own male contemporaries. What exactly was precolonial women's political domain and to what extent had colonial constructions of womanhood transformed the role of women in a postcolonial world? Early works by these writers examined the role of women within African historical space—exploring the role of women in their recently postcolonial world and in certain cases revisioning the past as to make their present viable, stripping away the colonial representations of womanhood. They also investigated the double-bind they found themselves in as women in the postcolonial era, and looked to the past for answers in demarcating African women's domain for the present.

From the early works in the 1960s until the writings of the '80s and '90s, the challenge of development and women's role in the political space of the (re)new(ed) West African nations remain a question. This essay is intended to examine this original project for demarcating African women's political domain, and then interrogate the changes in the writings of two of these authors, Nwapa and Aidoo, in more recent novels *One is Enough* and *Changes: A Love Story*. To do this, I examine the role of the younger woman in relation to her mothers, including grandmothers and older women, within the context of an African family and community. This relationship tells us a great deal not only about the position of women in a West African community, but also the contradictions in reconceptualizing women's role contemporarily. What is significant about this project is that these women writers do not leave us with a simple glorification of an African past, nor is their interest in the position of the precolonial woman "nostalgic": the aim of these writers is to somehow find a usable past in which to inform the present—a present, as we see with the most recent works, which has become increasingly more complicated in demarcating women's political domain.

It may be useful at this juncture to define my use of the term "political" within an African context, and present some background on the public role of women in a precolonial setting. I use the term "political" in the broadest sense of the word, connoting the range of women's roles—from citizens within a West African community, who affect the society's values and traditions, to a contemporary notion of women's space in the public sphere. From the more conventional role of women within the public arena of an Africa community and the religious life of her people, to the undocumented village women storytellers who educate and initiate future generations into the culture, women have played a major role in the formulation of the community, since they have not merely maintained the culture but often reformed it. As Filomina Chioma Steady contends in *The Black Woman Cross-Culturally*, "The woman ... represents the ultimate value in (African) life, namely the continuation of the group" (Steady 1981:32). And her service in continuing the group is intellectual, spiritual, and political as well as physical. In these matrifocal societies, women's place in the community is assessed in terms of "cultural elaboration and valuation as well as the structural centrality of mother roles" (Tanner 1974: 154). A West African adage goes, "If you educate a man, you educate an individual. If you educate a woman, you educate a nation." This concept, tied to the elaborate structure of a family compound in West Africa, attests to the predominance of woman's position as a political being in both family and community life.

Historically and today, a woman's function in the compound extends to the entire village communal life, but there have been changes which have limited women's roles as citizens in their own right. The balanced interrelationship between the woman and her community was disrupted during colonialism and that disruption has added to women's present-day second class citizenship. Niara Sudarkasa, in "Female Employment and Family Organization in West Africa," examines a precolonial system which, although male-dominated, incorporated women's power:

> "In traditional West Africa the compound was usually the unit of political organization... Thus wives, mothers, sisters, or daughters could exert direct political influence over males, or they themselves could play important roles by virtue of their position of authority, power or influence in their natal or affinal compounds." (Sudarkasa 1981:53)

Furthermore, in her well-researched study of Igbo women, *Male Daughters, Female Husbands*, Ifi Amadiume details not only the civic position of women within this West African society, but also the erosion of women's political domain with the advent of colonialism. However, not to reify this precolonial position, the relationship within the community was dialectical and remains so, framed by male privilege in precolonial Africa as well as the further restrictions imposed by colonialism and neo-colonialism.

Nwapa's *Efuru* (1966), Sutherland's *Foriwa* (1967), and Aidoo's *Dilemma of a Ghost* (1965) all focus on women's position in their West African communities. Since I have written in-depth about these three novels elsewhere,[1] I use these works cursorily to represent a view of African women at the beginning of the postcolonial moment and to situate the changes in the position of women in the contemporary works by Nwapa and Aidoo. In each of these works, there is a primary relationship between an older "mother" figure (who is not necessarily a biological mother), and her "daughter" that leads toward a resolution of conflict, and at times, a reinterpretation and acceptance of the traditional culture. In *Efuru*, Efuru's biological mother is dead, and some of her problems, especially in regards to her two worthless husbands, has been connected to that fact. However, Nwapa presents an almost precolonial African community, in which the mothering role is taken over by others in the community, because as the Igbo say: "The rearing of a child is not a job for one person nor is a child a child for only one person" (Okonjo 1984:1). For Efuru, whose mother is dead, other women including her first mother-in-law Ossai, her neighbors, and her first husband's aunt and confidante, Ajanupu, take on the role of familial teacher and prepare her for being a community mother to the next generation. In this novel, Efuru's most significant mother figure is Ajanupu. It is she who explains the ways of the community to Efuru in a beneficial way, unlike some others in Nwapa's fictionalized Oguta. She continues her role of mothering, even after Efuru has remarried, and she helps Efuru to work through her often problematic relationship with the community. Ajanupu stands up against second husband Gilbert's accusation that Efuru has been adulterous and supports Efuru as a mother would. This relationship, among others of the community, strengthens Efuru to take on a role in the public sphere as Uhamiri's worshipper and, by the end of the novel, Efuru is reintegrated into the community politic.

Although Nwapa presents the learning relationship of community mother-daughter as one aspect of women's citizenship in the West African communal world in which she was raised, Efua Sutherland, in *Foriwa*, poses the mother-daughter relationship in a more overtly politicized way. In this case, the relationship is between actual mother and daughter, but this short, activist play unmistakably addresses their political connection. *Foriwa* addresses the issue of disintegrating rural communities and the breakdown of traditional structures in developing African states, an issue which is still as relevant today. Sutherland, like her fellow Ghanaian Aidoo, centers in on women's role in nation-building in the process of decolonization. *Foriwa* demarcates this role of the African woman, identifying the place of generational continuity in the new African nation-states, the postcolonial world. In this regard, Sutherland's play functions at the time as an educational tool to unite traditional customs and modern technology through the collective process of a West African community.

Through the joined forces of the Queen Mother and her daughter Foriwa, along with the people of the decaying town of Kyerefaso, Sutherland designs an African-based development plan to revitalize rural communities and reconnects the traditional past with future generations. Relevant to this discussion, it is the resolution between the Queen Mother, who is desperate about the condition of her community, and the daughter that brings in the new life, that revives the town. The climax of the play is the revitalization of an important traditional festival, a ceremony of "New Life." The Queen Mother, with the help of her daughter Foriwa, decides to conduct a mock ceremony to point out how far the town has strayed from the original intent of the ceremony and the traditions. The reforming of the ceremony to awaken Kyerefaso to the real meaning of the festival reflects Sutherland's aim to arouse the audience so that they, too, will work to revitalize their own communities. Although Foriwa, the educated daughter, brings new ideas and is instrumental in the inclusion of the stranger Labaran (a Hausa from Northern Ghana, symbolizing the involvement of all Ghanaians in developing the country), the Queen Mother functions as a political and social leader for her daughter and the community, directing generations of young women to follow. In this way, Sutherland documents African women's unique contribution at an important juncture in postcolonial nation-building. The resolution at the end of *Foriwa* offers a positive statement which joins mother and daughter, young and old, tradition and technology in the possible future of contemporary African communities.

Ama Ata Aidoo, in her first published work, *The Dilemma of a Ghost*, blends her own version of nation-building and the position of women within an Akan community, integrating Nwapa's attention to traditional women's practices with Sutherland's activism. Furthermore, she connects the situation of the educated African "been-to" with the dilemma of the diaspora. Although the mother-daughter relationship in *The Dilemma of a Ghost* is both transatlantic and mother-daughter-*in-law*, Aidoo's play also offers a positive portrait of women's role in the political life of her community. Significantly, it portrays how one imparts traditions to those daughters lost in the slave trade. All of Aidoo's work demarcates the political nature of women's position within a Ghanaian community, and *Dilemma* is no exception. Even though she is quick to criticize male dominance in both traditional and contemporary society, Aidoo is equally clear about the political role women played in Akan society. In a recent interview, Aidoo comments that Akan society was/is "one of the most matriarchal societies in

West Africa," and states further: "Women were everything: they were supposed to hold the power.... Yet when a priestess had her period she couldn't approach her own shrine" (Maja-Pearce 1990: 17). As she demonstrates in *Anowa*, women's position in precolonial Akan society was a contested space, yet Aidoo also (re)places Eurocentric feminist bias in historical context.

Although not as overtly as in *Our Sister Killjoy*, the women in *Dilemma of a Ghost*, Esi Kom and the grandmother Nana, for instance, illustrate the powerful place of women in matrilineal Akan culture. The relationship between Esi Kom, her daughter Monka, and Nana exemplify a generational continuity that demarcates women's political position in the Yawson clan. In this regard, we see a working together of mother/daughter/grandmother, which is disputed in the later work, *Changes*. However, the most stimulating dynamic in the play is that between the Black American Eulalie and Esi Kom, since this conflict-resolution makes a major statement concerning women's polemical role in healing the rift of the diaspora. Although Esi is initially antagonistic to Eulalie, she (re)integrates Eulalie into the community. Esi Kom, by the end of the play, accepts Eulalie, and it is implied that Eulalie will gain a place among the women of the community (signified by the sympathies of the First Woman narrator). In the final confrontation between Esi Kom and her son Ato, the play clearly marks out a stand for African womanhood, the return of the lost daughters of the diaspora, and the importance of African family organization and communal values. The reconciliation of Esi Kom and Eulalie reflects not only a coming home for those in the diaspora, but clearly identifies in Esi's words and behavior a political act, reversing what Aidoo calls Africa's "amnesia" concerning its role in the Slave Trade.

Although I have not gone into the more problematic relationships set up in the '70s by Aidoo in *Anowa* or the many works of Buchi Emecheta[2]—nor are the examples I have cited here uncomplicated—I employ these first works to illustrate a positive view of the role of women envisioned for the postcolonial world. In each of the examples, there appears a resolution, a coming to terms of the postmodern situation and the traditional community, through the act and transmission of generational continuity. However, by considering two later novels—Nwapa's *One is Enough* (1981) and Aidoo's *Changes: A Love Story* (1991),[3] we witness, through the "changes" intimated in Aidoo's title, a larger challenge to questions of generational continuity and women's political domain in a so-called "liberated" environment. Obioma Nnaemeka, in a recent article on Nwapa, comments: "Feminists critics of African litera- ture focus primarily on where rebellious women liberate them- selves from, but it is equally, if not more, important to examine the politics of location that determine where they liberate themselves into" (Nnaemeka 1995:92). In *One is Enough* and *Changes: A Love Story*, Nwapa and Aidoo present a different picture of African woman's political domain, which resists the reconciliation between generations seen in the earlier works. In the rest of this essay, I interrogate some of the contradictions uncovered in these two nov- els of liberated African women of the '80s and '90s.

One is Enough, written in Nwapa's middle period, after she left Heinemann to start Tana Press, reflects many of the same concerns of both *Efuru* and *Idu*, but in an urban contemporary setting. The novel takes place after independence and the Biafran war, and it identifies many of the problems of postcolonial Nigeria. The main character, Amaka, like her predecessors, is a strong, competent woman, good at business, but is childless and in a marriage that restricts her. After being basically thrown out of her home in Onitsha by her mother-in-law, Amaka decides to give up on mar- riage and move to Lagos. Her life in Lagos details her rise to power as she turns her skills in the "attack trade" developed during the war to gain business "contracts" in the capitalism-gone-wild world of postcolonial Nigeria, and in the process, finally becomes preg- nant by seducing a priest. However, she decides that one husband is enough, and like Efuru, Amaka ends up alone and independent— although, in this case, less conflicted than her predecessor.

Amaka is a modern African woman, taking both from the tra- ditional role of the market women and a modern-day lifestyle of capital supply-and-demand business. However, there is an inher- ent problem attached to her individual rise to power and inde- pendence: What does Amaka's personal success mean to the growth and health of her nation? To what extent can there be female liberation when it is gained at the cost of the community? Nwapa, in *One is Enough*, clearly demonstrates that in a postcolo- nial setting, the politics of African women's cultural production is turned on its head, and the concept of generational continuity and women's political domain is transformed.

What I find especially ironic here is that, in the novel, indi- vidual advancement at the expense of the society in general is the complete reversal of what 'Zulu Ṣọfọla remarked about the basic tenets of an African community and one's responsibility to it: "One can object (follow one's individual notions) but not so far as to destroy the fiber of the society" (Wilentz 1984). Through the characters' actions, Nwapa demonstrates that the tenets that held together communities or clans do not seem to work in terms of an individual's commitment to the postcolonial nation. In her rise to power, Amaka thinks little about the fiber of her society and does what everyone else around her in Lagos is doing: she gets enormous kick-backs from government contracts. Like most of the men and women she meets in Lagos, she never questions the fact that the projects for the communities are done at exorbitant rates, or are paid for twice, or are paid for and not done at all! However, unlike Achebe's *A Man of the People*, there appears to be no authorial condemnation of these acts. As one of her first conquests in Lagos, Amaka begins dealing with an Alhaji, whom she meets through her sister's lover, a Permanent Secretary. They happily use each other: she gives him sex; he gives her contracts. At this same time, she has met Father McLaid (Izu, also an Igbo from Eastern Nigeria) through her friends, Mike and Adaobi. Realizing his attraction to her, she aims to seduce him for both fun and profit. As part of their affair (although in this case, they actually have feelings for each other), he also uses his power to secure her military contracts. In one incident, before she has wised up and still thinks that people get paid to do work, Amaka is given a half-million naira contract by Father McLaid to build a wall around some military barracks. When she arrives at the barracks, she sees the wall already erected. She asks one of the Brigadier's staff if she has made a mistake: "He told her that she must be foolish to talk that way. She should just send her bill for payment. Was she the only one who did not know what was going on? If she had met the Brigadier, he would just take the contract from her and give it to another person"(Nwapa 1992c:82). As she leaves, Amaka realizes she has just received 25% of a half-million naira for doing nothing (we wonder where the other 75% went), and we are told: "Amaka had finally arrived" (82).

Without authorial comment, there are few voices of resistance in the novel. One example of resistance in this world of individual achievement at the expense of society is Mike, the husband of Amaka's friend and contract-getter Adaobi. He is a civil servant who is honest and does not take bribes; however, he is hardly perceived as a hero in the novel. First of all, he is seen as a chauvinist who does not want his wife to succeed the way that Amaka has. Second, as in the above quote by the unnamed military official,

Mike is clearly identified as a "fool" for his attachment to values of honesty and integrity in his work. More significant, however, is the voice of Amaka's mother, who presents an alternative view to Amaka's. As in other Nwapa novels, the elder women often function as "custodians of the 'custom'" (Arhin 1983:94). And in this novel, Amaka's mother maintains this role in the family. The clash of traditional values versus the contemporary lack of values (except in terms of individual achievement) is exhibited throughout the novel by the conflict between Amaka and her mother. Early in the novel, Amaka is aware of the changes in attitudes with increasing Westernization and Christianity. She laments the loss of an earlier time period, when men respected the work of their wives, when her mother and mother's mother knew who they were in society: "Times changed, and men began to assert their masculinity over their industrious wives" (19). Amaka does not want the life of her mother, yet finds her own path unclear. Amaka's thinking reflects her confusion about her own role as well as her mother's less contradictory world-view. Amaka is stuck in her contemporary, Westernized lifestyle, yet is plagued by her inability to have a child to keep her marriage successful. The Western "ambition" of keeping a husband as the supreme success of female existence is an alien notion to her mother, despite what others of her "people" say:

> But Amaka knew from the behavior of her *illiterate* aunt and mother that they did not share in this belief of her people. Her mother brought them up to be independent, but she did not emphasize marriage. She had several children no doubt, but her emphasis was on self-determination and motherhood. She lacked the guts to ask her *formidable* mother how she was going to have children without being married. (26; my emphasis)

This passage not only demonstrates the transition from consanguineal to conjugal relations in this postcolonial society, but also the contradictions in respect to the elder women's knowledge. Simultaneously, Amaka perceives her mother and aunt as "illiterate" (a term that is fairly loaded) while, at the same time, her mother appears to Amaka—as fitting to her position in the community—as "formidable." Amaka, as well as her sister Ayo, pay deference to their mother's power and knowledge, yet at the same time, they see her as not comprehending the world of Lagos. However, through the fight between Amaka and her mother over whether she should marry Izu after the birth of her twins, Nwapa raises questions concerning the refusal of these "modern" women to value the voice of the elder generation's knowledge of the past.

On a cursory level, one might say that her mother is not only giving Amaka bad advice (to marry Izu even though Amaka is through with husbands), but also going against her own earlier advice—not to worry about a husband since the most important thing is to have a child, no matter what. However, in interrogating this section more carefully, we see the mother as not only defending the traditional values of family alliances, but more importantly, standing up for personal responsibility, a moral code lost in the world in which Amaka lives. Amaka's mother scolds her: "Amaka, did you not know he was a priest of God when you slept with him? He was only good as a lover, as a man who arranged contracts for you, and not good enough to be your husband?" (147). The mother, who grew up in a very different cultural setting, is frustrated in trying to determine what values to pass on to the next generation.

By the end of the novel, Amaka in some way replicates a more traditional role since she is a citizen in her own right and has extricated herself from a Western-style conjugal relationship. Nevertheless, the basic problem in the novel remains: Can we really see Amaka as a fully realized person if her self-determination as a woman and her public status is at the expense of the greater good of the society? There is a sense that the mother has a strength of purpose and vision that is not evident in either of the daughters. And despite the novel's apparent happy ending, we are left with an uneasy feeling about women's political domain and what kinds of values will be passed on to the next generation. While living in Nigeria during the Buhari coup d'etat and regime, I asked Nwapa after finishing the novel about the conflicts in the portrait of Amaka, and she responded characteristically: "Well, it is Amaka's story and it is her own story. There are many people who do this in our society. If the evils are relevant to the stories I am telling, I will include them; it does not mean I approve of it" (Wilentz 1984). For those of us who are more polemical in our creative writings and criticism, Nwapa's remarks are disturbing while resonating a certain truth. As in all of her works, Nwapa presents solely how women negotiate their positions in society; it is up to us as readers to make our own judgments.

Aidoo, a much more activist writer, is also more overt about the contradictions of the modern, "liberated" African woman and what has been lost in women's contemporary political space.

Aidoo's now famous opening "confession/apology" to the reader and critic of *Changes: A Love Story* is that she could never write about "lovers in Accra. Because surely in our environment there are more important things to write about." However, as we read the novel, her comment appears to be somewhat tongue-in-cheek. For it is here, at the most intimate of personal relations—love between man and woman—that Aidoo critiques the ironies in the changes in the neo/postcolonial world of the African nation-state since independence. In her interview with Maja-Pearce, Aidoo describes the irony of the present relationship with the West: "They shoved their language down our throats, we are wearing their clothes, driving their cars...They didn't come to understand us and [that] definitely had very negative results and effects on contemporary African women" (Maja-Pearce 1990:17).Therefore, if, in the novel, Aidoo challenges the continual loss of women's public space through the personal act of love and the community act of marriage, certainly she once again compels us to see exactly how the political is personal within an African context.

Esi, the protagonist of *Changes*, is the epitome of the modern African woman. She has a high-powered job, a husband and child, and is an independent woman. But she is not satisfied, to the astonishment of her mother and grandmother who conscribe marriage and family alliance in very different terms. In a rather contentious debate between grandmother and granddaughter, Nana keeps asking Esi what her husband Oko has done to her that she would want to leave him. They do not understand Esi's inarticulateness about her problem, since neither accept "not being happy" as a real issue. As the generations clash, the two women look at Esi as if she is insane. Finally, the grandmother tells her that she would not talk about it anymore, since "the matter sounded too much for her ears," and Esi's mother calls her "a fool" (Aidoo 1991:38-39). This scene poses a direct contrast to the mother/daughter/grandmother relationship presented in Aidoo's *Dilemma of a Ghost*. Unlike the earlier play, which wrestled with how to bring into the clan the lost daughter of the diaspora, this novel focuses on how lost the African daughters are. Esi, caught up in her Western, individualized lifestyle, does not listen to what her mothers are saying to her, breaking down that interrelationship developed over centuries. Despite their objections, Esi leaves her husband Oko, and ends up becoming a second wife to her lover, Ali Kondey, hence the "love story" subtitle of the novel. However, under the guise of a rather Euro-romantic narrative is an in-depth exploration of Nnaemeka's implied question stated earlier: "What are these women liberating themselves into"? In the interview already mentioned, Aidoo constantly challenges the notion that the "emergence into the modern world" actually helped women's position in Ghana (Maja-Pearce 1990:17), and this view is fictionalized in the novel.

Throughout *Changes*, the voice of the grandmother remains the voice of reason, and she questions the actions of everyone in this romantic farce of the second-time-around. In a recent essay, "Literature, Feminism, and the African Woman Today," Aidoo observes that in *Changes*, Nana "epitomises this capacity that the African woman has always had to formulate clear and critical opinions in order that she would understand her position and be able to deal with it" (Aidoo 1996:2). Ironically, Esi has lost this capacity, and her disastrous second marriage and inability to deal with her life are proof of this. Both her mother and grandmother try to convince Esi that there is no benefit in being a second wife, but Esi, caught in the contested space of contemporary relations, is again resistant to their advice and even incapable of dealing with her own misgivings. Her grandmother, in trying to explain things to her, notes in a voice that reflects a more cohesive world-view how it "used to be possible to talk and know that you and everyone else knew what you were talking about" (109). But in a world where language has been transformed by the remnants of a colonizing presence, there appears to be no way to continue any kind of helpful generational continuity. As Esi hears her mother and grandmother speaking to each other about her, Esi's lament connects with a larger political protest:

> "She could never be as close to her mother as her mother was to her grandmother...Why had they sent her to school...with no hope of ever meaningfully re-entering her mother's world...all this was too high a price to pay to achieve the dangerous confusion she was now in and *the country was now in.*" (114, my emphasis)

Here is where Aidoo ties in the romantic story with questions of how to live in this confused postcolonial world. Esi's own conflicts are further mirrored by her first co-wife, Fusena, who is forced into the arrangement as well (107). Moreover, Esi's inability to continue traditions handed down from mother to daughter is shown painfully here in the lack of a relationship with her own daughter, whom she mostly ignores. Esi, isolated from both the women before her and her own biological daughter, lives a lonely life in a miserable second marriage. The climax of this alienated life that she has chosen comes during the first holiday she spends alone. Ali is with his family, and her daughter Ogyaanowa has no particular interest in spending the holidays with her mother. She thinks that there is "no sense in taking a child from a house and a neighborhood full of children to the 'cemetery' that was where she lived" (142). Although she perceives her sterile life as one situated in a graveyard, Esi cannot even go home to her village to be with her own family, so ashamed is she of her predicament. So what is Esi's response? One well-known within the context of middle-class suburbia that her life has somehow inadvertently mirrored: "tranquilizers for her nerves." Aidoo adds, "Like any member of the late twentieth-century African and other world female elite and neo-elite, she had always known of tranquilizers" (143). Clearly, the treatment for her malaise is well prescribed among her class group. However, it is not how her grandmother might have dealt with her problem, with "clear and critical" analysis and opinions. Drugged up and miserable, Esi's life is quickly becoming something out of a melodramatic romance novel rather than the "love story" the subtitle suggests.

Changes: A Love Story, ironically titled, ends in stasis. Esi learns to live with her unhappy existence because she cannot bear the idea of going back to her grandmother and the village. The only answer they would have for her would be a "trip to the priestess" to find out "what it was that she really desired from this life" (Aidoo 1991:165). As readers, we may wonder why she finds that option so distasteful, since her other modes of interpreting her life have failed. Yet, we understand that to return to the village also signifies a kind of failure for Esi; therefore, she is caught without a way to discern the solutions to her contemporary problems. The ending of the novel leaves these questions of what values and traditions to pass on unresolved for Esi and her nation, but earlier on, she makes a prophetic comment. After listening to her grandmother and mother talk to her, she realizes that she cannot answer all the questions of her life and her nation by herself. She envisions a collective response, based on her community: "Hopefully a whole people would soon have answers for them. In the meantime, she would listen to her grandmother" (115). Unfortunately, Esi does not connect this comment to what her grandmother and the foremothers of her community have to tell her, and ironically, Esi winds up in precisely the bad situation her grandmother warned her about. In this novel, Aidoo clearly links listening to the grandmothers to the fate of a nation, but in this rather depressing, unresolved ending, she does not give us any clear-cut answers on how to proceed.

The contradictions of these two works—one of a successful modern woman who is in the process of helping destroy rather than rebuild her nation, and the other of a superwoman who is miserable because, despite ostensible changes, nothing much has really changed—leaves us with more questions than answers concerning women's contemporary political domain. Nwapa's last novel, *The Lake Goddess*, presents a kind of return to the voices that have guided the community, but *Changes*, Aidoo's most recent novel, complicates the voice that in earlier novels demarcated women's role as part of a community with traditions. Although the desire to reconnect to the past in order to understand the future is clearly not a nostalgic aim, the actuality of how to continue generational continuity in a postcolonial setting appears to exist in a domain without demarcations.

NOTES

1. For a fuller discussion of these three works, see the first half of *Binding Cultures: Black Women Writers in Africa and the Diaspora* (Wilentz 1992).
2. Although Buchi Emecheta has written extensively on women's role in West African societies, her vision is that traditional society was as restrictive towards women as the colonial one. In this regard, her vision is quite different from the three women writers I analyze in the beginning of this essay. For her view, see, for example, *The Slave Girl* and *The Joys of Motherhood*, whose title is an allusion to Nwapa's *Efuru* .
3. I am unable to create a perfect parallel structure in this essay because there is no correlating work by Efua Sutherland, who died in 1995. However, her powerful vision of mothers and daughters working together to improve their society, and the clear political domain of the Queen Mother in *Foriwa* led me to include this relevant work, nonetheless.

WORKS CITED

Achebe, Chinua. *A Man of the People*. London: Heinemann, 1966.

Aidoo, Ama Ata. *Changes: A Love Story*. New York: CUNY, The Feminist Press, 1991.

———. *The Dilemma of a Ghost* and *Anowa*. London: Longman, 1965.

———."Literature, Feminism, and the African Woman Today." African Literature Association Conference, Stony Brook, N.Y.: March 1996.

———. *Our Sister Killjoy: Or Reflections from a Black-Eyed Squint*. London: Longman, 1970.

Amadiume, Ifi. *Male Daughters, Female Husbands: Gender and Sex in an African*

Society. Atlantic Highlands, N.J.: Zed Books, 1987.

Arhin, Kwame. "The Political and Military Role of Akan Women."*Female and Male in West Africa*. Ed. Christine Oppong. London: George Allen, 1983: 92-98.

Emecheta, Buchi. *The Joys of Motherhood*. New York: Brazillier, 1979.

———. *The Slave Girl*. London: Allison and Busby, 1977.

Maja-Pearce, Adewale. "We Were Feminists in Africa First." Interview with Ama Ata Aidoo. *Index on Censorship* 19,9 (October 1990): 17-18.

Mere, Ada. "The Unique Role of Women in Nation Building." Unpublished paper, University of Nigeria, Nsukka, 1984.

Mudimbe, V. Y. *The Invention of Africa*. Bloomington: Indiana Univ. Press, 1988.

Nnaemeka, Obioma. "Feminism, Rebellious Women and Cultural Boundaries: Rereading Flora Nwapa and her Compatriots." In: "Special Issue: Flora Nwapa." Eds. Chikwenye Okonjo-Ogunyemi and Marie Umeh. *Research in African Literatures* 26.2 (1995): 80-113.

Nwankwo, Chimalum. "The Igbo World in Flora Nwapa's Work." In: "Special Issue: Flora Nwapa." Eds. Chikwenye Okonjo-Ogunyemi and Marie Umeh. *Research in African Literatures* 26.2 (1995): 42-52.

Nwapa, Flora. *Efuru*. Trenton, N.J.: Africa World Press, 1992a (1966).

———. *Idu*. Trenton, N.J.: Africa World Press, 1992b. (1970).

———. *One is Enough*. Trenton, N.J.: Africa World Press, 1992c. (1981).

———. *The Lake Goddess*. Trenton, N.J.: African World Press, 1995.

———. Personal Interviews. Enugu and Oguta, Nigeria: March - July 1984.

Ogunyemi-Okonjo, Chikwenye, and Marie Umeh. Eds. *Research in African Literatures*. "Special Issue: Flora Nwapa" 26,2 (1995).

Okonjo, Kamene. "The Place of Decision-Making in the Rural Igbo Family." Unpublished paper, University of Nigeria, 1984.

Oppong, Christine. Ed. *Female and Male in West Africa*. London: George Allen, 1983.

Sofola, 'Zulu. Personal Interviews. Ibadan, Nigeria: Feb 23 and June 16, 1984.

Steady, Filomina Chioma, Ed. *The Black Woman Cross-Culturally*. Boston: Schenkman, 1981.

Sudarkasa, Niara. "Female Employment and Family Organization in West Africa." In: *The Black Woman Cross-Culturally*. Ed. Filomina Chioma Steady. Boston: Schenkman, 1981. 49-64.

Sutherland, Efua. *Foriwa*. Accra: Ghana Publishing, 1967.

Tanner, Nancy. "Matrifocality in Indonesia and Africa and Among Black Americans." In: *Women, Culture and Society*. Eds. Michelle Rosaldo and Louise Lamphere. Stanford: Stanford Univ. Press, 1974. 129-56.

Wilentz, Gay. *Binding Cultures: Black Women Writers in Africa and the Diaspora*. Bloomington: Indiana Univ. Press, 1992.

———. "Flora Nwapa." In: *Twentieth Century Caribbean and Black African Writers: Dictionary of Literary Biography*. Ed. Bernth Lindfors and Reinhard Sanders. Columbia, S.C.: Bruccoli Clark Layman, 1993:178–184.

FLABBERWHELMED OR TURNING HISTORY ON ITS HEAD?

THE POSTCOLONIAL WOMAN-AS-SUBJECT IN

AIDOO'S *CHANGES: A LOVE STORY*

JULIANA MAKUCHI NFAH-ABBENYI

[The colonisers] shoved their languages down our throats . . .
they didn't come to understand us and definitely had very negative results and effects on contemporary African women. Ours has been the double quarrel. Not only as Africans but also as women. Colonised by the coloniser, then by our men, with their new power . . . .

-Ama Ata Aidoo, *In Their Own Voices*

Feminist critics of African literature have in the last decade been critical, and rightly so, of the stereotypical representations of African women either on the one hand, as voiceless, silenced victims, in short, as objects; or on the other hand, as Mother Earth,

Mother Africa, in short, as symbols for nationalist consciousness and (re)construction. They have been critical of the ways in which the African woman-question has often been blatantly subsumed under the nationalist-question. But literature is not the only culprit. Indeed, from Négritude to Fanon to contemporary postcolonial theories—all have also been guilty of not (adequately) problematizing the position of African and/or postcolonial women as acting, speaking subjects with agency. These theories have failed at historicizing and politicizing the identities and subjectivities of postcolonial women except when they fall within an essentialist category that serves as a convenient, albeit subversive symbol within the project of constructing national identity/nationhood. They have been censured for their androcentrism and/or gender neutrality. But this negligence or failure of postcolonial theories to deal effectively with the postcolonial woman-question, with postcolonial women's agency, is central to Aidoo's work as a writer, theorist and critic. Aidoo refuses to see African women only as symbols on which emergent African nations plant their patriotic flags. But this does not mean a rejection of nationalist thought on her part.

Aidoo has made no excuses about the fact that she is a Pan-Africanist and a nationalist. She has reiterated in interviews that one cannot claim to be an African nationalist without being a feminist, whether one is a man or a woman (Maja-Pearce 1990:17-18; Needham 1995:123-133). Her nationalism embodies many facets: she is a strong advocate of (affordable) education for all (especially for women, as witnessed in her essay, "Ghana: To Be a Woman")[1] and of gender equality (Aidoo 1988); she is distressed with current politics in Africa and demands that the leaders—African men—share power with African women but not only as tokens; she is concerned about health issues, the economy, in short, the future of Africa and more importantly, the future of Africa for women. Yes, she is a nationalist but she is also a staunch feminist, an African feminist who has spoken out against those critics who have been foolhardy enough to claim that African feminism was imported from abroad. Aidoo has maintained that being a feminist is "an ideological orientation" ("Profile" 1991:593). She has argued for the anteriority of an African feminism that does not owe its existence—or allegiance—to Western feminism. On the contrary, Aidoo has wryly noted:

I find this whole charge that African women have only borrowed feminist ideas from the West particularly painful. Those women who rioted against the colonial regime at Aba, in Eastern Nigeria, in the 1920s did not seek permission from Virginia Woolf. If anything, Western women have borrowed notions of women in struggle from us. Who started civil rights? The feminist movement was a kind of hijacking of the civil rights movement. (Maja-Pearce 1990:18)

Needless to say, Aidoo would be the first to chuckle at the title of Caroline Rooney's (1991) essay, "Are We in the Company of Feminists? A Preface to Bessie Head and Ama Ata Aidoo,"[2] for she has never had doubts about being a feminist. Aidoo is therefore both a nationalist and feminist, but her nationalism cannot, does not erase her womanhood; it cannot and should not consume her subjecthood. That is why she claims always to speak as an African, and as a woman, or vice-versa (Needham 1995:123; Maja-Pearce 1990:17). She has contended that West African women "have enjoyed a certain amount of the society's regard and respect, at least compared with the rest of the continent" (Maja-Pearce 1990:17), but has also in the same vein, decried the fact that these women have been discriminated against even in the most matriarchal of African societies because of their biology. When she says therefore that "ours has been a double quarrel," she is taking a nationalist shot at colonialism and proffering a feminist cry against the (gender) oppression of African women. It is no wonder that she sees herself placed at "an explosive junction of contemporary political history" (Needham 1995:123). It is the "refusal to begin from a basic acceptance of people's humanity and the validity of their historical and cultural experiences which continually seems to be a block to understanding," Aidoo tells interviewers Granqvist and Stotesbury (1989:14-15). Consequently, her representation of African women will be not only politicized but grounded in the historicity of their material, lived experiences. Aidoo's feminism finds itself embedded in and/or alongside her nationalism, both speaking to and feeding off each other.

I will, therefore, throughout this paper, use Aidoo's (non)fictional words as the theoretical foundation on which I will build my arguments given that I see her points of view as offering (gendered) indigenous theory[3] that overcomes some of the pitfalls with which

African criticism, feminist,[4] and postcolonial theories[5] have been plagued. The title, *Changes*, will be read contextually as an attack and subversion of entrenched hegemonies within African society, and discursively, as transgressing the meta-nationalistic language of postcolonial theories as it grounds and problematizes the materiality of postcolonial African women's construction of subjecthood and agency. This paper will focus on the modern, Western-educated African woman, with emphasis on the main protagonist, Esi Sekyi.

THE DOUBLE-DOUBLE QUARREL?

> Life on this earth need not always be some humans being gods and others being sacrificial animals. Indeed, that can be changed. But it would take so much. No, not time....What it would take is a lot of thinking and a great deal of doing....Are we human beings even prepared to try?
>
> —Nana, *Changes*

When *Changes* opens, we meet Esi Sekyi, the "new breed" of educated, professional African women, but that is only one reason our interest is piqued. We are confronted with an openly irritated Esi, reproaching herself for taking on a responsibility that is not part of her job description. At the heart of her anger is a potent issue of gender. Esi questions why her male colleagues would not do the job of the secretary while the latter is away but that *she*, Esi, would always "volunteer" to do it. Why does Esi feel the need to? Her words to Ali give us the answer: "I believe she must have sent in everything. I just thought I should come and check on the tickets and flight bookings" (Aidoo 1991:3). On the one hand, therefore, we have an educated woman who should know better how to assert herself with her male colleagues and not fall into the trap of predetermined gender roles/hierarchies that construct and position women at the bottom of power structures, but who, (un)consciously, does just that. Women are here constructed as those whose actions advance nation-building even as men do not value/validate their work. The little things women do provide the platform on which larger issues are conceptualized; men therefore abstract from the daily lived experiences of women. Secondly, Ali's fear at the end of chapter one that "the threatening storm might sweep [Esi] and her car away. They both looked so frail," is also very telling of Esi's predicament (4). Ali's I/eye(s) do not see a competent government statistician but an attractive, frail woman in dire need of protection, his protection. His gaze automatically constructs her as object for his consumption. By the same token, his maleness, manhood, and masculinity are constructed in opposition to her femaleness and "frailness"/powerlessness.

Similarly, when we meet Opokuya—Esi's best friend—for the first time in Chapter Three, we are also confronted with a registered nurse and midwife with many years of experience to her credit angrily, though pointedly, analyzing "the politics of population and fat" (15). Opoku lashes out at North/South relations and especially condemns "aid" policies that continue to enslave African leaders and reinforce the neocolonial status of their governments and people. But she is especially critical of the impact of these so-called benevolent Western handouts on the lives of African women and children. The proliferation of "pamphlets and samples for losing weight and contraception" (14) at even the remotest clinics to the detriment of basic drugs amply proves Opoku's arguments. These neocolonial programs have one objective: the control of African women's bodies, thereby, exerting control over African society and culture-gender relations, family systems, etc.). Furthermore, when one combines ideologies that inscribe the need to lose weight in women's psyches with the dreadful consequences—malnutrition, illness, even death—engendered by such a need, with the demand for fewer children, one would agree with Opokuya. This North/South exchange smacks of downright murder, a war engineered and waged by the North, the battleground of which is women's bodies in the South—genocide perpetrated on a society under the guise of humanitarianism.[6] We see Opokuya's resolve not only when discussing thorny issues that affect the individual and the collective, we also learn of her inner strength when it comes to her private life. "The politics of population and fat" have not made a dint on Opokuya. On the contrary, she is fat and not bothered by it, except when and if her health is at risk. Secondly, she wanted to have four children, had just that number, and tied her tubes. This act alone speaks to the strength of Opokuya's character, given that few African women—educated or uneducated—would actually undergo this operation after having "only" four children. Most would preferably stay on the pill rather than have a tubal ligation because these women would see the act of mutilating one's reproductive organs as a direct loss of womanhood, with the resultant loss of gender. It is an act that can be culturally read as de-sexualizing or masculinizing. What can be more terrifying for African women who are often socialized to view their womanhood as defined by or closely linked to motherhood? One therefore admires Opokuya, but just like in our first encounter with Esi, the chapter ends with a very frustrated, angry Opokuya "ready to bang" a car door shut. She has just lost the car to her husband who is driving it off to work, a car he will park in the Surveyor's parking spot for the entire day, unused; a car he drives away, "whistling, of course" (21). The triumph couched in Kubi's act of whistling stands in opposition to Opoku's loss. Kubi, who has stepped into the shoes of his former colonial counterpart—the home, Sweet Breezes Hill; the position of Surveyor; the car and fringe benefits that come with his government senior civil servant job—can wield this "new power" of African post-colonial male privilege in ways that his equally educated post-colonial wife cannot. Furthermore, it is no accident we are informed that when Opoku occasionally "wins" the car, she drives it "humming" all the way to work as opposed to Kubi whistling all the way to the regional administrative offices. Opoku's hums express how much she feels stifled, fighting over a car, one that for all practical purposes *should be used*, a vehicle that can grant her freedom of movement, of expression, the ability—incumbent on her gender roles as wife and mother—to manage her family and run her home in the face of multiple responsibilities. After all, as a state registered nurse with fifteen years of experience as a midwife, isn't her position and experience also deserving of a car, one might ask? Not only is she cheated by her husband, she is also cheated by a nation-state that allocates benefits in positions predominantly occupied by men. Her humming thus speaks eloquently of (un)spoken, suppressed emotions that one visualizes building up like a storm, raging within until they might force her to "explode" (no pun intended on Opoku's weight). In contrast, Kubi's whistles speak more of an act that is liberating, one that permits him to release, blow away any storms that might be raging or accumulating within. Whistling externalizes his feeling of freedom, meanwhile humming internalizes and re-enforces Opoku's feelings of frustration and near powerlessness.

We meet Fusena, the "other" woman, the third educated woman of *Changes* in Chapter Seven. Just like her counterparts, Fusena is an intelligent, "interesting" woman—a teacher who marries Ali, follows him to England where he goes to further his education. But Fusena is dissuaded from doing the same by her husband. She gives up her teaching career, gives up pursuing another degree, and spends her time being pregnant and taking care of her family. She returns to Africa where both she and her husband own and run successful businesses, but the chapter ends on a very sour note for Fusena. She is tortured by Ali's desire to make "a woman with a university degree his second wife. So Allah, what was she supposed to say? What was she expected to do?" (67). Fusena, I must say, is represented as the most stifled of these three modern African women. She is stifled and silenced at varying and multiple levels. First by her husband, who "takes away" her career, forcing her to construct her identity and womanhood through motherhood and in the shadow of his manhood, wealth and power; who imposes a second wife on her without the traditional respect for her position and duties as the first wife. Secondly, she is silenced not only by the patriarchs of Nima, but more importantly, by the sisterhood of "battle-weary" wives and sisters of these patriarchs who cannot/refuse to support/help her, all under the guise of women's universal, eternal victimhood in what they define as "a man's world. You only survived if you knew how to live in it as a woman" (107). I am reminded here of Ma'Shingayi's recommendation (Dangarembga 1989:16) to her daughter, Tambudzai, to "learn to carry [her] burdens with strength."[7] The painful irony here lies in the legacy of the "sisterhood" to Fusena (and Tambudzai): a sad lesson on women's naturalized place in the man's world. Thirdly, Fusena is silenced by Esi who usurps her right as first wife to give her consent or put her stamp of approval on the second wife. Lastly, Fusena is silenced by the text of *Changes* itself. Ali and the omniscient narrator, for the most part, speak her thoughts. Fusena is almost completely de-textualized but for a few words/phrases that directly escape her mouth and these in the form of questions, such as, "Why?" (65); "She has a university degree?" (99); "Is she also a Muslim?" (100) It is as if the text is, along with colonialism and patriarchy, colluding to practice an-other kind of epistemic violence on Fusena, one that the subversive nature of the title-text cannot redeem.

The double quarrel about which Aidoo speaks is clearly delineated through the dichotomies—their gender on the one hand and society on the other—that her representation of these women brings across when we first meet them. Western education has, on the surface, put these three women in advantageous social and class positions but they are still plagued by their gender(ed) roles, whether constituted or constituting. There are multiple examples sprinkled throughout the novel that reinforce this point, defining hyphenated selves and the bifurcated consciousness that these female characters need to navigate between their professional selves and their gender(ed) roles and responsibilities. Esi's husband and her male colleagues in the regional census office not only resent that she is over-qualified, they make no bones about the fact that "to cope with an over-qualified woman in any situation is a complete misfortune" (41).

But it is not only the men who can be accused of gender discrimination and this is where I propose an expanded reading of Aidoo's "double quarrel." In the spirit of Ghanaians (and West Africans, I might add) who "are good at simply turning English on its head" (35) to suit their own discursive practices, I contend that Esi's (ours) is, and should be a "double-double" quarrel that is both reflective and self-reflexive. Certainly, colonialism has "wreaked havoc" in the minds of contemporary African women through language and culture; certainly, African men have also colonized African women with their "new power," but how have modern African women also participated in their own colonization? Self-interrogation seems in order here. When Esi walks into Linga HideAways, she is "forced" to justify why she is even there. "I just thought I should come...," she says almost regretfully. Why did she have to come? She tells us she had to do it on the basis of a (c)overt "assumption," one that is predetermined by cultural practice or over-determined by her male colleagues. Ironically, she theoretically argues against her own actions but does not put that theory (rightfully) in practice. Another instance is one when Esi and Opoku bump into each other at Hotel Twentieth Century. Earlier, while having a drink alone, Esi reflects on what it would mean to see her, a single woman drinking *alcohol* in a hotel. Inferred here is the label of a loose woman, a prostitute, that is conferred on such a woman. Opoku joins her and much later, when a very late Kubi finally comes to pick her up, Opokuya takes Esi along with her to the car because it would "make it easier for her to explain how she had managed to spend an entire evening at the hotel, although the fact that she had had to was not even her fault" (53). These instances prove that "educated" African women have to re-think this double quarrel and make themselves an intrinsic part of such inquiry, they must subject themselves to self-analyzing practice as well.

Clearly, it is one woman's perceptive mind—Opokuya's—that pinpoints Fusena's predicament long before we meet her: "Men are not really interested in a woman's independence or her intelligence. The few who claim they like intelligent and active women are also interested in having such women permanently in their beds and in their kitchens" (45). This statement gains in import when we meet Fusena and the chapter ends with a distraught woman asking herself what she is "expected to do" with the bad news from her husband. But, is there not a helplessness that is framed by Opoku's statement, "No matter what anybody says, we can't have it all. Not if you are a woman" (49)? Nana's words: "Life on this earth need not always be some humans being gods and others sacrificial animals. Indeed that can be changed. But it would take so much," directly mimic and at the same time challenge Opoku's naturalization of women's oppression. Nana has earlier in the text called men, "devouring gods" (110), but proceeds in the next paragraph to speak about "humans" instead of "men." I infer from this switch that some of these humans can be/are women; and so, when Opokuya follows up her lament with the phrase, "Not yet," I also infer that the job of change lies both on the shoulders of men *and* women. Women have to learn/cease to be sacrificial animals, even though it will take time, as Nana cautions. It is important to note that Opokuya, Esi, and to a lesser extent, Fusena, do not necessarily conceive of themselves as "victims" but they are constantly aware of and do try to question those situations that potentially construct and position them as victims. The issue then lies with *how* they deconstruct and deal with what is at stake and what possible gains they can make for themselves. Discrimination inherent in their gender is only one dimension of the struggle for identity and self-definition. How can these women therefore learn to juggle to have it all? It would be useful to examine other issues that exist outside of and/or alongside gender, what I have argued is women's self-colonization, and the walls they erect that do stand in the way of their womanhood and strong subjectivity. The problems for these women will therefore be more complex in their relations with contemporary African men whom Aidoo maintains have colonized them "with their new power." A statement not to be read to mean they never "colonized" their women in the past. They did, but with a different kind of power—a power inherent in their patriarchal culture, one that has found ways to consolidate its gains with the new post-colonial power machine, thus posing more hurdles for the modern African woman.

THE PROBLEMATIC OF LANGUAGE, COMMUNICATION, AND GENDER RELATIONS

> One area of communication that made [Ali] feel sad
> were those walls that the different colonial experi-
> ences seemed to have erected between the differ-
> ent groups of Africans...especially when he hit them
> in relation to women.
>
> (Aidoo 1991:2)

Ngugi wa Thiong'o writes in *Decolonising the Mind* that any language "is both a means of communication and a carrier of culture"
(Ngugi 1986:13). Culture, he maintains, carries "the entire body of
values by which we come to perceive ourselves and our place in
the world....Language is thus inseparable from ourselves as a community of human beings with a specific form and character, a specific history, a specific relation to the world" (16). Ngugi pursues
his analysis of the imperialism of (the English) language even further in *Moving the Centre*, arguing that the languages of the colonizers never met with African languages as equals. "They met with
English as the language of the conquering nation, and ours as the
language of the vanquished" (Ngugi 1993:35). English, the language
of power, assimilated and imposed a condition of alienation on
those educated in the colonizer's language, a condition that Aidoo
says has "wreaked havoc" in the minds of modern African women
and thus threatens and continues to intrude in and shape gender
relations between contemporary, Western-educated, African men
and women.

This issue is raised on page two of *Changes* when Ali and Esi
meet for the first time. Whereas communication sometimes breaks
down between Esi and her colleagues because of the limitations
conferred on her gender; communication is lost in her encounter
with Ali because she seems to lack the necessary tools to master
the meanings that are overtly stated or implied by his words. When
Ali asks Esi whether he can sit down and Esi replies, "It is your
office and quite obviously your chair. Why ask me if you might sit
on it?" Ali is embarrassed and even hurt because he is only being
polite and respectful of the woman in front of him; whereas Esi's
response is grounded in her Western education that forces her to
recognize and assert Ali's individualism/ownership rather than an
African etiquette. Elleke Boehmer has suggested that "what is frequently ignored in postcolonial criticism is the difficulty or other-

ness of the postcolonial text: the implications for us as readers of its possibly untranslatable cultural specificity" (Boehmer 1995: 245). Certainly, the meanings rendered in Ali's "May I sit down?"—flirtation, respect, etc.—may be lost on (some) readers, but Esi ought to be competent in decoding what is culturally specific in Ali's statement. In this instance, missed-communication shrouds or impedes on gender relations, hence Ali's frustration and sadness.

Perhaps more important is the language that describes/inscribes the issue of marital rape between Oko and Esi in the story. Bola Makanjuola has argued that "Aidoo tentatively raises the issue...but never really dwells on the subject. It is as if both Esi and the author realize, that in an African society there could not possibly be an 'indigenous word or phrase for it'" (Makanjuola 1991: 474). Indeed, Aidoo does not dwell on the rape, but the act itself and its repercussions are sustained throughout the novel; after all, we are told that "[j]ust as earthquakes and floods become landmarks in the history of nations, the morning when Oko jumped on Esi became a landmark in their relationship: referred to thereafter by both of them as 'That morning'" (69). Secondly, I disagree with the assertion that the issue of rape is to be abandoned simply because there is no indigenous word or phrase for it. To maintain this line of thinking would mean falling into the same trap in which Esi-as-sociologist finds herself when rationalizing the relationship between language, ideas, and history to prove her point: "You cannot go around claiming that an idea or an item was imported into a given society unless you could also conclude that to the best of your knowledge, there is not, and never was any word or phrase in that society's indigenous language which describes such an item" (12). This takes us back to the issue of the untranslatability of cultural specificity, that is, the deliberated opacity of the postcolonial text that I contend is/can be translatable. The issue here is not so much the (non)existence of a word for rape in the indigenous language as the way in which language/(wo)men en-codes rape. In my language—Beba (Cameroon)—for instance, there is no word for "rape" *per se*, but there is an expression that literally says, "a girl/woman has been spoilt." Rape is thus captured in the language in "the act of spoiling" (read violating, dirtying). W.D. Ashcroft has argued that "the woman may not speak so much from the position of her *exclusion* from language as from the position of its inadequacy for her experience. In other words the woman and the postcolonial speak from the *margins* of language" (Ashcroft 1989:26).

If we move outside of Ashcroft's essentialist category that collapses "the woman" and "the post-colonial" and instead view Esi as an African woman with specific lived experiences in Ghana, we would on the one hand agree that there is no word in the indigenous language because of its inadequacy for her experience but, on the other hand, I would argue that this "inadequacy" can only be apparent at a superficial level. Her experience is inferred, is named in codes that are available in a heteroglossia that is culturally specific, culturally translatable to both Esi and Oko. If one were to give this rape and non-language in which it is portrayed a "polylectical" (Odamtten 1994:5) as opposed to dialectical reading, I would argue that herein lies the complexity of what/how Aidoo delves into marital rape. Granted, there might be no word in the indigenous language; granted, "sex is something a husband claims from his wife as his right" (12); but how about Oko's thoughts just before the act and his reaction just after he rapes his wife? Clearly, before he rapes her, we, the readers have a premonition that he would. On page six, Oko ogles his wife's body as she goes through the morning ritual of putting on her makeup. He muses on how Esi had not lost a bit of her "schoolgirl looks or schoolgirl ways. For a teacher in a co-educational school...this is a very dangerous thought indeed. He scolded himself." There are two things at work here. Oko commits mental rape. He relents and scolds himself. When the actual rape finally happens, we are told that Oko "was already feeling like telling Esi that he was sorry. But he was also convinced he mustn't" (10). Whether there is an indigenous word-phrase or not is here deflected and even erased by the obvious knowledge that Oko knows he has raped. He regrets it but will not apologize because an apology would undermine his use of rape as a weapon. Esi does not name the rape either but the shame she feels about her naked body (unusual for Esi) eloquently "names" the rape. There is therefore a language here, language as oppositional practice I might add, that exists outside of words and phrases—language that has clear meanings within Esi's and Oko's cultural script and it is a script they both participate in writing. Esi reacts against and effectively refuses to be "thingified" (Cesiare 1972:21) in any way by Oko or his actions. We are therefore not surprised when she also uses the rape as a weapon to leave her husband thirteen pages into the novel. But it is a break that propels her into a second marriage, as a second wife, a marriage that forces her to deeply question who she is, what she has become, and where she needs to take her life. The ultimate moment of self-reflection happens when Esi has to deal with an-other kind of language, one she overhears when her mother and grandmother reflect on their fears and hopes for the new generation of educated African women who do not seem to be doing much better than their uneducated foremothers. Esi is forced to question her education, the language of that "education" and the (apparent) alienated hybrid she seems to have become.

RE-ENTERING THE MOTHER'S WORLD

> Why had they sent her to school? . . .
> For surely, taking a ten-year-old child away from her mother, and away from her first language—which is surely *one of life's most powerful working tools*—for what would turn out to be forever, then transferring her into a boarding school for two years, to a higher boarding school for seven years, then to an even higher boarding school for three or four years, from where she was only equipped to go and roam in strange and foreign lands with *no hope of ever meaningfully re-entering her mother's world*...all this was too high a price to pay to achieve the dangerous confusion she was now in and the country now was in.

> (Aidoo 1991:114; my emphasis)

Aidoo has maintained that "education is the key, the key to *every thing*" (James 1990:11). If education is the key to everything and language is one of life's most powerful tools, then one can be sympathetic with Esi when she blames colonialism and the post-colonial era in Ghana for contributing to the confusion that she faces in her life. Here is a woman whose body has been bruised by her own husband; a woman who questions the fracturing of her identity and the (institutionalized) violence that colonial language and education have inflicted on her subjectivity. Deepika Bahri (1997) has rightly stated that "postcolonial theories of hybridity have been useful in many ways for theorizing both the anxieties and the potentially liberatory possibilities of displacement as well as challenging the authority of colonial discourse" (290). In *Changes* we note how years of displacement and dislocation from her "mother's world"—(women's) language, culture, women's networks—have molded Esi in ways that force her to make some grievous mistakes like opting for an "alternative lifestyle" without taking into consideration the many factors necessary for the success of such an enterprise: 1) her choice to become the second wife of a man whose first wife she does not even know, has not even met; 2) her "refusal" to listen to the voice of reason, and this not only from the women who support her, but also in her inability to read the (warning) signs from the very man she intends to marry.

Aidoo has said that in writing *Changes*, she wanted "to see what happens when a professional woman puts herself in the role of the other woman" ("Profile" 1991). I would like to argue here that even though Esi is the professional woman who puts herself in the place of the other woman, Fusena is as much Other(ed) by Esi as Esi is the other woman. There are many instances in the novel that attest to Esi's other-ness, but more alarmingly, are those moments when Esi others herself and does not either adequately gauge the ramifications or chooses to repress them. When Ali proposes to Esi, she asks him, "And your wife? Where does she come in?" (86). This is not the kind of question one might expect from a second-wife-to-be. "When do I get to meet your first wife?" would be a more appropriate question for it speaks to the knowledge of what marriage —polygamous marriage—as an institution means in her culture. Again when Ali gives her the engagement ring and wants her to wear it, Esi blurts out, "I thought I was *only* going to be your second wife" and Ali responds, "What difference does it make? And what is this about 'only a second wife'? Isn't a wife a wife?" (89; my emphasis). By juxtaposing Esi's statement and Ali's questions we see how much Esi is imputing (on herself) what I will refer to here as a kind of "social death."[8] On the one hand she loves this man, sees him as an equal, wants to marry him but on the other hand proclaims herself second-class, seems resigned to accept that she is only second best and can never be equals with Fusena, unlike Ali for whom "a wife is a wife." Is Esi underlining the fact that there can never be "equality" in a marriage of many wives, or is she failing to understand or accept the rules and conditions that govern a polygamous marriage even as she prepares to take the plunge? Yes, there is gender inequality, but the text also adequately demonstrates, and this includes Ali's thoughts on the matter, that the new generation of Africans have forsaken the rules that made such marriages work, hence their failures. In the words of Aidoo, "the factors which made polygamous marriages work have broken down in the urban environment" ("Profile" 1991:593) so much so that Esi can gallop into a marriage without even knowing what the first wife looks like and is not alarmed by it. It is almost as if the word-institution "polygamy" is erased from her consciousness. Esi continually treats Fusena as an absence, an Other, not even as an irri-table nuisance except when Ali does not come to see her or when he rushes off "home" instead of spending more time with her, plea-suring her body. Esi naively finds comfort in the enjoyment of her body, in fulfilling sexual relations with Ali, in short, in her sexu-ality. So long as Ali is there to satisfy her sexual needs then the rest does not matter. Good sex complements her other needs—her career. But for how long can this relationship woven mainly around sex/sexuality be sustained? Buchi Emecheta's words, "Sex is part of [African women's] life. It is not THE life" (in Petersen 1988:177), should serve as an eye-opener not only to Western feminists but as words of caution to Western-educated African feminists like Esi. I am also reminded here of Ann Rosalind Jones's (1986) critique of the *écriture féminine* and the concept of *féminité* that capitalizes on, and promotes *jouissance* to the detriment/erasure of women's differences and the historicity of lived experiences. Esi needs to inscribe her sexuality within the larger context of historical and cultural Ghanian practices that obviously do govern even a mod-ern "alternative lifestyle." She must learn to see her body as a con-tested terrain where sexuality and cultural politics converge and find expression in dialectical relation. Secondly, that her home has never been "home" to Ali should have been ringing alarm bells in Esi's mind but, in the same way that she selfishly marries Ali to shirk the responsibility of having to deal with a man who wants all of her time, so too she ignores the need for a co-wife relationship with Fusena. Is it therefore appropriate to blame her problems on a fragmented past and/or a hybrid identity-in-crises that contin-ues to bear witness to the violence of the colonial encounter, the psychopathology engendered thereof in the colonized about which Fanon so eloquently speaks? Is this what it means to be a "modern Western-educated African woman"?

I will submit that the answers lie partly in Esi's thoughts quot-ed at the beginning of this section. Her Western education has indeed made it possible for her to conceive of marriage in very individualistic, binary terms as if she were living with Ali in London or New York. Roaming for many years "in strange and for-eign lands" has taught her the ability to effectively cut herself off and dissociate herself from the community within which she lives. But Ali is the one subject in this story on whose body the discourses of colonialism and African patriarchal ideologies converge and are written. Ali, like the colonizer has "conquered many" African coun-tries, eight in all and has passports to prove it; he is a native of nowhere, of no one specific location; even his travel/tourist business, "Linga HideAways" is a metaphor for the selves Ali embodies that can "hide" and emerge when needed, in the same way that his command of English, French, and Koranic schools/education permit him to navigate in multiple directions. Ali, like his father, sees "intelligent" African women's bodies as territory to be conquered as he soars like a bird from border to border and across border(line)s. Ali therefore constitutes a cultural script that Esi should have read, should have been able to read. One must ask, how does a woman like Esi who has shown time and again that she can assess situations and make the right decisions for herself, fail to read Ali? She sticks to her career, a career she enjoys and will not give up, not even for a husband; she decides one child is enough, this despite all the curses labeled against her by her "families" and society; she openly enjoys her naked body and sexual pleasure in a context where sexuality has been repressed for various reasons—traditional contempt for the biology of women; Islamic suppressive ideas; English Victorian prudery and French hypocrisy imported by the colonizers—how can such a woman not see what Ali embodies?

I submit that coupled with her Western education is a selfish streak in Esi that only gives in when the stakes are in her favor. I see Esi's selfishness, some might say, her strong individuality, as being at the heart of some of her tribulations in the novel. Her mother, her grandmother, her best friend, all warn against the marriage but she does not listen. Even Ali "warns" her. Besides never considering Esi's home his home, there are other indications from Ali that provide ample warning. For instance, when he gives her his ring, Esi demands to know why it was necessary she wear the ring, and Ali responds: "To let the rest of the male world know that she is bespoke," and Esi responds, "That she has become occupied territory," and Ali concurs with her (91). Ironically, Ali who has on the one hand, forthrightly condemned the colonizers and their "concepts" proceeds with colonizing Esi with these same concepts of maleness and masculinity. We are told that Esi thought "the whole thing sounded so absolutely lunatic and so 'contemporary African' that she would save her sanity probably by not trying to understand it" (91). What is there not to understand about being occupied territory as Esi herself succinctly declares? It is my contention that Esi is not naive. On the contrary, she decides not to try to understand it under the guise of saving her sanity for very personal reasons. She does not want to be bothered by/with all these details. She wants Ali and that's that and not even the conventional wisdom that "no one ever made the mistake of thinking that any marriage was strictly the affair of the two people involved, one could never attempt to fight the war of marriage alone" matters (40). Esi chooses not to recognize the war that must evidently be fought on many battlefields. The war becomes a reality when Ali offers her the olive branch, a brand new car on New Year's Day. When she finishes inspecting and admiring the car, the first words that come out of Esi's mouth are, "But what will your wife say?" This question opens the window towards self-actualization, it represents the last straw in a complex struggle for self-determination. Esi finally realizes that she is Other, she is Object, she is and always has been just the concubine; she is indeed conquered territory on whose surface Ali will continue to dump and flaunt his wealth and parade his male-ness/power. She must save herself from the "mixture of emotional and physical exhaustion" that even tranquilizers cannot appease. If her marriage to Oko was one born "out of gratitude," what then is her marriage to Ali? She realizes that she must extricate herself from this "confusion" before it swallows her up and buries her alive and the one avenue open to her for self-(re)-construction is re-entering the mother's world. Esi does recognize that she could "never be as close to her mother as her mother was to her grandmother" (114), but re-immersing herself in her mother's world, in the language of the mother's world holds a number of advantages and especially points of reconciliation and reconstruction with/for this Western-educated African woman in search of a strong subjectivity and agency. Women have always been custodians of (traditional) history and knowledge and Esi must tap into this resource to fuel and regenerate herself.

FLABBERWHELMED OR TURNING HISTORY ON ITS HEAD?

> Hopefully a whole people would soon have answers for them. In the meantime she would listen to her grandmother. She would not pity herself. She would just relax and flourish in her mother's and her grandmother's peace.

—Esi Sekyi, *Changes*

A re-entry into the mother's world involves a process, one within which Esi would have to unlearn some of the ideals of individualism that have impeded her ability to construct and sustain fulfilling (love) relations with men. The mother's world would also offer her a (new) language; a language grounded within the women's network in the form of "gossip," the kind of gossip that she over- hears when her mother and Nana analyze her predicament. Odamtten has suggested that this gossip "creates the contextual frame that emphasizes the issues of a woman's place and her rela- tionship to another man or men by placing them within the larg- er network of neocolonial connections, while tracing their colonial and precolonial antecedents" (Odamtten 1994:165). This is pre- cisely therefore, the kind of (secret) language that is available to women *because* of their gender, and therein lie its strengths. It is a language that makes available to her the codes necessary for an African woman grounded in her culture and tradition to decode barriers, thus enabling the dismantling of some forms of patriar- chal and postcolonial male privilege. This is where I see Esi's edu- cation as a strength, a strength even more powerful than the comfort provided by economic independence and the freedom to pursue a career. When Esi can combine her ability to make per- sonal decisions about her career and her body with an ability to understand more fully the intricate fabrics woven by cultural prac- tice and then juggle/manipulate these to her advantage, then her education and her knowledge of tradition constructed through and with/in the women's material world stand to her advantage. Sure enough she will sometimes be overwhelmed by events; she will evidently continue to be occasionally flabbergasted by men—edu- cated or not—but ultimately, Aidoo's portrayal of the modern, Western-educated African woman of the text of *Changes* is not entirely doomed or flabberwhelmed. Thanks to Esi, Opokuya acquires a car, resolving the major point of contention in her mar- riage with Kubi. Fusena does not seem to have any desire to leave Ali, but she would have to(re)think the challenges she has to face as a Muslim-married-woman. These women do not wish to turn history on its head because that would only be suicidal or would continue to distort their daily lived experiences. But, they will con- tinue to re-write that history; they will continue to question and poke holes into the cultural scripts within which their identities and subjectivities are constructed. Tradition is not static, neither is it necessarily an enemy. Tradition is mutable, is in flux, just like their identities and it is their (gendered) duty as well to participate in shaping the changing faces of tradition in modern Africa. Similarly, modernity is dis-abling but it can also be en-abling, it can prove to be a valuable ally in this daunting enterprise.

We see an Esi by the end of the novel who knows that only she can save herself from the hasty way in which she galloped into her second marriage. Her education enables her to do without Ali's economic support, a guillotine that husbands often hold over the heads of poor, dependent women. Without the financial constraints that could have left her perpetually indebted to Ali, Esi has to make a decision that is primarily personal, emotional. Ali's "fashion of loving had proved quite inadequate for her" (165), and she breaks off the relationship. In both instances (the marriage and the break up), Esi has been the agent of her own self-destruction, self-reconstruction, and self-determination. She makes many mistakes, but eventually, she redefines herself in the context of her society's relations of gender. Although her's and Ali's type of modern free-floating relationship may not be the ideal for women, Esi's capacity to think and re-think issues centered on her body, her career, her marriage, and her ability to make choices for herself (though not always the right ones) becomes her strength. She has the ability as well as the means to enable her to assess the damage and move on in new and different directions (Nfa-Abbenyi 1997:57-61).

She might not know what all these directions are but they all have to combine both the personal, the collective, and the political, as the ending of the story clearly illustrates: Esi "comforted herself that maybe her bone-blood-flesh self, not her unseen soul, would get answers to some of the big questions she was asking of life" (166). Esi is aware that the answers she seeks cannot all come from her as an individual but hopefully from "a whole people." Her hopes are echoed by the words of her creator who has stated that whatever was left for Africans (after the onslaughts of the last five hundred years) to "recoup cannot be done unless we see ourselves as a people, as a nation" (Needham 1995:125). Aidoo's nationalism and feminism once again are inscribed as two sides of the same coin. Ben Okri has said that we can on the one hand "look at our condition in Africa in despair. On the other hand can look at it and say, 'Well, we are some of the luckiest people at this time because we've got so much to invent and fight for.' Time is actually a short thing and the future is all there to be created" (Wilkinson 1992:87). The narrative(s) of *Changes* can thus be seen to serve as "a socially symbolic mediation of the frustrations and hopes informing [African women's] experiences of postcoloniality" (Mohan 1992: 30). Aidoo is right to say that those Aba women did not need Woolf's permission (a contemporary who only dignified their existence with one word, "Negress" in her ground-breaking *A Room of One's*

Own) to go about the business of fighting colonial oppression. It is my contention that their post-colonial descendants know they cannot afford to forget their foremothers legacy of those histories of struggle and courage. Postcolonial African women are sometimes flabberwhelmed, will continue to make mistakes, but as they learn to assess their losses and capitalize on their gains, their strong subjectivities will continue to ground their strengths, not weaknesses, so long as, to paraphrase Aidoo, they approach issues from their position in life, in society, in history, as women.

NOTES

1. In Morgan 1984:128-65. See also Aidoo's profile in *West Africa* 3842 (April 22-28, 1991):593, in which she looks at the role she played in her bid to transform Ghana's educational system during the eighteen-month period she was Secretary for Education, and her interview with Adeola James in James 1990:8-27.
2. Head and Aidoo are the only two African women to whom paper is devoted in this book of essays on twentieth-century women writers in English. They seem to be granted this spot because they qualify as feminists alongside their white Euro-American counterparts.
3. I have discussed indigenous African theory at length in chapter 2 of *Gender in African Women's Writing*.
4. See Davies 1986; Mohanty 1991; Anzaldúa 1983; Lugones and Spelman 1983; and Lâm 1994.
5. See Mishra and Hodge 1991:408; Katrak 1980; Spivak 1986; and Chow 1993:27-54.
6. Gayatri Spivak (1996) has discussed how the creation of a transnational world has helped perpetuate "gynocide and war on women" (246) through aid packages that are linked to population control.
7. Tambudzai is rebelling against what she contends is the "question of femaleness. Femaleness as opposed to and inferior to maleness."
8. For a detailed definition of the concept of "social death," see Kalu 1994: 95.

WORKS CITED

Aidoo, Ama Ata. *Changes: A Love Story*. New York: (CUNY) The Feminist Press, 1991.

———. "Ghana: To Be a Woman." *Sisterhood is Global*. Ed. Robin Morgan. New York: Anchor/Doubleday, 1984. 258-65.

———. "To Be an African Woman—an Overview and a Detail." In: *Criticism and Ideology*. Ed. Kirsten Holst Petersen. Uppsala: Scandinavian Institute of African Studies, 1988:155-72.

Anzaldúa, Gloria. "Speaking in Tongues: A Letter to 3rd World Women Writers." *This Bridge Called My Back: Writings by Radical Women of Color*. Ed. Cherríe Moraga and Gloria Anzaldúa. New York: Kitchen

Table/Women of Color Press, 1983. 165-72.

Ashcroft, W.D. "Intersecting Marginalities: Post-Colonialism and Feminism." *Kunapipi* 11,2 (1989):23-35.

Bahri, Deepika. "Marginally Off-Center: Postcolonialism in the Teaching Machine." *College English* 59,3 (March 1997):277-98.

Boehmer, Elleke. *Colonial and Postcolonial Literature: Migrant Metaphors.* Oxford: Oxford University Press, 1995.

Booth, James. "Sexual Politics in the Fiction of Ama Ata Aidoo." *Commonwealth Essays and Studies* 15,2 (Spring 1993):80-96.

Césaire, Aimé. *Discourse on Colonialism.* Trans. Joan Pinkham. New York: Monthly Review Press, 1972.

Chow, Rey. *Writing Diaspora: Tactics of Intervention in Contemporary Cultural Studies.* Bloomington: Indiana University Press, 1993.

Dangarembga, Tsitsi. *Nervous Conditions.* Seattle: Seal Press, 1989.

Davies, Carole B. "Introduction: Feminist Consciousness and African Literary Criticism." In: *Ngambika: Studies of Women in African Literature.* Eds. Carole B. Davies and Anne Adams Graves. Trenton, N.J.: Africa World Press, 1986. 1-23.

Emecheta, Buchi. "Feminism with a small 'f'!" In: *Criticism and Ideology.* Ed. Kirsten Holst Petersen. Uppsala: Scandinavian Institute of African Studies, 1980: 173-85.

Fanon, Frantz. *The Wretched of the Earth.* Trans. By Constance Farrington. New York: Grove Press, 1963.

Granqvist, Raoul and John Stotesbury. Interview with Ama Ata Aidoo. "African Women's Writing." *African Voices: Interviews with Thirteen African Writers.* Sidney: Dangaroo Press, 1989. 12-15.

James, Adeola. Interview with Ama Ata Aidoo. *In Their Own Voices: African Women Writers Talk.* London: James Currey, 1990.8-27.

Jones, Ann R. "Writing the Body: Toward an Understanding of L'Écriture Féminine." *The New Feminist Criticism: Essays on Women Literature and Theory.* Ed. Elaine Showalter. London: Virago, 1986.361-77.

Kalu, Anthonia C. "Those Left Out in the Rain: African Literary Theory and the Re-invention of the African Woman." *African Studies Review* 37,2 (September 1994):77-95.

Katrak, Ketu H. "Decolonizing Culture: Toward a Theory for Postcolonial Women's Texts." *Modern Fiction Studies* 35,1 (Spring 1989):157-79.

Lâm, Maivân C. "Feeling Foreign in Feminism." *Signs* 19, 4 (Summer 1994):865-93.

Lugones, María C. and Elizabeth V. Spelman."Have We Got a Theory for You! Feminist Theory, Cultural Imperialism and the Demand for 'The Woman's Voice'." *Women's Studies International Forum* 6, 6 (1983):573-81.

Maja-Pearce, Adewale. Interview with Ama Ata Aidoo. "We Were Feminists in Africa First." *Index on Censorship* 19, 9 (October 1990):17-18.

Makanjuola, Bola. "A Modern Woman's Dilemma." *West Africa* no 3839 (1-7 April 1991):474.

McClintock, Anne."The Angel of Progress: Pitfalls of the Term 'Post-Colonialism'." *Social Text* 31-32 (1992):84-98.

Mishra, Vijay, and Bob Hodge, "What is post(-)colonialism?" *Textual Practice*

5, 3 (1991):399-414.

Mohan, Rajeswari. "Dodging the Crossfire: Questions for Postcolonial Pedagogy." *College Literature* 19,3 (October 1992)/20,1 (February 1993): 28-44.

Mohanty, Chandra T. "Under Western Eyes: Feminist Scholarship and Colonial Discourses." *Third World Women and the Politics of Feminism.* Ed. Chandra Mohanty et al. Bloomington: Indiana University Press, 1991.51-80.

Morgan, Robin. Ed. *Sisterhood is Global: The International Women's Movement Anthology.* Garden City, N.Y.: Anchor Press/Doubleday, 1984.

Needham, Anuradha D. "An Interview with Ama Ata Aidoo." *Massachusetts Review* 36,1 (Spring 1995):123-33.

Nfah-Abbenyi, Juliana M. *Gender in African Women's Writing: Identity, Sexuality, and Difference.* Bloomington: Indiana University Press, 1997.

Ngugi, wa Thiong'o. *Decolonising the Mind: The Politics of Language in African Literature.* London: James Currey, 1986.

Odamtten, Vincent O. *The Art of Ama Ata Aidoo: Polylectics and Reading Against Neocolonialism.* Gainesville: University Press of Florida, 1994.

Petersen, Kirsten H., Ed. *Criticism and Ideology: Second African Writers' Conference, Stockholm 1986.* Ed. Kirsten H. Petersen. Uppsala: Nordiska afrikainstitutet, 1988.

"Profile: Ama Ata Aidoo: Sharp-minded progressive." In: *West Africa.* 3842 (22-28 April 1991): 593.

Rooney, Caroline. "Are We in the Company of Feminists? A Preface to Bessie Head and Ama Ata Aidoo." *Diverse Voices: Essays on Twentieth-Century Women Writers in English.* Ed. Harriet D. Jump. New York: Harvester Wheatsheaf, 1991.214-46.

Shohat, Ella. "Notes on the 'Post-Colonial'." *Social Text* 31-32 (1992):99-113.

Spivak, Gayatri C. "Imperialism and Sexual Difference." *Oxford Literary Review* 8,1-2 (1986):225-40.

———. "Diasporas Old and New: Women in the Transnational World." *Textual Practice* 10,2 (1996):245-69.

———. *Moving the Centre: The Struggle for Cultural Freedoms.* London: James Currey, 1993.

West Africa." No. 3842 (22-28 April 1991):593.

Wilkinson, Jane. "Ben Okri." *Talking with African Writers: Interviews with African Poets, Playwrights* and *Novelists.* London: James Currey, 1992.76-89.

Woolf, Virginia. *A Room of One's Own.* London: Hogarth Press, 1929.

THE POLITICS OF MOTHERING:

MULTIPLE SUBJECTIVITY AND GENDERED

DISCOURSE IN AIDOO'S PLAYS

NAANA BANYIWA HORNE

No man claims to speak from the womb, women do. Their site of fertilization, they often insist, is the womb, not the mind. Their inner gestation is in the womb, not in the mind. The mind is therefore no longer opposed to the heart; it is, rather, perceived as part of the womb, (as) being "englobed by it."

Men name "womb" to separate a part of woman from woman (to separate it from the rest that forms her: body and mind), making it possible to lay legal claim to it. By doing so, they create their own contradictions and come round to identifying her with their fabrication: a specialized, infant-producing organ.

Women use "womb" to re-appropriate it and re-unite (or re- differ) themselves, their bodies, their places of production. This may simply mean beating the master at his own game. But it may also mean asserting difference on differences.

—Trinh T. Minh-ha, *Woman, Native, Other*

This paper explores the politics of mothering in Aidoo's two plays. In *The Dilemma of a Ghost* (1965), first produced in 1964, and *Anowa* (1970),[1] female subjectivity and agency are located in the contested socio-ecomonic and political terrains of the woman-nurturing, matrilineal kinship system of the Akan of Ghana and patriarchy with its penchant for oppressing women globally. Patriarchy, the system of male-dominance, is seen as a delimiting influence while matrilineal kinship, a mother-based system, is perceived as an enabler of female personhood. Mothering, which is sociologically defined as a historically and culturally variable relationship based in one individual nurturing and caring for another (Glenn 1994: 3),[2] is conceived to be the encompassing socio-political and spiritual foundation of human organization. This concept is explored beyond the context of birthing and caregiving, beyond women's biological and sociological functions, and opened up to encompass the political and spiritual ramifications of female agency within the context of human organization. However, contrary to Western liberal feminist perceptions of the womb as a vehicle that leads to the devaluation of female personhood,[3] this analysis acknowledges the womb as an enabling element and situates it at the center of female agency. It is through the agency of the womb that human societies are actualized. Thus by acknowledging mothering as the locus of social, economic, and political organization in the human community, through the tracing of descent and the inheritance of political power via the mother line, the matrilineal kinship system recognizes women's multiple subjectivity emanating from maternal agency.

Ghanaian woman writer Ama Ata Aidoo's commitment to her craft issues from a strong recognition of a gendered self that is female. Unlike some writers who have reservations about being designated women writers, she not only accedes to being a *woman*, but even acknowledges that feminism is integral to her artistic consciousness, as the following assertion indicates:

When people ask me rather bluntly every now and

> then whether I am a feminist, I not only answer yes,
> but I go on to insist that every woman and every
> man should be a feminist—especially if they believe
> that Africans should take charge of our land, its
> wealth, our lives and the burden of our own devel-
> opment. Because it is not possible to advocate inde-
> pendence for our continent without also believing
> that African women must have the best that the
> environment can offer. For some of us, this is the
> crucial element of our feminism. (Aidoo 1998:47)[4]

The author's descent from a matrilineage buttresses her belief that
women belong in the forefront of development and social transformation, a belief she brings to realization through her writings.
Her feminism colludes with her activism to render a multiple subjectivity and agency in female identity formation imperative to the
conception of womanbeing. The continued focus on the female
subject in her creative works—plays, fiction (long and short), and
poetry—is bolstered by a string of non-fiction titles which identify
womanbeing as subject.[5]

In the opening quotation, Trinh T. Minh-ha's words are deliberately framed into three distinct blocks/tropes to foreground *the womb*
as the locus of woman's layered identities—of her multiple subjectivity at the core of feminist excavations (African and Western) of
mothering as a biological experience, a socially constructed institution,[6] as well as an objectified being at the heart of patriarchy's reductionist figurations of womanbeing. The first trope is that of mothering
as the source of familial continuity engendered through the womb's
agency to "englobe." It inscribes matrilineal kinship and its enabling
of female personhood embodied in Nana and Esi Kom in *Dilemma*.
The second trope inscribes patriarchy and its conscription of the
womb in the service of male privilege represented by Ato and Kofi
Ako in *Dilemma* and *Anowa* respectively. These two tropes articulate a gynocentric and a phallocentric construction of female personhood. The third trope derives from the third frame and the issue
of women's re-appropriations of the womb. Though similar to the
first, it introduces the element of motive into the context, thereby
rendering the issue more complicated. Re-appropriation of the
womb, in this case, separates into actions motivated by a desire to
beat "the master at his [own] game" or to assert "difference on differences" (Trinh 1989:38). Women like Badua and The-Old-Woman-
Mouth-That-Eats-Salt-And-Pepper operate in manners that delimit

rather than foster female personhood. Their motives derive from ideological positions which, like patriarchal ideology, are manipulative and obsessed with power over and control of others. The third trope, therefore, inscribes the problematic of women's evocation of maternal agency in ways that are defeatist, because motivated by the divisive intentions undergirding patriarchy. In contrast, female re-appropriation of the womb, which assert difference on differences, fostering complementarity and interdependence as integral dimensions of gender relations, are already subsumed in the first trope and its inscription of mothering as the source of human continuity. Notably, females like Maami Esi Kom and Anowa, whose interventions foster maternal agency, re-appropriate the "womb" for purposes of "englobing."

Obioma Nnaemeka emphasizes "the importance of cultural literacy to any valid feminist theorizing of African literature" (1997: 1). Matrilineal kinship, the system underlying the society within which Aidoo's fiction and dramatic productions are constructed, I argue, lends intricacy to her articulation of womanbeing. Therefore, to truly understand the discursive terrains which come into constant contestation in her plays, it becomes imperative not only to examine constructions of personhood, gynocentric and phallocentric, but also how kinship systems inform gender politics. Human communities perpetuate themselves through procreation, with kinship at the core of human organization, providing a primary form of identification along maternal and paternal lines. In the contemporary world, while patriarchy, the rule of the fathers, has entrenched itself as the dominant mode of global organization, nature itself intimates that women are the natural nucleus of human organization. Pregnancy, gestation, birth, producing food for new life, and other forms of nurturance, all stem from the female body to affirm the organic centrality of the female in human organization. This ability to give birth and sustain life gives woman an undisputed natural authority which, because it is functional rather than artificially constructed,[7] points to the tracing of descent through the maternal line as the organic system of human organization. However, man, perceiving himself to be disadvantaged by nature in such a fundamental manner, resorted to force and other forms of manipulation, to wrest from woman her organic authority. Patriarchy, then, constitutes the institutionalization of the male subversion of the natural life-line established through the agency of the womb between mothers and children, a sabotaging of maternal agency as the organic root of social connectedness.

The so-called rule of the fathers is synonymous with male domination, with the exertion of control, often through coercive means, over others, primarily women and children.

Conversely, matrilineal kinship, a system which valorizes motherwork,[8] affirms the organic root of human organization by acknowledging woman as the producer and reproducer of the body politic. Barbara Katz Rothman, comparing mothering ideologies, asserts that in "a mother-based system, *a person is what mothers grow—people are made of the care and nurturance that bring a baby forth into the world, and turn the baby into a member of a society"* (1994: 141; emphasis added). Matrilineal kinship recognizes woman as the very source of intergenerational connectedness, the hub of human and social relationships. She is one who, in full knowledge of her agency in perpetuating humankind, asserts that agency for human continuity in a most fundamental sense. Aidoo sheds some light on matrilineal kinship and gender politics:

> It is now clear that most African societies were matrilineages lasting millennia, from the prepharonic period all the way down to a micronation like the Akans of Ghana. What changed the pattern in some areas were, first, Islam, and later, Christianity, since both religions were obviously patriarchal in orientation. *The African societies that retained vestiges of their matrilineages were also ones that met both Islam and Christianity with the greatest resistance.* These areas—for instance, coastal West Africa—are also where one finds some of the least oppressed women. (1998:42-43; emphasis added)

Thus, in spite of the intensified efforts to construct mothering into an instrument of gender oppression,[9] it nonetheless remains valorizing in organically rendering women prominent in the shaping of the lives of their children, the fruits of female labor. In the matrilineal kinship system, women's biological role as producers of humans gives them primacy in human society by positioning them organically to exert influence on human events.

In *The Dilemma of a Ghost*, the natural privileging of women on account of their biology is inscribed in Nana's person, particularly, and in that of the women in the Odumna household and in the community at large. In the Odumna family council, there are five women—Ato's grandmother, mother, two aunts, and his sister—and only two men, his two uncles. The general community is represented by two women, First Woman and Second Woman, who provide the community's perspective on the issues raised by the play. There is no male voice from the community. Furthermore, in the text four women characters—Maami Esi Kom, Eulalie and the two women neighbors—have prominent roles, while Ato is the only male character who is spotlighted. The prominence accorded women in the text affirms the fact that everyone, men included, is the child of some mother. This primacy is symbolically rendered by the Akan saying, *Wona wu a, na wo abusua asa.* (When one's mother dies, one is bereft of kinfolk.) *The Dilemma of a Ghost*, therefore, authenticates matrilineal kinship's inherent enabling of female personhood through the affirmation of maternal agency. *Anowa*, on the other hand, corroborates the insidiousness of patriarchy, drawing attention to specific ways in which female agency is subverted through force and co-optation.

Aidoo explodes gender configurations that automatically assign victimhood to females by focusing attention on the multiple subjectivity inherent in female personhood. In fact, she ruptures the oppressor/victim dichotomy characteristic of liberal feminist theorizing of mothering by demonstrating "that agency and victimhood are not mutually exclusive ... [for] victims are also agents who can change their lives and affect other lives in radical ways" (Nnaemeka 1997: 3). Consequently, in her plays, the mother is constantly portrayed mediating the roles of victim and agent. Mothering is situated at the cusp of limitation and transcendence. The mother is often shown crossing the borders within which patriarchy constricts mothering to emerge as an agent of transcendence, as one capable of making the world better for herself and her progeny through her re-inscription of female agency into human organization. Such is the nature of the mother in *Dilemma*. Ato's mother, Esi Kom, commonly referred to as Maami (the generic nomenclature for the Mfantse mother), rises above the victim status her son sets her up for, to reclaim her place as the agent of familial continuity.

On the other hand, Aidoo makes evident that victims are not always passive; for potential victims often stave off victimization to their person by becoming co-opted into oppressive institutions. They participate actively in oppressive practices or become instruments of oppression by subscribing to oppressive ideologies. On occasion, the mother is shown trapped, unable and unwilling to assert her agency for change, opting instead to settle for crumbs from the table of patriarchal privilege. She becomes party to the appropriation of female agency for the ultimate furtherance of patriarchy and gender oppression. Contrary to what critics say, namely that Aidoo demonizes males and depicts females in appealing light, she does not cast females only in nurturing roles but also delineates their corroboration of patriarchy's hegemony. For instance in *Anowa*, females like Badua and The-Old-Woman-Mouth-That-Eats-Salt-And-Pepper acquire notoriety on account of their support of patriarchal ideologies of gender. In the end, they become the strongest proponents of patriarchy and gender oppression through their support of Kofi Ako in his struggle to dominate Anowa, and acquire validation within the masculinist bourgeois context of success and its concomitant domestication of the female. Badua and the Old Woman legitimize patriarchy's constriction of female ingenuity. In fact, they are directly responsible both for the demise of Anowa and for what Kofi Ako ultimately becomes: the epitome of patriarchy, visibly surrounded by the indices of power and material success acquired through the ruthless exploitation of human flesh.

In *Dilemma* and *Anowa*, the multiple subjectivity and agency inherent in mothering at the core of gender politics are rendered central to Aidoo's artistic vision. She explores mothering from the vantage points of reproduction and production, that is, as biological experience and as it is socially constructed within the matrilineal kinship system with its gynocentric propensities and also as it is impacted by patriarchy. She makes evident that mothers produce human beings, and this act constitutes the most fundamental level of human production; for without the children produced by mothers, there will be no citizens, no workers, in fact, no humankind. This reality is tapped by Aidoo in scripting the multiple subjectivity embodied in female personhood. The multiple role of grandmother, mother, other-mother, birth-mother, wife, daughter, sister, barren woman, caregiver, proud parent, aggrieved parent, priestess, witch, slave mother, slave daughter, radical woman, conservative woman, nosy neighbor, tomboyish girl populate her dramatic productions, providing a multiple definition of female personhood derived through agency and victimhood. In fact, the very structuring of her plays affirms woman's multiple subjectivity.

In Aidoo's Prelude to *Dilemma*, the "Bird of the Wayside" is initially introduced as "The sudden scampering in the undergrowth, / Or the trunkless head / Of the shadow in the corner" (7). It is an enigmatic figure, genderless, elusive, defying identification, clearly more bird/owl than human, lacking a distinct human identity.

However, quickly, it acquires a multiplicity of female identities based in both agency and victimhood, primary among which is the "Asthmatic, old hag / Eternally breaking the nuts" (7), whose soup perennially nourishes the world. It assumes the identity of the female progenitor from whom the clan is descended and evokes the roles of nurturer and worker, entwined in the imagery of nuts.

The nuts referred to are palm nuts, from a tree that appropriately images the nurturance and resourcefulness of the Akan mother. The *abe* palm tree is celebrated in Ghana as the ultimate symbol of productivity. No part of the tree ever goes to waste. Palm nuts are the source of the Ghanaian staple, palm soup, the preferred choice of nourishment for nursing mothers and growing people because of its high nutritional value. It is considered a dish with soul, one that holds up the ribs, that is, keeps one sustained for a long time. Fufu and palm soup are, in fact, a mark of Akan hospitality. Akan women are also greatly respected for their resourceful handling of the palm nuts. After pounding the nuts in order to acquire the creamy pulp for the soup and palm oil, use is found for the residue. The washed out pulp is dried and used as fuel, and also as incense on account of its appealing smell; and the discarded nuts are cracked to separate the shell from the kernel which provide palm kernel oil, used for cooking, for cosmetics, and for lubrication. Often times, women and/or their children are seen cracking the nuts during what should constitute their leisure time, an action that supports the image of the mother as perennially working. Palm nuts, therefore, constitute a binding symbol of maternal agency, nurturance, and survival.

At the same time, the image of the Asthmatic, old hag eternally breaking palm nuts evokes Ghana's colonial history, palm nuts being intertwined with colonial/capitalist exploitation. During the colonial period, cracking palm nuts became associated with colonial oppression. Ghanaian school children were mandated to bring a stipulated measure of palm kernels to school regularly. It was explained that British industries needed them to produce oil for lubricating industrial machines and for making margarine. It was a kind of tax the colonized nation had to pay to the colonial nation, a tax of loyalty to the empire into which colonized nations were conscripted. Failure to deliver the stipulated measure of palm kernels resulted in whippings and even suspension from school.[10] Oftentimes, mothers ended up cracking the nuts for their children to ensure their escaping this brush with colonial oppression. Therefore, through her nut breaking, the "Asthmatic, old hag" evokes both the hard work that goes into mothers nurturing their children, and the colonial/capitalist exploitation of African womanhood.

The Asthmatic, old hag's eternal breaking of nuts is again reminiscent of Sisyphus and his eternal rolling of the boulder up the hill, only for the boulder to roll right back down and for the process to start all over again, imaging the never-ending repercussions of colonialism. The myth of Sisyphus also appropriately images motherwork, the business of nurturing the human race. Nurturing, granted, has a built-in gratification that comes from the sense of pride generated by caring, in meaningful ways, for people, and from the growth and the pleasure the nurtured derive from the care they receive, while the myth of Sisyphus connotes nothing but pure drudgery. Nonetheless, motherwork is also tedious and wearing on women; it is a never-ending process. Hence, the double-bind of agency and victimization inherent in mothering. This double-bind is epitomized by the two women in *Dilemma*, the nosy neighbors of the Odumna household through whom we find out all about Esi Kom's business. These two women, also subsumed in the image of the Asthmatic, old hag in the Prelude, constitute the community of women whose voices affirm the liveliness of the community, in addition to framing the boundaries for polarizing the politics of mothering through the portraiture of the overly fertile woman and her childless friend. Their representative nature is reflected by their not bearing personal names. 1st Woman, who is childless, envies 2nd Woman because she has a house teeming with children—the eleven she has given birth to herself, in addition to her husband's and her sister's children. While it is evident that the woman with children takes pride in her ability to have them, what is realized most strongly in the play is the fact that women in their role as mothers, other-mothers, and wives, bear the brunt of the burden of catering to the needs of their household. Throughout the play, the two women (one in her capacity as mother, other-mother, and wife, and the other as wife), are portrayed at work every time they appear: fetching water, gathering firewood, and returning from the market with food to cook for their families. The one exception is when at the end of the play they are roused from their sleep by the commotion in the Odumna house. We are constantly informed by the two women neighbors of the culinary activities going on in the Odumna house itself, betrayed by the enticing aromas emitting from the Odumna kitchen. In the play, these aromas come to signify Ato and his wife's visits with the family as well as those momentous occasions, such as the "Sprinkling of the Stools" by the family, on which the matrilineage, with the women in the forefront, confront those issues of life and death which cement the family unit.

Above all, the "Asthmatic, old hag" evokes Nana, Ato's grandmother, who is old at the time the drama unfolds, thus conflating this image with the symbol of intergenerational continuity in the matrilineage. A highly visible character in the text, Nana is the oldest living female of the Odumna clan or *abusua* in Akan language.[11] She is on the threshold of the ancestral world and the world of the living, visibly connecting the living with the ancestral world and with the world of the unborn, thus holding the Akan world together. Nana, being the most senior female and the one who has reproduced on the highest level, being grandmother, has considerable authority. Within the Akan family structure, the matrilineage, she is the living female through whom the *abusua*, the matrikin, traces its descent and ancestry. This is a primary source of identity formation for Nana, and Akan women, and it is acquired through the agency of the womb, that is, through women's ability to bear children who, in the matrilineal kinship system, are recognized as belonging to a core socio-political group that recognizes female agency in human organization. Nana's authority, deriving from her position as the living female through whom the Odumna *abusua* traces its family group, also conjures up wisdom. The "Bird of the Wayside" is conflated with the "Asthmatic Old Hag" to evoke the owl, that bird symbolizing wisdom and mystery. Significantly, no serious family deliberation takes place without Nana being present. The responsibility for the Odumna *abusua* falls squarely on her. Consequently, when Ato violates custom by not only shutting the *abusua* out of his marriage but marrying someone of questionable stock, to be precise, the "daughter of slaves who come from the white man's land" (19), Nana assumes full responsibility, physical and spiritual, for the survival of the clan. She articulates the imperative in her position as the custodian of the Odumna *abusua* and the peril she envisions to her spiritual well-being on account of what she perceives as her failure to ensure the continuity of the *abusua*. The primacy of maternal agency in human production, therefore, is depicted in *Dilemma* through the prominence that the subject of motherhood and the role of mother are given. Notably, even in her hour of distress, Nana asserts her connectedness to the ancestral world through her maternal line. It is to her spirit mother she appeals, lamenting that she (mother spirit) had failed to come for her (Nana/daughter) earlier, leaving her (Nana/daughter) to live to witness the desecration brought on the matrilineage. Moreover, it is Maami Esi Kom, Nana's daughter and link to the world of the living, who initiates the necessary action to bring about a healing of the rupture caused by Ato's action. Thus, the Akan world view is affirmed through the maternal line: Nana, her spirit mother, and her daughter, Esi Kom.

The conflicts inherent in *Dilemma* are fueled by a contestation between maternal agency (vested in Maami Esi Kom) and patriarchy (assumed by Ato); and the denouement is brought about through the assertion of the potency of that agency in harnessing patriarchy's threat to female personhood. By making his marriage his personal affair rather than the family's affair, that is, as an appropriate vehicle for consolidating family strength, Ato attempts to negate the agency vested by the matrilineage in its women in the building of family ties. Above all, he subverts Maami's maternal agency by depriving her of exercising one of the key maternal roles in matrilineal kinship—the mother's right to visibility in the choice of a spouse for her son. This privilege affords the mother of the groom the opportunity to pave the way for establishing a mother-daughter relationship with her son's wife, to lay down roots for a relationship founded in harmony, rather than risk the contentious relationship of in-laws with its built-in trap for generational and familial conflicts on which patriarchy thrives. Ato's actions mainly establish roots for the alienation between his wife and his people, threatening Eulalie's very survival within her new homeland. Especially with Nana close to the grave, nothing would be considered more fortuitous than a new birth to maintain the equilibrium of the Akan world, to affirm the continuum inherent in the world of the living, the ancestral world, and the world of the unborn; and Eulalie becoming the instrument for bringing about this realization will engender her connectedness to Ato's family, mitigating the alienating circumstances surrounding Ato's marriage. Yet, when Eulalie voices her apprehension about the negative implications of postponing having children after marriage within the African context, Ato downplays her uneasiness, making her believe that having children will be disruptive to their love. "Children, who wants them? In fact, they will make me jealous. I couldn't bear seeing you love someone else better than you do me. Not yet, darling, and not even my own children" (10).

Ato's perspective on marriage mirrors a clearly patriarchal

obsession with dichotomizing and hierarchizing relationships in order to ensure male privilege. He constructs maternity and conjugality into a conflictual relationship which abrogates complementarity and interdependence by depicting the male in competition with children for the love of woman. Woman as mother is vested with authority; but woman as wife is subordinated to male pleasure, a paradox located at the heart of phallocentric and gynocentric constructions of female subjectivity/objectivity, and an impetus for patriarchy to subvert maternal agency. Considering that we first encounter Ato on a university campus in America, the stronghold of patriarchal and imperial hegemony, a world notorious for inventing tools for enforcing hegemonic relationships and for objectifying women as toys for male pleasure and as beasts of burden catering to male whims, it is little wonder that he consciously crafts his actions to separate "a part of woman from woman" (Trinh 1989:37), in order to control and dominate her.

Apparently a good student of colonial education, Ato, in his intercourse with both his wife and his indigenous family, manifests a flair for dominance, for talking down to people and striking the pose of the enlightened/colonizer/male in the presence of the ignorant/native/female. The desire to dominate Eulalie culminates in his slapping her during their final confrontation towards the end of the play when Eulalie challenges him for hiding behind his people to oppress her. His flair for hegemonic discourse also reveals itself when his family confronts him about his secret marriage. Significantly, the matrikin's reaction is on the level of high emotions (weeping, enactments of horror, and great distress), while Ato's reaction is froth with the coldness Western/patriarchal ideology attributes to reason, a quality appropriated by men as a male prerogative. He strikes an academic pose, moving upstage to lecture his distraught people on African history. He is, in fact, appalled by their lack of reason in reacting so negatively to what he perceives as an enlightening move. Though the political expediency of his marriage is worthy of commendation, his handling of affairs reeks of the arrogance brewed by colonial education and the inculcation of patriarchal values. Neither is Ato above employing the imperialist tactic of divide and conquer: pitting his mother against his wife; mimicking the duplicity of the imperial powers who, to begin with, caused the rift between Africans on the continent and in the diaspora. Further, he paints his indigenous family as a primitive lot too rigid to accommodate difference, while condoning his family's perceptions of his foreign wife as a woman plagued by the superiority complex of whites.

Nevertheless, in *Dilemma*, patriarchy's impositions are shown to be contained by the women in the matrilineage. Ato's actions are constantly questioned, particularly by the women in the *abusua*. His mother stands up to him, unearths his divisive motives, and confronts him with his dubiousness. She then commences to pave the way for Eulalie's integration into her new world. In order to reclaim the maternal authority that Ato has attempted to wrest from his mother and his wife through his manipulation of the latter's ignorance of Akan society, Maami asserts the mother's agency in educating her children to bring about transformation. Eulalie, being an outsider, needs to be educated about Akan beliefs in meaningful ways to bring about her integration into her new world, a responsibility at which Ato has failed, making it imperative for his mother to take it on. While the search for a family has been a motivating factor in Eulalie's decision to marry Ato, she seems to need educating on the fact that in the African world, it is motherhood rather than wifehood that will bring about this realization. Full womanly stature is premised on motherhood. Marriage is primarily an instrument for laying the foundation for motherhood to happen, making wifehood, at best, a means to an end rather than an end in itself. For this reason even a "bad marriage" is considered redeemable by motherhood for the simple reason that "even from bad marriages / Are born good sons and daughters" (22).

By extending a maternal arm to Eulalie, Maami Esi Kom affirms maternal agency in human continuity by elevating her daughter-in-law to the stature of daughter, inducting her into the Odumna household, and bringing about the realization of the latter's prayer to acquire a new family through her marriage. Eulalie being doubly orphaned (first through the death of her mother, and second by being removed from America, her place of birth, where she, at least, has friends and is familiar with the way of life, into a world that is foreign to her), is in desperate need of a mother, not a mother-in-law. In the Akan matrilineage, woman as daughter is treasured. But as in most African societies, woman as wife is prone to victimization.[12] Maami's action affirms the truly African context of marriage as the consolidator of families. She also exerts political agency by re-inscribing the uprooted, dispossessed daughter of Africa into her motherland. This action is political because it bridges the estrangement that slavery/colonialism has forced between continental Africans and those in the diaspora. Maami subsumes the role of mother Africa by suturing the rupture of slavery and colonialism that has alienated Africa from her children. It is worth noting that Ato is the one who initiates this process by marrying Eulalie, an African American, and pledging to integrate her into his African family; however, he stalls the process through his identification with patriarchal and colonialist ideologies of divide and conquer.

At the end of the play, Maami Esi Kom overturns the divisiveness wedged by patriarchy between the African woman as mother and as wife that Phanuel Egejuru identifies as the "paradox of womanbeing" (1997:11-19), and by colonialism/slavery between the African woman as trueblood and as alienated daughter contesting for mother Africa's affection. When Maami reaches out to Eulalie by extending a maternal arm of support to the younger woman, the older woman's action is scripted as an act of englobing, spurred by the agency of the womb, to borrow Trinh T. Minh-ha's words (1989:37). Being a mother herself renders Maami sensitive to a daughter's need for a mother. When she cautions, "And we must be careful with your wife / You tell us her mother is dead. / If she had any tenderness, / Her ghost must be keeping watch over / All which happen to her ...(Aidoo 1987:52), Maami is impressing upon her son the potency of maternal agency as a physical and a spiritual phenomenon. This invocation is the obverse of the Akan saying cited earlier on: *Wona wu a, na wu abusua asa* (When one's mother dies, one is bereft of kinsfolk). Mothers, being the source of human connectedness, never die. And mothers never really stop mothering their children, regardless of how old they get.

Maternal agency is symbolically asserted and patriarchy undercut in the image of Maami Esi Kom and Eulalie, walking together in a manner befitting mother and daughter into the lighted old wing of the Odumna house, while Ato is left all alone in the new wing, floundering around in darkness like an impotent ghost. The mother must have strength and wisdom in order to protect the weak, maintain justice, and keep the victimizer at bay. Maami's action is a reminder to women to exercise fairness and good judgement. As mothers of sons, women by accepting their sons' wives as daughters, can foster bonds of solidarity and social kinship which can protect women from patriarchal assaults; they can unite against those divisive ploys men employ to keep women divided on all kinds of hierarchical levels, which in the end only facilitate patriarchy's control of all women. The beauty in this trope lies in its reclaiming of the agency of mothering as a female prerogative to "englobe," that is, to engender wholeness, thereby negating the perception of the womb as a vehicle for limiting, fragmenting, or handicapping female personhood.

Akan valorization of the womb as the site of connectedness does indeed challenge the patriarchal construction of the womb as a source of hysteria. Among the Akan, when young women manifest symptoms of hysteria, or schizophrenia, a primary recommendation for re-instituting wholeness is motherhood. It is believed that through the affirmation of a woman's centrality to procreativity, motherhood will exert a centering impact that will render the fragmented, dislocated, individual whole by re-inscribing her connectedness, through birth and caregiving, into the human community. This theme is explored with a twist in Aidoo's play, *Anowa*, the story of a young woman who fails to realize her ability to bear children and, in the end, goes insane and drowns herself. Some of the surface elements of the plot point to a connection between Anowa's childlessness and insanity and suicide. When she marries her lover, Kofi Ako, and the two leave home to build a life together, their relationship thrives in the early years of the marriage, fostering conjugality and business partnership. However, as they become successful and work plays a minimal role in their lives, Anowa grows restless, worrying more and more about children. Estranged from a husband who is threatening to send her back to Yebi, a place she had sworn never to return, loneliness and desperation eventually force her to lose her grasp on reality, and she drowns.

This reading, however, finds support only in the surface elements of the play, that is, in a simplistic reading of the plot. The play *Anowa* is a complexly crafted work of art in which multiple subject areas ingenuously intersect to establish Aidoo as a precursor of African women's creative theorizing of the multiple subjectivity and agency that inform human interaction within a gendered and class-stratified context of existence.[13] Davies notes that the "intersections of coloniality, male dominance, class prejudices, economic exploitation, power and gender dynamics ... explored in this play ... placed it ahead of its time" (1994:60). The intricacies in works like *Anowa* inspired Vincent Odamtten's (1994) book-length study of Ama Ata Aidoo and its polylectic/multiple readings of her themes. Childbearing, childlessness, homelessness, slavery, are placed in tandem in *Anowa* to force a confrontation of troubling issues that "[a]ll good men and women" would much rather forget (106). In a stroke of genius, all these conditions are discursively positioned in Anowa's person. Aidoo's unsettling message is that when the agency of the womb in ensuring intergenerational continuity is sabotaged and the womb becomes expropriated in the furtherance of the exploitative designs of patriarchy and male hegemony, mother nature fights back by withholding maternal bounty from humankind. Anowa's childlessness, within this context, then, represents an assertion of agency, the conscious curbing of a function to arrest its misappropriation.

Right from childhood, Anowa is considered wild. When the emerging young woman's wildness becomes a source of concern for her family, prompting suggestions of having her apprenticed to a deity to become a priestess, Badua objects, convinced that Anowa marrying and settling down to have children is the needed antidote to her wildness. What Badua articulates, in the words of Carole Boyce Davies, is "the classic mother's 'wish'" (69) for her daughter. The mother's convictions firmly ground her daughter's envisioned fulfilment as a "human woman" (72) in the stabilizing impact attributed to the womb's agency. Badua identifies motherhood as the key to her daughter's attainment of full personhood; nonetheless, her aspirations do not negate all other roles but that of procreating for her daughter. Multiple possibility, including leadership positions—taking one's place at meetings where clan decisions are taken, assuming a captainship in the army/*asafo*—offer opportunities for enhancing female personhood.

Much of the criticism of Aidoo's *Anowa* has focused on the constricting role opportunities for women in society. A critical but realistic look at the play, however, questions such a critique; for, men of the period are not shown doing much more than women except hatching intricate schemes for undermining women's agency. The last quarter of the nineteenth century, the approximate period in which the play is set, is definitely not the last quarter of the twentieth century, the period out of which criticism of Aidoo's plays have emerged. Nevertheless, the resourceful lives women lead is intimated by the roles women are depicted playing. Farming, trade and commerce, and active participation in the corporate organization that the family is considered to be, is quite well-documented by Gold Coast historians and also supported by Badua's catalog of possibilities.[14] Anowa, the heroine of the play, and her husband Kofi Ako, have a flourishing trading business, selling natural products to the Europeans on the coast. Trade and commerce constitute a viable segment of global economy that has, from time immemorial, been dominated by women in West Africa. Aidoo observes:

[T]here is one group of women almost peculiar to

West Africa. These women are in trade and commerce. Mostly, such women are referred to as "market women" or "market mammies" by non-West
Africans. But of course, not all of them actually work
from the markets, although the great majority do.
Their activities range from gem dealing and high
finance to "petty" trading. Therefore, their work-
places also range from highly sophisticated office
complexes to the pavements of the cities where
their kiosks stand. (Aidoo 1998:45)[15]

While the above quotation reflects the contemporary scene,
Ghanaian women's visibility in trade and commerce is of proverbial stature. Therefore, through Anowa, Aidoo pays tribute to the
industry and ingenuity of our foremothers. In fact, the story of
Anowa, symbolically, mirrors patriarchy's maneuvers to erode
women's effective participation in the global economy. Notably, in
the play, Kofi Ako comes to dominate the trading and commercial
enterprise he establishes with Anowa. Even though Anowa is the
brain behind the business, Kofi Ako eventually runs her out, vetoing her participation so that he can freely exploit slave labor to
build an economic empire. Therefore, while much attention has
been given to the issue of limited opportunities for women, and to
Anowa's barrenness as a tragedy, the crux of the issue in Anowa
is the politics of dispossession—that is, the disenfranchisement
resulting from patriarchy's systematic eroding of maternal agency, be it through husbands vetoing their wives' resignation from
the public sphere of work, or ruthless, power-hungry, men like Kofi
Ako making slaves of women's children.

In a similar vein, considerable discussion has centered around
Anowa's victimization on account of her assertiveness.[16] However,
a close scrutiny of the evidence intimates that assertiveness in a
woman, in itself, is not considered a justifiable ground for her
oppression, and that it is mainly in the position of wife that
assertiveness becomes constructed into a justifiable basis for
oppression. Assertiveness in Ghanaian women, I submit, is
encouraged, and there is ample support for this view. The "market woman" is the epitome of assertiveness. Aidoo talks about how
"these women make money to feed, clothe, and educate their children, and sometimes [even] support their men" (Aidoo 1998:46).
That assertiveness is positively perceived is also evident in the
nsabran (boast) of Ama Adoma, the Saturday female.[17] Ama is

hailed: *"Adoma ye ntsen"* (Adoma, the sassy one), and she responds: *" Na nkye me nye wo ba bi se""* (My sassiness is just like your child's), in other words, "I am your kin in sassiness." This interchange is normally between an older female and the younger Ama Adoma. Since every Ama is Adoma, and the signifier of Adoma is sassiness, it is a quality presumably possessed by every Ama. Ama being a very common female name, the significance, then, is that the trait embodied in the by-name is one that is predominant in females. Furthermore, the very existence of the boast itself subsumes a platform for the enactment of sassiness. Sassiness/assertiveness, therefore, is an attribute that is openly celebrated rather than suppressed in females. Notably, both of Aidoo's plays have more assertive women than docile ones. No female character in either text ranks in the docile department. Each of them, including the girl who plays ghost-ghost with the boy, can dish out more than she will take. In fact, in *Dilemma*, Monka, Ato's sister, is declared the "queen of sassiness" by the two women neighbors, the voice of the community. Not surprisingly, the context for raising the issue of Monka's sassiness is that of marriage; Monka's sassiness is highlighted as the inhibiter to her success in marriage.

Again, at the start of the play, the young, unmarried Anowa is a very different female from the later, married Anowa. She is sassy, spunky, energetic, and relatively free, free enough to risk choosing her own husband, and to set out with him, filled with the optimism that she can transform him into somebody. Until her marriage, though her wildness is talked about by her mother and everybody else, there is no urgency to make her act differently. The outright antagonism her wildness attracts comes later, when she marries Kofi Ako. It is only then it becomes intimated that her assertiveness will not stand her in favorable light as a wife. Badua, hearing about Anowa's unhappiness in her marriage volunteers: "Before she walked out that noon-day, she should have waited for me to tell her how to marry a man.... A good woman does not have a brain or a mouth" (Aidoo 1987:93). Substituting "wife" for "woman" would have been more appropriate. Anowa, herself, arrives at this realization too late. Towards the end of the play, she soliloquizes:

> Someone should have taught me how to grow up to
> be a woman. I hear in other lands a woman is nothing. And they let her know this from the day of her

birth. But here, O my spirit mother, they let a girl
grow up as she pleases until she is married. And
then she is like any woman anywhere: in order for
her man to be a man, she must not think, she must
not talk. O-o, why didn't someone teach me how to
grow up to be a woman? (112)

Again, substituting "wife" for the last "woman" throws a light on
Anowa's plight. What both plays confirm is that it is in the role of
wife that women are rendered the most vulnerable to patriarchal
assaults on personhood. Furthermore, gender oppression on that
level persists because of the support some women lend to the victimization of other women in the role of wife.

Contrary to *Dilemma* in which the womb's agency in ensuring
intergenerational continuity is affirmed, *Anowa* focuses on the collapse of maternal agency. In *Anowa*, images of rupture prevail.
Davies addresses this issue of rupture:

Anowa refigures the New World/Old World signs of
rupture, schism, opening and othering as it simultaneously embodies the critique of constructions of
the woman in society.... The material of the play
itself traverses boundaries that have to do with orality, writing and performance, gender, marginality
and the social construction of identity, the patriarchal assumptions that are generally allied with capitalist exploitation. (1994:59)

Patriarchy is what reigns supreme while maternal agency is shown
tottering on the brink of collapse. There are no nurturing grandmothers to intervene in mother-daughter fall-outs; daughters
brand mothers witches; mothers produce children they are left
impotent to save from the clutches of the enslaver and his dehumanizing atrocities; women become agents of patriarchal oppression, condoning the victimization of other women and supporting
patriarchal ideology. Badua and Anowa have a relationship befitting rivals, not mother and daughter; and The-Old-Woman-Mouth-
That-Eats-Salt-And-Pepper, contrary to the harmonizing image of
the grandmother, images rupture. She leads the crusade to perse-
cute Anowa. Anowa's failure to reproduce therefore becomes
symptomatic of a general failure of maternal agency to engender
human continuity.

Even Badua's desire for Anowa to get married is motivated

more by the mother's concern about her own image and well-being than by what is best for her daughter. For example, her continued objection to training Anowa to become a priestess stems from her conviction that that line of work offers limited options for prominence or material success. As she puts it, "a priestess lives too much in her own and other people's minds" (Aidoo 1987: 72). Living in the mind, ministering to the spirit, is not being in the limelight compared to living in the eyes of the world, flaunting one's material success, a hint at the bourgeois aspirations and lifestyles that were becoming entrenched among the indigenous populations through the European presence on the African coastline. Ironically, even though Badua realizes her aspiration of seeing her daughter married, that prospect becomes a source of serious discontent. Anowa choosing her own marriage partner, contrary to customary practices of her time, deprives the mother of her share of the fanfare the marriage of an only daughter is likely to be for her, not to mention the contravention of kinship hierarchies that such a move entails.[18] Badua's unceasing lament that her daughter has made her the laughing stock of Yebi by marrying a fool, coupled with her persistent forecast of failure of the marriage, leads to Anowa calling her a witch and leaving home with her husband to settle far away. Her farewell promise never to return to Yebi erases all possibilities for reconciliation between mother and daughter. So Anowa's marriage ironically dates the estrangement between mother and daughter that prevails till the end of Anowa's life, defeating the ultimate benefit in marriages to foster family unity.

Paradoxically, the maternal image that leaves a lasting impression in *Anowa* is that of the slave mother, poignantly imagined by Anowa in her dream and imaged through her body giving birth to children who are seized, dashed to the ground, and stamped upon to burst like ripe tomatoes. She is at the time a young girl who has probably just entered puberty, being no more than twelve years old, a time that is notorious for leaving lasting impressions about adulthood. Given the young Anowa's "prememory" of slavery, her failure to have children takes on the form of female resistance to expropriation of the female womb in the perpetuation of gender oppression. Since women are the reproducers and producers of the human body politic, abuses of women's reproductive agency should be met with women withholding their ability to reproduce.

The insidious manner in which patriarchy works to render women and others subordinated/disenfranchised is ingenuously explored by Aidoo through dialogue, particularly the interchange between Kofi Ako and Anowa in that unencumbered territory, the highway. Significantly, it is on the highway—that uncircumscribed, fluid space—that crucial negotiations of identity are located. It is the site of possibility as well as foreclosure. It is on the highway we see Anowa the happiest and the freest. It is also the site at which the crucial issues that come to govern her marital life and systematically dispossess her are unearthed (Davies 1994:63-64). A scrutiny of the dialogue between husband and wife in Phase Two, of the play, titled "On the Highway," is essential in bringing out the deftness with which Aidoo renders the interdepencies between words and other culturally loaded modes of communication such as body language and other ultra-verbal codes. She sophisticatedly milks the dialogism embedded in discourse (Bakhtin 1981: 276),[19] exposing Kofi Ako's perfidy, spurred on by his desperation to become the dominant male who will reduce Anowa to a subordinated wife. The raging storm which frames the couple's encounter on the highway presages the stormy gender relations that awaits their settlement in their new home on the coast. Ironically, it is when the storm is raging that husband and wife project the lighthearted bantering which has characterized their courtship, a camaraderie that they lose forever, once they traverse the highway and settle on the coast; for, the subsiding of the storm ushers in Kofi Ako's resolve to "be the new husband" and transform Anowa into "the new wife" (Aidoo 1987:87).

In their interchanges, Kofi Ako displays an underhanded talent for twisting Anowa's words into a noose around her neck. Anowa, for her part, counters Kofi's craftiness with verbal and intellectual acumen. For instance, he seizes on a joking reference she makes to taboos to reintroduce the subject of consulting diviners for protective medicines against their enemies. When Anowa voices an objection, he puts her on a guilt trip by craftily evoking her childlessness, a grave condition that mandates intervention, and insinuating that Anowa will not condone his consulting a diviner about that problem since she is against consulting diviners. Anowa's query, "Is it the same thing to ask an older person about a woman's womb as it is to contract medicines in pots and potions which would attract good fortune and ward off evil?"(86), points to the fact that she is not blind to Kofi Ako's verbal and psychological gimmicks of employing guilt as a weapon to compromise her resistance to his exploitative schemes.

In another instance, Anowa broaches the issue of infertility by asking Kofi if his friend the doctor has told him "what is wrong" with her (88). Rather than answer her directly, he exploits the occasion to derive both medical and spiritual authority for his perfidy: a calculated design to dislodge Anowa from the business as equal partner by forcing her out of the public sphere of employment with decision-making powers, in order to have a free hand to implement his diabolical plans of exploiting slave labor; to domesticate her by installing her in the private domain of the home as wife, as one dependent on the beneficience of her husband. He masks his perilous intentions by vocalizing instead a concerned husband's commitment to the well-being of his wife. He tells Anowa the doctor "says there is nothing wrong with your womb. But your soul is too restless. You always seem to be looking for things; and that prevents your blood from settling" (88). Aware of the Akan belief that it is the mother's blood that forms the human body, Kofi Ako insinuates that Anowa's childlessness is caused by her spiritual restlessness, which impedes her blood from settling to enable her to conceive. In fact, his construction of the case makes Anowa into an irrational woman who, because of some perverted sense of adventure, is blind to the risk to her health and spiritual well-being. A woman who does not reproduce does not see herself in the future, he reminds Anowa.

Kofi Ako's insidious machinations surface again when he draws Anowa back to an earlier conversation in which she had recommended a co-wife to join their family to augment its numbers, and then springs on her his intentions to procure slaves. He even attempts to justify his involvement in an institution that is exploitative and dehumanizing, by locating his practice of slavery in a humanized context, arguing that African slavery is not comparable by any yardstick to European chattel or even Arab slavery. "What is wrong with buying one or two people to help us? They are cheap...Everyone does it...does not everyone do it? And things would be easier for us. We shall not be alone..." (90). He proffers the usual excuses apologists of slavery on the African continent offer to diffuse attention from the fact that slavery as an institution, regardless of the logistics of it, is premised on the disenfranchisement of other human beings. However, through Anowa, Aidoo asserts that slavery "is wrong. It is evil" (90). Taking people away from their own people in order to assume total control of their lives and labor is dehumanizing. Calling a slave "a wayfarer, with no belongings either here or there" (96), only becomes "a painless way of saying [s]he does not belong. That [s]he has no home, no family, no village, no stool of his own; has no feast days, no holidays, no state, no territory" (97). Anowa's reactions to her husband's patriarchal and hegemonic rhetoric makes evident her conviction that all hegenomic structures are victimizing. She conflates patriarchy's subordination of women with the disenfranchisement of people as slaves, internalizing the sense of not-belonging and homelessness experienced by the slaves with whom Kofi surrounds them. When Kofi Ako attempts to erase that image, Anowa confronts him with "What is the difference between any of your men and me? Except that they are men and I'm a woman? None of us belongs" (96).

In *Anowa*, homelessness, exile, not-belonging, are multiply imaged as both dispossession and resistance. Having sworn never to return to her natal home, Kofi Ako asking her to leave, renders her homeless, with nowhere to go. Moreover, after all the years of toiling that finally put them on the way to success, he blatantly dispossesses her by asking her to leave. On the other hand, by choosing the identity of a wayfarer, of one who belongs to no one, Anowa reclaims selfhood. As she tells Kofi Ako, "One can belong to oneself without belonging to a place" (97). Homelessness, therefore, as a choice made by Anowa, signifies a process of disencumbering herself from compulsory domesticity, of liberating herself from condoning class oppression and the exploitation of other humans on which capitalism thrives, and of dissociating herself from the "Big House" and its opulent, indolent, lifestyle. Indeed, homelessness becomes a choice Anowa makes to disrupt both patriarchal dominance and capitalist exploitation (Davies 1994:66).

In a most poignant scene towards the end of the play, Anowa situates the taboo of childlessness against the plight of the slave mother. Contemplating the young twin slaves, Panyin-na-Kakra, fanning Kofi Ako's empty throne-like chair "so that by the time their lord enters, the space around it will be cool" (Aidoo 1987:111), Anowa soliloquizes that not reproducing is an act of mercy, for the blatant abuse of the fruits of human labor should not be condoned but resisted. In a dysfunctional world that offers one's progeny no hope save debasement, childlessness becomes a blessing when juxtaposed to the curse of losing one's children to slavery. Anowa's situation images that of slave women in the New World who took measures to interrupt their fertility to foil the enslavers' efforts to exploit their childbearing in maintaining that inhuman institution. When the preventive measures sometimes failed and they had children, these women engaged in infanticide rather than be party to breeding human beings who are fated to be victims. When Anowa objects to Kofi Ako's decision to buy people to exploit their labor, he dismisses her objections as womantalk. While his statement is intended as a pejorative, it nonetheless registers the fact that woman, being the one who bears the responsibility for human regeneration, should be one to speak out against the abuses of her progeny. Anowa, symbolically imaging a mother whose maternal agency is wrested from her through the victimization of her children, redefines maternal agency to entail non-production. That Aidoo exploits Anowa's childlessness more for its symbolic potential than just the physical condition of inability, falling short, a diminution, etc., is mirrored in the open-endedness of the play, the absence of closure it posits, and in Aidoo's attributing Anowa's childlessness not to a problem with her womb but to the restlessness of her soul. Her childlessness, then, speaks to resistance generated from within to counter actions which violate the sanctity of human life.

Aidoo's stage directions suggest possibly ending the play "with the final exit of Anowa" (63), a choice which erases her suicide to refocus the finale on her closing words, *"it matters not what the wise ones say, / For / Now, I am wiser than they"* (123, italics added). What earth-shaking truths has Anowa unearthed in the end that she dons herself the repository of wisdom? The answer, I submit, lies in the experience of living. Having lived her life, she comes to possess more knowledge about the affairs of her life than anybody else, legitimating her ideals and beliefs. Rejecting victim status, she fights viciously to reclaim her personhood when her husband decides to cast her away. She rejects the role of the reasonable woman who will settle for the best she can get out of a bad situation and refuses to leave quietly, to condone his dispossession of her. Furthermore, she involves the community of slaves in her resistance of victimization, an act which re-inscribes her as an agent of revolution, mobilizing the dispossessed to strike their oppressor down. It is no accident that in the end, she openly declares Kofi Ako impotent, holding him responsible for their childlessness. His impotence signifies patriarchal attempts to sabotage maternal agency through dehumanizing the product of female productivity. Hence, his identification as the enslaver who appropriates the female womb for his own benefit. In this ending, the emphasis is on Anowa as the agent of resistance as well as wisdom. She declares herself wiser than the people she is expected to look to for advice.

The earth-shaking truths Anowa learns are inspired by her personal life. Having lived with a man who, by succumbing to the pressures of patriarchal attributes of masculinity, is transformed from a gentle, fun-loving, kind, and companionable mate into a power-hungry despot, Anowa arrives at the realization that the slave-owning psyche must issue from a deep internalization of impotence. Those who are not productive often derive a perverse pleasure from erasing evidence of other people's productiveness. Kofi Ako, being impotent, grows nothing; he cannot contribute to the regeneration process. Instead, he functions as an agent of dehumanization; he diminishes human agency through exploitation. Anowa's final declaration is that Kofi Ako "is a corpse. He is dead wood. But less than dead wood because at least, that sometimes grows mushrooms" (122). Though harrowing, this statement poignantly mirrors the absolute absence of identification one must cultivate in order to be able to exploit others so unfeelingly.

In the play *Anowa*, Aidoo shrewdly introduces her young heroine as "a young woman who grows up" (59). Growing up for Anowa brings with it the realization of the dispiriting process that the transformation from woman to wife entails. Though the fights that Anowa and Maami Esi Kom wage in *Anowa* and *The Dilemma of a Ghost* respectively are on different levels, Aidoo, particularly through these two women, valorizes woman as thinker and as revolutionary. She is one who is entrusted with a natural responsibility to engender human regeneration, one who sees the imperative of fighting all forms of exploitation and oppression, to ensure a better world for future progeny.

NOTES

This writer is grateful to Indiana University Kokomo for the Summer Faculty Fellowship 1997, a grant which made possible the completion of this paper for puplication.

1. All references to these two plays will be to the Longman 1987 edition of both plays.

2. Evelyn Nakano Glenn's article, "Social Constructions of Mothering: A Thematic Overview" (1-29), introduces the anthology, *Mothering: Ideology, Experience, and Agency* (1994), edited by Evelyn Nakano Glenn, Grace Chang, and Linda Rennie Forcey. This anthology, which originated from the conference, "Contested Terrains: Constructions of Mothering," at the State University of New York at Binghamton, "brings together an interdisciplinary group of scholars 'to provide a variety of perspectives on

mothering as a socially constructed set of activities and relationships involved in nurturing and caring for people'" (ix).

3. Barbara Katz Rothman, in the essay, "Beyond Mothers and Fathers: Ideology in a Patriarchal Society" (139-157), discusses this dimension of liberal feminism in detail. Of particular interest is the following quotation: "Strangely enough, albeit for different reasons, both patriarchal ideology and liberal feminist thinking have come to the same conclusion about what to do with the problem of the uniqueness of pregnancy—devalue it; discount it so deeply that its uniqueness just doesn't matter" (153). Rothman delineates the strong links inherent in various ideologies—liberalism, capitalism, and technology—and their fostering of patriarchal ideology and systemic subversion of female personhood. A serious limitation Rothman locates in liberal feminism is its focus on fighting for women to be given the right to be just like men rather than the right to be women, and in the end short-changing women's right to their uniqueness as women, a problematic which becomes particularly evident when issues such as pregnancy and motherhood arise. Because, like patriarchal ideology, liberal feminism has its roots in liberal philosophy, it ends up corroborating the reductionism at the core of patriarchal constructions of female personhood through its failure to challenge the mind-body dualism posited by patriarchal ideology.

4. This essay, "The African Woman Today" (47), in Obioma Nnaemeka's important, recent anthology, *Sisterhood, Feminisms and Power: From Africa to the Diaspora*, is a reprint of Aidoo's essay first published in *Dissent* 39 (1992):319-25.

5. Some of these non-fiction titles are: "Ghana: To Be a Woman" (1980), "To Be an African Woman Writer—An Overview and a Detail" (1988), and "The African Woman Today" (1992).

6. Adrienne Rich, *Of Woman Born: Motherhood as Experience and Institution*. New York and London: W. W. Norton, 1986.

7. See Briffault's *The Mothers* (1927, reprinted 1969), cited in Rich's *Of Woman Born*. Refer also to Rich's text, particularly Chapters 3 (The Kingdom of the Fathers) and 4 (The Primacy of the Mother).

8. Patricia Hill Collin's "Shifting the Center: Race, Class, and Feminist Theorizing About Motherhood" presents a detailed discussion of motherwork and particularly the race and class dimensions of this subject in the United States.

9. Adrienne Rich engages in a thorough analysis of the elaborateness of the patriarchal scheme to subvert women's primacy in procreation through the institutionalization of the birthing process. Medicalization and hospitalization are focused on as practices that undermine birthing as a natural process to vest control of the birthing experience in male dominated institutions.

10. My father explains that the levy of cracking palm nuts imposed by Britain on its colony is the Gold Coast's contribution to the debt incurred by the British from the World War. As a young girl who attained school going age in the pre-Independence era, I remember having to turn in the equivalent of a pound of cracked palm nuts every Monday morning.

Oftentimes I fell short of this measurement and had to submit to lashes for my failure. In addition, I had to ensure I would make up the deficit by the next Monday, on top of that period's concession, or receive more lashes and still carry forward what I owed. This experience left a lasting impression on me of the long arm of British imperial power.

11. *Abusua* is the Mfantse word for the family, both in the extended context of all the people who trace their descent through a common ancestor, that is, those related by blood, and in the sense of those related by marriage and other social institutions. In this context, the consanguineous, extended family is the matrilineage. *Abusua* will therefore be used in this analysis in reference to the matrilineage in addition to the English terms clan and family when referring to the matrilineage or the extended family. (For a detailed discussion of this concept, see Ephrim-Donkor 1997: 33-37).

12. Ifi Amadiume's *Male Daughters, Female Husbands* (1987), and 'Molara Ogundipe- Leslie's *Re-Creating Ourselves: African Women and Critical Transformations* (1993) are two works which discuss the oppression of women which is predicated on their position as wives.

13. Carole Boyce Davies' essay, "Deconstructing African Female Subjectivities" (Chapter Three in her book *Migrations of the Subject* [1994]), offers a detailed discussion of this issue. She presents an inspirited analysis of subjectivity and agency as multiply articulated in Ama Ata Aidoo's play *Anowa*. In this chapter, she also devotes a considerable attention to the issue of witchery and madness in Aidoo's play.

14. Historical accounts of the life of the Mfantse people of the period, such as Margaret Priestley's *West African Trade and Coast Society* (1969), are informative on this subject.

15. In this essay, she presents quite a detailed discussion of African women's participation in the business world of commerce and the contemporary global policies that have undermined women's progress in the commercial world.

16. N. Jane Opoku-Agyemang, Tuzyline Jita Allan, and Carole Boyce Davies offer more recent perspectives on this issue.

17. Nketia, in *Funeral Dirges of the Akan People* (1969), engages in a detailed explication of naming among the Akan. He talks about day-names and by-names. The day-name derives from the day of the week on which the individual is born. And every day-name has a by-name bracketing it. By-name, based on Nketia's explication, embodies a personality trait that is believed to be possessed by people born on specific days. Ama is the day-name of the Saturday born female. And every Ama is Adoma, Adoma being the by-name of Ama.

18. Refer to Opoku-Agyemang (1997:22-23;29) for an illumination of the individual's commitment to kinship ties in marriage decisions.

19. Bahktin's discussion of dialogism is aimed specifically at the novel as a genre. Nonetheless, his comment regarding utterance illuminates the charged verbal interchange between Kofi Ako and Anowa in this particular situation.

WORKS CITED

Aidoo, Ama Ata. *The Dilemma of a Ghost and Anowa*. London: Longman, 1987.

———. "The African Woman Today." In *Sisterhood, Feminisms and Power: From Africa to the Diaspora*. Ed. Obioma Nnaemeka. Lawrenceville, N.J.: Africa World Press, 1998. 39-50. [Originally published in *Dissent* 39 (1992):319-325.]

———. "Ghana: To Be A Woman." UNITAR Seminar, Creative Women in changing Societies, July 9-13, 1980. Also in *Sisterhood is Global*. Ed. Robin Morgan. New York: Doubleday, 1985. 258-265.

———. "To Be An African Woman Writer—An Overview and a Detail." In: *Criticism and Ideology*. Ed. Kirsten Holst Petersen. Uppsala: Scandinavian Studies, 1988. 155-172.

———. "The African Woman Today." In *Sisterhood, Feminisms and Power: From Africa to the Diaspora*. Ed. Obioma Nnaemeko. Trenton, N.J.: Africa World Press, 1998:39-50.

Allan, Tuzyline Jita. "Afterword." *Changes: A Love Story*. Ama Ata Aidoo. New York: CUNY, The Feminist Press, 1993. 171-196.

Amadiume, Ifi. *Male Daughter, Female Husbands*. London and New Jersey: Zed Books, 1987.

Bakhtin, M. M. *The Dialogic Imagination*. Ed. Michael Holquist. Trans. by Caryl Emerson and Michael Holquist. Austen: University of Texas Press, 1981.

Collins, Patricia Hill. "Shifting the Center: Race, Class, and Feminist Theorizing About Motherhood." *Mothering: Ideology, Experience, and Agency*. Ed. Evelyn Nakano Glenn, Grace Chang, and Linda Rennie Forcey. New York and London: Routledge, 1994.45-65.

Davies, Carole Boyce. *Migrations of the Subject: Black Women, Writing and Identity*. London and New York: Routledge, 1994.

Egejuru, Phanuel A. "The Paradox of Womanbeing and the Female Principle in Igbo Cosmology." *Nwanyibu: Womanbeing and African Literature*. Eds. Phanuel A Egejuru and Ketu H. Katrak. Trenton, N.J.: Africa World Press, 1997.11-19.

Ephirim-Donkor, Anthony. *African Spirituality: On Becoming Ancestors*. Trenton, N.J.: Africa World Press, 1997.

Glenn, Evelyn Nakano. "Social Constructions of Mothering: A Thematic Overview." *Mothering: Ideology, Experience, and Agency*. Eds. Evelyn Nakano Glenn, Grace Chang, and Linda Rennie Forcey. New York and London: Routledge, 1994. 1-29.

Nketia, J. H. Kwabena. *Funeral Dirges of the Akan People*. New York: Negro Universities Press, 1969.

Nnaemeka, Obioma. "Imag(in)ing Knowledge, Power, and Subversion in the Margins." *The Politics of (M)Othering: Woman, Identity, and Resistance in African Literature*. Ed. Obioma Nnaemeka. London and New York: Routledge, 1997. 1-25.

———. Ed. *Sisterhood, Feminisms and Power: From Africa to the Diaspora*, Trenton, N.J.: Africa World Press, 1998.

Odamtten, Vincent. *The Art of Ama Ata Aidoo: Polylectics and Reading Against*

Neocolonialism. Gainesville: University of Florida Press, 1994.

Ogundipe-Leslie, 'Molara. *Re-Creating Ourselves: African Women and Critical Transformations.* Trenton, N.J.: Africa World Press 1994.

Opoku-Agyemang, N. Jane. "A Reading of Ama Ata Aidoo's *Anowa.'* *Nwanyibu: Womanbeing and African Literature.* Eds. Phanuel A. Egejuru and Ketu H. Katrak. Trenton, N.J.: Africa World Press, 1997. 22-31.

Priestley, Margaret. *West African Trade and Coast Society.* London: Oxford University Press, 1969.

Rich, Adrienne. *Of Woman Born: Motherhood as Experience and Institution.* New York and London: W. W. Norton, 1986.

Rothman, Barbara Katz. "Beyond Mothers and Fathers: Ideology in a Patriarchal Society." *Mothering: Ideology, Experience, and Agency.* Eds. Evelyn Nakano Glenn, Grace Chang, and Linda Forcey. New York and London: Routledge, 1994. 139-157.

Trinh T. Minh-ha. *Woman, Native, Other: Writing Postcoloniality and Feminism.* Bloomington/Indianapolis: Indiana University Press, 1989.

"STRANGE AS IT MAY SEEM":

AFRICAN FEMINISM IN TWO NOVELS

BY AMA ATA AIDOO

SALLY MCWILLIAMS

In a selection from *Critical Fictions: The Politics of Imaginative Writing*, Ama Ata Aidoo recounts an incident that occurred when she was part of a panel on African literature and issues confronting African women writers. Being challenged by white feminists on one side and African men on the other, Aidoo explains that "out of sheer exasperation, we [the African women panelists] told both the European feminists and the African men resident in Europe that, strange as it may seem, we African women are perfectly capable of making up our own minds and speaking for ourselves" (Aidoo 1991b:154).The theoretical speculation that her words foreground is countered by the materiality of the phrase's implicit meaning for African women writers like herself. Obviously, it does not seem strange to them that they are individuals who can think and speak for themselves. Aidoo's statement expresses the conviction that African women are not to be silenced, even by those who feel they have the African woman's best interests at heart. Writers like Aidoo are striving to awaken their critical constituencies to the oppressive effects of the protectionism expressed by European white feminism and African patriarchy; contemporary African women writers are encouraging critics and readers to shake off the "strangeness" through which they hear African women's voices. Critical attacks like the one which confronted Aidoo and her co-panelists on African women writers' abilities to represent their ideas and existence demonstrate the vestiges of colonialism and patriarchy involved in the reception of these women's writings[1] These stigmatized and outdated modes of interpretation act as barricades obscuring African women's lives, subjectivities, and narrative representations. In this essay, I discuss how Aidoo moves beyond the stifling binary oppositions established between Western feminist discourse and African male discourse of female identity through her representations of African feminism *in Our Sister Killjoy: Or Reflections from a Black-Eyed Squint* (1977) and *Changes: A Love Story* (1991).

Aidoo's assertion emphasizes the decision-making capacities and oratory abilities of her African sisters, and by returning to the phrase "strange as it may seem," we are given a provocative lens through which to consider Aidoo's two novels. Her phrase frames the historical and literary contexts that have shaped the reception of works by African women writers. In the past several decades the literary works of African women were deemed lacking when measured against those of their male compatriots in a critical arena dominated by European male academics and African male writers and intellectuals (Davies 1987:1-23; Steady 1981:1-41). Scholarly work on the societal impact of gender and the ideologies of postcolonialism have allowed critics to begin to recognize and appreciate that African women's narratives have always been sites where women were struggling against multiple oppressions to construct worlds of meaningful acts.[2] Unlike its European-American middle-class counterparts, African feminism does not look exclusively at gender oppositions, but provides insights into the role that colonialism and its concomitant exploitation have played in the oppression suffered by African women.[3] Cheryl Johnson-Odim writes: "While it is clear that sexual egalitarianism is a major goal on which all feminists can agree, gender discrimination is neither the sole nor perhaps the primary locus of oppression of Third World women" (Johnson-Odim 1991:315). She continues to explain that "Internationally orchestrated exploitation [that is, structural elements of imperialism, multinational exploitation, international family planning] bears on the oppression of women in the Third World as much as patriarchy does in their societies" (320). International exploitation, neo-colonial ideology, and patriarchal gender oppression shape the material lives of African women. Implicit in these various enterprises is the image of African women as sexual beings who need to be controlled for the productivity of the local and global economies, for the strength of the nation, and for the support and well-being of their male counterparts. The intersecting and often competing discourses of economics, motherhood, and racial solidarity shape the options available for African women's sexual politics. These discourses imply a compulsory heterosexuality that impacts the sexual identities of these women.[4] *Our Sister Killjoy* and *Changes* investigate how women's sexuality is circumscribed by (neo)colonialism, gender oppression, and compulsory heterosexuality.

SEXUALITY AND STEREOTYPES

In the little explored area of sexuality lies the potential for revolutionary changes to androcentric systems of power. Evelyne Accad explains that such change will occur with "a transformation of the traditional rapports of domination and subordination which permeate interpersonal, particularly sexual, relationships (such as power struggles, jealousy, possession). Change is fundamental at the level of sexual and familial intimacy" (Accad 1991:237). But any discussion of Black women's sexual identity and politics is fraught with historical and cultural baggage. Deborah McDowell's explanation of the African American women's situation elaborates on the situation of her African maternal predecessors: "Since the very beginning of their history running roughly 130 years, black women novelists have treated sexuality with caution and reticence, a pattern clearly linked to the network of social and literary myths perpetuated throughout history about black women's libidinousness" (xii). Like their sister and daughter writers of the African Diaspora, African women writers such as Aidoo[5] are cautious in their attempts to delve into the sexual waters for fear of reinscribing stereotypes that misrepresent the complexities of African women's subjectivities and lives.[6] In the case of Aidoo's two novels the shadows of two such stereotypes darken the paths to independence and sexual identity for the protagonists:

Stereotype 1: The Westernized-Sexualized-African Woman

- Neglecting her cultural roots and values, this African woman has assimilated European values
- She rejects the African concept of women's roles in society: wife and mother
- She substitutes Western values of individuality and autonomy to the loss of her African values of familial responsibility and collective decision-making
- She grants her sexual needs more importance than her familial duties and demonstrates a loose sense of morality
- Her career is more valuable to her than her maternal and conjugal duties
- She undercuts the support she should give her husband by putting her needs first

Result: A vixen cut from a Western cloth of sexual liberation.

Stereotype 2: The Ideally Africanized African Woman

- Her pride in a national identity is directly linked to her ability to procreate
- Her individual sexual desires and their satisfaction are seen as unimportant in light of the overriding importance of motherhood and its duties/responsibilities
- She thrives on the higher value granted to married women who have children
- Her devotion to her family drives her to shun single women who are seen as detrimental to society and the nation because they refuse to be wives and mothers

Result: A Mother of Africa cut from a cloth of Kente

I have employed exaggerated "results" to emphasize the excessiveness of these images. My intention is to highlight how the employment of these two stereotypes establishes a non-negotiable polarity between the monstrosity of an African woman who has rejected her identity in light of the West's sexualized spell and the equally unrealistic idealization of an African woman who has been inseminated by the exclusionary light of African nationalism. Reductionist readings of African female characters have instituted a debate that in actuality is a diversionary tactic.[7] The diversion works to maintain the anger directed at the colonial hierarchy (the negative attacks on the woman who seemingly favors the West over Africa in Stereotype 1) and the joy directed at the vaunted place of privilege granted motherhood (the positive remarks about the woman who sacrifices all for the good of her family and community in Stereotype 2). If we focus on this division our attention will be diverted from the workings of sexuality that Aidoo employs to re-situate her characters and narratives beyond this narrowly defined debate of hypersexuality/procreative sexuality.[8]

IMPERIAL DESIRE AND SEXUAL POLITICS

In its most imperial and confident guise colonialism presented itself through repetition as a complete ideology without fractures and gaps. It was, as Robert Young describes, "a machine of war, of bureaucracy and administration, and above all of power" (Young 1995: 98).[9] Young continues by explaining that this machine of war was also a machine of desire and fantasy. Expressing unlimited appetite for lands, cultures, and peoples, it forced territories, histories, and peoples together; "[i]n that sense it was itself the instrument that produced its own darkest fantasy—the unlimited and ungovernable fertility of 'unnatural unions'" (98). Thus one could say that colonial desire for a racialized Other came from a dialectics of loss-loss in terms of anxiety about control. Such fear manifests itself in the gap between the dialectic of plenitude and isolation. The performative qualities of colonial discourse, now signifying both the potentialities of loss *and* gain with neither fully present at any one time, carry over into neo-colonialist thinking. Whereas the agents of colonial ideology in Africa from the nineteenth century to the middle of the twentieth century were predominantly European men (and in the case of Ghana, British specifically), the practitioners of neo-colonialist ideology are African men whose behavior echoes with imperial patriarchal strains. At work in depictions of neo-colonialist agents are markers of assimilation, but with an assimilation that is never total. Just as British colonial ideology functioned because of its refusal to allow the colonized full and consensual participation in the administration of its ideology, so too the neo-colonial attitudes of certain African men preclude women's full participation even as they construct their ideology of power. Struggling to concretize a place in post-colonial African society, African men face the dialectics of loss—a loss best described in terms of fear of disempowerment and emasculation.

This masculinized anxiety creates the cultural and social back-drop against which Aidoo's female characters must move. To allay such anxieties the fiction of heterosexuality works to control women's sexuality while neocolonialism and patriarchy function to categorize and sustain discourses of race and gender. Heterosexuality aligns designations of gender and sex, maintaining a seemingly inextricable link between the two. Judith Butler explains the grid of cultural intelligibility through which bodies, genders and desires are naturalized: "For bodies to cohere and make sense there must be a stable gender (masculine expresses male, feminine expresses female) that is oppositionally and hierarchically defined through the compulsory practice of heterosexuality" (Butler 1990:151).[10] The heterosexual matrix demands a female body (gendered and sexed as "female") for a male body (gendered and sexed as "male"). Once this regulatory fiction is in place certain practices follow: heterosexuality becomes the frame in which the male/female dyad is the favored and primary (and exclusive) unit; sexual desire is based exclusively on the male/female couplet; political agency is premised on this coupling (and often the female partner in the dyad becomes the protected subject of the male component thus linking heterosexuality and gender oppression); decisions and resulting actions are based on the assumption of a nation/state/community functioning because of heterosexual units (for example, family structure premised on heterosexual relationships); motherhood becomes the site of productive heterosexual desire; and conjugal relationships are favored over blood relations. The regulatory capacity of heterosexuality must be unraveled in the light of neo-colonialist and patriarchal pressures for us to understand the feminism produced in Aidoo's fiction.

SISSIE AND "KNOWLEDGE GAINED SINCE"

I would like to return for a moment to Aidoo's interjection, "strange as it may seem." The marker "strange" usually presumes a standard against which something is judged; that which is being evaluated falls short of matching the criteria employed in the judgment. The now "foreign" entity is marked as different. And yet this difference, in Aidoo's textual representations, allows for slippage to occur—a movement that does not transcend the dualism of standard/foreign, but sidesteps the definition of difference as built on division so that readers might engage with this new territory of African literature by women in terms neither predetermined by

Western feminism nor African male literary tradition. In relation to sexual politics, this slippage may create "strange bedfellows"—a disturbance to the norms for female behavior and concerns in the ongoing discourses of heterosexuality, patriarchy, and neo-colonialism.

Our Sister Killjoy is a narrative of disturbance and transition. The hybrid narrative form foregrounds the text's resistance to abide by any one set of norms, be they literary or ideological. Just as the narrative mixes prose and poetry with oral traditions to create a new literary form, so too does the mixture of African and Western beliefs highlight the protagonist's entry into a world criss-crossed with competing systems of knowledge.[11] Sissie, the titular character, journeys from her homeland in West Africa into the vast ideologically complicated morass of Europe to her so-called imperial "motherland" of England; she then turns back to Ghana with new insights about the regulatory fictions of post-colonial society that shape her existence as a sexual and social female being.

Aidoo's interjection—"strange as it may seem"—points us to the first section, "Into A Bad Dream," from which we will exit into a space of potentiality and change as the discursive architecture of neocolonialism, gender oppression and institutionalized heterosexuality become sites of exploration and resistance. The nightmarish quality that develops throughout the opening section turns on the initial promise that "things are working out / towards their dazzling conclusions..." (Aidoo 1977:3-4; ellipsis in original). Closure may be suggested but is indefinitely withheld just as the metaphorical brilliance of that deferred unity becomes imprinted with a material reality that boasts both pleasure and pain, comfort and risk, old traditions and new possibilities. Sissie enters a bad dream that is presented to her by an African male peer as "a dress rehearsal for a journey to paradise" (9). Expectations of disaster (the "bad dream") seem oddly out of place given this promise of bliss by her countryman. And yet this disjuncture marks the larger project of the novel which is to unhinge easy estimations by revealing the underlying presuppositions of racial, gender, culture, and sexual inferiority ready to consume our protagonist, Sissie, if only she will partake of them. Are we to read this young Ghanaian woman chosen to travel to Europe as just a token within the patriarchal system of global beneficence bestowed by First World countries on needy Third World recipients, now reaching out to the secondary ranks of Third World women? Is she to be relished for her youthfulness, smooth dark skin and naiveté just like the plums proffered by the German housewife Marija? Instead of having the power to consume, is she to become an object to be consumed by international exploitation, neo-colonial ideology, and patriarchal gender and sexual oppression? The narrative resists such a denouement on a number of levels but most significantly through a twist of terminology that bespeaks a slippage away from a degenerating trajectory of oppression.

In his discussion of imagery and language, critic Kofi Owusu points out that the Akan word "di" means both to eat and to make love to (Owusu 1990:352). While Owusu's linguistic analysis focuses on the second section of the novel, "The Plums," and Marija's attempt to seduce ("eat/make love to") Sissie, I would like to suggest that earlier in the text we see a narrative pairing of the discourses of consumption with heterosexuality, which will affect the interpretation of Marija and Sissie's relationship later in the novel. In the first section the guests for the small dinner party in Sissie's honor are heterosexually coupled and by implication Sissie is to be paired with the single African man, Sammy, who represents an African already appreciative of the benefits offered by an European reality (Aidoo 1977:8). From his words Sissie sees how Sammy, a Ghanaian whose proper name is never used, both consumes and loves the imperial discourses of opportunity and universalism that are fed to him by his European hosts.[12] Sissie notes that "his voice, as he spoke of that far-off land, was wet with longing" (9). Sissie feels ill at ease with this sexualized desire to survive on that which is not African; her response echoes the critical narrator who feels frustrated by the so-called "moderate" African male who "can regurgitate only what he has learned from his bosses" (6). Recognizing the role she ought to play in this heterosexualized and colonial compact, Sissie's mouth fills with saliva when she confronts the face of her countryman whose views are reflections of the imperial project's infantilization of the "native" (9). The saliva does not indicate a healthy satisfaction with the discourses presented for her delectation, but rather it marks the vile taste produced by her countryman's internalized colonialism and paternalistic attitude towards her along with the decorous heterosexuality in which she is assumed to be a willing player. The elision, eating/making love to, sexualizes the act of appropriation implicit in Sammy's discursive attempt to create in Sissie a desire to give over her sites of female strength (her black body and mind) to a prejudiced and consuming white Eurocentric humanism.

For Sissie the "bad dream" of the first section isn't Europe *per se,* but the evidence of heterosexism, gender tokenism, and racialized difference perpetuated by the neo-colonial system of power in which Sammy lives and she is now implicated. The disaffection that this systemic power produces is inscribed in the sterile representation of heterosexuality and homosexuality enacted in the bedroom of the German housewife Marija whom Sissie meets during her stay in Germany. The productiveness of heterosexuality has ominously fascistic overtones when we learn that the husband's name is Adolf and sexist implications when the Germanic mother exclaims the importance of having had a boy child for the success of the marriage. And yet the benefits of such intercourse are emptied of their loving content when the narrative reveals the excessive loneliness of the woman in the household. Marija turns her attention to Sissie, a woman she categorizes as exotic as the Indians she once knew. Uneasy with Marija's devotion to her and yet unable to relinquish her own need to feel connected with someone, Sissie continues to spend time with Marija, even daydreaming of the "delicious love affair she and Marija would have had if one of them had been a man" (61). And yet this fantasy of transgendered and heterosexual delight is disrupted by the inclusion of violent images devolving from the discourse of miscegenation. Sissie imagines a romantically doomed heterosexual relationship and then remembers the prohibition of interracial/inter-cultural heterosexual relationships coached in gustatory language: "First Law: / The Guest Shall Not Eat Palm-Nut Soup" (61). The convergence of consumption with sexual desire takes a devastating turn in this scenario because the discourses of racialism and heterosexism overlap within the framework of imperial anxiety discussed earlier in the essay. The discourse of miscegenation brings together the fear and desire for the racialized and sexualized Other within the confines of compulsory heterosexuality. Sissie's imaginings are reconfigured when the narrator steps in to describe the horrors inflicted on the bodies of black men who have intercourse with white women: "Beautiful Black Bodies ... Buried in thickets and snow/Their penises cut" (62). When her romanticized heterosexual images have been supplemented by images of castrated black men, Sissie rejects Marija's offer of food (to eat) and concomitantly rejects her interracial heterosexual fantasy (to make love to), now indelibly marked by racialized violence.

Thus, two narratives frame Sissie's entrance into the master bedroom of Marija's house: the violence of interracial relations and the necessity of heterosexuality. From this backdrop of danger and compulsion the bedroom emerges as a site of insufficience. In its decoration and design Sissie reads the absence of love in Marija's marriage and the ominously unfulfilled primeval yearning for sexual connection and satisfaction. The presence of the two women does not put in abeyance the overwhelming absence embodied by the room. Absence disrupts the interaction between the two women. In this instance no mutual desire for one another exists. Instead of amorous and passionate desire we see a scene of morbidity and vacuity. Marija may be a lonely lesbian trapped in an unfulfilling life (Dunton 1989:432) but Marija's conception of Sissie subjects the Ghanaian woman to the role of exoticized Other, denying her agency and affections. And for Sissie the "giant white bed... waiting to be used" and the shelf loaded with the sexually feminized "bottled affairs from the beauty business...for a ferocious war" (Aidoo 1977:63) form the iconography of female isolation *qua* excessiveness and sexual emptiness. Marija's lesbian sexual advances awaken Sissie to the reality of her homelessness in Europe, the emptiness of Marija's motherhood, and the tragedy of colonialism's systemic imbalance of power relations as she thinks to herself.

> How did she get here? What strings, pulled by whom, drew her into those pinelands where not so long ago human beings stoked their own funeral pyres with other human beings, where now a young Aryan housewife kisses a young black woman with such desperation, right in the middle of her own nuptial chamber, with its lower middle-class cosiness? (66)

The treacherous interplay of racialism, neo-colonial oppression, and institutionalized heterosexuality leaves the women, both black and white, marked by loneliness and unfulfilled desires.[13]

However, rather than leaving Sissie's refusal of Marija's sexual overture as an outright rejection and violation of African women's sexuality, the narrative circles back to homosexual desire via a narrative interjection. While homosexual activity has been attributed to the West and identified with the exploitation enabled by the power relations of the colonial paradigm and thus alien to indigenous African society (Dunton 1989:422;424),[14] Aidoo's narrative questions the formation of homosexuality as a Western import. Her narrative demythologizes this reduction of homosexuality, and specifically lesbianism, to colonialism by playing with the power of language to control bodies. The slang expression "bush" allows for a double reading of the term as a marker of African rural space and female anatomy. In a critique of the imperial project practiced by missionary women who became headmistresses of African girls' schools, the narrator tells us the story of one such headmistress who had given her life "to educating and straightening out African girls" (Aidoo 1977:66). The project of "straightening out" is explicitly that of criminalizing homosexuality and imposing heterosexuality on the young, rural African women whom the headmistress discovers in bed together one night. Shocked by the sight of two females in bed the headmistress questions them as to whether or not they are "bush"; this inquisition results in outlandish giggles from the African girls. The scene allows for the double entendre of "bush" to disrupt the cold masculinist language used by their teacher. The girls reply that their parents are not bush, which could be interpreted as saying they are not from a rural section of the country, or perhaps it could mean their parents are not homosexual. But in either case the young African girls in the narrative interjection mimic their white missionary headmistress by saying that they understand that lesbianism is "not just b-u-s-h / But a / C-r-i-m-e / A Sin / S-o-d-o-m-y, From knowledge gained since" (67). Their mimicry deconstructs the imperial project of criminalizing a simple act like being in bed together by revealing that it is only through language previously imposed that the action can be condemned. This encoding of potential lesbian desire within the African experience suggests that lesbianism is not anathema to African societies, but rather is controlled and marked as felonious because of the colonialist fear that the desiring machine of imperialism is a sexualized system of power relations. The scene leaves open the interpretation of what being "bush" could mean: it is not the African girls' bodies and words that close off and prevent same-sex desire from circulating but rather the language of the imperial authority uttered by the headmistress.

Sissie's own narrative, however, returns to the confines of a compulsory heterosexuality, as she "looked at the other woman [Marija] and wished again that at least, she was a boy. A man" (67). Dunton aptly explains that Aidoo's representation of Marija does not stigmatize her as "another phenomenon of a degenerative and oppressive culture" (Dunton 1989:432); lesbianism is not simply described as another Western disease crippling the purity of African society. The narrative reveals, as Dunton argues, a common ground between the two women based on Sissie's ability to empathize with the German woman's sense of isolation. And yet we must recognize that even though a parallel is drawn between the two women's feelings of marginalization, there is no simple "sisterhood" to be understood. In fact, Aidoo's narrative is careful to craft the diverse effects of colonialism and heterosexuality on the two women. While Marija has been victimized by virtue of her culture's heterosexual paradigm, Sissie's experience of marginalization arises from the intersection of heterosexism, exoticism, and colonialism that has disenfranchised her and erased her individuality even in the eyes of another woman. My point is not to suggest that lesbian relationships would provide the answers to the disaffection demonstrated by a female character such as Sissie; rather, I am suggesting that as a discourse of control, heterosexuality works complicitly with colonialism and racism to restrict the conceptual and material options for African women. Dunton writes that the subject of homosexuality "is granted a greater capacity to disturb, to call questions" (423); I would agree in that Aidoo's inclusion of this relationship between Marija and Sissie allows us to see how women's sexuality is interlaced with the effects of hierarchical power relations marked by gender, race, and culture.

Women's sexuality, however, is not easily explained and fulfilled through heterosexual relationships. The narrative indicates that "time was to bring her many Sammys. And they always affected her in the same way..." (Aidoo 1977:9; ellipsis in original). This declaration foreshadows Sissie's encounters with expatriate Ghanaian and other African men during her time in London in the final section of the novel. She resists their arguments favoring expatriate living arrangements; her beliefs do not allow her to capitulate to the idea that as educated Ghanaians they are underappreciated and undervalued in their homeland. Her stance denies her admission to their inner circle, and as an outsider she is placed in the position of Other in relation to her countrymen. Sissie strives to be heard against their neo-colonialist discourse of expatriatism couched in the language of universalism. The words of the expert in gastric disorders exemplifies the attitude confronting Sissie; he claims that his annual visit home is "a very revitalising process" (128) but given the importance of his research she cannot expect him to go home and be frustrated by the lack of equipment, financing, and congenial atmosphere for research especially given that for him "wherever one feels at home must be home. This earth belongs to us all. We can perch everywhere" (129). Her objections to his avian analogy fall on deaf ears as he reminds her that by remaining in the West his presence "serves a very useful purpose in educating [the white Europeans] to recognize our worth" (129). Sissie refuses to concede this mission to him as she sees the Sammy-ness of his neo-colonialist discourse. She represents to this group of African men that difference which Sander Gilman describes as "that which threatens order and control; it is the polar opposite of [the] group" (Gilman 1985:21). And to contain such a disrupting difference, Sissie's arguments about the need for repatriation must be silenced and shown as impotent by being "projected on to the Other as frigidity" (24). This frigidity is projected onto Sissie when upon finishing her response to his borrowed rhetoric, she sees the gastric disorders expert holding hands with a white woman. Sissie's dismay is apparent when she writes to her beloved: "We are back to square one, yes? The superior monkey has got his private white audience for whom he performs his superior tricks. Proving our worth, eh? I was close to tears..." (Aidoo 1977:130; ellipsis in original). Her countryman's neo-colonialist discourse erases Africa in its reliance on the West as the standard against which cultures are judged; even his suggestion that he will be a model African to show the Europeans that Africans can be internationally recognized physicians is based on the dialectics of lack and racialism. And in the end the seemingly benign action of holding hands symbolizes the erasure of African women as desiring subjects within the heterosexually inscribed world of the expatriate intellectual black man.[15]

Sissie is rescued from this scene by her "Precious, My Own Something," and yet this intercession of one black man for another does not buy Sissie the comfort of mind, body and soul that it might have previously provided had she not already changed from her own "knowledge gained since." For his views have already echoed the cold tones of conservatism and alienation that Sissie questions in her reconsideration of having rejected his neo-colonialist, heterosexist paternalism. And yet in an ironic tone she reveals that certain "facts" about bowing to male pressure, to gender estimations, to heterosexual prescriptions, to female acquiescence, are strangely out of sync with the rhythm of her production of knowledge. Her "big mouth," as she playfully calls it, utters critical insights about the Victorian notions of gender and sexuality; these notions are holdovers being misapplied to African women by her "Precious" and other African men who want to mold African womanhood into a controlled objectivity and passivity. Sissie writes,

No, My Darling: it seems as if so much of the softness and meekness you and all the brothers expect
of me and all the sisters is that which is really western. Some kind of hashed-up Victorian notions, hm?
Allah, me and my big mouth!!
   See, at home the woman knew her position
and all that. Of course, this has been true of the
woman everywhere—most of the time. But wasn't
her position among our people a little more complicated than that of the dolls the colonizers brought
along with them who fainted at the sight of their
own bleeding fingers and carried smelling salts
around, all the time, to meet just such emergencies
as bleeding fingers? (117)

Sizing up these views in her black-eyed squint, Sissie asserts the
material and linguistic complexities and complications of African
women's lives that her African male counterparts would neither
allow nor avow as evidence of disturbances in the ruling ideology
of neo-colonial sexual politics.

   No longer an itinerant traveler in her country's "motherland,"
Sissie's narrative concludes with her in transit between countries
on her way back to Ghana. This site of relocation combines her
questions and insights into an emerging knowledge of feminist principles. Her letter of the final section opens up the discourse of heterosexuality by demonstrating how masculinized anxiety propels
African men into the role of protector of women's sexual and social
identities. Likewise, her intricate composition deconstructs the
destructive shortcomings of the patriarchal discourse presented by
Sissie's countrymen. The love letter forms the bridge connecting
her early concerns about sexual politics with her newfound determination to reintegrate with a difference into Ghanaian society:

She was never going to post the letter. Once written, it was written. She had taken some of the pain
away and she was glad .... She was going to let things
lie where they had fallen. Besides, she was back in
Africa. And that felt like fresh honey on the tongue:
a mixture of complete sweetness and smoky
roughage. Below was home with its unavoidable
warmth and even after these thousands of years, its
uncertainties. (133)

With Sissie on the verge of re-entry into Ghanaian society with her own "knowledge gained since"—a knowledge balanced on the willingness to take risks in the face of neo-colonialist and heterosexist ideologies—the novel dazzles us not with conclusions, but with its energetic hope for positive change for Africa through its female constituency. Aidoo's protagonist is in the transitional space from which awareness of oppressions turns into productive actions of female autonomy and strength.

ESI'S CHANGING STORY OF LOVE

Where *Our Sister Killjoy* unveils the complications of neocolonialism and sexuality for formally educated African women living abroad, Aidoo's second novel takes an inside perspective on Ghanaian society as its inhabitants confront changing views on power relations, gender roles and sexuality. *Changes* presents a challenge to the institutionalized politics of heterosexuality as the female protagonist, Esi Sekyi, strives to define a life that is fulfilling on its multiple levels: career, family, and personal. Taking a page from her countrymen's critique of her Ghanaian sister Sissie, Esi could be seen as the stereotypical Westernized professional West African woman. Yet like their misapprehension of Sissie, such a reductionist reading of Esi belies the intellectual and emotional struggles Esi confronts as she attempts to enact her beliefs about independent women and create a living arrangement that suits these principles. The novel leverages open questions of sexual identity, female autonomy and gender oppression through its orchestration of female characters. *Changes* is not Esi's story alone, but also the multi-voiced narrative of Opokuya Dakwa, Fusena Kondey, and their older female relatives. Through these various generations of women we begin to see that the sentimental narrative suggested by the novel's subtitle—*A Love Story*—is ironized and reevaluated when the popularized "happy ending" of heterosexual monogamous marriage is thrown out in the opening chapters of the narrative. Aidoo's text does not dramatize a simple boy-girl romance; it takes as its theme the ideological complexities conscripting West African women's lives as they encounter previously naturalized rules about gender and sexual politics. As suggested by the name of the hotel where Esi stops in for a drink, the Twentieth Century in Accra is criss-crossed with tensions and entanglements involving traditions and transitions that affect women's sexual identities.

While Sissie's sexuality became a site for political awakening to the limitations of compulsory heterosexuality, Aidoo's characterization of Esi Seyki demonstrates sexuality as a site for physical appreciation and acceptance. The stereotypical images of Westernized versus Africanized womanhood no longer compete for prominence in Aidoo's narrative. Esi's character draws vitality from her sexual being. Contrary to the negative discourse she received about her body when she was a girl, Esi now feels self-confident about her physical and sexual self. Rather than allowing a rhetoric of shame and Victorian prudery to circumscribe her feelings about her body, Esi recognizes and values her "bone-blood-flesh self." Her view of heterosexuality attempts to combine gender equality with sexual desire while displacing the negative hierarchy of male control over female desire. The regularity of arguments over sex and reproduction between Esi and her husband Oko is established in the opening scene of Chapter Two where their young daughter Ogyaanowa is isolated in her highchair and the radio is blasting from her parents' room to disguise their angry voices (Aidoo 1991a: 5). The scene reveals Esi's detachment from her husband Oko's feelings. Oko is unhappy and frustrated because Esi has opted to use birth control instead of consenting to have another child. He has started to give credence to his mother's and sisters' suggestion that he take an "outside" woman to get more children. His anger builds as he explains to Esi that his friends are laughing at him for not being able to control his wife's reproductive desire (8). His words demonstrate how masculinity for the modern West African man must repress emotional needs and instead function in terms of what Adrienne Rich describes as compulsory heterosexuality: "the enforcement of heterosexuality for women [is] ....a means of assuring male right of physical, economic, and emotional access" (Rich 1986:238). When Oko says that his friends are laughing at him, he understands that they see him as being less than a man because he does not control either the sexual politics of his married life or his wife's career.

To assert his masculine identity he pushes Esi on to the bed and forcibly has intercourse with her. By focusing on his actions and ascribing Esi to the role of passive object the passage emphasizes through its narrative structure the objectification of Oko's anxious need to exhibit his masculinity to Esi and, almost more importantly, to himself. Because she is unwilling to accede her sexual prerogative, he attempts to physically take it away from her to solidify his threatened gender identity. The incident of marital rape discloses the debilitating effects of static gender roles for both men and women against the field of heterosexual politics that exceed the confines of the bedroom walls. Similar in character to Sissie's encounter with the African physician who must support his masculine power through the erasure of African women's sexuality by having a white European girlfriend, Oko's violent response to his fear of emasculation reveals the tenuous and treacherous discourses of sexuality and gender for both men and women.

This scene underscores Oko's anxiety and need for control through the use of heterosexual and gender domination. For Esi, it acts as the catalyst for her confrontation with the sexual politics of her society. She wonders if she can name the act "marital rape" and thus pit it against her society's sexual politics if there is no indigenous word for such an act:

> The society could not possibl[y] have an indigenous word or phrase for it. Sex is something a husband claims from his wife as his right. Any time. And at his convenience. Besides, any 'sane' person, especially sane women, would consider any other woman lucky or talented or both, who can make her husband lose his head like that:
>
> What does she use?....
>
> And here she was, not feeling academic or intellectual at all, but angry, and sore... And even after a good bath before and after, still dirty... Dirty!...Ah-h-h-h, the word was out. (Aidoo 1991a:12; ellipses in original)

A female chorus criticizes Esi's actions and thoughts because she is stepping outside the narrowly prescribed role of the heterosexually accepting African woman. And yet these voices cannot contain Esi's rage at the moral indignity she feels at the expense of Oko's actions and ideology. Unwilling to compromise her body and her views, Esi refuses to acquiesce to the heterosexual politics of domination and submission in the "good" name of African womanhood. Like her sororal counterpart in *Our Sister Killjoy* who accepts being called crazy if it means resisting neo-colonial, heterosexist ideology, Esi would rather run the risk of being marginalized than submit to the coercive tactics of gender oppression and heterosexual violence in her own home.

Critical of the complicity among heterosexism, patriarchal standards, and violence against women, the narrative goes one step further in its unmasking of oppressions circumscribing African women's existence. With the entrance of Opokuya Dakwa a new line of criticism opens. Opokuya's first words in the novel are to deconstruct the politics of fat and population propagated by international organizations. Hers is the voice of counter-hegemonic critique when she expresses her conclusion "that those who are interested in women, especially African women, losing so much weight must be the same ones who are interested in women, especially African women, cutting down their birth rate" (14). Her incisive commentary condemns not only internationally orchestrated programs which undercut health programs designed by Africans for Africans, but also the dependency of neo-colonial African governments that "are behaving like all professional beggars... one of [the rules of effective begging being] never object to anything the giver likes. And they know the givers like one thing very much now: that there should not be too many of us [Africans]" (14-15). She refuses to concede control of her reproductive life and her physical size to the demands of the international and neo-colonial economics regulating women's body and sexual politics.

Quickly and expertly the narrative has disturbed the *status quo*, delineating how women should view their bodies, reproductive rights, gender roles, and sexuality. The disturbance continues as Esi and Opokuya flout society's conventions for decent women by staying and conversing in the lobby of the Hotel Twentieth Century, alcoholic drinks in hand. Wit, irony, and laughter pave the way for these women to explore their situations and those of their West African sisters. Marriage, divorce, motherhood, independence, and career ambitions are the topics of their discussion. Time and again the conversation comes back to the societal requirement that women marry, that historically the single woman, given no place in African society, was pressured:

> '—until she gave in and married or remarried, or went back to her former husband.'

> 'And of course if nothing cured her [of her desire to be single] they ostracized her and drove her crazy.'

> 'And then soon enough, she died of shame, loneli-

ness and heartbreak.'

> At this point, both Esi and Opokuya burst out laughing again. Almost hysterically. As they calmed down Opokuya said, 'Esi, it's not funny,' and Esi said, 'Opokuya, it's not funny.' (48)

Their double-edged laughter reveals the restrictive nature of society's heterosexual mandate for women. With motherhood being either devalued or controlled by international and patriarchal forces, sexuality being defined strictly by men, and gender roles mired in static cultural perceptions, female friendship becomes a network of support and an avenue of resistance. I will come back to this complicated issue of female friendship in the conclusion of my essay, but for the time being the value of their exchange is that it airs the matrix of problems confronting them as West African women friends. Although no answers are provided to their dilemmas during this meeting, Esi's and Opokuya's daring to express their views and their society's shortcomings breaks the culturally and socially imposed silences concerning female sexual, personal and social desires.

Esi and Opokuya's honest conversation stands in contrast to the silence that ultimately circumscribes the life of another female character in the novel, Fusena Kondey, the first wife to Ali Kondey. Fusena had approached her marriage to Ali as a marriage of equals; but after living in rain-soaked London where her livelihood involved buying food and drying wet nappies while her husband pursued and received his M.A., she realizes that by marrying "she had exchanged a friend for a husband" (66). Her understanding of this tradeoff and the position of women in society leads her to the conclusion that "she would rather be married than not, and rather to Ali than anyone else" (67). The narrative does not elaborate on how Fusena's Islamic faith affects her political perceptions of the gender disparity she inhabits, but from the story we see that she finds no specific comfort in her religion, although she is a practicing Muslim. She is a well-organized housekeeper who values a well-run household. And yet it is the other tradeoff, that of giving up her university studies, which haunts her. Where Opokuya strikes out against reproductive compromises and Esi against sexual ones, Fusena begrudges her decision to accede to Ali's wishes that she not continue her teaching profession and her post-secondary studies. Ali, in ignoring his first wife's wishes, has undercut Fusena's sense of self-confidence and her authority in her home. The expression of compulsory heterosexuality which keeps her in this marriage and Ali's usurping patriarchy that curtailed her education combine to form the backdrop against which she envisions Ali's new second wife as a "monster." The unfolding oppression quickly forces Fusena to relent and, like her female relatives before her, she falls silent with her acceptance that "it was a man's world. You only survived if you knew how to live in it as a woman" (107). The gendered survival skills at this juncture are acquiescence and submission as the text literally writes Fusena out of the story. We hear nothing more from her during the remaining one-third of the novel. Whereas Opokuya and Esi remain active questioners and actors in the changing landscape of sexual and personal relationships, Fusena remains a question mark—the silenced reminder that oppression remains in different corners of female society.

Our understanding of the complexity of women's experiences is enhanced by the older generation of women; the most significant among these is Esi's grandmother, Nana. She explains to Esi how the benefits of the matriarchal society have been forgotten and what is remembered is that men were the first gods, "devouring gods" (110). To excel the men had to have regular sacrifices made to them and these sacrifices came in the form of women's selves with marriage being the first of such sacrifices:

> 'But remember, my lady, the best husband you can
> ever have is he who demands all of you and all of
> your time. Who is a good man if not the one who
> eats his wife completely, and pushes her down with
> a good gulp of alcohol?' (109)

Nana is quick to point out that colonialism has demanded that Africans sacrifice their egos to Europeans (just as the narrator of knowledge in *Our Sister Killjoy* has stated), but it is the continuing sacrifice of women's identities that troubles her the most. In her "Afterword" to the novel, critic Tuzyline Jita Allan explains: "On the surface, Nana's account of male occupation of the female body seems approving.... Close inspection of this female griot's story, however, reveals a satirical edge undercutting the grandstand image of maleness" (Allan 1991:184).[16] The couplet of consumption and sexual desire (to eat/to make love to) that we saw in the earlier novel comes into play again through Nana's retelling of the male myth of domination through heterosexuality. The strength of men and the romance of heterosexuality are now framed by the excessiveness of alcohol. This storytelling detail satirizes and deflates the supposed prominence and control dictated by the men. Nana continues her "subversive rendition of the myth of male supremacy," to employ Allan's phrasing, by turning away from the sacrificial vein of women's lives to the potentiality they hold as agents of change for the world.

> Do I think it must always be so [that women must be consumed by men]? Certainly not. It can be changed. It can be better. Life on this earth need not always be some humans being gods and others being sacrificial animals. Indeed, that can be changed. But it would take so much. No, not time. There has always been enough time for anything anyone ever really wanted to do. What it would take is a lot of thinking and a great deal of doing. (Aidoo 1991a:111)

Nana's discourse, like Esi and Opokuya's laughter, proves double-edged: on the one hand, she counsels continued complicity in the heterosexual system that necessitates female submission to male egos; on the other hand, her words are a call to action to women for beneficial change that she deems possible if difficult to attain. Nana's satirical yet survivalist language echoes the joke Sissie shared with Marija in *Our Sister Killjoy*. Sissie wants to deflate Marija's desire to cook for her by explaining that men "are the only sex to whom the Maker gave a mouth with which to enjoy eating" (77). Marija does not understand the words or the fact that the seriousness of the statement masked what the narrative calls "a rather precious joke." This joke, like Nana's counter mythology about gender relations and sexuality, reveals that although women appear to be the ones who will always be devoured, it is women who will upset this dialectic through their keen abilities to see and act beyond the joke that marries male domination to neo-colonial relations through the strictures of an unrelenting heterosexism. In this manner, the primacy of the devouring gods (men) is undercut and revealed as excessively exploitative while the joke-tellers/griots (women), although implicated in the serious consequences of the joke, nonetheless hold the power of oration and the vision of change. Sissie and Nana empower Ghanaian women to see different worlds while their male counterparts become glassy-eyed from the alcohol they must swallow so as to consume (make love to and try to control) their women (109).[17]

This prospect of visualizing and instituting change emerges through Esi's and Opokuya's actions. The realm of change for Opokuya comes in the form of transportation; mobility has been a contested issue between Opokuya and her husband Kubi. Their daily battles over who should have the car epitomize the disparity between the value associated with prestige and that of practicality. Kubi feels he must be able to park the car in his parking space at work to affirm his status, while for Opokuya the car would mean easier completion of routine errands for the benefit of the family. When Esi decides to give Opokuya her car following the receipt of a new one from her second husband Ali, Opokuya asserts her need for independence by demanding that Esi allow her to buy the car (154). The car signifies a shift away from the politics of prestige that burden Opokuya's daily life with Kubi. No longer held to Kubi's need for control, Opokuya now can move freely to accomplish the material duties of her role as wife, mother and worker. Slipping outside of the patriarchal confines associated with the politics of transportation improves the viability of her marriage by contributing to her self-confidence, personal dignity, and autonomy.

While gaining the car opens the way for change in Opokuya's life, Esi's attempts for greater female autonomy are much more complicated and less easily satisfied. Having originally rejected the heterosexual confines of monogamy, Esi finally accepts the romantic overtures of Ali Kondey and agrees to marry him. Her acceptance comes with the ironic acknowledgment that she "has become occupied territory" (91). Recognizing what she deems the lunacy of the contemporary African discourse on marriage, she does not try to unwind the cross-cultural implications of wearing a ring and being considered "property" from the African male perspective. Instead she forges ahead trying to create for herself a space in which her sexual desires, her need for companionship, her counter need for freedom and her career ambitions can all coexist. She sees the potential for such coexistence within the realm of polygyny. And yet she fails to foresee how difficult for a full sense of well-being would be the act of compartmentalizing her life in such a way as not to demand too much from Ali or herself. She has even cut herself off from the support that could have been exhibited from her co-wife by acquiescing to Ali's acts of deceit towards his first wife, Fusena.

But it is Nana's voice that Esi hears when given the failure of polygynous marriage, she begins to consider the prospect of becoming a man's mistress. When Kubi, Opokuya's husband, tries to seduce Esi and she feels herself giving way to the power of the male ego and sex drive, her grandmother's words keep her from capitulating and highlight the enduring importance of female friendship:

> Opokuya's ample face came into view, beaming... humorous, but with Nana's voice, 'My lady Silk, remember that a man always gains in stature any way he chooses to associate with a woman—including adultery.... But, in her association with a man, a woman is always in danger of being diminished...' In any case, wasn't the need to maintain that friendship greater on her [Esi's] part? Maybe Opokuya could shed her. She, Esi, could not afford to shed Opokuya. (164; ellipsis in original)

By refusing to have sex with Kubi, Esi has enacted one moment of her grandmother's belief that change can come with "thinking and a great deal of doing" (111). Her rejection is an affirmation of female power against the masculinist heterosexuality exemplified by Kubi's act of unzipping his pants. Esi asserts her will against the coercive forces of heterosexuality that underpin gender oppression and proscribe certain emotional and material opportunities for women.

Both of Aidoo's novels return to the strength of African women as the transitional force to forge a way out of the confines of heterosexism and the infirmity of neo-colonialist thought. The novels recognize the potentially subversive powers exhibited by women who trust other women. Yet, sisterhood in itself does not produce change. Although I agree with Tuzyline Jita Allan's assertion that in *Changes* "the novel's culminating stance...offers female friendship as a site of resistance against the erotics of [male-dominated] control" (Allan 1991:184), such a conclusion sidesteps the novel's concern with women's sexuality. While neither narrative investigates the potential of a lesbian love affair between African women, in taking up the complications of interracial lesbianism in the one text and the struggles for a satisfying heterosexual relationship in the other, they propose a forceful critique of the various pressures delimiting visions of African feminism. Each contributes to the expanding discourses on African women's sexuality by pushing aside old contexts and providing new representations that take nothing at face value. To that end, Aidoo's assertion "strange as it may seem" aptly suggests the transgressive power of her texts. Her female characters are desiring subjects, and their desires, as depicted by Aidoo, take a variety of previously unexplored forms, objects, and trajectories. These narratives deliberately disrupt the powerful matrix of heterosexual, patriarchal, and neo-colonialist ideologies that mark the African literary landscape. Aidoo's representations need no external voices of affirmation or protection; they speak for themselves of the transformations being produced by the literary voices of African feminism.

NOTES

1. Given the multiple critiques of how First World feminists have employed a maternalistic attitude towards Third World feminists and women writers, I use the term "colonialism" to indicate how the European feminists in Aidoo's anecdote attempted to silence the African women writers in a manner analogous to the colonial powers' use of language to speak *for* the so-called "natives." See Chandra Talpade Mohanty's "Under Western Eyes: Feminist Scholarship and Colonial Discourses" for an early critique of Western feminism.

2. 'Molara Ogundipe-Leslie's work on gender and West African women is an important study that resonates with the literary work of her West African female contemporaries. Likewise the collection *Third World Women and the Politics of Feminism* has been instrumental to the development of the interconnecting discourses of post-colonialism, gender, and global feminism.

3. A parallel exists between the concerns of African feminists and North American feminists of color. Gender is now considered as only one vector among an intricate web of oppressions that these feminists explore in their writings. The material differences that occur because of the geo-economic spheres they inhabit do not make African women's realities the same as those of women of color from North America, but they do share such concerns as institutionalized economic inequities, inadequate health and educational resources, and racial and class biases among others.

4. The phrase "compulsory heterosexuality" is taken from Adrienne Rich's essay "Compulsory Heterosexuality and Lesbian Existence." In this essay Rich accounts for the domination of heterosexuality as not a naturally occuring phenomenon but rather a culturally constructed institution. In her 1982 "Foreword," Rich explains that the essay was written not only to increase lesbian visibility "but [also] to encourage heterosexual feminists to examine heterosexuality as a political institution which disempowers women—and to change it." It is in this sense that I am employing the term in this paper. Aidoo's narratives take up the challenge Rich proposes by investigating the pressures that heterosexuality exerts on women's lives and by calling into question the merits of such a political institution as it works in conjunction with patriarchy and neo-colonial

measures to silence women's choices and voices.

5.   Among West African women fiction writers, Flora Nwapa and Buchi Emecheta are two other courageous writers who carefully explore the sexual identity of their women characters. In Southern Africa, Tsitsi Dangarembga, Farida Karodia, and Sindiwe Magona are just a few who are investigating women's sexualities in their contemporary fiction. When I say that these writers are using care when exploring black women's sexualities in their writings, I am taking up the issue of reception as well as representation. The politics of reception is a treacherous arena. African writers whose works reach a predominantly white American and/or European audience must confront the negative constructions of blackness that surround any interpretation of "African." Sander Gilman takes up the psychological aspects of this issue in his book *Difference and Pathology: Stereotypes of Sexuality, Race and Madness* while Jan Nederveen Pieterse in *White On Black: Images of Africa and Blacks in Western Popular Culture* describes the racial backdrop against which African novels are read in contemporary Western societies.

6.   In her introductory essay in *Ngambika*, Carol Boyce Davies suggests that there is a continued need to study images of women in novels as a first step in African feminist criticism. I want to suggest that representations of women's sexuality become problematic when they are burdened with excessive idealization or stereotypical associations. For example, Mumbi in Ngugi wa Thiongo's *A Grain of Wheat* is figured as both the mother of Gikuyu society and a sexually irresponsible female. The tension between the two intertwined images pulls the reader to judge her against the purity of Gikuyu socio-historical mythology without a full exploration into her material reality in the aftermath of war-torn Kenya. Plus her relative isolation within the narrative (as the sole young female character that plays a significant role in the novel) marks her as a limited representative of Gikuyu womanhood in contrast to the varied characterizations of the Kenyan men who inhabit diverse ideological and material positions in the novel. Another example of a critical idealization of African womanhood that ultimately erases issues of women's sexuality and gender occurs in Femi Ojo-Ade's "Of Culture, Commitment, and Construction: Reflections on African Literature." In this essay Ojo-Ade comments that most women writers, other than Buchi Emecheta, "enjoy the support of their families and, rather than engaging in a war of sexes, seek to go beyond their particular conditions to attain the human" (1987:21). Such an evaluation is a mean-spirited devaluation of not only Emecheta's work but other autobiographical writing by African women, and by extension a misconstrued condemnation of the relation between gender and experience expressed in literature. Such a statement suggests that by eliminating gender women will be better capable of depicting human conditions because they will reach human (read: universal) situations. But such "universals" have been critiqued as man-made constructions from an European enlightenment era. Although Ojo-Ade's intent is to trumpet the literary accomplishments in a feminist light, especially the work of Aidoo, his language betrays his own commitment

to a patriarchal economy of literary representation *qua* repression that silences African feminists' concerns with the intersections of culture, gender, sexuality and economics. See also Davies' note 55 in her introductory essay on Ojo-Ade's earlier essay, "Female Writers, Male Critics."

7. In her introduction to *The Black Woman Cross-Culturally*, Filomina Steady cites an influential example of such reductionist readings in G.C.M. Mutiso's 1977 essay in which African women's sexuality is given little or no consideration in the traditional context, and in the urban context their sexuality dooms these women in terms of their morality as they "end up victims of suicide" (Steady 1981:14).

8. Aidoo refuses stereotypes that her literary brothers (for example, Armah in *The Beautyful Ones Are Not Yet Born* or Chindoya in *Harvest of Thorns*), have incorporated in certain instances into their fiction. Aidoo's literary work reflects the task articulated by Susheila Nasta:

> The post-colonial woman writer is not only involved in making herself heard, in changing the architecture of male-centered ideologies and languages, or in discovering new forms and language to express her experience, she has also to subvert and demythologize indigenous male writings and traditions which seek to label her. (Nasta 1992:xv)

9. Young's scholarship contextualizes British imperialism as a tripartite enterprise combining cultural and race theory with sexuality thus defining colonialism as a dual machine of war and desire. See, in particular, Chapter 4, "Sex and Inequality," in Young 1995.

10. See ch. 1, note 55 in Butler 1990. Or, in the words of another critic, Butler "argues that gender and sex become regulatory fictions, found and experienced today as binary relations consolidated through the practices of heterosexual desire" (L. Cream. "Resolving Riddles: The Sexed Body" In: *Mapping Desire*. Eds. David Bell and Gill Valentine. New York/London: Routledge, 1995. 38).

11. For a more detailed discussion of Aidoo's use of oral traditions in *Our Sister Killjoy* see Arlene Elder's (1987) essay, "Ama Ata Aidoo and the Oral Tradition: A Paradox of Form and Substance" in Jones 1987:107-118.

12. The lack of a proper name erases this Ghanaian's individuality; christened "Sammy," he takes on what might be Albert Memmi's "mark of the plural." But rather than being exclusively categorized by the imperial powers, the narrator of Aidoo's novel employs this moniker to underscore how "Sammy" is one of many "academic-pseudo-intellectual" African males who are even more dangerous than their colonial predecessors. The danger is their continued devotion to a set of beliefs that erase African culture and instead foster a belief that humanity is based on a Eurocentrism that masquerades as the language of "universal truth, universal art, universal literature and the Gross National Product" (Aidoo 1977:6).

13. See Frank (1987) and Innes (1992) for divergent readings of Aidoo's representation of the relationship between Marija and Sissie.

14. In *Lesbians Talk: Making Black Waves*, Eds. Valeria Mason and John and Ann Khambatta, the myth of homosexuality as a white colonial product is likewise deconstructed. Refer to the section "Out and About" (19-25).
15. There is also the ominous threat to erase the black man's life, given the images of lynching the narrative has provided, linking interracial sexual relationships with misegenation laws in the earlier encounter between Marija and Sissie.
16. Allan's "Afterword" provides a fine analysis of how Aidoo's narrative deconstructs the limitations of romance, both as a strategy for living and as a genre. Her analysis also presents a close look at the ways in which the novel brings together issues of gender and nationality.
17. Gay Wilentz makes an interesting assertion in the introduction to her study of the cultural connections between African women and their female "children" of the diaspora. In exploring Bernice Johnson Reagon's work on cultural workers, Wilentz asserts that a "mothering process" occurred between these workers, a process that "is a way of preserving (and dialectically, sometimes challenging) cultural and generational continuity. Who were the undocumented cultural workers who prepared the new soil to adapt the traditions" (xxvii). Nana and Sissie are doing this work for succeeding generations on Nana's part and for sororal peers on Sissie's. I agree with Wilentz's evaluation of Aidoo in her authorial role as "reflect[ing] the tradition of women storytellers and cultural advisors and tak[ing] that role into the modern political and social arena" (Wilentz 1992:42) through her contemporary representations of women's lives.

WORKS CITED

Accad, Evelyne. "Sexuality and Sexual Politics: Conflicts and Contradictions for Contemporary Women in the Middle East." *Third World Women and the Politics of Feminism.* Ed. Chandra Talpade Mohanty, Ann Russo and Lourdes Torres. Bloomington: Indiana University Press, 1991. 237-250.

Aidoo, Ama Ata. *Changes: A Love Story.* New York: CUNY, The Feminist Press, 1991a.

——-. *Our Sister Killjoy: Or Reflections from a Black-eyed Squint.* White Plains N.Y.: Longman, 1977.

——-. [Untitled essay] *Critical Fictions: The Politics of Imaginative Writing.* Ed. Philomena Mariani. Seattle: Bay Press, 1991b. 151-154.

Allan, Tuzyline Jita. "Afterword." *Changes: A Love Story.* By Ama Ata Aidoo. New York: CUNY, The Feminist Press, 1991. 171-196.

Bell, David and Gill Valentine. *Mapping Desire.* New York/London: Routledge, 1995.

Butler, Judith. *Gender Trouble: Feminism and the Subversion of Identity.* New York: Routledge, 1990.

Cream, L. "Resolving Riddles: The Sexed Body." In. *Mapping Desire.* Eds. David Bell and Gill Valentine. New York/London: Routledge, 1995. 22-41.

Davies, Carole Boyce. "Introduction: Feminist Consciousness and African

Literary Criticism." *Ngambika: Studies of Women in African Literature.* Ed. Carole Boyce Davies and Anne Adams Graves.1-23.

Dunton, Chris. "'Wheyting Be Dat?' The Treatment of Homosexuality in African Literature." *Research in African Literature* 20.3 (Fall 1989):422-448.

Elder, Arlene. "Ama Ata Aidoo and the Oral Tradition: A Paradox of Form and Substance." *Women in African Literature Today.* Ed. Eldred Jones. London: James Currey, 1987. 107-118.

Frank, Katherine. "Women without Men: The Feminist Novel in Africa." *Women in African Literature Today.* Ed. Eldred D. Jones. London: James Currey, 1987. 14-34.

Gilman, Sander. *Difference and Pathology: Stereotypes of Sexuality, Race and Madness.* Ithaca: Cornell Univ. Press, 1985:15-38.

Innes, C. L. "Mothers and Sisters? Identity, Discourse and Audience in the Writing of Ama Ata Aidoo and Mariama Bâ." *Motherlands: Black Women's Writing from Africa, the Caribbean and South Asia.* Ed. Susheila Nasta. New Brunswick: Rutgers University Press, 1992. 129-151.

Johnson-Odim, Cheryl. "Common Themes, Different Contexts." *Third World Women and the Politics of Feminism.* Ed. Chandra Talpade Mohanty, Ann Russo and Lourdes Torres. Bloomington: Indiana University Press, 1991. 314-327.

Jones, Eldred D. *Women in African Literature Today,* London: James Currey, 1987.

Mason-John, Valerie, and Ann Khambatta, Eds. *Lesbians Talk: Making Black Waves.* London: Scarlet Press, 1993.

McDowell, Deborah. Introduction. *Quicksand and Passing.* By Nella Larsen. New Brunswick: Rutgers University Press, 1986. ix-xxxv.

Mohanty, Chandra Talpade. "Under Western Eyes: Feminist Scholarship and Colonial Discourses." *Third World Women and the Politics of Feminism.* Ed. Chandra Talpade Mohanty, Ann Russo, and Lourdes Torres. Bloomington: Indiana University Press, 1991. 51-80.

Nasta, Susheila. "Introduction." *Motherlands: Black Women's Writing from Africa, the Caribbean and South Asia.* New Brunswick: Rutgers University Press, 1992. xiii-xxx.

Nederveen, Pierterse Jan. *White on Black: Images of Africa and Blacks in Western Popular Culture.* New Haven: Yale University. Press, 1995.

Ngugi, wa Thiongo. *A Grain of Wheat.* London: Heinemann, 1967.

Ogundipe-Leslie, Molara. *Re-Creating Ourselves: African Women and Critical Transformations.* Trenton N.J.: Africa World Press, 1994.

Ojo-Ade, Femi. "Of Culture, Commitment, and Construction: Reflections on African Literature." *Transition* 53. 1991.4-24.

Owusu, Kofi. "Canons Under Siege: Blackness, Femaleness, and Ama Ata Aidoo's *Our Sister Killjoy.*" *Callaloo* 13,2 (Spring 1990):341-363.

Rich, Adrienne. "Compulsory Heterosexuality and Lesbian Existence." *Blood, Bread, and Poetry, Selected Prose 1978-1985.* New York: WW Norton, 1986. Rpt. in *The Lesbian and Gay Studies Reader.* Ed. Henry Abelove, Michele Aina Barale, and David M. Halperin. New York: Routledge, 1993. 227-254.

Steady, Filomina Chioma. "Introduction." *The Black Woman Cross-Culturally*. Ed. Steady. Cambridge, Mass.: Schenkman Publ. Co., 1981. 1-41.

Wilentz, Gay. *Binding Cultures: Black Women Writers in Africa and the Diaspora*. Bloomington: Indiana University Press, 1992.

Young, Robert. *Colonial Desire: Hybridity in Theory, Culture and Race*. London: Routledge, 1995.

FREE BUT LOST:

VARIATIONS IN THE MILITANT'S SONG

PAULINE ONWUBIKO UWAKWEH

"Simply writing about women doesn't make anyone
a feminist writer. Feminism requires attending to
and offering a very clear perception of gender, class
and power relationships."
                    -Ama Ata Aidoo, *The Massachusetts Review*

BREAKING NEW GROUNDS

Ama Ata Aidoo's *Changes* (1993) is perhaps the most feminist novel
ever to surface on the arena of African female literature. It is
unique not only in its approach to the woman question, but also
in its underlying revolutionary vision of the modern African
woman. Indeed, *Changes* celebrates the modern woman's new status, her self-determining and independent spirit, her intellectual
and professional acumen. Above all, it projects her new self-awareness in the search for a self-fulfilling model of existence in her tran-
sient society. Aidoo acknowledges that to be feminist is, among

other things, to "celebrate the physical and intellectual capabilities of women and unfolding a revolutionary vision of their role" (Ezeigbo 1990:144). Furthermore, *Changes* fulfills Katherine Frank's criteria for the feminist novel in Africa, which "is not only alive and well, it is, in general, more radical, even more militant, than its Western counterpart" (Frank 1987:15).

The militant timbre of Aidoo's novel is unquestionable. Its militancy is conceived in terms of the heroine's self-determining actions, her resilience in the pursuit of goals or empowering ideals. Underlying the concept of militancy is the transforming potential of the heroine's choices. Change, emerging from those choices, is critical to the militant individual. Militancy thus requires that the individual be the "subject of action—those who know and act," rather than objects of action—those who are known and acted upon" (Freire 1973:169).[1]

Changes shares similarities with some African feminist novels such as Flora Nwapa's *One is Enough* (1982) and Buchi Emecheta's *Kehinde* (1994) to mention a few.[2] They are similar in their writers' portrayal of educated, professionally and economically independent heroines in an urban setting. These females exercise a degree of control over family affairs that complements the independence achieved outside the family setting in the course of their revolt. Polygamy or the prospects of it is central to the conflict in these writers' exploration. Indeed, it is made the engendering factor for their heroines' actions who remarkably gain powerful insights about their new status.

In contrast, however, *Changes* breaks new ground, veers off into a new feminist question that is yet unexplored in African literature. It all has to do with the issue of an alternative lifestyle in polygamy for Africa's modern woman.[3] Whereas polygamy has been a debatable issue among African writers and critics, it is refreshing but nonetheless explosive to witness on the literary scene the arrival of an iconoclast who gives the institution of polygamy an artistic second thought. Aidoo's foray into polygamy for its viability to the professional modern female goes "beyond what would be of general interest to the author herself, as well as her potential readership" (Aidoo, 1996:163). Her heroine's search asks these questions: Is a career-driven lifestyle compatible with monogamy? Does being career-driven make an African woman less African? The intensity of these questions lie in Oko's doubts about his wife's African identity: "Is Esi too an African woman?" The narrative voice affirms: "She not only is, but there are plenty of them around these days..." (Aidoo 1993:8). Aidoo seems to comprehend the exigent need for new modes of existence if the educated/professional female is to have a more self-enhanced life.

Therefore, she breaks new ground, primarily, in the area of choices that her heroine makes. Esi not only names marital violence as rape, but also seeks legal action on that grounds. She may be the first African heroine to seek divorce from husband for marital rape, a crime socially perceived as the husband's claim to his property rights. Esi's genuine feelings of disorientation following the rape incident clearly debunks any notion that marital rape is an imported feminist idea. It is worth noting that there are no indigenous words for rape in her culture. The authorial voice observes, "But marital rape? No. The society could not possibly have an indigenous word or phrase for it. Sex is something a husband claims from his wife as his right. Anytime. And at his convenience" (12). Esi does not euphemize marital rape, naming it a violent crime against womanhood. Her experience thus calls for a reassessment of this subversive mode of male aggression toward females, especially in the marriage partnership.

Secondly, Aidoo's protagonist wades into more controversial waters by questioning the husband's rights to his wife's time and space. Metaphorically, time and space connote autonomy, a concept hereby perceived as the heroine's ability to control or lay claim over her physical environs (the bungalow) and to pursue her interests (career) without undue restrictions.[4] It is in this sense that Esi's choice of divorce becomes a reappropriation of her time and space. Grandma Nana, Aidoo's choral voice, presents a traditional perspective on time and space, maintaining that the problem of womanhood lies solely with being woman:

> But Esi tell me, doesn't a woman's time belong to a man ? My lady Silk, that one is a very new and golden reason for leaving a man, if ever there was one.... But remember, my lady, the best husband you can ever have is he who demands all of you and all of your time. Who is a good man if not the one who eats his wife completely, and pushes her down with a good gulp of alcohol?... A good woman was she who quickened the pace of her own destruction. To refuse, as a woman, to be destroyed, was a crime that society spotted very quickly and punished swiftly severely.... It was not a question of being an

only wife or being one of many wives.... It is being a woman. (109-110)

Esi's choice of polygamy is striking. She is distinct from other feminist characters such as Amaka and Kehinde. Indeed, her choice of polygamy as opposed to monogamy may appear to detract from the writer's feminist commitment. Significantly, the novel's militant core lies in what Esi hopes to achieve in this marital institution—full devotion to career interests. It is ironical that while Nwapa's Amaka and Emecheta's Kehinde shun a polygamous lifestyle striking out alone to face the world as "single" women, Aidoo's Esi embraces this "alternative lifestyle" for its possibilities to her professional growth. Again, while moral laxity is the lot of our feminist heroines mentioned earlier, undoubtedly from their reaction to male maltreatment as one critic has observed (Ezeigbo 1990:154), Esi asserts her dignity, never yielding even at her weakest moment. Rather, she reassess her status in the polygamous relationship with Ali, thereby maintaining a marriage that is radically changed. Esi may indeed be the answer to the call for a new portrayal of the female whose assertion need not lie in separateness nor tagged with immorality (Chukwuma 1990:141). *Changes* is thus an *exposé* of new conflicts attending the modern African woman, who is not only married but also career-oriented. Ironically, this modern female chooses a traditional institution to resolve the conflicts of time and space in the monogamous relationship. Aidoo's focal shift to new questions about female claims to her time and space, concern with career growth within the marriage institution endow the novel with its characteristic revolutionary quality. Gone are the motherhood themes prevalent in female literature. In fact the heroine's motherhood is not at stake. What may be at stake is the claims of a mother over a child/children in the event of a divorce. This poses the biggest challenge to patriarchy. Esi's pioneering choice of an alternative lifestyle within polygamy makes her perhaps the most militant female ever to emerge in African female literature.

THE MAKING OF A MILITANT

Aidoo casts her protagonist in the role of militant, charting a new and unbeaten path, seeking a useful model of existence for the professional woman in marriage. Esi's tenacity is suggested in her slim physique as opposed to the robustness of Opokuya. By seeking divorce, she sees things clearly as they are. Esi is a "tough bird," well respected at work by colleagues. She is neither the weeping nor dependent type. Ali says to her, "you don't strike me as someone who'll miss anybody" (Aidoo 1993:86).

Esi's militancy is defined in terms of her choices, her self-awareness and resilience that transform her unwanted reality. Since militancy is realized in transforming action, the choices made by protagonists underline the revolutionary visions of their creators. However, that some choices may sometimes go contrary to social expectations does not make them any less militant.[5] Indeed, to perceive Esi as a militant, one needs to confront the meaning of her search for a new model of existence for the professional female. One needs to consider the power of her self-awareness which obviously comes from her intellectual capabilities. One needs to comprehend the challenge to patriarchy posed by her very act of unveiling marital rape against the background of tradition. Esi initiates her legal divorce despite the stigma attached to divorced women in African societies, thereby indicating that she values herself as a human being and not as an object for male ego gratification. In an insightful essay in which she explores the place of motherhood in African societies, Lauretta Ngcobo remarks:

> The image of divorced women in our society and our literature is negative. Only a handful may earn the understanding of the community such as in cases where the woman has a clean reputation which contrasts sharply with her husband's maltreatment of her. Only in a few cases do some women win the sympathy of the public. This is confirmed if they are seen to behave with dignity after divorce. On the whole a wife will do everything to endure even a stressful marriage, for in a divorce she comes out the loser: Even when her husband is the offending party, society sees her as having failed to hold him in place—therefore his failure is her failure as well (Ngcobo 1988:149).

Grandma Nana warns Esi on learning her intentions to enter a new marital relationship sharply contradictory to her elite status: "Remember a man always gained in stature through any way he chose to associate with a woman. And that included adultery.... Esi, a woman has always been diminished in her association with a man" (Aidoo 1993:109-110). Surely, there is a tension between her class status as an educated woman and the notion of polygamy as a traditional sexist institution. Without the backing of tradition, and skepticism from family members, Esi walks out of her tenuous marriage with Oko, thereby projecting her independent spirit. Notably, too, her economic viability makes her choice to leave possible. Esi's self-determination and resilience in the pursuit of goals complements her portrayal as a militant female.

Esi's choice distinguishes her from the other self-affirming female characters mentioned earlier. This is emphasized by her pioneering search for an alternative lifestyle capable of resolving the conflicts between a woman's career and her marital commitments. Esi's choices are not only a revolt, but one that carries with it social stigma. Her choice of polygamy goes against social expectations for the educated elite. Considering her economic independence, Nana wonders: "Leave one man, marry another. Esi, you can. You have got your job. The government gives you a house. You have got your car. You have already got your daughter. You don't even have to prove you are a woman to any man, old or new. You can pick and choose" (109).

Polygamy, as a lifestyle, has had its share of criticism basically for its assumed denigrating posture on the female. It is not only perceived as sexist at core but also scorned by women who consider themselves emancipated. When Buchi Emecheta dared to suggest that polygamy has merits for African women, she was soundly condemned for her notions.[6] Interestingly enough, she goes further to depict those merits in *Kehinde*, a novel whose purported message on polygamy is unclear. Note, for instance, Emecheta's views in this article, "Feminism with a small 'f'!" where she states:

> In many cases, polygamy can be liberating to the woman, rather than inhibiting her, especially if she is educated…. Polygamy encourages her to value herself as a person and look outside her family for friends. It gives her freedom from having to worry to be sure that he is in a good mood and that he is washed, and clean and ready for the wife, because the wife has now become so sophisticated herself that she has no time for a dirty, moody husband. And this in a strange way, makes them enjoy each other. (Emecheta 1988:179)

As I have argued elsewhere, her message in *Kehinde* is ambiguous because the writer simultaneously exposes Kehinde's humiliating experience in polygamy, a traditional institution that devalues women, while delineating its positive aspects in terms of extended kinship and sharing childcare responsibilities (Umeh, 1996: 399). In contrast to Emecheta's stated views, another female critic describes polygamy as "the most glaringly, inequitable and sexist feature of traditional African society" (Jones et. al. 1987:18). Significantly, polygamy engenders the heroine's choices in novels that dramatize the dilemma in this marital institution.

Aidoo's picture of urban polygamy is scarcely acknowledged in African literature. It is different from the rural-type polygamous structure where co-wives live together as a unit family. What makes this picture remarkable is her characters' modern views about polygamy. It is difficult to assess how far modernity can be superimposed on this traditional institution for it to yield its benefits to the participants. Ali contracts his marriage contrary to accepted traditional norms. He neither gets the consent of his wife nor does he inform his immediate family. Furthermore, he meets Esi's family with his employee as witness, an action that is condemned by the angered family members. In fact, Ali prioritizes his private engagement to Esi, for the sole reason that it transforms her into an "occupied territory." Significantly, the co-wives, Esi and Fusena never meet, preferring to live an existence separate from each other, while laying claims on the shared husband. Thus, Esi's "married but single" status marks the alternative lifestyle that she desires. It is this status that accords her control over her time and space—her bungalow where she operated as she pleased without undue pressures or restrictions. In contrast to Amaka and Kehinde, who reject this lifestyle, Esi embraces it for its benefits to her career interest. Aidoo offers a fresh way of looking at the benefits of this traditional institution to the career woman. However, through Esi's disillusioning experience with Ali, Aidoo warns about the emotional costs of such a lifestyle, thereby making the variableness of human nature an important lesson in this love story.

NEGOTIATING THE BATTLEFRONT

Changes is laden with images of war and conflict, an artistic ploy that denotes the marriage partnership as a conflict ridden zone, a battle front to be trodden with caution. Indeed, marriage is a core arena of feminist struggle where negotiation becomes either a weapon of survival or subjugation. For instance, Oko's violent physical abuse of his wife is intended to negotiate his way into power and subdue Esi into her role as wife. Note also that prior to this incident of abuse, communication between them had grounded to a halt and anything proved potentially "explosive." It is, therefore, not by chance that the rape incident becomes his wife's "assault weapon." The narrative voice clearly states that, "part of its fascination for her was its legal usefulness" (Aidoo 1993:36). Another interesting image of battleground is portrayed in Ali's engagement to Esi. She becomes an "occupied territory" by the mere fact of the engagement ring. Negotiation in this arena takes the form of expensive gifts subversively meant to be substitutes for the absentee husband, Ali. Further, in Opokuya and Kubi's marriage, conflict is projected in the perpetual "fight" for control over the family car. The car problem is one of the few cracks in the wall of their otherwise good marriage:

> Each morning's argument ended with one of them giving in. The winner drove the car. When it was Kubi, which was most days, he would deposit Opokuya at the hospital and then take the car, whistling all the way to the regional administrative offices. If Opokuya won, she would deposit Kubi in front of his office and drive away from there, humming all the way." (19)

Interestingly, Opokuya envied Esi's freedom of movement and realized herself "that in fact she had been thinking that for a very long time" (56). She seizes the opportunity to ask for a price on Esi's old car, thereby negotiating herself into mobility and earning a measure of control over her time. Esi's gift of a car to Opokuya is symbolic and critical to Aidoo's message on friendship. The car as symbol operates on two levels. It is as much a powerful symbol of negotiation in the marriage front-line as it is a symbol of mobility. Ali offers Esi a new car to bribe her into silence, an object that she understood as a substitute for his presence.

In contrast to the dynamism of Esi and Opokuya, Fusena accepts her fate as a first wife. As she sat before the group of older women who gathered to negotiate on Ali's behalf, her passivity becomes in fact a survival strategy:

> ...Those who had been first wives looked dignified, but clearly also battle-weary? She decided to make their job easier for them. "Yes, Mma. Yes, Auntie. Yes...yes...yes..." was all she said to every suggestion

that was made. The older women felt bad. Soon an understanding that had never existed between them was now born. It was a man's world. You only survived if you knew how to live in it as a woman. What shocked the older women though was obviously how little had changed for their daughters—school and all! (107)

Thus negotiation as a concept of survival or subjugation where the powerful gain the upperhand, even if temporarily, is strongly emphasized. The trio—Esi, Opokuya, and Fusena—respond to their battlefronts uniquely and, as characters, portray the varied images of the modern African woman. Each exercises a choice to stay within marriage or leave, to accept her lot or find a middle ground without causing undue turbulence to her marriage.

COUNTING GAINS AND LOSSES

Considering her emotional turmoil, to view Esi simply as a desolate lost female for whom freedom is unattainable detracts from the revolutionary import of her choices or her search for an answer to the professional woman's haunting problem in marriage. Esi emerges from her quagmire, never giving room to self-pity, but rather "teaching" herself to accept Ali as a good friend.

That relationship stopped being a marriage. They became just good friends who found it convenient once in a while to fall into bed and make love.

She never bothered to look for an annulment of the marriage....

So the marriage stayed, but radically changed. All questions and their answers disappeared. If Ali went to Esi's and she was not in, he tried not to question her about it when they next met. For Esi though, things hadn't worked out so simply. She had had to teach herself not to expect him at all. (164-165)

A recurring question surrounding female characterization in Esi's search for self-determination has to do with the problem of morality. A most common portrait tags the heroine's independence with sexual indulgence. Consequently, critics wonder if female assertion need lie in her sexuality or separate existence from the male.[7] In regard to such troubling female portrayals, Esi Sekyi stands out. One wonders if her choice of an alternative lifestyle may be the answer to the problem of separateness? Could her characterization be the answer to critics' call for a decent portrayal of the female who does not use sex as a means to an end? Esi, despite her disillusionment with Ali's fashion of loving, maintains her dignity. Even at her weakest moment, she rejects Kubi's sexual overtures. Here is a character best understood in terms of her pioneering effort in charting a new path and seeking a complementary model for career-enhancement in marriage.

In spite of the odds, Esi's success lies in her freedom-control over her time and space:

> Ali was not on her back every one of every twenty-four hours of every day. In fact, he was hardly ever near her at all. In that sense she was extremely free and extremely contented. She could concentrate on her job, and even occasionally bring work home.
>
> It was at this time that she confirmed what she had suspected about herself all along: she not only enjoyed the job she was doing, but she actually enjoyed working. She enjoyed working with figures—coordinating them, correlating and graphing. She also had more time to give to other aspects of her job. Like not only being able to be present at nearly all the important office meetings, but also sitting attentively through them and fully participating.
>
> Of course all this was different from how things had been in the past. Now she had almost lost the harassed feeling that had attacked her every late afternoon of every working day: that she had to hurry home, or to the market or the shops to buy something, or do something in connection with her role as a mother, a wife and a home-maker. Of course, when she thought of her daughter, she felt a little bad too. But there was no doubt at all that she enjoyed the fact that she was free to attend all the conferences, workshops, seminars and symposia on her schedule, whether they were held inside the country or outside. (138)

Esi's resilience is marked by her ability to transcend the dark side of her freedom, her sense of desolation which makes her a credible human character. Perhaps her greatest success lies in her insights about the nature of friendship. She realizes that friendship is also a fulfilling choice and perhaps the most constant relationship between two individuals. Thus friendship is uniquely idealized especially in the bonding between Opokuya and Esi. In a distinct sense, their bonding complements the writer's revolutionary vision of women. Esi's gift of her old but refurbished car to her immobile friend is a symbolic gift of freedom to a "caged bird". It enables Opokuya to appropriate more time for herself.

Charles Larson negates the value of Esi's freedom in this remark: "The freedom she sought is probably unattainable. Independence can be as painful as its opposite. In *Changes*, Ama Ata Aidoo presents an interesting variation on an age-old dilemma" (Larson 1992:389). This misperception of Esi's role in the story necessitates a female aesthetic canon that would adequately account for the peculiar female modes of addressing issues of male sexism. True to her artistic commitment, Aidoo raises questions that have no easy solutions. As do her other stories, *Changes* ends with a moment of crisis where the protagonist does not have clear alternatives. This creative flair affirms her belief that the responsibility of the artist is to expose social problems, entertain, inform, inspire and offer clear perceptions of gender, class and power relationships.

NOTES

1. On theorizing female militancy, see Uwakweh 1995:2-3, who argues that since violence in all its forms is a social reality of women worldwide, the study of female militancy as well as women's peculiar modes of addressing this reality is imperative in literary criticism. Her conceptual framework on militancy complements ongoing efforts to delineate a female aesthetic canon for interpreting women's actions in literature.

2. African female writers like Flora Nwapa and Buchi Emecheta shy away from the terminology "feminist" despite their obvious feminist concerns and approaches to the woman question. In contrast, Ama Ata Aidoo's position is unapologetic, as in this remark: "Feminism is an essential tool in women's struggles everywhere, and that includes African women. Every woman, as well as every man, should be a feminist. We African's should take charge of our land and its wealth, and our own lives and the burden of our reconstruction from colonialism and slavery. If Africa is to develop, then first African women must get the best that the environment can offer for their well-being and development; in primary

health care; shelter; adequate nourishment; accessibility to suitable career opportunities; freedom from sexual harassment in the workplace; freedom over their wombs, and the end to all other forms of marginalizations and tokenism. For some of us, the demand from society of these fundamentals constitutes the most important element in our feminist thought" (Aidoo 1996:163-164).

3. See for example Buchi Emecheta's novel, *Kehinde* (1994), which explores the polygamous institution. In contrast to Aidoo's heroine who embraces polygamy voluntarily, Kehinde repudiates such a lifestyle. Unlike Kehinde and Kike (co-wives who lived under the same roof), Esi and Fusena never meet, each preferring to live a separate existence from each other.

4. See Busia, (1988:4). Busia perceives space as a metaphor for autonomy and personal responsibility, a theme that is interwoven with women's search for security, financial independence from men, and total control of their spiritual and physical well-being.

5. Uwakweh (1995:9) argues that transformation is an important criterion for judging the success of an action emerging from the individual's choice. Therefore, a "failed" action could be militant by virtue of the transformation it brings to the militants, or to the oppressors, or society in general.

6. Carole B. Davies (1986:20) notes that at a 1984 California African Studies meeting, "African women in the audience, some feminists, were appalled at Emecheta's stand on polygamy. One has to admit, however, that Emecheta, who has written several novels which show polygamy in negative light would not have come to her position casually."

7. Cf., Ezeigbo, 1990:152, 154; Chukwuma,1990, 141.

WORKS CITED

Aidoo, Ama Ata. *Changes: A Love Story*. New York: CUNY, The Feminist Press, 1993.

———. "Literature, Feminism and the African Woman Today." In: *Reconstructing Womanhood, Reconstructing Feminism: Writings on Black Women*. Ed. Delia Jarrett-Macauley. London and New York: Routledge, 1996. 156-174.

———. "To be An African Woman Writer - An Overview and A Detail." In: *Criticism and Ideology*. Ed. Kirsten Petersen. Scandinavian Institute of African Studies, Uppsala: 1988. 155-172.

Busia, Abena. "Words Whispered Over Voids: A Context For Black Women's Rebellious Voices in the Novels of The African Diaspora." In: *Black Feminist Criticism and Critical Theory*. Eds. Joe Weixelmann and Houston Baker, Jr. Greenwood, Fla.: Penkeville, 1988. 1-41.

Chukwuma, Helen. "Voices and Choices: The Feminist Dilemma in Four African Novels." *Calabar Studies in African Literature: Literature and the Black Aesthetic*. Ed. Ernest Emenyonu. Ibadan: Heinemann, 1990. 131-142.

Davies, Carole B. "Feminist Consciousness and African Literary Criticism."

In *Ngambika: Studies of Women in African Literature*. Ed. Carole Boyce Davies and Anne Adams Graves. Trenton, N.J.: Africa World Press, 1986. 1-23.

Emecheta, Buchi. "Feminism with a small "'f'!" In *Criticism and Ideology*. Ed. Kirsten Petersen. Uppsala: Scandinavian Institute of African Studies, 1988, 173-185.

———. *Kehinde*. Portsmouth, N.H.: Heinemann, 1994.

Ezeigbo, Theodora Akachi. "Reflecting the Times: Radicalism in Recent Female-Oriented Fiction in Nigeria." *Calabar Studies in African Literature: Literature and the Black Aesthetic*. Ed. Ernest Emenyonu. Ibadan: Heinemann, 1990, 143- 157.

Frank, Katherine. "Women Without Men: The Feminist Novel in Africa." In: *Women in African Literature Today* 15. Eds. Eldred D. Jones, Eustace Palmer and Marjorie Jones, Trenton, N.J.: Africa World Press, 1987. 14-34.

Freire, Paulo. *Pedagogy of the Oppressed*. [1970] Trans. by Myra Bergman Ramos. Foreword. Richard Schaull. New York: Seabury, 1973.

Jones, Eldred D., Eustace Palmer and Marjorie Jones. *African Literature Today* 15. Trenton, N.J.: Africa World Press, 1987.

Larson, Charles. "Review of *Changes: A Love Story* by Ama Ata Aidoo." *World Literature Today* 66,2 (1992):389.

Needham, Anuradha Dingwaney. "An Interview with Ama Ata Aidoo." *The Massachusetts Review* 36,1 (1995):123-133.

Ngcobo, Lauretta. " African Motherhood—Myth and Reality." In: *Criticism and Ideology*. Ed. Kirsten Petersen. Uppsala: Scandinavian Institute of African Studies, 1988. 141- 154.

Nwapa, Flora. *One is Enough*. Enugu, Nigeria: Tana Press, 1982

Uwakweh, Pauline Ada. " To Ground the Wandering Muse: A Critique of Buchi Emecheta's Feminism." In *Emerging Perspectives on Buchi Emecheta*. Ed. Marie Umeh. Trenton, N.J.: Africa World Press, 1996. 395-406.

———. "The Dimensions of Female Militancy in African and African-American Women's Fiction: Buchi Emecheta, Nawal el Saadawi, Alice Walker, and Gloria Naylor." Diss., Temple University, 1995.

Sexual Politics and Phallocentric Gaze in Ama Ata Aidoo's *Changes: A Love Story*

Miriam C. Gyimah

My folk...have always been a race for theory."

-Barbara Christian

"My young lady, today you came here asking me a question. I shall try as hard as possible to give you an answer. I shall also try to make it my truth, not anybody else's. For in a world where lies are pampered like the only children and nephews of queens and kings, all we can do is to hold on to our own truths.... *These days, we are getting used to people saying big things when they mean so little or nothing at all!*"

-Nana, *Changes*

BLACK WOMEN: CHALLENGING AND THEORIZING

In her essay "The Race For Theory," Barbara Christian argues that theory is being manipulated by Western philosophers through a particular use of language, to "mystify rather than clarify." This "new takeover" (Christian 1990:335) is a means to prevent African scholars' participating in the critique of literature, even what is considered "minority discourse" (337). While this manipulation of language is crucial to the politics of exclusion, it implies that in order to be recognized as theorizing, one must prove her ability to engage in "rhetorical complexity." Christian argues that despite this new method of validation, African people have always theorized. The theoretical discourse of Africans, she maintains, have often been in narrative forms, in the stories they create, in riddles, proverbs and in the play with language (336). African women, she says, "continuously speculated about the nature of life through pithy language that unmasked the power relations of their world" (336). Christian maintains that these forms of theorizing by African people is different from Western use of abstract logic. Furthermore, Christian strongly holds that because the race for theory involves a monolithic and abstract approach to the world, she refuses to rush and develop a black feminist theory since it would be prescriptive and limiting (342).

While bell hooks in "Feminist Theory: A Radical Agenda," agrees with Christian that African people have always theorized, she disagrees with Christian's assertion that they do not employ abstract logic. hooks cites the Dogon people of Africa "who have very abstract logical schemas to support rituals that focus on creating gendered subjects" and continues by referring to Frigga Haug, who writes that "contrary to reputation, our everyday language is more than a little abstract: it suppresses the concreteness of feelings, thoughts, and experiences, speaking of them only from a distance" (hooks 1989:39). "All theory," hooks asserts, "emerges in the realm of abstraction, even that which emerges from the most concrete of everyday experiences" (39). Again, hooks critiques Christian's refusal to engage in a black feminist theory as devaluing theory because, according to hooks, while the concepts will still be abstract, they can be developed through "accessible language." Hence, there should be a "production of visionary feminist theory. Such theory emerges only from a context in which there is either an integration of critical thinking and concrete experience or a recognition of the way in which critical ideas, abstractly formulated, will impact on everyday life experience" (39).

On one hand, Christian's refusal to rush and develop a black feminist theory is defensible, even though it can be stifling the black woman's creativity and voice. On the other hand, hooks' argument for the need to theorize and employ accessible language, language which does not purposely exclude others' theoretical engagement, allows the space for black women's thoughts to be heard. Her argument follows in the tradition of Helene Cixous' "The Laugh of the Medusa." In this essay, Cixous refuses to comply with the muted position reserved for women as she refutes Freudian and Lacanian arguments about women's limitations. To Cixous, woman's writing is essential and it fulfills a purpose, that is the taking back of the body (Cixous 1991:335). She says, "Woman must write herself: must write about women and bring women to writing, from which they have been driven away as violently as from their bodies ....Woman must put herself into the text—as into the world and into history—by her own movement" (334). We argue that black women should employ any vehicle, creative, theoretical or otherwise, in order to claim the legitimacy of their voice. By engaging in theoretical discourse, black women claim for themselves as women and blacks their bodies and their historical place. It is important that women do not abstain from contributing to, and being a part of, theoretical discourse because of Eurocentric and phallocentric manipulations.

Black women demonstrate through various means their ability to philosophically engage in issues and questions of power, dominance and language. For example, they theorize via their creative texts, using a character or characters to engage in theoretical discourse as is pertinent to the plot. Secondly, the creative text itself can serve as not only a literary work telling a story, but a work which puts forth and attempts to grapple with the same questions that recognized theorists observe and discuss. In *Black Women, Writing, and Identity: Migrations of the Subject,* Carole Boyce Davies is reluctant to see any difference between what theorists and creative writers do:

> ...for Black women's writing, I believe it is premature and often useless to articulate the writer/theorist split so common in European discourses, for many of the writers do both simultaneously or sequentially. If we define theory as 'frames of intelligibility,' by which we understand the world, and

not as a reified discourse used to locate, identify and explain everything else, then we can pursue critically how we theorize.... *Theory in my view, ought not to be an impediment to movement but should be an enabling set of discourses.* (Davies 1994:35; emphasis mine)

Ama Ata Aidoo simultaneously and sequentially writes and theorizes. Her creative texts interrogate the lives of Africans, especially African women in regards to colonial, imperial and patriarchal domination. "To Be a Woman," one of her shorter essays, however, can be read as a theoretical work. The essay broaches the subject of female discrimination in a male dominated society. It gives a closer look at the life of a Ghanaian woman, particularly one who is educated and professional. Aidoo talks about the pain and struggle she encounters while attempting to function and survive in such a hostile space. In her novel *Changes: A Love Story*, Aidoo demonstrates that she can merge fiction and theory within the same text. By so doing, she confirms not only Boyce Davies' assertion about black women as theorists and writers but also Christian's and hooks' points of view concerning the historical role of blacks as theorists.

Changes substantiates the argument for race theory. With women such as Nana, Ena and Opokuya, Aidoo demonstrates in this novel that African people have always theorized and that theory is an important activity in which black women engage. The reader is exposed to a female community where women are able to discuss issues of hegemony, patriarchal privilege and sexual politics and then use that knowledge to impact everyday life. When Nana, Esi's grandmother, takes her short stool and sits in the company of her daughter and granddaughter, it is to begin the eloquent articulations of what she considers "truth," her truth, or perhaps what might be considered her version of theoretical discourse through what hooks calls "accessible" language. As far as Nana is concerned, because lies are always being pampered, all we can do is hold on to our truths (Aidoo 1991:109). She adds:

It used to be possible to talk and know what you and everyone else knew what you were talking about. It has stopped being like that for some time now. *These days, we are getting used to people saying big things when they mean so little or nothing at all.* They talk of pretty things when they intend ugly, and carry

dangerous deeds home that properly belong in the
bush. (109; emphasis mine)

From here, Nana begins her discourse on issues of power and
dominance as related to local and global politics. Nana's words
directly speak to Christian's discussion on the use of language to
exclude certain people. Aidoo is here using dialogic consciousness
to communicate her anxiety: the exclusion of African women's
texts from African literary criticism by Western and African critics alike. Furthermore, with Nana's words, it becomes evident that
the theoretical concepts of Western philosophers such as Michel
Foucault and Jacques Lacan are neither new nor are they too
"abstract," as their use of language makes them appear for everyday thinkers.

Just as Foucault talks about power and truth to professional
and academic audiences, so does Nana to her granddaughter within the home space for domestic applications. In *Power and
Knowledge*, Foucault postulates that:

Truth isn't outside of power or lacking in power...As
a thing of this world, truth is produced only by
virtue of multiple forms of constraint and induces
regular effect of power. Each society has its regime
of truth, its general politics of truth: that is the types
of discourse it accepts and makes function as true"
(Foucault 1980:131).

Foucault adds that power is co-extensive with the social body
and that relations of power are interwoven with other kinds of relations such as kinship, family and sexuality, for which power relations play at once a conditioning and conditioned role (142). After
Esi informs Nana, first of her intention to leave her husband Oko
because he demanded too much of her time, and second her desire
to enter into a polygamous marriage, Nana propounds her theory
that in society truths, which privilege men, are used to dominate
women, to establish power relations in society:

But Esi tell me, doesn't a woman's time belong to a
man?...You can pick and choose. But remember, my
lady, the best husband you can ever have is he who
demands all of you and all of your time. Who is a
good man if not the one who eats his wife completely, and pushes her down with a good gulp of
alcohol. In our time, the best citizen was the man

who swallowed more than one woman, and the more, the better...Esi, why do you think they took so much trouble with a girl on her wedding day? When we were young we were told that people who were condemned to death were granted any wish on the eve of their execution...Anyhow, a young woman on her wedding day was something like that. She was made much of, because that whole ceremony was a funeral of the self that could have been. (Aidoo 1991:109, 110)

Nana thus confirms what Foucault calls a normalized arrangement, which affects sexual politics, and (always) indicates one group's domination over another, domination which is "organized into a more-or-less coherent...strategic form..." (Foucault 1980:142).

Sexual politics in most societies is always about male domination of women. Maleness is privileged while femaleness is subordinated. In his *Three Essays on the Theory of Sexuality*, Sigmund Freud explains that this hierarchical relationship can be attributed to the male's possession of a phallus and the female's lack of the same. While the male is empowered, the female is disemboweled through castration (Freud 1965:92-93). Freud points that the phallus is the male sexual organ. Lacan disagrees in *Female Sexuality*, however, maintaining that the hierarchical relationship plays itself out in language, and this language which also represents power is easily accessible to the male, and not readily accessible to the female since the symbolic order (of language) is closely associated with the law of the father (Booker 1996:36). Jane Flax clarifies the silencing of women according to Lacan:

All speaking beings 'inscribe themselves' on the masculine side, no matter what their physical attributes might be. To speak one must enter into and become constituted by the realm of the symbolic—the play of signifiers and the signified and the 'universal signifier' (the phallus). Those who lack access to the phallus and hence to the world of culture and language (the symbolic) are called 'woman'... (Flax 1990:111).

It is therefore the lack of this phallus which prevents woman from having the same position as the man; he is the subject, she the Other. The argument that women lack a phallus, thus, language, according to Jane Flax, is in effect a deliberate silencing of women (118). Conversely, Flax and other feminist theorists such as Marlene Nourbese Philip argue that the power of language is something that women have always possessed. In "Discourse on the Logic of Language," Philip makes the point that it is the mother who gives language to her child:

> when it was born, the mother held her newborn child close: she began then to lick it all over...the mother turning it this way and that under her tongue, until she had tongued it clean of the creamy white substance covering its body. The mother then put her fingers to her child's mouth—gently forcing it open. She touches her tongue to the child's tongue, and holding the tiny mouth open, she blows into it- hard. She was blowing words—her words, her mother's words, those of her mother's mother, and all their mothers before—into her daughter's mouth. (Philip 1989:56 and 58)

With this analogy, Philip illustrates that the female possesses language and is able to impart it to another. She goes on to suggest in "Mother's Recipes on How to Make a Language Yours or How Not to Get Raped" that language as given by the mother to the daughter can be simultaneously used as a tool of empowerment and one against dominance.

Philip's reference to the tongue as a symbol of female nurturing and power is also corroborated by the friendship between Janie and Pheoby in Hurston's *Their Eyes Were Watching God*. Upon her return from "burying the dead" (Hurston 1990:1), Janie sits with her friend Pheoby and relates to her the experiences responsible for her new vision and insight of her person and womanhood. Entrusting Pheoby, another woman, with her story, she tells her "you can tell 'em what Ah say if you wants to. Dat's just de same as me 'cause mah tongue is in mah friend's mouf" (6). Janie's tongue, a symbol of the power of speech and her voice, is passed on as language to a trusted friend. By placing her tongue in her friend's mouth, she not only empowers herself by assuring the continuation of her own testimony, she also enables Pheoby to recognize this power, for Pheoby says after receiving Janie's gift that "lawd!...Ah done growed ten feet higher from jus' listenin' tuh you, Janie" (182). In her chapter "Other Tongues," Davies writes of Janie's passing her tongue to Pheoby and states that it is a critique of the privileging of language and a recognition of how articulations for the dispossessed can take place (155). Indeed, it is from hearing Janie's testimony that Pheoby decides to incorporate changes in her life. Therefore, by asserting their own truths through their theoretical discourse, black women writers and critics disprove racist sexist sociopolitical exclusionary theory which renders them without linguistic access and power.

By textually combating phallocentric suppositions embedded in male centered theory, black women writers reveal how they themselves resist the appropriation of such theory. This is a case of challenging dominant theory and practice. Because certain truths, as Foucault and Nana suggest, are the basis of power relations, these truths are depended upon for the activities of everyday life. Male supremacists either embrace Freud's and Lacan's positions pertaining to sexual politics or somehow, informed by their communities, accept concepts of their superiority over women. It is difficult to say this notion of superiority rests only on the concept of a phallus, either physical or linguistic, since Ifi Amadiume explains that certain societies, such as the Igbo of Nigeria, do not necessarily always determine their gender relations from sex, even though it is still common for males to exercise privileges over females. She states that there is an absence of the pronouns "he" or "she" in Igbo society, adding that some men can be addressed as "wives" and some women as "husbands." Amadiume argues that sex and gender alone do not determine who possesses power. Rather, power relations can determine one's gender without considering sex.

As men accept the "truths" about their position of power in sexual politics, they begin to perform their role as dominant persons and require that women conform as subordinates. This sexual politics begins the phallocentric gaze—not after the physical or emotional contact between men and women—as the male perceives himself as subject and locates the female as object. It is from this identification that the relationship is established. Furthermore, it is also here that Aidoo's depiction of African women's community becomes relevant. Aware of men's privileges in society, and therefore of the relationships established to actualize these judgments, Aidoo gives an account of some women's response to it. Nana, Aidoo's fictional character, becomes this author's persona. However we choose to read it, Aidoo is repeating the language and role of the female elder in society, that is the voice of the grandmother. Aidoo illustrates this by exposing Esi Sekyi's relationships with three different men. We see how sexual power roles are played out through visual contact, the phallocentric gaze.

SEXUAL POLITICS AND PHALLOCENTRIC GAZE IN *CHANGES*

> "...after his eyes had raked Esi's body...
> he had in fact concluded that he could sleep
> with her." (135)

Aidoo establishes that the phallocentric gaze, prompted by social truths and power relations, is without barriers. While Esi's experiences with men give a glimpse of the private affairs of Ghana's educated elite, they also confirm Nana's words regarding societal expectations of women. Nana hopes that Esi's scholastic training provides her with more options than she [Nana] had, but with the persistence of ideologies that protect male domination in a changing society, Nana admits that sexual politics has remained the same.

The personal lives of educated and career-minded Africans are perhaps expected to be different from the lives of those who have not had the privilege of higher education. In fact, it is assumed by the elders in this novel that this should be the case. The first pages of Aidoo's *Changes* appear to give the same impression when we see a career woman come in contact with her equal, in the person of Ali Kondey. As Esi addresses Ali about business matters, the two are presented as reciprocating professionals. But this reciprocity begins to fade when sexual politics invades the professional space. As they faced each other, Aidoo lets us know that "Esi became aware that something quite interesting was trying to make itself felt in that room that early evening..." (Aidoo 1991:3). Thus begins the love story of Esi and Ali.

But what Aidoo calls a love story is in fact a discourse on the complexities of the positions, relationships and lives of members of the Ghanaian neocolonial elite (Odamtten 1994:161). As Odamtten notes, "by suggesting that this is only a love story, Aidoo has set us up for a rather rude awakening, designed to disabuse us of our dearly held pre(mis)conceptions about love and marriage" (161). What Aidoo reveals with *Changes*, as she depicts these neocolonial elite, is that despite the so called formal education of the mind, the sexual politics between men and women is yet the same which governed their ancestors.

Some of the changes that Aidoo alludes to become obvious in

the beginning of the work. For one, Aidoo brings together a Ghanaian Southerner and Northerner without a dispute between their families regarding their different backgrounds, and she also discloses that educational "equality" has effected change in African women's lives. Esi's husband, Oko, regrettably admits that Esi "definitely put her career well above any duties she owed as a wife" and as a result, he questions if Esi and other women like her are still African women (Aidoo 1991:8). By noting this at the beginning of the work, Aidoo prepares the reader for a conflict of ideologies which has shaped the typical gender relations between men and women. With the dissolution of Esi and Oko's marriage, it becomes clear that failure to negotiate expectations between equally educated and professional couples will produce an often difficult and unsuccessful marriage. However, while this conflict between husband and wife is in fact important to the novel's theme of changes, it is only a manifestation of a more prevailing issue which is delicately woven throughout the text: the prevailing issue, which subtly begins with the meeting of Esi and Ali within the first pages of the novel and ends with the embrace of Esi and Kubi in the end, is the gaze.

When Ali's father, Musa Musa, looked upon Esi, he determined that "he could sleep with her" (135). Although he ruled it out because Esi was his daughter-in-law, he nevertheless determined she was an object of desire and that conquest was indeed possible. While Aidoo, the omniscient narrator, carefully describes and discloses his most private and intimate thoughts about Esi, or rather, Esi's body, what is re-presented here as the thoughts of an old man immersed in a culture that honors his maleness and celebrates his ability to "swallow a woman" (109), is also those of the other men within the work. Musa Musa's gaze and thoughts are the same as Oko's, Ali's and Kubi's. Aidoo demonstrates that for all these men, Esi is their object of desire. That Esi is desirable to these men is not the issue; instead, the issue is the motive behind their longing. It is this motive which precedes the gaze and it is the gaze and all that is implied with it that in turn initiates the performance of possession.

In "The Oppositional Gaze," bell hooks postulates that the gaze involves issues of power. She adds: "I thought again...about the ways power as domination reproduces itself in different locations employing similar apparatuses, strategies, and mechanisms of control" (hooks 1992:115). Echoing Foucault's words, hooks reveals that these strategies and mechanisms of control are daily manipulated in the intimate relationships of the sexes. Since traditional gender relations between men and women privilege the male, allowing him power over the female, the woman becomes the object of the phallocentric gaze, when this entitlement is acted out. Sexual politics is then a place of struggle where the man, at the moment of his gaze, begins to fulfill the advantages accorded to his maleness.

In *Changes*, the phallocentric gaze serves as the initial point of disguised compulsion. Throughout the work, Aidoo only overtly mentions this male gaze twice. The first is Oko's admiration of Esi's body before he rapes her. The second is in relation to Musa Musa. It is interesting that Aidoo shows the violence associated with the gaze in the beginning of the novel with Oko's raping of Esi, quite before she casually relates Musa's thoughts. In so doing, Aidoo first foreshadows the prevailing threat of the gaze within the work as it affects Esi's relationships with men. Furthermore, while dramatizing the rape scene early in the text, partly to further the plot of Esi's liberation from her marriage with Oko, and partly to permit the love story between Esi and Ali to materialize, Aidoo also foreshadows Musa's thought and gaze. The rape and Musa's gaze then foreshadow the final encounter between Esi and Kubi, a possible seduction or perhaps another rape! Then again, there is also evidence of a consistent gaze throughout the work. Although sometimes passively alluded to or often unmentioned, it nonetheless occupies a fixed space between the subject and the object of desire. Thus, upon Esi's encounter with any of these men, the presence of the gaze is silently noted.

The phallocentric gaze is always significant even when it is not mentioned, preceding the act of possession. All the men's intention in regard to Esi is to objectify her. This objectification can become realized through sexual contact. Gaining access to Esi sexually is not only an attempt to control her body but one to manipulate her as an individual, for Esi signifies the strong and challenging professional woman who many men perceive as a threat to their power. Clearly, this is the case with her first husband, Oko.

Though a victim, Esi is not without agency in her relationships with them, because she also engages in the gaze. But unlike the men in her life, she employs it toward asserting and celebrating her sexuality. For instance, upon seeing Ali at the Hotel Twentieth Century, Aidoo notes that "Esi on her part was following him with her eyes as he...went straight up to the front desk. She tried not to stare too hard. But there was no doubt that she was interested in whoever he was" (Aidoo 1991:51). Esi engages in what might be considered an oppositional gaze. hooks identifies this gaze as "an overwhelming longing to look, a rebellious desire" because it is a site of resistance that subordinates in relations of power have come to learn experientially (hooks 1992:116). In looking, Esi breaks down gender roles and privileges. It is a defiance against the passive space reserved for her African womanhood. Her rejection of such roles continues as she refuses to adhere to Opokuya's and Nana's advice about the expected behavior of an African woman. It is important to note that Aidoo explicitly notes that Esi also gazes, for in so doing she portrays her as a complex female subject requiring both a healthy professional and sexual life. She is not simply an appropriated sexual object, but an aggressive woman consciously claiming her sexual agency. Nevertheless, Esi approaches her sexual relationships with men as one of reciprocity and not a calculated manipulative arrangement.

But reciprocity, especially a sexual one, is not entirely welcome by the men in her life. In her marriage with Oko, Esi's focus and control of her self and career intimidates him and eventually challenges him to assert himself through dominance and violence. Oko complains of his wife's refusal to assume and fulfill the traditional role of an African woman. For Esi, marriage and motherhood should not conflict with or precede her career. In order to maintain what she may identify as a balance, she opts to have only one child despite the persistent oppositional views of her husband and his family. Esi's decisions about her life is a claim for the freedom that men, not bound by the obligations of motherhood, enjoy. Esi then consciously ignores the established truths and power granted to the male and begins to establish her own truths through the decisions she makes. Her freedom to choose is however an unacceptable challenge to her husband. Oko feels threatened and emasculated by the respect she receives from her colleagues, her insistence to remain on birth control, and the fact that the very bungalow they lived in came with her job (Aidoo 1991:8). At this point, he realizes that any authority that has been granted him via his society has been rendered void by Esi. Hoping he might receive some sympathy and perhaps understanding concerning his questioned manhood, he says to Esi: "[m]y friends are laughing at me...They think I'm not behaving like a man." But refusing to engage in a discourse and relationship which provides preferential treatment based on his maleness, she responds with "[w]e all make friends. They either respect us for what we are or they don't"

(9). Further angered by her words, Oko then counters Esi's refusal to be subordinated. In a desperate act to assert authority and reclaim his manhood, Oko violates Esi's body. Aidoo narrates that:

> Oko snatched [Esi's watch] from her and threw it...[he] flung the bedcloth away from him, sat up, pulled her down, and moved on her. Esi started to protest. But he went on doing what he had determined to do all morning. He squeezed her breast repeatedly, thrust his tongue into her mouth, forced her unwilling legs apart, entered her, plunging in and out of her, thrashing to the left, to the right, pounding and just pounding away. (9)

For Oko, masculinity insists on the subjection of a woman's body, even if it involves violence. But Aidoo demonstrates that the violence did not just stem from Oko's resentment of Esi's failure to fulfill her traditional role, but that it began at the point of the gaze. Aidoo clearly says that "...he went on doing what he had determined to do all morning" (9). Before the violent rape episode, we find Oko's eyes and mind fixed on Esi. Looking at her naked body with admiration, Oko associates Esi's naked body with that of a school girl. Aidoo records that:

> As she picked this up [toilet spray or perfume] and poured a bit of that into her palm and rubbed it on parts of her body, Oko looked at her. Lying down and watching her go through the motions of dressing was a pleasure he was fully enjoying this particular morning. *It occurred to him then, as it had occurred to him countless other mornings before, that Esi had not lost a bit of her school girl looks or school girl ways.*
>
> For a teacher in a co-educational school, and soon to be a headmaster of one, this is a very dangerous thought indeed. He scolded himself.... *I love this body. But it is her sassy navel that kills me, thought Oko, watching the little protrusion, and feeling some heating up at the base of his own belly.* (6; italics mine)

Still looking at her, Oko begins to reflect on their frustrating marital difficulties.

> Thinking of how much he had invested in the mar-
> riage with Esi, and how much he had fought to keep
> it going made him feel a little angry and a little
> embarrassed. With all that was going on in his head,
> his penis, which had then become really big and
> hard, almost collapsed. But since his eyes were still
> on Esi's navel, the thing jerked itself up again. (7)

With an erect penis and still looking at Esi, Oko continues to think and agonize about their relationship. It is the result of his eyeing Esi's body and his further thoughts about her refusal to conform that produces the explosive rape scene.

While looking at Esi's nakedness, Oko's mind and body respond to a complexity of feelings ranging from admiration, pleasure, resentment, anger and finally violence. Beginning with admiration and pleasure, he positions Esi as a school girl and he the school master. In so doing Oko attempts to occupy a safe ground for himself where his authority and stature are not threatened but acknowledged. Within his mind and their marriage, Esi must remain the school girl and he the headmaster. Oko's insistence to perceive Esi as always the school girl makes it difficult for him to see her assume another identity beyond what he has established for her. Because if he does, it will in turn mean a reidentification of himself. There can be no headmaster without a school girl. His fantasy is disturbed by the reality of their married life. Thoughts of Esi's resistance to his construction continues to resurface in Oko's mind although it is apparent that he would rather reflect on the hierarchical relationship he prefers. Note again that Aidoo says, "[w]ith all this going on in his head, his penis, which had by then become really big and hard, almost collapsed. But since his eyes were still on Esi's navel, the thing jerked itself up again" (7). It is Oko's attraction toward Esi and his frustration and anger about his threatened position as a figure of authority by this school girl which leads to the rape. Here, the act of rape is to reestablish the proposed hierarchical order. It is an act against the image of the school girl turned independent career woman. Oko's actions speak to his fear of changing roles that destabilize his position as a man, perhaps more importantly, an African man. Furthermore, his scolding himself for sexually positioning Esi as a school girl is not genuine, because following this supposed scolding, he enacts with the rape: the worst possibility of an encounter between a school girl and her headmaster.

Interestingly, Oko's violent response to Esi is not out of order. Both Foucault and hooks acknowledge in their discourse on power and hegemony that specific strategies are employed to ensure the established social order. Included in this strategic plan is the use of violence. It was the use of violence that warned potential Emmett Tills about looking, much less whistling. Expressing the same sentiments, Nana warns Esi about the repercussions of not passively falling into the role required of women. Society does not grant protection and support to one challenging its structure. For according to Nana, "[a] good woman was she who quickened the pace of her own destruction. To refuse, as a woman, to be destroyed, was a crime that society spotted very quickly and punished swiftly and severely" (111). Thus, with the authority given Oko by society, he asserts his right to Esi's body violently through rape.

While Oko claims domination over Esi, Ali, on the other hand, subtly approaches his purpose. Aidoo constructs the text in a manner that is ironically self-fulfilling. A feminist writer and critic, she approaches the work often portraying the sensitive male professing genuine love and respect for his woman. These new African men, educated and aware of the feminist activities of their women, seem to prefer the educated woman, perhaps as an equal. However, *Changes* illustrates that the claim to love and respect is no more than a guise concealing a desire for patriarchal control. Aware of this, Opokuya discloses to Esi that "men are not really interested in a woman's independence or her intelligence. The few who claim they like intelligent and active women are also interested in having such women permanently in their beds and in their kitchens" (45). Opokuya's revelation precedes Ali's encounter with Esi in The Hotel Twentieth Century. Although Esi and Ali have already met, this second encounter symbolically marks his entrance into Esi's life. As Opokuya describes "everyman," Ali enters and falls into character.

If we go by Opokuya's concept of "everyman," a man who claims equality but yet subscribes to male domination, then Ali, like Oko, is also "everyman." My use of the term "everyman" is not an effort to grossly generalize, but one to specifically identify Ali as one of the men to whom Opokuya refers. It is also a means to confront the obvious ideological disposition of many, if not all, as Opokuya would argue. However, Ali's true stance is not recognized by Vincent Odamtten. In Odamtten's effort to render a critique that portrays Ali in a more favorable light in comparison to Oko, he falls short of understanding Opokuya's words. Odamtten takes for granted that Opokuya's statement is only in reference to Oko (Odamtten 1994:163) and therefore goes on to critique only Oko's behavior as if Ali's is not relevant. Although Ali's troubles with Esi are not the same as those of her previous marriage to Oko, it does not negate the fact that both men similarly ascribe to a male dominant ideology. Ali is indeed included in Opokuya's words, after all, he is a colonizer of female bodies.

Ali's decision to provide Esi as his "occupied territory" (Aidoo 1991:91), his exact words, was formed when he first met her. While their meeting was prompted by a professional agenda, it soon becomes clear in the end that their brief moment had gone beyond professionalism. Although Aidoo explicitly points to Esi's gaze, stating that she notices "a very handsome face," and while Ali's gaze is implied, we are yet able to read his gaze through his thoughts. Watching Esi depart from his office, Ali concludes that "there was only one way to interpret his encounter with this fascinating woman: a gift from Allah.... If it was His will, things would right themselves in the end" (4). At this point, we see Ali making decisions hoping for God's approval without even bothering for a moment to ask or assume whether Esi is already married. Ali's behavior is representative of the phallocentric and colonialist attitude which holds that a women, like a vacant land without history, can be freely claimed, occupied and appropriated. At the moment of this conception, "the southern sky was ripped by massive lightning, followed by a heavy boom of thunder. As he got into his solid and luxurious vehicle, Ali had only one fear; that the threatening storm might sweep that woman [Esi] and her car away. They both *looked* so *frail*"(4). These last lines of the chapter confirm Ali's position as a patriarchal (pseudo-) colonialist engaging a phallocentric gaze that identifies the object of desire as weak and frail. His identification of Esi in these terms enables him to undertake the task of possessing her. Moreover, Ali's decision is captured by the symbolism of the storm that might "sweep" Esi away.

Ali's means of sweeping Esi away, making her "occupied territory," resonates Oko's positioning of himself as headmaster and Esi as student. Oko's failure to understand his wife frustrates him into using force against her body. Ali, however, constructs a similar relationship between he and Esi, a manipulative one without the obvious appearance of force. Esi once again becomes the school girl and he the "sugar daddy" who woos her with his expensive foreign gifts. Ali's behavior throughout the text is consistently contradictory. Unlike his father, he claims to prefer older women and not young girls who are not free from their father's influence. His avowal is a form of escape, a means to disassociate himself with his father's sexual desires for young girls, images of his young mother. By so doing, he will not be implicated in the activities which led to her bloody death. But Ali is not able to escape this fully. While he professes his dislike for young girls, what he really means is that he prefers them but that he must be the only significant masculine force in their lives. It is his compulsion to have young girls that leads him to construct a space that enables him to manipulate a form of hierarchy in his relationship with Esi. While he might not be comfortable or able to perform with young girls at a physical level, he does so psychologically. Buying school-girl clothes, jewelry, and other "goodies" for Esi secures his position in her life. Ironically, Aidoo narrates the text in a way that Ali's intentions seem as if they are gestures of true love. But Aidoo's comic and satirical style is furthermore revealed when Esi—a strong, independent, educated woman, careful to make and defend unconventional decisions regarding motherhood and marriage—permits such a manipulative relationship.

Once Ali establishes this relationship, he realizes that he must maintain it in order to keep Esi as a wife. Their relationship never moves beyond this point. It is one sustained with sexual gratification and material bribery. We see that Ali always situates himself in this manipulative position demonstrating that it is the only way that he can function with people. He indiscriminately buys presents for his elders, Esi's mother and grandmother, his contemporaries, Fusena, Esi and her friends, and children. Whether the gifts are in the form of candy, toys or a brand new car, they speak of Ali's inability to approach a relationship maturely. The adults clearly see his gestures as bribes calculated to win affection, but it seems Ali is clueless about his approach. By always employing this means to attain a favorable ground in people's lives, Ali demonstrates that he is not able to move to a level that involves emotionally and mentally approaching others on an adult level. His constant construction of himself as not necessarily a provider but a supplier, a perpetual "sugar daddy," provides him the safe ground to manipulate everyone like children. Engaging in a gaze that objectifies women, Ali casually relates to his women just as he does material objects. Women here are indiscriminately treated as replaceable commodities. Aidoo reveals with these characters and situations that the personal is very political.

Still Aidoo allows for a level of humor in this text and this is produced when Aidoo as narrator encourages the men in their belief and portrayal of themselves as good and genuine. Odamtten allows himself to become a victim of this false presentation by receiving Aidoo's sarcasm as truths. He accepts that Oko is a good man who "actually loves Esi, in his own way, but has adopted uncritically many petty and chauvinistic social attitudes" (Odamtten 1994:163). Odamtten also declares that "unlike Ali, he [Oko] is insensitive" because "he is unable to understand either Esi's needs or the implications of his own actions until it is too late" (163). That Ali is sensitive and understands Esi's needs is inaccurate. The text undoubtedly demonstrates that Ali is only sensitive towards meeting his own needs. His neglect to consult Fusena about intending to marry Esi, failure to understand Esi's need to have him do more than conveniently fall into bed and make love with her (164), and his extramarital affairs are far from what qualifies a person as sensitive. In addition, Odamtten judges these men by measuring them against each other, posing them as opposites. Simply because Ali does not sexually violate Esi does not mean that he does not rape her. Their relationship, as hierarchically positioned by him, rapes her emotionally and results in her need to take medication. Describing the emotional and physical toll of the relationship, Esi thinks:

> [b]y now she could not believe the mess she was in. She tried to sit and think things through, but she was getting nowhere at all. She finally decided to have a drink, a fairly strong one, and slept the rest of the day through.

> By New Year's Eve, Esi, [one who has always believed that taking certain pills was a sign of weakness], had decided that she needed some tranquilizers for her nerves. (Aidoo 1991:143)

The argument is not whether Ali is a better man than Oko, rather the question is what prompts their different actions, because their acts are nevertheless meant to accomplish the same task. As Odamtten notes, their backgrounds have been influential. Oko resorts to physical violence because he has women in his family who endorse patriarchal manipulation and therefore his asserting his masculine authority even through physical force. After all, to these women, Esi is a "semi barren witch" (70) who is depriving their son and brother of happiness. She is also a property of the man. So although Oko had attempted to be sensitive in the past, because of the ideologies, the truths embedded in him, he inevitably resorts to violence to claim his power. And while not articulating an obvious discourse on violence, Ali's background also encourages him to treat women as property. Islam and traditional practice including polygamy, automatically grant that Ali be an owner of women. His family, as opposed to Oko's, appears calmer, providing him with both female and male advisers. Besides, Ali's strategy is that of a beguiling lover. Although the two men's strategies are different, in the end their intentions are the same.

Finally, Opokuya's husband Kubi also locates Esi through the phallocentric gaze. Like Ali and Oko, he too objectifies Esi, therefore privileging himself in their relationship. Suspicious about the unspoken discomfort between Kubi and herself, Esi comes to discover that their relationship is sometimes comparable to that of an uncle/niece and at other times, a brother/sister. Either relationship is based on a hierarchy with Kubi occupying the dominant position. The uncle/niece relationship is one of adult and child, similar to Esi's relationship with the other men. The brother/sister association also provides Kubi as the head. Esi admits that he often acted like an irritated and disapproving older brother (163). Kubi's relationship with Esi is emotionally and mentally incestuous. Whether performing the role of uncle or brother, Kubi nevertheless identifies Esi as an object of desire. Aidoo suggests throughout the work that there is an unsettling energy between the two. This energy is the gaze and the desire that rest between the subject and the object. As illustrated with Oko and Ali, the purpose of engaging the gaze is to fulfill the desire of possession by claiming the body. Claiming the object of desire requires a performance of power relations. Subordinated and objectified, an "extremely vulnerable" Esi, then, must succumb to male authority (163). It is here that Aidoo dramatizes a final meeting between subject and object. She says, "Kubi took her hand...[t]hen, as though he had taken a quick decision just in that minute, he turned to face her and hold her closer and hard....He began to kiss her face, her neck and all over...Esi could feel Kubi's manhood rising" (163). Aidoo narrates that earlier, feeling vulnerable, Esi "did not feel like offering any resistance," but as her "mind snapped open" (163), she freed herself from the embrace, refusing to be victimized once again. It is here, in the final pages of the work, that Esi awakens and reclaims her subjectivity. Remembering her grandmother's words but seeing Opokuya's face, she finally understands that "a man always gains in stature any way he chooses to associate with a woman—including adultery....But, in association with a man, a woman is always in danger of being diminished..." (164).

Clearly, Nana's words are not only practical, they are undoubtedly theoretical. They confirm Christian's argument that her folk have always been a race for theory, as well as hooks' that black women do theorize and they can and should communicate it through accessible language. Although not formally educated, Nana espouses the very ideas that major theorists present. In the communal space, she educates her grand daughter about subjectivity and objectivity in power relations. Her discourse will be located within what is considered (black) feminist theory. By allowing the supposed passive African woman of old come to voice, Aidoo not only presents black women's theoretical discourse but reveals another irony within the text: that with all her education, conferences and traveling, it is from her grandmother that Esi learns to resist dominance.

With *Changes*, Aidoo makes several points regarding black women's writing. She demonstrates, as I argued earlier, that creative and theoretical texts cannot always be separated but that they can be merged into one text. Thus, she substantiates Davies' position that the writer/theorist split should not be quickly articulated as black women's writing is concerned. The text can be read as an unfolding of Nana's words. While Nana articulates her understanding of the workings of power in the social relations of men and women, the plot unveils as we are presented Esi's dilemmas. Furthermore, by presenting Nana as she does, Aidoo demonstrates the importance of possessing the power of language. Nana disputes the phallocentric argument on language. By seizing her agency to use this tool, she influences Esi's final claim to her subjectivity. Thus, the production of *Changes* by Aidoo illustrates that the use of language leads to the claiming back of one's body as Cixous puts forth. It is essential that black women resist imposed limitations and exclusion in order to continue their various forms of writing and therefore claim back their words and bodies which have been stolen and appropriated. Their participation in theory is important for *Changes* presents that this engagement, whether articulated in the home space or through written works, is particularly empowering for black women themselves.

WORKS CITED

Aidoo, Ama Ata. *Changes: A Love Story*. New York: The Feminist Press, 1991.

―――."To Be A Woman." In: *Sisterhood is Global*. Ed. Robin Morgan. New York: Anchor Doubleday, 1985. 258-65.

Amadiume, Ifi. *Male Daughters, Female Husbands: Gender and Sex in An African Society*. London: Zed Press, 1987.

Booker, Keith M. *A Practical Introduction to Literary Theory and Criticism*. New York: Longman Publishers, 1996.

Christian, Barbara. "The Race For Theory." In: *Making Face, Making Soul*. Ed. Gloria Anzaldúa. San Francisco: Aunt Lute Books, 1990. 335-345.

Cixous, Hélène. "The Laugh of the Medusa." In: *Feminisms*. Eds. Robyn Warhol and Diane Price Herndl. New Brunswick, N. J.: Rutgers University Press, 1991. 334-349.

Davies, Carole Boyce. *Black Women, Writing and Identity: Migrations of the Subject*. London: Routledge, 1994.

Flax, Jane. "Signifying The Father's Desire: Lacan in a Feminist's Gaze." In: *Criticism and Lacan: Essays and Dialogue on Language, Structure, and the Unconscious*. Eds. Patrick Colm Hogan and Lalita Pandit. Athens: The University of Georgia Press, 1990. 109-119.

Foucault, Michel. *Power/Knowledge. Selected Interviews and Other Writings, 1972-1977*. Brighton, Sussex: Harvester Press, 1980.

Freud, Sigmund. *Three Essays on the Theory of Sexuality*. New York: Avon Books,1965.

Henderson, Mae. "Speaking in Tongues: Dialogics, Dialectics, and the Black Woman Writer's Literary Tradition." In: *Changing Our Own Words*. Ed. Cheryl Wall. New Brunswick, N.J.: Rutgers University Press,1989.16-37.

hooks, bell. "Feminist Theory: A Radical Agenda." In: *Talking Back*. Boston, Mass.: South End Press, 1989.

―――. "The Oppositional Gaze. Black Female Spectators." In: *Black Looks. Race and Representation*. Boston, Mass.: South End Press, 1992.

Hurston, Zora Neale. *Their Eyes Were Watching God*. New York: Harper and Row Publishers,1990.

Lacan, Jacques. *Feminine Sexuality: Jacques Lacan and the Ecole Freudienne*. Eds. Juliet Mitchell and Jacqueline Rose. London: The Macmillan Press Ltd., 1982.

Odamtten, Vincent. *The Art of Ama Ata Aidoo: Polylectics and Reading Against Neocolonialism*. Gainsville, Fla.: Univ. of Florida Press, 1994.

Philip, Marlene Nourbese. *She Tries her Tongue. Her Silence Softly Breaks*. Edward Island, Canada: Ragweed Press, 1989.

The Multifaceted Aidoo:

Ideologue, Scholar, Writer, and Woman

In order to fully comprehend the life and work of Ama Ata Aidoo, it is important to grasp the constant tension between Aidoo the intellectual, Aidoo the ideologue, and Aidoo the revolutionary. This tension has made Aidoo known as a forceful and passionate writer in literary circles and has also harmed her with those among the critics who find her just too aggressive and brash for a woman writer.

In her theoretical essays, Aidoo confesses her awareness of the phenomenon of critics' silence to her works. Especially in "Unwelcome Pals and Decorative Slaves," she says, "They had always told me that I wrote like a man" (Aidoo 1982:21). The implication of this statement is that she is far too bold, too revolutionary and too loud for her sex; that she has subverted her gender and so has upset most yardsticks by which her artistry as a writer, who is a woman, may be measured. Aidoo, however, scorns male appropriation of linguistic aptitude, "political awareness, sensitivity to social issues, and vulnerability to mental and physical pain" (21). This is a revolutionary stance for a woman, given that most men still believe that women are inferior to them and that men should first be given a chance at the good, hard and lofty things and positions in society before women.

THE IDEOLOGUE

Behind the revolutionary is an original thinker whose vision of a better African continent in the future cannot be divorced from the survival of African nations in the modern era, a reunion with African diasporans, and the progress of women on the continent and in the diaspora. Speaking to Adeola James during an interview, Aidoo said: "The survival of our continent hinges on the woman question" (James 1990:13).

How did Aidoo's revolutionary orientation come about? It came from her parents, who were politically aware both of the ravages of colonization on the continent and of the importance of women in the struggle to reestablish African civilization; from her grandfather, who actually died in a colonial prison; from an aunt who sensitized her to the subjugation of women, urging her to embrace formal education as a means of mitigating the imposed inferiority of women. The foundations for a revolutionary in Aidoo were then laid very early in her life. And she struggled hard during her own administrative tenures—first with the Ghanaian government as Education Minister (1982), and then as director of the Ghana Arts Council, Ghana Broadcasting Corporation, and the Medical and Dental Council—to turn Ghanaian society around, until her activism was forced to end, due to circumstances arising from the lack of acceptance of women in political office in her time (Allan 1993:191-193). Reacting to the hegemony of African men who refuse to acknowledge women's ability to contribute meaningfully to society, Aidoo states:

> Over the last five hundred years we've had African men in leadership positions, certainly since Africa's collusion with the western world. Isn't it clear that the African man alone isn't able to cope with our relationship with the West and the rest of the World? (Maja-Pearce 1990:18)

Is it any wonder, then, that Aidoo should see a correlation between the evils of colonialism and the forces of patriarchy? Both conspire, she says, to support with social structures and institutions endemic male sexism on the continent. Aidoo has become the mouth of those women who have no mouth to speak for themselves. This is significant and is principally the reason why critics say that Aidoo refuses to have heroines who see themselves as victims.

On the regional level of the world, Aidoo has assumed the responsibility to be the spokesperson for Africa still suffering from its position on the periphery of a global system, which places it in a third world of poverty, want and indignity. According to Aidoo's authorial ideology, the survival of the nation goes hand in hand with feminism in the African sense. That is to say, women taking active part in nation-building, benefiting from its God-given natural resources for the good of Africans. For this to happen, imperialism needs to be banished from world political, social and economic spheres.

Aidoo cannot rail too often against the evils of imperialism as an ideology, because she sees it as wrong. Some critics have debated the morality of the empire and continue to wonder why people keep going on against imperialism in the world today (Hodgart 1977; Wright 1976). After all, they say, Africa had its own share of empires and kingdoms in its medieval history, including Mali, Ghana, Axum, Kush, Songhai, Zulu, Oyo, Kanem Bornu, Bini and others. What is more, most countries of the world which were under colonization are now independent to a lesser or greater degree politically, though sometimes not economically as in the case of Africa. Yet, the dominance of Westernism makes Aidoo doubt that Africa will ever regain itself, unless Africans themselves take steps to ensure that Africanism is affirmed.

All through Aidoo's writings, especially in *Our Sister Killjoy* and to a lesser extent in *Changes*, we see imperialism linked closely with issues having to do with neo-colonialism and international economics. Africa is tired of being a raw materials base, and at the same time a dumping ground for industrial waste (Gore 1993). Africa would be better off developing its own modern technology, Aidoo implies, when she decries experimentation with population control, economic expansion, scientific research, and discoveries of all sorts, which claim to place Africa at the receiving end of technological breakthroughs. For a better future, Africa needs to look into capital formation, rather than importation or exportation—unless for reason of generating capital—which are parasitic in

401

intent and dependent in practice. The recognition of human potential both in women and in men is therefore of the utmost urgency.

On the issue of brain-drain, from Africa towards the metropolis, which continues relentlessly to beckon, Aidoo bemoans the unfortunate situation of a continent. De Blij and Muller, two well-known and informed international geographers, explain the predicament of Africa, making Aidoo's anguish more understandable. These eminent geographers see the global capitalist economy in a core/periphery system in which the core is made up of the West and Japan and the periphery by the countries of the Third World, including Asia, Africa, South America, the Caribbean and the inner cities of North America. The core, they add, is "the foci of human activity that function as the leading regions of control and change" (De Blij and Muller 1993:41). This core area, insist De Blij and Muller, will always have needs and demands for its life of affluence and enjoyment, which the periphery willingly or by force will be constrained to give. They add:

> The countries of the periphery, therefore, confront severe problems of many kinds. They are pawns in a global economic game whose rules they cannot touch, let alone change. Their internal problems are intensified by the aggressive involvement of core-area interests. Their resource use is strongly affected by foreign influence. They suffer far more than core-area countries do from environmental degradation, overpopulation, and mismanagement. They possess inherited disadvantages that have grown, not lessened, over time. The widening gaps that result between enriching cores and persistently impoverished peripheries clearly are a threat to the future of the world" (De Blij and Muller 1993:42).

The geography of economic development, which is the crux of international geography that De Blij and Muller deal with, takes into account the present structure of the globe in terms of developed/advantaged and undeveloped/disadvantaged nations. It considers the level of modernization of each individual nation-state, the means by which people earn their living, produce and move products and services. Economic geography, its first sub-field, looks at how environment influences living patterns and their impacts on subsistence and commercial agriculture and deforestation. The second sub-field, the geography of development and modernization, deals with the indexes of underdevelopment. It also explains the core-periphery relationship of the rich and poor nations of the world. The predicament of Africa and its diaspora as parts of the Third World is better understood in the face of East-West *rapprochement* after the Cold War. The supranationalisms of the First and Second Worlds are seen as attempts to consolidate the head start given them by European chattel slavery, colonization and neo-colonization. Therefore, such groupings as NATO (North Atlantic Treaty Organization), GATT (General Agreement on Tariffs and Trade) signed recently by one hundred twenty-six nations of the world on April 15, 1994, APEC (Asian-Pacific Economic Commission), NAFTA (North American Free Trade Agreement), EC (European Community), EMU (European Monetary Union), to name only these few, are seen as economic apparatus for conquering the world, politically and economically. And, as always, it is to the advantage of the North and to the disadvantage of the South, which can only hope to spend more and buy more of the North's finished goods, producing or selling little or nothing itself (De Blij and Mueller 1992).

In apparent agreement with the geographers, two educators Pansye S. Atkinson and Frederick L. Hord lament the ignorance of peoples of African descent at the approach of the twenty-first century about how international politics oppresses people all over the world. They stress: "Its purpose is to maintain the present societal and global structures. For people of African descent not to know what is happening is to be ahistorical; not to care is to be iniquitous (Atkinson and Hord 1983:21-22). Aidoo's views on the rough deal that is the lot of Africa in international politics appear as valid as they were in 1977 when *Our Sister Killjoy* was published. When the little that Africa possesses is being taken away from her, this sensitive author explodes:

> So, please,
> Don't talk to me of the
> Brain—-
> Drain—-
> which of us stays in these days?
> But those of us who fear
> We cannot survive abroad,
> One reason or another? (Aidoo 1970:32)

Aidoo blames African leaders the more for failing to keep the brains at home on the continent. Services, where they exist at all, are inadequate. Workers are not paid decent salaries to help them take care of their personal obligations without having to embezzle from the coffers of the state (that is, when they are paid at all). It is not uncommon to have civil servants go for long months without pay. Thousands of professionals, including teachers, nurses, accountants, lawyers, engineers, and doctors are in self-exile abroad, due to the apparent planlessness of their nations' governments. The leaders have betrayed the trust bestowed on them by the electorate. While "things are falling apart," as the roof is caving in on the inhabitants of the burning house, the same leaders are chasing after rats fleeing from the conflagration, they are busy lining their pockets with the dollar, the mark, and more lately the yen. They stash away unbelievable sums of money in Swiss, American and French bank accounts with complex codes, which even they themselves sometimes forget and forever are unable to retrieve their money. Should they die suddenly, their heirs are unable to reach the money. Aidoo laments it all in *Our Sister Killjoy*:

> From all around the Third World,
> You hear the same story;
> Rulers
> Asleep to all things at
> All times—
> Conscious only of
> Riches, which they gather in a
> Coma—
> Intravenously— (34).

Nigeria, Burkina Faso, and in particular Ghana have come under rebuke for failing Africa. Why has Aidoo singled out these three West African countries in *Our Sister Killjoy*? In the case of Nigeria, rich and the most populous black nation on earth, Aidoo is angry that she blew her chance to lead Africa, thanks to her incessant political and economic instability. Alternating between French and English, the incensed author exhorts the reader to behold how the mighty hath fallen: "Mon ami/household quarrels of/Africa become a/WAR in/Nigeria" (53). In a recent report, Stephen Buckley of The Washington Post, in an article entitled, "Zaria: Nigeria," summarized the woes and disappointment of Nigeria in recent years:

At Ahmadou Bello University, students hunch over battered textbooks and squeeze into classrooms with broken seats and smashed, cobwebbed windows. They strain to focus on their professor as the stench of urine wafts into the room.

Their textbooks are typically more than 10 years old. Dormitory rooms, usually built for three, often must hold double their capacity. Laboratories have no chemicals for experiments. The main library has gotten no new funding for four years.

It was not always this way at the school, once one of sub-Saharan Africa's premier institutions of higher learning in a national system formerly regarded as among the best on the continent.

But in recent years, Nigeria's 38-school university system has collapsed from under-funding, mismanagement and constant labor strife, leaving students with understaffed, unkempt campuses that lack basic tools of learning.

"If I had known things would be like this I would not have returned," said Paul Izah, 45, head of Ahmadou Bello's political science department, who came back after earning a doctorate from Northwestern University. "Students cannot get materials. Teachers cannot do research. It is a very, very difficult existence."

Professors and students say military rulers have destroyed the university system in Nigeria, sub-Saharan Africa's most populous nation, with more than 100 million people. They accuse military regimes, which have controlled the country for 25 of its 35 years of independence, of ignoring higher education to maintain and tighten their grip on power.

"There has been inadequate funding and mismanagement of funds because they have not made upkeep and maintenance of the universities a priority it should be," said one education expert, who asked not to be named.

"It is not in the best interest of these military governments to educate their people," said Wale Deyemi, a doctoral student at the University of

Lagos. "They do not want people to be able to challenge them."

Nigeria's university system began to slide more than a decade ago, as the government failed to keep pace with unprecedented growth in enrollment. Ahmadou Bello's enrollment has tripled over the past 10 years to an estimated 45,000 students.

On many campuses, shortage of money left buildings unfinished and aging structures not replaced. Schools were left without laboratory equipment, and professors' salaries plunged.

As Universities deteriorated, top professors fled to schools in the United States and Europe or turned to other careers. Parents who could afford it sent their children to schools abroad.

Lengthy labor strikes had added to the universities struggles, shutting down campuses for months, wrecking students' academic plans and delaying graduations.

Schools were paralyzed for months following the government's 1993 annulment of presidential elections and subsequent arrest of businessman Moshood Abiola, the candidate who reportedly won the contest.

Government statistics on education spending are elusive, but foreign donors say under-funding continues to hubble Nigeria's universities. Four years ago, the World Bank pumped some $40 million into the ailing university system, a loan designed in part to make up for lack of funding, World Bank officials said.

Conditions at Ahmadou Bello University, 550 miles north of Lagos, epitomize the system's failures.

Lawns across the spacious campus have gone unmowed for weeks. Some buildings are falling apart; others are clearly in need of paint. Mounds of garbage lie between buildings. Roofs leak. A stomach-churning odor from perpetually broken toilets fills the corridors.

When Izah returned from Northwestern, Ahmadou Bello boasted an experienced staff, known for strong teaching and sophisticated research. But money for research has vanished, many experienced professors have left and the university is understaffed. Only 30 percent of the teaching staff has more than five years' experience, and the teacher-student ratio is 1 to 45.

Sitting in his clustered office, Izah, a friendly, soft-spoken man, pointed to his bookshelf. "The most recent journal up there?" he asked, "1989."

He pointed to a textbook on American government and politics on his desk. "1985," he said. "That's the latest thing we have available to us."

A professor came into Izah's office with complaint. He had no paper on which to copy a test for some 800 students. "What can I do,?" asked Izah. "You know we do not have the paper. Maybe you can borrow it from somebody." He said later that he gets just over $100 a year to spend on paper for his department.

Most demoralizing, Izah said, is that most professors' salaries do not support their families. They typically make less than $100 a month.

Izah supports his wife and four children by supplementing his income through data analysis and word processing work. Other professors often skip lectures or neglect course work because of moonlighting opportunities.

"We are at the bottom," Izah said, My entire [teaching] salary cannot buy food for my family for one week. I came home because I felt obligated," he added. "I never foresaw things would come to this state."

Over the past several years, Ahmadou Bello has suffered crippling strikes, as its staff has protested the school's conditions and accused administrators of mismanaging funds. Since 1992, students have lost 22 months of school to strikes.

Professors allege that the administration has squandered hundreds of thousands of dollars in grants for research and teaching materials.

"Yes, we are under-funded," said Tanimu Abubakar, a professor of comparative literature and leader of the teachers' union. "But if we were properly using the money we have been given, we would not have the crisis we have at this university today." University administrators have described charges of wrongdoing as "untrue and misleading" and accuse the teachers' union of making unsubstantiated charges. School officials contend that the university's primary problem is inadequate funding.

Last month a government panel spent two weeks at the school to address its problems and investigate allegations of mismanagement. It has not yet reported its findings. Caught in the middle are demoralized students, worried that the value of their diploma sinks daily.

Vivian Uzomah, 22, an English major, describes life at the school as "very hard." She said faculty strikes have drained her enthusiasm for school and will force her to graduate at least a year late.

"I was supposed to finish this year, but I can't because so many months of classes have been canceled,: she said. "When school is out, I try to keep reading, but it is hard to stay focused."

Uzomah, who hopes to find a job in the media, fears that she will not find work after graduation because Nigeria's economic woes have dried up the job market. She said one friend, an industrial engineering major, has spent four years looking for work in his profession.

"I do not want that to happen to me. As soon as I graduate, I have to find a way to leave Nigeria," she said. "The situation in the country is very frustrating. Right now, there are very few opportunities."

Back in Izah's office, the professor was equally pessimistic. He said that the future of the nation's universities hinges on whether Nigeria's political and economic situation stabilizes and improves.

"I was once very hopeful," he said. "Now I am doubtful about whether we as a society can rise above corruption and mismanagement. And that scares the hell out of me" (Buckley 1994:A27).

The story of Nigeria is about Africa's betrayal in the twentieth century. Although Africans always take reports from foreign correspondents with a grain of salt—and indeed this report should carry the same caveat, especially in its lurid details—yet suffice it to say that the likes of this report by Stephen Buckley have been reliably confirmed at other occasions. The foregoing Buckley account helps explain why Aidoo bemoans the loss of leadership of African nations for which Nigeria showed such early promise, and why she links the survival or downfall of Nigeria and the future of the African continent.

Nigeria.
Nigeria our love
Nigeria our grief.
Of Africa's offspring
Her likeness —

O Nigeria.
More of everything we all are,
More of our heat
    Our naiveté
    Our humanity
    Our beastliness
    Our ugliness
    Our wealth
    Our beauty

A big mirror to
    Our problems
    Our tragedies.
    Our glories. (Aidoo 1977:52-53)

As for Burkina Faso, despite the biennial African film festival which draws several thousands of participants from around the world to its capital city, Ouagadougou, the country seems incapable of assuming its own identity apart from the French. The same infrastructures left by the French at the inception of political independence still continue to remain with no modification by the people and their leaders: "The French, with/characteristic contempt and/Almost/childish sense of /Perfidy had/A long time ago, tarred two/narrow/Strips of earth for motor vehicles./Each wide enough for/One tyre" (54). When the leaders of the country finally wake up from slumber and to their responsibility, adds Aidoo, all they do is fall right back into the lap of the ex-colonial masters: "Now we hear the road is/First class to Ouagadougou. Done up with borrowed money from/Those who know where to sow/—even in a wilderness—/To reap a millionfold" (59). This scenario could easily be extended to every other West African Francophone country.

The fall of modern Ghana is perhaps the most painful to our author, partly because it is her own country, and partly because of the reversal of fate that the former empire has suffered. Growing up in Africa in 1960s, it was not difficult to feel the renown of Ghana all around one. While traveling in London as a student in 1974, I sauntered into a neighborhood store to browse. An English housewife who ran the store wanted to know from which country of Africa I was. Upon learning that I was from Nigeria, she proceeded to ask me whether it was a part of Ghana. To my answer in the negative, and still in her effort to place me, she wanted to know if Nigeria was a part of the Commonwealth. It was my positive answer to that final question that convinced her that I was a friend that could be trusted in her store. Ignorance of this sort was not uncommon even in the '70s in Europe and elsewhere about Africa. In *Africa, History of a Continent*, Basil Davidson corrects some erroneous beliefs about African history in general by refuting the belief that Africa was in a savage chaos before the arrival of the Europeans:

> The belief so dear to nineteenth century Europe that all of Africa was in savage chaos before the coming of the Europeans still lingers here and there, but historians concerned with Africa know better. Far from being a sort of museum of barbarianism whose population stayed out of the human growth and change through some natural failing or inferiority, Africa is now seen to possess a history which demands as serious an approach as the history of any other continent. (Davidson 1966:9)

On the history of Ghana particularly, Mary Penick Motley writes in *Africa: Its Empires, Nations and People*:

> In 1957 the Gold Coast gained its long-sought independence from the fading British Empire. It dropped its relatively new name, Gold Coast, which referred to the trade in slaves, gold, and ivory that had flourished there over a hundred years ago, and took a

name with historical meaning for its people, dating
back many centuries, Ghana. Ghana or Kumbi (...),
as the Arabs called it, existed over 1500 years ago.
It is thought to be the earliest Western Sudan state
that rose to fame and glory.

Ghana grew from a small state to an empire
because the people of the original state of Ghana
were the first, in their immediate area, to learn how
to smelt iron ore. With this knowledge they
equipped themselves with bows, arrows, swords,
and lances and began to conquer their neighbors.
The superiority of the Ghanaian weapons was obvious, and by ninth century Ghana was well on its way
to becoming a powerful empire. Mali, or the land of
the Mandingoes, was one of the areas taken into this
growing empire. (Motley 1969:86-87)

The Arabic language became Ghana's first written language, adds
Penick, when the Arabs who had settled along the border of the old
Ghana state were conquered, intermarried with their conquerors,
and for the first time Ghana's history could be written down by contemporary writers. The king, or emperor, was always of the original
Soninke tribe who were Ghana's empire builders. Pagan, they lived
side by side with Moslem Arabs, who were allowed to establish
mosques and to participate in the empire's swiftly expanding commerce. In the tenth and eleventh centuries, Ghana the capital city
was luxurious and full of beautiful buildings and the empire extended to the Upper Niger, south to the Atlantic Ocean and north to the
Sahara. There was gold in the south, and this tempted invaders.
However, for centuries, Ghana kept its lands intact, what with an
organized government and an army of some 200,000 men. In the
eleventh century, Ghana was still the foremost kingdom of the
Western Sudan, having reached its peak in the ninth and tenth centuries. The people raised sheep and cattle and crops. They worked
in metal, spinning, and weaving. Caravans crossed the Sahara to
trade with them, often bartering salt for gold. Ghana began to wane
in the eleventh century, due to a geological or climatic change.
Ghana's productive land suddenly began to dry up, and a large part
of it became wasteland. Then the Almoravides, Moslem fanatics,
many of whom were from the Senegal River area, struck the empire,
determined either to convert the Ghanaians to their religion or to
destroy their empire. Slowly at first, their determination was later

increased by their awareness of Ghana's great wealth. As the Ghanaian empire began to crack, subject countries, like Mali, began to break away, much in a similar way that the countries of the former Russian empire did in the twentieth century. The invaders also caused the ethnic groups of present-day Ghana, a much reduced version of the former empire that crumbled in the thirteenth century, to move southwards: the Akan; the Ashanti; the Fanti; the Akims; the Akwapims; the Akwamus; and the Gyamans (87-9).

Aidoo weeps in *Our Sister Killjoy*, not only because the greatest Medieval West African empire is gone, but also because in modern times its involvement in the global capitalist economy has exacerbated the situation of the present-day Ghana and her people:

> And Ghana?
> Ghana?
>> Ghana?
>> Just a
>> Tiny piece of beautiful territory in
>> Africa—-had
>> Greatness thrust upon her
>> Once.
>> But she had eyes that saw not—-
>> That was a long time ago ...
>> Now she picks tiny bits of
>> Undigested food from the
>> Offal of the industrial world ...
>> O Ghana. (Aidoo 1977:53)

In the May-June 1993 issue of *Africa Report*, Ghana's so-called economic recovery in the 90s—the so-called great twentieth-century African miracle—is debunked when Ruby Ofori explains that the remedy is cosmetic rather than deep-seated. A lot of foreign aid was poured into the country to help it to withstand the strains of trade liberalization, he explains, a shift away from import substitution schemes, correction of overvalued exchange rates, improvement of public finances, and cutting of inflation and privatization of state enterprises (Ofori 1993a:12). In the September-October issue of the same year, in an article with an eloquent title, "Ghana 2000 and Beyond: Ghana's Mixed Messages," Ruby Ofori again asks, with utter skepticism, about Ghana's future: "Can Ghana make the leap from poverty and dependency on donor aid, to the sort of prosperity seen in the newly industrialized Southeast Asian States? That's the major question facing policy makers in the West African state today" (Ofori 1993b:70-71). It becomes clearer at this point why Aidoo eventually immersed herself in politics in general, and in Ghanaian politics in particular, rather than the love stories in her earlier writings. As she had confessed to Adeola James in an often-quoted interview this gentleman had with her in London: "I cannot see myself as a writer, writing about lovers in Accra because you see, there are so many other problems" (James 1990:19).

By focusing attention on the leaders as colonialism recedes and even as neo-colonialism is on-going, Aidoo is rejecting the notion put forth by such Westerners as De Blij and Muller that the source of Africa's problems lies entirely in the fact that it is a pawn in the hands of the West and its agencies—the banks, multinational corporations, and other capital-making financial institutions. Aidoo rather declares that Africans should take their fate into their own hands, accept their shortcomings, and work towards a change in their social, economic and political institutions. Africans certainly are in need of an enlightened leadership in every one of the fifty-four nation-states as the globe moves towards the millennium (Gordon and Gordon 1996:5).

Education is, therefore, also high on the list of issues that gained Aidoo's attention. In different African countries, the items on the curriculum do not seem to be geared towards fostering African values, though children do not seem to learn from the wisdom of their grandparents anymore. According to Fred Inglis, who quotes Atkinson and Hord, "Curriculum should be understood as an ensemble of stories told by one generation to the next about what the possibilities are for the future and what it may be going to be like to attempt to live well at the time" (Atkinson and Hord 1983:142). Since curriculum is the means by which a society transmits its values and power, it follows that the educational systems of African schools need a major and urgent overhaul if the people are mindful of maintaining African mores and values. In *Killjoy*, Aidoo wails, "Look at them returning with grandchildren/whom she can't communicate with, because/they speak only English, French, Portuguese/or even German, and she dosen't" (Aidoo 1970:123).

If Aidoo appears to belabor the point about rural exodus in Africa and the exodus of African youth to the West to study in foreign universities, it is all from first-hand knowledge about the cultural damage to these young minds and their loss to their countries, just as other youth were lost to Africa in the Atlantic slavery period. Aidoo is also saddened by the situation at home, where universities are closed for more months of the year than they are open.

With a good dose of irony she complains: "EDUCATION HAS BECOME TOO/EXPENSIVE. THE COUNTRY CANNOT/AFFORD IT FOR EVERYBODY./Dear Lord,/So what can we do about/Children not going to school ..." (57). Aidoo is also aware of the damage that can be done to young minds subjected to new ideologies, as John A. Hobson intimates in the following confession:

> The real determinants in education are given in these three questions: "Who shall teach? What shall they teach? How shall they teach?" Where universities are dependent for endowments and incomes upon the favor of the rich, upon the charity of the millionaires, the following answer will of necessity be given: "Safe teachers. Safe studies. Sound (i.e. orthodox) methods." The coarse proverb which tells us that "he who pays the piper calls the tune: is quite applicable here as elsewhere, and no bluff regarding academic dignity and intellectual honesty must blind us to the fact." (Hobson 1976:41)

Aidoo laments that African youth who have been educated abroad on foreign scholarships become acculturated to their host countries. They either refuse to go home thereafter or, if they are able to extricate themselves, they have become virtual strangers to their own country and people:

> Post graduate awards
> Graduate awards (...)
> Awards? (...)
> Dainty name to describe
> This
> Most merciless
> Most formalized
>
> One
> Thorough,
> system of all time:
>
> For a few pennies now and a
> Doctoral degree later,
> Tell us about
> Your people
> Your history

Your mind. (...)
Tell us (...)
How
We can make you
Weak
Weaker than you've already
been. (Aidoo 1970:86-87)

It was Jean Paul Sartre who, in his preface to Fanon's *The Wretched of the Earth*, speaking in a similar vein to Ama Ata Aidoo, explained how this rush to the mother country all started:

The European elite undertook to manufacture a native elite. They picked out promising adolescents; they branded them as with hot iron, with the principles of Western culture; they stuffed their mouths full with high-sounding phrases, grand glutinous words that stuck to the teeth. After a short stay in the mother country they were sent home, whitewashed. These walking lies had nothing left to say to their brothers; they only echoed." (Fanon 1963:7)

Aidoo speaks in a similar language in *Our Sister Killjoy*:

What is frustrating, though, in arguing with a nigger, who is a 'moderate' is that since the interests he is so busy defending are not even his own, he can regurgitate only what he has learnt from his bosses for you. Like:
The need for law and order;
The gravest problem facing mankind being hunger, disease, and ignorance;
On hijackings as a deliberate attempt to hold decent society to ransom;
The sanctity of the U. N. charter;
The population explosion;
—the list is endless.
Nor does anything he has to say have to be logical responses to questions posed. (Aidoo 1970:6)

Aidoo speaks particularly about Sammy, a typical example of what she calls a "nigger"—his master's voice—who was invited to the going-away party for Sissie to help sing the praises of Europe into Sissie's ears:

> Sammy laughed all the time: even when there was nothing to laugh at. Or when she thought there was nothing to laugh at.
>
> And when he was not laughing loudly, he carried a somewhat permanent look of well-being on his face, supported by a fixed smile.
>
> Sammy had obviously been to their country before and seemed to have stayed for a long time. He was very anxious to get her to realise one big fact. That she was unbelievably lucky to have been chosen for the trip. And that, somehow, going to Europe was altogether more like a dress rehearsal for a journey to paradise.
>
> His voice, as he spoke of that far-off land, was wet with longing.(9)

It is safe to say that Aidoo's personal ideology is her fight against neo-colonialism and imperialism in all their guises. Vincent Odamtten has made the politics of Aidoo a large part of his seminal book, *The Art of Ama Ata Aidoo*. Our own contribution to the discourse is to say that Aidoo would like to see a vehement reassertion of African values and communal social systems. She urges a return to African roots as a way of transcending the lingering effects of European chattel slavery and colonization. This involves a rejection of foreign lures, no matter how tantalizing, and a glorification of all that promote African unity, and all that present Africa and Africans as noble all over the world.

How will these dreams be realized? By hard work on the part of Africans or by sheer grace of God? God seems to be absent in Aidoo's world. Consequently, she reposes the fate of the continent on the people themselves. Aidoo's religion approaches a Marxist materialism which sees no defense and no refuge against the power of modern technology. Not even the ancestors can stand up against these machines.

In conclusion of this first part of Aidoo's life and work, it is evident that Aidoo's revolutionary ideology is three-pronged: It is very vehement against isolationism; it is passionate about knowledge based on reason, and it is adamant about pan-Africanism. Aidoo's commitment as a writer can be summarized simply as a drive against the political and economic exploitation of Africa by forces of imperialism, and a praise of the beauty and glory of a return to Africa and her sense of human values.

THE SCHOLAR

Aidoo's scholarship did not happen overnight, as one might expect. It is a combination of age, experience, travel, natural (read native) intelligence, and an avid love of reading and research. In 1958, when Chinua Achebe published his classic, *Things Fall Apart*, Aidoo published her first written work, a Christmas short story based on the Nativity, entitled "To Us a Child is Born," which won a competition prize from *The Daily Telegraphic* (Allan 1993: 192). Aidoo later confessed that Achebe's publication raised her awareness that it was all right to try to recover Africa's greatness in writing, amidst all the colonial verbiage being bandied around at the time in the name of African literature. After her second short story, "No Sweetness Here," she found herself hobnobbing at an African Writers' Workshop at the Cambridge University College of Ibadan, Nigeria, with veteran artists like Chinua Achebe, Wole Soyinka, Christopher Okigbo, Ezekiel Mphalele, and Langston Hughes (Allan 1993: 192). Aidoo would later dedicate three poems to Chinua Achebe in *An Angry Letter in January*: "A Modern African Story," "Questions," and a series of three poems "New in Africa." At the young age of twenty-two, Aidoo had already published her first drama and book, *The Dilemma of a Ghost*, to be followed later by another play, *Anowa*. These works exhibit her firm knowledge of Ashanti mythology, African and world history, African religion, not to mention an enviable command of the English culture, civilization and language enough to create in it as a medium.

What is evident is that history is the basis of understanding all human civilizations. In recalling history, what is important for Aidoo is that the lessons of the past need to be learned for an understanding of the present and a better projection of the future.

In *Killjoy*, Aidoo debunks the state of academics in the universities by putting up a representative of this group for ridicule:

> Oh no. The academic-pseudo-intellectual version [of a nigger] is even more dangerous, who in the face of reality that is more tangible than the massive walls of the slave forts standing along our beaches, still talks of universal truth, universal art, universal literature and the gross National Product.
>
> Finally, when he has emptied his head of everything, he informs you solemnly that your problem is that you are too young. You must grow up.

> Without doubt, the experience is like what a
> lover of chess or any mind-absorbing sport must feel
> who goes to a partner's for a game, but discovers he
> has to play against the dog of the house instead of
> the master himself. (Aidoo 1977:6)

Looking especially at the last five lines of the quotation above, it is clear why some readers have a dislike for Aidoo's style of writing. But that is beside the point we intend to make here. What is also evident is her high intellectual ability, her love of making abstractions from the concrete and coming up with perfectly original analogies. Several years of university teaching in Africa and abroad—Ghana, Xavier, Richmond, Florida, Oberlin—to mention only these few, have taught her that you do not always find the best brains on university campuses. It is on record that, in Africa, male academics on several occasions tried to silence her so that they might all the more shine. They tried on numerous occasions to banish her to the kitchen—in a man's house, of course—to no avail. She simply refused to believe that a woman's place is necessarily in a kitchen rather than in the classroom.

In the face of the polarization of the world towards the millennium into the North and South, the Haves and the Have-nots, Aidoo has added a new chapter to this division by distinguishing between the oppressed and the oppressors. Among the oppressed of the earth are Africans, Jews, African Americans, Amerindians, Germans and the Irish. She goes further to divide this group into the more Oppressed and the less Oppressed. Africans, African-Americans, Amerindians and Jews belong to the "more wretched of the Earth" group while the "less wretched of the earth" group, at least in recent history, are the Germans and the Irish (Aidoo 1977:93-94).

The case of the Germans is rather controversial and problematic for Aidoo, given past German history with racism, Nazism, the Jewish pogrom and modern Germany's reputation as a world leader in technology. Still, for the German professor in the humanities Sissie held a conversation with, Germany ranks among nations of the world that have been oppressed in the past: "Ja, our people have been oppressed for many many years, since the First war," a reference to the redistribution of German holdings-cum-spheres of influence in West, Central, and East Africa to France and Britain, following her defeat at the end of the First World War. The author's persona, Sissie, African to the core that she is, disagrees with Marija, the Aryan housewife who has befriended her, on whether Germans and Africans could ever be put on the same footing when their vicissitudes in recent history are recounted (93). The one group belongs to the Third World and the periphery of the world global and capitalist economy, the other to the First World and the core.

As we have already noted, European chattel slavery resulted in some one hundred million of young and skilled Africans being removed from the continent at its most vulnerable period in historical and technological development. Aidoo's agenda in recalling knowledge about African history appears to stem from her eagerness to see that Africa be reinstated in world history and accorded reparations for past wrongs by the First World. Her personal philosophy could thus be construed as being a fight against all odds, no matter how overwhelming, against all forces that put Africa and its peoples down.

THE WRITER

It is difficult to divest the ideologue, the revolutionary, and the scholar from the writer. As a writer, Aidoo is at once a fighter and an artist who knows her craft. Her ability to cross genres for effectiveness has by now become her signature tune. Right in the same prose work, it is common to find a bit of poetry, anecdote, letter, myth, journalistic jottings and all. It is this manner of holistic text treatment that prompted Odamtten's polylectic reading of her body of works.

Aidoo had also dabbled into unorthodoxy to the extent that a love letter is no longer what it purports to be. A love letter does not necessarily have to be romantic only in the sense of singing about love between two human beings. A love letter can be romantic in the sense that it is a patriotic letter, from a concerned citizen about the motherland or fatherland. It could be a love letter about Mother nature and about the cosmos and the environment:

> She sat quietly in her seat and stared at the land unfolding before her. Dry land, trees, a swamp, more dry land, green, green, lots of green. She had to check herself from laughing aloud. (...) she was back in Africa. And that felt like fresh honey on the tongue: a mixture of complete sweetness and smoky roughage. Below was home with its unavoidable warmth and even after these thousands of years, its uncertainties.
>
> 'Oh, Africa. Crazy old continent...' (Aidoo 1977:133-134).

But for a cursory lament of her unrequited love for an unnamed medical practitioner residing in London, Sissie spends the rest of the letter discussing African politics in a global perspective. Among the serious issues discussed are the exile of Africans abroad and how it is hurting Africa's normal pace of development, and a comparison of black-on-black and white-on-black oppression. Aidoo concludes that the West owes enormous reparations to Africa, becoming, perhaps, the first African voice in recent times to broach the issue of reparations for past wrongs, including slavery and colonization. She drives the issue home when she reenacts in *Killjoy* the horror of slavery for many an African woman and a man: "once before they (slave masters) died, they slept with an/African woman. And if the titillation was/supreme if they could have her brother/watching helplessly on—a bonded man, Lord/what we've been through" (123).

The careful use of "we" in the last line makes the reader leap from the distance of four hundred years ago into the nearness of recent times as the author links the past to the present, bringing back the past of history into the present of literature. It was the French psychiatrist-cum-novelist, George Duhamel, who sought to explain human behavior by stating that history is literature in the past as literature is history in the present (Popkin and Popkin 1977: 365-372).[1] What seemed like a happening in ages past in the cotton fields in the New World immediately becomes an event of the present day in Aidoo's fiction. In the reader's mind are conjured images of violence, rape and murder in contemporary world societies. It is in this way that Aidoo identifies with Sissie as a fellow woman who has always suffered at the hands of men, whether under slavery, colonialism, or patriarchy.

Looking back, Aidoo's implicit call for reparations makes her a precursor for all the eminent people now doing the same. It is pertinent to note that twelve eminent African men, including Ali A. Mazrui, among others, have drawn up a testament calling for reparations for slavery and colonization for Africans. In the diaspora, specifically in the House of Representatives of the United States of America, a bill was introduced in January 1993 by some twenty representatives which was referred to the Committee on the Judiciary. It read, *inter alia*:

> To acknowledge the fundamental injustice, cruelty, brutality, and inhumanity of slavery in the United States and the 23 American colonies between 1619-

1865 and to establish a commission to examine the
institution of slavery, subsequent de jure and de
facto racial and economic discrimination against
African Americans, and the impact of these forces
on living African Americans, to make recommen-
dations to the Congress on appropriate remedies,
and for other purposes. (Lumumba, Obadele, and
Taifa 1993:93).

Even the seating Pope, John Paul 11, has maintained that whites
must continue to ask forgiveness from blacks and Amerindians for
past injustices: "This demand for forgiveness has to be made above
all to the first inhabitants of the New World, the Indians, and also
to those who were deported as slaves from Africa for heavy labor"
(*Jet* 1992; Browder 1992:41).

It is pertinent to observe that between *Killjoy* and *Changes*, Aidoo
has seemingly, above all else, transformed from a cursing writer-
activist to a plaintiff for romantic love. Is there an anomaly here,
especially given her earlier pronouncements to the effect that she
could not be caught talking about love when there are serious human
issues to discuss? If indeed we take literally on its face value her
ironical confessional epitaph on the first page of *Changes* as an exercise in word-eating, would there be other reasons for Aidoo's present preoccupation with love? Might it all be due to life's experiences
themselves? Has she had time to ruminate on what older professors
at the University of Cape Coast once told her, namely that she was
too young to understand that life was not only about solving political problems, and that she needed to grow up? Does this apparent
shift in sensibility, from treating hard-core politics alone to doing it
on the bedrock of romantic human relationships, mirror anything
else other than a devotion to her own brand of radical feminism,
where the political is also personal, where the woman question is
implicated in the survival of the collectivity? We attempt to answer
these questions as we discuss her career as a woman who writes.

THE WOMAN

I have been happy
being me:

an African
a woman
and a writer. (Aidoo 1992:25)

421

Aidoo's women characters fight for their sovereignty in the African context. These are women engaged in a very hard struggle because the boundaries erected around them are so rigidly constructed that most women succumb at the altar of self-actualization. The new woman, formally educated and having a career and therefore her own money, finds herself with many choices, which are hard to grapple with. Worse, men are collectively not prepared to budge an inch. Relationships with men are very unstable. Often, the woman is undecided as to whether to follow tradition or follow her own fantasy. On this dilemma about her identity and the pull to aspire for her own freedom and self-fulfilment, Beatrice Stegerman explains:

> The new Woman represents a theory of personhood where the individual exists as an independent entity rather than her kinship relations, where she has a responsibility to realize her potential for happiness rather than to accept her role, where she has indefinable value rather than quantitative financial worth, and where she must reason about her own values rather than fit into a stereotyped tradition. (Stegerman 1974:92)

On the same issue, Maria Ros Cutrefelli has this to say in *Women of Africa: Roots of Oppression*:

> The new characteristically urban figure of the new male-amputated, husband-less single woman has significantly taken shape: and in the light of the traditional view of celibacy as a social failure, even a crime against society, the consciously deliberate rejection of marriage on the part of an increasing number of urban women appears to be a courageous, indeed a daring deed. (Cutrefelli 1983:31)

Feminism for Aidoo is about gender, but also about her radical point of view and her localization in the world as a Third World person. She does not write about women simply because she is a woman writer, but rather because she is insistent that African women should demand their rights as human beings. Although reticent about prescribing modes of behavior and thought for the modern woman, she has nonetheless experimented with suggesting new options for women, like a loose association with men for the career woman, following the example of Esi Sekyi in *Changes*, who sees her husband when it is convenient for both of them, much like a boy friend and a girl friend would do. Feminism is also about women being politically conscious and taking on significant roles in the politics of the day.

What we have tried to do in this chapter is summarize the life and works of Ama Ata Aidoo, in order to establish her as an interesting person to know, a politically-minded individual, and a serious writer of fiction. From our findings, we can say that she is a woman of many facets who vibrates in her own right. Perhaps, unknown to herself, she might have furnished 'Molara Ogundipe-Leslie with material for her famed manifesto on the commitment of an African woman writer. We extend the following paragraph from Ogundipe-Leslie, to describe to the letter the accomplishments we make of Aidoo as an ideologue, a scholar, a writer, and a woman:

> ... the female writer cannot usefully claim to be concerned with various social predicaments in their countries or in Africa without situating their awareness and solution within the larger global context of imperialism and neo-colonialism. For what is it that makes us so dismally poor? What forced our individuals to schizophrenic cultural confusion? Why are the national ruling classes so irresponsible, criminal and wasteful? Because they sold out? To whom? A deep female writer who has anything worthwhile to say must have these insights .... (Ogundipe-Leslie 1987:11-12).

NOTES

1. The actual famous words of George Duhamel (1884-1966), psychiatrist-turned-novelist, whose novels are based on the Europe of the years 1920-1930, are:

   "La littérature est l'histoire du présent,
   l'histoire est la littérature du passé."

   Duhamel's death ended his years of torture as he saw the peaceful world he knew become something else—violent. Human beings, he regrets, are incapable of learning from past mistakes, because they are so swollen up with turmoil that they are unable to assimilate their feelings of anger and hatred. Instead, they level aggression on their neighbors by way of expelling their harsh feelings. Bettina L. Knapp summarized Duhamel's life and work thus:

"Duhamel's major works fit into our contemporary fad-mad, psychedelic world mainly as counterweights. He is a representative of the heart of feeling, understanding, balance, harmony, and stability. These character traits are so submerged in today's violent, ebullient, ruthless society as to be virtually nonexistent. One gazes at Duhamel's works, therefore, with a twinge of nostalgia, longing, and melancholy...." (*Georges Duhamel*, New York: Twayne Books, 1972. 174-176)

Works Cited

Aidoo, Ama Ata. *Our Sister Killjoy*, New York: Longman, 1977.
———. "Unwelcome Pals and Decorative Slaves." *AFA Journal of Creative Writing* 1 (Nov. 1982):34-43.
———. *An Angry Letter in January*. Coventry, Sydney/Aarhus: Dangaroo Press, 1992.
———. *Changes: A Love Story*. New York: CUNY, The Feminist Press, 1994.
Allan, Tuzyline J."Afterword." *Changes: A Love Story*. Ama Ata Aidoo, New York: CUNY, the Feminist Press, 1993.
Atkinson, Pansye S. and Frederick L. Hord. "The Best System: Black Academic and Cultural Retention (Save the Children)." Frostburg, M.: Panfre Productions, 1983. 21-22.
Browder, Anthony T. *The Nile Valley Contributions to Civilization*. Intro. by Dr. John Henrik Clarke. Brentwood, Maryland: International Graphics, 1992.
Buckley, Stephen. "ZARIA, Nigeria." *The Washington Post*. October 6, 1994: p. A27, WORLD NEWS Section.
Cutrefelli, Maria Ros. *Women of Africa: Roots of Oppression*. London: Zed Books, 1983.
Davidson, Basil. *Africa, History of a Continent*. New York: Macmillan Co., 1966.
———. *The Lost Cities of Africa*. Boston: Little Brown, 1959).
———. *The Search for Africa: History, Culture, Politics*. New York: Randon House, 1994.
De Blij, Harm J. and Peter O. Muller. *Geography: Regions and Concepts*. Revised Seventh Ed. New York: John Wiley and Sons, Inc., 1993.
Fanon, Frantz. *The Wretched of the Earth*. New York: Grove, 1963.
Forde, D and P. M. Kaberry. Eds. *West African Kingdoms in the Nineteenth Century*. London: Oxford University Press, 1967.
Gore, Al. *Earth in the Balance: Ecology and the Human Spirit*. Boston/New York/London: Houghton Mifflin Company, 1992.
Gordon, April A. and Donald L. Gordon, Eds. *Understanding Contemporary Africa*. Boulder/London: Lynne Rienner Publishers, 1996.
Hobson, John A. "Imperialism: A Study." Ed. In: *The New Imperialism: Analysis of Late Nineteenth Century Expansion*. Harrison M. Wright. Lexington, Mass: D. C. Heath and Co., 1976.
Hodgart, Alan. *The Economics of European Imperialism*, New York: W. W.

Norton & Company, Inc, 1977.

James, Adeola. "Ama Ata Aidoo." In: *In their Own Voices: African Women Writers Talk.* London/Portsmouth: Heinemann, 1990.

Jet Magazine, November 9, 1992.

Jones, Eldred Durosimi. Eustace Palmer, and Marjorie Jones. *Women in African Literature Today,* 15. London: James Currey/Trenton: Africa World Press, 1987.

Kimble, David. *A Political History of Ghana: 1880-1928.* London: Clarendon Press, 1963.

Knapp, Bettina L. *Georges Duhamel.* New York: Twayne Books, 1972.

Lumumba, Chokwe, Imari Abubakari Obadele & Nkechi Taifa. *Reparations Yes!: The Legal And Political Reasons Why New Afrikans-Black People In The United States Should Be Paid Now For The Enslavement Of Our Ancestors And For War Against Us After Slavery.* Third ed. Baton Rouge, La: The House of Songhay, 1993.

Motley, Mary Penick. *Africa: Its Empires, Nations and People.* Detroit: Wayne State University Press, 1969.

Ngara, Emmanuel. *Art and Ideology in the African Novel.* London: Heinemann, 1985.

Ofori, Ruby. "Business Briefs." *Africa Report*: Southern Africa, Troubled Transition, May-June 1993:p.12.

―――. "Ghana 200 and Beyond: Ghana's Mixed Messages." *Africa Report*: Africa's Wars: The Costs of Intervention. September-October, 1993: 70-71.

Ogundipe-Leslie, 'Molara. "The Female Writer and Her Commitment." In: *Women in African Literature Today.* Ed. Eldred Durosimi Jones et al. Trenton N.J.: Africa World Press, 1987.

Pellow, Deborah. *Women in Accra: Options for Autonomy.* Michigan: Reference Publications, Inc., 1987.

Popkin, Debra and Michael and Duhamel, Georges, *Modern French Literature.* Eds. New York: Frederick Ungar Publishing co., 1977.

Sartre, John Paul. "Preface." In: Frantz Fanon, *The Wretched of the Earth.* New York: Grove Press, 1963.

Stergerman, Beatrice. "The Divorce Dilemma: The New Woman in Contemporary African Novel." *Critique: Studies in Modern Fiction* 15, 3, (1974).

Wright, Harrison M. *The New Imperialism: Analysis of Late Nineteenth Century Expansion.* Lexington, Mass: D. C. Heath and Company, 1976.

Part Five

CONVERSATIONS WITH AMA ATA AIDOO

FACING THE
MILLENNIUM:

AN INTERVIEW WITH AMA ATA AIDOO

ADA UZOAMAKA AZODO

The day was March 30, 1996; the place, Hauppauge, New York. It was the last day of the Nineteenth Annual African Literature Association (ALA) conference, convened by Professor E. Anthony Hurley at the State University of New York, Stony Brook. A beautiful morning it was! You imagined you were hearing the birds singing in the trees, even though there were no trees and no birds in sight, nor within ear shot. The venue of the conference was the superb Radisson Hotel Islandia, just the right ambiance, the inspiring environment to make one think of doing very ambitious things, of undertaking very great endeavors. So beautifully decorated were all the open areas, so inviting were they that, towards the closing of the conference, when it dawned on me that sooner or later, indeed much sooner than later, I would have to catch my train back to Rochester, New York, I started to dream of capturing the essence of the conference, taking something lasting about it away with me, something loftier than merely presenting a paper and chairing a panel of students of the State University of New York College at Geneseo, where I was teaching at the time, discussing the place of the novel and the short story in the continued quest for pan-

Africanism. Although now that my paper has been accepted for publication in a collection of essays arising from the proceedings of that conference, my participation no longer seems so banal to me as it was at the time.

But, like a flash it came! Like the proverbial muse, a still, small voice whispered to me: "Do a book on Ama Ata Aidoo!" A confirmation, perhaps, of the saying that great ideas first come to their originators in the form of a dream! Einstein first dreamt of relativity before he propounded it as a theory, which would later stand the rigors of scientific experiments. French philosophers of the Age of Enlightenment were dreaming of going to the moon long before it happened, two whole centuries later!

Marie Umeh had just published the first book in the Africa World Press series, *Emerging Perspectives,* on Buchi Emecheta. And there it was sitting pretty on the Africa World Press stand! And she was vigorously working on the second in the series, on Flora Nwapa. I knew about the forthcoming book, because I had contributed two articles to that volume. The day before my sudden awakening to edit a new book, Aidoo had presented herself very well at the many appearances she made: at the opening ceremony of the conference as keynote speaker, the women's caucus luncheon as guest speaker, the CUNY Feminist Press stand as special guest and where she signed autographs, and the evening forum on African reality where she appeared together with Zimbabwean Shimmer Chindoya and Egyptian Nawal el Sadawi, who was the keynote speaker for the evening. And I was teaching *Our Sister Killjoy* that Spring semester! And I had announced to my students before my departure that I was actually going to see our author in flesh and blood! And I made sure I took some photographs of and with Aidoo when we met (see photos), in anticipation of a show-and-tell session with my students when I saw them again on my return! There seemed therefore to be every good reason for me to do the third book in the *Emerging Perspectives* series on Ama Ata Aidoo.

As soon as I made the decision, I went to speak to Mr. Elias Gebrezgheir, the Staff Editor of Africa World Press. He was very cordial, as people from his region of Africa are wont to be. In addition, he was very encouraging, asking me to contact him as soon as I returned to my post. Before I left him, I bought myself a copy of Marie Umeh's book on Buchi Emecheta. Then, I immediately began to scout for prospective contributors. Fearing that many members of the Association were already beginning to leave the conference, I proceeded to speak to a number of participants whom I had heard present on a number of panels I had attended.

Fortuitously, I ran into Dr. Gay Wilentz at the entrance to the Ladies, who was bounding in as I was leaving. We had a brief conversation, for she was decided not to miss her place on the long line. (It is now proverbial, the story about lobbies to the Ladies, namely that one must be prepared for a long wait most of the time). Even though she bade me not to bother, adding that she would certainly bump into me again to finish the discussion, she had said enough to arrest my curiosity. I thought, how incredible that two people could be thinking of the same matter without having said a word to each other! Telepathy? So, rather than go away, I found myself hanging around the loo, waiting for Gay to come out, in order to find out the rest of her plans to edit a book. Simply put, Gay and I discovered that we were thinking along the same lines, about writing a book on Aidoo, though in her case she was planning to co-edit it with another colleague and merely wanted to know if I could contribute to the volume. I then proceeded to inform her that I had already gone ahead of her and spoken to Mr. Gebrezgheir. I then invited Gay to join with me in a partnership, if she did not mind dropping her earlier plan. Then Gay and I went back to Mr. Gebrezgheir to inform him that the said proposal I would send him was going to be on behalf of Gay and myself. Mr. Gebrezgheir agreed. The rest is history ....

The next task was to find Ama Ata Aidoo. I went in search of the author with the objective of asking her to grant me an interview. Without much ado, she consented. I thanked my lucky stars. I remembered what my people always said, that when you are on your right path of destiny all obstacles fall away as if by magic. Even brick walls vanish at your approach. Yes, that was just what it was like. I found Aidoo to be the most cooperative famous person with whom I ever had dealings. Not only would she talk without first asking me how much I would pay her for speaking with me, she agreed to meet me over breakfast the following morning for our rendez-vous in the open area of the hotel lobby which was doubling, perhaps during that conference only, as a restaurant. That was going to be my paltry attempt at offering her an honorarium.

I had extracted a promise from Ama Ata Aidoo to grant me an interview! Unbelievable! The Heavens do work in mysterious ways!

Then I realized that I had not brought along my tape-recorder to the conference! And I must have one to record the interview! Talk about not being prepared in case of eventuality! I had definitely disregarded the wise caution of my Igbo people, never as a hunter to leave home without my hunting bag. In the bush, one never knows what luck or destiny may bring along as venison. So, I had to ask around until I found one, courtesy of Keiko Kusunose and her husband Masaoki Miyamoto. My luck bolstered my intuition that the work I was about to embark on was a celestially determined mission.

The morning of the interview, Aidoo was held up for a short time from coming down at the appointed time. She had earlier called to let me know that she had to await a call from a brother, but would join me as soon as possible. Then, on her way to our interview venue, many people had besieged her on many issues which needed immediate resolution.

When we finally sat down to breakfast and to talk, what we did not realize we would have to contend with was that the crowd which had waylaid Aidoo earlier would continue to pursue her, very nearly ruining our plans, but certainly turning our beautiful morning into something else that was unprecedented. They interrupted our breakfast intermittently, to the point that several times Aidoo ordered me to "kill" the recorder, so that she could attend to that party or the other. Given what is the norm, it is a near wonder that I have the text of the interview presented below.

It took an interviewee of such exceptional skills, experience, and maturity as Aidoo's to deftly handle interview questions in the kind of situation in which this interview was realized. Therein is a lesson for all those theoriticians who advocate elaborate preparations for recording sessions, far away from the earshot and eyesight of everyone else but the parties involved in the interviewing process. If the interviewee is experienced, there is perhaps no need for isolation and extreme quiet while conducting an interview. Or should I say that if the interviewee is an African, in which case she should be used to taking a short time away from one listener to speak to another without considering it an act of rudeness, then there is perhaps no need to screen off everyone else but the interviewer and the interviewee.

Many times, people stopped, oblivious of the interview going on, to ask Aidoo to have a cup of tea on them, or merely to say hello, or to discuss administrative issues. And I had to kill the recorder each time! Throughout the interview, there was also a continuous background noise of laughter, talking, music and clinking of cutlery and glasses and all, almost a din. In short, Aidoo and I were doing the interview under stressful conditions. Aidoo was certainly worse off, if we must use such a term, since my prepared questions were hitting her relentlessly. So, the text of the interview is full of "hmms" and "ehs," abandoned thoughts and expressions, which have been made smooth in places in the edited form. In reality, the interview took a little over two hours. A good portion of this time was taken up by trespassers. And these interruptions would go on for five to ten minutes. In one case, it must have gone on for some twenty minutes. What was remarkable, however, was that Aidoo always came back to the moment with such presence of mind, as if there had been no interruption at all. For my part, I had a list of questions I meant to exhaust and so was in a better position than she was. Even though I was in sympathy with her, I was nonetheless dogged about getting all I could from the interview, since I could not tell when next the Heavens would again butter my bread. Otherwise, I might have been frustrated. We barely finished before I had to rush to catch my train back to Rochester.

* * * * * *

Azodo: How did you begin to write?

Aidoo: Well, it was more an awareness that I wanted to write from when I was about fifteen. My literature teacher asked me what I wanted to do as a career. And I said I wanted to write poetry. So, that's how far it goes.

Azodo: What are the difficulties you have faced as a writer?

Aidoo: Well, I think basically, for me, these are difficulties I became aware of later, not when I started. Just the whole business of having space, space and time to write, without having to do other things, you know. What I mean is the whole business of not having structures, supporting structures, precisely because of the neocolonial nature of our society. Unlike an American or a Scandinavian, you don't have access to things like funds, things like fellowships or grants. So, you always have to work. You always have to do other work, in order to survive. I mean, I've had to teach and that takes away writing time. So, that has been for me one single most pressing problem, all my life.

Azodo: What is your advice to budding women writers?

Aidoo: Well, to go on writing, in spite of the problems.

Azodo: How do female writers compare with their male counterparts, in your estimation?

Aidoo: In terms of what?

Azodo: In terms of production, in terms of depth of understanding of issues?

Aidoo: Well, I think it is an unfair question, because different writers have different depths of understanding. I don't think we can characterize the issue of depth of understanding on a gender basis. Because I am a woman, and it is very tempting to me to say that we have more understanding than men. Everybody knows that. But, I don't think that will be fair, you know. As far as the production is concerned, women are constrained by all the forces that take part of our attention. I mean, as mothers, as wives, and so on and so forth. We have to farm away part of out time. And of course that reduces the volume of our work. I mean at least the quantity of it, enormously. So, men are luckier than us in that respect.

Azodo: Okay. Your writing is remarkable for criss-crossing genres, as you well know.

Aidoo: Hmm.

Azodo: Novel to poetry, poetry to short story to drama. Which side of you seems to be dominant over the others?

Aidoo: Well, that's for the critic to say, really, because as I am a poet (well, I hope I can say I am a poet), the novel takes a lot more time. I haven't written as many novels as I would want because a novel takes so much time. And then I haven't done as many plays as I probably would want to, because, for the past twenty years or so, I have not led a stable existence. And without a certain kind of stability, you can't do drama on the move. You need a stage. You need maybe a company that could produce your plays on stage, and so on and so forth. So, again, my output as a dramatist has been terrifyingly ....

Azodo: Well, I have read *Anowa* and *The Dilemma of a Ghost*, and I think they are excellent books.

Aidoo: Thank you. But, I am not talking about the quality. But I mean the quantity. *The Dilemma* was published in 1965, and *Anowa* was published in 1970. And since then, apart from a radio play, I haven't done drama. That's what I mean. That's what I'm saying. Well, I am not even in a position to judge the quality of a few of my works. But I'm saying, in terms of the sheer volume, I haven't done as much as I would want, because of the way my life has seemed to have worked out.

Azodo: In the future, which direction do you see yourself leaning?

Aidoo: Well, you know, me, I am a writer. When I say I am a writer, what I'm saying is, depending upon the m-a-t-e-r-i-a-l and how it strikes me, or how the material presents itself, then I write a poem. For instance, I have just written a new short story, two weeks ago. I would like to happily announce it, because it was nice. Because I had been teaching full-time for the past three years, I hadn't really written much. So, it was very nice that I should sit down and write a story. So, in the mean time, I am working on a novel. Again, I can't see myself doing plays for the reason I have outlined. But I do hope that I'll be writing more and more. That sort of thing.

Azodo: In reading your works, I see that the grandmothers have a significant role. With changes in society, and young women moving away from home ... with modern life and travels, and the young people moving around, what or who do you see replacing the grandmother?

Aidoo: You mean the grandmother in her role as grandmother?

Azodo: As the custodian of tradition, and ...

Aidoo: Well, then, there is no replacement. I mean, I think that we are looking at a society which, by and large, has been in a process of collapse and disintegration, as a result of colonial intervention for some time. That is, if we are looking at it in terms of very original, very traditional structures. But, you see, I think that societies, even our own, are dynamic in their own way. And it is quite possible that not all the changes are going to be negative. I suspect grandparents will be there. They may not fulfill the same roles in our lives as they've done. But the choice is ours entirely to make—whether we let the present process, which more or less sidelines grandmothers, continue or whether we do something to stop this disintegration. And I think that to a certain extent, we can intervene. We don't have to simply let everything collapse. But, what we need is a certain measure of energy. And what is really bothersome is whether we have this energy, whether we have energy at all. But the kind of energy that we need to intervene in the disintegration of the role of the grandmother as we know it is the same kind of energy we need to reorganize other areas of our life. Like making the education system more meaningful, and so on and so forth. Like tackling the issue of African languages and what we want to do about that. You see what I am saying. I see that energy as central to all our future, because the issue of the decay or the disintegration of the role or the function of the grandmother in our life is not separate from all the other developmental issues facing us as a people.

Azodo: Nawal el Sadawi, only a few days ago, was saying that a committed artist must be an activist. I wonder what your opinion is on that issue?

Aidoo: I think she is right. You know, the committed artist has to be an activist. The thing is that if you are committed, you will be an activist, whether through the mode of writing or other areas. I know that Nawal was categorical in thinking that what we artists do is not enough. We need to be out there. And I cannot agree with her more, because I tried, you know, to even enter what I then perceived as revolutionary politics. So, I agree with her. If everything were equal, we wouldn't be asking the writer and the artist to also be going out there actively participating in the struggle. But, we know that everything is not equal where we come from.

Azodo: In reading *Changes*, sometimes I wonder what the changes are.

Aidoo: Well, you are the c-r-i-t-i-c. That's okay. I also titled my book *Changes*. I was trying to see how one young woman, or one woman perceived herself in a non-stable environment. Do you see? I mean, in our environment, as we keep coming back to the issue, as a result of colonial intervention, what you would see under any circumstances as normal societal development was interfered with. So now, we have all these forces going on around us. And, in the mean time, we are not living in a vacuum. We are also living in a world which is impacted on by other forces outside itself. I called the book *Changes*, because I see primarily a character like Esi, the protagonist, as being a part of those who are trying to redefine, or even define woman as a lover, as a wife, as a mother, even as a daughter, as a granddaughter. Do you see? So, that's why I called the book *Changes*. In the meantime, it was fascinating to note that, for instance, my Dutch publishers titled the Dutch version of the book *Choices*. So, they saw her as somebody who had to deal with the issue of choices.

Azodo: Very good. Tuzyline, whom you know, in the "Afterword" to *Changes*, did mention that your major characters usually do not portray, what she called, "a drama of victimization." Do you see yourself as an advancement on your predecessors, Flora Nwapa or Buchi Emecheta?

Aidoo: Well, that's again an unfair question, because I don't want to position myself as an advancement. That is for the critic to decide. Well, I would want to think that I do not see my women as victims. Although even that statement cannot be wholly true. For instance, in terms of a woman like Anowa, who refused to be a victim, but finally, eventually, had to submit and commit suicide. Committing suicide is pretty nihilistic, you know. I mean, you have to be confronted with despair, which is so total you cannot see any other way out. Right? I mean, when a person, if a person gets into that kind of hole, that's being victim. She succumbs. The thing is that not all but some of my women escape being victims. Right? I would like to think that I do try to prevent victimization. If people see that as an advancement on Nwapa and Emecheta, for instance, fine. But, I wouldn't go characterizing my work in that kind of way. You know what I am trying to say.

Azodo: Yes. Let me get back to *Changes*. I really like that novel. Do you see a certain kind of oxymoron ...? Do you see yourself shifting on issues that you had categorically dealt with in, say, *Our Sister Killjoy*?

Aidoo: Like?

Azodo: There is no question about how you feel about things. And my students really say, "Oh, my God, she's so angry!" But in *Changes*, you seem to...let me use the word...waffle a little bit on issues.

Aidoo: Like what?

Azodo: Like polygamy.

Aidoo: No. But I don't waffle on it. You just can't stay angry all the time. In *Killjoy*, I was dealing with very hard public issues, political issues, like colonization, what happened to us as a people. *Changes* is much more easy. I deal with love, personal relationships. You can't take up an angry posture over issues to do with love and marriage. I mean, you have to be calm about it. Do you see what I'm saying?

Azodo: Turning now to feminism as such, African feminism. Cherie Register has spoken of American feminism as suffering from a "biological putdown" on women. Do you see any such attitude of male writers on women in African literature?

Aidoo: Well, I definitely think it is a characteristic, rather than an attitude. Because I don't think they do it deliberately. It is just their perception of society. And they can't go beyond what they see as a *status quo*. So, you get these women who are not very assertive and so on and so forth. But, I wouldn't use the term "attitude," because when you say that, it means they do it deliberately. But an attitude needn't be deliberate. Yet, it is there. But, we have to also understand it in terms of how they perceive contemporary society. I think it is there.

Azodo: Years ago in Stockholm, you reluctantly accepted the label of a feminist. And I know that many African women writers prefer womanism to the term feminism. How do you yourself define womanism? What does that mean to you?

Aidoo: Well, my understanding of womanism is like feminism. But, because of us being African and black, because of our particular position in history, womanists believe that special component makes it a little difficult for us to say we are feminists. Womanism adds the added understanding of our position in history to the discourse. You know that we can be feminists. But, you know, on the other hand, we bring more to the discourse, which makes us womanists. But, like you heard me say yesterday, for me, that's also problematic, because it is essentializing our situation, which brings its own limitations. I think it is a very complex issue.

(Aidoo is motioning to me to wrap up the interview.)

Azodo: Okay. What do you feel about Alice Walker's *Possessing the Secret of Joy? (Laughter).*

Aidoo: (*Laughter*) You know perfectly well that we don't have too much time. What I mean is, this is a big issue that needs time. And, I think it needs its own interview. My position is that, unlike other people, I disagree with the position that Alice has no right to talk about these things. I think, as the author of *The Dilemma of a Ghost*, which has a main character who is African American, I think that if I can write a play with an African American as a main character, then Alice can talk about that. What I mean is that the relationship between Africans and African Americans is too ... We are relatives, conflictual, but also familiar. What I mean is, we are cousins, so we can not say that we can't talk about issues to deal with one another. What I find problematic in Alice's handling of the issue is the way Africa got demonized in the process. Older African women got demonized, you know. I think that's very unfortunate. You see. And as a person who has a bad leg, I think I have a problem with *Possessing the Secret of Joy*, because the older woman who does these things has a limp. And, for me, that's saying something there that I don't ... that I find too heavy. Do you see?

Azodo: Yes. Do you think we should have canons among literatures by African women?

Aidoo: Well, a canon develops. Right? Like every literature, like every art, there's bound to be a canon. But who determines the nature of that canon is r-e-a-l-l-y who determines it. And what eventually emerges as the canon is what we have to be clear about and try to deal with. But, there is bound to be a canon.

Azodo: How would you define a literature that is good from a feminist perspective, in regard to African literature?

Aidoo: Well, again, I wish it were something that I could deal with in a more substantive way. Literature that deals with women's issues, I mean with women and our position in history, but goes beyond just being about women. First of all, we have to decide what a feminist would consider literature and good literature. But I think that a literature that affirms women, representing us as articulate, three dimensional beings, not flats, not caricatures, a literature that dosen't portray us as being dumb or inactive. You know what I am saying?

Azodo: Yes.

Aidoo: A literature that affirms women, that for me is good feminist literature.

Azodo: Would you characterize the African feminist novel as radical, Marxist, liberal or militant? (*Laughter*).

Aidoo (*Laughter*) Well, if it is a feminist novel, then it is bound to be radical. It is probably bound to be militant. It should be socialistic. I don't know about Marxist. If it is socialistic, it is probably Marxist as well.

Azodo: Don't you see any kind of class consciousness among African women?

Aidoo: What do you mean? First of all, we have to clarify that. The fact that a novel is written by a woman dosen't make it feminist. That is what I was saying yesterday. A book written by a woman is just a book written by a woman. It dosen't make it feminist, because feminism is a specific category, is an ideological overview. It is an ideology. Feminism is an ideology. So a woman writer is just a woman writer. A book written by a woman is just a book written by a woman. When we say that literature is feminist, then we are speaking specifically of a literature produced from a feminist view point. And that means that literature, if it is feminist, has done more. It affirms women. If you write a book about women, which portrays women as being silly, giggly, ineffectual characters, that's not feminist.

Azodo: I understand where you are coming from. How does the African woman today negotiate her space between the claims of tradition or traditionalism and modernization? I am thinking specifically of Esi's dilemma. At the end, despite her praxis, she ends up as a second wife, who is not much regarded, from what we see, not even by her new husband. So, how does the career woman juggle relationships with men?

Aidoo: Well, she tries to juggle. But, the thing is that it is not a situation that's going to be easily resolved. Right? I think that the African woman who is like Esi, a woman with high education, who has a career, is going to have a hard time of it. But, I suspect that she's not going to have a harder time than any woman in that kind of position anywhere. The added detail is that our society is at a stage where it is a little less tolerant of this dilemma than may be the West. But, mind you, the greater sections of our world are in the position of Esi. Do you see what I'm saying? But for me, what is interesting to me is her willingness to even struggle. Do you see? Yes, for me, life itself is dynamic. And when people say, "but Esi does not end up anywhere," I say, "but she has done part of the journey." And for me, the willingness to even put her emotions out there, her mind, her desires, is in itself a good thing, a positive thing.

Azodo: This question is almost redundant. But what is your idea of romantic love? (*Laughter*).

Aidoo: (*Laughter*) Oh, I suppose romantic love is precisely that, romantic love. As long as we know it represents an almost unattainable ideal, it is okay.

Azodo: Yes.

Aidoo: And it is only when women delude themselves into thinking that romantic love is life that we get into trouble.

Azodo: Hmm.

Aidoo: I mean, it exists in every society. Different versions of it.

Azodo: Hmm...

Aidoo: In the West, in Africa, if you listen to our songs, it is there! You see what I'm saying.

Azodo: Hmm.

Aidoo: Yeah. And we need it to take us out of the humdrum also.

(Aidoo is motioning to me again to end it. And I am pleading, equally with gestures, to be allowed a little more time.)

Azodo: Okay. I am almost finishing, because I see we are taking very long. You have spoken very strongly against brain-drain from Africa. Do you see a way we can transform the status quo positively?

Aidoo: If we get good, confident leadership, a leadership that has confidence in itself and in us as African people, so that we would undertake the development of our environment meaningfully, not only will we be needing our brains, but we will create structures that would make the people with expertise want to stay. Do you see?

Azodo: Hmm.

Aidoo: That's the only way we can. We can't do it by complaining about it.

Azodo: Okay. There are already thousands out ...

Aidoo: Exactly.

Azodo: How can they help Africa from here?

Aidoo: Ah, well, that's another story.

Azodo: What can we do to transform the negative into the positive? I mean, being already here, what can we do?

Aidoo: Well, Nawal gave you one of the best possible answers, that people become organized, and collectively strong, so that at least, those issues that can be handled, from this end, will be handled. For instance, one of the ways I thought we could operate from the West, meaningfully, is for us to pool our resources, so that we become some kind of a pressure group, which is also what Nawal was saying.

Azodo: Hmm

Aidoo: So that people do not take us for granted. So that people do not go abusing us and get away with it. So that people, like Dennis has been doing, can't say they are coming to re-colonize Africa without us protesting. Do you see?

Azodo: Hmm

Aidoo: Because so much of the negative impulses and stimuli coming from the West may not be entirely taken care of. But, they can be handled, a little, from here.

Azodo: Okay. That explains your position that the survival of the nation is implicated in feminism?

Aidoo: Of course.

(Aidoo makes gestures to me again to round up.)

Azodo: Okay. Do you see any way we could really combat the evils of imperialism in the world today?

Aidoo: Well, there must be. For every problem there is a solution. And so, if we look hard, we will find answers. We would be able to combat imperialism.

Azodo: Oh! Thank you very much.

Aidoo: You are welcome.

Afterword:
Interviewing and Transcribing
a Writer-Oral Artist

Ada Uzoamaka Azodo

The interview transcribed above mirrors two kinds of questions. First, those discussing issues raised by Ama Ata Aidoo in her body of work, including how she started writing and her advice to aspiring women writers. Second, those others which are more comprehensive, probing the author's views on literature, feminism, and African, Western, and global societies.

I have used two styles—directive (when I wanted specific responses to particular questions, issues or points) and non-directive (a sort of free-association style, when at a simple question I allowed the author to go on and on, with hardly any interruption, for as long as she wanted to express her views and opinions on the issues). All I did was encourage her to continue by interjecting at the appropriate pauses "Hmm." I found the non-directive questions to be harder for Aidoo to respond to, perhaps due to her emotional state during the interview, or due to inadequate amount of time to treat a complex issue in the way she would have liked. Aidoo's emotional turmoil could be seen in her hesitations, interrupted thoughts, abandoned phrases and sentences. It was indeed easy to see that Aidoo was stressed. The long days of keeping up appearances were finally beginning to take their toll, perhaps.

At the end of the interview, I still wanted to play back even a minute of the recording, in order to be sure I really had the game in the bag. It appeared that the recording did not start right at the beginning of the tape. First of all Aidoo aloud, and then myself with internal trepidation, were momentarily alarmed that there might not have been any recording at all, after all! But, thank God, we were quickly reassured and relieved when my voice posing the first question came on....

I quickly packed my bag, bade Aidoo goodbye, and rushed off to the train station. Half-way to the station, I realized that in my hurry I had forgotten to pay our bill for breakfast. Now, for an interview that was granted on a platter of gold, abandoning the breakfast bill for her to pay was going to be the height of treachery! I told the driver to turn around and return me to the hotel, immediately. Missing or not missing my train was no longer the question, for the time being. I was resolute not to be counted among the opportunistic lot whom Aidoo kept saying were taking advantage of her. Throughout the interview, at every opportunity, when the recorder was killed, she repeatedly mentioned that people were taking advantage of her, had always taken advantage of her. She was perhaps referring to her discussions with some of the groups who interrupted our interview. Who knows?

Back to the narrative. When I returned to the hotel and rushed into the restaurant, Aidoo was still seated at our table. I was relieved to see her still sitting there. This time, she was talking with another lady. I found out she had settled our bill. I pleaded with her to accept my reimbursement and was only happy when she eventually did. Off I disappeared again towards the train station and luckily still caught my train, just as the doors were about to close.

After I got home, I was very cautious not to lose the treasure, I mean the interview recording. I moved the cassette tape from one safe place to another, until I was sure that I was going to finish by not remembering where I had put it away. My document retrieval system is not known to be one of the best anyone could have. My greatest worry was how to safeguard it throughout the summer months as my family relocated from New York to Indiana. Even to make a duplicate copy was a hard decision for me to make, lest an inattentive attendant erased the tape instead of copying it! And so the duplication was not done until Fall. Even then I waited for the completion of the process with anxious, almost religious, expectancy.

Transcribing the interview was an equally hard task. It had to be done safely and as faithfully as possible for three reasons. One, to recreate the circumstances and fidelity of the occasion. Two, for the sake of the book at hand, of which it is to form a major part. Three, and perhaps most important, for the sake of adding a new chapter to human knowledge about this illustrious daughter of Africa, Ama Ata Aidoo. For many hours, I sat down close to my tape deck trying to decipher some of the voices which were quite faint or muffled behind the din that was going on in the recording ambiance. If it proved impossible to make out a word after playing it over and over again, I would simply leave a blank space, intending to return to it as soon as I could. And sometimes this did not happen before the end of the period of a week. Meanwhile, in-between preparing classes and teaching and family, time was often a very precious commodity.

The more I listened to the tape, the more I was able to recreate the occasion and recall the entire experience in my mind's eye. At a point, I felt it was grossly inappropriate to continue to transcribe the interview in prose format, though it be the norm to which the reading public is used: a text shorn of all speech redundancies. In my opinion, I would be failing in my duty as Aidoo's transcriber, if I did not set things down in the manner they were performed. Yes, I really felt I had been part of an oral performance, a sort of accompanist-audience to a speech act, which is quite different from ordinary everyday speech.

Having taken the decision to keep to the habitual prose format, I have however retained a small verbatim portion of interview text as it was captured by the recording apparatus at the end of this essay, so that readers may get a glimpse of what it was like for me to interview Aidoo on the fateful day. For that short section, I have transcribed all that the tape recorder captured, all that have a chance of helping readers get into the feel of what the morning was like for both Aidoo and myself. I felt that nothing should be left out; interjections, questions, answers, asides, laughter. What I would encourage readers to do is to try to put themselves in the shoes of Ama Ata Aidoo when they see in parenthesis "Interruption." They should try to imagine how Aidoo must have felt when she came back to continue an interrupted answer, or even worse, to face a new question from me for which the foregoing did not prepare her. When readers see the annotation,"laughter," I would like them to think about the subject under discussion, especially about their implications in African literature and social life.

More generally, the reader should be able to grasp the full dimensions of the interview as an oral speech act, which it was. Aidoo's responses especially mirror her emotional rythmn. Sometimes her answers were short, at other times long. Sometimes she spoke quite fast, at other times she was quite slow. Sometimes her voice was high, at other times her voice was low, almost imperceptible on the tape. It is our hope that others will try our transcription style, in order to make interviewing a more rewarding and exciting experience, not only for the interviewer, but also for the reading public. Contextual factors can be of great artistic merit to the interview and the documentation of the interview.

Why have we rendered the "candid camera" portion of the interview in verse rather than in prose? It is because we believe something is lost in the prose version which we had edited, in order to drastically reduce the instances of repetition, redundancies and all, which peculiarly characterize this interview. So, in this "exhibition" version, we have used the verse form with line breaks at the end of the line, which correlate with breath stops either of the interviewer or of the interviewee. In this way, the reader will better grasp a little bit of the complex moods of the interviewer and interviewee, as well as the emotionally charged atmosphere and cacophony of background music, noise and laughter from conference participants at the restaurant that morning. For comparative purposes, we have also reproduced an excerpt from *Our Sister Killjoy* and another from the book of poetry, *An Angry Letter in January*. Readers will be able to see that Aidoo writes many times according to the rythmn of her speech. Perhaps, what critics see as her ability to criss-cross genres is nothing more than her natural way of speaking, or by extension could be anybody's natural way of speaking.

In the end, the texts that follow approach the dimensions of Tedlock's practice of rendering all spoken accounts in verse form, as if they are dramatic poetry (1971;1983). His argument is that people usually speak with an ebb and flow, which follow not only the breath of the speakers but also the emotional rythmn of the content of the speech (Okpewho 1992). We have used the following appropriate elements of oral literature transcription to differentiate the variety of emotional and mood changes that characterize this interview:

1. Stage directions to annotate interruptions during the interview
2. Boldface for words said in a high voice or with stress
3. Italics for words said in a soft, low voice
4. Roman type for ordinary voice
5. Verse line breaks to indicate breath stops or normal pause in speech
6. Ellipses (...) to indicate hesitations, redundancies
7. Dashes to indicate words that were said extremely slowly—almost spelled out—for added emphasis

* * * * * *

A. Verbatim transcription from Aidoo interview tape.
A slice only.

Azodo: Which side of you seems to be dominant over the others?

Aidoo: Well, that's really for the critic to say, really,
because I am a poet.
Well, I will ...
I hope I can say I am a poet.
Er ...
The novel ...
because it takes a lot more time,
er ...
that ...
you know ...
I haven't written as many novels as I would want
because, you know,
because for the past twenty years or so,
I have not led a stable existence.
And without a certain kind
em ...
stability,
you know ...
I mean ...
Without ...
You can't do
you can't do drama on the move.
You need a stage.
You need ...

You know,
may be a company that would produce your plays on stage,
and so on and so forth.
So, again,
my ...
my output has been terrifyingly,
em ..., em...
you know ...
Azodo: Well, I have read *Anowa* ...
Aidoo: **Yeah!**
Azodo; ... and *The Dilemma of a Ghost,*
and I think they are excellent books.
Aidoo: **Thank you**.
But, I am not talking about the quality.
But, I mean the quantity.
You know,
The Dilemma was written,
was published in 1965,
and,
Anowa, was published in 1970.
And since then,
apart from a radio play,
I haven't done drama.
That's what I mean.
What I'm saying is ...
Well,
I am not even in a position to judge,
Azodo: Hmm
Aidoo: ... You know, the quality of my work ...
Azodo: Hmm
Aidoo: A few of my books ...
But I'm just saying ...
Just in terms of the sheer volume, you know ...
Azodo: Hmm
Aidoo: You know ...
Er ...
I haven't done as much as I would want,
because of the way my life has seemed to have worked out.
Hmm ...
Azodo: In the future,
which direction do you see yourself leaning?
Aidoo: Well, you know,

Me, I am a writer.
When I say I am a writer,
what I am ...
What I'm saying is,
you know,
I ...
depending upon the m-a-t-e-r-i-a-l
and how it strikes me,
you know,
or how the material presents *itself*,
then I write a poem, and I do ...
For instance,
I have just written a new short story,
two weeks ago ...
Azodo: Hmm! ...
Aidoo: You know,
I would like to happily announce it,
because it was nice ...
You know ...
I mean, because I had been teaching full-time for the past
three years,
I hadn't written much.
So, it was very nice,
er ...
that I should sit down and write a story.
You see,
er ...
So, in the mean time I am working on a novel.
Again, I can't see myself doing plays for the reason ...
For the reason ...

(Interruption as a steward finally brings Aidoo some tea.)

For the reason ...
that I have outlined ...
you know ...
But I ...
I do hope that I'll be writing more and more.
That sort of thing ...
Azodo: In reading your works,
I see that the grandmothers are ...
have a significant role,

em ...
Aidoo: Hmm ...
Azodo: Yeah.
   Em ...
   With changes in society,
   And young women moving away
   From home, er ...

(Interruption as Aidoo calls "Carol!" to get the attention
of Carole Boyce Davies. I kill the recorder on Aidoo's orders).

Azodo: Okay.
   We were on the role of grandmothers.
Aidoo: Hmm ...

* * * * * *

B. Excerpt from *Our Sister Killjoy* (25-27):

   Mary?
   But that is an English name, said Jane.
   Maria ... Marlene.
   That is a Swedish name, said Ingrid.
   Marie is a French name, said Michelle.
   Naturally
   Naturellement
   Natürlich!
   Mary is anybody's name but ...

   Small consolation that in some places,
   The patient, long-suffering
   Missionaries could not get as far
   As
   Calling up to the pulpit
   A man and his wife who
   Fight in the night
   and
   Whip them
   Before the
   Whole congregation of the
   SAVED.

But my brother,
They got
Far
Enough.
Teaching among other things,
Many other things,
That
For a child to grow up
To be a
Heaven-worthy individual,
He had
To have
Above all, a
Christian name.

And what shall it profit a native that
He should have
Systems to give
A boy
A girl
Two
Three names or
More?
Yaw Mensah Adu Preko Oboroampa Okotoboe

Ow, my brother ...
Indeed there was a time when
Voices sang
Horns blew
Drums rolled to
Hail
yaw
     —For getting born on Thursday
Preko
     —Just to extol Yaw
Mensah
     —Who comes third in a series of males
Adu
     —A name from father
after venerable ancestor,

Okotoboe
    —For hailing the might of Adu.

No, my brother,
We no more
Care for
Such
Anthropological
Shit:

A man could have
Ten names.
They were all the same—
Pagan
Heathen
Abominable idolatory to the
Hearing of
God,
Who, bless his heart,
Is a rather
Nice
Old
European
Gentleman with a flowing white beard.
... And he sits
Flanked on either side by
Angels that take the roll-call for
The Elect

Lord,
Let us Thy Servants depart in peace
Into our rest
Our oblivion and never
Dare expect
Angels who take roll-calls in
Latin—most likely—
To twist rather delicate tongues
Around names like
—Gyaemehara
Since, dear Lord, Your
Angels, like You, are
Western

White
English, to be precise.

Oh dear visionary Caesar!
There are no other kinds of
Angels, but
Lucifer, poor Black Devil. (25-27)
* * * * * *

C. Excerpt from *An Angry Letter in January*, (24-25):

"An Angry Letter in January"

Dear Bank Manager,

I have received your letter.
Thank you very much:
threats,
intimidations, and all.

So what,
if you won't give me a loan
of two thousand?
Or only conditioned by
special rules

and regulations?

Because I am *not*

white
male *or*
a 'commercial farmer'?

(And in relation to the latter,
whose land is this anyway?)

I know that but for what I am not,
you could have signed

away
two solid millions, and

453

not many questions asked.

Of course I am angry.

Wouldn't you be if you were me?

Reading what you had written
was enough
to spoil for me
all remaining eleven months of the year,
plus a half.

But I wont let it.

I had even thought
of asking God
that the next time round,
He makes me
white, male, and a 'commercial' farmer.

But I wont.

Since apart from
the great poverty
                    and
the petty discriminations,

I have been happy
being me:

an African
a woman
and a writer.

Just take your racism
              your sexism
                    your pragmatism
                          off me;

overt

covert or

internalised.
And
damn you!

WORKS CITED

Aidoo, Ama Ata. *Our Sister Killjoy*. London: Longman, 1977.
———. *An Angry Letter in January*. Coventry/Sydney/Aarhus: Dangaroo Press, 1992.
Johnson, John William. *The Epic of Sonjara: A West African Tradition* (Text by Fa-Digi Sisoko). Bloomington and Indianapolis, Indiana: Indiana University Press, 1992.
Okpewho, Isidore. *African Oral Literature: Backgrounds, Character, and Continuity*. Bloomington and Indianapolis: Indiana University Press, 1992.
Tedlock, D. "On the Translation of Style in Oral Literature." *Journal of American Folklore* 84 (1971):114-133.
———. *The Spoken Word and the Work of Interpretation*, Philadelphia: University of Pennsylvania Press, 1983.

SELECTED BIBLIOGRAPHY

OF AND ON

AMA ATA AIDOO

Adams, Ann, Ed. *Fifty African and Caribbean Women Writers: A Bio-Bibliography.* Westport: Greenwood Press, 1996.

Adelugba, Dapo. "Language and Drama: Ama Ata Aidoo," *African Literature Today* No.8. Ed. Eldred D. Jones. 72-84; Africana, 1976. London: Heinemann, 1976. 72-84.

Agovi, Kofi. "Is There an African Vision of Tragedy in Contemporary African Theatre?" *Presence Africaine* (1984):133-134.

Aidoo, Ama Ata. *Our Sister Killjoy: Or Reflections From a Black-Eyed Squint.* Lagos/New York: NOK Press, 1979. Harlow, U.K.: Longman, 1977.

____. "Ghana: To Be a Woman." UNITAR Seminar, *Creative Women in Changing Societies*, Oslo, July 9-13, 1980. Also in *Sisterhood is Global.* Ed. Robin Morgan. New York: Anchor Doubleday, 1985. 258-265.

____. *Someone Talking to Sometime.* Harare: The College Press, 1985.

____. *Anowa.* London: Longman, 1970. Harlow, U.K.: Longman, 1985.

____. *The Dilemma of a Ghost and Anowa.* Essex: Longman, 1965, 1970; Harlow, U.K.: Longman, 1985.

____. *The Eagle and the Chickens and Other Stories.* Enugu: Tana Press, 1987.

____. "Unwelcome Pals and Decorative Slaves," *AFA Journal of Creative Writing* 1 (November 1982):34-43. Originally in: *Medium and Message.* Proceedings of the International Conference on African literature and the English language, University of Calabar, Nigeria, November 1982. Also in *Literature and Society: Selected Essays on African Literature.* Ed.

Ernest Emenyou. Lagos, Nigeria: Zim Pan-African Publishers, Lagos, Nigeria, 1986, Roth, 1990.

_____. "On Commitment." *Burning Issues in African Literature.* Vol. 1. Cape Coast University English Department, 1981.

_____. "Sisterhood is Global." *Essence* (March 1985):12-13, 15, 134, 137.

_____. *Birds and Other Poems.* Harare: The College Press, 1987.

_____. "To Be an African Woman Writer—An Overview and a Detail." In *Criticism and Ideology.* Ed. Kirsten Holst Petersen. Uppsala, Sweden: Scandinavian Institute of African Studies, 1988. 155-172.

_____. "- For Kinna VII." *West Africa* March 6-12, 1989):357.

——. *No Sweetness Here.* Essex, 1970. London: Longman; 1971, 1972. New York, Doubleday, 1989.

_____. "Nowhere Cool." *Callaloo* 13,1 (1990): 62-70.

——. *Changes: A Love Story.* New York: CUNY, The Feminist Press, 1991.

——. "Modern African Stories 1" and "A Path in the Sky or 7 A. M. and Airborne." *Literary Review* (Summer 1991):434-436.

_____. "Whom Do We Thank For Women's Conferences?" *Ms.* (January/February, 1991):96.

_____. "Changing her Tune." Interview with Maya Jaggi. *Guardian,* (April 2, 1991).

_____. [Untitled Essay.] 1991. In: *Critical Fictions: The Politics of Imaginative Writing.* Ed. Philomena Mariani. Seattle, Washington: Bay Press, 1991. 151-154.

_____. "Change of Art," Interview with Deirdre Forbes. *Voice* (April 9 and 18, 1991).

——. "The African Woman Today." *Dissent* 39 (1992):319-325.

_____. *An Angry Letter in January.* Coventry, U.K.: Dangaroo Press, 1992.

_____. *The Girl who Can And Other Stories.* Legon, Ghana: Sub-Saharan Publishers, 1996.

——. "Literature, Feminism and the African Woman Today." Address to the Women's Caucus of the African Literature Association, State University at Stony Brook, New York, 1996.

_____. "Facing the Millenium." Interview with Ada Uzoamaka Azodo. In: *Emerging Perspectives in Ama Ata Aidoo,* Eds. Ada Uzoamaka Azodo and Gay Wilentz. Trenton, N.J.: Africa World Press, 1998.

Allan, Tuzyline Jita. "Afterword." *Changes: A Love Story* by Ama Ata Aidoo. New York: CUNY, The Feminist Press, 1991.171-196.

Andrade, Susan. "Rewriting History, Motherhood, and Rebellion: Naming an African Literary Tradition." *Research in African Literatures* 21,1 (Spring 1990): 91-110.

Azodo, Ada Uzoamaka. "Issues in African Feminism: A Syllabus." *Women's Studies Quarterly: Teaching African Literatures in a Global Literary Economy* xxv, 3&4 (Fall/Winter 1997):201-207. Ed. Tuzyline Jita Allan.

——. "Introduction: A Breath of Fresh Air." In: *Emerging Perspectives on Ama Ata Aidoo.* Eds. Ada Uzoamaka Azodo and Gay Wilentz. Trenton, N.J.: Africa World Press, 1998.

——. "*The Dilemma of a Ghost*: Literature and Power of Myth." In: *Emerging Perspectives on Ama Ata Aidoo.* Eds. Ada Uzoamaka Azodo and Gay

Wilentz. Trenton, N.J.: Africa World Press, 1998.

——. "The Multifaceted Aidoo: Ideologue, Scholar, Writer, and Woman." In: *Emerging Perspectives on Ama Ata Aidoo.* Eds. Ada Uzoamaka Azodo and Gay Wilentz. Trenton, N.J.: Africa World Press, 1998.

——. "Facing the Millennium." Interview with Ama Ata Aidoo. In: *Emerging Perspectives on Ama Ata Aidoo.* Eds. Ada Uzoamaka Azodo and Gay Wilentz. Trenton, N.J.: Africa World Press, 1998.

——. "Afterword: Interviewing and Transcribing a Writer-Oral Artist." In: *Emerging Perspectives on Ama Ata Aidoo.* Eds. Ada Uzoamaka Azodo and Gay Wilentz. Trenton, N.J.: Africa World Press, 1998.

Bell, Roseann P. "The Absence of the African Woman Writer," *College Languages Association Journal* 21,4 (1978):491-498.

Bell, Roseann. Bettye J. Parker, and Beverly Guy-Sheftall. Eds. *Sturdy Bridges Visions of Black Women in African Literature.* New York: Doubleday, 1979.

Berrian, Brenda F. "The Afro-American West African Marriage Question: Its Literary and Historical Contexts." *Women in African Literature Today.* No. 15, London: James Currey, 1979. 152-159.

——. "Bibliographies of Nine Female African Writers." *Research in African Literatures* 12, 2, (Summer 1981):214-236.

——. "African Women as Seen in the Works of Flora Nwapa And Ama Ata Aidoo." *College Language Association Journal* 25,3 (March, 1985):331-339.

Bishop, Rand. "The Only Ones Who Need To Know." Review of *Our Sister Killjoy: Or Reflections From a Black-Eyed Squint. Obsidian: Black Literature in Review* 6, 1 and 2 (1980):251-154.

Boehmer, Elleke. *Colonial and Postcolonial Literature.* New York: Oxford University Press, 1995.

——. "Stories of Women and Mothers." In: *Motherlands, Black Women's Writing from Africa, the Caribbean and South Asia.* Ed. Susheila Nasta. New Brunswick, N.J.: Rutgers University Press, 1992.

Booth, James. "Sexual Politics in the Fiction of Ama Ata Aidoo." *Commonwealth Essays and Studies.* [Dijon, France], 15, 2 (1993): (Spring 1993):80-96.

Brown, Lloyd W. "Ama Ata Aidoo: The Art of the Short Story and Sexual Roles in Africa."*World Literature Written in English"* 13 (1974):172-183.

——. "The African Woman as Writer." *Canadian Journal of African Studies* 9,3 (1975): 493-501.

——. *Women Writers in Black Africa.* Westport, conn.: Greenwood Press, 1981.

Burner, Charlotte H. "Child Africa as Depicted by Bessie Head and Ama Ata Aidoo." *Studies in the Humanities* 7, 2 (1979):5-12.

Burness, Donald. "Womanhood in the Short Stories of Ama Ata Aidoo." *Studies in Black Literature* 4, 2 (summer 1973):21-24.

Busia, Abena. "Whispered Over Voids: A Context for Black Women's Rebellious Voices in the Novel of the African Diaspora." In: *Black Feminist Criticism and Critical Theory.* Eds. Houston A. Baker and Joe Weixelmann. Studies in Black American Literature, Vol. 3, Greenville, Fla.: Penkewill, 1987.

——. *Testimonies of Exiles.* Trenton, N.J.: Africa World Press, 1990.

Butler, Judith. *Gender Trouble: Feminism and the Subversion of Identity.* New

York: Routledge, 1990.

Chapman, Karen C. "Introduction." *The Dilemma of a Ghost by Christiana Ama Ata Aidoo*. New York: Collier, 1965.

____. "Introduction." *The Dilemma of a Ghost. In Sturdy Bridges: Visions of Black Women in Literature* 2 (1965):33-34.

Chetin, Sara. "Rereading and Rewriting African Women: Ama Ata Aidoo and Bessie Head." *Dissertation Abstracts International*, 1 53, 3 (Sept. 1992): 808A.

____. "Reading from a Distance: Ama Ata Aidoo's *Our Sister Killjoy*." In: *Black Women's Writing*. Ed. and Introd. Wisker, Gina. New York: St. Martin's Press, 1993. x, 146-159,189.

Christian, Barbara. *Black Feminist Criticism: Perspectives on Black Women Writers*. New York: Pergamon, 1985.

Collins, Patricia Hill. *Black Feminist Thought*. New York: Routledge, 1991.

Condé, Maryse. "Three Female Writers in Modern Africa: Flora Nwapa, Ama Ata Aidoo, and Grace Ogot," *Presence Africaine* 82 (1972):132-143.

Cooke, Michael G. Ed. *Modern Black Novelists* Englewood Cliffs, N.J.: Prentice-Hall, 1971.

Coussy, Denise. "Is Life Sweet? The Short Stories of Ama Ata Aidoo." In: *Short Fiction in the New Literature in English: Proceedings of the Nice Conference of European Association for Commonwealth Literature and Language Studies*." Ed. Jacqueline Bardolph. Nice: Faculté de Lettres et Sciences Humaines de Nice. 1989. 1111, 290.

Davies, Carole Boyce. *Black Women, Writing and Identity: Migrations of the Subject*, New York: Routledge, 1995.

Davies Carole Boyce and Ann Adams Graves. "Introduction: Feminist Consciousness and African literary Criticism," *Ngambika: Studies of Women in African Literature*. Trenton, N.J.: Africa World Press, 1987.

Dunton, Chris."Wheyting Be Dat?" The Treatment of Homosexuality in African Literature." *Research in African Literatures*. 20, 3 (Fall 1989):422-448.

Du Pleissis. Rachel Blau. *Writing Beyond the Ending: Narrative Strategies of Twentieth Century Women Writers*. Bloomington, Indiana: Indiana University Press, 1985.

Eke, Maureen N. "Diasporic Ruptures and (Re)membering History: Africa as Home and Exile in *Anowa* and *The Dilemma of a Ghost In: Emerging Perspectives on Ama Ata Aidoo*. Eds. Ada Uzoamaka Azodo and Gay Wilentz. Trenton, N.J.: Africa World Press, 1998.

Eko, Ebele. "Beyond the Myth of Confrontation: A comparative Study of African And African-American Female Protagonists. " *Ariel: A Review of International English Literature*. 17, 4 (October 1986):139-152.

Elder, Arlene A. "Ama Ata Aidoo and the Oral Tradition: A Paradox of Form and Substance." *Women in African Literature Today*. No. 15. Ed. Eldred Jones et. al. London, James Currey, Africa World Press, 1987. 109-118.

——. "Ama Ata Aidoo: The Development of A Woman's Voice." In: *Emerging Perspectives on Ama Ata Aidoo*. Eds. Ada Uzoamaka Azodo and Gay Wilentz. Trenton, N.J.: Africa World Press, 1998.

Etherton, Michael. *The Development of African Drama*. New York: Africana,

1982. 227-238.

Fairbairns, Zoe. "Book Review." *Everywoman* (May 25,1991).

Frank, Katherine. "Women Without Men: The Feminist Novel in Africa," *Women in African Literature Today.* Ed. Eldred Durosimi Jones, Eustace Palmer and Marjorie Jones. London: James Currey, Africa World Press. 1987. 14-34.

Gourdine, Angeletta. "Slavery in the Diaspora Consciousness: Ama Ata Aidoo's Conversations." In: *Emerging Perspectives on Ama Ata Aidoo.* Eds. Ada Uzoamaka Azodo and Gay Wilentz. Trenton, N.J.: Africa World Press, 1998.

Grant, Jane W. *Ama Ata Aidoo: The Dilemma of a Ghost-A Study Guide.* Harlow, U.K: Longman, 1980.

Gyimah, Miriam C. "Sexual Politics and Phallocentric Gaze in *Changes: A Love Story.* In: *Emerging Perspectives on Ama Ata Aidoo.* Eds. Ada Uzoamaka Azodo and Gay Wilentz. Trenton, N.J.: Africa World Press, 1998.

Harrow, Kenneth. *Thresholds of Change in African Literature.* Portsmouth, N.H.: Heinemann, 1994.

— —. "Of Those Who Went Before." In: *Emerging Perspectives on Ama Ata Aidoo.* Eds. Ada Uzoamaka Azodo and Gay Wilentz. Trenton, N.J.: Africa World Press, 1998.

Henderson, Mae. "Speaking in Tongues: Dialogics, Dialectics, and the Black Woman Writer's Literary Tradition." In: *Changing Our Own Worlds.* Eds. Cheryl Wall. New Brunswick, N. J.: Rutgers University Press, 1989. 16-37.

Herdeck, Donald. *African Authors.* Washington D.C.: Black Orpheus Press, 1973. 29- 30.

Heywood, Christopher. Ed. *Perspectives on African Literature.* New York: Africana, 1971.

Hill-Lubin, Mildred A. "The Relationship of African-Americans and Africans: Recurring Theme in the Works of Ama Ata Aidoo." *Presence Africaine* 124, 4 (1982):190-201.

____. "The Storyteller and the Audiennce in the Works of Ama Ata Aidoo," *Neohelicon* 16,2 (1989):221-245.

— —. "Ama Ata Aidoo And the African Diaspora: Things 'all Good Men and Women Try to Forget,' But I will Not Let Them." In: *Emerging Perspectives on Ama Ata Aidoo.* Eds. Ada Uzoamaka Azodo and Gay Wilentz. Trenton, N.J.: Africa World Press, 1998.

Holloway, Karla F. C. *Moorings and Metaphors: Figures of Culture and Gender in Black Women's Literature.* New Brunswick N.J.: Rutgers University Press, 1992.

hooks, bell. "Feminist Theory: A Radical Agenda." In: *Talking Back,* Boston Mass. South End Press, 1989.

Horne, Naana Banyiwa. "Ama Ata Aidoo." *Twentieth-Century Caribbean and Black African Writers.* Ser. 1, Vol 117. Ed. Bernth Lindfors and Reinhard Sander. Detroit: Gale Publishers, 1992, 34-40.

____. "Ama Ata Aidoo." *Dictionary of Literary Biography.* Vol. 117. Detroit: Gale Publishers, 1992. 32-40.

— —. "The Politics of Mothering: Multiple Subjectivity and Gendered

Discourse In Aidoo's Plays." In: *Emerging Perspectives on Ama Ata Aidoo.* Eds. Ada Uzoamaka Azodo and Gay Wilentz. Trenton, N.J.: Africa World Press, 1998.

Innes, C. L. "Mothers or Sisters? Identity, Discourse and Audience in the Writing of Ama Ata Aidoo and Mariama Bâ," In: *Motherlands.* Ed. Susheila Nasta. New Brunswick, N.J.: Rutgers University Press, 1992.

Irele, Abiola. *The African Experience in Literature and Ideology.* Bloomington, Ind.: Indiana University Press, 1990.

Jahn, Jahnheinz. Ulla Schild, and Almut Nordenas. *Who's Who in African Literature,* Tubingen: Erdmenn Publishers, 1972. 25-26.

James, Adeola. *"Ama Ata Aidoo."* In: *In Their Own Voices: African Women Writers Talk.* London and Portsmouth, N.H.: Heinemann, 1990.

Jones, Eldred Durosimi. "Ama Ata Aidoo: *Anowa.*" Book review. *African Literature Today,* No. 8. Ed. Eldred Durosimi Jones. New York: Africana, 1976. 142-144.

_____. Ed. *African Literature Today.* No. 8. New York: Africana, 1976.

Jones, Eldred Durosimi. Eustace Palmer, and Marjorie Jones. Eds. *Women in African Literature Today,* No. 15. Trenton, N.J.: Africa World Press, 1987.

Julien, Eileen. "Of Traditional Tales and Short Stories in African Literature."*Présence Africaine* (1st Quarter, 1983): 125.

Kern, Anita. "Review of *Our Sister Killjoy.*" *World Literature Written in English.* 17, 1 (1978):56-57.

Killam, G. D. Ed. *African Writers on African Writing.* New York: Africana, 1973.

Kilson, Marion. "Women and African literature." *Journal of African Studies* 4, 2 (1977):161-166.

K. W. "Review Article." *West Africa.* (January 30, 1971):133.

Korang, Kwaku Larbi. "Ama Ata Aidoo's Voyage Out: Mapping the Coordinates of Modernity and African Selfhood in *Our Sister Killjoy.*" *Kunapipi* [Aarhus, Denmark] 14,3 (1992):50-61.

Lautré, McGregor Maxine. "Interview with Ama Ata Aidoo." In: *African Writers Talking.* Eds. Dennis Duerden and Cosmo Pieterse. New York: African Publishers, 1972. [Also under Maxine McGregor] 19-27.

Lindfors, Bernth. "The Image of the Afro-American in African Literature." *Literary Criterion* 12,1 (1975). Also in: *Association for Commonwealth Literature and Language Studies Bulletin* 4, 3, (1975):19-26.

Lionnet, Françoise and Ronnie Scharfman. Eds. "Post/Colonial Conditions: Exiles, Migrations and Normadisms." *Yale French Studies* 1, 2, (1993): 82, 83.

Lurdos, Michelle. "Une Situation-cliche renouvélée: L'Epouse occidentale dans *The Dilemma of a Ghost* de Ama Ata Aidoo.*" Visages de la féminité.* St Denis: Université de Réunion, 1984. 283.

Maja-Pearce, Adewale. "We Were Feminists in Africa First." *Index on Censorship,* London, 19, 9 (October 1990):17-18.

McCaffrey, Kathleen. "Images of Mother in the Stories of Ama Ata Aidoo." *African Woman* 23 (1979):40-41.

McGregor, Maxine, Interview with Ama Ata Aidoo. "*African Writers Talking: A Collection of Radio Interviews.*" Eds. Cosmo Pieterse and Dennis Duerden. New York: Africana Publishing Company, 1972.

McWilliams, Sally. "Strange as It May Seem: African Feminism in Two Novels by Ama Ata Aidoo." In: *Emerging Perspectives on Ama Ata Aidoo*. Eds. Ada Uzoamaka Azodo and Gay Wilentz. Trenton, N.J.: Africa World Press, 1998.

Mohanty, Chandra T. "Under Western Eyes: Feminist Scholarship and Colonial Discourses. In: *Third World Women and the Politics of Feminism*. Eds. Mohanty Chandra et al. Bloomington, Indiana: Indiana University Press, 1991. 51-80.

Mohanty, Chandra T. Ann Russo, and Lourdes Torres. *Third World Women and the Politics of Feminism*. Bloomington, Indiana: Indiana University Press, 1991.

Morgan, Paula. "The Risk of (Re)membering My Name: Reading *Lucy* and *Our Sister Killjoy* as Travel Narratives. In: *Emerging Perspectives on Ama Ata Aidoo*. Eds. Ada Uzoamaka Azodo and Gay Wilentz. Trenton, N.J.: Africa World Press, 1998.

Morgan, Robin. *Sisterhood is Global*. New York: Anchor Doubleday, 1985.

Mphalele, Ezekiel. "Introduction." *No Sweetness Here*, by Ama Ata Aidoo. Second edition. Garden City, New York: Doubleday, 1972. xix-xx.

Nagenda, John. "Generations of Conflict: Ama Ata Aidoo, J. C. deGraft, and R. Sharif Eastmon." *Protest and Conflict in African Literature*. Ed. Cosmo Pieterse and Ian Munro. New York: 1970. 101-108.

Nandakumar, Prema. "Another Image of Womanhood." *Africa Quarterly* 13,1 (1973):38-44.

Nasta, Susheila. "Introduction.": *Motherlands: Black Women's Writing from Africa, the Caribbean and South Asia*. New Brunswick, N.J.: Rutgers University Press, 1992. xiii-xxx.

Needham, Anuradha Dingwaney. "An Interview with Ama Ata Aidoo." *Massachusetts Review*, 36, 1 (Spring 1995):123-133.

Nfah-Abbenyi, Juliana Makuchi. "Flabberwhelmed or Turning History on its Head?: The Postcolonial Woman-as-Subject in *Changes: A Love Story*. In: *Emerging Perspectives on Ama Ata Aidoo*. Eds. Ada Uzoamaka Azodo and Gay Wilentz. Trenton, N.J.: Africa World Press, 1998.

Niara, John. "Review of *Our Sister Killjoy*." *African Woman* 12 (!977): 65-66.

Nicholas, Mary Naana. "The Affirmation of African Womanhood in the Works of Ama Ata Aidoo." unpublished Master's Thesis, 1983.

Nketia, J. H. *Drumming in Akan Communities*. London: Thomas Nelson Publishing, 1963.

Nkosi, Lewis. *Tasks and Masks: Themes and Styles of African Literature*. London: Longman, 1981. 180

Nwankwo, Chimalum. "The Feminist Impulse and Social Realism in Ama Ata Aidoo's No Sweetness Here and Our Sister Killjoy, In: *Ngambika: Studies of Women in African Literature*. Eds. Carole Boyce Davies and Anne Adams Graves. Trenton N.J.: Africa World Press, 1986. 151-59.

Odamtten, Vincent, Okpoti. "The Developing Art of Ama Ata Aidoo." *Dissertation Abstracts International* 50,5 (Nov. 1989):1303A.

——. "Ama Ata Aidoo," In: *Fifty African and Caribbean Women Writers*. Eds. Anne Adams. Westport, Conn.: Greenwood Press, 1996.

____. *The Art of Ama Ata Aidoo: Polylectics and Reading against Neocolonialism.*

Gainesville: University of Florida Press, 1994.

— —. "The Bird of the Wayside: From *An Angry Letter* to ... *The Girl Who Can*. In: *Emerging Perspectives on Ama Ata Aidoo*. Eds. Ada Uzoamaka Azodo And Gay Wilentz. Trenton, N.J.: Africa World Press, 1998.

Ogede, Ode. "The Defence of Culture in Ama Ata Aidoo's *No Sweetness Here*: The Use of Orality as Textual Strategy." *International Fiction Review* 21,1-2, (1994):76- 84.

Ogunba, Oyin. "Modern Drama in West Africa." In: *Perspectives on African Literature*. Ed. Christopher Heywood. New York: Africana, 1971.81-105.

Ogundipe-Leslie, 'Molara. *Recreating Ourselves: African Women and Critical Transformations*. Trenton, N.J.: Africa World Press, 1994.

Ogunyemi, Chikwenye Okonjo. "Womanism: The Dynamics of the Contemporary Black Female Novel in English." *Signs: Journal of Women in Culture and Society* 2.1 (1985):63-80.

Ojo-Ade, Femi. "Female Writers, Male Critics." In: *African Literature Today* 10, Ed. Eldred Durosimi Jones. London: Heinemann, 1979. 158-179.

_____. "Of Culture, Commitment, and Construction: Reflections on African Literature." Transition 53 (1987):4-24

Okonkwo, Juliet. "The Talented Women in African Literature." *Africa Quarterly*, 15, 1-1 (1975):36-47.

Opoku-Agyemang, Jane, Naana. "Lest We Forget: A Critical Survey of Ghanaian Women's Literature." *Asemka* (1995) 8:61-84.

— —. "Narrative Turns in Ama Ata Aidoo's *No Sweetness Here*. In: *Emerging Perspectives on Ama Ata Aidoo*. Eds. Ada Uzoamaka Azodo and Gay Wilentz. Trenton, N.J.: Africa World Press, 1998.

Owusu, Kofi. "The Fictionalizing as Fiction-Analyzing: A Study of Select 'Critical' Fiction by Ayi Kwei Armah, Wole Soyinka, Ama Ata Aidoo and Chinua Achebe." *Dissertation Abstracts International* 50,11, (May 1990):3584A.

— —. "Canons under Siege: Blackness, Femaleness, and Ama Ata Aidoo's *Our Sister Killjoy*." *Callaloo* 13, 2(Spring 1992):341-363.

Phillips, Maggi. "Engaging Dreams: Alternative Perspectives in Flora Nwapa, Buchi Emecheta, Ama Ata Aidoo, Bessie Head and Tsitsi Dangarembga's Writing." *Research in African Literatures* 25,4 (Winter 1994):89-103.

Pieterse, Cosmo, and Dennis Duerden, Eds. *African Writers Talking: A Collection of Radio Interviews*. New York: Africana, 1972.

Rand, Bishop. "The Only Ones Who Need to Know." *Obsidian: Black Literature in Review* 6, 1-2 (1980):151-154.

Rea, C. J. "The Culture Line: A Note on *The Dilemma of a Ghost*." *African Forum* 1, 1 (1966):111-113.

Ridden, Geoffrey M. "Language and Social Status in Ama Ata Aidoo." *Style 8* (1992):452-462.

Rooney, Caroline. "Dangerous Knowledge and the Poetics of Survival: A Reading of *Our Sister Killjoy* and *A Question of Power*." In: *Motherlands: Black Women's Writing from Africa, the Caribbean and South Asia*. Ed. Susheila Nasta. New Brunswick N.J.: Rutgers University Press, 1991.

Sackey, Edward. "Oral Tradition and the African Novel." *Modern Fiction Studies*, 37,3 (Autumn 1991):389-407.

Samantrai, Ranu. "Caught at the Confluence of History: Ama Ata Aidoo's

Necessary Nationalism," *Research in African Literatures* 26, 2 (1995):140-157.

Sarpong Peter A. *The Sacred Stools of the Akan*. Tema: Ghana Publishing Corporation, 1971.

Simonse, Simon. "African Literature between Nostalgia and Utopia: African Novels since 1953 in the Light of the Modes of Production Approach." *Research in African Literatures* 13,4 (Winter 1982).

Stegerman, Beatrice. "The Divorce Dilemma: The New Woman in Contemporary African Novel." *Critique: Studies in Modern Fiction* 15, 3 (1974).

Stewart, Danièle. "Ghanaian Writing in Prose: A Critical Survey." *Presence Africaine* 91 (1974):73-105.

——. "New Life in Kyerefaso," *Ghanaian Writing Today*, I. Ed. B.S. Kwakwa. Accra, Ghana: Wolei Publishers, 1974. 80-86.

——. *Le roman africain anglophone depuis 1965: d'Achebe à Soyinka*. Paris: L'Harmattan, 1988.

Stine, Peter. "The Language of Endurance in the Short Stories of Ama Ata Aidoo." In: *Emerging Perspectives on Ama Ata Aidoo*. Eds. Ada Uzoamaka Azodo. Trenton N.J.: Africa World Press, 1998.

Strong-Leek, Linda. "Inverting the Institutions: Ama Ata Aidoo's *No Sweetness Here* and Deconstructive Theory." In: *Emerging Perspectives on Ama Ata Aidoo*. Eds. Ada Uzoamaka Azodo and Gay Wilentz. Trenton: Africa World Press, 1998.

Sutherland-Addy, Esi. "Narrative Technique and the Role of Commentators in Ama Ata Aidoo's Works." *Research Review* 5,2 (1989).

Sutherland, Efua. *Foriwa*. Accra: Ghana Publishing, 1967.

——. "New Life in Kyerefaso." In: *An African Treasury*. Ed. Langston Hughes. New York: Bram Publishing, 1960. 11-117.

Taiwo, Oladele. *Female Novelists of Modern Africa*. New York: St Martin's Press, 1984.

Thies-Torkornoo, Suzanne. "Die Rolle der Frau Afrikanischen Gesellschaft: Eine Betrachtung von Ama Ata Aidoos *Anowa* und Efua T. Sutherlands *Foriwa*." *Matatu* 1, 1 (1987):53-67.

Utudjan, Elaine. Saint-André. "Ghana and Nigeria." *Post-colonial English Drama: Commonwealth Drama since 1960*. Ed. Bruce King. New York/London: St. Martin's/Macmillan, 1992.

Uwakweh, Pauline O. "Variations in the Militant's Song." In: *Emerging Perspectives on Ama Ata Aidoo*. Eds. Ada Uzoamaka Azodo and Gay Wilentz. Trenton: Africa World Press, 1998.

Vincent, Theo. "Form in the Nigerian Novel: An Examination of Aidoo's *Our Sister Killjoy* ... and Okpewho's *The Last Duty*. Paper presented at the African Studies Association, Philadelphia, October 7, 1980.

——. Seventeen Black and African Writers on Literature and Life. Lagos: Cross Continent Press, 1981.

Wilentz, Gay. "African Woman's Domain: Demarcating Political Space In Nwapa, Sutherland and Aidoo." In: *Emerging Perspectives on Ama Ata Aidoo*. Eds. Ada Uzoamaka Azodo and Gay Wilentz. Trenton: Africa World Press, 1998.

——. *Binding Cultures: Black Women Writers in Africa and the Diaspora.* Bloomington: Indiana University Press, 1992.

——. "Introduction: A Breath of Fresh Air" In: *Emerging Perspectives on Ama Ata Aidoo.* Eds. Ada Uzoamaka Azodo and Gay Wilentz. Trenton: Africa World Press, 1998.

——. "The Politics of Exile: Ama Ata Aidoo's *Our Sister Killjoy*," *Studies in Twentieth Century Literature* (Special Issue. Africa: Literature and Politics) 15,1 (1989):159-173. Rpt. "The Politics of Exile: Reflections of a Black-Eyed Squint in *Our Sister Killjoy*:" In *Emerging Perspectives on Ama Ata Aidoo.* Eds. Ada Uzoamaka Azodo and Gay Wilentz. Trenton: Africa World Press, 1998.

——. "Reading the Critical Writer." In *Emerging Perspectives on Ama Ata Aidoo.* Eds. Ada Uzoamaka Azodo and Gay Wilentz. Trenton: Africa World Press, 1998.

——. "Toward a Diaspora Literature." College English (April 1992): 385-405.

Yan, Haiping. "Transnationality and Its Critique: Narrative Tropes of 'Borderland' in *Our Sister Killjoy*." In: *Emerging Perspectives on Ama Ata Aidoo.* Eds. Ada Uzoamaka Azodo and Gay Wilentz. Trenton, N.J.: Africa World Press, 1998.

NOTES ON CONTRIBUTORS

Maureen Ngozi Eke, Assistant Professor of English at Central Michigan University has a Ph D. in Comparative Literature from Indiana University, Bloomington. She teaches African, African American and World literatures, and the literary dimensions of film. She has research interests in Black women's writing, drama, African cinema, postcolonial literatures and theory. Dr. Eke has published in *Callaloo, Visual Anthropology,* and *South African Theater Journal.* Her publications include, "Revisioning Drama to include the Female Voice: Fatima Dike, a Revolutionary Dramatist;" *Doing Feminism: Teaching and Research in the Academy* (Michigan State University Press, 1997); "From the Heart: Women and Liberation in New Writings by Black South African Women," Working Papers, Women and International Development (Michigan State University, 1993); "Sociopolitical Awakening in Ken Saro-Wiwa's *Sozaboy"* (Lynne Rienner Publishers, forthcoming). She co-authored "Towards a Theory of Orality in African Cinema, (RAL 26,3 (1995); "Secondary Orality in South African Film" (IRIS 18 1995). Dr. Eke was formerly the Associate Outreach Coordinator and Director of the African Media Program at Michigan State University, East Lansing.

Arlene A. Elder, Professor of English and Comparative Literature at the University of Cincinnati, teaches and writes on African, Australian Aboriginal, and Ethnic U.S. literatures and ora-tures. She is a member of the MLA Executive Committee for the Study of Multi-Ethnic Literature in the United States, and was a member of the Executive Committee of the African Literature Association in 1976-77. She was a Senior Fulbright Lecturer at the University of Nairobi and has published *The Hindered Hand:*

Cultural Implications of Early African-American Fiction as well as articles, chapters, and encyclopedia entries.

Angeletta KM Gourdine is an Assistant Professor of English at Louisiana State University. Specializing in African, African American and Caribbean women's writing, she is currently completing a book project on *Diaspora Consciousness in Black Women's Fiction.*

Miriam C. Gyimah was born and raised in Ghana. She came to the United States of America in 1979 where she completed her primary education and continued on to college. She received her B.A. in English in 1992 at the University of Maryland Eastern Shore, her M.A. in English Literature at Southern Illinois University in 1994 and is now a Clark Fellow at the New York State University at Binghamton where she is working towards a Ph.D. in Comparative Literature, with a focus on Diaspora (Africana) literature and cross-cultural and black feminist theory. Gyimah is now an A.B.D. doctoral student and is writing a dissertation on the works of Ama Ata Aidoo. She intends to be a professor of literature and a creative writer.

Kenneth W. Harrow had his Ph.D. from New York University, and is a Professor of English at Michigan State University. He is a past president of the African Literature Association, and has edited two volumes on Islam in African Literature, *Faces of Islam in African Literature* (Heinemann, 1991)and *The Marabout and the Muse.* He co-edited *Crisscrossing the Boundaries of African Literature* and has also published *Thresholds of Change in African Literature: Emergence of a Tradition* (Heinemann/Currey, 1994). Dr. Harrow has published widely in African literature and film.

Naana Banyiwa Horne, an Assistant Professor of English at Indiana University Kokomo, is a native of Ghana. She obtained her Ph.D. from the University of Wisconsin-Madison, and has contributed poems and articles on African and African American literature to a variety of anthologies and journals. Her scholarly works have appeared in *Sage: A Scholarly Journal on Black Women; Ngambika: Studies of Women in African Literature; Dictionary of Literary Biography, Volume 117; Twentieth Century Caribbean and Black African Writers; and Emerging Perspectives on Flora Nwapa,* published by Africa World Press.

Mildred A. Hill-Lubin, a member of the English Department and an affiliate member of the Center for African Studies, University of Florida, Gainesville, teaches African and African American Literature. She received her Ph.D. in English and African Studies from the University of Illinois, Urbana-Champaign; her M.A. in English from Western Reserve University, Cleveland; her B.A. in English from Paine College, Augusta, Georgia. She is the author of several articles on Ama Ata Aidoo, the co-editor of the 1980 ALA Selected Papers, *Toward Defining the African Aesthetic* (1982), and co-organizer of the 1990 meeting of the African Literature Association in Gainesville. She has hosted Ama Ata Aidoo as Visiting Professor and Writer at the University of Florida (1979 and 1994). Hill-Lubin was the first female and the first African American to serve as president of the African Literature Association, 1987-88.

Sally McWilliams received her Ph.D. from the University of Washington in Seattle. She is currently an Assistant Professor of English at Montclair State University in New Jersey. Her scholarly interests include International women's writing, Lesbian literary studies, and the Pedagogy of teaching world literature in the US classroom.

Paula Morgan lectures in the Department of Liberal Arts, University of The West Indies, St. Augustine, where she teaches introductory prose, poetry, and drama, Women's Literature, West Indian and American Literature. Dr. Morgan is also attached to the University of the West Indies Centre for Gender and Development Studies, and the Distance Education Centre. She is a member of the Women and Development Studies Group (WDSG), for which she has served as Deputy Coordinator and Head of Publications Group. Her primary research interest is in women's literature of the African diaspora. She has done numerous conference papers and published several articles in this subject area. Paula Morgan has edited the WDSG Newsletter and is currently the editor of the Centre for Gender and Development Studies' *Working Papers Series*. At present, Dr. Morgan is writing a language course for distance delivery, *Language Proficiency for Tertiary Level*.

Juliana Makuchi Nfah-Abbenyi is an Assistant Professor of English and Post-Colonial Literatures at The University of Southern Mississippi and author of *Gender in African Women's Writing:*

Identity, Sexuality, and Difference (Indiana University Press, 1997). She has contributed chapters to books such as *Our Own Agendas: Autobiographical Essays by Women Associated with McGill University* (McGill-Queen's University Press, 1995), *The Politics of (M)Othering: Womanhood, Identity, and Resistance in African Literature* (Routledge, 1996), *Post-Colonial African Writers: A Bio-Bibliographical Source book* (Greenwood Press, 1997); and *The Garland Book of Nature Literature* (Garland, 1998, forthcoming). Abbenyi has also published in scholarly journals such as *Canadian Woman Studies, Notre Librairie, Comparative Literature in Canada*. Her fiction has also appeared in *Callaloo* (Fall 1996), *Crab Orchard Review* (Spring/Summer 1997), and *The Toronto Review of Contemporary Writing Abroad* (Summer 1997).

Vincent O. Odamtten, who taught at the University of Cape Coast, Ghana, won the 1976 Valco Fund Literary Award for Poetry. He holds a doctorate from the State University of New York at Stony Brook. His award-winning dissertation on the work of Ama Ata Aidoo has been published as an acclaimed book, *The Art of Ama Ata Aidoo: Polylectics and Reading Against Neocolonialism* (1994). He has contributed articles to a number of critical anthologies, including *Of Dreams Deferred, Dead or Alive: African Perspectives on African-American Writers* (1996) and *Language in Exile: Jamaican Texts of the 18th and 19th Century* (1990). Currently, Odamtten is collaborating on a critical text on narrative. He is the Director of the Africana Studies Program at Hamilton College, New York.

Naana Jane Opoku-Agyemang is a Senior Lecturer in the Department of English, University of Cape Coast, Ghana. She received her Ph.D. in Commowealth Literature from York University, Toronto, Canada. She has published in *Asemka, The Journal of the Council of Black Studies, Nwanyibu: Womanbeing in African literature* and *Women Re-Writing Women*. Her current area of research is literature by women from Ghana and Africa.

Peter Wilfred Stine, a native of Michigan, is Professor of English Language and Literature at Gordon College in Wenham, Massachusetts. He began teaching African Literature in 1986, soon after his first trip to Kenya. In 1988, with the help of Kellogg faculty development funds, he traveled to Ghana, Cote d'Ivoire, Zaire, Kenya, and Ethiopia. In 1990, he spent a week in Senegal on his way to a teaching Sabbatical in Kijabe, Kenya. He returned to Kenya with a student drama troupe in 1993. He is interested in writing further on the image of missionaries in African literature. Professor Stine received his A.B. from Asbury College, his M.A. from Northwestern University, and his Ph.D. from Michigan State University.

Linda Strong-Leek is an Assistant Professor of English at Florida International University. She co-edited a volume of essays, *Winds of Change: The Transforming Voices of Women* (Peter Lang Publishers, 1997), on writings from the 1996 International Conference of Caribbean Writers and Scholars. Strong-Leek has also published a chapter in *Emerging Perspectives on Flora Nwapa* (Africa World Press, 1998) and is currently revising *Excising the Spirit*, an analysis of the issue of female circumcision from various cultural and political perspectives. Dr. Strong-Leek was awarded a Fulbright scholarship and is spending the 1998 academic year teaching at the University of Zimbabwe, Harare.

Pauline Onwubiko Uwakweh earned her Ph.D.(1995) from Temple University, Philadelphia. Formerly, she taught in the Department of English and Literary Studies at the University of Calabar, Nigeria. She is the author of *Running for Cover*, a novel on the Nigerian civil war. Her literary interests include the militant tradition of African and African-American women, theorizing female militancy, and children's narrative literature. Dr. Uwakweh has published articles in various literary journals and anthologies. Currently, she is an independent scholar and is working on a novel about female rebellion in a fictional African setting.

Haiping Yan is an Assistant Professor of Theater and Comparative Literature at the University of Colorado, Boulder, and an Adjunct Professor of Literary and Cultural Studies at Tsinghua University, Beijing, China. She received her B.A. in Chinese literature from Fudan University and her Ph.D. in theater and critical theory from Cornell University. Her research focuses on twentieth-century drama and critical theory. She has published in the areas of drama, women's theater, and cross-cultural issues. She is the author of several dramatic and literary works including a prize-winning historical drama *Li Shimin, Prince of Qin* and a collection of prose narratives on gender, culture, and global politics.

ABOUT THE EDITORS

Ada Uzoamaka Azodo, B.A. (Hons.), University of Ife; *Diplôme d'études supérieures françaises*, Université de Dakar; and M.A. and Ph.D., University of Lagos, has teaching and research interests in French Studies, African Studies, Women's Studies and International Studies. Dr. Azodo's *magnum opus, L'imaginaire dans les romans de Camara Laye* (Peter Lang Publishers, 1993) explores the symbolic, shady and mysterious African world which that classical author inhabited. Azodo has also published in *Journal of Religion in Africa*; CUNY, The Feminist Press; and Africa World Press. Azodo was elected Secretary of the ALA Francophone Caucus 1998–1999. She was also elected member of the MLA African Studies Committee 1998-1999, will become secretary to the committee in the year 2000, and will succeed to the office of the president in the year 2002. She is currently affiliated with Indiana University Northwest as Adjunct Associate Professor of African Studies and French Studies, and is presently working on a novel temporarily titled, *Afuda: Or, Meditations.*

Gay Wilentz, Associate Professor of English and Director of Ethnic Studies at East Carolina University and Adjunct Professor at University of Belize, was born in New York and attended Rutgers University, North Carolina State University, and University of Texas. She was a Fulbright scholar to Nigeria in 1984, and received her doctorate in English in 1986. Her teaching and research interests include African, African-American, and Caribbean literatures, Ethnic Studies, and Women's Studies. She has published in *College English, African American Review, Research in African Literatures, Twentieth Century Literature*, and *MELUS*, among others. She is the book editor of Jewish immigrant writer Anzia Yezeierska's 1923 novel, *Salome of the Tenenments.* Her germinal critical work, *Binding Cultures: Black Women Writers in Africa and the Diaspora*, was one of the earliest full-length studies to examine women's role in the transmission of culture on both sides of the Atlantic. She is presently working on a book, *Curing Dis-Ease*, exploring the relationship of ethnicity and healing in cross-cultural women's writing.

INDEX

HR
Gift FIPSE)

466B21 FM 1009
12/05/06 44400 MC

(329800) 17.5

Gramley Library
Salem College
Winston-Salem, NC 27108